D0875676

Re-Envisioning
Egypt
1919-1952

Hugh Roberts
Boston
December 3, 2012

Re-Envisioning
Egypt
1919-1952

Edited by

Arthur Goldschmidt
Amy J. Johnson
Barak A. Salmoni

The American University in Cairo Press
Cairo   New York

Copyright © 2005 by
The American University in Cairo Press
113 Sharia Kasr el Aini, Cairo, Egypt
420 Fifth Avenue, New York, NY 10018
www.aucpress.com

All rights reserved. No part of this publication may be reproduced,
stored in a retrieval system, or transmitted in any form or by any means,
electronic, mechanical, photocopying, recording, or otherwise,
without the prior permission of the publisher.

Dar el Kutub No. 16560/04
ISBN 977 424 900 3

Designed by Fatiha Bouzidi/AUC Press Design Center
Printed in Egypt

Contents

**Part V: Art, Cinema, Literature, and
Historiographical Memory**

Illustrations

Contributors

Tewfik Aclimandos is an Egyptian political scientist and historian working for the Centre d'Études et de Documentation Économique, Juridique et Sociale (CEDEJ), a French center based in Cairo. The subject of his doctoral thesis at the Institut d'Études politiques de Paris is on political activism in the Egyptian army. He has been working on the political activism of Egyptian officers for the past nineteen years and has published a dozen articles on this and related issues They include: "Officiers et Frères Musulmans," working paper, CEDEJ, 2002; "Les ingénieurs militaires égyptiens" in *Maghreb Machrek* 1995; "Regard réstrospectif sur la Révolution égyptienne," in *EMA* 4/5; and "Nationalismes machréquins et nassérisme" in *Taguieff*, Delannoi: "Nationalismes en perspective," *Berg*, Paris, 2001.

Malak Badrawi is an honorary university fellow at the Institute of Arab and Islamic Studies at the University of Exeter, U.K. He received his B.A. from Cairo University and his M.A. from the University of London. Badrawi is the author of *Isma'il Sidqi: Pragmatism and Vision in Twentieth Century Egypt* (Curzon Press, 1996) and *Political Violence in Egypt, 1910–1925: Secret Societies, Plots, and Assassinations* (Curzon Press, 2000).

Andrew Flibbert earned a Ph.D. in political science from Columbia University in 2001. His dissertation is now a book manuscript entitled *Commerce in Culture: States and Markets in the World Film Trade* and his research focuses on the political economy of cultural production. He is currently an adjunct professor of politics at New York University and a visiting assistant professor at Trinity College in Hartford, where he teaches comparative and international politics.

Nancy Gallagher is chair of the Middle East Studies Program and a professor of history at the University of California, Santa Barbara. Her publications include *Egypt's Other Wars: Epidemics and the Politics of Public Health* (The American University in Cairo Press, 1993); *Medicine and Power in Tunisia, 1780–1900* (Cambridge University Press, 1983); "Apostasy, Feminism, and the Discourse of Human Rights," in Sherifa Zuhur, ed. *Women and Gender in the Middle East and the Islamic World Today* (University of California Press, 2003); "Learning Lessons from the Algerian War of Independence," *Middle East Report*, 225 (Winter 2002); and "The International Campaign against Gender Apartheid in Afghanistan," *Journal of International Law and Foreign Affairs*, 5, 2 (Fall/Winter, 2000–2001).

Arthur Goldschmidt is professor emeritus of Middle East history at Pennsylvania State University. He received his Ph.D. in history and Middle Eastern Studies from Harvard University in 1968. His main area of research has been nineteenth- and twentieth-century Egyptian history; he has recently completed revisions of his *Historical Dictionary of Egypt* and *Modern Egypt: The Formation of a Nation-State*. Originally a specialist in political history, his interests have moved in the direction of social, intellectual, and cultural trends in modern Egypt.

Mervat F. Hatem is professor of political science, Howard University, Washington, D.C. She obtained her Ph.D. from the University of Michigan in 1982. Her interests include the study of gender, discourse and politics in Egypt and the Arab Middle East. Her latest publication is "The Nineteenth Century Discursive Roots of the Continuing Debate on the Social Contract in Today's Egypt," Mediterranean Programme, Robert Schuman Center for Advanced Studies, European University Institute Working Papers (no. 2002/13), Florence, Italy.

Misako Ikeda is associate professor at Koryo International College, Aichi, Japan. She received her Ph.D. in history and Middle East Studies from Harvard University in 1998. Her research interests include social and intellectual history in modern Egypt, particularly social debates prior to the 1952 Revolution.

Amy J. Johnson was an associate professor of history at Berry College. She earned her Ph.D. in history and Middle Eastern Studies from Harvard University in 1998. Her research interests included rural development, social history, and gender issues. She wrote extensively on Middle Eastern and North African history, and her most recent work is entitled *Reconstructing Rural Egypt: Ahmed Hussein and the History of Egyptian Development* (The American University in Cairo Press, 2004).

Anne-Claire Kerbœuf is a Ph.D. candidate in history at the Université de Provence (Aix-Marseille I). She is an associate researcher at the Centre d'Études et de Documentation Économique, Juridique et Sociale (CEDEJ), Cairo. Since September 2002, she has been a recipient of the French Foreign Affairs Minister Lavoisier scholarship. Her major research interest is in social and urban Egyptian modern history. Her most recent publication is: "La 'racaille' et les intrigants. Étude comparée de deux émeutes: Alexandrie, 11 juin 1882 / Le Caire, 26 janvier 1952," in *Égypte/ Monde Arabe*, n° 4–5, 2003.

Samia Kholoussi is assistant professor at the University of Ain Shams, Cairo, Egypt. She has taught at UCLA and the University of Arizona, and received her Ph.D. from the University of Ain Shams. Her publications include "The Revolution that Failed: A Study of Radwa Ashour's *Siraj* and Nadine Gordimer's *July's People*," *Philology XXII Literature and Linguistics Series*, eds. Salama M. Soliman el al. (Cairo: Al Alsun Faculty Press, 1994); "Cracks in the Edifice of National Consciousness: Tawfik al Hakim's Bird of the East and Elizabeth Bowen's The Last September," in *Literary Inter-Relations: Ireland, Egypt, and The Far East* (Gerrards Cross: Colin Smythe, 1996); "Laying Bare the Artifice of Fiction: Al Qa'id's *The Grievances of the Eloquent Egyptian: The Apathy of the Wealthy* and Nabokov's *The Real Life of Sebastian Knight*," in *Essays in Honor of Louis Morcos* (Cairo: Dar al-Kutub, 1998). Current research interests include English literature, Arabic literature, gender studies, colonialism, and the politics of poetics.

Hanan Kholoussy is a joint doctoral candidate in the Departments of History/Middle Eastern Studies at New York University (expected 2005/ 2006). She holds a joint B.S./M.A. in Foreign Service/Arab Studies from Georgetown University (1998/1999). Her research interests include gender, nationalism, and law. Her publications include, "Stolen Husbands, Foreign

Wives: Mixed Marriage, Identity Formation, and Gender in Colonial Egypt, 1909–1923," in *Hawwa: Journal of Women in the Middle East and the Islamic World* 1, 2 (July 2003).

Fred H. Lawson is professor of government at Mills College. He received his doctorate in political science from the University of California, Los Angeles, in 1982. During 1992–93, he was Fulbright lecturer in international relations at the University of Aleppo; in the spring of 2001, he was Fulbright lecturer in political science at Aden University. He is the author of *The Social Origins of Egyptian Expansionism during the Muhammad 'Ali Period* (Columbia University Press, 1992) and *Why Syria Goes to War* (Cornell University Press, 1996). He is presently finishing a book-length study of the emergence of sovereign states in the modern Middle East.

Shaun T. Lopez received his M.A. in Middle Eastern Studies from the University of Utah and his Ph.D. in history at the University of Michigan (2004). His dissertation research focuses on the relationship between the proliferation of *akhbar al-hawadith* (news about domestic mayhem) and the gendering of a mass-mediated popular culture in Egypt after World War I. His article, "The Dangers of Dancing: The Media and Morality in 1930s Egypt," has appeared in *Comparative Studies of South Asia, Africa, and the Middle East.* He is now a post-doctoral fellow at the University of North Carolina at Chapel Hill.

Scott David McIntosh received his B.A. in history and English from Berry College in 2001, where his studies focused on Egypt and Sudan. He worked for two years as program coordinator for the National Council on U.S.-Arab Relations in Washington, D.C., and contributed to its online journal *GulfWire Perspectives.* He is currently on staff at CHF International, an NGO that provides technical expertise and leadership in domestic and international development initiatives in more than one hundred countries.

Roger Owen is A.J. Meyer professor of history at Harvard University, and directed Harvard's Center for Middle Eastern Studies from 1996 to 1999. He is a leading authority on Middle Eastern economic history in the nineteenth and twentieth centuries. His publications include *Cotton and the Egyptian Economy, 1820–1914: A Study in Trade and Development* (Oxford University Press, 1969), *The Middle East in the World Economy, 1800–1914* (Methuen, 1981), *A History of Middle East Economies in the Twentieth Century* (with Sevket Pamuk, Harvard University Press, 1998), *State, Power and Politics in the Making of the Modern Middle East* (2nd ed., Routledge, 2000); and *Lord Cromer: Victorian Imperialist, Edwardian Proconsul* (Oxford University Press, 2004).

Lucie Ryzova is a junior research fellow at St. John's College, University of Oxford. She specializes in the social and cultural history of Egypt under the monarchy, with attention to the emergence of urban mass culture and the media. She is the author of *L'Effendiyya ou la modernité contestée* (CEDEJ, 2004).

Barak A. Salmoni is deputy director of the Center for Advanced Operational Culture Learning, U.S. Marine Corps Training and Education Command, in Quantico, Virginia. Until May 2005 he was assistant professor in Department of National Security Affairs, Naval Postgraduate School. His dissertation was titled "Pedagogies of Patriotism: Teaching Socio-Political Community through 20th-Century Turkish and Egyptian Education" (Harvard University, 2002). His research interests include collective identity in the Middle East; military, polity, and society in Middle East and Central Asia; Turkish foreign relations; and American interests in Middle East. He has published articles and book reviews in *Middle Eastern Studies, Turkish Studies Association Bulletin, History of Education Quarterly, Turkish Studies Journal, Comparative Studies in South Asia, Africa, and the Middle East, Journal of Strategic Studies, Journal of Political and Military Sociology, Current History*, and *Middle East Review of International Affairs*.

James Whidden is assistant professor of history and classics at Acadia University, in Wolfville Canada, previously having taught at Murray State University in Murray, Kentucky. He received his Ph.D. from the University of London, and currently has a book manuscript on 1920s–30s Egyptian political life under review.

Caroline Williams holds an M.A. degree in Middle East history from Harvard University and a degree in Islamic art and architecture from the American University in Cairo. Her work on *The Islamic Monuments of Cairo* (The American University in Cairo Press, 2002) led to a study of nineteenth-century Orientalist depictions of Cairene urban life, and most recently to an exploration of Egypt's twentieth-century visual expressions.

Preface

Barak A. Salmoni and Arthur Goldschmidt

The editors of *Re-Envisioning Egypt* wish to acknowledge the support of several individuals. Robert Vitalis, director of the University of Pennsylvania's Middle East Center, was encouraging at the beginning of the venture, as was James Jankowski, recently retired from the University of Colorado. Mona Russell of the Massachusetts Institute of Technology and then Framingham State University and Lisa Pollard of the University of North Carolina at Wilmington, were instrumental in alerting us to scholars in diverse fields, encouraging them to contribute, and reading drafts of chapters. In addition to contributing a conclusion, Roger Owen worked to continually assure the editors of the need for such a volume, suggested potential contributors, and read draft chapters. The editors thank Lucie Ryzova for sharing her immense collection of 1919–52 Egyptian imagery, from which the cover illustrations for this volume come. We would also like to acknowledge Amy Johnson's two research assistants at Berry College, Jennifer Carman and Zachary Greene, who were integral to this book's completion. Tremendous gratitude is due to Barak Salmoni's wife, Alicia Salmoni, who continually encouraged her husband, while editing his and several other chapters on very short notice.

Re-Envisioning Egypt originated in a series of conversations among the editors at academic conferences, over the telephone, and in the halls of Harvard University's Center for Middle Eastern Studies. Still, this book is in many ways the brainchild of Amy Johnson, who first suggested both the scholarly collaboration and the topic. It is thus with a most profound sense of sorrow that we mourn her premature passing on the night of 2 December 2004, from injuries sustained in an automobile accident while returning to Berry, Georgia from the Middle East Studies Association conference. Amy was the consummate colleague: ever-attentive, diligent, and concerned to help other scholars both to pursue their interests to completion and to integrate them with the intellectual world around them. She was also a peerlessly conscientious teaching scholar, putting equal effort and concern into educating her students in and out of the classroom. As her contribution to this volume with Scott McIntosh shows, Amy took quite seriously her mission of academic and educational mentoring. Likewise, her chosen subject of academic inquiry—social reform, and governmental as well as societal efforts to alleviate the suffering and disenfranchisement of Egyptian masses—is a clear testament to her commitment to use her scholarly prowess to further her sensitive intellectual mission.

It was as a friend, however, that Amy made the greatest impact on us, and it is as a friend that we will miss her most dearly. She was able to balance intellectual ambition with an unpretentious personality, unfettered by the pursuit of status, visibility, or self-promotion. Amy's concern to always prove a genuine, unselfish, and supportive friend thus both endeared her to others and encouraged those lucky enough to know her to better themselves. Her legacy will be a renewed effort on our part to be humane, intellectually honest, and mentally engaged for the benefit of friends we have yet to meet.

Re-Envisioning Egypt is dedicated to the memory of Amy Johnson, 1969–2004.

Introduction

Barak A. Salmoni and Amy J. Johnson

As visitors to Egypt soon learn either from billboards or taxi drivers, *Misr umm al-dunya*—Egypt is the mother of the world.[1] Of course, this Egyptian assertion must compete with those of other Middle Easterners: some Iranians claim their country is the "pivot of the universe," while Turks might assert that their ancestors spread civilization from Central Asia to all points on the compass.[2] Still, Egypt has proven central to marking out the key dynamics of the Middle East in the past two hundred and fifty years. The first Middle Eastern region to experience European territorial encroachment during the 1798–1801 Napoleonic invasion, Egypt then went on under Muhammad 'Ali (r. 1808–48) to set a pattern of relatively successful regime-led, authoritarian military-bureaucratic reform. Such reform also strived for a state-driven, autarkic economy, with tremendous power politics dividends. As a result, the valley of the Nile again attracted the interest of Europeans, whose military muscle-flexing and manipulation of indigenous leaders determined the course of regional politics, with implications for the European balance of power. Not only did such experiences in Egypt again herald future trends, but the 1850s–80s dynamics of civilian modernization, with concomitant indebtedness to western creditors and eventual bankruptcy, also exemplified processes elsewhere in North Africa, the Ottoman center, Iran, and, to a lesser extent given lesser means, the Central Asian Muslim khanates.[3]

The end of the nineteenth century and beginning of the twentieth century brought European occupation. Here, too, Egypt saw dynamics later to emerge in other parts of North Africa and the Levant. These included domestic power relations entangling anti-colonialist nationalist

1

intellectuals, foreign overlords, and local elites who compromised with the latter; the emergence of a highly variegated, sociopolitically aware, and didactic press; and the flowering of a movement for the reform and increased societal application of a modernized Islam.[4] In these last two cases, Egypt even served as a gathering point for like-minded people from other Middle Eastern lands, in addition to functioning as a radiating point for such ideas.[5]

Jumping ahead, it has rightfully become commonplace for discussions of post-World War II history, politics, and socioeconomic change in the Middle East to begin with Egypt. The Free Officers coup-turned-revolution of 23 July 1952 opened the Arab world's era of nationalist liberation, replacing politically ineffective and societally inattentive ruling elites with self-consciously progressive regimes emerging from popular social classes via the military academies.[6] Taking the cue from Gamal 'Abd al-Nasser, young military men in Iraq, Syria, Libya, and elsewhere purposefully, if uncertainly, sought to recraft societies, polities, and economies. Likewise, the failure of Egypt in the 1967 June War symbolized for the rest of the Arab world a seeming need to reassess the conceptual and ethical foundations of politics. And, while the post-1973 experience of Egypt diverges in certain respects from that of Syria, Iraq, and other North African countries, it still has exemplified larger Middle Eastern patterns. Sadat's eventual eschewal of direct military conflict with Israel has indeed been emulated by other Arab states, just as steps toward economic opening and privatization have also been seen in other statist Middle Eastern economies.[7] More recently, and perhaps most fundamentally, the ossification of political orders and emergence of a newly energized Islamist spectrum sidestepping or challenging incompetent states can be observed throughout the Arab world, but most starkly in Egypt.[8]

If it is true that Egypt exemplifies Middle Eastern trends, it is also true that the above perspective ignores a tremendously important period of Egyptian history, one perhaps more significant for Egypt's post-1952 century than any other. This is the era between 1919, when a self-appointed delegation of Egyptian elites—the *wafd*—visited the British high commissioner and spurred the 'revolution,' and the 1952 coup. The coup itself is often interpreted as indicative of the monarchy's social, political, intellectual, and economic failure. Yet, though it continues to receive insufficient scholarly attention, the period from 1919 to 1952—referred to variously as Egypt's 'liberal experiment,' 'parliamentary era,' 'monarchical period,' or 'constitutional monarchy years'—exhibits a cultural vibrancy, societal dynamism, and intellectual-political legacy requiring a renewed intensity of focus.[9] The present volume provides this renewed intensity, emphasizing the ways in which the period was crucial to later twentieth-century events.

From one perspective—once popular among western writers and cultivated by the post-1952 regime—1919–52 was indeed a failure. According to this view, Egyptian politics had been mired in corruption, incompetence, and internecine wrangling from the outset. The machinations of the political parties, individual politicians, the monarch, and the British ensured that no government lasted its full term. In this scurry for self-enrichment, little time, inclination, or effort was devoted to confronting Egypt's massive challenges of economic development, education, and social welfare. Demographically growing and urbanizing sectors of the population were thus excluded by a culturally European elite out of tune with the mindset of the people. Sociopolitical exclusion thus led to extra-legal mobilization. Meanwhile, British-curtailed sovereignty barely increased over twenty-five years, so that failure in Palestine in 1948 and rising street violence during the next four years symbolized the bankruptcy of the existing sociopolitical regime, and the need for a strong hand to obviate politics for a while.[10]

Seen from another perspective, the constitutional monarchy era is much more important, and exhibits key accomplishments as well as enduring challenges. Among countries joining the Arab League in 1945—headquartered in Cairo—monarchical Egypt was the most sovereign state, especially after the conclusion of the 1936 Anglo-Egyptian Treaty, which further reduced the British role in Egyptian politics. Even from 1923, British-granted limited independence meant that all spheres of domestic affairs unrelated to security and strategic communications became the preserve of Egyptians themselves. With the arguable exception of Saudi Arabia, Egypt was thus quite distinct from other Arab states. Likewise, though political triangulation of the monarch, the British, and the political parties rendered representative rule dysfunctional, a parliamentary system did indeed exist. Among other characteristics, it featured lively debate, vociferous challenging of ministers, and vetting of legislation.[11] Several chapters of *Re-Envisioning Egypt* bear out this parliamentary vitality, especially those by Malak Badrawi, Hanan Kholoussy, and Misako Ikeda.[12] And, while deputies and ministers often exhibited great attachment to nepotism and narrow sectoral interests—normal in open political systems—more remarkable was the enduring commitment among most of the political elite to maintaining parliamentary government, limiting temporary forays into rule-by-decree,[13] and upholding the Constitution as a touchstone of maturing political life. Growing judicial efficacy and an attachment to the courts' autonomy were also important in this regard.[14] At the beginning of the twenty-first century, as Egyptians contemplate a more open political life in the next decades, some have thus looked back to the constitutional era with nostalgia—rightly or wrongly, as Anne-Claire Kerbœuf shows in her chapter.

Also during the post-World War I era, Egypt continued modest, though real, private sector-led economic development, all the while maintaining financial solvency.[15] Due to global circumstances as well as indigenous activity, Egypt remained debt free, in contrast to its current situation. Likewise, a small group of native Egyptian entrepreneurs emerged, as did infant industries that met local and regional needs. New economic directions, and concomitant geographic mobility for some Egyptians, also entailed greater prominence of new social formations. These included an urban working class, the laboring rural sector, and a newly educated white-collar stratum who sought to synthesize their particular understandings of tradition and modernity.[16] Lucie Ryzova and Samia Kholoussi analyze both these new social classes and larger attitudes toward them, while Andrew Flibbert's chapter explores one aspect of entrepreneurial expansion into new realms.

Perhaps because of its manifest shortcomings in the past thirty years, some of the more under-studied achievements of the 1919–52 years relate to education. After decades of British neglect, state educational efforts underwent a gradual revolution under the constitutional monarchy. This included an expansion in numbers of schools, their geographic distribution, and the provision of female education.[17] Likewise, pedagogical professionalism continued to increase, such that by the 1940s, Egyptian educational experts were firmly integrated into global pedagogical trends and activities, and were increasingly conscious of the ideological potential of schooling, as the chapter by Barak A. Salmoni demonstrates. To be sure, problems and disagreements persisted, particularly in terms of equality of educational opportunity between genders and among different social classes and geographical regions. Further, the purpose of education for these groups, and thus the curricular substance appropriate in schools, was never fully determined. Yet these very issues—advertised by the post-1952 regime as the new order's priorities and monopoly—topped the agenda of professional educators and legislators alike from the 1920s, with small yet concrete achievements being made before 1952, as Misako Ikeda's essay illuminates.

Just as indicative of the importance of this era in Egyptian history—and likewise neglected in most writing—are the initiatives taken in the fields of foreign policy and social reform. Though Egyptian leaders did not possess untrammeled independence in this realm, Fred Lawson shows that they demonstrated real and growing interest in events in North Africa, the Levant, and the Arabian Peninsula, especially from the 1930s. As such, by the mid-1940s and with the establishment of the Arab League in Cairo, the monarchical era had set the parameters for the post-1952 regime's search for regional involvement and dominance.

A consistent criticism of parliamentary Egypt has focused on the inadequate concern demonstrated for social affairs and for full social inclusion of different sectors of the population.[18] While Egypt's elites were for the most part derelict in this regard, this historiographical approach needs to be moderated. As noted previously, from the 1920s, Egyptian educators had spoken of the need for schooling to address the needs of rural and impoverished Egyptians in particular, for the sake of the nation as a whole. Further, socialist and Marxist intellectual trends, as studied by Samia Kholoussi, demonstrate that such concerns were articulated beyond the pedagogical milieu. The establishment of a Social Affairs Ministry in 1939, as well as key legislation at the end of the 1940s and beginning of the 1950s, brought a renewed concern for these matters.[19] As Amy J. Johnson and Scott David McIntosh show in their chapter, societal elites themselves began to actively pursue initiatives for the economic and social uplift across broader strata of Egyptian society, in cooperation with the state. Here too one finds patterns the post-1952 state adopted, using some of the same personnel.

As highlighted by Johnson and McIntosh's chapter, as well as Nancy Gallagher's contribution, increasing both opportunities for, and the autonomous agency of, women was integral to social reform. Though reflecting energized advances in gender studies more than a focus on the 1919–52 period itself, Egypt's women's movement during these years has received substantial attention.[20] In this context as well, Egypt during the first half of the twentieth century was a pioneer. Women and men debated the roles and self-identities of both genders in a modernizing country under European colonial control. Later, urban elites of the parliamentary era exerted continual efforts to mold a modern, nationalist woman able to contribute to Egypt's uplift, while navigating between liberation into the public sphere and maintenance of traditional, male-serving roles. As such, during the constitutional era consensus was never achieved on what a modern, nationalist, and matronly woman meant across different social strata, with women's advocates often providing mixed messages, as chapters by Mervat Hatem and Nancy Gallagher reveal. Still, the mechanisms for crafting new Egyptian womanhood were many throughout this period, including, among others, education, mass culture as depicted by Shaun Lopez, the literature and social reform efforts covered by Johnson, McIntosh, and Hatem, and law, as Hanan Kholoussy illuminates.

An enduring characteristic of Egypt since the nineteenth century has been the variety of cultural and intellectual expression, and either through their sources or topical foci, virtually every chapter in this volume reveals that the constitutional era emerges as Egypt's most vibrant period in this respect. Assertions and sources used by Ryzova, Kholoussi, Lopez, and others show that freedom of the press and the continuing emergence of new print-media outlets provided an arena for ever-diversifying economic, sociopolitical, and religio-cultural attitudes. These new avenues also served a multiplicity of societal sectors, featuring authors from an ever-broadening array of backgrounds. Likewise, periodicals and journals, though sometimes quite contentious, evinced growing intellectual sharpness, particularly as regards matters of education, social welfare, and science. As shown by Arthur Goldschmidt, Egyptian historians were also quite active in this period, bequeathing to subsequent students a rich body of knowledge, as well as insight into nationalist intellectuals' political attitudes.

Print media was accompanied by a flourishing associational life, only intermittently interdicted by the state prior to the late 1940s. Though certain manifestations—Young Egypt, the Muslim Brotherhood—at times became obstacles to public order, Egypt's associational life approximated quite well what scholars in the 1990s referred to as 'civil society,' so often lacking in the contemporary Middle East.[21] Here, intellectual, cultural, and organizational pluralism appears to have been a positive conviction. As such, and in light of the picture briefly sketched out here, this book invites the reader to reconsider the accepted wisdom on 1919–52 Egypt. Rather than being a period of creeping decay, these years emerge as integral to modern nation-state formation and social transformation. Though perhaps an over-burdened polity and society by the 1950s, it is equally likely that in the absence of the stresses of World War II and the Palestine

War—primarily external issues with internal reverberations—Egypt would have moved much more gradually toward the kind of political inclusion, economic development, and social progress to which the coup-makers of 1952 aspired, but which they could not effect. In this view, Egypt belongs in the category of the more sovereign Middle Eastern countries between 1920 and the early 1950s, such as the Republic of Turkey and Reza Khan's Iran. Egypt was closer to Turkey in its greater degree of lasting sovereignty, economic vitality, and infrastructural development. Like Iran, however, Egypt was still hemmed in by the British and possessed a monarch who attempted to control parliamentary politics while co-opting economic elites—which Reza Khan did much more successfully. Yet Egypt also diverged from both Turkey and Iran in its much more open sociopolitical arena and capitalist economy.[22]

Re-Envisioning Egypt, 1919–1952 therefore joins a growing body of literature reassessing the post-World War I political and social transformations in the Middle East's first sovereign states.[23] And, as these other recent works have done, the present volume both implicitly and explicitly shows that much of what is associated with post-1952 Egypt as a break from the past actually emerged from processes whose roots go back to the 1930s. Likewise, the 1919–52 years possess so many legacies for today's Egypt that the era must be re-envisioned. The intellectual dynamics of the 1919 Revolution itself, as analyzed by James Whidden, have continued to resonate for the past eighty-five years, just as Lawson's coverage of Egyptian foreign relations reveals the kernel of approaches more fully developed in later periods.[24] Likewise, nearly the entire agenda and ideological intentionality of Egypt's educators from the 1930s on was taken over by the Free Officers' pedagogues—who in the 1950s and 60s were often the same pedagogues of the earlier era.[25] This continuity from the constitutional to Nasserist era is also visible in the primacy of rural issues as seen in Johnson's work, both here and elsewhere.[26] Of course, as investigated so well by Tewfik Aclimandos, the evolution of the Egyptian officer corps into a coup-ready instrument was a long-term process, the social background of which reaches back into the 1930s. Finally, as mentioned above, Kerbœuf teaches us that even the events leading to the 1952 coup itself, such as the Great Cairo Fire, continue to resonate for key social strata in Egypt today.

This volume examines topics neglected by previous examinations of Egypt, uses new sources and methods to reassess matters familiar to Egyptian historiography, and augments the literature on topics that have attracted greater scholarly attention in the last decade. In so doing, it brings together an international group of senior and younger scholars from various disciplines. *Part I: Reassessing Polity and Diplomacy* begins with a chapter examining political ideologies and formations in the 1920s–30s. James Whidden focuses on the self-proclaimed embodiment of 1919 and the Egyptian national soul, the Wafd Party. He counters the view that the Wafd was an elitist, only superficially liberal grouping. Exploring Egyptian political party documents, British government archives, and memoirs, he highlights the ideologically dynamic nature of the 1920s, when ideas of nationhood, citizenship, cultural orientation, labor, and gender remained hotly contested. Ultimately, rather than an elite-driven political consensus during the first decade of Egyptian independence, Whidden finds that the Wafd adopted approaches of pre-World War I Egyptian nationalists, and was thus much more radical than scholars have assumed.

In chapter two, Fred Lawson introduces readers to the largely uncharted territory of Egypt's foreign relations during the 1920s and 1930s, questioning traditional scholarship which assumes little interest from Cairo in relations with surrounding states during these years. By contrast, Lawson locates several occasions when the Egyptian government displayed considerable regional initiative, including its actions on the issue of Palestine. Investigating in particular Cairo's resistance to Italian attempts to redraw the boundary with Libya in early 1925 and its efforts at Saudi-Yemeni mediation during the crisis of 1934–35, he illuminates Egyptian diplomatic activism at the height of the monarchy, throwing new light on the strategic calculus characterizing Egyptian diplomacy in spite of limited independence from Britain.

Chapter three, Tewfik Aclimandos' "The Activists in the Egyptian Army, 1936–52," is a major contribution to reshaping our perspective on a topic of tremendous importance to both the monarchical era and Egypt's post-1952 years. The 1936 military reforms facilitated the entry of Gamal 'Abd al-Nasser and Anwar al-Sadat into the Officer Academy. Exploring the broad, long-term impact of these reforms on the Egyptian officer corps, he challenges the accepted wisdom that the army was a Turco-Circassian institution before 1936, which the Egyptian petite bourgeoisie then took over. He finds that, even before 1936, native Egyptians of wealthy families as well as soldiers of modest origins already provided a large component of the officer corps. As such, the 1936 reforms produced a *relative* democratization of the admission to the academy but less promotion from the ranks, and a corresponding rise of officer susceptibility to politicization.

Aclimandos also examines the organizational dynamics of the clandestine officers' groups that ultimately led to the fall of the monarchy in 1952. While other scholars have pointed to one large group, he finds several, with the Free Officers who led the 1952 coup emerging as a fusion of nationalist and Muslim Brotherhood-inclined officers. Thus, in addition to providing a much-needed corrective, the author analyzes the implications of pre-1952 military dynamics for the struggles characterizing the first years of the 'Abd al-Nasser regime after 1952.

Part I concludes with Malak Badrawi's chapter on Egyptian public finances during the constitutional era. Examining a topic usually overlooked, Badrawi's chapter suggests that Egyptian administrators and politicians remembered quite well the lessons of the national bankruptcy from 1876–82. Key leaders affirmed throughout the period that successful financial management was a requirement for proving Egypt no longer needed foreign tutelage. Through parliamentary debates and various organs of public opinion Egyptians could indeed manage their own finances and maintain budget discipline, and were motivated by a nationalist economic intentionality—so much so that the coup-makers of 1952 were astonished to find Egyptian finances in quite good shape, with the treasury possessing a foreign currency surplus. Yet, political maneuvering among palace and parliamentary factions often determined the motives for, and tenor of, debates on the economy and budget. More mundane or self-serving political interests therefore combined with a larger nationalist desire to remain solvent. The fiscal tightfistedness which has been viewed as the culprit behind insufficient expansion of education and social services thus emerges in a new light.

Part II: Reconstructing Society, Recasting History opens with Lucie Ryzova's investigation of the 1930s–40s new *effendiya* phenomenon, often portrayed as a newly urbanized and educated middle class, with more traditional approaches to religion and cultural identity. For the first time shedding empirical light on this rising group, Ryzova demonstrates that while not an economic middle class, the new *effendiya* comprised an emerging public of educated young men from modest backgrounds, who viewed modernity through a Muslim and Arab lens. Just as important, however, they saw themselves as distinct from both the traditionalists and the westernized upper classes. In defining themselves in this way, they promoted new understandings of Egypt as a national community. Ryzova's examination of novels, memoirs, cinema, popular press, and other materials illuminates the new *effendiya*'s dual revolution, both against the traditional world from which they rose and the Egyptian upper class, whom they condemned on nationalist and socioeconomic grounds. Highlighting a specifically Egyptian modernity 'from below,' this chapter puts into sharp relief the social foundations of post-revolutionary Egypt. It thus engages in a fruitful critical dialogue with other emergent literature of the past decade.

Turning to the ideological component of the pre-1952 Egyptian state's modernization project, Barak A. Salmoni in chapter six shows how nationalist pedagogues employed education to cultivate a consciousness of civic duty and Egyptian greatness based on particular interpretations of Egypt's ancient and contemporary history. By and large, scholars have yet to systematically examine educational substance as ideological communication to rising generations during the constitutional monarchy. Key historiographical claims about an elite-focused and ideologically unconcerned state, or the 1930s–40s evolution of nationalist reorientations to the East and Islam, thus remain untested in a central arena for mass socialization. Yet pedagogical inquiry demonstrates that the state was indeed concerned about reaching the masses, utilizing conscious ideological communication to provide present-relevant lessons from a history which throughout the 1920s–52 period focused most of its curricular time on the pharaonic era and reign of Muhammad 'Ali, the latter serving as the continuator of meta-historic Egyptian glory and whose traits young Egyptians were expected to emulate.

In chapter seven, Anne-Claire Kerbœuf shifts from state institutions' functions in creating collective memory to the political and ideological role of a decisive event, the 26 January 1952 Cairo fire. The fire discredited the regime, prepared the way for coup six months later, and has been passionately debated by Egyptian journalists and historians. Yet the event still lacks detailed academic inquiry. Through new evidence and fresh interpretation, Kerbœuf argues that more than political plotting or elite intrigue, the Cairo fire manifested mass nationalist protest and was the first blow to the regime for reasons still under-appreciated. This is only a component of the story, however. In an insightful demonstration of ways the pre–'Abd al-Nasser years are variously remembered in Egypt, Kerbœuf illuminates how the nostalgia of today's 'liberal elite' for the former *Belle Époque* motivates them to commemorate the fire as the dramatic end of the monarchy, and not as a mass revolutionary day heralding the delegitimation of the Egyptian elites themselves.

The chapters in *Part III: Social Action, Social Discourse* reorient our perspective on Egypt before 1952 by highlighting the concern of Egyptians for socioeconomic reform and enfranchisement. Misako Ikeda returns in chapter eight to the domain of education, arguing that although Nasser-era policies regarding free public education and a unified primary curriculum receive much attention, the roots of these approaches emerged in the 1930s and 1940s. Discussing parliamentary, press, and professional pedagogical debates about equality of educational opportunity and the use of education to lessen socioeconomic gaps, Ikeda also shows the striking diversity of opinions, while she reminds the reader of the dynamism of professional pedagogical expression as well as the Wafd's role in these debates. As the post-1952 regime in many ways co-opted earlier efforts, this chapter again forces us to reassess the constitutional monarchy era.

In the same vein, Amy J. Johnson and Scott David McIntosh's chapter entitled "Empowering Women, Engendering Change: Aziza Hussein and Social Reform in Egypt" challenges the view of the pre-1952 period as bereft of meaningful governmental reform programs, while revealing women's social reform activism in Egypt during these years to have transcended upper class urban issues. In their revisionist approach based on painstaking research and Johnson's extensive interviews with Aziza Hussein and her colleagues, the authors examine the Cairo Women's Club under Aziza Hussein, which founded the country's first rural day-care center and spearheaded literacy campaigns, family planning, and rural industry. As against the notion of decaying social organs and an unconcerned government, the project involved active cooperation between the private and public sector, while setting a new standard for women's activism by empowering rural women as development agents. Not only does this chapter expose readers to Aziza Hussein as a pioneer in Egyptian social reform, but it also shows how these activities set a pattern of social reform followed after 1952.

Moving into another segment of society, chapter ten by Samia Kholoussi focuses on the 'mud bearers' of Egypt's 'liberal age.' These were the country's rural inhabitants, known as *fallahin*. During the 1920s–40s, they became many things in the literary, academic, and cinematographic imaginings of many people. For some, the Egyptian peasant embodied the authentic contiguity of the Egyptian character, from the days of the pharaohs to the twentieth century. In the eyes of others, peasant difficulties represented all that was wrong socioeconomically with Egypt, exposing the lack of concern for society among elites. For still others, the rural arena became a place to envision and re-envision dynamics of religion, gender, and development. Kholoussi examines all of these facets of how Egyptian writers and artists represented and imagined *fallahin* during the constitutional monarchy era, highlighting what they included while reminding us of what they excluded. Her work encourages us to conceive of the category of 'peasants' and elite imaginings about them in a more regionally comparative fashion.[27]

Part IV: Engendering a Modern Nation extends empirically and conceptually one of the most dynamic categories of Egyptian historiography that related to gender roles. Though studies of Egyptian nationalism posit a binary opposition between the 'public,' nationalist domain of male politics and the 'private,' cultural sphere of marriage and the family, in chapter eleven Hanan Kholoussy directs our attention to the post-1919 state's unparalleled intervention in marital relations. Making extensive use of debates in the press, in the legislature, and among intellectuals, Kholoussy argues that Egyptian nationalist reformers sought to redefine marriage in order to create a nuclear family as the foundation for a nation free of the perceived social ills of polygamy and male-initiated divorce. Likewise, she reveals how Egyptian writers used marriage to critique their society through prescriptions for modernity. This chapter contributes to our historical understanding of marriage in monarchical Egypt; it also demonstrates how this important social institution can be used to reconceptualize Egyptian nationalism, with theoretical ramifications for other national contexts.

Linking up with themes in Johnson and McIntosh's chapter, in chapter twelve Nancy Gallagher makes an important contribution to Egyptian social history before and during the parliamentary era by exposing the important role of female health workers *(hakimat)* in modern Egypt. Women in Egypt entered the medical and health professions much earlier than their counterparts elsewhere in the Middle East as a by-product of Muhammad 'Ali's modernization programs. Later, in the first half of the twentieth century, Egyptian women with the same societal commitment as Aziza Hussein worked in clinics, hospitals, and public health programs. In the context of a broad review of related literature, Gallagher evaluates Egyptian women's medical contributions, arguing for these accomplishments to attain a more prominent place in contemporary recastings of Egyptian social dynamics in the 1919–52 period.

Like Kerbœuf's work, Shaun Lopez's "Madams, Murderers, and the Media" (chapter thirteen) assesses the profound effects of a particular incident, this time to illuminate the role of the press in both reinforcing an Egypt-wide interest in quotidian events, and helping to craft a gendered mass culture. The 1920 Raya and Sakina serial murders attracted national attention, and the great number of Egyptians who followed press coverage of the murders underwent a re-examination of gender, class, and national identifications. Though usually discussed in the post-1952 context, as early as 1920 the beginnings of a 'mass-mediated' popular culture began to percolate through Egypt based on notions of acceptable public behavior.

Shifting to a different type of literary representation, in chapter fourteen Mervat Hatem examines the biographical writing of Mayy Ziyada, whose writings on Malak Hifni Nasif and 'A'isha Taymur sought to remind a mobilized public of women's contributions to the nation. Still, Ziyada reinforced ambivalent attitudes to women, since her biographies apportioned a derivative role to women in Egyptian national history. By critically reconsidering Ziyada's output and the activities of her chosen subjects, Hatem alerts readers to the problematic incorporation of women into the Egyptian nation, through the devaluation of gender difference and a stress on national homogeneity. Her contribution is important in its own right, but it also highlights the importance of viewing other geographical contexts in the Middle East and beyond through a similar analytical and methodological prism.

Part V: Art, Cinema, Literature, and Historiographical Memory integrates important topics into the mainstream of early twentieth century Egyptian history. Caroline Williams' general overview of 1919–52 visual artistic expression depicts how painting and sculpture were critical to the articulation of a national image. She also provides valuable insights into the *cursus honori* of Egyptian artists during these years, who emerge as truly international figures. Artistic pioneers of the 1920s and 1930s viewed Egypt in ways distinct from the Orientalists who preceded them. In the process, they established Egypt as unique among Arab countries. By also examining 1940s approaches expressing the subjective, psychological world of the masses, Williams demonstrates Egyptian artists' intensifying social concerns toward the end of the monarchy, rendering the visual arts a key barometer of societal dynamics.

Most studies of Egyptian cinema focus on the years after 1952; scholars thus know little about the development of Egyptian filmmaking.[28] Still, the golden age of Egyptian cinema largely preceded the 1950s, and its films are still popular today. Using one of the largest personal collections of film-related source materials outside of Egypt, Andrew Flibbert, in chapter sixteen, illuminates the problematics of moviemaking beyond the Euro-American ambit. In particular, he focuses on the relationship between state authority and filmmaking, as well as the role of foreign residents in Egyptian cinema, in order to point to the sources of the industry's early success. Through this political economy of cinema, Flibbert questions the conventional wisdom that the Egyptian monarchy was disinterested in film and revises contemporary historiography downplaying the significance of foreigners. Finally, Flibbert explores the origins of the 1940s 'crisis of the film industry' in Egypt, plotting out linkages among mass culture, economics, and politics in 1920s–40s Egypt through the prism of a heretofore underappreciated domain.

In the volume's final substantive chapter, Arthur Goldschmidt puts the preceding essays into larger historiographical perspective by discussing the most prominent historians of the period and highlighting the most dominant themes in scholarly coverage of 1919–52 Egyptian history, in English, French, and Arabic works. Examining the major themes and biases as they have evolved over time, Goldschmidt also provides an important guide for both beginning and advanced scholars and suggests paths for future research. He reminds us that both earlier and later works of scholarship, memoir, and popular history are equally important to conducting research today. As such, Goldschmidt's chapter embodies the intent of the volume as a whole. No single volume can investigate all aspects of a generation's worth of Egyptian history; yet by introducing new approaches to both underappreciated and popular categories of analysis—including domestic politics, foreign policy, the military, education, social reform, gender, class, popular media, art, and literature—*Re-Envisioning Egypt, 1919–1952* casts the period as fundamental to the country's twentieth-century trajectory, encouraging more inquiry into this era.

Notes

1   See Nelly Hanna, *Misr, umm al-dunya: qissat al-Qahira fi 1300 'am* (Cairo: Dar al-Fatah al-'Arabi, 1992).
2   See Abbas Amanat, *Pivot of the Universe: Nasir al-Din Shah and the Qajar Monarchy, 1831–1896* (Berkeley: University of California Press, 1997); Graham E. Fuller, *Center of the Universe: The Geopolitics of Iran* (Boulder: Westview Press, 1991); Busra Ersanli Behar, *Iktidar ve Tarih: Turkiye'de Resmi Tarih Tezinin Olusumu, 1929–1937* (Istanbul: AFA, 1992); Hugh Poulton, *Top Hat, Grey Wolf and Crescent: Turkish Nationalism and The Turkish Republic* (New York: New York University Press, 1997).
3   For aspects of these Egyptian processes demonstrating its explanatory centrality for the rest of the Middle East, see Afaf Lutfi al-Sayyid Marsot, *Egypt in the Reign of Muhammad Ali* (Cambridge: Cambridge University Press, 1984); Ehud R. Toledano, *State and Society in Mid-Nineteenth-Century Egypt* (Cambridge: Cambridge University Press, 1990); Khaled Fahmy, *All the Pasha's Men: Mehmed Ali, His Army, and the Making of Modern Egypt* (Cambridge: Cambridge

University Press, 1997); Kenneth M. Cuno, *The Pasha's Peasants: Land, Society, and Economy in Lower Egypt, 1740–1858* (Cambridge: Cambridge University Press, 1992); Nelly Hanna, ed., *The State and Its Servants: Administration in Egypt from Ottoman Times to the Present* (Cairo: The American University Press, 1995). For aspects of international relations and "Eastern Question" diplomacy, see L. Carl Brown, *International Politics in the Middle East: Old Rules, Dangerous Game* (Princeton: Princeton University Press, 1984); Fred Lawson, *The Social Origins of Egyptian Expansionism During the Muhammad Ali Period* (New York: Columbia University Press, 1992); David S. Landes, *Bankers and Pashas: International Finance and Economic Imperialism in Egypt* (Cambridge: Harvard University Press, 1979); Juan R. Cole, *Colonialism and Revolution in the Middle East: Social and Cultural Origins of Egypt's 'Urabi Movement* (Princeton: Princeton University Press, 1993).

4 For the press, see Ami Ayalon, *The Press in the Arab Middle East: A History* (New York: Oxford University Press, 1995) and Beth Baron, *The Women's Awakening in Egypt: Culture, Society, and the Press* (New Haven: Yale University Press, 1994); for intellectual change, see Albert Hourani's classic *Arabic Thought in the Liberal Age, 1798–1939* (London: Oxford University Press, 1962) as well as Louis Awad, *The Literature of Ideas in Egypt* (Atlanta: Scholars' Press, 1986).

5 One may note that though written in Zoya, Russia, the seminal manifesto of early Turkish nationalism, Yusuf Akçura's *Üç Tarz-i Siyaset* ("Three Styles of Politics") was published in the periodical *Türk* of Cairo, in 1904.

6 See Joel Gordon, *Nasser's Blessed Movement: Egypt's Free Officers and the July Revolution* (London: Oxford University Press, 1992); Kirk Beattie, *Egypt During the Nasser Years: Ideology, Politics, and Civil Society* (Boulder: Westview Press, 1994); James Jankowski, *Nasser's Egypt, Arab Nationalism and the United Arab Republic* (Boulder: Lynne Rienner Publishers, 2002); P.J. Vatikiotis, *Nasser and His Generation* (New York: St. Martin's, 1978).

7 Kirk J. Beattie, *Egypt During the Sadat Years* (New York: Palgrave, 2000).

8 Eberhard Kienle, *A Grand Delusion: Democracy and Economic Reform in Egypt* (New York: I.B. Tauris, 2001); Carrie Rosefsky Wickham, *Mobilizing Islam: Religion, Activism, and Political Change in Egypt* (New York: Columbia University Press, 2002).

9 Afaf Lutfi al-Sayyid Marsot, *Egypt's Liberal Experiment, 1922–1936* (Berkeley: University of California Press, 1977).

10 This sentiment is expressed quite well in Joel Gordon, *Nasser's Blessed Movement*. For Egypt in the 1948 Palestine War, see Fawaz A. Gerges, "Egypt and the 1948 War: Internal Conflict and Regional Ambition," in Eugene L. Rogan, ed., *The War for Palestine: Rewriting the History of 1948* (London: Cambridge University Press, 2001), 151–77.

11 Marius Deeb, *Party Politics in Egypt: The Wafd and its Rivals, 1919–1939* (London: Ithaca Press, 1979).

12 Misako Ikeda, "Sociopolitical Debates in Late Parliamentary Egypt" (Ph.D. diss., Harvard University, 1998).

13 For the Isma'il Sidqi interlude of rule-by-decree, see Malak Badrawi, *Isma'il Sidqi, 1875–1950: Pragmatism and Vision in Twentieth-Century Egypt* (Richmond: Curzon, 1996).

14 See Nathan J. Brown, *The Rule of Law in the Arab World: Courts in Egypt and the Gulf* (London: Cambridge University Press, 1997).

15 See Roger Owen and Sevket Pamuk, *A History of Middle East Economies in the Twentieth Century* (Cambridge: Harvard University Press, 1998), 30–50, 127–30.

16 Eric Davis, *Challenging Colonialism: Bank Misr and Egyptian Industrialization, 1920–1941* (Princeton: Princeton University Press, 1983); Robert Vitalis, *When Capitalists Collide: Business, Conflict, and the End of Empire in Egypt* (Berkeley: University of California Press, 1995); Roger Owen and Sevket Pamuk, *A History of Middle East Economies in the Twentieth Century* (Cambridge: Harvard University Press, 1998); Robert L. Tignor, *Capitalism and Nationalism*

at the End of Empire: State and Business in Decolonizing Egypt, Nigeria, and Kenya, 1945–1963 (Princeton: Princeton University Press, 1998); idem., State, Private Enterprise, and Economic Change in Egypt, 1918–1952 (Princeton: Princeton University Press, 1984); Zachary Lockman and Joel Beinin, Workers on the Nile: Nationalism, Communism, Islam and the Egyptian Working Class, 1882–1954 (Princeton: Princeton University Press, 1987).

17 See Barak A. Salmoni, "Pedagogies of Patriotism: Teaching Socio-Political Community in Twentieth-Century Turkish and Egyptian Education" (Ph.D. diss., Harvard University, 2002).

18 Joel Beinin, "Egypt: Society and Economy, 1923–1952," in M.W. Daly, ed, The Cambridge History of Egypt, volume 2: Modern Egypt, from 1517 to the End of the Twentieth Century (Cambridge: Cambridge University Press, 1998), 309–33.

19 Amy J. Johnson, Reconstructing Rural Egypt: Ahmed Hussein and the History of Egyptian Development (Syracuse: Syracuse University Press, 2004).

20 Margot Badran, Feminists, Islam, and Nation: Gender and the Making of Modern Egypt (Princeton: Princeton University Press, 1995); Baron, The Women's Awakening in Egypt; Marilyn Booth, May Her Likes be Multiplied: Biography and Gender Politics in Egypt (Berkeley: University of California Press, 2001); Lynn Haney and Lisa Pollard, eds., Families of a New World: Gender, Politics, and State Development in a Global Context (New York: Routledge, 2003); Clarissa Lee Pollard, "Nurturing the Nation: The Family Politics of the 1919 Egyptian Revolution" (Ph.D. diss., University of California at Berkeley, 1997); Mona L. Russell, "Creating the New Woman: Consumerism, Education, and National Identity in Egypt, 1863–1922" (Ph.D. diss., Georgetown University, 1997).

21 Augustus Richard Norton, ed., Civil Society in the Middle East (New York: E.J. Brill, 1996); Richard P. Mitchell, The Society of Muslim Brothers (London: Oxford University Press, 1969); James Jankowski, Egypt's Young Rebels: "Young Egypt," 1933–1952 (Stanford, CA: Hoover Institution Press, 1975).

22 For a long-awaited study comparing Turkey's Kemalist modernization to approaches in Reza Shah's Iran, see Touraj Atabaki and Erik J. Zurcher, Men of Order: Authoritarian Modernization under Ataturk and Reza Shah (London: IB Tauris, 2004).

23 Sibel Bozdogan and Resat Kasaba, eds., Rethinking Modernity and National Identity in Turkey (Seattle: University of Washington Press, 1997); Stephanie Cronin, ed, The Making of Modern Iran: State and Society under Riza Shah, 1921–1941 (New York: Routledge Curzon, 2003).

24 See Yehoshua Porath, In Search of Arab Unity, 1930–1945 (London: Cass, 1986); Barry M. Rubin, The Arab States and the Palestine Conflict (Syracuse: Syracuse University Press, 1981).

25 For crossover educational personnel of this type, see M. Khayri Harbi, Education in Egypt (U.A.R.) in the Twentieth Century (Cairo: General Organization for Government Printing, 1960); Abu al-Futouh Ahmad Radwan, Old and New Forces in Egyptian Education (New York: Bureau of Publications, Teachers College, Columbia University, 1951); Isma'il M. al-Qabbani, Dirasat fi masa'il al-ta'lim (Cairo: Maktabat al-Nahda al-Misriya, 1951); idem., Dirasat fi tanzim al-ta'lim bi-Misr (Cairo: Maktabat al-Nahda al-Misriya, 1958); Amir Boktor, School and Society in the Valley of the Nile (Cairo: Elias Modern Press, 1936).

26 Johnson, Reconstructing Rural Egypt.

27 For comparisons within the region during this era, see M. Asim Karaömerlioglu, "The People's Houses and the Cult of the Peasant in Turkey," Middle Eastern Studies 34: 4 (October, 1998), 67–91.

28 For the post-1952 years see Joel Gordon, Revolutionary Melodrama: Popular Film and Civic Identity in Nasser's Egypt (Chicago: University of Chicago Press, 2001).

Part I

Reassessing Polity
and Diplomacy

1   The Generation of 1919

James Whidden

Nineteen-nineteen was a critical year in Egyptian history. Early that year a national delegation *(wafd)* issued revolutionary proclamations demanding Egypt's complete independence from the British Protectorate. But the *wafd* was more than a challenge to the British occupation. The proclamations also questioned the authority and legitimacy of the ruling dynasty, as represented by Sultan Ahmad Fu'ad. Massive demonstrations in March and April of 1919 legitimized the emergent *wafd*'s claim to represent the national will, beginning a political battle between liberal or democratic nationalists and the more conservative monarchists. By 1924 the monarchists had introduced Islamist ideology into politics, transforming Egypt's political and cultural landscape.

Likewise, the events of 1919 altered relations between the British and the Egyptians. The British government delegated Lord Milner, the colonial secretary, to head an inquiry into the causes of what was popularly referred to as the '1919 Revolution.' In a remarkably bold move, Milner initiated negotiations on a treaty that would recognize Egypt's independence while safeguarding Britain's strategic interests.[1] However, when the negotiations split Egyptian political society between moderates and radicals, the British responded with the unilateral declaration of Egyptian independence in 1922. Shortly afterwards a constitutional commission was convened by moderate politicians acceptable to the British. The 'liberal constitution' of 1923 declared Egyptian national sovereignty, the supremacy of the national will through elected parliaments, and established the principles of individual civil and political rights. As a consequence, studies of this period have remarked upon the dramatic shift of Egyptian political identities from the old regime as represented by the Muhammad 'Ali dynasty toward the idea of Egypt as a nation. According to these interpretations of the 'revolution,' the 1920s witnessed the apogee of political consensus upon liberal nationalism before the emergence of Islamism and Arab nationalism in the 1930s and 1940s.[2] The emergence of these later forms of nationalism has been credited to the international context, particularly the persistence of French and British colonialism in the region.[3]

Beginning with the formation of a modern political society over three generations, this chapter traces the development of rival ideological parties in the years after 1919. Formed in 1922, the moderate character of the Liberal Constitutional Party marked continuity with the pre-war period. Emphasizing continuity in this section of the chapter underlines the radicalism of the Wafd Party. During the first sessions of parliament in 1924 issues such as class and gender, as well as treaty negotiations, intensified political contests. The final section is a consideration of the Union (Ittihad) Party. This party deepened ideological cleavages by making monarchy and Islam the symbols of the new Egyptian nation state.

Less emphasis has been placed upon ideology than other factors in the analysis of Egyptian politics in this period.[4] Nationalists argued that in a kind of divide and rule strategy the British strengthened the position of Egypt's ruling dynasty to weaken the Wafd and subsequently the British contributed to the formation of the Liberal Constitutional Party and the Ittihad Party for the same purpose.[5] This argument has been echoed in works of scholarship, according to which the "hopes of 1919" were crushed by the alliance of colonial power with parties that represented large landholding interests and the ruling dynasty.[6] However, British power was not so overwhelming. The British only exploited ideological differences that already existed within Egyptian political society. The British did not invent or even control these forces. Secondly, it has been argued that political parties were vehicles for the political interests of elite politicians, without any basis in ideological politics. Accordingly, the Wafd did not represent a revolutionary political program; rather, its character as an elite organization immobilized it as a force for radical change.[7] Emphasis upon elite politics tends to discount the importance of 1919 as a moment of political change. Indeed, it is worth considering how a nationalist organization that championed lower class groups, women, and youth in 1919 was co-opted to an elite type of politics. To what degree was this outcome determined by the elite structure of Egyptian political society? This chapter will argue that the co-optation was the result of political party rivalries and ideological contests and not determined by colonial interference or elite social structures. Also, these conclusions question the assumption that the 1919 Revolution established ideological consensus within Egyptian political society. Rather than consensus, it intensified debates upon Egypt's political identity. It is this disputation that defines the generation of 1919 — the inability to find consensus on what should be Egypt's modern political identity. Nineteen-nineteen was thus a most important turning point, after which the articulation of Egypt's identity revolved around questions of Islamism and secularism, democracy and authoritarianism.

Political Generations

Historical research on nineteenth-century Egypt demonstrates that a modern political society evolved over three generations, expanding and integrating new social groups throughout the century. The first generation of Egypt's modern political society formed during the reign of Muhammad 'Ali, securely under the patronage of the ruler and therefore marked by a great degree of loyalty to the ruling house. The second generation formed with the development of a landholding class that had gained more autonomy from the ruler.[8] The third generation emerged with the creation of a modern type of bureaucratic state that included professional and administrative sectors. As Lucie Ryzova shows in the opening sections of chapter five, this third generation of political society is collectively known as the *effendiya*, partially correlated with the middle classes, but in particular the liberal professions.[9] This third generation — the *mutatarbishun*, or tarboosh wearers — was particularly open to intellectual and cultural change and was largely responsible for making the revolutionary calls of 1919.

Karl Mannheim has said that age cohorts fragment into rival "generation units" and that these units compete for cultural dominance.[10] Changes in the composition of Egyptian political society over three generations created distinctly different political groups and ideologies by the early twentieth century. Many of the most influential members of political society in 1919 gained status and power from close association with the monarchy. Indeed, a leading representative of political society in 1919, 'Adli Yakan, was descended from a first generation political family. Reformists and liberal nationalists were more often descended from second and third generation families that had profited from land reforms in the mid-nineteenth century, as well as the sale of lands belonging to the ruling family after the British occupation in 1882. With the emergence of Egypt's third generation, middle class families entered into political society. These families profited from the expansion of the bureaucracy, the professions, and the educational system. The third generation produced more radical and anti-colonial types of political tactics and ideologies by the early twentieth century. This process of change meant that fundamental ideological cleavages divided political society. The popular demonstrations of 1919, followed by constitutional reforms afterwards, highlighted these cleavages.

1st Generation		2nd Generation		3rd Generation
Muhammad 'Ali Dynasty			Ahmad Fu'ad (b. 1868)	
Yakan Family			'Adli Yakan (b. 1864)	
			Sa'd Zaghlul (b. 1860)	
			Lutfi al-Sayyid (b. 1872)	
			Mustafa Kamil (b. 1874)	
1800	**1825**	**1850**	**1875**	**1900**

Political generations during the Muhammad 'Ali Dynastic Period

Egypt's third political generation included men born in the 1860s, such as Sa'd Zaghlul, 'Adli Yakan, Husayn Rushdi, and Muhammad Sa'id, who attended new western-type schools and took up positions within the bureaucracy or professions. These men witnessed the deposition of the Egyptian ruler, Khedive Isma'il, in 1879 and the imposition of a new ruler, Khedive Tawfiq, under pressure from the French and British. During the colonial period (1882–1922) some of these men called for a restoration of the pre-colonial status quo, as it had existed during the later stages of Isma'il's rule when Egypt was an autonomous part of the Ottoman Empire. Others looked forward to the creation of a 'new Egypt,' that is to say a territorial nation-state governed according to the principles of liberal nationalism. This was particularly true of younger men born in the 1870s, such as Mustafa Kamil and Ahmad Lutfi al-Sayyid.[11] But even Kamil and Lutfi al-Sayyid diverged on tactics to achieve that goal. The nationalist historian 'Abd al-Rahman al-Rafi'i suggests that the divergence was implicit in political programs alternately defined by the concepts of evolution (*nahda*) and revolution (*thawra*).[12] Normally translated as renaissance or awakening, al-Rafi'i interpreted *nahda* in this way to underline the correspondence between cultural change in Egypt and cultural develop-ments in Europe, notably Social Darwinism. Perhaps more important for al-Rafi'i were tactical differences. In the period before 1919 the People's (Umma) Party represented the evolutionary orientation, calling for orderly social progress rather than revolutionary change. Tactically this meant accepting the British occupation as a necessary stage in Egypt's evolution. Kamil's Nationalist (Watani) Party demanded immediate independence and thus represented the revolutionary alternative, although tactically he chose ideological persuasion rather than force.

In 1919, the divergent political paths of evolution and revolution were not subsumed into a single, national 'movement,' but continued to repre-sent alternate ideological orientations. As a prominent representative of Egypt's third generation of politicians, Sa'd Zaghlul was a supporter of the Umma Party and a proponent of liberal nationalism. On 13 November 1918 Zaghlul, together with 'Abd al-'Aziz Fahmi and 'Ali Sha'rawi, visited the British high commissioner, Sir Reginald Wingate, demanding that Egypt's case for independence be heard at the post-war peace conference in Paris. Wingate responded with the standard evolutionary argument that Egypt's high illiteracy rate made it unprepared for self-government. Fahmi replied that even in Britain only a handful of ministers had the confidence of the nation. Similarly, in Egypt a government could be formed from among the elite, which he described as a thousand capable men.[13] Discussions between Egyptian politicians and British agents in Egypt were thus made within a common evolutionary discourse. Another indicator of the evolutionary, rather than the revolutionary, orientation of the Wafd at its inception was that it had the support of leading representatives of first generation fami-lies, such as Prime Minister Husayn Rushdi and his ministers, 'Adli Yakan and 'Abd al-Khaliq Tharwat. These men's families had taken an active part in the formation of an autonomous Egyptian state from the early nine-teenth century. Politicians with a pedigree traceable to first generation families were, however, conservative. In particular, they were concerned that the powers of the ruler not be purely symbolic, since their own power was linked with the dynasty.[14]

After massive demonstrations in 1919, the British government replaced Wingate with General Edmond Allenby. In early 1920 Allenby reported to the Foreign Secretary, Lord Curzon, that Zaghlul was a nationalist com-mitted to independence and a representative type of government. Allenby contrasted Zaghlul to Muhammad Sa'id, who served as prime minister from May to November 1919. "The one [Sa'id] is a Turk with pan-Islamic sympathies; the other [Zaghlul] has founded a movement on purely Egyptian lines and pretends to be disinterested in the fate of Turkey."[15] Allenby's report suggests that Zaghlul represented a transformation from Ottoman and Islamic to liberal and nationalist political identities. However, this transformation was incomplete. Sa'id's attitudes suggest that some prominent members of political society were loyal to the ruling dynasty and suspicious of more radical nationalists. From April 1919 Husayn Rushdi and 'Adli Yakan emerged as the leaders of a conservative opposition to Zaghlul. After negotiations were opened with the British in 1920, Rushdi and Yakan rejected Zaghlul's uncompromising nationalist stance in the negotiations. When Yakan formed a ministry in March 1921 and opened treaty negotiations with the British, Zaghlul complained that Yakan was a "Turk" and families like his would "lose in the end."[16]

One important source of conflict within Egyptian political society was the issue of treaty negotiations with the British. Yet political differences went beyond the nationalist issue. First and third generation families represented different political principles and tactics. A common critique of Zaghlul was that in his bid for power he courted lower class groups, which the more conservative politicians regarded as aberrant behavior. Muhammad Sa'id accused Zaghlul of betraying all those with whom he had ever formed an alliance, an opinion shared by many liberal nationalists.[17] The prominent liberal intellectual Taha Husayn argued in his memoirs that Zaghlul was not motivated by any political principle, but simply his own desire for power. Tactically, Zaghlul rejected compromise and bilateral negotiations with the British while courting the masses.[18] As a result of these tactics Yakan and Rushdi allied with the younger liberals to form a powerful opposition to the Wafd. The opposition did not seek to re-orient Egypt toward the Ottoman Empire, since the empire was dying with the triumph of the Turkish nationalist leader, Mustafa Kemal Ataturk. Rather, its aim was to establish the new Egyptian nation-state on principles acceptable to conservatives and the Muhammad 'Ali dynasty, while establishing a bilateral basis for negotiations with the British over independence.

The coalition of conservatives and liberals took shape with the British unilateral declaration of Egyptian independence on 28 February 1922. The declaration created a sovereign Egyptian state under the grandson of Khedive Isma'il, Ahmad Fu'ad, who took the new title of king. At the same time, the declaration allowed liberals and conservatives to work out the details of the political system through a constitutional commission. The declaration also safeguarded British interests, known as the 'four reserved points' (Egyptian foreign defense policy, the Suez Canal, the Sudan, and the 'rights' of foreign nationals and minorities residing in Egypt), which were to be set aside for the moment and discussed in future negotiations.

The Liberal Constitutional Party

The liberalism of the 1920s was a continuation of a political ideology begun by the Umma Party in the pre-war period. The leading ideologue of the Umma Party, Ahmad Lutfi al-Sayyid, adopted the liberalism of John Stuart Mill as a model of 'advancement' from a 'traditional' to a 'modern' society and political system.[19] As Charles D. Smith has argued, Egyptian liberals were concerned with orderly social progress and the establishment of a modernizing nation-state.[20] Egyptian liberals and British agents found common cause on the principle of evolutionary 'advancement.' Colonial authorities looked favorably upon liberal nationalism because it strongly identified with modern, western culture and submerged the religious and ethnic characteristics of the nation, which British agents regarded as threats to the British occupation. Strongly evolutionary in their assumptions, colonial agents in Egypt emphasized the need to develop a 'modern' individualistic society. Edward Said's *Orientalism* has shown that these types of 'orientalist' descriptions enabled Europeans to represent western modernity as fundamentally different and superior to non-western cultures.[21] Lord Cromer, the British consul general in Egypt between 1883 and 1907, claimed that Egyptian mentalities were essentially irrational as compared to the 'rational' West.[22] Political systems were also compared. Lord Dufferin, who wrote Egypt's 'organic law' in 1883, contrasted European 'constitutional government' to Middle Eastern 'despotism.'[23] Yet, it should be underlined that some Egyptians also assumed that society had to 'evolve' modern types of social and political institutions before self-government was practical. Like the conservative monarchists, many liberals abandoned the Wafd after it adopted violent tactics that posed a threat to political and social order.

After 1919 the principles of evolutionary 'advancement' and 'progress' continued to inform British analysis of Egyptian society and politics. Lord Milner's report on the causes of the demonstrations of 1919 claimed that social evolution in Egypt was 'atrophied' because the population was ninety-two percent illiterate and lacked "social and moral training." Therefore, "parliamentary government under the present social conditions means oligarchical government, and, if too little controlled, it would be likely to show too little regard for the interests of the majority of the

Egyptian people."[24] Milner's report nevertheless advised a restoration of Egyptian self-government, claiming that the radical nationalists of the Wafd had won the support of the majority of the population. Allenby and other British agents in Cairo supported Milner's analysis of the political situation. Reginald Patterson, the adviser to the Ministry of Education, said that the pre-war policy of educating *fallahin* (Egyptians of peasant origins) had undermined the hereditary authority of the 'pashas' (elite politicians of Ottoman origin). By *fallahin* he referred to second and third generation Egyptians, like Zaghlul, who had been integrated into a ruling group of first generation families. Likewise, the adviser to the Ministry of Justice, Maurice Amos, described Zaghlul as representative of a new 'middle class.'[25] Patterson and Amos saw Lord Cromer's policies in the pre-war period as bringing about social and ultimately political change, which undermined the authoritarian politics of first generation political families, notably the ruling dynasty itself. For Amos, Egyptian political society was no longer dichotomous, divided between two nations, 'Turkish' and 'Egyptian,' aristocratic and peasant, but a nation divided between two political parties. According to Amos, 'Adli Yakan's party included the "more educated and older members of the professions" whereas Zaghlul's party consisted of the "Azharians ['ulama'], the students and the younger and less reflective members of the bar and other professions."[26] In consideration of these reports from his advisers, Allenby warned the Foreign Office that there was a serious risk of "revolution" if concessions were not made to the nationalists. When Allenby offered his resignation, the Foreign Office in London relented and allowed Allenby to issue his unilateral declaration of independence in February 1922.[27]

It is important to recognize that Allenby and his advisers redefined Egyptian politics in terms of party and ideological politics. Taken together with treaty negotiations, this marked a new stage in British-Egyptian relations. However, Allenby's tactics after 1922 also show some remarkable continuities with the pre-1922 period. According to Patterson and Amos, the British occupation of Egypt had always depended upon the cooperation of Egyptian politicians. The problem was how to restore the pre-1922 British-Egyptian relationship in the context of the post-1922 constitutional system of representative government and electoral politics. Allenby's reports to the Foreign Office in 1922 proposed the formation of a "party of order" composed of the "more level-headed of the professional classes" and the landowners, large and small, "who are not however a politically-minded class." The combination of professionals and rural landlords would, according to Allenby, result in "the election of a strong candidate in nearly all of the rural constituencies" in future elections.[28] These reports indicate that Allenby actively supported the formation of a party of landholders and professionals, which took the name Liberal Constitutional Party when it was formed on 30 October 1922. The party included prominent representatives of the new generation of Egyptian politicians, such as 'Abd al-'Aziz Fahmi, Ahmad Lutfi al-Sayyid, Muhammad Mahmud, and 'Ali Mahir, as well as representatives of the old 'Turkish' elite, notably 'Adli Yakan.

British support for a new party to counter the Wafd in elections might be viewed as colonial divide and rule strategy. However, it could be argued that party politics was a product of fundamental ideological differences among the Egyptians. Egyptian liberals had to confront the same sort of problems that troubled colonial agents, namely the problem of maintaining political order in the context of social and political change. Allenby described the new electoral law of 1923 (drafted by Egyptians, with European legal advisers) as designed to leave the "final selection of members [of parliament] in the hands of a few who would be susceptible to the pressure of rich reactionaries."[29] The electoral law was not designed to give a free expression to the popular will, but to control political participation and electoral results. According to Allenby, the new electoral system favored rural landlords who were, in Allenby's words, "ignorant and reactionary," while the intellectuals and radicals were concentrated in the cities.[30] Allenby's comments suggest that radical ideologies were a product of the urban middle classes, which British agents and Egyptian liberals wanted to counter-balance with the rural vote where landlords held great sway over their tenants and small landholders. That British agents and Egyptian politicians sought to reconcile democratic elections with political patronage indicates a type of political discourse current in Britain and Egypt in the 1920s. In each case new political parties had arisen that challenged historic types of power structures. In Egypt the Wafd represented that challenge; in England, the Labour Party. To meet the challenge in Egypt the Liberal Constitutional Party took the idea of patronage as the organizational basis of the party, as Allenby's commentary has already indicated.

Clearly, some Egyptians wanted to restrict political participation to the few. Consider the response of the Liberal Constitutional Party to the electoral victory of the Wafd Party in 1924. Galavanized by a Wafd-led purge of Liberal Constitutional politicians and supporters from all government positions in early 1924, the Liberals joined a coalition against the Wafd Party in 1925. The coalition was formed after the 1924 assassination of the British governor general of the Sudan, Sir Lee Stack, which resulted in the collapse of the Wafd government. Afterwards, the Liberals took up positions in the government of Ahmad Ziwar, a monarchist, who relied upon them to assist in the redrafting of the electoral law. An electoral commission was formed that included 'Abd al-'Aziz Fahmi, the president of the Liberal Constitutional Party, Muhammad 'Ali 'Alluba, and Tawfiq Doss. The draft law drawn up by the committee resembled electoral laws in Italy, Spain, Holland, and Denmark and was therefore designed to conform to the more conservative states of Europe. The law proposed to increase the minimum voting age from twenty-one to twenty-five years and apply restrictive property qualifications, which would disenfranchise ten to fifteen per cent of the existing male electorate.[31]

The task of arguing the case for electoral reform fell to 'Abd al-'Aziz Fahmi in a speech to the National Bar of the Court of Appeal on 17 March 1925. In a commentary that paraphrased and supported Fahmi's argument, Muhammad Husayn Haykal, the editor of the Liberal Constitutional Party paper *al-Siyasa* claimed that "Western democracy had proven to be 'too rich' for Egyptian stomachs."[32] Haykal claimed that the electoral law should be modified to conform to the "nature of the Egyptian nation." This idea indicates the influence of Herbert Spencer's Social Darwinism, as well as Hippolyte Taine's theory of 'naturalism.' Taine had argued that societies and cultures were determined by natural forces. An important study of Muhammad Husayn Haykal's thought by Israel Gershoni and James P. Jankowski suggests that Haykal developed his understanding of naturalism to establish the connection between the territory of Egypt and a specifically Egyptian mentality. According to their interpretation, Haykal argued that the "natural environment" of the Nile Valley molded a homogeneous "race," characteristically calm, benevolent, and obedient, which bred an unchanging social and political culture.[33] But naturalism served quite a different purpose in 1925. It amounted to a defense of authoritarian politics. Haykal and 'Abd al-'Aziz Fahmi claimed that an electoral law that restricted the vote to the few was the one most fitting to Egypt's stage of social and political evolution.[34] By applying evolutionism and naturalism to the issue of electoral reform Haykal could argue that a new electoral law would "guarantee the representation of the vital elements of the Egyptian nation" and "enable the nation to enjoy its constitutional rights according to its physical system and nature."[35] Naturalism, like Social Darwinism, demonstrated that politics should fit the 'real' nature or historical evolution of Egypt. To understand that 'nature,' Haykal rephrased the old colonial question: What was the evolutionary stage of Egyptian society and what political system best corresponded to it? 'Abd al-'Aziz Fahmi made a similar observation in his speech to the national bar: "I worked with the constitutional commission . . . but practice has proved that the government is too big for the body."[36]

The Wafd Party journal, *al-Balagh*, highlighted the correspondence between Egyptian liberalism and British colonialism by claiming that Fahmi's argument for a new electoral law echoed Reginald Wingate's response to the demand made by the Wafd for self-government in 1918. Wingate had said, "If an infant were given more food than necessary he would suffer from indigestion."[37] The article in *al-Balagh* asked if the "vital powers" of the nation consisted of the educated class alone, noting that the new electoral law would deny the vote to the agricultural and laboring classes, that is to say 90 percent of the population.[38] *Al-Balagh*, framed its argument in socialist language, arguing that politics was not a means for the elite to establish its hegemony, but a struggle between classes. Society, in this argument, was not a product of nature, but of a political struggle. According to the critiques in *al-Balagh* the electoral commission planned to restrict the vote to the narrowest possible 'social circle,' eliminating representatives of the lower classes completely at the final stage of voting.[39] The electoral law would undermine the 'social system' and, according to the writer in *al-Balagh*, revive a system of "caste distinctions" in these "communistic times." Thus, the "aristocrats" of the Liberal Constitutional Party were engaged in a kind of "class warfare," by distinguishing in the "text of the constitution" between the rich and the poor.[40] The argument in *al-Balagh* also illustrated that the liberal "aristocracy" was not hereditary, but the product of a generation that had gained social prominence in the latter part of the nineteenth century with the formation of a new educational system and an expanded bureaucracy. The Wafd paper reminded its readers that Fahmi was hardly of aristocratic pedigree. He was the son of a *qadi* (judge) authorized to write marriage contracts. Similarly, 'Alluba was the son of a legal secretary and Doss the son of a bookseller in Asyut.[41]

Although the Liberal Constitutionals represented a new generation of politicians, they nevertheless defended the privileges of the elite. The content of their ideology suggests that the liberals had been integrated into elite political society and thus defended its privileges and interests. Haykal's theories on the social system, whether expressed in the language of naturalism or evolutionism, had a political purpose. They were designed to block the election of a Wafd government and the democratic type of politics it represented. Likewise, when the Wafd ideologues employed the concept of 'aristocracy,' it was not meant to describe a social class because the members of the Liberal Constitutional Party and the Wafd Party were mostly from the same 'class.' Rather, the term 'aristocratic' designated a style of politics. The juxtaposition of aristocracy and democracy represented a political contest between 'generation units.'

The Wafd Party

Regardless of the upper class or elite social status of its political leadership, the Wafd represented a class-based and democratic political program in opposition to the elitism of the Liberal Constitutional Party. And although the Wafd claimed a special status as a national delegation, ideological and tactical differences with the liberals meant that the Wafd took shape as a distinct political party by 1923. On constitutional issues the Wafd was to the left of the Constitutional Liberal Party, although the Liberals denied this. The liberals claimed that the Wafd did not have an ideological position; rather the Wafd exploited religious symbols to control popular opinion. Echoing liberal critiques, historical research on the Wafd Party has attempted to prove that its tactics were designed to fit into existing sectarian, lineage, or regional social structures. It has been argued that these tactics emptied nationalist ideology of its liberal content.[42] According to these critiques, the Wafd Party became a vehicle of class or group interests variously described as elite, bourgeois, and landholding. Yet between 1919 and 1926 the Wafd was not the party that represented elite interests explicitly. Rather, as this chapter has shown, this was the distinctive trait of the Liberal Constitutional Party. Nor did the Wafd Party explicitly represent religious politics. The Ittihad Party represented that tendency, as will be argued.

Although the Wafd was triumphant in the national elections of 1923 and 1924, the issue of treaty negotiations, as well as cultural and ideological differences, continued to divide political society. The British were not indifferent to the potential for political discord. Shortly after the Wafd's electoral victory, the English-language press predicted that the Wafd Party would divide between those "discontented with the existing state of things and those with an instinctive distrust of change." The voice of the British community in Egypt, the *Egyptian Gazette*, argued that the election of "fallahin" and "Egyptians of urban ancestry" threatened the status of the old Turkish "ruling caste."[43] The new prime minister and leader of the Wafd Party, Sa'd Zaghlul, was also aware of the problem of political division. He thus attempted to form a coalition cabinet that safeguarded the interests of the monarchists. Notably, he appointed Muhammad Sa'id to the cabinet and allowed the king to block the appointment of more radical nationalists, such as 'Ali Shamsi, who was a former member of the Watani Party. Yet, it is striking how rapidly the Wafd government unraveled after the convening of parliament in March 1924.

Shamsi resented Zaghlul's concessions to the monarchy, which had frustrated his own political ambitions. As a result, he led a faction in the parliament that orchestrated the election of Ahmad Muhammad Khashaba as the vice-president of the lower house. The vote amounted to a personal defeat for Zaghlul, who had supported the candidacy of Wisa Wasif. Shamsi and Khashaba mustered the support of Wafdist deputies from rural Upper Egypt. These rural landlords (*fallahin*) formed a coherent group with considerable leverage within the parliament.[44] Moreover, they were resentful of the power of the urban *effendiya* at the core of the Wafd Party, many of whom, like Wasif, were Coptic Christians. Cultural issues were thus an important consideration. At the same time, the deputies from Upper Egypt were highly nationalistic. Thus, by claiming that Zaghlul had surrendered Egyptian national interests in negotiations with the British, Shamsi could sway the parliament away from Zaghlul. Members of the formerly influential Watani Party also saw this issue as an opportunity to revive their political fortunes. For instance, Amin al-Rafi'i joined the opposition to Zaghlul by demanding a statement of principle on the issue of negotiations with the British.[45] Shamsi and Rafi'i attacked Zaghlul principally on the issue of the reserved points, which were described as an illegal imposition upon the nation's natural right to self-determination. The king also exploited this issue when he entered into the contest by making a reference to the complete independence of Egypt and the Sudan in the speech from the throne. The speech won the king a resounding cheer from the assembled parliamentarians: "Long live the king of Egypt and the Sudan." In a revealing passage, a Foreign Office report conjectured that the king had introduced the issue of the Sudan to "wreck the Wafd government on the rock of British imperialism."[46]

The sessions of parliament that followed the speech from the throne resulted in uproarious debates, led by Rafi'i, on the language of the speech and its implications for negotiations. Zaghlul responded by first lecturing the deputies on parliamentary procedure and then threatened to resign from office on 19 March. In a cartoon entitled "The illiterate deputies take their parliamentary examination," the satirical journal *Kashkul* depicted the parliament as a classroom, with Zaghlul dressed in the effendi attire of suit and tarboosh lecturing an unruly 'class' of rural notables dressed in *gallabiya* and turban (fig. 1.1).[47] The cartoon played upon cultural differences between the westernized effendis and rural notables wearing Egyptian dress, who were clearly suspicious of the *effendiya*. The episode suggests that politicians could manipulate cultural differences between the effendi and the rural notable to build political factions, even after the triumphant victory of the Wafd Party in popular elections.

Another way to assess the impact of cultural values upon national politics is to consider the reaction of the Wafd Party to feminist demands. Huda Sha'rawi, founding member of the Wafdist Women's Committee and the Egyptian Feminist Union in 1923, could make her demands for female suffrage within the framework of universal civil and political rights enshrined in the Constitution of 1923. Yet her demands had complex cultural and political ramifications. She recalled in her memoirs that Wasif Ghali attempted to dissuade her from her public unveiling at the port of Alexandria in July 1923 because, as he had warned, "the people would never accept it." The unveiling of Sha'rawi's face (not hair) occurred on the ship that returned Zaghlul to Egypt after his exile. But while Zaghlul supported Sha'rawi's demonstration and was personally in favor of women's emancipation, his own wife, Safiya, disembarked the ship wearing a veil.[48] Sha'rawi's memoirs indicate that Zaghlul and Ghali were aware that prevalent cultural values did not correspond with their own. Unveiling could be accepted in principle, but not in society. Therefore, although Sha'rawi led a female demonstration at the opening of parliament in March 1924 demanding the vote for women, the Wafd Party stalled in its reform of the electoral franchise and ultimately revised the electoral law in August 1924 to the exclusion of women. Clearly the Wafd Party was sensitive to prevailing cultural values on this question, even if this meant a tactical retreat from liberal nationalism.

Zaghlul's policy alienated Sha'rawi. As a result, after a debate in parliament on 25 May on the question of treaty negotiation, Sha'rawi rebuked Zaghlul for failing to make an unequivocal statement concerning the status of the Sudan. Although she voiced her dissent on treaty negotiations, her position was certainly influenced by Zaghlul's stance on women's political rights. Sha'rawi did not renounce her commitment to the national cause as a result of the Wafd Party's position on the women's issue. Instead, she became a vocal critic of Zaghlul on nationalist issues, placing the women's movement securely on the side of unflinching patriotism while challenging Zaghlul's nationalist credentials. The contest between Zaghlul and Sha'rawi was depicted by *Kashkul* in a cartoon that showed Zaghlul as an old, tired organ grinder parading in the street, while Sha'rawi leaned from the window of her residence emptying a slop bucket on his head. The image enraged Zaghlul, who had the editor of the journal arrested and imprisoned. The cartoon is noteworthy because the image itself reinforced patriarchal notions of women's place within the home, as opposed to aging patriarchs, who paraded in the public street.[49] Nevertheless, the cartoon indicates that Sha'rawi had made Zaghlul pay a political price for his retreat from liberal principle on gender issues. Thus, the cartoon indicated the way politics had made patriarchy more than just a system of cultural values, but a political issue that fitted into national debates.

Zaghlul's betrayal of the feminists indicated the compromises on liberal principles the Wafd made to build consensus within political society. While apparently oriented toward the issue of national independence, political contests revealed a subtext of cultural values. Sha'rawi, like Shamsi and Rafi'i, had her own motives, yet assailed Zaghlul on the issue of treaty negotiations. This tactic pushed Zaghlul toward a unilateral position in negotiations with the British. Reverting to the militant tactics characteristic of the years between 1919 and 1921, the Wafd organized assaults upon estates of former government officials in the provinces of Gharbiya and Minufiya, which occurred in March and April 1924. Carrying banners, the revolutionaries proclaimed the redistribution of land to the less privileged classes. Also, in Alexandria, there were industrial disturbances heralded by manifestos with republican and communist tones.[50]

It is difficult to determine to what degree Zaghlul controlled these events. British intelligence reports claimed that Zaghlul described the parliamentary opposition as "*très rouge*" (very red) and that the revolutionaries "bound his hands" in any future treaty negotiations.[51] Allenby reported to the Foreign Office that Zaghlul would overcome the virulent radicals in the parliament if the British government withdrew British troops from Egypt and conceded sovereignty of the Sudan to Egypt. However, the Foreign Office denied that Allenby's private discussions with Zaghlul on the treaty negotiations had any bearing upon government policy. Meanwhile, a War Office committee of imperial defense advised the establishment of air bases at Heliopolis and Helwan, which were suburbs of Cairo.[52] Without any substantial concessions on the part of the British, it would appear that Zaghlul defended his political status as national leader by radicalizing his own position.

The events of the summer of 1924 were indicative of this trend. Before departing to London for treaty negotiations in July of 1924, Zaghlul made a speech honoring the leaders of the tramway workers union, particularly 'Abd al-Rahman Fahmi, who had been made responsible for organizing labor organizations. Attending also was Hasan Nafi, a lawyer similarly involved in labor politics. Joel Beinin and Zachary Lockman have described Fahmi and Nafi as indicative of the "developing relationship between the bourgeois nationalism of the Wafd and the emerging working class."[53] While this might be an accurate assessment of the social groups involved, it hardly does justice to the political stakes. By appearing in this venue and identifying his party with the working classes, Zaghlul identified himself with the *"rouges."* Because this was a political meeting, there were no workers present. Rather, government officials, notables, merchants, and students gathered to praise the working class (*ra'a*, or *canaille*, as it appeared in the French translation) to underline the relatively radical, democratic principles of the Wafd Party. The point was to reestablish Zaghlul's claim to the leadership of a revolutionary party founded to destroy colonialism in Egypt, and thus neutralize his opponents on the left. In the speech Zaghlul reinterpreted the term *ra'a*, which had had the derogatory meaning of riff-raff in Egypt's customary political discourse. In Zaghlul's speech, the term came to represent the Wafd Party as a class-based party. Zaghlul claimed that this class (*tabaqa*) had a "natural" attachment to the principle of patriotism (*mabda' al-wataniya*). In his rhetorical declaration "I am one of you," Zaghlul identified his party with revolutionary change and uncompromising commitment to national independence.[54]

In sum, Zaghlul's compromises with elite politicians from January 1924 were designed to improve his chances in bilateral negotiations with the British. But a moderate position was increasingly hard to sustain after the convening of parliament. Discord within the Wafd Party began when revolutionary nationalists, like Shamsi, exploited the issue of treaty negotiations to undermine Zaghlul's authority. This strategy also won the support of radical reformists, like Huda Sha'rawi. As subsequent events revealed, these episodes were particularly instructive for liberals and conservatives, who marshaled the support of those jealous of the power of the Wafd Party and fearful of the radicalism of labor and feminist groups tied to the Wafd Party. Liberals and conservatives certainly did not underestimate the implications of the speech to the tramway union bosses. Even a rhetorical identification with the working class was considered aberrant to conservative monarchists and liberals, more so given the demonstrations in Alexandria and in the provinces of Gharbiya and Minufiya throughout the spring of 1924. Allenby also noted the revolutionary implications of Zaghlul's speech, pointing to Zaghlul's reference to the divergent roles of the "Pasha class" and the "workmen" in the national struggle.[55] In the opposition press, Zaghlul was dubbed "King of the riff-raff."[56] Al-Siyasa viewed Zaghlul's speech as a "direct incitement to Bolshevism and as being designed to stimulate class hatred."[57] Shortly afterwards, an unknown assailant attempted to assassinate Zaghlul.

The Ittihad Party

Before 1922, Egyptian politics was defined to a large extent by colonial power, and the evolutionary or revolutionary responses to it. As the British retreated from the political arena, more fundamental issues, such as electoral law and the Constitution, divided Egyptian political society. While a constitution had been written in 1923, this was only the beginning of a process. Defining the political system according to liberal principles highlighted deep divisions on such issues as democratic elections, gender, and class. That the Liberal Constitutional Party attempted to redefine the electoral system in 1925 indicates that constitutional issues remained unresolved. Likewise, the ambivalent attitude of the Wafd Party toward gender issues betrays the sort of problems confronted by the liberal-minded politician. Tensions within the ranks of the Wafd Party created an opening for conservative monarchists, which were fully exploited after the assassination of Sir Lee Stack in November 1924. Newspaper reports claimed that the assassins were men wearing effendi dress. Within Egypt's political culture, the effendi signified the leadership of the Wafd Party. Blaming the Wafd Party, Allenby compelled Zaghlul to resign and imposed severe financial and territorial penalties (the Sudan was effectively separated from Egypt).[58] In many accounts this act has been taken as yet another demonstration of colonial power.[59] Yet, it is more likely that radical right-wing nationalists initiated the crisis by planning and executing the assassination. Evidence collected in the subsequent trial of the assassins pointed to a plot masterminded by the king's political agent Hasan Nash'at—whom Malak Badrawi discusses in terms of economic intrigue in chapter four.[60] Thus, intense ideological ferment brought about the collapse of the Wafd government in 1924, and not gunboat diplomacy, which was a reaction to it.

Indeed, the assassination followed a dramatic contest between the Wafd Party and the monarchy. To enhance the political role of the monarchy, King Ahmad Fu'ad built a base of support within the 'ulama', particularly at the religious university of al-Azhar. The king's agents exploited the grievances of the religious students of al-Azhar against government school students, who were a core group within the Wafd Party. The tactics of the monarchists resulted in open clashes between the government and religious students. At the same time Hasan Nash'at initiated the formation of a monarchist political party, the Ittihad Party, by encouraging some Wafdist parliamentary deputies to denounce Zaghlul and defect by November 1924.[61] That many of those who defected were large landholders might support the idea that the Ittihad Party represented an elite group only. Likewise, the role of the *'ulama'* might indicate that the party had a basis in 'traditional' culture. Yet, younger effendis played a prominent role in the party. Nash'at, 'Ali Mahir, and Mahmud Abu al-Nasr were typical of Egypt's third generation. These men had been educated in government schools and had begun their political careers in the Watani or Wafd parties. Nash'at and Abu Nasr had been involved in the militant groups mobilized by the Wafd in 1919, while Mahir had traveled to Paris with Zaghlul in 1919.

It is important to note the diversity of the Ittihad Party membership, if only to guard against its usual description as a party of rural landlords tied to a monarchy easily manipulated by British agents. Indeed, while Allenby and Foreign Office officials supported the formation of a "counter-organization" with a solid base of support in the rural notability, the Ittihad Party was not manipulated.[62] It sought independent political power by mobilizing diverse constituencies in street demonstrations and electoral contests. The increasingly religious content of Ittihad ideology, as well as the campaign of the monarchists to mobilize the *'ulama'* and religious students was as destabilizing as were the activities of the left-wing radicals. Thus, whereas the radicals had spoilt Zaghlul's attempt to build consensus and coalition in 1924, the religious orientation of the Ittihad Party spoilt the attempt to build national consensus on conservative principles in 1925.

The Ittihad program called for a complete reform of al-Azhar University and Mosque to prepare its graduates to occupy "dignified" positions in the Ministries of Justice and Education.[63] The king also expanded his control over the Ministry of Awqaf (Religious Endowments). Monopoly over the distribution of public and private endowments *(waqf ahli* and *waqf khayri)* provided immense resources of patronage for the monarchy, since the *awqaf* comprised perhaps one-tenth of Egypt's cultivable land. Control of the *awqaf* also had an impact upon social values, as the *awqaf* included mosques and charitable societies. In 1925 the king was involved in setting up an asylum, a home for strays and waifs, and a workmen's dispensary in Bulaq, which was a working class district of Cairo. The charitable societies later attracted Islamists, such as Hasan al-Banna of the Muslim Brotherhood, which recruited through the Jam'iyyat al-Shubban al-Muslimin (Young Men's Muslim Association). The YMMA was founded under royal patronage, notably through royal 'connections' *(wasta)* in the Ministries of Awqaf and Education.[64]

The king exerted his influence over appointments to al-Azhar to bring about a reorganization of its highest council. The council restored the supervision of the school for *qadi*s (Islamic judges) to al-Azhar. In a contest with the Ministry of Education for a contract to supervise government schools in 1925, the *'ulama'* again triumphed over the bureaucrats. New schools were founded under royal patronage, normally in districts with candidates running for the Ittihad Party, who of course profited from such displays of royal patronage. Rules for state pensions were redrafted so that *'ulama'* that served in religious institutions were eligible for state pensions. By these measures, the king enhanced the role of the *'ulama'* in the state bureaucracy against the entrenched privileges of the *effendiya*. The cultural implications were shortly manifested when the *'ulama'* attempted to restrict the extension of *effendiya* culture in the school system. For instance, the students at the Dar al-'Ulum teachers' college were warned that they would be expelled and their positions taken by students from al-Azhar if they did not adopt Egyptian dress. That campaign provoked students at the government schools to debate whether the hat should be worn, instead of the tarboosh, as a sign of the 'true' effendi. The king supported the campaign against both the tarboosh and the hat, which resulted in a *fatwa* that "bristled with warnings against assimilation to foreigners." The *fatwa* said that the hat was an improper headdress. It also said that Muslim women must not marry non-Muslims, and that women must not be given equal rights to men in matters of inheritance.[65] Thus, the policies of the monarchists went against the westernizing trends of effendi reformers in the Wafd Party and the Liberal Constitutional Party, indicating a fundamental divergence of cultural and ideological orientations. Policy differences were most apparent on gender issues. The Wafd had already declared that the improvement of the status of women (particularly in the area of maternity or child-rearing) was a keystone of its political program.[66] In chapter eleven of this volume, Hanan Kholoussy has described in greater detail the 'nationalization' or politicization of the family in this period. As already indicated in this chapter, the Wafd Party took a moderate stand on gender and other cultural issues, refusing to challenge *fatwa*s issued after the Ittihad Party came to power. Indeed, Hasan Yasin, the leader of the Wafd Party's student executive, led the campaign to ban the wearing of hats in favor of the tarboosh at Dar al-'Ulum.[67]

The monarchist campaign was highly ideological. It touched upon fundamental issues of Egypt's political constitution and national identity. The religious campaign of the palace emboldened Muslim activists to challenge the government on political as well as cultural issues. For instance, students from al-Azhar signed a petition for the universal application of *sharia* (Islamic law) instead of civil law in January 1926.[68] This demand followed upon the highly publicized controversy that followed upon the publication of 'Ali 'Abd al-Raziq's *al-Islam wa usul al-hukm* (Islam and the Bases of Governing). This book was a straightforward refutation of the Islamist ideal of harmonizing the political community with *sharia*. 'Ali 'Abd al-Raziq explicitly challenged the idea of an Islamic state and implicitly the monarchy's cultural program by applying the logic of Taha Husayn's doctoral thesis, also published in 1925, to the caliphate issue. Like Taha Husayn, 'Abd al-Raziq rejected the idea that religion was a legitimate principle of political authority, using historical analysis to show that the caliphate had been neither religious nor just. 'Abd al-Raziq took the example of Abu Bakr, the first caliph, who he said founded a state on the basis of Arab *'asabiya* (ethnic solidarity). As well, 'Abd al-Raziq argued that the Prophet Muhammad had not intended to found an Islamic state and that Islam constituted a unity of faith and not of politics. As he said, "If we were to collect all his [the Prophet's] direct teachings on the question of government, we would get little more than a fraction of the principles of law and organizations needed for maintaining a state."[69] In this way, 'Abd al-Raziq argued for a liberal, individualistic political society and the effective exclusion of religion from politics.[70] As the European Department at the Ministry of the Interior reported, 'Ali 'Abd al-Raziq's education "led him to discard accepted ideas on religious questions and seek for facts, by going back to the fountainheads, the Koran and the Traditions. In the mingling of civil and political authority, with the latter always predominant, in Moslem countries throughout the ages, Shaykh 'Ali sees the principal reason for the failure of Mohammedan nations to advance as Christians have done."[71]

The publication of 'Abd al-Raziq's book provided the king with an excellent opportunity to establish the Ittihad Party and the monarchy as defenders of 'tradition.' For the king, this was perhaps a pretext because it enabled him to strengthen his power by weakening the 1923 constitution, as well as building broad-based popular support against the Wafd Party. However, the king's strategy also highlighted a cultural war between secularists and Islamists. Relying on the support of the "great mass of the illiterate population" on any religious question, the king and Nash'at supported, and probably encouraged, the condemnation of 'Abd al-Raziq by the 'ulama'. This was the opinion of the acting high commissioner, Neville Henderson, who said that the growing support for the Ittihad Party in the rural electoral constituencies emboldened the monarchists.[72] The condemnation of 'Abd al-Raziq was made by the Caliphate Commission of al-Azhar, which was actively lobbying for the king's candidacy as caliph of the Muslim world after the Turkish nationalists abolished the Ottoman caliphate in 1924. The al-Azhar Caliphate Committee appealed to the Council of al-Azhar to condemn 'Abd al-Raziq. As a result, the council issued a *fatwa* on 14 August 1925 that compared 'Abd al-Raziq to the Kharijites, who had seceded from the "majority" Sunni community after the murder of Caliph 'Uthman.[73]

The *fatwa*, like 'Abd al-Raziq's book, seemed loaded with a political message, comparing the *fitna*, or civil war between Sunni and Shi'a of Islamic history, to the present party conflicts in Egypt. The council accused 'Abd al-Raziq of unorthodox views and expelled him from the 'ulama', as well as depriving him of his post as *qadi* in the Shari'a Court of Alexandria. 'Abd al-Raziq appealed the ruling on the principle of "absolute freedom of belief" guaranteed in the 1922 Constitution.[74] But the council based its decision on the legal right of al-Azhar to discipline any member of the 'ulama'. Therefore, the council could declare that the constitutional right to freedom of opinion could not supersede the religious rulings of al-Azhar. In this way, the caliphate issue came to represent a conflict of political principles between liberal nationalists and Islamists, which shortly turned into a conflict between the Liberal Constitutional and Ittihad ministers in Ziwar's government. Significantly, the controversy placed religion at the center of political debates.

The controversy came to a head while Prime Minister Ziwar was on holiday in Europe. The acting prime minister, Yahya Ibrahim, communicated the decision of the Council of al-Azhar to 'Abd al-'Aziz Fahmi, the minister of justice. Fahmi's interpretation of the al-Azhar regulations was that the ruling of the 'ulama' on such an issue conflicted with the authority of the minister of justice. Fahmi claimed that employees of the religious and national courts were government officials and therefore fell under the authority of the Ministry of Justice. At a cabinet meeting, Fahmi refused to dismiss 'Abd al-Raziq and instead referred the issue to the legal department of the Ministry of Justice to determine if the Constitution safeguarded citizens from a charge of "false opinion." Ibrahim protested that the legal department included Europeans, who were incompetent on religious issues, and threatened to resign.[75]

After consulting with Henderson at the British Residency, who cautioned him to preserve the coalition government, Ibrahim visited the king. Although 'Abd al-'Aziz Fahmi had in the meantime agreed not to submit the issue to the legal department, Ibrahim summarily dismissed Fahmi and appointed 'Ali Mahir to the Ministry of Justice in his place. The political principle that Ibrahim defended, backed by the king and the Ittihad Party, was that the liberal declarations of the Constitution did not supersede the historic role of religion in Egypt's political community. Shaykh Muhammad Shakir, a former vice-chancellor of al-Azhar, who had quit the Wafd Party for the Ittihad Party, stated the principle in the journal *al-Ittihad*: "It was inadmissible that a decision of the Grand Ulama should be referred to Christian lawyers. In disapproving the verdict of the religious leaders of Islam, the State religion, the Minister of Justice attacked Islam and the constitution. We are surprised the he did not ask the Contentieux [legal department] their opinion on Islam as the State religion."[76]

Joining the debate, *al-Siyasa* responded in an editorial that Shakir should vent his anger at the "Egyptian legislator who put aside the penalties provided by the Moslem Shariah and replaced them by our penal and Civil Codes taken from the French Law."[77] On 8 September the Liberal Constitutional Party met and declared that the dismissal of Fahmi was "unconstitutional and not in accordance with political tradition."[78] This opinion indicates that the political principles that divided liberals and monarchists went to the very foundations of the constitutional system. As a result, the liberal ministers resigned from the cabinet in early September.

The 'Abd al-Raziq controversy enabled the Ittihad Party to assert the historical rights of the *'ulama'* and secure Islam as a symbol of the new Egyptian state. To be sure, Shaykh Muhammad Bakhit announced in the press in October that the Constitution was inconsistent with *shari'a*.[79] The secretary general of the Ittihad Party, Mahmud Abu al-Nasr, led a straightforward campaign on the religious issue. In a speech on 11 November 1925 Nasr condemned 'Abd al-Raziq's deceitful *(kadhib)* and skeptical *(mutashakkik)* interpretation of Islamic legal traditions *(hadith)*. He claimed that the fatwa of the *'ulama'* against 'Abd al-Raziq, on the other hand, was founded on verifiable *hadith*. Nasr claimed that Islamic law could not, by definition, be unconstitutional. Rather, when 'Abd al-Raziq and 'Abd al-'Aziz Fahmi claimed that the Qur'an was full of inconsistencies and required interpretation they set out to create disturbances within the Islamic community. Nasr concluded, "We should hold to religion first." The speech was followed by another from a lawyer in the *sharia* courts of Alexandria that praised Nasr's words as an example of "true nationalism" (*al-wataniya al-haqq*).[80]

The campaign of the Ittihad Party indicates that the monarchy took center stage in political and cultural contests. Just as 'Abd al-'Aziz Fahmi and 'Abd al-Raziq insisted upon a secular, liberal interpretation of the Constitution, the monarchists gave a boost to the Islamists. Through a cultural campaign that involved patronage over religious and educational institutions, and the production of literary works, the monarchy redefined Egypt's modern political community in religious terms. A monarchist, Zaki Fahmi, published his treatise on the Islamic prince, *Safwat al-'Asr* (The Elite of the Age), in 1926 to contest the secular vision of the liberals.[81] Barak Salmoni's chapter on schooling in this volume reveals that the monarchy also exerted its influence on the content of school curricula, as well as the scholarship of Egypt's first professional historians, including Muhammad Shafiq Ghurbal.[82] In short, the monarchy took a key role in shaping politics and the national identity.

Conclusion

The defeat of the Wafd government in 1924 and its weakened state afterwards might be viewed as the result of colonial interference or tactical maneuvers within an elite political society. Certainly, these factors cannot be dismissed altogether. Yes, the national government of Sa'd Zaghlul was wrecked on the rock of British imperialism. Yet its course was steered there by radical nationalists. This suggests that we should carefully consider cultural and ideological factors in our analysis of Egyptian politics in the period after 1919. Other examples underline this conclusion. For instance, the coalition of monarchists and liberals in 1925 was undermined by the religious commitments of the Ittihad Party. The liberal orientation toward evolutionary social progress meant that the liberals could hardly accommodate the religious politics of the Ittihad Party, any more than they could the class-based, revolutionary politics of the Wafd. Each of these parties, Wafd, Liberal, and Ittihad, were founded by third-generation politicians. Because this generation was particularly open to change and was familiar with western cultural and political models, ideological conflicts were intensified. These conflicts demonstrate that Egyptians failed to achieve consensus on even the most basic principles of Egypt's national identity, such as a clear definition of Egypt's territorial borders, civil and political rights, and the supremacy of civil law over religious law. The political generation of 1919 was far from cohesive, but divided culturally and ideologically. Thus, liberal nationalism and elite politics hardly defined or unified the 1920s. Rather, intense ideological discord marked the generation of 1919.

Notes

1   Miles Lampson Killearn, *Politics and Diplomacy in Egypt, The Diaries of Sir Miles Lampson 1935–1937*, ed. Malcolm Yapp (Oxford: Oxford University Press, 1997), 18.

2   Albert Hourani, *Arabic Thought in the Liberal Age*, 2nd ed. (Cambridge: Cambridge University Press, 1983), passim. For Hourani, liberal nationalism in Egypt reflected the cultural dominance of Europe in the liberal age (1798–1939).

3   Israel Gershoni and James P. Jankowski, *Egypt, Islam and the Arabs: The Search for Nationhood 1900–1930* (New York: Oxford University Press, 1986), 271. Gershoni and Jankowski underline the dramatic shift of cultural and political orientations from the Ottoman Empire and Islam to the Egyptian nation after 1919.

4   Although academic works on the period often show an appreciation for one of the ideological persuasions that I discuss in this paper, there are few works that give a balanced consideration of each ideological position. To give just two examples, Marius Deeb, *Party Politics in Egypt: the Wafd and its Rivals* (London: Ithaca Press, 1979), shows that the Wafd Party was more than simply a vehicle for elite politicians. Rather, it was a highly developed party organization with constituencies in society. Deeb does not, however, consider the Liberal Constitutional Party or Ittihad Party in any way comparable. Secondly, Afaf Lutfi al-Sayyid-Marsot, *Egypt's Liberal Experiment 1922–1936* (Berkeley: University of California Press, 1977), gives a sympathetic appreciation of the liberals, yet argues that in 1919 Egypt's social structures were not conducive to party politics, and dismisses the Wafd Party's leader, Sa'd Zaghlul, as demagogic.

5   This of course refers to the theme of collaboration, which is a hallmark of nationalist political rhetoric and literature. It began very early in the Egyptian context. In 1921 Wafd manifestos referred to the moderate politicians involved in negotiations with the British as infidels *(murtaddin)*. Although the use of religious terminology in this context is significant, the term should probably be understood in the nationalist sense of traitors to the cause. See *Parliamentary Papers*, vol. 42, no. 24, Egypt no. 3 (1921), Military Court of Inquiry into the Alexandria Riots, May 1921: 240.

6   Very many examples might be given of academic scholarship influenced by the nationalist narrative. The reference given here is to Jacques Berque, *Egypt: Imperialism and Revolution* (London: Faber, 1970), 312–24, 363–402.

7   Louis Joseph Cantori, "The Organizational Basis of an Elite Political Party: The Egyptian Wafd" (Ph.D. diss., University of Chicago, 1966), 215 and 423–25. See also Malcolm Yapp, *The Near East since the First World War* (London: Longman, 1991), 55. The elite model of politics has been most influential in the historical study of modern Egypt, see for example, Leonard

Binder, *In a Moment of Enthusiasm: Political Power and the Second Stratum* (Chicago: University of Chicago Press, 1978) and Robert Springborg, *Sayyid Mar'i: Family, Power and Politics in Egypt* (Philadelphia: University of Pennsylvania Press, 1982).

8   Robert F. Hunter, *Egypt Under the Khedives: From Household Government to Modern Bureaucracy* (Pittsburgh: University of Pittsburgh Press, 1984), 82–83.

9   Ehud Toledano, "Social and economic change in the 'long nineteenth century,'" in *The Cambridge History of Egypt*, 2 vols., ed. M.W. Daly (New York: Cambridge University Press, 1998), 2: 264–65.

10   Karl Mannheim, *Ideology and Utopia: An Introduction to the Sociology of Knowledge* (New York: Harcourt, Brace & Co., 1936), 237–80.

11   Hourani, *Arabic Thought*, 193–221. See also Gershoni and Jankowski, *Egypt, Islam and the Arabs*, 94.

12   'Abd al-Rahman al-Rafi'i, *Thawra sanat 1919: tarikh Misr al-qawmi min 1914 ila 1921* (Cairo: Dar al-Ma'arif, 1987), 263.

13   Cantori, *Organizational Basis*, 174. Fahmi's argument was well-informed; for instance Barrington Moore Jr. has said that the ruling class of Britain in the early nineteenth century included no more than 1,200 persons, mostly gentry and aristocracy. Barrington Moore, *The Social Origins of Dictatorship and Democracy: Lord and Peasant in the Making of the Modern World* (Boston: Beacon Press, 1966), 33.

14   When the British proclaimed the protectorate in 1914 they made the representatives of the Muhammad 'Ali dynasty sultans, rather than khedives, to legitimize the break with the Ottoman Empire. The wartime cabinet of Rushdi, Yakan, and Tharwat accepted this new arrangement in spite of political protests, whereas Muhammad Sa'id resigned his post as prime minister in 1914. A series of memorandums in 1917, when Ahmad Fu'ad acceded to the throne as the sultan, indicate that Rushdi's government intended that the ruler's power should be limited and responsible to his ministers yet without compromising the ruler's symbolic authority. See "Accession of Ahmad Fuad" FO141/620/5603/6 and FO141/620/5603/21 and FO/141/620/5603/29. See also *Journal Officiel*, 86 (10 October 1917).

15   Allenby to Curzon, February 1920, FO371/4978 431/93/16.

16   FO371/6294 6037/260/16.

17   FO371/7741 1039/61/16.

18   Taha Hussein, *The Days* (Cairo: The American University in Cairo Press, 1997), 400–402. Originally published as *al-Ayyam* between 1929 and 1939.

19   Hourani, *Arabic Thought*, 171–73.

20   Charles D. Smith, *Islam and the Search for Social Order in Modern Egypt* (Albany: State University of New York Press, 1983), 23–24.

21   Edward W. Said, *Orientalism* (London: Routledge, 1978), 1.

22   Ibid., 40.

23   British Foreign Office (FO), 26 April 1883, File FO78/3568, "Lord Dufferin's Scheme for the Reorganisation."

24   Report of the Special Mission to Egypt, February 1920, FO371/4978 5168/6/16.

25   Maurice Amos, "The Constitutional History of Egypt," *Publications of the Grotius Society* 14 (1929): 131–35.

26   Allenby to Curzon, April 1920, FO371/6295 4919/260/16.

27   In November 1921 Allenby warned the Foreign Office that there was a "serious risk of revolution" and "complete administrative breakdown" if concessions were not made to the nationalists, FO371/6307 12656/260/16 and FO371/6307 12666/260/16. Allenby offered his resignation in January and Curzon relented, FO371/7730 466/1/16 and FO371/7730 467/1/16 and FO371/7731 1482/1/16.

28   FO371/7730 11477/1/16.

29   FO371/8963 10383/10/16.

30   FO371/8973 4591/351/16.

31   FO371/10889 3628/29/16.

32   *Egyptian Gazette* (1 April 1925).

33   Gershoni and Jankowski, *Egypt, Islam and the Arabs*, 35–39. For an interpretive study of Haykal's thought see Smith, *Islam and the Search*, passim.

34   Charles D. Smith, "The 'Crisis of Orientation': The Shift of Egyptian Intellectuals to Islamic Subjects in the 1930s," *International Journal of Middle East Studies* 4 (1973): 382–410.

35   *Egyptian Gazette* (1 April 1925).

36   Ibid.

37   Ibid.

38   Ibid.

39   *Egyptian Gazette* (2 April 1925).

40   Review of Press, Allenby, 20 April 1925, FO371/10087 1142/29/16.

41   *Egyptian Gazette* (1 April 1925).

42   Cantori, *Organizational Basis*, 2 and 79.

43   *Egyptian Gazette* (14 January 1924).

44   Binder, *In a Moment of Enthusiasm*, 248 and 300.

45   FO371/10020/3102/22/16 Allenby, 29 March 1924, refers to outbursts in the parliament over the issue of the Sudan. Outside the parliament Zaghlul's supporters attacked the offices of *al-Akhbar*, the Watani Party newspaper, denouncing the "traitor" Amin al-Rafi'i.

46   Murray to Ingram, 5 January 1924, FO371/10020 3532/22/16.

47   Allenby to Murray, 12 April 1924, FO371/10020 3532/22/16. *Kashkul* was described as the most popular Egyptian journal, with double the circulation of any daily because it appealed to the "illiterates." Allenby's commentary on the events in the house of deputies can be found in a file of 22 March 1924, FO371/10020 2853/22/16.

48   Margot Badran, *Feminists, Islam, and Nation: Gender and the Making of Modern Egypt* (Princeton: Princeton University Press, 1995), 80–81.

49   Allenby to FO 12 April 1924, FO371/10020 3532/22/16.

50   Allenby, 12 April 1924, FO371/10020 3534/22/16.

51   Allenby, 22 April 1924, FO371/10040 3651/368/16.

52   It appears that Foreign Office officials believed that Allenby was advocating a policy of withdrawal; however, the evidence suggests that Allenby fell short of openly advocating that policy. Certainly Allenby was regarded by some British officials as taking too conciliatory a line with the nationalists. See Murray, Oliphant and Ingram, 22 April 1924, FO371/10040 3563/368/16. On the aims of the War Office to increase Britain's military presence in the Nile Valley see Cabinet, 16 April 1924, FO371/10040 3785/368/16.

53   Joel Beinin and Zackary Lockman, *Workers on the Nile* (Princeton: Princeton University Press, 1987), 127, 157–58.

54   *Al-Ahram* (5 July 1924).

55   Allenby, 14 July 1924, FO371/10021 6081/22/16.

56   Press Reports, FO371/10022 11524/22/16.

57   Allenby, 21 July 1924, FO371/10021 6249/22/16.

58   Political Developments in Egypt prior to the murder of Sir Lee Stack, FO371/1044 10208/368/16.

59   Selma Botman, "The Liberal Age, 1923–1952", in Daly, ed., *Cambridge History*, 2: 291.

60   Lloyd, 13 March 1926, FO371/11582 637/25/16 and FO371/10887 2337/29/16. The latter report claims that Shafiq Mansur, who was convicted of the crime, was "screaming in his cell" that Nash'at had masterminded the assassination.

61   Letter dated January 1925, Egyptian National Archives, 'Abdin Files, Review of Parties, Hizb al-Ittihad, Box 218 and FO371/10887 1257/29/16.

62 Henderson, 6 December 1924, FO37110022 11614/22/16.

63 Egyptian National Archives, 'Abdin Files, Box 219, "Note."

64 Egyptian National Archives, 'Abdin Files, Box 207 and FO/371/10888 2674/29/16.

65 Lloyd, 19 April 1926, FO371/11582 908/25/16. The *fatwa* was issued 28 March 1926.

66 Egyptian Nation Archives, 'Abdin Files Box 219, "Note," unsigned.

67 Lloyd, 13 March 1926, FO371/11582 693/25/16.

68 Lloyd, 23 February 1926, FO371/11582 637/25/16.

69 Jamal Mohammed Ahmed, *The Intellectual Origins of Egyptian Nationalism* (London: Oxford University Press, 1960), 118.

70 Leonard Binder, *Islamic Liberalism: A Critique of Development Ideologies* (London: University of Chicago Press, 1988), 131–36.

71 Report of European Department, Ministry of Interior, 28 September 1925, FO371/10888 2825/29/16.

72 Neville Henderson, 11 September 1925, FO371/10887 2664/29/16.

73 C.C. Adams, *Islam and Modernism: A Study of the Reform Movement Inaugurated by Muhammad 'Abduh* (London: Oxford University Press, 1933), 266.

74 FO371/10888 2825/29/16.

75 FO371/10888 2990/29/16.

76 Henderson, 21 September 1925, FO371/10888 2748/29/16.

77 FO371/10888 2825/29/16.

78 Henderson, 12 September 1925, FO371/10888 2746/29/16.

79 FO371/10888 2919/29/16.

80 *Al-Ittihad*, 11 November 1925.

81 Zaki Fahmi, *Safwat al-'asr* (Cairo: Matba'at al-I'timad, 1926). That Zaki Fahmi rehabilitated the thought of Ibn Khaldun suggests that his argument was designed as a riposte to Taha Husayn's doctoral thesis and 'Abd al-Raziq's celebrated critique of the caliphate. While Husayn and Raziq were critical of Ibn Khaldun's claim that ethnic solidarity and religion were useful categories of political analysis, Zaki Fahmi made these concepts the very basis of his theory of the Islamic monarch.

82 See also Yoav Di-Capua, "'Jabarti of the 20th Century': The National Epic of 'Abd al-Rahman al-Rafi'i and other Egyptian Histories," *International Journal of Middle East Studies* 36 (2004): 429–50.

2 Reassessing Egypt's Foreign Policy during the 1920s and 1930s

Fred H. Lawson

Egyptian foreign policy during the years between the revolutions of 1919 and 1952 remains largely unexplored. Existing scholarship asserts that political leaders in Cairo exhibited little if any interest in diplomatic and strategic relations with surrounding states prior to the signing of the Anglo-Egyptian Treaty of Alliance in August 1936.[1] The one partial exception to this general rule concerned the steadily escalating conflict between the Zionist movement and the Arab inhabitants of Palestine. Egyptian officials took steadily increasing notice of developments in Palestine as the 1920s drew to a close,[2] and they committed themselves to play a more active role in the dispute in the lead-up to the 1931 General Islamic Congress in Jerusalem.[3] But such sustained attention and activism with regard to external affairs is generally held to have been a pronounced anomaly.

More typical, in the conventional view, was the apathy demonstrated by the Egyptian authorities when units of the Ottoman armed forces seized control of the strategic harbor at Taba in early 1906.[4] In the same vein, officials in Cairo persistently refused to intervene in the fighting between Sultan 'Abd al-'Aziz al-Sa'ud and his northern and western neighbors that raged throughout the 1920s.[5] The Egyptian government proved equally reticent to express any overt criticism of the brutal measures that were adopted by the French to suppress the 1925 revolution in Syria.[6] In all of these cases, Cairo's pervasive passivity has been interpreted as a sign of the monarchy's fundamental unwillingness to engage in foreign relations to a degree commensurate with Egypt's power and prestige in the Arab world—a failing that was to be quickly rectified by the post-1952 leadership.

This commonly held view of Egyptian diplomacy ignores a number of occasions during the two decades after 1919 on which the government displayed a considerable degree of activism in regional affairs. In the winter of 1931–32, for instance, Cairo raised strong objections to a Turkish proposal that the former Khedive 'Abbas Hilmi be considered as a candidate for the position of king of Syria. Itamar Rabinovich reports that King Fu'ad's undisguised animosity toward the proposal generated friction in the relations between Egypt and Turkey, which in turn "led to an angry exchange of letters in [early] 1932."[7] Six years later, Egyptian officials riposted by championing the candidacy of Prince 'Abd al-Mun'im for the post. In Rabinovich's words, the suggestion "was not an isolated episode but part of a new and more active Arab policy which the young king [Faruq] launched under the guidance of 'Ali Mahir and 'Abd al-Rahman 'Azzam. As a result of this policy, Egypt became a full and active partner in the nascent system of inter-Arab relations and developed a greater interest in the course of Syrian politics."[8]

More intriguingly, Elie Podeh points out that King Fu'ad in early 1929 launched a campaign to improve relations with Imam Yahya of Yemen. The Yemeni ruler welcomed the overture, and immediately offered to draw up a formal treaty of friendship with Egypt "along the lines of the 1926 Italian-Yemeni accord."[9] In mid-July, a delegation of five Yemeni notables traveled to Cairo to finalize the agreement.[10]

Such episodes suggest that Egyptian foreign policy during the 1920s and 1930s could at times be more energetic than is usually portrayed. The question is why the authorities in Cairo adopted an active posture at certain times and assumed a more passive stance at others. Two divergent instances of Egypt's foreign affairs in the years before 1936 shed light on this puzzle: Cairo's firm resistance to Italian attempts to redraw the boundary with Libya around the oasis of al-Jaghbub in 1924–25, and its apparent unwillingness to become involved in mediating between Saudi Arabia and Yemen during the prolonged 'Asir crisis of 1933–34. Both of these cases represent, if the conventional wisdom is to be believed, a sharp reversal of the Egyptian government's earlier stance toward the issue at hand. Moreover, each illustrates the complex dynamics and strategic calculations that characterized foreign policymaking at the height of the monarchy.

This chapter will lay out the most important aspects of these divergent episodes. It will then offer an explanation for the policy that Egypt pursued in each case in terms of struggles among powerful actors for control over the domestic arena. Finally, it will suggest two implications of this analysis for our overall understanding of Egyptian foreign relations during the era of the monarchy, a period whose most neglected segment stretches from the series of negotiations that accompanied the end of the First World War to the flurry of initiatives that broke out during the Second World War and culminated in the formation of the League of Arab States.[11]

Defending al-Jaghbub, 1924–25

Located some 100 miles south-southwest of Sallum on the Mediterranean coast, the oasis of al-Jaghbub was notable at the beginning of the twentieth century as the site of the tomb of Sayyid Muhammad bin 'Ali al-Sanusi, the founder of the influential al-Sanusiya fraternal order. In the course of the 1911 invasion of Libya, Italian military commanders asserted exclusive claim to the entire region of Cyrenaica, as far as the twenty-seventh degree of longitude east. British officials in Cairo riposted that the strategic port at Sallum lay inside Egyptian territory and quickly dispatched a detachment of troops to garrison the town. The British notified the Italian authorities that al-Jaghbub likewise stood inside the borders of Egypt. Four years later, however, as part of the April 1915 treaty whereby Italy allied itself with Great Britain, France, and Russia in fighting against Germany, Austria-Hungary, and the Ottoman Empire, London stipulated that if important German territories were to change hands as a result of the war, Rome could "claim some equitable compensation, particularly as regards the settlement in her favor of the questions relative to the frontiers of the Italian colonies of Eritrea, Somaliland, and Libya and the neighboring colonies belonging to France and Great Britain."[12] This arrangement was reaffirmed in July 1916, when British representatives once again indicated that the final determination of the territorial boundary between Egypt and Cyrenaica would be postponed until after the war.

At the 1919 Paris Peace Conference, Lord Milner proposed to transfer title to al-Jaghbub to Italy in exchange for a pledge on Rome's part to recognize Egyptian sovereignty over Sallum. The Italian government replied in April 1920 that it would indeed accept Egypt's right to govern Sallum, "so long as al-Jaghbub is included within Italian territory."[13] The Foreign Office signaled a willingness to go along, and incorporated the bargain into a draft treaty that was submitted to the Italian foreign minister, Count Vittorio Scialoja, in April 1921. Egyptian officials were not informed of the treaty's provisions until two months later, and then refrained from making any public comment on the proposed exchange of territories. For its part, the government in Rome offered no response to the draft treaty until April 1922, by which time London had already granted formal independence to Egypt. British officials consequently refused to accept the Italian counter-proposal, on the grounds that the question of delimiting the frontier had become a matter for the authorities in Cairo and Rome to hammer out between themselves.

During the spring of 1924, simmering popular unrest in Cyrenaica concentrated attention on al-Jaghbub. Italian military commanders charged that Bedouin tribes based in the oasis were responsible for organizing popular resistance to Italian rule, as well as for smuggling sizable quantities of weapons across the border to support the rebel cause. A series of armed skirmishes in eastern Cyrenaica in June and July brought Italian ground and air forces into areas adjacent to the oasis. The officers in charge of Egyptian units patrolling the border worked out a modus vivendi with the Italians, whereby limited incursions into Egyptian territory would be tolerated if Italian troops were engaged in hot pursuit of Bedouin insurgents.[14] Meanwhile, Italy's ambassador in Paris persuaded Prime Minister Sa'd Zaghlul to reconsider the question of permanently demarcating the border during the course of the latter's recuperative visit to Europe that summer. Zaghlul's cabinet collapsed in November, however, before any firm steps to address the boundary question could be taken. At the end of the month, the Italian minister of colonies expressed concern that the problem be handled in an expeditious fashion. Nevertheless, discussions between the two governments did not resume until February 1925, in the context of sharply escalating Italian military operations in the desert south of Sallum.[15] There were persistent reports during the course of these operations that Italian forces had taken up positions inside Egyptian territory, particularly in the district of al-Shaqqa.

On 20 February, Italy's ambassador to Cairo submitted a formal request that Egypt cede control over al-Jaghbub, prompting an emergency series of closed-door meetings of the council of ministers, chaired by Prime Minister Ahmad Ziwar Pasha.[16] The premier emerged from these meetings to announce that any permanent arrangement regarding the border could not be concluded at that time, due to upcoming parliamentary elections and the generally unsettled nature of the country's "internal and external conditions." He recommended that the two sides instead undertake "a provisional delimitation of the Egypt-Tripoli frontier, pending a definite settlement of the question in accordance with the preamble of the so-called Milner-Scialoja agreement" of April 1921.[17] Egyptian news-papers, incensed at what they took to be a preemptory demand on Italy's part, printed articles and editorials that adamantly rejected any move to reconfigure the border. Rumors then started to circulate in Cairo that Italian troops had already occupied the oasis.[18] The ensuing public outcry proved so hostile that the foreign ministry in Rome issued a statement denying that it had suggested anything other than a resumption of nego-tiations concerning the final delimitation of the border.[19]

As March opened, the Egyptian press began to demand that the govern-ment dispatch an expeditionary force to protect al-Jaghbub. It was widely reported that the inhabitants of the oasis had earlier urged the authori-ties in Cairo to establish a permanent military presence in the area, but that the request had fallen on deaf ears.[20] Meanwhile, *al-Ahram* reported that the Egyptian garrison at Sallum had been attacked by local Bedouin, prompting the hurried deployment of fresh troops to the town.[21] These movements accompanied heightened Italian pressure to bring the dispute to a resolution. In response, the Egyptian council of ministers appointed a special commission to investigate the problem. It was reported in early April that members of the commission were about to depart for al-Jaghbub in order to "visit all the leading men [in the district] to ascertain their views as to the political future of the oasis."[22] This plan was sharply criticized by the pro-Wafd newspaper *al-Balagh*, which charged that the Ziwar govern-ment was acting "in a dangerous way." "What is meant by consulting the inhabitants of Jaghbub regarding the destiny of the district?" the paper asked. "Such consultation is out of place unless we admit that the present Ministry has no decisive opinions on the question."[23] *Kawkab al-sharq*, a 1920s and 1930s Wafdist daily newspaper edited by Ahmad Hafiz 'Awad, added that if the current government agreed to cede the oasis to Italy, it would in effect be taking sides against the guerrillas *(mujahidin)* who had long been struggling against imperial domination in Cyrenaica. In this way, Egypt "would help in subjugating these brave fighters, and so deviate from the neutrality she has kept since the beginning of the fight between the Tripolitans and the Italians."[24] Such reporting led the undersecre-tary of state for the interior, Gamal al-Din Pasha, to summon a group of prominent journalists to his office and admonish them to "do nothing to aggravate the difficulties of the situation."[25]

Public sentiment in London, by contrast, tended to favor the Italian position. Influential newspapers expressed the hope that negotiations between Egypt and Italy would proceed in an orderly, amicable fashion, and that Rome's view of the matter would ultimately prevail. The *Daily Mail* went so far as to affirm that "Egypt never did possess the Jaghbub Oasis; it has been really a no man's land occupied by some Senussi."[26] More moderate publications pointed out that Cairo was attempting to disavow earlier understandings concerning the disposition of al-Jaghbub, while at the same time soliciting British backing in the dispute; "Thus Egypt wishes to have it both ways, but Great Britain has no intention of being made such a catspaw."[27] British officials patiently explained to the London correspondent of *al-Ahram* that Egypt had never shown any real interest in al-Jaghbub, and would only benefit by exchanging control of the oasis for "a definite right to valuable elbow room on the seacoast in the vicinity of Sollum [sic]." They went on to declaim that "while it has no objection naturally to the Egyptian Government obtaining by negotiations some modification of this frontier line in favor of Egypt, the British Government holds that the Milner-Scialoja line is the only possible existing basis on which an agreement can eventually be reached and considers, moreover, that the Egyptian Government should have no difficulty in so presenting the matter as to enable the Egyptian public to realise the material advantages accruing from such a settlement."[28]

Egyptian nationalists rejected out of hand the logic of the British viewpoint. When it was announced at the end of April 1925 that the Egyptian military units that had been ordered to withdraw from the Sudan were to be stationed at al-'Arish, there were widespread calls for the troops to be deployed instead to "the threatened frontiers in the West."[29] Britain's willingness to acquiesce in a territorial settlement that was fundamentally in line with Italy's stated demands led *al-Balagh* and *Kawkab al-sharq* to conclude that London was acting in accordance with its own strategic interests, which had now diverged from those of Egypt.[30] This opinion gained credence when the findings of the special commission on the border question were disclosed in early May 1925. The commission concluded that al-Jaghbub was "indispensable to Egypt from the strategic point of view, and that the territory proposed to be given to Egypt in its stead on the coast will be of little value to this country for military purposes."[31] These findings exacerbated the difficulties confronting the Ziwar government, which found itself increasingly torn between growing popular insistence that the oasis be retained and heightened British pressure to conciliate Rome. Stalling for time, the council of ministers asked the special commission to provide further clarification regarding a number of points addressed in its report.[32]

In the face of Cairo's apparent hesitation, and encouraged by intimations that London backed his government's claims, Benito Mussolini on 21 May 1925 declared that al-Jaghbub rightfully belonged to Italy.[33] Jolted into action, the Egyptian foreign ministry notified its counterpart in Rome that Egypt was now "prepared to go into negotiation with it on this question, on the condition that negotiation will be free from all restrictions, and the result will be submitted to the Egyptian parliament."[34] When this overture led to even more unequivocal statements of Italy's right to the disputed territory—the minister of colonies, for instance, replied to the call for talks by proclaiming that "Italy's rights over Jaghbub are indisputable"— Egyptian newspapers of all stripes castigated Britain for strengthening the Italian leadership's resolve. British officials responded by reiterating the strategic importance of Sallum and belittling "the insignificant oasis of Jaghbub, hidden in its mystic distant desert setting." Of the two districts, there was no question which one military planners in London considered to be more important: "In these days of mechanical transport the undisputed possessor of the Sollum area holds Siwa as well, and Siwa blocks the way into Egypt through the southern chain of oases."[35]

Britain's expressed preference for a settlement in which Egypt would relinquish control over al-Jaghbub severely weakened Cairo's bargaining position vis-à-vis Rome. At the same time, the rapid approach of parliamentary elections made it impossible for the unpopular Ziwar government to focus its attention on negotiations with Italy. Consequently, officials at the Egyptian foreign ministry floated an ingenious proposal: that a Free Zone be set up along the Egyptian-Libyan border, "which both parties would undertake not to enter."[36] The Italians were not impressed, and the dispute dragged on into the summer.

In mid-August, Egypt's influential minister of the interior, Isma'il Sidqi, traveled to Rome in an attempt to restart talks. Sidqi met personally with Mussolini on the sixteenth, but the two men merely restated their respective governments' positions on the matter.[37] At the conclusion of the meeting, Sidqi issued a press release in which it was announced that an Italian-Egyptian Mixed Delimitation Commission would be formed in October to deal with the boundary problem. When the commission convened, the Egyptian delegation put forward three major proposals: that the border be drawn some seven miles to the west of al-Jaghbub; that certain sites in the oasis be designated as holy places open to Muslims from Egypt and Libya, but closed to the Italians; and that Italy assume full responsibility for maintaining security along the border. The Italian representatives to the commission grudgingly accepted the second and third of these items, but flatly rejected the first.

By late November, growing popular disorder sparked by the disputed outcome of Egypt's parliamentary elections led the British high commissioner in Cairo, Sir George Lloyd, to pay an official call on King Fu'ad and warn him "that he personally would be held responsible if the negotiations failed."[38] The king promptly ordered Prime Minister Ziwar to reinstate Sidqi as minister of the interior, and to bring the negotiations with Italy to a rapid conclusion. The premier wasted no time in carrying out the king's wishes. According to the terms of a protocol signed on 6 December 1925, Cairo recognized Italian sovereignty over al-Jaghbub and, in return, gained full control over a strategically situated strip of territory northwest of Sallum. Bedouin caravans calling at the oasis were exempted from customs duties levied by either state, and freedom to visit the tomb of Sayyid Muhammad was guaranteed to all Muslims. The complicated question of conferring citizenship on the nomads who frequented the oasis was left to further deliberation on the part of the Mixed Delimitation Commission.[39]

Egyptian nationalists reacted to the agreement with sharply worded speeches in parliament and essays in the press. *Al-Balagh* averred that al-Jaghbub was as much a part of Egypt as Alexandria or Cairo; *Kawkab al-sharq* lamented that the agreement would "disgrace Egypt in the eyes of Islam."[40] Students at a number of prestigious secondary schools in the capital and the university's Faculty of Arts took to the streets in protest in the days immediately after the agreement was announced. The scale of popular opposition convinced the council of ministers not to bring the protocol before parliament for ratification. At the same time, the Ziwar government adopted a revised electoral law designed to weaken the Wafd and strengthen rival parties, such as the Liberal Constitutionalists and the Unionists, whose programs tended to coincide with the interests of the palace.[41] Public outcries against the new voting regulations quickly eclipsed nationalist displeasure over the loss of al-Jaghbub.

Two thousand Italian troops at last set out for the oasis at the beginning of February 1926. While the 350-vehicle column moved south, Italian military aircraft dropped leaflets over al-Jaghbub promising that all holy sites in the area would be respected.[42] The massive expedition encountered no resistance along the way, and reached the neighboring oasis of Musalla after only five days. Here the heads of the major Bedouin clans in the area presented themselves before the commander of the expedition and pledged that they and their followers would submit to him. The next morning, 7 February, Italian soldiers marched into al-Jaghbub itself, where they were greeted by a delegation of local notables, who formally professed their allegiance to the authorities in Rome. Ceremonies ended with the raising of Italy's national flag over the center of the community.

'Abd al-Rahman 'Azzam captured the significance of the moment in a commentary that appeared in *al-Ahram*: "With the disappearance of al-Jaghbub from the map of Egypt, gone too is Egyptian peace and security. Now more than ever before we must rely on British assistance."[43] The government of Ahmad Ziwar Pasha, along with its political allies in the Liberal Constitutionalist and Unionist parties, emerged from the episode in disgrace, and thus weaker than ever both with regard to the British administration and to the palace.

Side-stepping Arabia, 1933–34

During the summer of 1931 and again in November 1932, jockeying between followers of the King of Najd and the Hijaz, 'Abd al-'Aziz al-Sa'ud, and forces loyal to the Zaidi Imam of Yemen, Yahya Hamid al-Din, for control of the southern marches of 'Asir flared into armed skirmishes. On both occasions, direct negotiations between the two rulers produced provisional agreements that not only halted the immediate fighting but also raised the prospect of a peaceful future between their respective states.[44] In May 1933, however, Zaidi forces overran strategically important districts of northwestern Najran, bringing them into proximity to areas of the 'Asir highlands that had risen in open revolt against Saudi control. When Imam Yahya refused to order these fighters to pull back, King 'Abd al-'Aziz mobilized troops and supplies and moved them into northern 'Asir;[45] in November a large number of Saudi troops took up forward positions in eastern Najran and along the Tihamah coast.

A final attempt to resolve the crisis through bilateral talks collapsed in February 1934, and on 20–21 March Saudi forces initiated a two-pronged offensive aimed at enveloping southern 'Asir and northern Najran and cutting these regions off from the Imam's heartland in the mountains around Sa'da and San'a.[46] At the end of an address in Mecca that spelled out the reasons for the offensive, King 'Abd al-'Aziz remarked:

> More than ten months have elapsed during which period we have
> been negotiating with Yahya on the points at issue. The news of
> our disagreement was broadcast to the world. No move emanated
> from the Muslims, whether from their monarchs, Emirs or political

parties. No one approached us for a reconciliation or for the purpose of learning the point of disagreement between us and Imam Yahya and to find out who was the liar or the truthful person. We have only received telegrams of good wishes which do not bring any material results. When the Austrian incident occurred, certain great powers immediately interfered and did everything possible to avert the disaster of war, whereas the Muslims and Arabs remained indifferent and their activities did not depart from mere wishes.[47]

At almost the same time that the Saudi ruler was decrying the apparent lack of concern over the fighting among Muslims, the General Arab Union in Cairo convened a public meeting to discuss measures that might be undertaken to defuse the conflict.[48] The meeting had initially been planned for mid-March, but had been called off on news that Saudi and Yemeni representatives were conferring in Abha. The collapse of the bilateral talks rekindled worry among members of the Union, who recommended forming two separate commissions to investigate the reasons for the war and possible ways to respond. Among the names that were proposed to be members of the dual commissions were Muhammad 'Ali 'Alluba Pasha, who had just resigned from the Liberal Constitutionalist Party, Shaykh Muhammad Mustafa al-Maraghi, who had attempted to mediate between Cairo and Riyadh during the 1920s concerning disputes over the official Egyptian caravan to the pilgrimage in Mecca, and 'Abd al-Rahman 'Azzam, one of the most outspoken proponents of co-operation among Arab countries.

After a prominent lawyer, 'Uthman Murtada Pasha, instructed the gathering that it "had no legal right to discuss the subject from a legal point of view, seeing that it was not yet known which of the two sovereigns was responsible for the existing difference," the Union decided to draft telegrams to the two rulers, "suggesting that the points of difference should be referred to an arbitration committee, similar to the Hague Court, and that members of the arbitration committee should be chosen from among the Muslim Kings." Following considerable debate, a less precise communiqué was adopted: "The meeting expresses indignation that war should take place between two Muslim groups, especially in the Houroum [sic] months, a thing which is inconsistent with the commandments of God and His Messenger—and a war in which Muslims will kill one another while they are brothers who believe in God's Book. The meeting further asks the two sovereigns to fear God regarding themselves and the Muslims, to avoid bloodshed, and to submit to God's order regarding arbitration."[49] An eight-person delegation was then charged with delivering the document to the Saudi and Yemeni governments. King 'Abd al-'Aziz's private secretary replied almost immediately: "His Majesty remained patient for ten months during which he made endeavors to maintain peace, but the Imam Yahya continued in his aggression. No intermediation by the Muslims has taken place to bring about reconciliation between the two sides. His Majesty having resorted to all peaceful means, but without avail, cannot but defend the country and prevent any aggression on it."[50] The Imam's response was somewhat more hopeful. He recommended that the Union appoint a representative to accompany a Yemeni delegation to Mecca to discuss the situation. Dr. 'Abd al-Hamid Sa'id was promptly nominated to carry out the assignment.[51] But his mission was scuttled when the Saudi authorities denied that any such delegation existed.[52]

On 3 April, the leader of the Wafd, Mustafa al-Nahhas, sent telegrams to the two rulers, in which he urged them in the name of "the Egyptian people in particular and the Muslims in general" to do everything in their power "to avoid Muslim bloodshed and to avoid war between two neighboring Muslim countries."[53] King 'Abd al-'Aziz thanked al-Nahhas for his message, but reiterated that the Yemenis had acted aggressively and it was his duty to defend his "country and position."[54] The Imam returned an equally polite but uncompromising defense of his actions.

Meanwhile, the General Islamic Congress in Jerusalem began to take steps to intervene in the conflict. The president of the Congress, Sayyid Muhammad Amin al-Husayni, dispatched a cable to Prince 'Umar Tusun, asking him to get in contact with the Saudi and Yemeni rulers.[55] At the beginning of April, the Congress's Executive Committee appointed a peace delegation to mediate between the belligerents.[56] The four-person team, consisting of al-Husayni, Muhammad 'Ali 'Alluba, Amir Shakib Arslan and Hashim al-'Atasi, arrived in Mecca on 14 April. It was welcomed by King 'Abd al-'Aziz, who not only agreed to take advantage of its good offices but also authorized it to use the Saudi government's telegraph facilities to communicate with the Imam. Exchanges of cables under the auspices of the delegation facilitated concessions on both sides, which resulted in the composition of a draft peace treaty. The document was made public on 12 May, setting the stage for a pair of lavish celebratory banquets in Taif hosted by the Saudi ruler on the evenings of the twelfth and thirteenth; closed-door negotiations concerning the precise terms of the agreement commenced on 15 May.

Bickering between Saudi and Yemeni representatives over the issue of reparations caused the talks to stretch out for more than a week.[57] As the days passed, King 'Abd al-'Aziz's misgivings grew, and on 22 May he ordered his commanders to take steps to resume military operations if the Imam did not promise to carry out the provisions of the draft treaty by the twenty-fourth.[58] On that day, there were reports that the Yemeni ruler had given orders to his own officers to prepare to resume hostilities. Incensed, the Saudi king told a special correspondent of *al-Jihad*: "This time I shall not stop the march toward San'a and shall not sheathe the sword: either victory with the will of God or defeat, may God forbid it. It will then be up to the Muslim world to give the final judgment, and nobody can then accuse me of having not used wisdom, patience, toleration, indulgence and frankness in settling the differences between me and the Imam Yahya."[59] Still the Imam offered no direct reply. Instead, he proposed that a special commission made up of representatives from Muslim countries be appointed to orchestrate the disengagement, and that the withdrawal of Saudi forces from the Tihama and Yemeni forces from 'Asir be supervised by a select group of Egyptian and Iraqi military officers. *Al-Muqattam* reported that Imam Yahya had even written a letter to a retired Egyptian general, who had previously served in the Ottoman army in Yemen, inviting him to take charge of the Yemeni armed forces.[60]

Clashes broke out north of al-Hudayda on 26 May. *Al-Jihad* reported that advance units of the Saudi army initiated the fighting by launching attacks on fortified Yemeni positions in the mountain passes along the road to San'a. The newspaper received a cable from Mecca on the twenty-eighth, advising that a large-scale push toward the Yemeni capital would begin the following day.[61] But in a sharp reversal, the Saudi news agency in Cairo released a communiqué on 30 May which stated that Imam Yahya had agreed to the terms specified in the draft treaty and had taken steps to implement them. The Imam blamed unavoidable delays in communicating his orders to the battlefront for the apparent lack of responsiveness. In light of these circumstances, the communiqué continued, King 'Abd al-'Aziz had extended the truce for an additional few days. Furthermore, the king had received a telegram from the Yemeni ruler, "in which the latter expressed his resentment of the violent attack made by Prince Sa'ud's army on the Far' District. His Majesty, in reply, however, emphasized to the Imam that he also was dissatisfied with any violation of the truce and [assured him] that measures have been taken to avoid a recurrence."[62]

On 11 June 1934, King 'Abd al-'Aziz received a further cable from Imam Yahya informing him that the treaty would arrive in San'a for ratification the next day. In expectation that the pact was going to be finalized in the near future, the chief Yemeni negotiator left Ta'if for al-Hudayda, where he planned to meet with both the Peace Delegation of the General Islamic Congress and the commander of Saudi forces in the Tihama. Meanwhile, Amir Muhammad bin 'Abd al-'Aziz al-Sa'ud arrived at Abha in northern 'Asir with a fresh contingent of Saudi troops.[63] On 14 June, the Jidda correspondent of *al-Ahram* reported that the Imam was now expected to sign the treaty "within a week."[64] The ratified document was at last released to the public on 23 June.[65]

Imam Yahya's senior adviser traveled to Cairo in early July. He brought with him a letter to King Fu'ad, expressing the Yemeni ruler's interest in establishing formal diplomatic relations between San'a and Cairo.[66] The overture elicited no reply. In fact, the Cairo government's silence throughout the months of the crisis proved deafening. On at least two separate occasions, the Imam appealed directly to King Fu'ad to act as mediator; each request was ignored. Prominent Egyptian nationalists, including 'Abd al-Rahman 'Azzam, published passionate commentaries in the local press urging the council of ministers to assume an active role in resolving the dispute, to no avail. Nonpartisan civic and cultural societies, most notably the Young Men's Muslim Association, campaigned for some sort of official Egyptian intervention, but had no impact in policy-making circles.[67]

Given all this activity, it would be a mistake to conclude that Egypt was apathetic or unconcerned about the Saudi-Yemen crisis of 1933–34. What prevented Cairo from playing an active part in mediating the dispute was not a lack of strategic or popular interest, but rather the complex configuration of conflicting interests harbored by the country's major political actors. It was only when these interests aligned so as not to cancel one another out that the Egyptian government found itself able to carry out significant foreign policy initiatives.

Explaining Foreign Policy under the Monarchy

Egypt's foreign policy in the era of the monarchy was determined by the confluence of several overlapping, and most often incompatible, interests. The broad limits of what was feasible for the government in Cairo to undertake were set by British imperial authorities. From 1882 until the Second World War, British political and military officers exercised tight control over key components of the Egyptian administration, with special attention to external and internal security matters. But it would be misleading to infer that London's preferences dictated how Egypt dealt with diplomatic and strategic affairs within these boundaries, particularly after the country was granted de jure independence in 1922.

Egypt's response to external challenges during the 1920s and 1930s can therefore best be explained in terms of the conflicting interests of four key actors: the palace, the Wafd, the Wafd's primary rivals, and the British. For the palace, the highest priority was to enhance the influence and prestige of the institution of the monarchy; a secondary interest lay in placating the country's British overlords, at whose pleasure the king remained in office.[68] The Wafd, as the nationalist organization that consistently enjoyed the greatest degree of popular support, had an overriding interest in promoting Egypt's independence from Britain, and a secondary interest in gaining control of the council of ministers. Other political parties, like the Liberal Constitutionalists and the Unionists, were primarily concerned with blocking the Wafd from consolidating power; their secondary interest lay in implementing fundamental reforms in the domestic political order and amending the Constitution of 1923 upon which the system was based. Finally, the principal interest of British officials, both in London and in Cairo, was to maintain order inside the country; a secondary interest was to advance the empire's strategic interests in Middle Eastern affairs.

Why Egypt Resisted Italy over al-Jaghbub

As the confrontation between Cairo and Rome for control over the oasis at al-Jaghbub escalated during the late spring of 1924, circumstances in Egypt predisposed the government of Sa'd Zaghlul to respond in an accommodative fashion to Italy's demands. The Wafd had triumphed handily in parliamentary elections that January, and the prime minister had received a further boost in stature and popularity as a result of an unsuccessful attempt on his life in July.[69] The organization's leadership therefore embarked on a campaign to moderate the tone of its rhetoric and the scope of its immediate demands, in hopes of convincing the British that it could act as a responsible partner in the complicated and risky process of devolution from imperial rule. Rival parties, by contrast, turned up their pronouncements, and denounced the Wafd for softening its position regarding total independence. British officials complained that efforts by smaller parties to undermine the Wafd threatened to destabilize the country, but generally tolerated the heightened friction that permeated

Egyptian politics during the summer and fall. Faced with Zaghlul's unprecedented strength, the palace kept to itself.

In light of Britain's evident preference for a settlement that sacrificed al-Jaghbub for territory around Sallum, the Wafd expressed a willingness to accommodate Rome. This policy not only avoided antagonizing the Italians, who had fielded a substantial military force along Egypt's western borders, but also and more importantly signaled to London that a fully independent Egypt would pose no danger of contradicting Britain's strategic interests. Smaller parties, which might have objected to a deal, were tightly constrained by the British administration, while the palace saw no advantage to be gained from coming out against a minor readjustment of the country's legal boundaries.

Before a settlement could be reached, however, circumstances in Egypt changed dramatically. Pushed to the breaking point by his rivals and stung by British charges that he had been complicit in the assassination of the commander of the Egyptian armed forces (the Sirdar), Zaghlul unexpectedly resigned as prime minister in November 1924. Seizing the opportunity to reassert the king's influence, the palace nominated the head of a smaller party to the premiership. The new council of ministers included no members of the Wafd, but consisted entirely of Liberal Constitutionalists, Nationalists, and independents. Minister of the Interior Sidqi quickly proclaimed that the government's first priority would be to restore internal order.[70] At the same time, the Ziwar government accepted British demands that it pull Egyptian troops out of the Sudan and pay a heavy indemnity as retribution for the death of the Sirdar.[71] The Wafd thus reassumed its longstanding role as outspoken critic of both the palace and the British. The organization's antagonism toward the government soared in the wake of the March 1925 elections, when the palace first re-appointed Ziwar as prime minister (despite another overwhelming Wafdist victory at the polls) and then dissolved the parliament.

Under these circumstances, the leadership of the Wafd adopted an exceptionally hard line toward the existing order and its British underpinnings. Newspapers associated with the organization insisted that the nation's rights and territorial integrity be defended at all costs; local offices of the Wafd mobilized popular demonstrations against the government and in support of complete independence. The coincidence of strategic interests between London and Rome became no longer a reason to accommodate Italy's demands, but rather good grounds to forcibly resist them. Caught off guard by the shift, smaller parties represented in the council of ministers scrambled to conform to public opinion concerning the disposition of al-Jaghbub. The ministers delayed making a firm decision as long as possible, and thereby permitted the Wafd to set the terms of the debate. Similarly, the king refrained from taking a public position on the issue, until the British high commissioner (now called ambassador), worried that popular unrest would spread and concerned that the leadership of the Wafd was preparing to seize control of the government with the support of the Liberal Constitutionalists,[72] issued the November 1925 ultimatum compelling him to do so.

At that point, Cairo's resistance to the Italian campaign to seize al-Jaghbub collapsed. The Ziwar cabinet, entirely dependent upon the palace for its incumbency, quickly fell in with Britain's expressed wishes. The Liberal Constitutionalists initially objected to the proposed settlement, but lacked the popular backing necessary for it to have an impact on policy-making. The Wafd, whose affiliates had been most vocal and active in opposing the transfer of sovereignty over the oasis, turned its attention away from foreign affairs to concentrate on proposed changes in the election law that had immediate consequences for the organization's continued ability to prevail at the polls. A resolution of the crisis in Italy's favor therefore emerged by default, and the government even found itself too vulnerable to bring the draft treaty to parliament for formal ratification.

Why Egypt Failed to Intervene in Arabia

Escalating tensions between the Saudis and Yemenis accompanied a major reshuffling of Egyptian politics. The draconian government of Isma'il Sidqi fell in September 1933 and was replaced with one headed by the former minister of foreign affairs, 'Abd al-Fattah Yahya, who had at one time been a senior figure in the People's Party.[73] This cabinet lacked the capacity to stand up to the palace, which quickly reasserted control over governmental affairs.[74] In an unusual twist of fate, however, the newly arrived British ambassador, Sir Miles Lampson, set out to impose strict limitations on the political prerogatives enjoyed by the king. The Wafd, meanwhile, found itself increasingly divided over a wide range of fundamental issues, including whether or not to take part in coalition cabinets with smaller parties, and whether or not to tolerate the use of violence to promote complete independence.[75] Deepening internal fissures prevented the organization from taking advantage of the sudden collapse of Sidqi's government to augment its influence in policy-making.

Egyptian politics throughout the fall and winter of 1933–34 were driven by the cabinet's persistent efforts to resist British pressure, combined with repeated calls by the Wafd to hold elections for a new parliament. Growing friction between the prime minister and high commissioner led the cabinet to adopt "attitudes of intransigent nationalism" with regard to a variety of matters.[76] Nevertheless, the ministers found themselves unable to cultivate ties to any of the established political parties, all of which considered the selection and appointment of the premier and his colleagues to have been illegitimate. Finding itself increasingly marginalized, the Yahya government had no interest in building bridges either to Britain's new-found ally on the Arabian peninsula, King 'Abd al-'Aziz, nor to King Fu'ad's putative ally, the Imam Yahya. At best, the cabinet was favorably disposed toward Italy's half-hearted attempts to intervene in the fighting: a larger and more active Italian presence in the Red Sea could be expected to weaken British predominance in the region, while at the same time containing the rising Saudi state. Such sentiments contributed to British hostility toward Yahya's cabinet, and the prime minister finally submitted his resignation in early May 1934.[77]

Pro-Italian sympathies were shared by the palace, which was smarting under heightened British surveillance and interference.[78] Since Rome had provided military assistance to Yemen, it was not surprising that the imam turned to King Fu'ad as the crisis erupted into war. But even their increasing aggravation at the actions of the high commissioner could not lure the king and his advisers into responding favorably to Yemeni overtures, since doing so would put the palace at odds with Britain's regional interests. London was already suspicious of King Fu'ad for dismissing the Sidqi government without explicit British authorization.

Furthermore, as Wafdist critics were quick to point out, any effort on Egypt's part to mediate between the warring parties was precluded by the absence of working relations with King 'Abd al-'Aziz. Cairo's relationship with Riyadh, which appeared to be amicable at the beginning of the decade, had suffered a number of serious setbacks as the 1920s passed, due to recurrent conflicts over the terms under which the official Egyptian caravan could take part in the annual pilgrimage to Mecca.[79] As a result, al-Jihad commented, Cairo found itself in an unenviable position:

> All the Muslims in the world have unanimously expressed the desire
> that the differences existing between King Ibn Sa'ud and the Imam
> of the Yemen should be settled amicably in order to avoid Muslim

bloodshed. Meanwhile, they have felt the danger of the interference of non-Muslims in these differences and have gone as far as to warn the Christian Powers against interference in the matter which concerns the Muslims alone. The Arab world wishes to see Egypt taking the lead in intermediation to settle the differences between the two Arab sovereigns and the Muslim world wishes to see her rising to occupy the position which conforms with her capacity as a leader of the Muslim countries. On the other hand, Egypt states that Islam is her official religion and that Arabic is her official language. Also there exists in Egypt the University of al-Azhar which asserts that it is the greatest guardian of Islam. Hence it was expected and it was only reasonable that Egypt should be the first to respond to the appeal of the Muslims throughout the world and to intercede with the two Arab sovereigns in an attempt to settle their differences amicably, thereby earning the satisfaction, appreciation and admiration of the Muslim world. But because the government in Egypt does not recognize the government in Mecca, Egypt has kept silent and has refrained from taking an interest in a matter which preoccupies the attention of the Muslims and Arabs in all parts of the world, and even occupies the attention of the Egyptians themselves.[80]

Given these circumstances, King Fu'ad kept his attention narrowly focused on domestic affairs. He emerged, to the public's surprise, as a staunch advocate of restoring the 1923 Constitution.[81] In addition, the king took unprecedented steps to curb political intrigue and corruption on the part of the palace.[82] But wrestling simultaneously with his advisers, the British administration and the Wafd steadily sapped his health, and in August 1934 the king fell victim to a severe illness. Medical specialists were summoned, and "gave such a gloomy prognosis that his demise was expected within a matter of weeks."[83] Any lingering possibility that the palace might play an active part in mediating the war in Arabia thereby evaporated.

Conclusion

Existing studies of Egyptian diplomacy in the 1920s and 1930s err in asserting that Cairo stood aloof from the outside world prior to the 1936 Treaty of Alliance with Britain. Government officials, nationalist leaders and other influential public figures took a lively interest in international affairs, and debates in parliament and the press over the country's role in the Arab and Muslim worlds frequently ignited heated controversy. Furthermore, within the broad parameters laid down by British imperial authorities, successive Egyptian governments pursued a number of diplomatic and strategic initiatives, some of which directly contravened the expressed preferences of the country's de facto overlords.

Moreover, explanations for Egyptian foreign policy during this period in terms of what students of international relations call the 'rational actor model' are almost certain to prove misleading. No single agent decided or implemented the country's responses to external challenges during the years of the monarchy. Instead, foreign policy resulted from the complex interaction of at least four influential actors: the palace, the Wafd, the smaller parties that competed with the Wafd, and the British administration. Cairo's dealings with the outside world seldom, if ever, reflected the preferences of any one, or indeed any combination, of these agents, but instead represented an unintended consequence of clashes among all four of them. This makes it impossible to posit any single rationale behind Egyptian diplomacy in the 1920s and 1930s, not even the quest for full independence.

These findings have two noteworthy implications for future scholarship on Egyptian foreign policy. First, the task of making sense of a country's variegated dealings with the outside world, which tends to be difficult and susceptible to oversimplification and post hoc reasoning under the best of circumstances, will be even more demanding in this particular case. Stipulating that foreign policy can best be seen as the unintended consequence of domestic conflicts remains an unconventional and counterintuitive proposition, despite a growing body of literature that demonstrates the fruitfulness of this approach. Besides, linking foreign policy to the interests, objectives, or perceptions of a single actor appears to conform to the widely accepted methodological principle known as Occam's Razor. The simplest answer, however, is not always the most profound, and may by its very obviousness lead the unwary to problematic conclusions.

Second, studies of Egypt's external relations during the 1920s and 1930s will profit greatly from paying careful attention to a broad range of internal developments that are not usually associated with diplomatic history. Trends in gender relations covered most notably by Hanan Kholoussy and Shaun Lopez in this volume, or educational matters which Misako Ikeda explores in chapter eight—all things that might be considered irrelevant to diplomacy in other contexts—can be expected to provide important insights into the societal struggles that had a major impact on Egyptian foreign policy during the last three decades of the monarchy. As a country that remained subject to de facto imperial control, but boasted a highly mobilized citizenry fighting almost continuously for national independence, monarchical Egypt represents a state in which changes in the content of history textbooks covered by Barak Salmoni in chapter six, or the imagery displayed in public sculpture covered in chapter fifteen by Caroline Williams, all indicate trends that intimately connect to foreign relations. Future scholars will also need to plot out the connections between diplomatic initiatives, on the one hand, and the internal politics of Egypt's social groups on the other, to include army officers whom Tewfik Aclimandos explores in this volume's next chapter, or the 'new' *effendiya* illuminated by Lucie Ryzova in chapter five. Ultimately, explanations that focus exclusively on the embassies and conference rooms where 'high politics' takes place will most likely overlook subtle dynamics that are crucial to our understanding of how Egypt actually interacted with its neighbors during this long-neglected era.

Notes

1   James Jankowski, "The Egyptian Wafd and Arab Nationalism, 1918–1944," in Edward Ingram, ed. *National and International Politics in the Middle East* (London: Frank Cass, 1986); Israel Gershoni and James P. Jankowski, *Redefining the Egyptian Nation 1930–1945* (Cambridge: Cambridge University Press, 1995), 147; Ralph M. Coury, *The Making of an Egyptian Arab Nationalist: The Early Years of Azzam Pasha, 1893–1936* (Reading: Ithaca Press, 1998), 392–93 and 441–42; Nabih Bayyumi 'Abdullah, *Qadaya 'arabiya fi al-barliman al-Misri 1924–1958* (Cairo: al-Haya al-Misriya al-'Amma li-l-Kitab, 1996). A tangential issue that periodically attracted the attention of successive Egyptian rulers was the matter of what to do about the Islamic Caliphate, particularly after that institution was abolished by the Turkish nationalists in March 1924; see Elie Kedourie, "Egypt and the Caliphate, 1915–1952," in his *The Chatham House Version and Other Middle-Eastern Studies* (Hanover, NH: University Press of New England, 1984).

2   James Jankowski, "Egyptian Responses to the Palestine Problem in the Interwar Period," *International Journal of Middle East Studies* 12: 3 (August 1980); Abd Al-Fattah Muhammad El-Awaisi, *The Muslim Brothers and the Palestine Question 1928–1947* (London: Tauris Academic, 1998), chapter 2; Basheer M. Nafi, *Arabism, Islamism and the Palestine Question 1908–1941* (Reading: Ithaca Press, 1998), chapter 4; Rif'at al-Sa'id, *al-Yasar al-misri w-al-qadaya al-filistiniya* (Beirut: Matba'at al-Farabi, 1974).

3   Thomas Mayer, "Egypt and the General Islamic Conference of Jerusalem in 1931," *Middle Eastern Studies* 18: 3 (July 1982); Uri M. Kupferschmidt, "The General Muslim Congress of 1931 in Jerusalem," *Asian and African Studies* 12 (March 1978); H.A.R. Gibb, "The Islamic Congress at Jerusalem in December 1931," in Arnold J. Toynbee, *Survey of International Affairs 1934* (London: Oxford University Press, 1935); Ralph M. Coury, "Egyptians in Jerusalem: Their Role in the General Islamic Conference of 1931," *Muslim World* 82 (January–April 1992).

4   See Gabriel R. Warburg, "The Sinai Peninsula Borders, 1906–47," *Journal of Contemporary History* 14 (October 1979).

5   Jankowski, "Egyptian Wafd and Arab Nationalism," 167; Martin Kramer, "Shaykh Maraghi's Mission to the Hijaz, 1925," *Asian and African Studies* 16 (March 1982); Israel Gershoni and James P. Jankowski, *Egypt, Islam and the Arabs* (New York: Oxford University Press, 1986), 239–45.

6   Jankowski, "Egyptian Wafd and Arab Nationalism," 167–168; Gershoni and Jankowski, *Egypt, Islam and the Arabs*, 245–47.

7   Itamar Rabinovich, "Inter-Arab Relations Foreshadowed: The Question of the Syrian Throne in the 1920s and 1930s," in *Festschrift in Honor of Dr. George S. Wise* (Tel Aviv: Tel Aviv University, 1981), 246. See also Elie Podeh, "The Emergence of the Arab State System Reconsidered," *Diplomacy and Statecraft* 9 (November 1998), 61–62.

8   Rabinovich, "Inter-Arab Relations Foreshadowed," 246.

9   Podeh, "Emergence of the Arab State System," 54.

10   U.S. National Archives, Record Group 59, 783.90j/3, 17 July 1929. The agreements with Yemen preceded Egypt's Treaty of Friendship and Bon Voisinage with Iraq by some two years. Cf. Gershoni and Jankowski, *Redefining the Egyptian Nation*, 147.

11   Yehoshua Porath, *In Search of Arab Unity 1930–1945* (London: Frank Cass, 1986).

12   Arnold J. Toynbee, *Survey of International Affairs 1925: The Islamic World Since the Peace Settlement* (London: Oxford University Press, 1927), 185.

13   Yunan Labib Rizk, "A Deal That Was Never Ratified," *Al-Ahram Weekly*, 30 November–6 December 2000.

14   *Egyptian Gazette*, 20 February 1925.

15   *Egyptian Gazette*, 13, 16, and 17 February 1925.

16   *Egyptian Gazette*, 20 and 21 February 1925.

17   *New York Times*, 21 February 1925.

18   *Egyptian Gazette*, 2 March 1925.

19   *Egyptian Gazette*, 23 February 1925.

20   *Egyptian Gazette*, 3 March 1925.

21   *Egyptian Gazette*, 3 March 1925.

22   *Egyptian Gazette*, 7 April 1925.

23   *Egyptian Gazette*, 9 April 1925.

24   *Egyptian Gazette*, 12 April 1925.

25   *Egyptian Gazette*, 16 April 1925.

26   *Egyptian Gazette*, 17 April 1925.

27   *Egyptian Gazette*, 18 April 1925.

28   *Egyptian Gazette*, 28 April 1925.

29   *Egyptian Gazette*, 29 April 1925.

30   *Egyptian Gazette*, 1 and 7 May 1925.

31   *Egyptian Gazette*, 9 May 1925.

32   *Egyptian Gazette*, 9 and 20 May 1925.

33   *Egyptian Gazette*, 22 May 1925.

34   *Egyptian Gazette*, 25 May 1925.

35   *Egyptian Gazette*, 26 May 1925.

36   *Egyptian Gazette*, 29 June 1925.

37   Malak Badrawi, *Isma'il Sidqi (1875–1950): Pragmatism and Vision in Twentieth Century Egypt* (Richmond: Curzon, 1996), 41–42.

38   Afaf Lutfi al-Sayyid-Marsot, *Egypt's Liberal Experiment: 1922–1936* (Berkeley: University of California Press, 1977), 88.

39   Toynbee, *Survey of International Affairs 1925*, 187.

40 Gershoni and Jankowski, *Egypt, Islam and the Arabs*, 239.

41 Al-Sayyid-Marsot, *Egypt's Liberal Experiment*, 89.

42 *New York Times*, 9 February 1926.

43 Rizk, "A Deal That Was Never Ratified."

44 Toynbee, *Survey of International Affairs 1934*, 310–316.

45 U.S. National Archives, Record Group 84, Confidential Correspondence: Aden, 1933–39, vol. 163, Fox to Secretary of State, 31 July 1933.

46 Toynbee, *Survey of International Affairs 1934*, 316–17.

47 U.S. National Archives, Record Group 84, Confidential Correspondence: Aden, 1933–39, vol. 163, Knabenshue to Secretary of State, 3 May 1934.

48 *Egyptian Gazette*, 30 March 1934.

49 Ibid.

50 *Egyptian Gazette*, 1 April 1934.

51 *Egyptian Gazette*, 3 April 1934.

52 *Egyptian Gazette*, 4 April 1934.

53 *Egyptian Gazette*, 9 April 1934.

54 Ibid.

55 *Egyptian Gazette*, 1 April 1934.

56 Gibb, "Islamic Congress at Jerusalem," 109.

57 *Egyptian Gazette*, 24 May 1934.

58 *Egyptian Gazette*, 25 May 1934.

59 *Egyptian Gazette*, 26 May 1934.

60 *Egyptian Gazette*, 28 May 1934.

61 *Egyptian Gazette*, 29 May 1934.

62 *Egyptian Gazette*, 31 May 1934.

63 *Egyptian Gazette*, 13 June 1934.

64 *Egyptian Gazette*, 16 June 1934.

65 *Egyptian Gazette*, 25 June 1934.

66 *Egyptian Gazette*, 6 July 1934.

67 Coury, *Making of an Egyptian Arab Nationalist*, 330.

68 See Charles D. Smith, "4 February 1942: Its Causes and Its Influences on Egyptian Politics," *International Journal of Middle East Studies* 10: 4 (November 1979).

69 *Egyptian Gazette*, 15 July 1924.

70 *Egyptian Gazette*, 15 December 1924.

71 Al-Sayyid-Marsot, *Egypt's Liberal Experiment*, 82.

72 bid., 88.

73 Badrawi, *Isma'il Sidqi*, 109.

74 Al-Sayyid-Marsot, *Egypt's Liberal Experiment*, 171–72.

75 Ibid., 161; Marius Deeb, *Party Politics in Egypt: The Wafd and its Rivals 1919–1939* (London: Ithaca Press, 1979), 246–48.

76 Deeb, *Party Politics in Egypt*, 252.

77 Jacques Berque, *Egypt: Imperialism and Revolution* (New York: Praeger, 1972), 453.

78 Al-Sayyid-Marsot, *Egypt's Liberal Experiment*, 172–73.

79 Toynbee, *Survey of International Affairs 1925*, 319; Berque, *Egypt: Imperialism and Revolution*, 447.

80 *Egyptian Gazette*, 3 May 1934.

81 Berque, *Egypt: Imperialism and Revolution*, 454.

82 Deeb, *Party Politics in Egypt*, 252–53.

83 Al-Sayyid-Marsot, *Egypt's Liberal Experiment*, 172.

3   Revisiting the History
   of the Egyptian Army

Tewfik Aclimandos

This chapter recasts political activism in the Egyptian army between 1940 and 1952 and demonstrates the evolution of the social composition of the officer corps. Historians have so far not treated these two themes convincingly. The social history of the Egyptian army has not been successfully written, and the first attempts strayed off course. Academic conventional wisdom identifies 1936 as the decisive turning point. Most scholars believe that before that year, most officers had Turco-Circassian origins or came from well-to-do families.[1] According to this general consensus, following the 1936 Anglo-Egyptian Treaty the Military Academy was reformed, its admissions criteria were democratized, and a new recruitment strategy was adopted. As a result, the social composition of the officer corps changed, with the admission, for the first time, of persons of Egyptian background who came from the lower and middle strata of the bourgeoisie or from small or middle landowning families. According to these views, this evolution led to the rise of nationalism in the army, which would eventually cause the fall of the monarchy.

Lately, these views have come under scrutiny. For example, the Egyptian historian Ra'uf 'Abbas admitted at a conference in 2003 that those views were unacceptable, given a lack of evidence to sustain the construction of a sharp dichotomy based on ethnicity. He proposed a subtler interpretation, trying to salvage the idea of a decisive and radical turning point situated in 1936, perhaps through analogies to conclusions of research he had conducted on the history of the Egyptian university. His idea might be summarized as follows. Before 1936, a native Egyptian of modest social background who wished to find a job or to be admitted to any governmental institution had to beg for it—to find and implore an upper class sponsor.[2] After 1936, this was no longer necessary. Egyptians of modest background had gained the *right* to join the military. The monarchical regime could no longer block young nationalists' admission to governmental institutions (even if they were not embedded in clientelist networks).

This approach seems more reasonable, but remains problematic. For instance, it is clear that the dichotomy between the 'holder of a right' and a beggar, while interesting in theory, breaks down in practice: even after 1936 an applicant still needed the intervention of a strong protector. 'Abd al-Nasser and Sadat had to pursue intercession, and they were not alone: even aspirants of considerably higher status had to ask for intervention. The organization of the admissions procedure gave the authorities discretionary powers enabling them to eliminate an unwanted candidate: the exam named *kashf hay'a* was, of course, a test of the aspirant's psychological readiness and general culture.[3] But its main purpose was to check the candidate's social origins, in order to eliminate the "unworthy."[4] Ra'uf 'Abbas's comments, however, do indicate a change of *perception* after 1936: for young people of middle class and petty bourgeois backgrounds, admission to the military academy now *seemed* possible, albeit still difficult. And this perception had *consequences*. Still, other factors might be at least as central. For instance, a careful examination could confirm that the army's rising demand for personnel led the authorities to abandon their implicit political conditions for admission or to relax controls on the students' political background (this is especially true after the big 1935 uprising, which mobilized the majority of educated youth). We must also remember that after 1936 the monarchy was seeking an alliance with young educated nationalists against domestic political opponents.

The academic conventional wisdom of 1936 as the watershed of change also contradicts participants' memories. Ten years ago, I asked a dozen old officers, some of them officers' sons, whether the corps was totally or predominantly 'Turkish' before 1936. I also asked whether, at the beginning of their career, the senior officers were of Turkish descent. *All* the people polled found the questions comical. Wafiq Draz, a Free Officer (born in 1931) and a son of a high-ranking officer (Amiralay Abu al-Futuh Draz) told this writer, for instance, that, as far as he remembered, *all* his father's colleagues and friends were of Egyptian descent, and wondered how a historian could be incapable of making distinctions between Muhammad

'Ali's and Fu'ad's armies. 'Abd al-Ra'uf Nafi' (Free Officer, born in 1916), answered more charitably: "Like us. Egyptians. Maybe some of them had a Turkish mother. But this is also true for our generation."

To approach this question, one must first address some methodological issues. First of all, it is impossible to determine scientifically a person's ethnic origins, especially if the sample studied is large. Let us take the example of a prototypical officer. One has to determine his parents' origins. This is neither easy nor sufficient. It is necessary, in order to identify his parents' origins, to determine those of his grandparents. Confronted with this problem, the Nazis—self-styled experts on racial issues—tried to solve it by adopting different criteria:[5] they looked at people's religions and decided that a set of family names proved their ethnic origins. The first criterion does not help: Turco-Circassians were Muslims, just as were Egyptians. Paradoxically, it only points to a Coptic presence in the army. The name criterion matters little, for the majority of Egyptians do not have family names. We may assign to officers having peculiar first names, such as "Khamis," a purely Egyptian descent, or limit ourselves to those few who have family names. But it is clear that a sample so selected would not represent the whole officer corps, for it will be composed of higher status persons. Rather, one might examine a sample of holders of family names, by interrogating the sources, consulting the press, and collecting examples. Though the result remains partial and open to further investigation, in the present chapter it serves as a key principle of selection.

Another problem is that a dichotomy 'before vs. after 1936' obscures the fact that the two periods considered are not homogeneous. History is not static, either before or after that crucial year. We cannot rule out some important evolutions or significant discrepancies between the two eras. Unfortunately, our data do not suffice to draw an exhaustive picture. Here, however, is an illustrative example: at least two persons of relatively modest background, both of them admitted to the Military Academy in 1938, both Free Officers and later RCC members, claimed in public statements that they gained admission despite poverty and lack of connections. This may seem impossible, as even quite wealthy young people had to look for support. But one of these sources (Hasan Ibrahim) had a plausible explanation: a few days before the new academic year began, rumors spread of an impending world war.[6] Many new cadets, of *ibn al-dhawat* (affluent) background, got cold feet and withdrew their candidacy. The authorities, lacking time to prepare another set of exams, accepted the first candidates to show up; alternatively, they admitted candidates who had passed all the exams but the *kashf hay'a*. It would be interesting to know whether this cohort (receiving degrees in November 1939) was an exception or the pioneer class in the process of greater democratization that occurred during the war years. The data do not suffice, but the available evidence points to the first explanation.

The third methodological problem can be stated briefly: in Egypt of the thirties, especially during the crisis years, there was no correlation between social status and wealth, or between wealth and well-being. For instance, 'Abd al-Nasser's father's income should have sufficed to guarantee a very decent livelihood for a small family.[7] Unfortunately, he had many children.

From a random sample of officers, one may draw three conclusions.[8] First, the democratization of admission procedures after the 1936 reforms must not be overestimated. The (Wafdist) legislators may have wanted a radical rupture with the past but facts were more elastic and subtle. For instance, the pre-1936 army was hardly aristocratic, and the officer corps already had an extremely important native Egyptian component. Some of the officers came from truly modest backgrounds, originating as enlisted or non-commissioned officers (NCO) and then promoted. Indeed, one must not forget that before 1936 the Military Academy was not the sole producer of officers. The post-1936 officer corps still came predominantly from well-to-do backgrounds, from middle and upper-middle class families, rather than the petite bourgeoisie—the latter being a trend seen in the early 1960s. 'Abd al-Nasser and Sadat were *exceptions*, not representatives of a pattern. After twenty years of fieldwork, this writer has not found any son of a landless peasant or of a worker in the post-1936 cohorts.

If this chapter's sample of Free Officers represents the social origins of the whole corps, they are predominantly of middle and upper-middle class status. According to the officers' conventional wisdom, their peers of this generation generally came from "good families."[9] The fees for the Academy were high (£E 60, according to Hamrush).[10] Stories abound that cadets of relatively poor background (like 'Abd al-Nasser, though he was not technically poor) were the object of occasional or persistent teasing.[11] Candidates for admission far outnumbered the available places,[12] criteria such as physical fitness and good health played an important role, and connections *(wasta)* were often crucial. Such a situation generally favors the sons of resourceful and rich families.

Academy admission did become easier after 1936 and a real, albeit limited, democratization of its procedures was perceptible. For instance, the requirements related to the financial status of the civilian father of a candidate became less rigid. But it is difficult to measure the real impact of this change because it was matched by another one that held back social mobility: the Academy became the main producer of officers and fewer officers rose from among the enlisted. Data do not suffice to determine the weight of the two trends, though at least three officers told the author that the 1936 reforms caused an *amelioration* of the social origins of the officer corps, which was not the legislation's supposed purpose. To say the least, trends were not as clear-cut as previously thought. As seen below, the presence of officers' sons who became officers challenges the idea of a socioethnic earthquake in the post-1936 army.

The second conclusion is that it is highly doubtful that the alleged 'Egyptianization' of the officer corps led to a rise of political activism. The very idea of 'Egyptianness' is vague and difficult to verify, and, as previously stated, the army already had a very strong Egyptian component before 1936. In fact, this ethnic divide, Egyptian vs. Turkish and Circassian, can be construed in two different ways. We can understand it as an opposition between an aristocracy and the rest of the people. In that case, we have propositions that can be tested, and they are simply wrong. Before 1936, and even around 1900, the officer corps was not aristocratic.[13] The other manner of constructing the ethnic divide is much more vicious, and cannot be scientifically tested. It implies either that only pure ethnic Egyptians are nationalists, or that they are much more patriotic than everyone else. Prima facie, this racist thesis is wrong. This chapter has already high-lighted the presence of an important Egyptian component in the army. For instance, Muhammad Naguib, Rashad Mihanna, Muhammad Haydar, al-Mawawi, the Sayf al-Yazal Khalifas, the Rimalis, Mitwalli Sawi and his sons, 'Abd al-Mun'im 'Abd al-Ra'uf, and al-Rahmani were Egyptians. There is no correlation between the Egyptian component and political activism. More significant still, Egypt has an honor roll of prestigious nationalists who were not purely ethnic Egyptians. Examples include 'Abd al-Rahman Fahmi,[14] one of the heroes of the 1919 uprising, 'Aziz 'Ali al-Misri, the activists' spiritual father,[15] and Ahmad 'Abd al-'Aziz, the legendary hero of the 1948 war,[16] were not purely ethnic Egyptians. In the younger generation, Wajih Abaza was not a purely ethnic Egyptian. This is but a portion of a long list.

Moreover, it is impossible to prove a person's origins; the number of practical and logical problems that have to be solved is staggering. For instance, we cannot assume that a person of provincial background is purely Egyptian: such a person can be of Arab, Turkish, Syrian, or Caucasian descent. For example, 'Abd al-Nasser and Salah Nasr had Arab blood.[17] Last but not least, such ethnic classification neglects Egypt's social geography and the important rise of interethnic marriages during the fifty years preceding 1936. The classification of the son of a rural notable and a Turkish mother, a rather common case, is problematic. To cite another relevant example, a branch of the al-Shahids, a Turkish family that consistently gave many of its sons to the army, had Sudanese ancestry.[18]

In the rest of this chapter, any person born in Egypt who does not belong to a self-identified Turkish family or to the Turkish aristocracy, who has at least one parent regarded, rightly or wrongly, by the conventional wisdom as 'purely' Egyptian, and whose mother tongue is Arabic will be considered a pure Egyptian. Furthermore, it is simply wrong to claim that the Egyptian countryside (rif) was not represented in the army before 1936.

The third conclusion is that the rise of political activism in the army cannot be ascribed to 'Egyptianization.' The class structure seldom explains ideological and political choices. But we might test the idea of a change in the class origins of the officers' corps, explaining the rise in nationalist activity by the slow replacement of officers of modest backgrounds by younger officers from middle-class origins. In effect, then, the rise of politicization would result from the opposite of democratization. But the data, for the time being, are unavailable: we do not know the real importance of the phenomenon of officers rising from the ranks, either before or after 1936, and therefore we cannot measure the impact of its decline. And claiming that one class is not patriotic seems unfair; other explanations are more plausible.

Social Reproduction

Let us now briefly focus on the social reproduction of the military, in a critical evaluation of the conventional academic wisdom. This phenomenon has been grossly underestimated by Hamrush, who wrote, for instance, that no Free Officer with the exception of Naguib was the son of an officer. His assertion is wrong. Although he acknowledges that military families existed, they are not integrated into his analysis. He states that the officers' sons did not follow the career of their fathers, but he only gives one example, a military man (Muhammad Mahir) whose sons had to choose their career at the turn of the century, in a period of Egypt's history when the officer corps did not attract ambitious young men.[19]

There were a striking number of cadets admitted to the Military Academy after the 1936 reforms, who had a father, older brother, or cousin who belonged to the officer corps. This fact should have drawn the attention of historians, and deterred them from accepting the 'Egyptianization' thesis. A few examples suffice: Zakariya Muhi al-Din's cohort (the first one after the reforms) had in its ranks a majority of officers' sons.[20] If we consider the Free Officers as a sample, we find a limited number of officers' sons, but many of its members had uncles, older brothers, or cousins in the officer corps. Officers' sons include Naguib and Yusuf Mansur Siddiq (both admitted to the Academy before 1936), Tharwat 'Ukasha, Ahmad Kamil, Amin Shakir, Ma'ruf al-Hidri, Rashdan, Mustafa Kamal Lutfi, and Wafiq Draz. Many Free Officers had older relatives in the corps: Siddiq had a maternal uncle, Salah Nasr was the nephew of another officer and the cousin of General 'Uthman al-Mahdi,[21] 'Abd al-Hakim 'Amir's mother was Haydar Pasha's cousin,[22] 'Abd al-Ra'uf Nafi' was the General 'Umar Tantawi's cousin,[23] Abu al-Fadl al-Jizawi had an officer uncle, 'Ali Fahmi Sharif had a considerably older brother who was commander of the artillery branch,[24] and the young Hasan Mahmud Salih had a much older brother officer.[25]

If we broaden the scope of our examination to cover the other members of these generations, the results are even more impressive. All of the following were officers' sons: the future chief of the Mukhabarat (Intelligence), Hafiz Isma'il (admitted to the Academy before 1936); 'Abd al-Mun'im 'Abd al-Ra'uf (also admitted before 1936); 'Abd al-Mun'im Riyad, the famous chief of staff who died in 1969 on the front line;[26] Jamal 'Askar, founder of the Central Agency for Public Mobilization and Statistics (CAPMAS);[27] Muhammad Ahmad Sadiq, Sadat's second defense minister;[28] General 'Abd al-Rahman Fahmi; Mustafa Mukhtar, who became a diplomat after the Revolution; Yahya Khudayr;[29] and Sa'ad Mitwalli were all officers' sons.[30]

Moreover, obituaries published in *al-Ahram* reveal the existence of old Egyptian and, of course, Turkish military dynasties. The Egyptian ones include al-Battuti, Sawi, Fahmi, Khudayr, Humayda, Muji, Hajjaj, Qusi, Shukri, and Rimali dynasties. In his autobiography, 'Abd al-Mun'im 'Abd al-Ra'uf wrote that he was born into a family of *'ulama'* and officers. He had a father, many uncles, and an elder brother belonging to the officer corps. In his often neglected study of the social origins of the officers who fell in the 1948 War, Eliezer Be'eri showed that the dead were often sons, nephews, or cousins of high-ranking officers.[31]

Further proof follows that the Egyptian presence in the army must not be underestimated. First, the majority of the army commanders during the 1948 War were non-Turkish, and they had chosen their career before 1920 (examples include Haydar, al-Mawawi, Sadiq, 'Uthman al-Mahdi, Sa'd al-Din Sabbur, Sayf al-Yazal Khalifa, Naguib, al-Sayyid Taha, and Hafiz Bakri). Second, at least two of the stars of the Military Academy teaching staff,

'Umar Tantawi and Muhammad Fattuh, were not Turkish, and had familial roots in the countryside.[32] Third, one of the most celebrated Egyptian poets of the beginning of the century, Hafiz Ibrahim, was an officer of purely Egyptian descent. His peers (poets and officers) Muhammad Tawfiq 'Ali, 'Abd al-Halim Hilmi al-Misri, and Muhammad Fadil, were also Egyptians. Muhammad Bayyumi, the first Egyptian moviemaker, was also an officer of 'Egyptian descent' with roots in the countryside.[33] Fourth, though 'Ali and Ahmad Mahir were the sons of a 'Turco-Circassian' officer, their maternal grandfather was an Egyptian officer (who married a Turkish woman).[34] Salih Harb and Mahmud Labib, both older than Naguib, were also officers of Egyptian descent. Fifth, Prince 'Umar Tusun published a list of the officers who were serving in Sudan and protested against the British government's measures following the murder of the Sirdar in November 1924. Of course, it is impossible to determine the "ethnic origins" of the majority, but for those who can be documented (the case for a sizeable minority) the officers are Egyptian.[35] Finally, Muhammad Naguib;[36] Ahmad Shawqi; Yusuf Siddiq; and 'Abd al-Mun'im Amin, who played a crucial role during the 1952 coup; Rashad Mihanna, the future regent; 'Abd al-Mun'im 'Abd al-Ra'uf and his brother 'Abd al-Qadir; Sidqi Mahmud (the air force commander during the 1956 and 1967 wars); 'Abd al-Khaliq Kamil (the last four names mentioned were, as well as Siddiq, officers' sons);[37] 'Abd al-Wahhab al-Bishri ('Abd al-Nasser's defense minister); and Ahmad Fahim Bayyumi were all of Egyptian descent and admitted to the Academy before 1936.

Let us conclude this discussion with two general points. First, in 1882, when Lord Dufferin began to reorganize the army after 'Urabi's defeat, he decided to bar foreign elements, including Albanians, Anatolians, and Circassians, but allowed the Egyptianized (i.e., assimilated) Turks and the Egyptians of Turkish descent to choose this career. The 'pure' ethnic Egyptians had a strong presence and the British never obstructed their promotion, lest an 'Urabi uprising recur.[38] This policy endured throughout the British occupation. It is thus impossible to speak of a Turco-Circassian elite before 1923. Second, to quote a wise observer of military matters, the late Hafiz Isma'il: "My father joined the officer corps when it was built up again in the last decade of the nineteenth century. . . . When the time came, a great number of officers sent their sons to the Military Academy, thus creating a new tradition in the Egyptian army."[39]

The 1936 reforms were very important, but they must be described properly. From available evidence, the real changes can be summarized into three main points. First, degree requirements were raised, a trend that preceded the 1936 reforms. In 1928, a decree stipulated that the cadet should have completed some secondary studies. Before that, graduating from primary school was enough. In 1917, the admission tests were quite rudimentary: some gymnastics, math exercises, and dictation. By the end of the forties, the admissions criteria, although more relaxed than those for western academies, were rigorous by local standards.[40]

Second, the officer corps was more professional. After 1936, the quality of the education and training improved slowly but markedly. The war school was founded in 1938. Up to 1940, the instructors were highly competent British officers, and the Academy's rector was Brigadier G. Austin.[41] In theory, the studies lasted three years, but this was not the case for the first classes. Their studies were shortened to meet the pressing needs of the army.[42] It is also interesting that the officers belonging to the post-1936 generations of cadets, when they criticize their elders of the pre-1936 cohorts, blame them for their incompetence,[43] their servility toward the British,[44] and sometimes for their alcoholism,[45] but almost never frame their criticism in ethnic terms.

Finally, there was a marked increase in the recruitment of cadets, coming mainly from middle class families, who were always well-represented in the army, but with a possibly growing minority of sons of the lower middle class. But representation of this class in the officer corps remained weak until 1952, and possibly even 1961.[46] According to General Ibrahim Shakib, the army counted in its ranks 607 officers in 1936; 664 in 1938; 1,421 in 1939; 1,633 in January 1942; 1,962 in October 1942; 2,029 in January 1944; and 2,206 in January 1946, amounting to a 300 percent increase in ten years. The military career became a serious option for middle class young men. Some Egyptian families that did not have a single officer before 1936 saw their sons admitted to the Military Academy, a brother leading another into the career, and a young man persuading his classmates to enter the officer corps.[47] In this chapter's sample, this recurs often, as in two striking examples: the class of future RCC member Kamal al-Din Husayn in the Ibrahimiya Secondary School contained twenty students, of whom ten became officers.[48] In his autobiography, Hamrush recalls that seventeen students of the Tawfiqiya School, all of them belonging to the class that preceded his, were admitted to the Academy.[49]

The overwhelming majority of the newcomers were ethnic Egyptians. After the 1936 reforms, the young nationalists, generally from middle class background, could hope for better advancement prospects. Joining the army became an interesting option: a well-paid job in the service of the nation, contributing to its strength and modernization. It is hard to know if before 1936 the army was the refuge of unworthy sons of notable families.[50] But after 1936, the officer corps included many bright, young professionals and fervent nationalists—many of whom detested the political practices and realities of the times.[51]

Thus, after 1936, we see a limited democratization of admission to the Academy (easing the stated financial conditions for admission), coupled with curricular reforms. The Academy's role in producing officers grew, while the incidence of officers rising from the ranks fell. Available evidence does not suffice to describe the processes in terms of profound changes in the ethnic composition, or of a democratization of the officer corps' social origins. What really changed was the institutional and structural framework. The army now had to be ready to defend the land and tried to strengthen itself for that purpose. In order to achieve this, it recruited more and more cadets, probably from the same sources, and it provided much better instruction. An eventual opening to the lower classes may have occurred, but it remains to be proven. The variable possibility for a son of the petite bourgeoisie to be admitted to the Academy was offset by the declining commissioning of officers from the ranks.

Explaining Activism

Therefore, we must seek another explanation for the rise of political activism. Let us consider briefly some theories of frustration. Economic or materialist grounds were irrelevant. The officers were well-paid and the regime paid close attention to their material requests and grievances.[52] King Faruq and his men courted them. We may, however, partially accept the 'professional frustration' thesis: the discovery of the real world, so different from the ideal one taught by the curriculum and prescribed by the value system, was often a great shock.[53] There is also a structural problem: the Military Academy was producing officers following a plan based on the army's *needs* and not its *resources*.[54] The plan assumed that the British wanted to have an efficient Egyptian army and would help them achieve this goal. Yet, Britain's interest in this project was varied and depended on good will (the needs of the British army got priority and the pro-Axis leanings of the king and of the young officers were frightening), on bad attitudes (colonial administrations were simply incapable of being generous), and on the evolution of the situation. The practical consequences were that the officer corps grew too rapidly, and the arms supply and other means were too scarce.

This remains a secondary factor. All the accounts and testimonies available strongly point to nationalism as the main cause for political engagement, though scholars tend to look for materialistic explanations and deconstruct any discourse. We must not overlook the fact that if all the discourses are constructed, particular ones are believed and legitimate. We must not forget that motives for human actions, especially in religious societies, are not always based on self-interest. Many soldiers' accounts relate an experience, which may be personal or based on another's narrative, with a foreigner, British, Greek, French, or other, constructed as behaving in a racist, greedy, haughty, or lofty way. This bad experience structures the narrator's world-view and ultimately leads him to become a firm nationalist. It is tempting and easy to deconstruct these incidents and to point out that the Egyptian upper class and the actors themselves were often guilty of the same behavior. What really matters is the actor's perception: for him, the Egyptian (the narrator or another victim) is maltreated because he is Egyptian. What is relevant is the phenomenon of self-identification with the victim, integrated with specific experiences of living under occupation and the daily humiliations inflicted on the natives by foreigners.[55]

The *younger* generations and political activists did not have a monopoly on nationalism, nor did they alone experience strong national feelings. For instance, it is clear that Muhammad Naguib, Muhammad Haydar, 'Aziz al-Misri, Ahmad Fu'ad Sadiq, Sa'd al-Din Sabbur, Salih Harb, Ahmad 'Abd al-'Aziz, Muhammad Kamil al-Rahmani, Mahmud Labib, and Rashad Mihanna[56] had similar passions. So why did this factor (nationalism) suddenly become crucial? But this amounts to asking two different questions: What happened before 1936? Why did the situation change in the late thirties? To answer the first question, though the 1922–36 period can be only briefly addressed, we do have evidence of episodic activism at the end of the nineteenth century, after the proclamation of the protectorate in 1914, and during the 1919 uprising, with an active participation of officers. Traces of passive resistance or of expressed dissatisfaction were evident during this period.[57]

Further, the 1922–36 period was not one of absolute calm. In 1924, before and after the sirdar's assassination in November, friction increased between Egyptian and British officers in Sudan, and a real conflict broke out between them after the murder. In July, the Egyptian officers protested after one of them was locked up in a jail instead of being held prisoner in a military garrison. They deplored the sudden ban by the British on the traditional acclamation of the Egyptian king's name. They wrote letters of protest against a British magistrate, who they accused of using insulting terms against the Egyptian king, in the grounds for a judicial decision published in the press. And after the sirdar's assassination and the British ultimatum, some Egyptian battalions mutinied, in a well-known episode.[58] Brigadier Rif'at, in relating the incidents, describes the officers' feelings as "sincere and real nationalism" (wataniya sadiqa). Yet, despite occasional resistance or expressions of dissatisfaction, the Sudan mutiny was rather the exception. Some individual initiatives did occur. Shakib wrote that some Egyptian officers were subjected to courts-martial, after having refused to obey vexatious British commands.[59] But this is not activism.

An Egyptian scholar has explained this passivity before 1936 by the strong British presence in the army, combined with the absence of Egyptians from the top of the hierarchy.[60] The situation, according to him, made it impossible for patriotic Egyptian officers to act. This is a strange explanation. A strong foreign presence and the obstruction of paths to promotion should have led to activism. The historian may be confusing action by the army with that by its officers. Or he may assume that the British exercised tight political control. According to Hamrush, the British officers were keeping a close watch over the army's political activities.[61] This sounds highly plausible, but Naguib, who plausibly claimed to have been politically active, does not mention such a control. No control, however stringent, can block political activity. Besides, the Egyptian army did not threaten the British and could at best slow down an invader. Moreover, the probability of a military coup was almost nil, due to the overwhelming presence of British troops and the vivid memories of 'Urabi's attempt.

An interesting explanation may be the lack of civilian support. In his autobiography, Naguib writes that after King Fu'ad dissolved the Wafdist parliament and forbade the MPs to assemble in 1929, he met with the Wafdist leader, Mustafa al-Nahhas Pasha. He told him that the army supported him and was ready to "do anything ordered by him." He even made a concrete proposition: "The battalions protecting and monitoring the Senate and Assembly's meetings won't bar access. Moreover, they are ready to help you to force the door." Al-Nahhas declined the offer, saying that he "wanted to keep the army out of political life: the nation should be the sole source of sovereignty." The largest Egyptian party, which could at the time seriously claim that it represented the nation, was, whatever its motives, legalist.[62]

The contrast in the 1940s is striking: the radical wing of the National Party, the Muslim Brothers, the Marxist organizations, and maybe Misr al-Fatat favored or even warmly welcomed officers' offers of collaboration. This became important over time, as activists in the army knew they acted in accordance with the beliefs of important segments of the population. They could secure assistance and help from civilians, had reliable and valuable sources of information, and even in some cases foot soldiers. We can thus combine these different elements with the volatile *Zeitgeist*. During the twenties, the mixture of Wafdist legalism, the political agenda of the times (securing British evacuation by peaceful and legal means), remembering the disastrous consequences for Egyptian nationalism of Sir Lee Stack's assassination, and the impossibility of securing a foreign power's support for the Egyptian cause ruled out political action by the Egyptian officers.

The situation changed greatly after 1936. The political forces challenging (if necessary by force) the status quo in Egypt were numerous and powerful. Charles Tripp and George Kirk brilliantly showed that Egypt's monarchy tried to secure the support of these new forces and of young constituencies to outbid the Wafd, to gain a new and Islamic legitimacy, and to impose new modes of action.[63] King Faruq, his men, and his allies frequently used nationalist demagogy, trying to capitalize on the weaknesses of the 1936 Treaty. The palace was no longer a moderating factor. World War II and the emergence of the Axis powers were seen as opportunities for Egypt by many forces, even by some wise statesmen. Last but not least, the war had an unintended and unwelcome consequence: an abundance in Egypt of available and quite sophisticated weapons. At least one political force and many clandestine organizations were now better armed than the police force.[64] The use of force could now more quickly become an option.

A Brief Story of Political Activism in the Army

The first young people admitted to the Military Academy after 1936 belonged to a generation marked by a strong political experience: the 1935 uprising.[65] They also had an idol: General 'Aziz 'Ali al-Misri, who became chief of staff shortly before the war.[66] Some of them would also seek guidance from other nationalist militants. Like many other Egyptians, they were thrilled by the Nazis' initial successes. Their attitude to King Faruq is not clear, their autobiographies and other testimonies offering contradictory evidence.[67] The officers who would become activists espoused a cult of force, sport, and nationalism. They enjoyed reading historical books, searching for inspiration, studying biographies of great men and national liberation movements (such as the Irish one).[68] Politically speaking, the activists were anti-Wafdist and anti-British, though there were differences among officers. Most of them were deeply aware of the social problems of the countryside, and favored an authoritarian solution to Egypt's ills. However, it is doubtful that political action against the regime was on their agenda.

Two 'triggers' could have affected them. The first was al-Misri's failure, which had a strong impact. The second was a collective mobilization at Marsa Matruh (September 1940), to prepare resistance against an attempt, real or imagined, by the British to disarm the Egyptian troops.[69] During the 1940–42 period, two main actors emerged. One was a more or less structured organization, founded by four air force officers, led by 'Abd al-Latif al-Baghdadi and Wajih Abaza. This group recruited 16–25 air force officers, plus Sadat. This is quite impressive: it means that a third or more of the air force officers joined the organization. The other was a loose constellation of young officers, gravitating around al-Misri. The most important ones were Wajih Khalil (deceased in 1948), Anwar al-Sadat, and 'Abd al-Mun'im 'Abd al-Ra'uf (who, although an air force officer, did not belong to Baghdadi's organization).

Two points deserve emphasis: first, before 1944, 'Abd al-Nasser was not politically active. Second, more crucially, the idea that al-Misri's clique, acting under 'Ali Mahir's instructions, founded a mega-organization whose purpose was to create a new order to back Faruq has very little support.[70] Even a superficial examination of the evidence suggests a different picture: there was no mega-organization. The young officers founded their own small groups and only then asked al-Misri for guidance. The general played a complicated game, probably without any real strategy: he tried to avoid undesirable organizational commitments and to play the nice and cost-free role of spiritual father. Occasionally, he used them. It is highly improbable that he was acting on Mahir's behalf.

These officers tried two *coups de force*. In the second, Sadat and 'Abd al-Ra'uf tried to arrange al-Misri's escape, which failed.[71] The air force group tried to hand maps of British bases in Egypt over to the Nazis, which succeeded.[72] These groups suffered some severe setbacks, first in 1941 with the arrest of 'Abd al-Mun'im 'Abd al-Ra'uf and then in 1942 with the death of Sa'udi Abu 'Ali, who tried to reach the Nazi forces in his plane, and finally with the arrest of Sadat and Hasan 'Izzat, also in 1942. After Britain's victory at al-'Alamayn, they lost hope and suspended their activities.

After the British victory, it was almost impossible to seek the support of a foreign power (except for the very few ready to embrace communism). Instead, two patterns emerged: the terrorist option without a clear political objective—killing Egyptian traitors or British soldiers; and the coalition-building option, either by joining the most important political force of the scene (the Muslim Brothers) or by organizing a collective action to mobilize as many nationalist officers as possible. Some officers oscillated between the two options.

The Muslim Brothers were the main proponent of the coalition-building option, trying to recruit the greatest number of officers. They had tried and failed to do so with the air force organization and Sadat. Al-Misri had warned the young officers against Supreme Guide Hasan al-Banna's hidden agenda,[73] and their personal admiration for him was matched by their suspicions of his motives. They had a problem with his personality: his answers were never clear and he demanded obedience. But in 1942 the Muslim Brothers succeeded in recruiting 'Abd al-Mun'im 'Abd al-Ra'uf some months after his release and transfer from the air force to the army. 'Abd al-Ra'uf in the next two-and-a-half years recruited six other officers: 'Abd al-Nasser, Khalid Muhi al-Din, Kamal al-Din Husayn, Sa'd Tawfiq, Salah Khalifa, and Husayn Hammuda. These seven went on to form the first cell affiliated with al-Banna's organization. It must be noted that only the last two (and 'Abd al-Ra'uf) were true Islamists. The others were primarily nationalists, who were impressed by the Brothers' power, their members' dedication, and al-Banna's presumed selflessness. One of the supreme guide's advisers, Mahmud Labib, who was modern, popular, and likeable, had persuaded his boss to forgo his preconditions for admission and to accept patriotic officers, provided they were ready to act.

The story of this complicated relationship cannot be fully told here. These seven officers recruited fifty to seventy-five of their peers. In February 1946, the members of the first cell joined the secret apparatus of the Islamist group and swore an oath. 'Abd al-Nasser, the number two man in the military section (and probably its strongman), and Khalid Muhi al-Din had strong doubts. According to the latter, promising to blindly obey an unknown person beyond consultation, who might order an assassination, was no small matter. The relationship between the officers and the Brotherhood slowly soured. Al-Banna's support of Prime Minister Sidqi Pasha and his acrimonious break with al-Sukkari (both in 1946), and the Islamists' indiscriminate use of force during 1947–48, alienated many officers. After the Palestine War, more specifically, in September 1949, a strong quarrel arose between 'Abd al-Nasser and the organization over their recruitment strategies (with 'Abd al-Nasser seeking more flexibility) and the Brotherhood's "fanatical mentality." This quarrel resulted in a break between the majority of the officers and the Islamist organization.[74]

Between 1945 and 1948, between sixty and a hundred nationalist officers were active. A loose conglomeration soon emerged. At least three different groups of friends (not including Sadat and Hasan 'Izzat, who were at the time discharged from the armed forces) adopted the terrorist option, trying either to kill British soldiers or to intimidate or assassinate pro-British Egyptian political leaders. Other cells, born independently during 1945–46, tried to cobble together a new group. Their members agreed to found an organization that they called the 'officer's movement.'[75] They accepted and recruited officers, regardless of their ideological leanings. They all wanted a strong regime, imposing reforms to better the lot of the poor, restoring the nation's greatness, and purifying its political life. The major issue was whether they could achieve these reforms with King Faruq or without him. They agreed to disagree.

In 1947 some fifteen officers and three NCOs were arrested. They belonged to various organizations, including the Muslim Brothers. It seems that they had attended a meeting discussing the unification of some movements, and that an NCO recruited by one of the groups denounced them.[76] However, most of them were affiliated with the officers' movement. Their incarceration didn't last: some enemies of the chief-of-staff, Ibrahim 'Atallah, used this affair to convince the king that 'Atallah's great unpopularity posed a growing danger to the regime, and that a better strategy would be to appease the nationalists. The arrested officers were released, and some of them were recruited by the king to join what became the infamous Iron Guard.[77] Convinced that the king was the best ally of the anti-Wafdist and anti-Marxist nationalists, they agreed to kill his enemies for money. They at some time joined Sadat, who had probably since 1945–46 been on the king's payroll. This period also saw the first communist attempts to infiltrate the army, with very limited success. The Marxists had to overcome objections to their atheism and lifestyle (notably, a reputation for easy sexual relations). Much of their work was ruined by their support for the Zionists in Palestine.

The Free Officers organization, founded by 'Abd al-Nasser at the end of 1949, was at its birth, the result of a coalition between 'Abd al-Nasser's friends (the dissidents from the Muslim Brothers and some of the officers who had served at al-Faluja) and the bulk of the officer's movement. They were soon joined by Baghdadi and his air force colleagues. Many young officers were enrolled later. On the night of the coup, the organization had, according to the official estimate, more than 280 members, and another count put the number at more than 340. The ambiguities of the reunification explain the great divergences among the different accounts, some of which assume (wrongly) that a group of older activists actually hijacked the officer's movement. According to this version of the story, the organization that staged the 1952 coup was born in 1945, accepted a new leader and his friends in 1949, and changed its name in 1950. This author prefers the unofficial version of the large group of older officers who successfully created a structured *organization* instead of a *loose coalition*, and who displayed incredible skill in dealing with the other political forces. But the other version was an important *perception*, shaping some actors' behavior.[78]

'Abd al-Nasser's genius lies in his perception that the terrorist option was fruitless, and that a change could only come through the nerve-racking path of coalition-building, probably with the aim of toppling the regime.[79] He needed considerable skill and luck, as the challenges were formidable. The main one was the pressure coming from the base of the movement, which wanted immediate action. For the young recruit, the situation could quickly become unbearable: he was joining a secret organization, taking considerable risks, and perhaps even jeopardizing his military career—and the movement's command wanted him to stay quiet and wait for the proper occasion, which seemed never to come. Opting out of the movement often seemed a rational choice for the young members. 'Abd al-Nasser had to find a delicate balance between avoiding an early confrontation with the regime and keeping the young officers busy. The result involved decisions that must have sounded bizarre: diffusion of tracts, participation in elections, and the misguided assassination attempt against Sirri 'Amr, which could have had dire consequences for the young officers. Another problem was the need to secure the support of a high-ranking officer, whose name could attract young men or middle-ranking officers slightly older than 'Abd al-Nasser (like Yusuf Mansur Siddiq, for instance). Hence the command's secrecy and its frantic search for an older officer—and their eventual choice of Muhammad Naguib.

Another problem was the neutralization of the security services' surveillance. It is not clear how 'Abd al-Nasser and his friends managed this. This problem has not received close attention. The infiltration of military intelligence by the Free Officers has been documented,[80] but does not provide a complete explanation. Incredibly, despite the defections, *nobody* ever denounced a Free Officer until the last 24 hours of the monarchy. Many high-ranking officers knew at least one Free Officer: Naguib, Haydar Pasha himself, Fu'ad Sadiq, al-Rahmani, and al-Sawwaf.

Some writers implausibly attribute this fact to treachery by the king's close collaborators, either Nahid Rashad or Haydar Pasha, who had been harmed by Faruq and were taking revenge (or at least turning a blind eye).[81] Reality is more complex. Indeed, Haydar[82] did choose to engage in a dialogue with the movement's leaders, making concessions in order to use them.[83] His strategy toward the movement undeniably played a role in the regime's demise, but it had a rationale: on one hand, he probably thought that the clandestine movement was too weak to pose a serious threat, and we must not forget that 'Abd al-Nasser's diagnosis was identical, that he was *forced* to act. On the other hand, it was difficult, and politically risky, to arrest an unknown number of officers who were just circulating tracts.[84] Moreover, the tracts were quite popular, for they reflected the feelings of the officer corps. Arrests could have backfired. More fundamentally, it appears the officer corps basically agreed with the tracts' content. The silence of those who knew and who should have issued a warning, as well as the absence of any denunciation, pronounce a terrible verdict on Faruq's last years in power.

The last six months leading up to the coup are critical. The list presented by the movement won a crushing victory at the December 1951 elections for the administrative council of the Officers Club. It is easily overlooked that the movement received the support of the top brass. These elections were more an "army versus king affair" than a challenge by the movement to the military authorities.[85] This success had a positive impact on recruitment, which accelerated and became easier after that.

In chapter seven, Anne-Claire Kerbœuf has shown the burning of Cairo on 26 January 1952 to be central to the post-1952 regime's claims to revolutionary authenticity. Functionally, however, the fire itself incited the Free Officers movement to accelerate preparations for a coup and to contemplate action sooner than previously planned. For this, 'Abd al-Nasser[86] was quite sure of American neutrality: he had indirect contacts with American intelligence officers, who had noticed the movement's existence, probably during the December elections. The movement also tried to multiply contacts and to negotiate a deal with the Muslim Brothers.[87] Somewhere between February and March 1952, 'Abd al-Nasser clinched a deal with the Brothers, negotiated with Salah Shadi and Hasan al-'Ashmawi. The terms were favorable to 'Abd al-Nasser: the Brother negotiators agreed to support a military regime and accepted his argument asking for a sine die postponement of the adoption of Islamic law, because the international and local constraints were too numerous. This is strange: either the negotiators were inept, thought that after the coup succeeded the Brothers would sooner or later take control, or were among the Brothers who gave priority to the fall of the monarchy and the British evacuation, regardless of the means and the costs.

Having secured this deal, 'Abd al-Nasser waited for the proper moment. He had two constraints. First, he needed to minimize the risks of British intervention, and thus had to wait for the political temperature to cool down. Second, he needed to have enough army units commanded by Free Officers in Cairo, and this depended on the chances of the rotation of the battalions and divisions.

In March, the authorities, finally noting that military intelligence could make little progress in investigating the Free Officers' organization, decided to turn the matter over to the political police.[88] Within a few months, this force succeeded in identifying some of the Free Officers, including 'Abd al-Nasser.[89] Furthermore, at the beginning of the summer, 'Abd al-Nasser received increasingly worrying reports telling him that Haydar had lost the political battle for the king's soul, and that the time of repression was nearing, with a probable nomination of the organization's foe, Husayn Sirri 'Amr, as war minister. The king then made the decision to dissolve the administrative council of the Officers Club. He could not let the officers' incendiary speeches go unpunished without endangering his credibility. This decision cost him the throne, for the movement, already nervous, made a similar calculation about the timing of their actions: delaying reaction would undermine the organization's prestige and could lead to major defections.[90]

The movement tried to mobilize its troops and verify the validity of its deal with the Muslim Brothers. Despite unavoidable defections and unforeseen difficulties, it succeeded brilliantly in achieving the first task. However, an unpleasant surprise awaited 'Abd al-Nasser. The Brothers' negotiators asked for the consent of Hasan al-Hudaybi, the supreme guide. Discovering how vague the officers' commitments really were, Hudaybi demanded more specificity. Cornered, 'Abd al-Nasser felt he had to accept the new conditions, but never considered himself bound by them.[91]

On the last afternoon before the coup, 'Abd al-Nasser informed the Marxist officer Ahmad Hamrush that the operation was scheduled for that night and asked him to send some specific instructions to the Free Officers serving in Alexandria. He knew that Hamrush would inform HADETO, the Marxist organization. Hamrush met with its leaders, and, despite all his later claims, missed the last train and never transmitted 'Abd al-Nasser's orders. Hamrush may have received instructions from his communist leadership to disengage, which seems highly probable. Such a decision would have been rational: the operation was too risky, with little chance of success, and Marxist officers were a scarce resource, not to be used for another organization's sake.[92]

The rest is history. Though the movement's forces were limited, the coup attempt succeeded. Nobody wanted to defend the regime. The Free Officers succeeded in preventing most of the high ranking officers from reaching their troops, and in persuading the few who managed to do so to let them finish the job. Of course, the movement was lucky. But it also helped secure that luck. The Free Officers felt their cause was just: they viewed good luck as a proof of their convictions' rectitude, and paid no attention to misfortune. The narratives of all the concerned parties strongly exaggerate the role of good fortune, as did the Free Officers: for them, it proved their divine election.

Notes

1 Ahmad Hamrush, *Qissat thawrat 23 yulyu*, vol. 1, 85; al-Biyali, *al-Safwa al-'askariya wa al-bina' al-siyasi fi Misr* (Cairo: General Egyptian Book Organization, 1992), 276; P.J. Vatikiotis, *Nasser and his Generation* (London: Croom Helm, 1978); Vatikiotis, *The Egyptian Army in Politics: Pattern for New Nations?* (Bloomington: Indiana University Press, 1961). Muhammad Sabir 'Arab, *Hujum 'ala al-qasr al-malaki: hadith 4 fibrayir 1942* (Cairo: General Egyptian Book Organization, 2003), 301.

2 'Abbas did not elaborate his views but he gave examples of *ibn al-dhawat* intervention in favor of persons from modest backgrounds, drawn from his studies on the Egyptian university. He may have overstated his point, but he seemed to think that the young Egyptian had to give guarantees of loyalty to the regime if he wanted to secure the support of the protector.

3 See *al-Musawwar*, 29 October 1948, 18, for a description of this exam and its requirements.

4 Hamrush, Qissat, 85. Salah Nasr, *Thawrat 23 yulyu bayna al-masir wa-l-massir* (Cairo: Mu'asasat al-Ittihad li-l-Sahafa wa-l-Nashr, 1986), 21.

5 Olivier Reboul, *Langage et idéologie* (Paris: Presses Universitaires de France, 1980), 107.

6 Hasan Ibrahim interview in *al-Jil*, 6 June 1954. The other source is Salah Salim. See for instance Muhammad al-Mu'tasim, *Salah Salim* (Cairo: Dar al-Qawmiya li-l-Tiba'a wa-l-Nashr, n.d.), 10.

7 On his father's income, see 'Abd al-Nasser's interview with Morgan (for the *Sunday Times* in 1962), quoted in 'Abdallah Imam, *al-Nasiriya: dirasat fi fikr Gamal 'Abd al-Nasir* (Cairo: Dar al-Sha'b, 1971).

8 Used for this random sample were: a) the obituaries in *al-Ahram*, b) studies, accounts, and published autobiographies, collecting all the information available on the officers named, c) the author's personal contacts, d) the press, studied on a systematic basis.

9 Wafiq Draz and Sa'id Halim (Free Officers) interviews with the author. Kirk Beattie has collected similar information. See Kirk Beattie, *Egypt during the Nasser Years: Ideology, Politics and Civil Society* (Boulder: Westview Press, 1994).

10 Hamrush, *Nasij al-'umr* (Cairo: General Egyptian Book Organization, 2003).

11 Mustafa Bahjat Badawi, *Hikayat Siptimbir 42: 'ala hamish 'uhud Faruq, 'Abd al-Nassir wa-l-Sadat* (Cairo: al-Ahram, 1990), 61. 'Abd al-Ra'uf Nafi' interview with the author.

12   For instance, for the Sadat/Zakariya Muhi al-Din cohort, more than 1,000 candidates
     applied, only 52 were admitted.

13   See, below the composition of the top brass during the 1948 War. These officers had started
     their careers before 1936. Cf. Hamrush, *Qissat thawrat 23 yulyu*, 2: 41. He writes that, during
     the forties, only one member of the royal family was an officer and not a single high-ranking
     officer came from a "feudal" family. See also 'Abd al-'Azim Ramadan, *al-Jaysh al-misri fi-l-siyasa:
     1882–1936*, (Cairo: General Egyptian Book Organization, 1977), 74 (on the officer corps at
     the turn of the century). He wrote that the "Egyptian officers did come from middle-class
     families having Turkish, Kurdish, and Circassian origins."

14   On the family background of 'Abd al-Rahman Fahmi, see 'Abd al-'Alim Khallaf, *al-Hay'a
     al-sa'diya* (Cairo: 'Ayn li-l-Dirasat wa-l-Buhuth al-Insaniya wa-l-Ijtima'iya, 1999), 207 (note 3),
     but also 215–16, where Khallaf examines the background of Ahmad Mahir (who later became
     prime minister). Mahir was Fahmi's nephew.

15   See Sabri Abu al-Majd, *'Aziz 'Ali al-Misri wa suhbatuhu: bunat al-wihda al-'arabiya wa al-islamiya*
     (Cairo: General Egyptian Book Organization, 1990), 30, 71.

16   Information given to the author by 'Abd al-'Aziz's son. Ahmad 'Abd al-'Aziz too had
     Egyptian blood.

17   According to his brother (admittedly unreliable), Sadat was not a "pure Egyptian." He of
     course had a Sudanese mother, but his father had also "Syrian origins." See 'Ismat al-Sadat,
     al-Haqiqa al-gha'iba (Cairo, 1991), 153.

18   Information given by the son of Colonel Fu'ad al-Shahid (1920–60). He added that King Fu'ad
     had once joked with his chamberlain, a member of the family, that the Shahids were so numerous
     in the army that he was afraid they might attempt a coup. Note also that one of the Shahid
     officers had served in Sudan and married there.

19   Hamrush, *Qissat thawra*, 2: 40–42.

20   Zakariya Muhi al-Din and 'Imad 'Askar interviews with the author.

21   Hamrush, *Shuhud thawra* (for Siddiq, 'Ukasha, and Kamil); Hilmi Sallam, *Ana wa thuwwar
     yulyu*, (Cairo: Dar Thabit, 1986), 203 (for al-Hidri, who was the son, grandson, and brother
     of officers); Amin Shakir's interview with Tariq Habib; Nasr, *Thawrat 23 yulyu bayna al-masir
     wa-l-massir*, 91 (for Rashdan). Obituary of Wafiq Draz's sister in March 2003 and Wafiq Draz's
     interview with author. Nafi' interview with the author (for Lutfi). Yusuf Mansur Siddiq also
     married his cousin, 'Aliya. His father, Mansur Yusuf Hasan al-Azhari, was an army officer, son
     of a judge, and grandson of *'ulama'*. Siddiq's mother came from a "pure Arab" family *(dima'
     'arabiya khalisa)*, originating from the 'Usayrat tribe. Mme. Siddiq's father, who was also the
     maternal uncle of the celebrated Free Officer, and his father's first cousin, graduated from
     Military Academy in 1899. See 'Aliya Tawfiq, *Yusuf Siddiq, Gamal 'Abd al-Nassir wa ana* (Cairo:
     al-Ahram, 2000), 7–9; or Muhammad Tawfiq al-Azhari, *Yusuf Mansur Siddiq, munqidh thawrat
     yulyu: ankarahu al-zayf wa ansafahu al-sha'b* (Cairo: Maktabat Madbuli, 2000), 18. Salah Nasr's
     paternal uncle was just a few years older, so some relatives wrongly assume that he was the
     elder brother. See Nasr, 19. Nasr was the grandson of two *'umda*s; the family, of Arab origin,
     entered Egypt soon after the Arab conquest. Nasr, 11.

22   Sa'id Halim and 'Abd al-Ra'uf Nafi' interviews with the author.

23   'Abd al-Ra'uf Nafi' interview with the author. Tantawi, during the thirties, was the Military
     Academy's chief of staff.

24   Nasr, 30; Ahmad Kamil, *Min awraq ra'is al-mukhabarat al-misriya al-asbaq: Ahmad Kamil
     yatadhakkar, bi qalam Ahmad 'Izz al-Din* (Cairo: Dar al-Hilal, 1990), 111.

25   Sa'id Halim interview with the author.

26   Hafiz Isma'il, *Amn Misr al-qawmi fi 'asr al-tahadiyyat*, (Cairo: al-Ahram, 1987), 15; 'Abd al-
     Mun'im 'Abd al-Ra'uf, *Arghamtu Faruq 'ala al-tanazul 'an al-'arsh: mudhakkirat 'Abd al-Mun'im
     'Abd al-Ra'uf*, (Cairo: al-Zahra li-l-I'lam al-'Arabi, 1988), 15; 'Abd al-Tawwab 'Abd al-Hayy. *Nisr*

Misr 'Abd al-Mun'im Riyad, hayan wa shahidan (Cairo: Dar al-Hilal, 1971), 52. Riyad's paternal grandfather was a middle-ranking *muwazzaf*.

27 Interview by 'Imad 'Askar (Jamal's brother) with the author.

28 Obituary in *al-Ahram*.

29 Bahjat Badawi, 17, 99, 63.

30 'Abd al-Ra'uf Nafi' interview with the author. Three times as many examples can be cited. For instance, *al-Jil* magazine evoked, during the 1956 war, many families with a great number of members serving in the army. See *al-Jil*, no. 259, 10 December 1956, describing a military family saga, which tells that the grandfather, the father, the uncle, and the sons were officers and served in wars. The eldest, Bahjat Muhammad Abu al-Hasanayn, was the first officer. His career seems to have started during the last decade of the nineteenth century. He had two sons, both of them officers, 'Abd al-Majid Bahjat and Muhammad Bahjat. Muhammad Bahjat had four sons, two of them officers. His three daughters married officers. His widow explained the social reproduction by evoking the virtues of a 'military education' (nationalism, toughness, discipline, and early rising, often due to the great distance between home and school). See Hamdi Lutfi, *al-'Askariya al-misriya fawqa Sina'* (Cairo: Kitab al-Hilal, 1976), 322–23. This concept of 'military education' is used in another context, that of relations between officers and soldiers, in 'Abd al-Rahman Zaki, *al-Tarbiya al-'askariya: al-khuluq al-'askari wa ruh al-qiyada* (Cairo, 1944). Here, it is the teaching of the love of the motherland, of military life, of order, discipline and selflessness, useful virtues both in military and civil life, instilled into the children. According to Bahjat's widow, her late husband had spent forty years forming officers and he did the same thing at home. The daughters' husbands were General 'Abd al-Majid Ahmad, Brigadier 'Abd al-Rahman Amin, and Mustafa Bahjat (the officer's nephew). The patriarch's second son, 'Abd al-Majid, had his three sons opt for a military career. His two daughters married officers, Lieutenant Sayyid Zaghari and Captain Muhammad al-Safi. Another issue of *al-Jil* (cover page lost, but probably dated 1956 or early 1957) describes the al-Masiri dynasty. The father was a 77-year-old retired brigadier, Muhammad al-Masiri, who left the army in 1933. He told the reporter that the al-Masiri family was a dynasty of army officers. His oldest son was then (1956) a lieutenant colonel *(bikbashi)* and the younger were lieutenants. Two were air force officers, one served in the infantry, another in the cavalry, and the last in artillery. All his daughters were married to officers, a brigadier, a colonel, and a lieutenant colonel. The patriarch also told the reporter that he was the nephew of two naval officers.

31 'Abd al-Ra'uf, 125; Eliezer Be'eri, *Army Officers in Arab Politics and Society* (New York: Praeger, 1970), 484.

32 Information on Tantawi from his nephew and from 'Abd al-Ra'uf Nafi'. For Fattuh, born in a village near Quwaysna, see Amin Huwaydi, *50 'Aman min al-'awasif: ma ra'aytuhu qultuhu*, (Cairo: al-Ahram, 2002), 18.

33 'Aliya Tawfiq, *Yusuf Siddiq, Gamal 'Abd al-Nassir wa ana* (Cairo: al-Ahram, 2000), 9–10. See also the documentary produced on Bayyumi. See especially Muhammad 'Abd al-Fattah Ibrahim, *Shu'ara'una al-dubbat*, ed. (Cairo: Matba'at 'Abd al-Halim Husni, 1935). The author, an officer, and son of an officer, would, some years later, be part of the first class in the War College, with Naguib, al-Rahmani, 'Ali 'Ali 'Amir, Shawqi 'Abd al-Rahman, and 'Abd al-Qadir 'Abd al-Ra'uf ('Abd al-Mun'im's brother). See *al-Musawwar*, 23 July 1953.

34 Khallaf, 216.

35 Cf. General Muhammad Pasha Labib al-Shahid, and Brigadier Ahmad Bey Rif'at, *Mudhakkiratan 'an a'mal al-jaysh al-misri fi al-Sudan wa ma'sat khurujihi minhu* (Alexandria: Matba'at al-Mustaqbal, 1936). We can find other lists of officers serving during the first decades of the twentieth century in 'Abd al-Rahman Zaki, *Ma'arik misriya fi al-qarn al-'ishrin* (Cairo: Matba'at Wizarat al-Difa' al-Watani, 1943), 21; Here also the names seem to be purely Egyptian with a few exceptions.

36 In his memoirs, Naguib provides biographical information on some of his friends, who are Egyptians. Muhammad Naguib, *Kuntu ra'isan li Misr* (Cairo: al-Maktab al-Misri al-Hadith, 1984), 12.

37 Sidqi Mahmud's obituary in *al-Ahram*; general knowledge; and Khalid Muhi al-Din, *Wa al'an atakallam* (Cairo: al-Ahram, 1992), 46 (for Kamil).

38 Ramadan, *al-Jaysh al-misri*, 32, 34, 30. Dufferin rejected khedivial suggestions to recruit mercenaries and also opposed creating a purely Egyptian army.

39 Isma'il, 15.

40 Hamrush, *Qissat thawra*, 1: 69; Naguib, *Kuntu ra'isan li Misr*, 22; (Amiralay) Muhammad Ibrahim, "Talabat al-kulliyyat al-harbiya," in *Sahifat al-kulliya al-harbiya al-malikiya*, no. 8, June 1951, 69; The general consensus is that the officers were not good professionals. For a dissenting opinion, see Rif'at's book, probably written in the late twenties or in 1930, cited earlier. Rif'at is clearly on the defensive and oscillates between denying the existence of a problem and admitting it. He acknowledges a negative perception of the officers' competence and deplores that view. He states that command is an "art" that requires practice, not studies. He claims that officers are often better administrators than civilians and gives many supporting examples this. Cf. Rif'at al-Shahid, 76. He writes that the army cannot progress as long as the British command it (77). He offers some proposals to ameliorate the officers' training. He favors the development of creativity and autonomy in the officers. They must learn the art of commanding and of conceiving plans (111). He restates that military arts and skills are acquired through practice (111). Then he denies that the officers are ignorant. The sources unanimously think that as a general rule the accusations about the incompetence of older generation, are unfounded, with some bright exceptions, and more numerous than previously thought.

41 Shakib, *Harb Filistin 1948: ru'ya misriya* (Cairo: Maktabat al-Zahra' li-l-I'lam al-'Arabi, 1986), 141, uses British documents and an interview with Muhammad Kamil al-Rahmani. Zakariya Muhi al-Din, in an interview with this writer, was of the same opinion, with some nuances. See also 'Abd al-Wahhab Bakr Muhammad, *al-Wujud al-britani fi al-jaysh al-misri: 1936–1947* (Cairo: Dar al-Ma'arif, 1982), 172.

42 See, for instance, Mustafa Bahjat Badawi, 20.

43 Yusuf Mansur Siddiq, *Awraq Yusuf Siddiq* (Cairo: General Egyptian Book Organization, 1998), 61; Anwar al-Sadat, *Asrar al-thawra al-misriya: bawa'ithuha al-khafiya wa asbabuha al-saykulujiya* (Cairo: Kitab al-Hilal, n.d.), 152.

44 Nasr, 30; Sadat, *Asrar*, 152.

45 Nasr, 30; Sadat: *Asrar*, 152.

46 Ramzi Hanna and Muhammad 'Abd al-Halim al-Zarqa, interviews with the author. Sons of the petite bourgeoisie rarely appear in this writer's random sample. See also my argument above. The barriers to admission were still too high.

47 See Badawi, 133, who gives as an example one of his comrades, the brother of three officers. The magazine *al-Jil*, during the second half of 1956, published a series of articles, each one presenting a family with many brothers belonging to the officer corps. See, for instance, no. 256, 19 November 1956, about the Rifa'i family: three out of four brothers were officers. For other details on the same family, including the father's occupation (police officer), see Lutfi, *al-'Askariya*, 314. For instance, we learn that military training, the influence of living in an environment where men wore uniforms, and the stories told by the maternal grandfather, himself an officer, influenced the brothers' career choice. Another issue, no. 258, dated 3 December 1956, treated the Mahdi family, where a grandfather and his cousins were officers. The generation studied by the article included the elder brother, Bikbashi 'Abdallah Mahdi. Other brothers were also officers. The mother explained her sons' choice by their nationalist values and by the elders' example. One of the two sisters was also married to an officer. Issue no. 260, dated 17 December 1956, introduced the six sons of a civil servant. The first three

were officers and the others were still in high school. Their father thought that the sons' choice was dictated by nationalist values and their love of sports. The mother declared that the transmission of nationalist values was the best explanation.

48 See the article on Kamal al-Din Husayn's cohort from Ibrahimiya Secondary School, published in *al-Jil*, 23 January 1961.

49 Hamrush, *Nasij al-'umr*, 20.

50 Hamrush, *Qissat thawra*, 2: 42.

51 Zakariya Muhi al-Din interview with the author. His diagnosis, a "phenomenon distinctive of this generation," is shared by many actors, for instance 'Ali Sabri, in Muhammad 'Uruq, *Qira'a fi awraq 'Ali Sabri* (Cairo: Dar al-Mustaqbal al-'Arabi, 1992), 23. See also Khalid Muhi al-Din, 25–26, on the causes of his application for admission to the Military Academy; and 'Abd al-Fattah Abu al-Fadl, *Kuntu na'iban li ra'is al-mukhabarat* (Cairo: Kitab al-Hurriya, 1986), 29–30. Abu al-Fadl's motives: 1) his admiration for 'Urabi; and 2) the thought that the army enables the young man to serve his country, in an institutional framework beyond politics. 'Ali Sabri, in his "confession" published by Ghali Shukri, said something similar. His father was patriotic and voted for the Wafd, but he nevertheless hated the factionalism of the multiparty system. See Ghali Shukri, *al-Muthaqqafun wa-l-sulta fi Misr (1): Nassir, al-Sadat, Khalid Muhi al-Din, 'Ali Sabri, Fathi Radwan, Tawfiq al-Hakim, Zaki Najib Mahfuz, Louis 'Awad* (Cairo: Akhbar al-Yawm, 1991), 148. For another similar account, see Nasr. He discovered, during his studies at high school, that the political leaders there were paid by the political parties and their decisions were by no means related to the national interest. He was also shattered by the corruption of the civil service and by the behavior of MPs. This person looked down on the peasants and respected the opinion leaders. Nasr had also a strong dislike for foreigners who capitalized on economic crises. So he convinced himself that the army was the best solution.
The following point should be strongly underscored: not all older officers were incompetent; most of them supported new developments regarding force structure and military education. For instance, Hafiz Isma'il cites 'Umar Tantawi's happiness when he greeted the first class of new cadets after the 1936 reforms. See Isma'il, 19. Al-Sayyid Faraj relates another anecdote: he wanted to study law, but changed his mind after an encounter with Tantawi, who accosted him during a condolence visit: "He sat next to me . . . and asked me . . . about my occupation. [I answered] and he interrupted me with a thundering voice: 'Lawyer? Why? This country is full of lawyers! A young fellow like you, as athletic and as quick-minded, should be an officer in the army! Come and see me tomorrow. . . .'" See Faraj, *Hayati bayna al-sayf wa-l-qalam* (Cairo: al-Dar al-Dawliya li-l-Nashr wa-l-Tawzi', 1994), 79.

52 In an important and little-noticed article, 'Abd al-Nasser emphasizes this point. See *al-Musawwar*, 23 July 1953.

53 Zakariya Muhi al-Din and Jamal Mansur, interviews with the author.

54 See Bakr Muhammad's work cited earlier, or Jabr 'Ali Jabr, *al-Quwwa al-jawiya bayna al-siyasa al-misriya wa-l-israiliya, al-juz' al-awwal: 1922–1952* (Cairo: al-Maktaba al-Akadimiya, 1993).

55 See Anwar al-Sadat, *al-Bahth 'an al-dhat*, 3rd ed. (Cairo: al-Maktab al-Misri al-Hadith, 1979), 18, 20, etc. His Englishman is ugly and barbaric. Cf. 'Uruq, *'Ali Sabri*, 18, where the central theme is the disdain of the wealthy foreigner toward the destitute Egyptian. 'Abdallah Imam, *Wajih Abaza: safahat min al-nidal al-watani*, vol. 1, (Cairo: 'Arabiya li-l-Tiba'a wa-l-Nashr, 1995), 110. Khalid Muhi al-Din, 25–33, quickly evokes the British occupation, recounting British troops' seizure of Egyptian tanks, a major trauma. Husayn Hammuda, *Asrar harakat al-dubbat al-ahrar wa-l-ikhwan al-muslimun* (Cairo: Maktabat al-Zahra' li-l-I'lam al-'Arabi, 1985), 19. 'Abd al-Mughni Sa'id, *Asrar al-siyasa al-misriya fi rub' qarn* (Cairo: Kitab al-Hurriya, 1985) and Nasr's work, cited earlier, are interesting: the authors' animosity toward the British was in contrast with a real admiration for them. According to Jean Lacouture, this also true for 'Abd al-Nasser. See Lacouture, *Nasser* (Paris: Éditions du Seuil, 1971), 314.

56 This is obvious for Naguib, 'Aziz al-Misri, Labib, and Harb, who were involved in early anti-British activities. It is also well-known that Sadiq and al-Rahmani were jailed during World War II for anti-Wafd and anti-British activities. Sabbur helped the anti-British guerrillas in the Canal Zone during the 1951–52 autumn and winter. The cautious Mihanna, while avoiding serious commitments, was always close to the nationalists.

57 'Isam Diya' al-Din al-Saghir, *al-Hizb al-watani wa-l-nidal al-sirri: 1907–1915* (Cairo: General Egyptian Book Organization, 1987), 19. Note that, for instance, Salih Harb and Mahmud Labib did rebel and join the Ottoman forces. See biographical information in Husayn Hammuda, 28, or in Ahmad 'Atiyatallah's introduction to Salih Harb, *al-Watan wa-l-jaysh* (Cairo: Maktabat al-Anglo-misriya, 1940). Also important, many operations against British troops showed a tactical skill proving officers' involvement. Cf. Ramadan, p 137–138; Hamrush, *Qissat thawra* 1: 75; Fahmi, *Mudhakkirat 'Abd al-Rahman Fahmi* (Cairo: General Egyptian Book Organization, n.d.).; Naguib, *Kuntu ra'isan*, 35.

58 Al-Shahid, 27–32; Ramadan, *al-Jaysh al-Misri*, 171.

59 Cf. Hamrush, *Qissat*, 1: 77; Naguib, *Kuntu ra'isan*, 38; Shakib, 141.

60 Al-Biyali, 246, writing about the 1882–1936 years.

61 Hamrush, *Qissat*, 1: 77.

62 Naguib, 44 et seq. Fear of mass activism became the Marxists' favorite explanation. See for instance Hassan Riad, *L'Égypte nassérienne* (Paris: Les Éditions de Minuit, 1964), 204. Also, the disastrous consequences of Stack's assassination were a strong inducement to caution.

63 Charles Tripp, "'Ali Mahir and the Politics of the Egyptian Army," in Tripp, ed., *Contemporary Egypt through Egyptian Eyes: Essays in Honour of J. Vatikiotis* (London: Routledge, 1993), 45; George Kirk, *The Middle East in the War*, 3rd ed. (London: Oxford University Press, 1954), 34.

64 Muhsin Muhammad, *Man qatala Hasan al-Banna?* (Cairo: Dar al-Shuruq, 1987), 93, in which he quotes British diplomatic telegrams.

65 A good introduction to the uprising is Sabri Abu al-Majd, *Sanawat ma qabla al-thawra: 1930–1952*, vol. 1 (Cairo: General Egyptian Book Organization, 1987), 393–479, 508–516, 605–673.

66 See, for instance: *Mudhakkirat al-Baghdadi*, vol. 1 (Cairo: al-Maktab al-Misri al-Hadith, 1977); Sadat, *Asrar*; Imam, *Wajih Abaza: safahat*; Hamdi Lutfi, *Thuwwar yulyu: al-wajh al-akhar* (Cairo: Kitab al-Hilal, 1977).

67 Compare for instance Abaza's version, in a letter to his wife, published in 'Abdallah Imam, *Wajih Abaza wa-l-'amal al-fida'i* (Cairo: al-Maktaba al-'Arabiya li-l-Tiba'a wa-l-Nashr, n.d.), 181, Hassan Izzat's one, in *Qissati ma' al-'amaliqa wa-l-aqzam al-sab'a wa thaminuhum haykal* (Rome and London, 1985), 186, with Baghdadi's version in Baghdadi, 10, or with Sadat's account in *Asrar*.

68 See for instance al-Baghdadi's interview in Lutfi, *Thuwwar*, 59; also 'Izzat, *Qissati*, 186.

69 For this episode, see Isma'il, 23. See also 'Abd al-Mun'im Amin's testimony in Hamrush, *Qissat thawrat 23 yulyu (4): shuhud thawra yulyu*, 2nd ed. (Cairo: Maktabat Madbuli, 1984), 247. Abu al-Fadl, *Kuntu na'iban*, 42. Majdi Hasanayn interview in al-Siyasi, 7 August 1988, and testimony in Hamrush, *Shuhud*, 358. See Sadat's comical version, *al-Bahth 'an al-dhat*, 36, and a more serious one in Sadat, *Asrar*, 39.

70 Set forth in Charles Tripp, "'Ali Mahir and the politics of the Egyptian army," in Tripp, ed., *Contemporary Egypt through Egyptian Eyes*, 45.

71 See for instance Sadat, *Asrar*, 98; 'Abd al-Ra'uf, 29; Baghdadi, 16. Abu al-Majd in *Sanawat ma qabl al-thawra: 1930–1952*, vol. 3 (Cairo: General Egyptian Book Organization, 1989), 395, 433.

72 Imam, *Wajih Abaza: safahat*, 117–20; Baghdadi, 21–23. Baghdadi's testimony in Hamrush, *Shuhud*, 215; 'Izzat, *Qissati*, 177.

73 See Abaza's letter published by Imam, *Wajih Abaza wa-l-'amal*, 189. For a study of relations between Muslim Brothers and activist officers, see Tewfik Aclimandos, *Officiers et Frères Musulmans* (Paris: CEDEJ, 2002).

74 Khalid Muhi al-Din's interview with the author.

75 On this coalition, see for instance Abu al-Fadl, cited earlier, or Mustafa Nusayr; 'Abd al-Hamid Kafafi; Sa'd 'Abd al-Hafiz; Jamal Mansur, *Thawrat yulyu wa-l-haqiqa al-gha'iba* (Cairo: General Egyptian Book Organization, 1997), but these two books overestimate the group's cohesiveness. See other accounts, such as those of Muhsin 'Abd al-Khaliq. See his long testimony in Rashad Kamil, *'Abd al-Nassir alladhi la ta'rifuhu* (Cairo: al-Jiddawi li-l-Nashr, 1990).

76 Nusayr, Kafafi, 'Abd al-Hafiz, and Mansur, 45–6; See Jamal Hammad in *Uktubar*, 19 April 1992. Other sources give different estimates, but Hammad had access to the files.

77 On the Iron Guard, see 'Abd al-Majid's testimony in Hamrush, *Shuhud* or Sayyid Jad, *al-Haras al-hadidi: kayfa kana al-malik Faruq yatakhallas min khusumihi* (Cairo: al-Dar al-Misriya al-Lubnaniya, 1992).

78 For more details on this issue, see Tewfik Aclimandos, "Regard rétrospectif sur la Révolution de juillet 1952," in EMA 4–5: *L'Égypte dans le siècle: 1901–2000* (Cairo: CEDEJ, 2003), where I evaluate multiple versions of stories. In particular, erroneous ones that turn out to be legitimate perceptions are critical, as they explain behavior of some actors, and reveal the complexity and ambiguities of the situation.

79 Khalid Muhi al-Din interview with the author.

80 Sa'd Tawfiq, a member of the movement, was a military intelligence officer. 'Ali Sabri and 'Abd al-Mun'im al-Najjar often helped the movement. See 'Uruq, and al-Najjar's testimony in Hamrush, *Shuhud*.

81 See, for instance, Rashad Kamil, *al-Mar'a allati hazzat 'arsh Misr* (Cairo: Markaz al-Raya li-l-Nashr wa-l-I'lam, 1994).

82 Haydar was highly popular in the officer corps, even among the nationalist activists.

83 Khalid Muhi al-Din interview with the author.

84 See Husayn al-Shafi', *al-Tahrir*, 8 April 1953.

85 Sa'id Halim interview with the author. See also 'Ukasha, 80.

86 For instance Salah Shadi, *Safahat min al-tarikh: hasad al-'umr*, 3rd ed. (Cairo: Maktabat al-Zahra' li-l-I'lam al-'Arabi, 1987), 216.

87 See Aclimandos, *Officiers et Frères Musulmans*.

88 Maraghi's memoirs, quoted in Muhammad al-Jawadi, *'Ala masharif al-thawra: wuzara' nihayat al-malakiya 1949–1952* (Cairo: Dar al-Khayal, 2001), 155.

89 Jamal Mansur interview with the author.

90 Muhammad Hasanayn Haykal, in *Wijhat nazar*, November 1952; Khalid Muhi al-Din, in *al-Musawwar*, 25 July 1958, and interview with the author.

91 Aclimandos, *Officiers et Frères Musulmans*.

92 Sa'id Halim and 'Abd al-Ra'uf Nafi' interviews with the author. The late Hamdi Lutfi had also collected many accounts, with similar conclusions. See Hamdi Lutfi, *Thuwwar*, in the section devoted to the Free Officers of Alexandria. Other Marxist officers, Khalid Muhi al-Din, Yusuf Mansur Siddiq, and 'Uthman Fawzi *(inter alia)* did not inform HADETO, a fact that strongly supports their claim that they were not affiliated with this formation.

4   Financial Cerberus?

The Egyptian Parliament, 1924–52

Malak Badrawi

Although a great deal has been written about Egypt's political history between 1923 and 1952, few scholars have written about Egypt's parliament at that time, or to how it dealt with the sensitive—but vital—question of money. This chapter will show how members of parliament between 1924 and 1952 questioned the government about the misuse or misappropriation of public funds.[1] It will examine what may have motivated questions and consider whether these were wholly devoid of ulterior motives, or whether they were inspired by partisanship or bias. Thus, both the timing and implications behind questions were relevant, as was the tone used when deputies denounced extravagant expenditures, and tried to protect parliament's reputation for integrity and civic responsibility.

The first elected and 'independent' parliament was inaugurated on 15 March 1924, with the prime minister, Sa'd Zaghlul, making the speech from the throne. Not surprisingly, like most educated Egyptians who had witnessed Egypt's bankruptcy, with the subsequent establishment of the *Caisse de la Dette* in 1876, followed by Great Britain's occupation of the country, Zaghlul was wary about public expenditure and exceeding the budget. He therefore affirmed that the financial plan for the coming year 1924–25 had been carefully calculated, and that reserves in the treasury were sufficient to improve the country's reputation, but he cautioned against unnecessary expenditure.[2]

Throughout that session, questions put to the government regarding corruption showed that members of parliament understood their roles.

On one occasion, a deputy, Muhammad Amin Nur, asked the deputy interior minister whether he had read the newspaper account relating how the inspector general of prisons had had a tarmac road built leading from Abu Za'bal Prison to the country property of a friend at the expense of the prison administration. The deputy pointed out that if the report proved accurate, it would affect the reputations both of the prison administration and that of the government officials working there. The inspector general was also reported to have had a special telephone line installed between Abu Za'bal Prison and this country property, thus saving the owner of this latter the cost of a telephone line from Cairo. If the account was true, this was money lost to the government; and, if so, had there been an investigation? Then, what had been the result of this investigation, and what were the procedures followed to penalize the inspector and guarantee that this sort of thing did not happen again? The deputy interior minister answered that his ministry had initiated an inquiry, and that the case had been placed in the hands of the public prosecutor who would determine the guilty party. Moreover, certain prison officials who had read the accusations directed against their administration had demanded an investigation, as they considered that the accusations affected their reputations as well.[3]

On another occasion, a question put to the minister of finance concerned the purchase by the land survey office, or cadastral administration (*maslahat al-misaha*), of metal plates. A newspaper report had claimed that these were made of cast iron, cost £E 300,000, and had been placed in storage after proving unusable; the cost of each plate had been estimated at 80 piastres, whereas the ton was now only worth 30 piastres. The deputy wanted to know who was responsible for this speculation with public funds, if there had been an investigation, whether the person responsible had been reprimanded or not, and whether or not the administration could return the plates to the supplier. The deputy was told that the cadastral administration had acquired the street signs, which were not made of cast iron, for £E 61,000, and not for £E 300,000. The cadastral office required these signs to be fixed to the ground to gauge lots of land marked off for sale. The government had bought the plates because they were cheap and, once fixed to the ground, they were difficult to remove. Each sign had cost 46.5 piastres, as compared to others bought earlier, which had cost 114 piastres apiece.[4]

Perhaps it was a measure of Zaghlul's control over the parliamentary majority, or possibly the weakness of the opposition during parliament's first term, or indeed the fact that the budget had been carefully planned, that it scarcely elicited a debate during that first session, except over the Sudan. The opposition consisted mainly of members of the Watani Party. They were consistent in their efforts to speak their minds, and to discharge their parliamentary duties effectively, despite the majority's scoffing attitude.[5] It was probably the nationalistic intransigence for which they were renowned that prompted 'Abd al-Latif al-Sufani, a senior member of that party, to demand an explanation for the £E 750,000 from the draft budget for 1924–25 intended for the government officials employed in the Sudan.[6] This deputy explained that previously both the Consultative Assembly and its successor, the Legislative Assembly, had received a detailed budget for the Sudan, and he could not understand why this budget was not as thoroughly justified as the preceding ones. Sufani, whose approach was typical of his party, objected that Egyptians had no supervision over the Sudan, even though its budget came out of the Egyptian treasury. Zaghlul, apparently lacking patience with Sufani, asked the deputy if he wanted the Egyptian government to negotiate with the administration in the Sudan, in order to tell that administration that the Egyptians had the right to know the exact purpose for the money being sent there. Zaghlul's sally was welcomed by laughter from the Wafd majority. The president of the Chamber, Ahmad Mazlum, suggested that, should Zaghlul go to the Sudan, he should take Sufani with him.

It may also have been a sense of patriotism, or justice, which induced a deputy to ask why no disciplinary action had been taken against a Mr. Anthony, the director of the administration of state property (maslahat al-amlak al-amiriya). Action had been taken against the Egyptian undersecretary for agriculture, when it was discovered that a plot of land had been deliberately substituted for another during a transaction. The response was that the investigation showed that those responsible for this fraud had led Mr. Anthony astray, so as to facilitate the completion of the transaction. Zaghlul added that, in any case, as a foreigner, Anthony would have been answerable only to a special commission, known as the Committee of Six, all of whom were foreigners. They would have handled the inquiry, as well as any legal action against the said Mr. Anthony.[7]

There was also a question from a member of the Liberal Constitutional Party addressed to the minister of war, inquiring why his ministry had purchased Indian rice, which was more expensive and less fine than Egyptian rice. This question may have been motivated by self-interest, owing to the fact that the deputy asking the question, 'Abd al-Halim al-'Alayli, was from Damietta, which cultivated rice. The response given was that although the war minister wished to encourage Egyptian production, Rangoon rice no. 3

was good quality and cheaper than Egyptian rice.[8] Observing that some parliamentary questioners expressed more nationalism than fiscal sense, a modern reader should note that members viewed themselves as the ones most responsible to the Egyptian people and especially their own constituencies. Naturally, they acted on press reports or rumors pertaining to expenditures by the palace, the military, or other groups less answerable than they to the Egyptian electorate.

Parliament and Royal Budgetary Concerns

A new session of parliament was inaugurated on 15 November 1924. Yet, because Zaghlul's popularity and parliamentary legislation bothered the king, the palace tried to undermine Zaghlul and to suspend parliament indefinitely, following Sir Lee Stack's assassination, the British ultimatum to the prime minister, and his resignation. However, the two feats proved impossible to achieve. Owing to strong public pressure, new parliamentary elections took place; these included candidates from the new Ittihad Party, established by the palace to oppose Zaghlul and the Wafd. The outcome was a coalition government. The Wafd still retained a majority, with Zaghlul as president of the Chamber of Deputies, but now there were articulate people from all parties, including members of the Liberal Constitutional Party.

It may be that the suspension of parliament for several months exacerbated members' irritation at this adjournment. Thus, one of the most noteworthy characteristics of that session was the joint effort to curb palace expenditure.[9] This began with criticism from the Chamber of Deputies' finance committee during its financial report for the proposed budget for 1926–27. Heading this committee was Isma'il Sidqi, a former cabinet minister, who drew the Chamber's attention to the fact that the estimate for the royal budget was £E 866,979, which was £E 56,917 more than what it had been in 1925, and £E 61,650 more than that of 1924. Sidqi offered several observations about the costs incurred by King Fu'ad's private cabinet. He pointed out that these costs had risen steadily from £E 82,603 to £E 169,308 between 1914 and 1919. However, there had been a marked increase starting in 1920, so that by 1926 these costs amounted to £E 603,699. Moreover, there was an unwarranted increase of the royal guard, whose number had grown slowly from 536 guards and officers in 1914 to 1,119 in 1926.[10] The Finance Ministry informed Sidqi that during the war years more guards had been needed to secure the royal palaces, but that subsequently no recruitment had taken place until 1925. The head of the finance committee considered this answer unacceptable, because in 1914 there had been only two palaces to guard, and the 526 guards on duty at the time had been adequate. The finance committee therefore recommended decreasing the number of guards, and instead raising the number of soldiers in the army, as the upkeep of the latter was less of a strain on the budget.[11] The use of army recruits would be more economical; furthermore, the king was not only their commander-general, but both the cavalry and infantry were at his absolute disposal. Sidqi suggested mentioning this cost-cutting measure to the king. Sidqi's insistence on reducing appropriations to the palace would contribute to King Fu'ad's attempts to undermine him years later.

Furthermore, the salaries of officials in the king's cabinet exceeded the salaries of employees in other government administrations. Moreover, the regulations for appointing and promoting officials in the king's cabinet were left to his majesty's discretion; this system did not conform with regulations for drafting the budget. The committee therefore recommended that rules for the employment of civil servants should be comparable to those for palace employees. In this way, when palace officials were transferred to other administrations, their pensions and system of promotions would not be affected.

The committee had also noticed that reserve funds had been created for almost each category of palace servant, and that in 1926, these added up to £E 6,302. Yet this arrangement had not existed before 1921, and the Finance Ministry explained that in the interval, the situation had called for salary raises or for creating new positions. The royal cabinet had, therefore, adopted the practice of including a reserve fund in its draft budget to pay the expenses resulting from salary raises or new appointments. This had been in compliance with the royal command (al-irada al-saniya). The committee judged that, nevertheless, all officials and servants had to be treated equally, whether employed by the palace or by the government. It also called for the abolition of that extra credit.

The next item mentioned was the royal Nile steamboat, the frame and machines of which initially were to have been built in England and then brought to Egypt to be assembled. A credit of £E 30,000 had been opened for this purpose. It was then decided most likely by the palace, to complete the steamboat in England, thus raising the price to £E 88,000, a difference of £E 58,000, to which the sum of £E 26,000 was added, as the price of furniture and accessories, now making the total price £E 114,000. A careful examination of these new items was required, owing to the great differences between the first and last estimates in the costs of this steam-boat. The committee also suggested using the staff of the royal yacht, instead of appointing new people.

The list of outstanding royal expenditure further included repairs on the royal palaces, at an estimated £E 402,759; these were to be paid over five years, starting in 1920. The committee had accepted that approxima-tion and addressed a note to the Chamber of Deputies recommending that these sums be paid. However, additional amounts up to £E 113,000 in 1926 had been spent by the Finance Ministry. These new expenses were due to changes to the condition of the land on which buildings were constructed, as well as modifications made to the original plan of 1920, which meant that they had exceeded the original estimate; finally, there was the fact that Muntazah and Qubba palaces both required refurbishing and altera-tions to render them suitable residences for the king. Sidqi judged this to indicate the need to shift the responsibility for these buildings from the royal cabinet back to the general administration of government buildings in the Works Ministry.

When Sidqi finished reading the finance committee's report, three deputies, 'Abd al-Rahman 'Azzam, Ahmad 'Abd al-Ghaffar, and 'Abd al-Khaliq 'Atiya proposed to address a note to the king:

> The Chamber of Deputies considered that royal expenses had grown
> very rapidly over the last few years, so that these had by far exceeded
> the previsions for the yearly budget, and had gone beyond the costs
> estimated as regards the wealth of the country, and its position among
> other nations. Yet with that, and out of loyalty to the homeland and
> respect for the august standing of the sovereign, and out of desire for
> His Majesty's understanding and sense of justice, the Chamber had
> decided not to cut it. Instead, the Chamber appealed to His Majesty
> to give these expenses his impartial consideration, so as to reduce
> the burdens on the state treasury, and to allow it to set an example of
> sound management and good economy to the nation.[12]

One deputy retorted that the matter needed to be treated with great delicacy, so that the message should include a clause affirming the depu-ties' loyalty to the king. Such apparent toadying only disguised the deputy's hope to reduce the king's budget. Sidqi therefore told the Chamber of Deputies that the committee had agreed not to grant the credit of £E 6,302 required for the aforementioned reserve fund, and the Finance Ministry had cut £E 2,500 from the credits for travel, uniforms, etc. The motion to address the note to the king was therefore passed, the only objection coming from the deputy who wanted to impose the cuts.[13] Attacking King Fu'ad personally could lead to severe repercussions against the offending member of parliament.

This outcome proved only minimally effective, because during the debate on the budget for the following fiscal year 1927–28, the deputy Muhammad al-'Abd protested that moneys allocated to the royal household had become burdensome on the budget; it was preferable to use this money on hospitals, schools, and other public utilities.[14] Ahmad 'Abd al-Ghaffar, a member of the Liberal Constitutional Party, pointed out that the previous year, when the Chamber had been presented this budget, which included the privy purse, as well as the expenses of the royal household, the majority of the Chamber had seen these costs as inconsistent with the state budget and revenue. However, out of respect for the person on the throne, the Chamber had agreed not to amend the proposed plan. Deputies had expressed the hope that, in the following year, the royal budget request would better reflect the state's financial condition.[15]

Showing his disappointment, 'Abd al-Ghaffar remarked that this year even the letter from the director of the king's cabinet, which traditionally demonstrated dexterity or suppleness, failed to meet even the simple rules of civility or respect for the authority of the state, implying that the palace's budget was not the Chamber's concern. It gave no information about the estimates for repairs and maintenance on the palaces, nor had the director of the royal cabinet, Tawfiq Nasim, even considered the Chamber's suggestion of reducing by two-sevenths the royal guard. The deputy remarked that this financial plan was characterized by boundless dissipation and extravagance, showing that the finances of the state were of no consequence to its drafters. This budgetary item of £E 743,478 was still inconsistent with state receipts of approximately £E 36 million, especially when compared to the British royal budget request, which never exceeded 563,000 pounds sterling, although this was from a revenue of 801 million pounds sterling.[16]

'Abd al-Ghaffar further contrasted the costs of Muntazah and Qubba palaces, which amounted to £E 9,100 and £E 2,500 respectively,[17] with corresponding costs in 1920, when the tender offered for the repairs and maintenance of all the palaces had been £E 400,002. Also, the expenses incurred by the sovereign's cabinet had risen from £E 82,000 in 1914 to £E 620,000 in 1926—a tremendous increase. In 1927, the budget of this bureau was £E 480,000. Then there was an increase in palace salaries and the cost of equipment. Accordingly, how could the person seated on the throne permit the state itself to cover these expenses? Such a situation might have been acceptable in 1919 when the royal income had been inadequate, but it was unsuited to a proper constitutional regime.[18] 'Abd al-Ghaffar blamed Hasan Nash'at, the assistant director of the king's private cabinet, for facilitating personal rule in the country, as he "wanted to show the people that cabinet ministers were ministers of the country, whereas the palace had another government."[19]

The deputy concluded by saying that he could make no suggestions to the Chamber, and that what had driven him to make his remarks was his commitment to the king, who had granted Egypt its constitution. When these disingenuous words caused a commotion, he added that some people with opinions about drafting the budget considered adherence to constitutional rule to conflict with loyalty to the throne: "We tell them from the top of this podium that we are most loyal to the throne, and most supportive of it, but at the same time we are the staunchest believers in the Constitution, because [through it] all authority emanates from the nation."[20] Everyone knew that king hated the 1923 constitution, which he believed had been forced on him by the British.

Another deputy, Muhammad Kamil al-Asyuti, lamented that present-day policy was focused on rank consumerism. The budget was being considered at a time when government salaries had been frozen; yet officials' rights did need to be considered. He wanted to know whether the responsibility for the heavy burden lay with the Finance Ministry, the Chamber, or both? He added that he was "absolutely convinced that if his majesty were informed of the dangers surrounding the national budget, he would be no less generous or honorable than those kings who had relinquished part of their allowances to avert a threat to their nation." Al-Asyuti nevertheless believed that as parliament had the power and the responsibility for the country, it had to act with aggressive fiscal restraint. He suggested cutting the £E 35,780 intended for the palace furniture and related items from the royal budget.

Other deputies added their comments, and most discussed palace officials. A Watani Party member, Mustafa al-Shurbagi, deplored the fact that one-eighth of agricultural income tax receipts was being frittered away on the king's cabinet. This deputy also severely criticized fees paid for the upkeep of royal yachts, which had been lying idle between 1921 and 1926, although more than half a million pounds had been spent on them.[21]

Among the motions mooted was one to present comments made by the Chamber to the king, who would then act as he saw fit, while the Chamber ensured that, in the following year, the council of ministers would maintain and repair the palaces. Another proposal was to return the draft budget to the Chamber's finance committee, which would then reduce the royal budget to what it had been between 1915 and 1918.[22] The palace's profligacy must have angered many deputies at a time when state revenues were still quite small (for example, tariffs on imported goods were low) and many state expenses (e.g., the British military occupation and the government of the Sudan) could not be controlled by parliament.

Tightening the Purse Strings on the Religious Establishment

Nash'at's name had been evoked a few days before the above debate. On that occasion, an interpellation, remarkable for its sharply inquisitive tone, was addressed by a deputy to the minister of *awqaf*, who administered religious charitable endowments. The minister was asked whether he had read a newspaper report concerning the receipt between 1924 and 1925 of several installments of money, valued at about £E 3,000, by the rector of al-Azhar from the charitable foundations (*awqaf*). Had the minister checked official records to see whether the rector had actually received this money? If so, where had the rector spent it, and who had authorized him to use money from the charitable endowments? Moreover, was it within the rector's authority to spend such sums, and had he done so before 1924, i.e., from when he was appointed to the rectorship? And, if that was the case, was it not the minister's duty to request an accounting from the rector, demand that he settle accounts to include reimbursements, and make an inquiry about who had authorized the rector to spend this sum without a valid reason?[23]

Taking the Chamber podium, the deputy, Khalil Ibrahim Abu Rihab, emphasized the seriousness of his interpellation: the rector of al-Azhar had officially requested £E 2,500 from the Ministry of Awqaf, claiming operating costs of religious institutes. The rector also asked for the sum to be excluded from the expense account of these institutes. Yet the religious institutes had no need for the money; the rector had used them as an excuse to spend money without informing the Ministry of Awqaf. Indeed, the rector wanted to spend that sum freely on what was referred to as the Congress for the Caliphate. Did the honorable deputies know how this sum was spent?

[It] went into a sumptuous summit intended for an undeserving few and for purposes which were mind-boggling; thus, al-Sayyid Rashid Rida was awarded the sum of £E 568.860 to reward him for his few months' supervision of the magazine covering the congress. Did the honorable deputies know how many issues of the magazine had appeared? Were they aware of what this supervision had entailed? Only nine issues of this magazine had appeared, no more, which meant that the supervision for each single issue had cost the state £E 65.

The deputy had brought copies of this publication to show the Chamber. He said that one issue, published two years before, in 1925, had been devoted to the topic of Shaykh 'Ali 'Abd al-Raziq, author of the controversial *al-Islam wa usul al-hukm*. Rashid Rida had also been paid to supervise the reprinting of that issue. The deputy observed derisively that such a heavy work load must have been exhausting for Rashid Rida.[24] Readers may recall that the political parties were deeply involved in the 1925 controversy because 'Abd al-Raziq had argued in his treatise that Islam did not require a caliphate at a time when King Fu'ad—despite his disclaimers—wanted the office for himself. Many Egyptian Muslims, especially Azharites, wanted to restore that ancient institution and bring it back to Cairo.

He itemized other expenses incurred over the congress, which included £E 164 and 258 milliemes taken by one Shaykh Abu-l-'Uyun for mounts (horses or, more likely, donkeys), while another *shaykh* had taken possession of £E 116 and 786 milliemes for the same purpose. The deputy told the Chamber not to disregard these milliemes because, he said with scathing sarcasm, they symbolized the honesty and precision of the two aforementioned *shaykh*s, which prevented them from accepting one millieme over the sum owed to them. He was also willing to "swear" that neither *shaykh* had ever spent half that sum on mounts. The same "honesty" also influenced the numerous other *shaykh*s who had offered their services for free as secretaries to the congress. Abu Rihab specified two, 'Abd al-Baqi Surur and Muhammad Farag al-Minyawi, the first of whom had helped himself to the sum of £E 172 for carriage transport, and the second to £E 170.64 for the loan of mounts. There was also the sum of £E 156.490 to print the magazine of the congress. Finally, one *shaykh*, 'Abd Rabbuh, had taken £E 30 without any explanation.

What was amazing, continued the deputy, was that £E 2,519 and one millieme had been spent on this Congress for the caliphate, yet the amount paid to the rector of al-Azhar had been exactly £E 2,500. The congress secretary, Shaykh Husayn Wali, had personally paid out the extra £E 19.001. The deputy contrasted this *shaykh*, who had tried to compensate for the deficit in the costs of the congress from his own pocket, with the others who had seized this money with the lamest excuse. From this account, the honorable deputies learned how much money belonging to the *awqaf* had been extravagantly wasted in the service of the caliphate, and saw the zealousness of the *shaykh*s who had taken this money. Was this incident therefore not compelling enough to indict those who seized public funds, and present them to the prosecutor's office? The pretext had been their need to spend these funds on religion, whereas it had been spent on feasting, drinking, and living a luxurious life, by those such as Shaykh Abu-l-'Uyun and Shaykh Muhammad Qandil al-Rahmani, the *shar'i* advocate.[25] The deputy therefore begged the Chamber to ask the minister of *awqaf* to institute an inquiry with the rector of al-Azhar and the other *shaykh*s, or else demand that the cabinet minister report these activities to the prosecutor's office.

The deputy's scornful explanation had been met with hilarity throughout, while the minister of *awqaf*, Muhammad Nagib al-Gharabli, resented the deputy's irreverence. Gharabli said he had already reported this occurrence to the Chamber during an earlier session by citing correspondence with the al-Azhar rector. He further asserted that Khalil Ibrahim Abu Rihab had spoken about an establishment which, regardless of the behavior of its members, was worthy of respect and honor. Did not the other deputies agree with him? Did it, therefore, still expect a statement from him? To the minister's chagrin, the deputies indicated that they indeed wanted an explanation.[26]

Gharabli said he would explain the rector's actions, without necessarily agreeing with him. What could be held against the rector, he believed, was that he had requested the installments for religious institutes, whereas it was clear from the records he had presented to the Ministry of Awqaf that he had spent the money on the congress. Yet the rector saw no inconsistency in this. Indeed, the caliphate issue had become important to Muslims throughout the world by 1924–25; it was the obligation of every Muslim to express his concern about the matter. After the abolition of the office in Turkey, the Muslims no longer had a caliph. According to the rector, the *shari'a* obliged Muslims to meet and discuss this important matter. Moreover, the rector believed that Egyptian *'ulama'* should head these pious efforts.

Since the *'ulama'* of al-Azhar were considered the vanguard of Islamic thought, they had decided to organize a conference on the caliphate with Muslims from other regions, and it was on this meeting that the aforementioned sums had been spent. This, then, was the rector's view: he had spent the money on the congress out of a sincere belief that he was helping the religious institutes. Gharabli asserted that the rector had been extremely surprised by the accusation that his spending the money for the congress was inappropriate to his request for its use on *awqaf*, because he solemnly believed that he was actually spending it justifiably.

As to the proposal that the minister of *awqaf* should force the rector to stand trial for his action, Gharabli pointed out that the religious institutes were not connected to his ministry, so that, even if an employee of these institutes were found guilty of misconduct, it was neither Gharabli's business nor his prerogative to undertake disciplinary action. He also reminded the Chamber that, though it was the rector's duty to prepare official correspondence, he oversaw others who actually wrote the letters, so that the rector was not responsible for the exact wording of correspondence. Besides, he was an elderly man, and the demands of his profession prevented him from writing official letters.

Hedging his bets, Gharabli added that when he had been minister of *awqaf* in Zaghlul's cabinet,[27] he had never been told that the money appropriated for religious institutes was linked to the Congress for the Caliphate. He also stated formally that he had found no documentation in the ministry indicating any such link. Presently a dispute existed between the ministry and the administration of religious institutes over the money. The ministry argued that the funds had been misspent, though the administration of religious institutes insisted that they had been used for the purpose requested.

Further, Gharabli pointed out that if the Chamber's chief preoccupation was to restructure and thus improve the religious institutes, it could achieve its objective by drafting a new directive giving the government, and hence parliament, the right to oversee and administer the budget of these religious institutes. This, more than the pursuit of the guilty parties, would, in his view, achieve the desired aim of reform.[28]

Ahmad Ramzi, the deputy who spoke after Gharabli, said that the scheme of re-establishing the caliphate came up in 1924 with no resistance. Apprehensive about this, he had asked Prime Minister Zaghlul what was understood by the caliphate, because in reality no one wanted another pretext—like the Suez Canal—to prolong the British occupation of Egypt. Zaghlul had replied that King Fu'ad had renounced the idea of becoming caliph. However, Muslim jurists continued to hold endless meetings throughout the country until parliament was dissolved in November 1924. As a result, members of parliament found themselves without a platform from which to express themselves. Ramzi had therefore used the medium of the press to attack the idea of the caliphate. He recalled a violent verbal attack from a colleague, Hafiz 'Awad, chief editor of the newspaper *al-Mahrusa*, who insisted that the caliphate was essential and should perhaps be located in Cairo. Ramzi had been uneasy, pointing out that it could not benefit the country in any way. Ramzi mentioned all of this to show the Chamber that, in spite of parliamentary uncertainty about the caliphate, the rector had not hesitated to ask for sums of money on one pretext, and spend them on other matters. Ramzi also criticized the minister for explaining that the issue had to be interpreted according to the rector's mentality. The money was gone, and the question was whether to demand it from the rector, or to remain silent in fear of denunciations planted in the press.[29]

The next deputy to speak was a lawyer, Yusuf al-Gindi, who had read all the papers regarding the case in order to establish responsibility for the misspent money. Gindi had discovered that the first letter, dated 31 March 1924, requesting the loan of £E 500, had been sent by the rector, not in that capacity, but as head of the Higher Council for al-Azhar. This was relevant, as Gindi would reveal to the deputies. According to the letter, the rector wanted this money to cover the running costs of religious institutes. Yet it was striking that the letter had been signed by the under-secretary of *awqaf*, Hasan Nash'at, who was now the assistant director of the king's private cabinet. Nash'at obtained the sum from the Ministry of Awqaf. Gindi drew the Chamber's attention to the speed with which all these transactions had taken place; this indicated that there were unknown factors, and that the rector was not the sole schemer in the matter. Gharabli could not be held responsible, because the cabinet minister had only just been transferred from the Justice Ministry to the Awqaf. Nash'at was therefore solely responsible.[30]

The fact that the rector had misspent the money was quite a serious matter; the by-laws of the mosque prevented the rector, or head of the Higher Council of al-Azhar, from asking for money for one venture but spending it on another. Indeed, the by-law stated that he was the supervisor of religious officials' personal ethics and responsible for the preservation of their reputations. It was also true that the rector's behavior had not adversely affected religion or any religious organization. What did affect religion, however, was permitting incorrect behavior. It was unbecoming for a man of the rector's status to behave as he had. The desire to save the institution of the caliphate was legitimate; however, if the rector believed this was necessary, it had to be at his expense, because using funds from endowments was absolutely unacceptable. Another detail mitigating the rector's responsibility was that letters addressed to the Ministry of Awqaf had been signed by the head of the Higher Council, which meant that it was the Council's decision, not the rector's alone. Furthermore, the requested sums had been immediately placed in the *awqaf*'s safe, and the other *shaykh*s had helped themselves to them. Thus, on 16 December 1924, £E 500 had been taken from the *awqaf* funds at the request of the head of the Higher Council of al-Azhar; yet, curiously enough, on 7 December, Nash'at, as undersecretary for *awqaf*, had asked whether money was available from the endowments, suggesting that others were also trying to obtain funds for the Caliphate Congress.[31]

The next deputies[32] proposed a course of action. The Chamber subsequently voted unanimously, first to ask the government to investigate the matter, pursue it legally, and then demand that the rector return the money, after the inquiry proved his responsibility; second, to have religious institutes placed under the control and supervision of the prime minister, and then to require the government to explore improving the administration of these institutes in order to fulfill the general desire for reform.[33] It is unclear from these debates to what degree the deputies, who were landowners and professional men, respected the *'ulama'*, but certainly they viewed them as manipulated by the palace.

Although not mentioned directly, the king was hardly a puppet. The deputies who knew him personally probably realized that Fu'ad was clever, manipulative, and inclined to surround himself with sycophants. Nash'at was one, and Tawfiq Nasim, the director of the king's cabinet, was another. Neither man was popular, but Nash'at was certainly more devious and politically active. The end of the Ottoman Empire in 1923 had fueled King Fu'ad's ambition to become caliph. Most of the educated Egyptian public had opposed the notion of the caliphate, but Nash'at had been active in promoting the king's cause. As undersecretary for *awqaf*, he was in touch with most important *'ulama'*. He approached these scholars, trying to get them to endorse the caliphate idea. Hence the congress was undertaken, to which various influential *'ulama'* had been invited, backed by an extensive newspaper campaign.

Nash'at was unpopular, and his polished facade concealed a cunning propensity to intrigue.[34] Zaghlul apparently told him that as under-secretary for the *awqaf*, Nash'at was "a government servant with defined duties." He had warned him not to go beyond these duties, adding that the whole country detested Nash'at, who would do well "to remedy that state of things."[35] Zaghlul had opposed the caliphate, perhaps because, as a progressive, he believed that the institution of the caliphate had outgrown its usefulness; furthermore, he probably felt King Fu'ad's autocratic ambitions, like his absolutism, needed to be checked. He had made his views known to the king, who later declared that he had renounced the idea of becoming caliph. In the meantime, Zaghlul's popularity and his obduracy toward the king had caused Nash'at to arrange for al-Azhar students to demonstrate in favor of King Fu'ad. This was extraordinary, given that demonstrators usually took to the streets shouting the slogan "Zaghlul or revolution." Zaghlul later moved to retire Nash'at, whereupon he was appointed assistant director of the king's private cabinet. Referring to this appointment, Zaghlul later told his party he had no wish to be stabbed in the back.[36] As an inconclusive denouement, the king was later persuaded to appoint his crony Nash'at as minister at the Egyptian Legation in Tehran.

After Zaghlul

Despite Sa'd Zaghlul's intransigence, his conviction that only he was right, and his initial attempts to limit other parties' participation both in government and in parliament, he had ultimately understood the benefit of involving his rivals. Indeed, up until his death in 1927, foreign observers commented on the method, order, and calm of the Egyptian members of parliament in the first few years of its performance.[37] In contrast, his successor, Mustafa al-Nahhas, nearly always opted for his party's supremacy, without considering that the absence of effective opposition in parliament undermined the legislative process. Most relevant for this chapter was the impact on parliament's fiscal watchdog function. Moreover, the enduring popularity of the Wafd under al-Nahhas led other parties to regard its predominance in parliament as a tyranny of the majority. This induced prominent Egyptians—backed by the king—either to suspend parliament, or to modify the constitution. One of these was Isma'il Sidqi.

Corniche Mismanagement
or Royal Anti-Sidqi Backlash

Sidqi had no definite party affiliation. He had long feuded with Zaghlul, and was remembered for his strong-arm tactics as interior minister in 1925. He became prime minister in September 1930, and his appointment came at a time of global financial crisis. Although Sidqi was generally distrusted by politically articulate Egyptians, his talents as a financier, his understanding of the Egyptian economy, and his ability to balance Egypt's national budget were commonly acknowledged, leading to his appointment. Apart from the premiership, he held the finance and interior portfolios. He remained in office for three years, during which he rewrote the constitution and practically banned the Wafd. He also took repressive measures against the Liberal Constitutional Party when it turned against him. He founded his own party, the Sha'b, and then fabricated a parliament out of its members, in addition to representation from the Watani Party and the Ittihad Party, which was allied with the king. In September 1933, he resigned due to perceived royal betrayal. He refused to fade into the background, though, sitting with the opposition in parliament.

Shortly after this, rumors were circulated—probably by the king's entourage—of Sidqi's corruption. Likewise, the new cabinet blamed him for cotton transactions he had supervised. Thus, to prevent speculation on the market when he was finance minister, he had sold all the government-held cotton secretly, without his ministers' advice, yet with unreserved royal approval. Sidqi's speculation had cost the country £E 20,000, though his raising the price of cotton had realized for Egypt's cotton market a profit of £E 300,000. This allowed him to vindicate himself to parliament, but the attack had sullied his name. Added to his mounting disquiet, both the king and prime minister held him responsible for the outstanding cost of the Alexandria corniche. This was after the estimate for building a road that would extend the entire length of Alexandria's coastline had risen from £E 80,000 to £E 450,000. Rumors spread that the corniche commission's report criticized Sidqi.[38] He was also accused of offering state land at reduced prices to two high-ranking government officials, in exchange for the capital value of their pensions. He scornfully denied this allegation.[39] The king knew full well that Sidqi was unpopular and probably took revenge for his past efforts to curb questionable palace spending.

Sidqi's successor as premier, 'Abd al-Fattah Yahya, had been chosen because he would obey the king blindly. When Yahya had been acting premier in the summer of 1932, the corniche had first drawn public attention. Yahya, desiring monarchical support for personal ends, had taken an interest in the matter and,[40] after Sidqi resigned, consistently attacked him. Yahya knew that this would please the king, who wanted to see the former premier accused of corruption.

The Watani Party, which sat in the parliamentary opposition with Sidqi, repeatedly attacked Yahya's government. Hafiz Ramadan, the Watani Party president, took on the role of parliamentary 'conscience.' He reminded his fellow members that he had opposed Sidqi, and criticized the latter's policies when everyone else had flattered him. Nonetheless, he had not questioned the man's capabilities then, nor did he like attacking him now that he was no longer in power.[41] Sidqi's case was probably the only instance in which a parliamentary opposition took a stance defending a party against accusations made by the government. This was because of serious doubts about the palace officials involved in the attack against the former premier, and particularly about Ibrashi. He, like Nash'at before him, was one of the king's all-intrusive henchmen.

Sidqi was annoyed because, instead of investigating the reasons for the extraordinary cost of the corniche, the commission of inquiry merely collected accusations against Sidqi as ex-minister of the interior. His motive had been to beautify Alexandria, especially the side overlooking the sea. Moreover, the air there was refreshing. When his cabinet came to power, the corniche's fifth section, the cost of which was currently under investigation, was being built. The project had created thousands of jobs. Besides, his desire to persuade wealthy Egyptians to spend their money inside the country led him to focus on Alexandria as an ideal summer resort.[42] He had also hoped to fulfill King Fu'ad's urgent ambition to see the corniche extend from Stanley Station to his palace at Muntazah.[43] As a conclusion to events, on 25 May 1934, a scathing newspaper editorial condemned the investigation on the costs of the corniche. Sidqi had not been permitted to defend himself, and this situation was a threat to simple citizens who were defamed by newspapers. Furthermore, "evidence" collected by the commission comprised only recorded statements, mere selections of which had been published.[44]

Al-Nahhas and the *Black Book*

The war years, which witnessed a huge influx of British Empire and other foreign soldiers, food shortages, and price inflation, facilitated much corruption in Egypt. To protect their interests in the region, and because they suspected the new King Faruq of harboring Nazi sympathies, the British government decided to impose a Wafd cabinet on Egypt. In the '4 February 1942 incident,' pregnant with consequences for historical memory, British Ambassador Miles Lampson instructed Faruq to approve a Wafd-led cabinet, though the king opposed al-Nahhas as premier. To persuade Faruq, Lampson had 'Abdin palace surrounded by British tanks, whereupon the king accepted the ultimatum. When accused by other politicians present at the time of agreeing to form a cabinet with the protection of British tanks, the Wafd leader claimed that the situation compelled him to accept the mandate. Al-Nahhas subsequently postponed parliament until new elections were carried out, thus muzzling the current session.[45] The Wafd cabinet then mobilized its supporters to ensure that public opinion remained unaware of the circumstances of its appointment. Al-Nahhas also categorically refused to allow the Liberal Constitutional Party opposition more than a quarter of the seats in parliament. Consequently, the party whose presence could have helped to restrain the Wafd's excesses decided to boycott the elections.[46]

Historians and contemporary witnesses who did not back the Wafd agree that, until the fall of al-Nahhas' cabinet, corruption was rampant within the party.[47] Moreover, al-Nahhas' term as prime minister was marked by the *Black Book* scandal, an affair which began with the breach between al-Nahhas and Makram 'Ubayd, his finance minister. 'Ubayd, who had been closely associated with Zaghlul, was a long-standing member of the Wafd. Indeed, the choice of al-Nahhas as Zaghlul's successor was largely due to 'Ubayd's efforts. The two men were close friends, and the mutual trust between them had grown after they had been deported to the Seychelles islands together with Zaghlul in the early twenties. They had subsequently become inseparable; it was Makram 'Ubayd who had helped al-Nahhas to choose his wife, and the two wives had become good friends. This went on until May 1942, when a rumor circulated that al-Nahhas had asked Makram 'Ubayd to resign, and the latter had refused. King Faruq himself had tried to resolve the dispute, but to no avail. Al-Nahhas had therefore presented the resignation of his cabinet, and immediately formed a new one which did not include Makram 'Ubayd. According to Muhammad Husayn Haykal, a member of the Liberal Constitutional Party who witnessed these incidents, everyone was surprised by this change.[48]

After 'Ubayd left office, he wrote an exposé of his former Wafdist colleagues, accusing them of corruption and abuse of power, and it was published as *al-Kitab al-aswad* ("The Black Book"). When the *Black Book* began to circulate, al-Nahhas was asked in April 1943, during a parliamentary session while he was prime minister, if the allegations made against him by Makram 'Ubayd were correct. A deputy had asked him whether it was true, as the *Black Book* asserted, that al-Nahhas' life style had become extravagant and wasteful. According to the book, al-Nahhas had demonstrated this by accepting a £E 3,000 car, a Packard, ceded to him by the Greek millionaire Kotsika.[49] Moreover, the prime minister had reportedly moved to the Mena House Hotel, which had cost him over £E 1,000;

furthermore, he had rented a villa in Garden City even though he resided in Heliopolis. These expenses, as well this new life style, undoubtedly cost a great deal. How would he respond to Makram 'Ubayd's attacks?

Al-Nahhas went to the podium accompanied by fervent clapping,[50] which leads one to believe that al-Nahhas himself may have instigated the question in order to embarrass Makram 'Ubayd by showing that he had unquestioning Wafd support. He declared that 'Ubayd had distorted facts, invented figures, and blackened his book with imaginings and hallucinations. The deputies roared appreciatively at the quip. Al-Nahhas then turned to 'Ubayd's allegation that as premier, minister for the interior, and foreign minister, al-Nahhas had been assigned three cars for his private and public use, but that he had decided to buy a Packard, to be distinct from other, more "democratic," cars. The prime minister explained that the government cars allocated to him were constantly breaking down, so he had decided to purchase a Packard super limousine, after approval by the council of ministers. This was in April 1942, and Minister of Finance 'Ubayd had advised al-Nahhas to get the car appraised by the government. When al-Nahhas told the dealer that he wanted another car for his private use, the only other car available was one ordered by the Greek millionaire, which the latter proved willing to cede. 'Ubayd then advised al-Nahhas to appeal to the dealer to keep the car until the government paid for the first one. Al-Nahhas decided then that he would keep the first car for his private use, and the second car would become the government car. The owner of the agency then demanded the price of seven cars intended for government use. The bill ran to £E 12,700, and the prime minister's invoice for his car was £E 3,075. In July, the owner of the car agency was asked if he would accept £E 5,282.500. After he refused, a transportation ministry committee estimated the cost of all seven cars at £E 7,540. The owner of the car agency still demanded £E 8,090. Finally, to resolve the problem al-Nahhas paid £E 1,550 for his car, while the committee head paid the extra amount of money charged by the agency owner. Al-Nahhas denied Makram 'Ubayd's accusation of automotive extravagance. It had nothing to distinguish it from other cars, except that its windows opened automatically, and it did not break down in the middle of the road.

As for the ninety-four days he had spent at the Mena House Hotel, this was because his house in Heliopolis was being refurbished. And, it had not cost him over £E 1,000, as Makram 'Ubayd claimed, but £E 323.315, plus £E 40 for gratuities. Besides, he habitually stayed at large hotels and resorts in Cairo, Alexandria, Upper Egypt, and Europe, as they reflected his status and suited his self-respect and dignity. He had spent his life doing this, for relaxation and as a health requirement. Was he unfairly using his authority, or was he blameless, living an irreproachable, honest life, so that God had blessed and protected him? Makram 'Ubayd had also alleged that al-Nahhas had rented the house in Garden City for the conspicuously opulent sum of £E 50 a month. Al-Nahhas could have excused anyone but Makram 'Ubayd, the book's author, for saying this, because no one could know anything about al-Nahhas' private life. 'Ubayd was well-informed on al-Nahhas's private affairs, through their wives, and certainly knew that al-Nahhas had risen from humble origins. Al-Nahhas would have known that 'Ubayd, as a Copt, lacked his own popular base.

Throughout his speech, al-Nahhas supported his defense by citing the numbers of the invoices and checks paid, and telling the Chamber that these were available for the Senate's scrutiny. His riposte was greeted with thunderous applause, which suggests he was widely believed to be innocent of corruption—no matter how serious or wounding were the accusations made against him—or that the Wafd would stand by its leader against any accusations.[51]

After that interpellation, hardly a day passed without questions about accusations in the *Black Book* from the Senate to the prime minister or members of his cabinet named therein. For instance, al-Nahhas was asked about the pious project *(mashru' al-birr)* begun by his wife Zaynab al-Wakil. The question stated that "in the book distributed by Makram 'Ubayd, there was more than one reference to the fact that aims behind the pious project were to force the payment of unofficial taxes, as well as to confer titles and medals on the rich contributors and to repay the employees involved in that benevolent project." Al-Nahhas responded by denouncing Makram 'Ubayd's lies, and explaining that in 1942, on the occasion of the anniversary of the king's accession (11 February), they had considered it "their duty to invite the rich and affluent Egyptians and foreigners to contribute to a great valuable action which would lighten the burden on the poor who were seeking their daily bread and facing the difficulties of life." The project entailed collecting contributions and membership fees, distributing stamps labeled "the piastre for piety" *(al-qirsh li-l-birr)*, holding expensive parties, and selling badges and flowers. On 20 July 1942 the contributions from the various activities amounted to £E 98,041.144, which were placed in the bank, minus £E 1.56, which were kept in the treasury. By 15 April 1943, the deposit at the Cairo branch of Banque Misr amounted to £E 101,750.406. The project had cost £E 584.340. Al-Nahhas indicated that only twenty from among the hundreds of contributors had complained that their contributions had not been mentioned, but this problem had been solved. The project had been so successful, continued al-Nahhas, that his wife had decided to establish it as a permanent charity. Among the members in the charity committee were Amin 'Uthman, Dr. 'Abd al-Wahid al-Wakil, who was al-Nahhas' father-in-law, and the British ambassador's wife, Lady Lampson.[52]

Many observers criticized this charity: Haykal's *Memoirs* implies that al-Nahhas' wife, Zaynab al-Wakil, had established it to feather her own nest.[53] Nevertheless, the senator asking the question, 'Abd al-Magid al-Rimali, thanked al-Nahhas for his detailed answer.[54] The fact that al-Nahhas managed to emerge with his reputation unscathed and his popularity intact suggests how irrelevant personal ethics had become in Egyptian public service. This tendency would grow.

The fawning attitude of the senators toward the Wafd cabinet and its leader during that session may help to explain why 'Ubayd, who eventually addressed an interpellation to the prime minister,[55] failed to make an impression on the Senate. The former secretary of the Wafd, who showed considerable courage by standing up for his accusations, spoke for almost two sessions. However, al-Nahhas' abusive manner enabled him to get Makram 'Ubayd's extremely lengthy interpellation rejected and dismissed by the Senate.[56] It is also curious that the opposition Watani Party never entered the debate on the *Black Book*, nor did it question or interpellate the government about corruption. Makram 'Ubayd's book ultimately resulted in his expulsion from parliament. Shortly thereafter, al-Nahhas decided that his activities were harmful, and he could not remain at large. As Egypt was under martial law, al-Nahhas was able to order 'Ubayd's internment. The latter remained in prison until October 1944, when a new coalition cabinet, headed by Ahmad Mahir, was formed.[57]

Al-Nahhas' cabinet was forced out of office on 8 October 1944, and he soon became the target of questions in parliament.[58] Some of these concerned Amin 'Uthman, chief government auditor in al-Nahhas' cabinet.[59] The questions asked in the Chamber of Deputies dealt with reports that 'Uthman had traveled with his wife on private trips to Palestine at Egyptian government expense, and that al-Nahhas similarly had taken his wife, her brother, and a retinue to Palestine in 1943, on planes belonging to Banque Misr, using official funds. There were also allegations that al-Nahhas had ordered a military plane to transport a nurse from Port Said to Alexandria to care for his mother-in-law. If all this was true, parliamentarians asked how the government would restore the funds taken from the state treasury. Naturally, both al-Nahhas and 'Uthman were targeted once the Wafd was out of power, but 'Uthman was resented by Egyptians for having publicly said that Egypt and Britain were bound together in a "Catholic marriage."

Now finance minister in Mahmud Fahmi al-Nuqrashi's cabinet, Makram 'Ubayd pointed out that all three questions dealt with misuse of state funds for private purposes. He added that the matter went beyond the deputy's query, since Amin 'Uthman had extended the Egyptian government's benevolence to members of his family, who had returned with him on the same plane, and the government had paid for their transport. The former minister's two journeys with his family had cost £E 250. In his capacity as minister of finance, Makram 'Ubayd had then sent a letter asking 'Uthman whether the ministry should consider his trips official, and if so, which administrative agency was responsible for the reimbursement of this money. In response, 'Uthman implied that his trip had been official and secret, and that 'Ubayd had no right to know, because "these matters had to remain undisclosed to the present government."[60]

Makram 'Ubayd had therefore gone back to official records, finding that 'Uthman had lied. On 2 July 1942, four passengers, i.e., Amin 'Uthman and his family, boarded a plane bound for Israel [sic].[61] Four days later, an empty plane left from Cairo, returning on 7 July, with Amin 'Uthman as sole passenger. These trips had cost the Egyptian government £E 137. On 11 August, 'Uthman embarked once again from Cairo on an empty plane, returning on 15 August with his wife, daughter and his wife's sister. On this occasion, the journeys had cost £E 113. Official records showed that 'Uthman had traveled with a normal passport, not a diplomatic one. Makram 'Ubayd said he had already initiated proceedings, so that in accordance with Law 17 (1918), a quarter of the former auditor general's monthly pension was to be withheld to return the money to the government.[62]

The matter of al-Nahhas and his wife was just as shameless. She had traveled with her brother to Palestine at the end of May 1943. Al-Nahhas joined them later, at the beginning of June. They had all spent a few days together, and then returned to Cairo. After their return, the Palestine railways system had demanded the payment of £E 156. Instead of paying for the costs of his trip, al-Nahhas had obtained funds from the Ministry of Finance. The letter sent to the Finance Ministry only mentioned al-Nahhas himself in the travel voucher. The sum had been paid in total by the state treasury, without legitimate right or reason. Makram 'Ubayd had therefore initiated proceedings against al-Nahhas. In addition, the former premier had assigned a military plane to travel between Cairo to Port Sa'id and then to Alexandria on the same day, to fetch a nurse to care for his mother-in-law. Al-Nahhas should have been able to find a nurse in Alexandria, but 'Ubayd remarked that the ex-prime minister needed to brag and show the generosity of the state. Steps had already been taken to prosecute al-Nahhas.

The minister of finance then told the Chamber that al-Nahhas had chartered trains without paying for the costs to the tune of £E 4,882. He observed that when a junior government official committed a minor offense he was expelled from his job, whereas those prominent gentlemen who had been in power had focused their attention on financing private affairs with state funds, moneys that had been entrusted to them. As a further insult to the people, they then claimed to be honest and upright.[63]

At the End of the Monarchy

The Wafd returned to power in January 1950; its new strategy was to appease the palace. This was reflected in the parliament's business, and one interpellation would have dire consequences for the monarchy. On 8 May 1950, a senator, Mustafa Mar'i, who was an Independent, addressed the prime minister, inquiring into the motives for the resignation of Mahmud Muhammad, a man of unimpeachable reputation who had headed the government audit office.[64] Consequently, al-Nahhas warned Muhammad Husayn Haykal, the president of the Senate, against dealing with this issue too openly.[65] A stickler for parliamentary procedure, Haykal did not understand al-Nahhas' admonition, and eventually concluded that the prime minister was telling him that the interpellation should in no way involve the king.

On 29 May 1950, the senator, Mustafa Mar'i, voiced his dissatisfaction at length, explaining that he had already asked why the head of the government audit office had resigned, because Mahmud Muhammad had given no motive in his resignation. Mar'i knew Muhammad, as did the other senators; he was independent, rational, and balanced in his views, and it was unlikely that he should have resigned without a reason. Mar'i had therefore addressed his question to the government, which had given him an answer in two parts. In the first, the government had declared that Muhammad had only indicated private circumstances, which made it very difficult for him to remain as head of the audit office. Here Mar'i had concluded that the word "private" did not mean personal, but that the resignation was due to his work as head of the audit office. Mar'i's guess was supported by the government's statement that the audit office would continue to supervise by legal means the state's resources and expenditures. Moreover, Muhammad had indicated in an interview that his resignation was not due to personal reasons.[66] Mar'i observed that the government, as well, had neglected to fulfill its duties, because it could actually have supported the man and protected him when he had tried to do his job.

As for the second part of the government's reply, it indicated that Mahmud Muhammad's resignation was related to observations made by the head of the audit office about the government's expenditure in the Palestine campaign, and about its financial support to al-Muwasa Hospital. Here Mar'i pointed out that the ninth clause of Law 52 (1942) dealt with the establishment of this government audit office, stipulating that it had full authority to give its views on the expenditure of credits. The law further affirmed that any difference of opinion between the audit office and a government department had to be referred to the council of ministers.[67] A senator thereupon asked when and under which cabinet these irregularities had taken place; Mar'i retorted that partisanship and the different cabinets that came and went had nothing to do with the matter, since the country was the loser because of this partisanship. He asked the senators to take their duties seriously when they considered his interpellation.[68]

He explained that, in fact, Ahmad al-Naqib, director of al-Muwasa Hospital, had presented Karim Thabit, the king's press attaché, a man of dubious reputation who was suspected of encouraging King Faruq's excesses, with the sum of £E 5,000. This was in January 1948, when Thabit had been chief editor for al-Muqattam. No explanation had been given for this gift. The audit office criticized this in its annual report.[69] Al-Nahhas' cabinet had asked the head of the audit office to omit the phrases of disapproval from the report, but Mahmud Muhammad refused. A crisis ensued which soon reached the palace. When the deputy head of the king's cabinet indicated that the conduct of the audit office had offended Faruq, Mahmud Muhammad tendered his resignation, and it was immediately accepted.

Mar'i stressed that the £E 5,000 check had been offered to Thabit without the consent of the hospital's administration; indeed, its board had only given its approval after the interpellation had been presented. Here Mar'i said that the hospital's board needed to be told that approving a crime did not eliminate it. Moreover, if £E 5,000 were given to a person, was it given as a general fee, or as a commission? If given as a fee, then a tax had to be taken from it; if taken as a commission, then this too was liable to commercial and industrial taxes. Consequently, wasn't the pasha (Naqib), who had paid the money to the other pasha (Thabit), required to pay taxes like the senators? Accordingly, where was the tariff payable to the state?[70]

The government replied on the following day. The cabinet minister present in the Senate on behalf of al-Nahhas was Fu'ad Sirag al-Din, the interior minister. Sirag al-Din's speech on behalf of the government was even more aggressive than the interpellation. Sirag al-Din pointed out that his party had nothing to do with this action, as another cabinet, under Mahmud Fahmi al-Nuqrashi had been in power at the time. He also maintained that the former head of the audit office had insisted on submitting his resignation, even though al-Nahhas and Sirag al-Din had tried to prevent it. At some point during the proceedings, Sirag al-Din declared that the seat that accommodated the president of the Senate was shaking; President Haykal understood this to mean that his position was at risk because the interpellation was taking an awkward turn.[71]

On the following day, a newspaper reported that Karim Thabit had tendered his resignation as royal press attaché, but that the king had refused to accept it, because he trusted Thabit completely.[72] When Sirag al-Din went to see Haykal, the Senate president reproached him for defending Thabit in his speech. Sirag al-Din relented, and criticized Thabit for his constant meddling in affairs of state; Sirag al-Din nevertheless added that the Wafd had been out in the political cold for several years, a condition that had almost destroyed the party. They had therefore had every excuse to come to an agreement with the palace and accept its policies.[73] Shortly afterwards, Haykal and the senators involved in the interpellation involving the king's press attaché learned that their tenure in the Senate would not be renewed, presumably on orders from the king.[74]

Although al-Nahhas' cabinet did not remain in power for long, it is noteworthy that in 1953, shortly after the Free Officers coup, the Karim Thabit case was tried before a court composed of both civilians and military. When asked about why the case had reached such proportions, a witness, the ex-Senator Ibrahim Bayumi Madkur indicated "we were not concerned with the resignation of the head of the audit office; rather, the principles were important, and we attached importance to what had taken place. It was a catastrophe."[75] Both Thabit and Naqib's lawyers, however, managed to shift responsibility for any irregularities that had taken place to Faruq, who was now in exile.[76]

Conclusion

The drafting of a constitution and the convening of a parliament had been a long-standing Egyptian dream, because it was felt that Egypt's bankruptcy in the nineteenth century could have perhaps been prevented by a reasonable legislative system. However, the Egyptian parliament between 1919 and 1952 proved to be an effective watchdog only when its members were completely independent from partisan or other considerations. The Wafd had initially been known as the party of the people. Under Sa'd Zaghlul's strong leadership, members of parliament had spoken out against corruption or the misappropriation of public funds. Nevertheless, under al-Nahhas, the successive resignation of most of that party's fearless, efficient, and dedicated members left an empty shell. Also, the Wafd became more introverted, and regarded any opposition to its policies in parliament with suspicion. Eventually, its partisans became so absorbed in adulating their leader, al-Nahhas, that they neither criticized nor denounced the government, no matter how blatant the issue that had instigated interpellations. Consequently, the monitoring role that the Wafd members of parliament should have played vanished. As for the Watani Party, despite its presence in all sessions of parliament, it was too engrossed in its program of opposing Great Britain's presence in Egypt to devote any time to attacking corruption. The Liberal Constitutionalists were probably the most effective party, but were not popular. Moreover, although its leader, Muhammad Husayn Haykal, certainly understood parliamentary procedure, he apparently was not strong enough to control the Senate.

In a deeper sense, these incidents are indicative of an underlying clash of attitudes. Members of Egypt's parliament thought that, under the 1923 Constitution, they had the power to set the government's budget. Those who had been honestly elected, notably the Wafdists, viewed themselves as the guardians of the national interest. Kings Fu'ad and Faruq disdained the Constitution and resented deputies' and senators' efforts to intervene in their patrimonial prerogatives as rulers of the country. Their appointees, such as Nash'at, Ibrashi, and Thabit, shared these sentiments. Because the kings and parliament competed for popular favor, interpellations like those described in this chapter angered the palace and led to reprisals against the questioners. But their corrosive effect on palace prestige contributed to the 1952 military coup.

Notes

1   I would like to thank Walter Armbrust for his generous help during all stages of writing this paper.

2   *Al-Dawla al-misriya, madabit majlis al-nuwwab*, 15 March 1924.

3   *Madabit majlis al-nuwwab*, 7 April 1924.

4   *Madabit majlis al-nuwwab*, 19 April 1924.

5   The Wafd won 90 percent of the 214 seats in the Chamber of Deputies, as well as the majority of the seventy-one Senate seats. Zaghlul's opponents, and those who did not support his policy, all failed in the elections. The historian, 'Abd al-Rahman al-Rafi'i, who was a member of the Watani Party, mentioned that the failure of Yahya Ibrahim, the previous prime minister, to win a seat in the Chamber of Deputies was indicative both of the man's integrity, and of the freedom of the elections. The Liberal Constitutional Party won only six seats, whereas the Watani Party obtained four. 'Abd al-Rahman al-Rafi'i, *Fi a'qab al-thawra al-misriya: thawrat 1919*, vol. 1 (Cairo: Dar al-Ma'arif, 1987), 72, 185. Before the elections, Muhammad Husayn Haykal, the editor of the Liberal newspaper *al-Siyasa*, and a fervent Liberal Constitutionalist, believed that despite the Wafd's popularity, the Liberals could win a respectable number of seats. He was, needless to say, extremely disappointed with the results of these elections. Muhammad Husayn Haykal, *Mudhakkirat fi-l-siyasa al-misriya*, vol. 1 (Cairo: Dar al-Ma'arif, 1978), 146. Indeed, al-Rafi'i would say that the aim of the four deputies representing the Watani Party was to use its opposition to uphold the country's rights and guide the government to undertake reform in all domains.

6   *Madabit majlis al-nuwwab*, 7 June 1924.

7   Ibid.

8   *Madabit majlis al-nuwwab*, 13 April 1924.

9   When parliament was convened on 15 November 1924, rumors of a pending cabinet crisis had abounded, and Zaghlul handed in the resignation of his ministers, as the palace was making life difficult for them. It had instigated demonstrations at al-Azhar and the religious institutes, and an observer remarked that they would probably have never become involved in demonstrations without the palace's prompting. Zaghlul's second motive was the appointment of Hasan Nash'at on 8 November 1924 to the assistant directorship of the king's cabinet without Zaghlul's, or his cabinet's, knowledge. The palace had further been instrumental in the resignation of Tawfiq Nasim, Zaghlul's finance minister, in the middle of November. Nasim's servility to the king was well-known, and Nash'at was identified as the source of the plots hatched against the cabinet. Accordingly, Zaghlul's cabinet regarded his appointment by King Fu'ad as encouragement to organize intrigues. 'Abd al-Rahman al-Rafi'i, *Fi a'qab al-thawra al-misriya*, 1: 227–29.

10 *Madabit majlis al-nuwwab*, 11 August 1926

11 Here Sidqi explained that a soldier cost £E 27 per annum, whereas the expense of a *sawari*, or cavalryman, was £E 50.

12 *Madabit majlis al-nuwwab*, 11 August 1926.

13 Ibid.

14 *Madabit majlis al-nuwwab*, 16 May 1927.

15 Ibid.

16 Ibid.

17 Ibid.

18 Ibid.

19 Ibid.

20 Ibid.

21 Ibid.

22 Ibid.

23 Ibid.

24 Shaykh Muhammad Rashid Rida (1865–1935) was the author of a treatise on the caliphate, *al-Khilafa aw al-imama al-'uzma* ("The Caliphate or the Great Imamate"), published in 1922. See Mahmoud Haddad, "Arab Religious Nationalism in the Colonial Era: Rereading Rashid Rida's Ideas on the Caliphate," *Journal of the American Oriental Society* 117: 2 (April–June 1997), 253–54.

25 *Madabit majlis al-nuwwab*, 11 May 1927.

26 Ibid.

27 Ibid.

28 Ibid.

29 Ibid.

30 Ibid.

31 Ibid.

32 Ibid.

33 Ibid.

34 *Al-Siyasa al-usbu'iya*, 10 March 1926.

35 F.O. 141/786/17329/3. Emile Khuri's views on the attempt on Zaghlul's life, 18 July 1924.

36 *The Egyptian Gazette*, 18 November 1924.

37 Émile Selim Amad, *La question d'Égypte (1841–1938)* (Paris: Les Éditions Internationales, 1938) 105. Cited in Marcel Colombe, *L'évolution de l'Égypte 1924–1950* (Paris: G.P. Maisonneuve et Cie, 1951), 19.

38 F.O. 371/17977. British Consul-General Heathcote-Smith (Alexandria) to His Excellency the High Commissioner for Egypt and the Sudan (Cairo). Confidential. No.R.54. 20 April 1934. J1095/9/16.

39 *Madabit majlis al-nuwwab*, 11 April 1934.

40 Ibid.

41 *Madabit majlis al-nuwwab*, 8 January 1934.

42 Isma'il Sidqi, "Mas'alat al-kurnish," *al-Ahram*, 14 December 1933.

43 F.O. 371/17997. p.156; F.O. 371/17996. Heathcote-Smith to Lampson. No.R.37. 4 April 1934. J900/71/16.

44 *The Egyptian Gazette*. 25 May 1934.

45 Haykal, 2: 211

46 Haykal, *Mudhakkirat*, 2: 214. The Liberal Constitutional Party was joined in boycotting the elections by Ahmad Mahir's Sa'dist bloc.

47 'Abd al-Rahman al-Rafi'i, *Fi a'qab al-thawra*, vol. 3.

48 Haykal, *Mudhakkirat*, 2: 225.

49 Kotsika was the founder of a large hospital in Alexandria.

50 *Madabit majlis al-nuwwab*, 21 April 1943.

51 The *Black Book* was banned from circulation by martial law.

52 *Madabit majlis al-shuyukh*, 17 May 1943.

53 Haykal, *Mudhakkirat*, 2: 226.

54 *Madabit majlis al-shuyukh*, 17 May 1943.

55 *Madabit majlis al-shuyukh*, 18, 19 May 1943.

56 Ibid.

57 Haykal, *Mudhakkirat*, 2: 244–45.

58 It appears that al-Nahhas made it a habit to offer his patronage freely to any number of people. Although he did this to boost his popularity, it may not have occurred to him that it was reprehensible, or even unethical, to use state funds to pay the salaries of officials who would later back him and offer him their support. Members of the opposition wished to draw the Chamber's attention to this. Both Muhammad Husayn Haykal and 'Abd al-Rahman al-Rafi'i also mention that the Wafd was in the habit of getting rid of government officials who opposed the party.

59 Amin 'Uthman had been educated in Great Britain, he was married to a Briton, and he was also a friend of Miles Lampson. He had helped the British ambassador to prepare the ultimatum presented to King Faruq on 4 February 1942: he eventually paid for it with his life, as he was shot in January 1946. According to 'Abd al-Rahman al-Rafi'i, the court followed a tendency to encourage assassinations and crime, and the killer and his associates received sentences which left them almost free of blame. Al-Rafi'i, 3: 273.

60 *Madabit majlis al-nuwwab*, 2, 3, 4 July 1945.

61 Although Israel as a state had not yet been founded, that was the word used in the text.

62 *Madabit majlis al-nuwwab*, 2, 3, 4 July 1945.

63 Ibid.

64 Mahmud Muhammad was the son of former Prime Minister Muhammad Mahmud (1877–1941) and came from a wealthy Upper Egyptian family.

65 Haykal, *Mudhakkirat*, 3: 89.

66 Ibid., 3: 90.

67 Ibid., 3: 92.

68 Ibid., 3: 93.

69 The report was also very critical of the money expended by the government in 1948 on weapons and ammunition during the Palestine campaign. However, due to space limitations, no mention will be made in this article about that part of the interpellation. '

70 *Madabit Majlis al-Shuyukh*, 29 May 1950.

71 Ibid.

72 *Al-Ahram*, 31 May 1950.

73 Haykal, *Mudhakkirat*, 2: 299.

74 Haykal, *Mudhakkirat*, 2: 300.

75 "Fi mahkamat al-ghadr," *al-Musawwar* 1494, 29 May 1953, 16.

76 "Fi mahkamat al-ghadr," *al-Musawwar* 1496, 12 June 1953, 18–19.

Part II

Reconstructing Society, Recasting History

5 Egyptianizing Modernity through the 'New *Effendiya*'

Social and Cultural Constructions of the Middle Class in Egypt under the Monarchy

Lucie Ryzova

The term effendi (pl. *effendiya* or effendis) figures prominently in all accounts of political development in modern Egypt as a group central to both the nationalist movement[1] and to the emerging radical movements in the 1930s and 1940s.[2] However, the effendis are rarely acknowledged as simply 'effendis.' They are often covered by other terms such as 'students,' 'modernizing elites,' or 'radical movements.' This is both imprecise and misleading. The concept effendi as such is well worth attention. No study has focused on the emergence of the new *effendiya*, or the effendis in general, as a distinct social phenomenon, linked to wider processes of modernity and social transformation.[3]

The absence of the effendis as a sociocultural category from historical writing is caused partly by the problem of defining the term. 'Effendi' is most conventionally defined as the stratum of western-educated town-dwellers. In its collective form, *effendiya*,[4] the term is often used to mean some kind of a middle class. It is, moreover, sometimes (over) character-ized as the reading public,[5] or (under) characterized as the bureaucratic class.[6] Whether the effendis can be taken for middle class is problematic, and the latter two definitions are equally misleading.

The term effendi meant two things. In one sense it was a conceptual category, a label for people who outwardly manifested certain diacritics of dress or manner. In this sense an effendi was closely related to status, and was defined by culture, often the result of formal (western) education, and, often but not necessarily, by position in the state bureaucracy. The other sense of the term was the sociological group associated with it. The social group of effendis, the *effendiya*, changed considerably over time, as did the perception of what it signified in cultural terms. The term effendi is taken for granted by historians. At the same time it appears virtually everywhere in historical sources, from newspapers and magazines to images (fig. 5.1).

The most blatant example is the use of the title effendi in names and thus by definition also in all orthodox historical documents. Effendi is visual, it is textual, it is everywhere. It is also distinctly present as a certain ethos, as effendi identity, in most narratives whether literary, cultural, or political, of the interwar period.

The usage of the term effendi changes considerably over time. It was first an honorific title, which, in the nineteenth century, came to signify a category of western educated bureaucrats from privileged backgrounds who were sent to khedivial schools or to Europe. Around the turn of the century the effendis assumed the role of the nation's liberators. Starting from the 1930s, academic literature speaks of the "new *effendiya*,"[7] and links it to the emergence of some kind of indigenous middle class, or to the radical movements from whose ranks the critique of the liberal establishment was waged. While at the turn of the century the term implied considerable social status, in the course of the interwar period the term lost most of its glamour and became more associated with the articulate but poor urban male.[8] By this time effendi could very easily be taken as an insult rather than as a term of respect.

It is not only the changing meaning and social usage of the term that poses a problem in conceptualizing the effendi. A related problem is that the effendis constantly tend to overlap with other social categories such as merchants, rural middle classes, the professionals, the bureaucrats, or the students. It can be said that the effendis are always in the process of becoming something else. They might have something in common with all of these categories without being quite any of them; they lie at the intersection of the merchant and the bureaucrat, of the rural second stratum and the professional, or even the national elite, yet they were distinct as effendis, and what makes them stand apart as a category is precisely their being effendis.

The concept effendi is not a class situation but a cultural term, and one that is related to social mobility, but more importantly, to passages from non-modernity to modernity in its many forms. The category of

'middle class,' while sometimes useful to locate some specific generation of effendis in its socioeconomic milieu, is limiting in our attempt
to understand the effendis as a phenomenon and as an emerging social
group. The effendis as a group have to be understood in relation to the
historical moment in which they are located, as well as in relation to other
social categories against which the term effendi is constructed. Effendis
were a heterogeneous group, but they were united by the way in which
they distinguished themselves culturally from the rest of the urban population, and from their often 'traditional' fathers. They practiced new
modes of socialization and of consumption, and new forms of identity
were spreading among them.

Functionally and conceptually, 'effendi' is linked to modernity. The purpose of making effendis is first informed by the state's will to modernize.
However, the transition toward modernity has many forms. In Egypt,
most generally, this transition was sparked from two directions—first
by the khedivial state, and later by more 'bottom-up' processes of social
change both evident in mass culture, and constitutive of it. Exemplified
in the rise of mass politics, in the transformation of values and new social
and cultural practices, the 'subaltern subject' becomes a 'modern citizen.'
The *effendiya* of the interwar period—a growing public constituted from
among the unprivileged, but not destitute, urban and rural social groups—
was the product of struggles for education and literacy, rather than a group
generated from above.

It can be said that the meaning of *effendiya* is related to both its position toward the modernizing state—as the producer and consumer of the
effendis—and, organically, to the country's social structure as transformed
under the impact of modernity. These two 'modernities'—top-down
modernity as imported and imposed technique, and bottom-up modernity as new practices adopted by social actors—interact. They also provide
for the contradictions that inform the meaning of the conceptual effendi.

The contradiction between effendi as a cultural construct versus
effendis as a social group suggests two different processes, one of
which was taking place on the level of discourse, reflecting the state's
modernizing project, and the other defined by the structure of income
distribution within the post-1923 state, which resulted in a social group
characterized by frustration. The conceptual effendi was constructed
through a harmonious imagery of middle class existence; the socioeconomic effendi was formed by a contest over who was to be included in the
modernist project. These two apparently contradictory processes were

culturally productive, and essential to the creation of modern Egyptian bourgeois culture and national identity.

This chapter will address primarily the question of what constitutes somebody as an effendi and how, 'becoming an effendi' shapes one's social and cultural identity. Starting with an outline of the historical development of the concept, this chapter will focus on the effendis' cultural identity and self-perception. It will attempt an interpretation of the cultural and social meanings of the conceptual effendi—both for those who attribute the term to themselves, and those who attribute it to others. I will use a variety of cultural sources, such as popular magazines and the cinema, to which the effendi was both the principal author and consumer. Such sources reveal a vision of modern Egyptian society through the lenses of the unprivileged, but articulate, urban citizen.

Historical Development of the Conceptual Effendi
From 'Executors of Modernity' to Makers of Modern Egypt
Originally of Greek origin, the term 'effendi,' originally meaning 'master, seigneur,' was used by the Ottomans as the title of address for various dignitaries and important functionaries.[9] In nineteenth-century Egypt, the title effendi took on a specific meaning that was organically linked to the building of a modern state, and related to both the emergence of modern bureaucracy as well as to the secular and Egyptian character of its elite.

While Muhammad 'Ali's elite was composed primarily of his personal entourage *(ma'iya saniya)*,[10] the future transformation of that elite also lay in the very policies Muhammad 'Ali put in motion: the building of modern schools on the western model, sending students to missions, and enrolling children from the provincial notability to attend these schools. This was an expression of a distinct view of the function of the state,[11] as well as a modernizing project that was to continue under his successors, notably Isma'il, with renewed force. Indeed, the change was slow and gradual, but, in Hunter's words:

> During Muhammad 'Ali's reign, a cadre of "new men"—physicians, engineers, geographers, metallurgists, printers—began to emerge. Employed by Muhammad 'Ali in various jobs, from translating French law codes to managing medical dispensaries in the countryside, these young men worked their way through the ranks of the bureaucracy until by the 1860s many had become part of Egypt's administrative elite . . . they became the cutting edge of new society.[12]

These 'new men,' were recruited on the basis of their professional skills or knowledge of a European language.[13] An intimate connection developed between administrative service and scientific knowledge, but also, between them and the state's modernizing project. They were all broadly committed to reform, "which in the most general sense meant the introduction of European knowledge or know-how."[14]

The recruitment and training of these new men took decades to be codified. The process of creating such men became increasingly associated with the effendis, as products of the specific western curriculum sponsored by the state. These effendis were drawn predominantly from the provincial notability[15] and assumed offices in state service just below the highest ranks of pasha and bey.[16] They were distinguished not only by their jobs, but also, by their specific "culture": their western manners, signified by their 'European' dress in the first instance, and their distinct perspective on the society in which they lived. In roughly 1910, this is how Sayyid 'Uways—later to become Egypt's pioneer sociologist—described his aunt, daughter of an effendi, a phenomenon never seen before in their family:

> My uncle Mahmud's wife originated from a different socioeconomic background than the one of my parents. . . . [She] brought with her a different culture and different human experience. She was greatly proud of her father, 'Ali Effendi, because he was an effendi. . . . She used to mix up with effendis, her father's friends, and learned a great many things from listening to them. She was aware of their lifestyle and the life of her father was for her a model of social relations and behavior. This effendi lifestyle she considered an ideal one, and it differed enormously from what she encountered after her marriage. But what could she do?[17]

The lady here was not necessarily from a family richer than that of Sayyid 'Uways. The difference lay in their culture. Similar testimony can be found in al-Muwailihi's famous sketch of Egyptian society at the close of the nineteenth century, in which the "new officials" were parodied as being "town bred and often educated in Europe and with European ideas and manners, [who] felt themselves superiors to those below them."[18] These characteristics derive from the status these officials enjoyed within their society, the kind of education and employment, which placed them 'above' the rest of society, as well as from their structural relationship to the modernizing state, as both products and agents of the kind of modernization in process. As this project progressed, the relationship to the state was to become more complex and ambivalent.

While in the mid-nineteenth century, effendi meant simply a bureaucrat who was associated with implementing the state's modernization agenda, toward the end of the century the effendi road was taken mostly by provincial families in their rise to the national-elite level.[19] Under Khedive Isma'il the highest administrative titles of bey, and sometimes pasha, could be bestowed upon a rural notable who had risen up through the provincial hierarchy, such as the illiterate Muhammad Sultan Pasha. Starting with the new century a pattern was gradually established, in which the road to bey and pasha—and thus to the social and increasingly also the political elite—led through the effendi, through graduation from one of the governmental higher institutes.[20] While in the 1880s one would still hesitate whether to send his son through the Azhari curriculum or a secular one, and would ideally combine both, at the beginning of the twentieth century the more well-to-do families started leaving al-Azhar for the government secondary schools and higher institutes, which offered much better career prospects, and came increasingly to be regarded as gates of entrance to "power and influence."[21]

The rise in status of provincial families, as well as their inclusion into the national elite hierarchy, was exemplified in their assumption of titles previously reserved, with few notable exceptions, such as 'Ali Bey Mubarak, for the Turco-Circassian elite.[22] As the relationship among provincial families, offices and land became more substantial, they also started to intermarry into the Turco-Circassian aristocracy.[23] Simultaneously, some effendis from these Egyptian provincial families began to occupy important positions in politics on the national level.[24]

By the turn of the twentieth century, the profile of the *effendiya* changed in several respects. First, with the emergence of new occupations and professional schools, the effendis ceased to be solely associated with the state bureaucracy. While the majority of these new professionals continued to be employed by the state, they were no longer simply bureaucrats, but came to represent new urban society, new social institutions, and new ways of life. The effendi was now an engineer, a lawyer, a doctor, but also a journalist and, increasingly, a political activist.[25]

This emerging secular elite came to represent a new social type known as the *mutarbashun*, 'tarboosh-wearers,' who would eventually clash with the *mu'ammamun*, 'turban-wearers' (*'imma*: turban), usually Azhari curricula graduates, over issues of career.[26] More than this, it was a clash of two knowledge hierarchies, one religious and one secular, over the question of inclusion and exclusion, which developed around what would be perceived as the interests of the new society: what medical practitioner should one visit, a *shaykh* or a medical graduate; and where should one send his child for schooling, to al-Azhar or to a modern school? Again, we can get a glimpse of how such a divide was perceived by a young graduate of al-Azhar in Taha Husayn's well-known autobiography:

> The young man realised his long-cherished dream of entering
> the world of the tarboush, just when he was sick to death of the
> turban and all that it implied. But in this society he met
> the wealthiest and most influential of men, while he himself was
> a poor man from a middle-class family, whose situation in Cairo
> was miserable in the extreme.[27]

Second, but in close relation to the first point, around the turn of the century the effendis assumed yet another dimension, that of being 'Egyptians' in national terms.[28] The effendis emerged in moments of crises as the defenders of Egypt's independence and speakers for the nation.[29] The decisive factor in this new self-identification of the effendis as the defenders of the national cause was the British occupation, in 1882. After its first decade, the British occupation started taking a decidedly permanent outlook, manifested, among other things, in British penetration of the institutions of the state accompanied by the influx of British trained personnel into positions of control and authority.[30] As the articulate, secular urban Egyptian elite, wherever the effendis looked, they found doors blocked in front of them: the British occupying high administrative and skilled positions in the state bureaucracy, the Levantines occupying those of the free professions.[31] Should they want to enter private businesses, the effendis were discriminated against by the fact that foreign companies paid lower taxes as result of the capitulations.[32] The feelings of frustration this generated among the educated urban Egyptians are again described on the pages of al-Muwailihi's *Hadith 'Isa Ibn Hisham*,

> The British earn huge salaries and have extensive authority, they have
> grabbed the reins of power and are keeping us shut out. The gates to
> promotion are shut in our faces, and the wherewithal of progress is
> cut off. If only France could regain her former power and might . . .
> then we could begin to run our government with our own hands.[33]

The 'New Citizens' and the 'Trouble-Makers'

Independence in 1922 brought about a new kind of order,[34] comprising not only a new institutional and legal framework, but also a regrouping of social forces resulting in new alliances. Political elites and institutions became Egyptian, and the state bureaucracy was significantly expanded, as well as extensively Egyptianized.[35] With the eclipse of foreign elites from public life, though not from economic or political power, many of their former strongholds were taken over by Egyptians.[36] The transfer of power that took place after 1923 thus turned the bomb-throwers of 1919 into state-makers, and the 'old' effendis became beys and pashas—that third generation of modern Egyptian political society to which James Whidden refers in chapter one of this volume.[37] Yet, what about the 'new' effendis, those effendis growing up in the new state?

A state-building project based on liberal ideology and institutions needs a middle class. In conceptual terms, the effendi became the ideal citizen of the state who also fulfilled the role of a modern 'public.' "The institution of a modern national state . . . entailed creation of new political subjects—citizens—and new political entitlements—rights."[38] The neglect of education was a major grievance of Egyptians under the British occupation,[39] and education was subsequently one of the priorities of the post-1923 Egyptian state.[40] As Misako Ikeda demonstrates in chapter eight, the numerical and administrative expansion of education was marked in comparison to the British era. Western-style education, says Beinin, not only expanded the ranks of the *effendiya*, but also provided a vocabulary for imagining Egypt as a political space comparable to European nation states. "Thus empowered, the *effendiya* presented themselves as bearers of national mission."[41] The school curricula instituted by the liberal establishment was filled with ideas of citizen rights and duties, and all that this implies in terms of political participation.[42] This was true not only of the curriculum, but also of the whole ethos of the liberal establishment: in the legal language of the elite, and the central role of the Constitution, which made the nation "the source of all power."[43] As Barak Salmoni explores in chapter six of this volume through the lens of history materials in primary and secondary schooling, the curriculum echoed the concept of popular sovereignty and participation, and the perception of political rights and obligations as "ethical values."[44] A symbol of such a modern citizen was 'al-Misri Effendi,' a cartoon character that became prominent on the pages of several magazines through the 1930s and 1940s (fig. 5.2).[45] He was usually portrayed as standing on the side and commenting on current political events. He was meant to represent the 'average' Egyptian. Dressed in a European suit and depicted holding prayer beads, he was both modern and Muslim.

Policies and discourses of the post-1923 Egyptian state were contradictory. The language of the political elite urged rights and duties for all citizens, and the state's priority was the spread of education. The regime's organic intellectuals, however, diffused a vision of society, in which the 'enlightened intellectuals,' in possession of the right kind of knowledge, were to lead the masses toward progress and modernity.[46] They represented a clearly delineated elite, in control of political institutions and economic resources.[47] In the cultural realm this elite was dangerously close to an imagery based on Pharaonism and westernization, rather than Arab and Muslim aspects of Egypt.[48]

Egypt in the inter-war period was characterized by important processes of social and economic change, which have been described as, essentially, those of population growth, urbanization, and the spread of modern education.[49] By 1946 the number of secondary and university students quadrupled over that of the 1920s.[50] Some authors, Gershoni and Jankowski among them, have taken this data as evidence for the emergence of an Egyptian middle class. The rise of the student population in cities was of major importance to politics,[51] but this was not just a function of numbers. Education, far from leading unquestionably to a middle class *existence* as was the case two decades before the period in question, represented a source middle class *status*. Middle class status is not the same as a middle class material existence. In respect to education, other issues, such as increasing differentiation in the levels of education and literacy, particularly with the advent of new forms of literacy geared to media, radio, and cinema, as well as practices of reading, should be considered. New practices of literacy articulated with new modes of consumption, socialization and politics, which were no longer confined to the educated elite.

Economic development was another crucial element in the equation. The Egyptian economy, after a relatively successful 1920s, experienced a more or less continuous decline starting from the early 1930s.[52] Owen characterized it as "development without growth," to illustrate the real drop in the general standard of living of everybody except the elite.[53] While students in the 1930s and 1940s had to cope with the unemployment of graduates, the position of existing or emerging middle class groups and households ought to be described as one of chronic instability.[54] Far from strengthening the Egyptian middle class, industrialization, depression in the 1930s, and ultimately World War II only exaggerated the winners and losers on both sides of the social divide. The numbers of university and high school graduates cited above are important, but not because they define the parameters of a class. Rather, they suggest a growing number of attempts at a middle class existence. We must take into account the crucial difference between 'shopping' for the accoutrements of a middle-class life, and 'window-shopping' for them—between being something and aspiring to be something, or having the status of the thing without actually being it.[55]

Returning to al-Misri Effendi, the cartoon character, he represents an 'average Egyptian,' but the image is not necessarily about the middle class as a socioeconomic category. Al-Misri Effendi, more than any social or economic position, represents a *concept of national identity* symbolized by the very fact of his being an effendi. The 'social middle'—the location of different middle class groups and identities—can be thought of as an aggregate of processes—social, economic, and cultural—characterized by both fragmentation and homogenization. Sociologically speaking, the middle class position was chronically unstable, with groups as well as households and individuals entering and leaving. On the other hand, the 'middle' is also viewed as a conceptual zone, not only between the rich and the poor, and not only, or ideally, defined by a middle class living situation, but also, in more abstract terms, as a site of the construction of modern national culture and identity.[56] The *effendiya* might be considered the primary claimant to the social and cultural 'middle,' as both a would-be modern middle class and the carrier of national middle class culture.

Yet, as result of the economic and social factors mentioned above, the *effendiya* were constantly buffeted by change. In one respect the effendis were not quite a middle class, but were rather the *idea* of it. In another respect, we must consider the likelihood that from the effendi's own perspective the crucial feature of effendi identity was not a desire to create a conceptual middle, but the desire to be upwardly mobile in terms of both status and material well-being. It was the liberal nationalists who required a middle class; the *effendiya* themselves were potential liberal nationalists, and would-be elites at the same time.

An Outside Perspective

An interesting and useful insight to the appearance of effendis of the 1930s and 1940s can be grasped from British Embassy documents. Officials in Cairo and across the Middle East had been paying increasing attention to what they came to call "the effendi problem."[57] "The effendis," as Walter

Smart, the oriental secretary at the British Embassy in Cairo, summarized in one of his reports, "are the class which must exercise the predominating influence in the future political development of their country."[58] Bevin, who had been receiving these dispatches, wrote in response,

> I have been giving thought to the problem of the effendis . . .
> I think the term is justified, for reports give the impression that the effendis (by which I mean the educated and semi-educated products of Eastern universities and schools) . . . are in a state of transition. They seem to be rapidly developing into a professional middle class destined to claim for itself a definite position in the social order in the Arab world and to play an increasingly important part in shaping the political destinies of the Middle East.[59]

The British officers had a strong interest in understanding what they observed as the emerging "effendi class." They described the effendis as a "new" phenomenon, essentially a product of modern education. They were also "in transition," as expressed perhaps in the tension between their expectations (they "claim" a role) and the "poor opportunities," which their countries were able to offer. They also seemed to be generally "suspicious and hostile" toward Britain, and communist propaganda among them was spreading. Because of their skills, education, and western culture, the effendis were perceived as a political force. It was therefore of extreme importance to British interests in the Middle East to develop friendly relations with them.

Behind the debate over how to "handle" the effendis and make them "more friendly" to Britain, the reports give more interesting, and analytically valuable, clues about them. In the exchange of dispatches that circulated between London and British embassies in the Middle East, each official focused on his "own" *effendiya*. Lebanon did not have the same problem, nor did Saudi Arabia, which had fewer effendis due to its lack of universities, coffeehouses, and club-life.[60] In Iraq, the analytically minded H.S. Bird distinguished among three types of effendis, a perspective that has much value for Egypt. Effendis from sufficiently wealthy families could obtain the better jobs in government or commerce: from this group came the ministers, directors-general, and *mutasarrif*s, provincial governors. The second group was made up of army officers, "now in very friendly relations with us," said Bird. The third effendi group, representing the "vital body of opinion," was made of the rest of "the 'literate town-dwellers' . . . the teachers, clerks, shop assistants, lawyers, and journalists." Moreover, con-cluded Bird from Baghdad, it really was a problem of money: if only the British could supply enough books, as the effendis ostensibly love to read, but make these editions cheap, as they ostensibly have no money.[61]

Another interesting insight came from Beirut. Here, the effendis could in no way be described as emblematic of a "professional middle class" as the term was used there rather pejoratively, as it was in some Egyptian contexts. "The successful doctors, lawyers and other professional men would not be flattered by being included as effendis ... who, being 'semi-educated products' would include unsuccessful professional men, the lower grade of civil servants, clerks in commercial houses and to some extent the student body." True effendis were "have-nots, whose salaries are small and who have little hope for the future."[62] Among the suggestions Houston-Boswall, in Beirut, sent to London to learn how to win over these "have-not" effendis was the idea of providing, again, more cheap books in Arabic, more lectures, and more scholarships to Britain. Moreover, he suggested, British films should be cheaper, to compete with American and French films, as the Lebanese public is very cinema-minded.

Reports from Egypt were less perceptive as to habits, but focused more on socioeconomic factors in the making of the *effendiya*. Walter Smart described the Egyptian effendis as "suffering under a strong social griev-ance," with their "growing realization of the social inequalities of the society in which they live."[63] W.F. Crawford writing from Cairo tackled the eco-nomic dimension of the *effendiya* even further: "The real effendi problem is that of the poorly-paid government officials, the commercial clerks and the 'out of work' graduates. There are too many of them," said Crawford, "as the output of universities is greater than the demand for their products ... these countries have not the commerce, industry and the social structure which can take up large numbers of graduates and diploma-holders.... The universities are poisoned by politics.... Then there is the present high cost of living." Crawford ended his dispatch by suggesting that tennis parties at the embassy and, again, lots of cheap books, would do the job.[64]

To summarize, what is learned about the effendi from these sources, though sometimes humorous in retrospect, is highly suggestive, and res-onates in our examination of the *effendiya* in Egypt: despite similarities with the upper class in outlook and education, the "true effendi" was a "have-not," who could hardly be associated with a professional middle class. They were only "developing into middle classes," as Bevin percep-tively said, and they were "in transition." The effendi not only lived under "strong social grievance," in a constant threat of unemployment, poverty, and high cost of living, but was also conscious of it. The effendi should also be understood as a political being, a fact reflected in the British concern with winning him over to their side. Finally, the effendis' cultural and consumer habits were crucial: the university, the coffeehouse, or the clubs. He read, played sports, and went to cinema.[65]

Looking at those effendis of the 1930s and 1940s through Egyptian sources, similar assumptions were made by the Egyptian mass media producers who targeted their products to the effendis, the would-be middle class. Their objective, however, differed from that of the British in that they commercialized the emerging effendi identity.

Reading the Effendi in the 1930s and 1940s
'Effendification': Avenues of Better Future

In *Qindil Umm Hashim*, an autobiographical novella of Yahya Haqqi, Shaykh Ragab was a migrant from the countryside, a *fallah*. He settled near the mosque of Sayyida Zaynab and opened a small business there. The business grew and the grandfather could afford sending his third son to school:

> [There] remained the youngest son, my uncle Isma'il, the last jewel
> of the family, for whom fate, and grandfather's profit, were preparing
> a brighter future. When the father induced him to memorize the
> Qur'an he thought he would be sent to al-Azhar and was scared,
> because he used to hear the chidren at the square running after the
> 'imma wearing youths and calling them those unflattering words:
> Shidd al-'imma shidd, taht al-'imma qird [take down your turban,
> there is a monkey below it].[66]

But Shaykh Ragab, with his heart full of hope, finally enrolled the lad in the *amiriya* (governmental) school. Although handicapped at first by his religious education and provincial origin, he soon distinguished himself by his good manners, his contemplative nature, and earned the respect of his teachers for his politeness and patience. He might have lacked elegance but did not lack cleanliness. He was, moreover, more articulate than his colleagues, called *awlad al-effendiya*, who were generally poorly articulate in Arabic. Soon he had surpassed them, "and all hopes of the entire family were concentrated on him."[67] This quote encapsulates what becomes a recurrent theme of many similar narratives, novels, films, memoirs, which I call narratives of 'becoming' effendi, or 'effendification.' The pattern of such narratives is that first, a provincial or urban family, not rich, not poor, but unprivileged and 'traditional,' struggles to send one of their sons to school, specifically to a governmental, or *amiriya*, school, in which a western curriculum is the standard.[68] Second, the son becomes an effendi. Next, the family dreams of a better future for him, often exemplified in the ideal of the *miri* (high office) or the *wazifa* (employment, job), though this imagery was changing during the interwar period. Finally, the effendi becomes prominent; or, conversely, in the 1930s and 1940s, he actually ends as unemployed and becomes a political activist. The first of these is the act of becoming an effendi.

In the preceding story, the simple fact of sending the boy to a governmental school generated "high hopes" on the part of the family. The young man, by virtue of attending the school, enjoyed high prestige usually accorded to the family elders.[69] Once Isma'il received his high school diploma, and thus became an effendi, his father sent him to Europe at enormous sacrifice on the part of the whole family. He does so because, as he himself describes it, he dreams of seeing his youngest son "in the first ranks."[70]

Becoming effendi, or making one's son an effendi, was associated with a certain repertory of meanings reflected in people's ways of life, from the way they dressed—the turban versus the tarboosh in Taha Husayn's words, or as the *gallabiya* (long traditional shirt) versus the *badla* (western suit) in the inter-war period—to their manners, occupations, localities, and even languages. The urban *hara*, a traditional neighborhood, of which the Sayyida Zaynab neighborhood mentioned in the preceding quote is a commonly invoked exemplar, is one of a number of localities associated with the 'non-modern' and 'backward' ways of life; the *rif*, or the Egyptian countryside, has a similar significance. The urban *hara* is inhabited by the *awlad al-balad* (traditional town-dwellers, often conflated with lower classes), while the *rif* is inhabited by the *fallahin* (peasants).[71] These are not in the first instance categories of class, but of culture, and they occupy the lowest level in the Egyptian representational hierarchy that was taking shape during the inter-war period—though, as Samia Kholoussi depicts in chapter ten, nationalists, social critics, and literati would also fasten upon the *fallahin* as the repositories of eternal Egyptian truths and contemporary dysfunctionalities. Why was the *shaykh* not content with keeping his son in the family business, which was obviously prosperous to the point of being able—though with difficulty—to send his son to Europe? 'Effendification,' as a strategy on the part of many middle-income families of urban or rural backgrounds—but crucially, of those labeled 'traditional'—amounted to an act of social mobility, which could be interpreted, in material terms, as a future prestigious job, the *wazifa*. But because the families were not a priori poor or in need, it can best be understood in more status-related terms, as moving from marginality to centrality.

The latter perspective is evident in the film *al-Duktur* ("The Doctor," 1939, Niyazi Mustafa). This is the story of a couple who cannot get married because of the perceived social gap that separates the lovers. The woman is a daughter of a pasha and the young man is a sucessful medical practitioner in Cairo. He is, however, of provincial origin, and the parents of the young lady thus consider him a *fallah*. The young doctor is by no means poor; his parents are medium to rich landowners. The conflict that stands in the way of the young couple's happiness is not about wealth, but about culture, expressed here in geographical terms as the *rif*, the countryside, versus the town. At one point the young man's father, a village *shaykh*, visits the pasha-father, in Cairo. When told that the union is impossible because of the social difference that separates the two young people, the *shaykh*-father responds, "Allow me to ask you a question, my pasha. Who was *your* father or grandfather? Was he not a *fallah*? And then he brought you up and educated you till you became a pasha? Me too, I have brought up my son and educated him, *saraft 'alaihi damm qalbi*, and he became a doctor. And tomorrow, he'll become a pasha!"[72]

The hero of this film, Dr. Hilmi, is an effendi.[73] His father is a *fallah* and the young man is just about to enter into the Cairene world of "power and influence" (to use Taha Husayn's expression above). He will eventually marry the woman in question; the pasha's ancestors have indeed been *fallah*s, and the perceived social difference will be renegotiated through the film and resolved in favor of the young couple. The same dilemma occurs in the film *Layla bint al-rif* ("Layla, Daughter of the Countryside," 1941, Togo Mizrahi). A young doctor from Cairo, played by Yusuf Wahbi, visits his provincial mother, also here a rich *fallaha* landowner, who wants to marry her son to his cousin, Layla (played by Layla Murad). When he steadfastly refuses to comply, saying that he, a Cairene man of society, cannot marry a *fallaha*, the mother replies, deeply offended: "And who are you? Is not your mother a *fallaha*?" These movies suggest that along with developments covered by Andrew Flibbert in chapter sixteen, a certain evolution of class—or better yet, status—aspirations shaped the political economy of movie-making in 1920s–40s Egypt.

A similar idea of social progress as status mobility is conveyed by this 1945 advertisement for a pastry manufacturer, exemplified in such diacritica as the head covering, which is laden with significance as used here. The image shows the "al-Rashidi al-Halawani Family." The grandfather wears a turban, the father a tarboosh, and the son is bareheaded, which—by the mid-1940s—simply signified a 'modern man' (fig. 5.3).

These narratives remind us that the native Egyptian bourgeois society, which is being consolidated with the creation of the new state is, in large part, only recently urbanized. From Sa'd Pasha to Sidqi Pasha, the indigenous elite have all been effendis at some earlier date, themselves sons of provincial notability.[74] The emerging bourgeois society consciously dissasociates itself from the *rif*, constructing it as distant as a foreign country.[75] Both the countryside and the urban lower class are therefore contructed as the effendi's internal others.

Narratives like *al-Duktur* illustrate the function of the effendi as a transitional state between the 'backward' or 'non-modern' *rif* and the modern world exemplified here in the person of the pasha. This cultural hierarchy, structured as an opposition of the *fallah*, or *ibn al-balad*, to the effendi, bey, or pasha, is a version of discourses known from other spheres and projected into the representational economy of the emerging Egyptian public sphere, which was taking shape through new media. Messages diffused by a variety of discourses—political, social, educational, and cultural—had a common message for the public: it is only through culture that a person can alter one's fate, it is through education that progress can be achieved. Both the *rif* and the urban *hara* remain equally banished from the modern world and damned to backwardness unless refined through the effendi road. Making one's son an effendi, or struggling to be one, is often associated with breaking away from backwardness into the realm of knowledge and new society.[76]

The narrative of *al-Duktur*, a popular film, is much like that of Taha Husayn who, in the above-mentioned passage dreamt about leaving the world of the turban, which made him "feel sick," and enter into the world of the tarboosh, where he would meet "the most influential of men." Shaykh Ragab—the father in *Qindil Umm Hashim*—who wished to see Isma'il "among the first ranks," makes the same point. So does the famous *Cairo Trilogy* by Nobel laureate Naguib Mahfouz which, like *Qindil Umm Hashim*, is largely autobiographical. In the Mahfouz epic chronicling the fortunes of a Cairene family between the two World Wars, the merchant-patriarch Sayyid 'Abd al-Gawwad, initially the focus of the story, represented a social elite of his neighborhood. In national terms, however, he was increasingly marginal. Although rich and respectable, he wears a *gallabiya* not a *badla*, rides a *caretta* not a car, and stores his money in a safe, not in a bank.[77] All three of his sons will become effendis. They will not be willing to continue his once prosperous business and by the end of the three novels 'Abd al-Gawwad, old and sick, is compelled to close down the business.[78] The novel suggests clearly that although the three sons are effendis—one works as a government clerk, one as a teacher, and one dies while a student during the nationalist revolution of 1919—they are actually *poorer* than their father was. In nationalist terms, however, they are more 'central' than their father could ever have been: 'Abd al-Gawwad's martyred son Fahmi Effendi actually becomes a national hero.

Similarly Shaykh Ragab in *Qindil Umm Hashim*, as previously mentioned, was not poor. He was, however, marginal in terms of the national modernizing project. For these people, becoming an effendi or making their son an effendi, represents upward mobility and access to real or imagined social and political power. The social mobility that is in question here is not solely, or perhaps even primarily, about improving their socioeconomic status. It is about upward mobility in status, and the inclusion of increasingly marginalized groups into the national culture and economy of modernity. The transition from a *fallah* or a merchant to the successful professional or bureaucrat, or ultimately a pasha, imbued with incontestable status, can only lead through the effendi road because the effendi is in possession of the right tools of inclusion into the national modernist project. This is his 'appropriate' culture, his cultural capital symbolized formally by his diacritica of dress, and generated most commonly, but not exclusively, by his formal education in a western curriculum. An effendi became increasingly defined not by institutional access, but by the 'modern' habits and practices associated with being an effendi—and signified by the tarboosh in the first place. The culture of 'being modern' functions here as a value judgment and as a gatekeeper to social status and mobility. Their cultural capital gave effendis the possibility, at least theoretically, to gain access to spheres to which a merchant, or a *shaykh*, as Taha Husayn's turban discourse reminds us, could never aspire.[79] This was doubly the case for *fallahin*, who ironically were held by some to embody the essential Egypt, as seen in Kholoussi's chapter.

Ambiguities of Modernity
The effendi became synonymous with the adoption of the quality of 'being modern,' and ever-larger numbers increasingly sought this prize. Modernity was thus a conscious choice of rather marginal actors. If the

effendi emerged first as a product of a modernist project already in progress, one generated by the state, then these narratives mark both the continuation of the modernist project as well as its evolution. We see a shift, roughly, from state-created effendis to society-created effendis—or a fourth political generation, to borrow Whidden's typology from chapter one. Starting originally, as a top-down project articulated and diffused through authoritative discourses, in the inter-war period we observe a re-appropriation of this process by non-privileged groups, which is evident in their daily choices as expressed in their educational and career choices.

Let me return to the famous cartoon character al-Misri Effendi mentioned earlier. Al-Misri Effendi was actually dropped from the pages of *al-Ithnayn* in 1941, "because it represented the lowest class of government official, that is the effendi class, or petty bureaucrats."[80] But al-Misri Effendi not only represented the petty bureaucrats. The figure also stood for a growing body of school graduates at various levels of their education.[81]

The effendi in the later 1930s became an increasingly disputed identity as well as an ambiguous social state. Narratives from that period betray an effendi who, far from enjoying the social mobility of the previous generation, was often poorer that his putatively marginal and 'backward' neighbours from the *hara*. If the effendi in the first quarter of the twentieth century signified the road to the world of "wealth and influence," as exemplified in the narratives of Taha Husayn or *Qindil Umm Hashim* mentioned above, than the 1930s and 1940s are a different matter.

On the other hand, the effendis had no choice. Being an effendi was a one-way street, or at least was constructed as such in narratives, for instance, of Sayyid 'Abd al-Gawwad's three sons in Mahfouz's *Trilogy*, none would return to the father's business. The effendis, whether they were coming from the countryside or from cities, were not from poor backgrounds. They were often sons of merchants or medium landowners, but their movement to town for study and subsequent unemployment often seem to have amounted to an actual *deterioration* in their living standard.

An Effendi Career: From the Miri to the Uniform

A well-known Egyptian proverb says, "*In fat lak al-miri, itmaragh fi turabuh*," if you fail [to be] a *miri*, then roll in the dust he leaves behind. *Miri* signifies the all-powerful government official, and on a more abstract level, the effendi as the *miri* symbolizes the power of the state. The 'classic' effendi occupations seem to confirm this hypothesis. An effendi is usually a bureaucrat, a tax collector, or a land measurement agent for example. Such occupations are the points of intersection, or interference, of the state with daily lives of ordinary people. Perception of the effendi by less elite people necessarily spans a wide range of reactions and images of respect and co-optation, wanting to be one of them, or in good terms with them, but also of fear and mockery, reflected in this song by Sayyid Darwish, "*Ista'gabu ya affandiya, litr ghaz bi-rubiya, thaman litr zaman bi-safiha, wa-illi yatulo al-yom bi-fadiha.*" This could be translated as, "Be amazed you effendis: a liter of kerosene is now a rupee (money unit); before a liter was a *safiha* (another money unit); being able to afford it today is something unheard of."[82]

The effendi as a *miri* harkens back to an older version of the popular perception of the effendi as the arm of the *hukuma* (government, state). The term itself is of Turkish origin. In the inter-war period, if not earlier, the term was being dropped for a new term, the *muwazzaf*, an 'employee,' someone with a *wazifa*, a job. The term *miri* still appears in films, but carries relatively archaic, Ottoman, associations. But in the 1930s, even the *muwazzaf* had lost his prestige, as exemplified in the discarding of the al-Misri Effendi cartoon character. People dependent on a fixed salary were among the most stricken by the economic crisis and general drop in the standard of living. Increasingly, young men in the 1930s and 1940s no longer dreamed about a career as a *muwazzaf*. They dreamed about the uniform instead, whether as police or army officers.

In 1939, one of my informants, 'Aziza, daughter of a rich merchant from Benha, married a young police officer stationed there. She expressed her family choice in the following words, "I would not have married an effendi, but he was an officer, it's a different matter."[83] Officers do not differ from effendis in essence, but rather in terms of scale. Officers might be considered a specific group within the *effendiya* at large. After 1936, they were recruited from secondary school graduates, and were actually called effendis until a certain rank. They were increasingly a privileged group within the *effendiya*. While the prestige of an average effendi as an employee declined, the prestige and salary of the officer corps grew in proportion to the growing public interest in the army.[84] As seen in chapter three of this volume, access to the officers rank remained, in practice, if not in theory, restricted to sons from well-off families.[85] In symbolic terms though, the uniform offered what the *miri* track, or government schools generally, had offered earlier in the century: the single possible path to social ascent for sons of modest but not poor families.[86]

Moreover, the army track for many a young man in the 1930s and '40s was increasingly informed by an imagery of their duty to liberate Egypt, as exemplified in the words of 'Abd al-Latif al-Baghdadi: "The youths around fifteen years of age, or slightly more, dreamt big dreams and harbored great hopes; they spent lots of time doing sports in order to build their physical strength. We all dreamt about joining the army and becoming an officer."[87]

If the effendi as *miri* at the beginning of the twentieth century represented a distant state that disciplined its subjects, then the effendi-as-officer is an image of distinctly national identity. The state becomes the nation, and the effendi takes the affairs of the state-as-nation in his own hands. In the meantime the state, as institutions and elites, became increasingly dissociated from the nation. The state no longer represented the nation. The *effendiya* did, perhaps displacing the peasants of chapter ten, and increasingly imagined itself as the appropriate defender against things gone wrong in the hands of the state elites. This point will become clear through the final section, as the *effendiya*'s self-appointed guardian-ship of the state converges with another important process, namely the articulation of a distinctly new effendi identity and self-identification.

Egyptianizing Modernity

Modernity Starts in the *Hara*

If 'effendification' in the first quarter of the twentieth century was about upward status mobility, in the second quarter of the century being an effendi increasingly meant entering a transitional state to another transitional state. Instead of leading to power and influence, becoming an effendi ends in a social impasse, where markers of a comfortable existence are unattainable. In the later 1930s and 1940s, the effendi starts building for himself an independent identity, making use of the emerging field of mass cultural production, such as the cinema and the popular press, of which he is also the principal consumer.

The film *Ibn al-haddad* ("Blacksmith's Son," Yusuf Wahbi, 1944) is a story of Taha Effendi, son of a blacksmith who has a small workshop in the indigenous part of Cairo. The father has sent Taha to modern schools, and the boy eventually completes his education abroad, earning a prestigious diploma in engineering. Upon his return to Cairo and to his native *hara*, a big party is arranged by the family and the neighbors to welcome Taha, "their" effendi. After the celebration, Taha has a serious talk with his father:

Father: You will now be able to get a good job (*wazifa*) worth at least
12 pounds a month."

Taha: No, father, I don't want a *wazifa*, I want to be my own master.

Father: What? Are you crazy? I have spent on you the blood of my
heart to be proud of you. To see Taha Effendi, son of Mu'allim
Salah,[88] walking in and out of the *diwan* (ministry). I have been
spending penny after penny and sent you [for study] to Europe,
to enable you to work as a *miri*.

Taha: But father, this is an old approach. I want to be free, to earn
every penny on my proper merit (by my own sweat) and be my
own master.

Father: Do you want the people to laugh at us?

Taha: The world has changed, father. The world belongs to those who
work.[89] Come out with me and I will show you the great buildings
and fabulous bridges. Who has built them? Those who work. I am
the son of a blacksmith and I want to remain one.

Father: And what about all your diplomas?

Taha: I shall make use of my knowledge and benefit my brothers.
Look at this small workshop where I grew up and learned the
basics of the profession. This was my first school and you were
my first teacher. I will mix my knowledge with hard work, and
tomorrow my struggle will start. Half of my job will be my
faith and commitment to work.[90] Tomorrow, father, you will see
this small workshop of yours get bigger and bigger, till it becomes
a great factory employing thousands of my kind, and sons of our
profession. I will make their lives better and make them join in my
success. And I shall never forget to kiss the hand of the one who
taught me all this (my teacher and my benefactor): you, father.

The story of Taha Effendi begins much like the stories of 'effendi-fication' of merchants, artisans, and medium landowners' sons discussed above. Originating in the *hara*, to which his father represented a social elite, Taha had been sent at considerable sacrifice to complete his education, and his father now dreams of a career for him as a *miri*, but Taha refuses this as old-fashioned.

What happens to Taha Effendi after his return to Cairo, after the above dialogue takes place, is less typical of the social realities that faced new effendis than it was of an ideal effendi self-representation. Taha Effendi succeeds in his independent business and, in so doing, he restructures the balance of power in society and creates a new effendi identity in which material realities match the imagined ideal.

Taha Effendi pulls down the workshop and builds a modern plant in its place. The business prospers and Taha becomes a big industrialist. His success and fortune enable him to lead a comfortable existence, yet he refuses to sit in his office and keeps supervising production from the workplace, dressed as one of the workers. He enjoys affectionate relationships with them, and even runs evening educational classes, in which he teaches them modern technology, using references to Prophet Muhammad:

> And now, dear friends, I shall explain to you how this new engine works. Before all I would like you to know that God has created the knowledgeable to teach others *(rabbena khalaq al-muta'allim 'ashan ye'allim ghayruh)*. And tomorrow I want to see you all on good terms [with each other], our master Muhammad said God's hand is with those who are united *(yaddu-llahi ma'a-l-gama'a)*. The engine consists of six parts. . . .

This speech reveals two major themes, social justice and Muslim identity. More importantly, the themes are presented as interdependent. Knowledge is authenticized as not western in origin, despite Taha's having obtained his diploma, his formal certification of expertise in culture-neutral technique, in Europe. It is, at the same time, prescribed by Taha's religion. Islam, properly interpreted, is also the basis of social justice. In the context of the preceding quote, Muslim ethics, the basis of both knowledge and social justice, is turned into a quasi-Protestant work-ethic, and put in service of industrialization. Taha at one point even speaks of industrial renaissance, *nahda sina'iya.*[91]

Taha Effendi, whom success has elevated to the rank of the upper class—the *dhawat*—soon gets patronized by them and eventually finds himself married to a daughter of a pasha. His new in-laws reproduce a typical example of how the upper class was portrayed in cinema of the period: they are idle, greedy, and indulge in dubious leisure pursuits, which duly contrast with Taha's work ethic.[92] They speak French among themselves and blame Taha for speaking Arabic to his small son. Taha's wife, the daughter of a pasha, drinks and dances to late hours with strange men, neglecting her son. Their house is a place of never-ending dance parties duly provisioned with alcohol. This kind of clash constantly emerges between them:

Decadent son-in-law: Are we not celebrating Christmas this year?
Taha: You have spent all your lives in this country yet you celebrate
    the festivals of other religions? This year, we will celebrate
    the birthday of the Prophet (*mawlid al-nabi*).

The way characters are constructed in this narrative, which is by no means unique in Egyptian cinema of the 1940s, informs Taha Effendi's trajectory.[93] The purpose of his pious but passive father, and indeed of the whole *hara*, is to stress the roots of Taha's modernity. Taha had kissed the hand of his father in the first dialogue mentioned above, an overt nod to patriarchal culture which could never be understood as consistent with modernity in a western context, but is indispensable in disconnecting modernity from its western associations in an Egyptian context. Taha transforms the sleeping capital of his father into success partly due to his technical expertise brought back from Europe, but what really enabled his success was, besides his entrepreneurial spirit, the nature of his authenticity: it is Muslim, as is social justice, and the quest for knowledge. All are integral parts of the process of becoming modern. All was blended together into a national modernist developmentalist ethos, at times bordering on industrialist propaganda.

From what has just been said we should by no means imagine Taha Effendi as merely an 'Islamist.' Taha was fully grounded in bourgeois etiquette, even using French words when appropriate. A crucial point in Taha Effendi's character, moreover, was the fact that he was played by Yusuf Wahbi, a foremost bourgeois idol and a heart-throb of Egyptian cinema, commonly associated with highbrow imagery and even aristocratic characters.[94] Wahbi's familiar persona links the film to the rest of his oeuvre, and creates associations with mainstream bourgeois imagery of the Egyptian commercial cinema of the period.

The purpose of Taha Effendi's in-laws in the plot is to make a moral judgment about modernity. Both Taha and his in-laws share the diacritica of modernity, yet the difference between them is made in terms of opposing interpretations of what makes up its content. The tension between them and Taha is not about being modern or not, but about correcting modernity gone corrupt, misinterpreted as *jouissance*, perversion or excess, irresponsibility and abuse of others. Modernity interpreted the right way, as Taha does, is then no longer a result of the appropriate degree of westernization. It has been fully appropriated, domesticated, and justified through local, Muslim, Arab, and Egyptian references. Taha Effendi's modernity is constructed as a critique of the excessively westernized *bashawi* imagery, and it is built around the themes of cultural authenticity and social justice.[95] A modernity gone wrong and interpreted as *jouissance* echoed what was by then public knowledge, the presumed reason for the political and economic failure of the elite. To this, Taha proposes a solution, an emerging bourgeois nationalist ideology. The clash between Taha Effendi and his *dhawat* in-laws, which in this film is articulated as a conflict over the ownership of modernity—"whose modernity?"—is a metaphoric representation of another conflict—"whose state?"

The Generation of Young Men

In November 1935 a wave of demonstrations across Egypt's major cities, the likes of which the country had not seen since 1919, achieved what the politicians were incapable of doing. At the forefront of these demonstrations was the Executive Committee of University and Secondary School Students. This body, consisting mostly of students, managed to pressure political leaders into forming the Unified National Front, which demanded the restoration of the 1923 Constitution and the beginning of negotiations with the British. In a clash with the British forces, several students had been killed, but their objectives had been achieved.

In December 1935, a variety magazine called *Kull shay' wa-l-dunya* published a special issue dedicated to the students. The cover picture showed two students embracing each other on the occasion of the restoration of the Constitution (fig. 5.4). The issue included various articles concerning student life and activities. It included articles about student martyrs during the November 1935 demonstrations, student political activities such as the Piastre Project or the Village Project, special festivities and conferences organized by and for the students. Other magazines quickly followed. *Al-Hilal* published a substantial 130-page issue devoted to youth in April 1936, again featuring articles on the youths' activities and interests, discussing, among other things, their virtues and mission.[96]

The point in mentioning this sudden interest of the press in all things young, and the students in particular, is to emphasize that during the 1930s the urban youth emerged as a distinct social force with which to be reckoned. These are the effendis, or the "effendi problem," which preoccupied British intelligence in the documents discussed at the beginning of the chapter. The British might have been naïve in thinking that an emergent Egyptian national identity could be coopted by providing suitably genteel social and cultural activities, but they were certainly right in seeing the *effendiya* as a distinct social group. It was a loose group, sociologically speaking, but one with a distinct generational profile, as well as with distinct sense of their own active role in the public affairs of Egypt. Here is a testimony of one of this generation, a "mission statement."

> It was the year 1935 and I was a student in Mansura Secondary School. We were a generation older than its age, a generation singled out by its seriousness *(jiddiya)*, its hardness *(khushuna)* and its virility, and by its interest in nationalism since its adolescence. We would listen to stories about [the revolution of] 1919, during which most of us were born, about the court cases the British launched against the revolutionaries from among the people, and about the executions they had ordered by the dozen, about prison sentences and beatings of hundreds, stretching from the south *(Sa'id)* to Alexandria. This all has generated in us a profound hate for the English and has filled us with patriotic sentiments.[97]

Or, in the very similar words of Khalid Muhi al-Din, which also resonate with what was said earlier about the ethos of the uniform: "We, the youth of that period, were motivated by patriotic and national feelings. We felt that Egypt was in need of a real army able to defend it. An army that would serve the nation and not any other power. I was gripped by the idea of entering the Military College and, after long opposition from my father and decisive determination on my part, I did so."[98]

This specific generational profile of the new *effendiya* was articulated on several levels. A distinct identity constructed as a cultural synthesis between local authenticity and the corrected, or rightly interpreted, modernity as social practice exemplified in the persona of Taha Effendi above, was only one of them. Another was the ongoing process of "attack against fathers." If Taha Effendi, as a metaphor for his generation, rises to save his country from failure incurred in the hands of the pashas, his in-laws, he must *both* pay respect to his father, the pious but passive Mu'allim Salah, and liberate himself from him. What is implied in the 1935 demonstrations mentioned above is that while the authenticity of the fathers is a crucial component of modernity, at the same time the kind of politics performed by the fathers' generation has failed.[99] The mid-1930s saw a steady rise of a cult of the student-martyrs, as well as a celebration of all things young, again observable in films and novels, as well as in posters distributed by illustrated magazines (fig. 5.5).

The dilemma inherent in these narratives is whether to see 'fathers' just as senior politicians—the discredited *dhawat* of the screen—or, rather as the pious Mu'allim Salah, Taha Effendi's father. In *The Blacksmith's Son* Taha Effendi resolved this dilemma by simultaneously refusing his father's will to go and work as *miri*, and kissing his hand. Naguib Mahfouz captured the dilemma of an effendi caught between loyalty to his father, and more generally to older male authority, and his conviction of their being desperately non-modern, and thus by definition an obstacle to "progress," in this dialogue between his two alter egos: Ahmad, the patriarch 'Abd al-Gawwad's grandson, announces to his uncle Kamal that he has started working in a leftist magazine, *The New Man*.

> Do whatever you want, but avoid offending your parents."
> Ahmad laughed and commented, "I love them and revere them, but . . . ."
> "But what?"
> "It's a mistake for a man to have parents."
> Laughing, Kamal asked, "How can you say that so glibly?"
> "I don't mean it literally, but insofar as parents represent bygone traditions. In general, fatherhood acts as a brake. What need do we have of brakes in Egypt when we're hobbling forward with fettered legs?"[100]

The effendis of the 1930s and 1940s construct their identity against their fathers, whom they see as traditional, backward, and passive, as well as against the existing political generation: old versus new reads also as old versus young in a much more local sense. This generation felt that it had the right to make its own rules because the laws of the fathers had failed.[101] Being young and being an effendi became conflated; the simple fact of being young in those years could potentially take a revolutionary dimension. According to some, the demonstrators of late 1940s chanted, among other things, a verse by Umm Kulthum: "It is not enough to dream about your dreams, the world is to be taken by force."[102]

Conclusion

It is unsurprising that a status group defined by shared culture and forms of identity, and having a structural affiliation with the institutions of a modernizing state, is a potential political force. The British officials knew this well, and neutralizing the effendis was thought a task of major importance. Cultural capital of the effendis was ultimately linked to the state, as the major producer and consumer of effendis. The ambiguous position of the *effendiya* lies between its position on the conceptual vanguard of modernization on one hand, and on the other hand, a state increasingly unable, or unwilling, to absorb the mass of graduates, not to mention an economic situation unfavourable to the emergence in material terms of a genuine middle class. The rise of mass politics is, therefore, better understood not necessarily through the emergence of a numerically significant social group, but crucially, of one with new political identities and practices, which indeed claimed for itself a role in the post-1923 establishment. In other words, the new *effendiya* in the 1930s and 1940s is not just the result of growing numbers of graduates, but of the articulation of a specific effendi identity, which converges with national meanings and takes on national imperatives.

In thinking of the *effendiya* as a social group, historical conjunction, as well as the effendis' relationship to the centre of power, is crucial. The social, political, and cultural landscape of the three decades of the Egyptian monarchy might be productively understood as a clash between two generations of effendis. One is the *effendiya* of the early twentieth century, known as the "bearers of national mission,"[103] of whom many after 1923 became state-makers, pashas and beys, and who are also known as the "liberal generation," the "generation of 1919" for whom chapter one of this volume is named. The other is the so-called "new *effendiya*" — the "troublemakers" of the 1930s and revolutionaries of the 1940s who worked to undo the liberal order. The difference between the two generations should be understood not in terms of the "new effendis'" rural, and therefore traditional or reactionary, background, because the "liberal" effendis were from predominantly rural origins as well, but in respect to their position toward the modernizing state and its elites.[104] 'Effendification' was about taking on the markers of modernity as a conscious choice of social actors. For historians of modern Egypt this might mean that liberalism on the one hand, or working class activism on the other, are not the only possible forms of modernity. The new effendis were really new in the sense that they represented a generation that grew up under, or was brought up by, the new state. In this respect, the challenge the new effendis posed to the liberal establishment was not an attack on the modernizing project—it was not about *whether* to be modern—it was an attempt by those who saw themselves as the vanguard of modernity, to *redefine* modern Egyptian society in terms of "whose society—and state—is this going to be?"

Notes

1　Joel Beinin, "Egypt: Society and Economy, 1923–52," in *The Cambridge History of Egypt*, ed. C.F. Petry (Cambridge: Cambridge University Press, 1998), 309; Robert Tignor, *Modernization and British Colonial Rule in Egypt 1882–1914* (Princeton: Princeton University Press, 1966), chapter 8.

2　Joel Beinin and Zachary Lockman, *Workers on the Nile: Nationalism, Communism, and the Egyptian Working Class* (London: Tauris, 1988), 67; Richard Mitchell, *Society of the Muslim Brothers* (London: Oxford University Press, 1969), 216, 239. On the radical movements—the Muslim Brotherhood, the Young Egypt *(Misr al-Fatat)* party and the communists—see also James P. Jankowski, *Egypt's Young Rebels: Young Egypt, 1933–52* (Stanford, CA: Hoover Institution Press, 1975); Selma Botman, *The Rise of Egyptian Communism, 1939–70* (Syracuse: Syracuse University Press, 1988).

3　With the partial exception of Israel Gershoni and James Jankowski, *Redefining the Egyptian Nation, 1930–45* (Cambridge: Cambridge University Press, 1995). They, however, identify the effendis too straightforwardly as middle class and see them mostly as professionals. The notion of effendi as not primarily a class concept is discussed throughout this chapter.

4　*Effendiya*, however, is not always *only* the plural form of effendi. I tend to use the English plural form effendis to designate a group of individual effendis. The Arabic plural *effendiya*—especially in the first decade of the twentieth century—is often charged with meanings associated more with the ideal image of the effendis as bureaucrats, free professions, or uniformed officers; in the 1930s and 40s, the term *effendiya* tends to mean a specific, 'rebellious' generation.

5　Gershoni and Jankowski, 1.

6　Sawsan El-Messiri, *Ibn Balad: A Concept of Egyptian Identity* (Leiden: E.J. Brill, 1978), 5.

7　A term used, for instance, by Gershoni and Jankowski, *Redefining the Egyptian Nation*, and Michael Eppel, "The Elite, the Effendiyya, and the Growth of Nationalism and Pan-Arabism in Hashemite Iraq, 1921–58," *International Journal of Middle East Studies* 30/2 (1998): 227–50.

8　The effendi is technically always a male. It is in fact the sole social category in modern Egypt that lacks its female counterpart: each of the *ibn al-balad* (traditional urban strata, often conflated with lower classes), the *fallah* (peasant), the *khawaga* (foreigner), or the *awlad al-dhawat* (bey and pasha—the elites) do have their female forms *(bint al-balad, fallaha, khawagiya,* and *bint al-basha* or *hanem)*. The effendis are males by definition, because they are constructed by the categories of education and employment, both being problematic for women. The relationship of effendis to their female counterparts, their wives, mothers, and sisters, as well as their matrimonial strategies—what kind of women they fantasize about in their narratives, and whom do they marry at the end—is an arresting issue, which, however, cannot be discussed here. It is the subject of a chapter in my dissertation, dealing with the construction of an "effendi woman" (understood as a modern middle class woman) through cultural channels, a process parallel and largely synonymous with debates over the 'New Woman' in Egypt.

9　For the origin and Ottoman use of the concept, which in the nineteenth century came to differ significantly from its use in Egypt, see B. Lewis, "Effendi," *The Encyclopaedia of Islam*, vol. II (Leiden: E.J. Brill, 1965), 687. In Egypt, the term 'effendi' became increasingly associated with the third rank in the state bureaucracy and with graduates of modern schools (i.e., those not using an Azhari curriculum). However, the term also continued to be used in other contexts too: in the sense of 'seigneur' to designate important personalities, such as in the case of Muhammad Sharif Pasha *Affandi*, cited in Robert F. Hunter, *Egypt under the Khedives, 1805–1879: From Household Government to Modern Bureaucracy* (Pittsburgh: University of Pittsburgh Press, 1984), 81. The meaning 'seigneur' persisted also as appellation for the khedives, often called *effendina* (such as, for instance the khedive Isma'il) again cited in Hunter, 75, or (this time about Abbas II) in Naguib Mahfouz, *Palace of Desire* (London: Black

Swan, 1991), 186. The title 'effendi' was also used well into the twentieth century to designate rabbis and important personalities of the Jewish community (such as the founder of the large commercial establishment Omar Effendi), and, least not last, it was used among members of sufi orders, see Khaled Mohi El Din, *Memoirs of a Revolution* (Cairo: The American University of Cairo Press, 1995), 7. All of these cases are exceptional, in the sense that they derive from the original Ottoman usage (as 'seigneur') and thus differ substantially from how the meaning of effendi developed in the mainstream society. Its mainstream, social, and cultural usage is discussed through this chapter.

10 "Noble entourage" formed by family members and former Mamluk slaves. On Muhammad 'Ali's elite and its transformation see Hunter, 22 and onward.

11 Hunter, 17.

12 Hunter, 113. According to him, under Muhammad 'Ali these new men were not only rare phenomenon, but also subservient to the *ma'iya saniya* elite which occupied the highest ranks. This balance shifted increasingly in the favor of the "new men," who were helped by processes such as the consolidation of land ownership, emergence of a new, educated Turkish elite and ultimately, toward the end of the nineteenth century, gradual erasing of difference between the Turkish and the Egyptian element within the *dhawat* elite. For the phenomenon of "new men" see also Tignor, *Modernization*, 25, 34–5, and Eric Davis, *Challenging Colonialism: Bank Misr and Egyptian Industrialization, 1920–41* (Princeton: Princeton University Press, 1983), chapter 2. Authors agree that the development of administration, modern schooling, and landed estates were all consequences of cotton-related processes of Egypt's integration to the world economic system.

13 Hunter, 83.

14 Hunter, 144, also Tignor, 25. What we see here is the emergence of a specifically "effendi" perspective on problems, wrapped into a reformist discourse which will manifest itself in the subsequent generations of effendis: a secular approach (though not anti-religious), characterized by a technocratic-scientific approach to reality, by advocacy of gradual change through education, and by stress on the maintenance of the existing social order. See, for instance, the life and works of Muhammad Husayn Haykal, in Charles Smith, *Islam and the Search for Social Order in Modern Egypt. A Biography of Muhammad Husayn Haykal* (Albany: State University of New York Press, 1983).

15 Some of them came from urban backgrounds, but those seem to have been less numerous. Use of officials from the provincial notability rather than urban strata (from *'ulama'* and *a'yan*) is argued in Davis, 19–20, and again 28–31. See also Hunter 39, 41, 85–8. Provincial notables, though often lacking formal education, did also serve in the administration and eventually some of them made it to the 'parliament,' the Consultative Chamber of Delegates and subsequent bodies. However, provincial notables served in the provincial administration while their sons, the effendis, served in the central administration, i.e., on the 'national' level. Hunter, 88.

16 The holding of office came to be increasingly associated with the ownership of land, and the relationship between high office and land was further strengthened. These officials had also developed interests of their own, says Hunter, 67. The emerging state in fact co-opted the rural notability for specific purposes. They accumulated land as rewards and soon started sending their children to school to make them effendis. Both the state and the native elite thus rise and consolidate simultaneously, and interdependently. See Hunter, 72–74, for how Khedive Isma'il granted land to his new officials in the framework of his struggle for succession.

17 Sayyid 'Uways, *L'histoire que je porte sur mon dos* (Cairo: Centre de recherche et de documentation économique, juridique et sociale/CEDEJ, 1989), 42.

18 Roger Allen, *A Period of Time. A Study and Translation of Hadith Isa Ibn Hisham by Muhammad al-Muwailihi* (Reading: Ithaca Press, 1992), 77. *Hadith 'Isa Ibn Hisham* became a standard school textbook during the monarchy period.

19   This was not necessarily the outcome of a conscious calculation. It was however certainly the consequence of a process of constituting a specifically Egyptian elite (constituted here jointly through land, the *effendiya*, urbanization, and intermarriage with Turco-Circassian aristocracy). However, the movement from local, provincial elite perceived by the center as *fallahin* (peasants), to a national elite with its share in political institutions, I think, explains the immense popularity of the "Law school track," discussed in Donald Malcolm Reid, "Educational and Career Choices among Egyptian Students, 1882–1922," in *International Journal of Middle East Studies* 8 (1977): 351–53. While Reid dwells extensively on the law school role and popularity, he somehow fails to explain *why* the law school was so popular among the sons of the rural notability.

20   For the Egyptian landowning families, making one of their sons an effendi—sending him to the state curricula, rather than to al-Azhar, and eventually to one of the higher institutes— amounted to a move from marginality to centrality: from local, provincial notability toward a national elite living in urban centers and socializing with the Turkish aristocracy. However they were not quite "equal" to the Turco-Circassian elite yet. Many an Egyptian politician was called a "*fallah*," or peasant, and most notably Sa'd Zaghlul, who capitalized on this appellation politically to raise his national credentials. Equity between Turkish and Egyptian notability was not achieved until the Monarchy period; we still find the term "Turkish" then, but it is increasingly used as insult. As for the point of rising to the ranks of bey and pasha through the effendi road, this was both the ideal and the most commonly used strategy. In practice, however, the titles of bey and pasha were sometimes bestowed upon the holder by either the king or the post-1923 politicians in exchange for various favors and services. These titles could also be bought. See, for instance, Naguib Mahfouz, *Midaq Alley*, trans. Trevor Le Gassick (Cairo: The American University in Cairo Press, 1992).

21   While sons of the Egyptian elite had previously three choices—the military, state bureaucracy and the army—it was now the bureaucracy which became their preferred choice. Reid, 353–54, writes that the more one decided to leave his Azhari past behind, the better career prospects he had. Reid also describes an interesting "transition" period, in which many an Egyptian father sent his son(s) to both al-Azhar *and* modern schools, to delay the moment of decision; fathers also often diversified the family prospects by sending one son to each. This strategy was, however, short-lived, before it became clear that Azhari graduates had few prospects for future career advancement. The Turkish elite had a different attitude, and for the most part did not send their children to these new schools, writes Reid. The shift in preferences with respect to educational and career strategies among the better-off Egyptian families was paralleled by the codification of school degrees, as well as that of access to bureaucratic jobs, and indeed—in general terms—by emergence of new occupations, the free professions. See also Tignor, 34, 43, and Allen, 89–91.

22   Davis, 46–48. Davis has assessed the progress in social status among the rural delegates in the Egyptian "parliament" between 1866 and 1914. In 1866, 8 percent of the delegates held the title of effendi, 4 percent that of bey, and none of them was a pasha. By 1914 there was already 66 percent of beys and several pashas. Simultaneously, the distinctly rural titles such as '*umda*, as well as the Turkish title of agha, virtually disappeared from the records, which means that rural titles give way to titles of national significance (Hunter speaks about the same, calling it "bureaucratic rationalization"). The title effendi among the Egyptian delegates to the Chamber started at 8 percent in 1866, reaching its peak through the 1880s when 58 percent of delegates bore this title. Then its occurrence started to decline with only 13 percent of effendi titles in the 1914 parliament. These are often the same people, or same families, so what we observe here is the changing status of rural delegates projected into their titles, says Davis.

23   Many authors discuss this point; see, for instance, Davis, 27–29, 39–50.

24 The first Egyptians in high office were Sa'd Zaghlul, who became minister of education in 1906; and Isma'il Sirri, who became minister of public works in 1908. See Reid, "Educational and Career Choices."

25 It is interesting to note that most of the nationalist leaders from among the *effendiya* of the turn of the twentieth century were private lawyers, not bureaucrats. Many of those who worked for the Parquet as state attorneys had resigned and opened their private cabinets. See Reid, "Rise of Professions."

26 Government schools took away from al-Azhar graduates the function of teachers; secular law courts took away their judicial role, Reid, 352. There were cultural clashes too. The *shaykh*s saw modernization and the reformist discourse led by the effendis as a threat to Islam itself. The *shaykh*s objected to the way in which the tarboosh wearers dared to "discuss, argue and disagree with turbaned shaykhs about their learning," writes Muwailihi in Allen, 90. The effendis, for their turn, regarded the *shaykh*s as a backward element, and thus somehow inferior; see Reid 353–54. Mocking of the 'turbaned *shaykh*' was common in popular literature, see Marilyn Booth, *Bayram al-Tunsi's Egypt: Social Criticism and Narrative Strategies* (Exeter: Ithaca Press, 1990), 404, note 1. New schools that accepted Azhari graduates and gave them the rudiments of western education, or "recycled" them for state service, such as Dar al-'Ulum or the School of Qadis, were established to ease this conflict. See also Donald Malcolm Reid, "The Rise of Professions and Professional Organization in Modern Egypt," in *Comparative Studies in Society and History* XVI (1974): 25–26, and Reid, *Cairo University and the Making of Modern Egypt* (Cairo: The American University in Cairo Press, 1990), 34–35. While the divide between the 'tarboosh' and the 'turban' is in many narratives constructed as fixed, it was in practice rather fluid. At the end it often depends on pure 'disguise,' i.e., what one chooses to wear: the turban or the tarboosh. Among those who 'crossed' the imaginary divide are such prominent personalities as Rifa'a al-Tahtawi, Muhammad 'Abdu, Sa'd Zaghlul, or Taha Husayn.

27 Taha Hussein, *The Days*, trans. Kenneth Cragg (Cairo: The American University in Cairo Press, 1997), 225. Taha Husayn perceived his struggle to enter the world of the tarboosh as—among other things—entering the world of the wealthy and the influential, which would no longer be true a couple of decades later, as will be discussed below. The point from this quote is also how immense the divide between the 'turban' and the 'tarboosh' seemed to him then.

28 Both Hunter and Tignor point at the link between the new effendi elite and the 'Urabi revolution. Their interests lay in a greater opening of the army (the officer corps) and the bureaucracy to native elements. Hunter, 35–36, 51–52, 78–80.

29 On the effendis' involvement—their leadership actually—of national politics around the turn of the twentieth century, see Tignor, chapter VII; Marius Deeb, *Party Politics in Egypt: The Wafd and its Rivals, 1919–1939* (London: Ithaca Press, 1979), 43, 53; and Beinin, "Egypt," 309–11.

30 Tignor discusses this issue extensively; see, for instance, Tignor, 178 and 180–84. After the crises of 1892–94, the influx of trained British personnel into the Egyptian administration was accelerated. The trend was again increased after 1905. When the Milner commission visited Egypt in 1920 to study the reasons for the "disturbances," they found that less than one-fourth of higher government posts were occupied by Egyptians; Tignor, 181, and Morroe Berger, *Bureaucracy and Society in Modern Egypt: A Study in the Civil Service* (Princeton: Princeton University Press, 1957), 32.

31 For problems facing the new professionals of Egyptian origin see again Reid, "Educational and Career Choices," 365, and his "Rise of Professions," 25 and 29; also Tignor, chapter VI.

32 'Capitulations' were privileges to foreign residents and companies in Egypt, guaranteed by a series of bilateral treaties signed since the sixteenth century between the weakening Ottoman empire and the European powers. In Egypt, they were only abolished (de jure) by the Montreaux Treaty in 1937 (de facto 1949).

33 *Hadith 'Isa bin Hisham*, Allen, 85–86.

34 Beinin's expression, Beinin, "Egypt," 309.

35 Posts in state bureaucracy rose by 61 percent, Morroe Berger, "The Middle Class in the Arab World," in *The Middle East in Transition*, ed. W.Z. Laqueur (London: Routledge & Kegan Paul, 1958), 82; see also Robert Vitalis, *When Capitalists Collide: Business Conflict and the End of Empire in Egypt* (Berkeley: University of California Press, 1995), xiv–xv.

36 For instance, journalism; Gershoni and Jankowski, *Redefining*, 13.

37 Badrawi brings interesting examples of radical nationalist effendis-turned-state-makers. Among the bomb-throwers investigated by police in respect to incidents before and during the 1919 Revolution were such figures as Mahmud Fahmi al-Nuqrashi or 'Abd al-Hadi al-Miliji, both prime ministers two decades later. Malak Badrawi, *Political Violence in Egypt, 1910–1924* (London: Curzon Press, 2000), 135, 142. But see also the Egyptian popular press: a glimpse of any periodical from the period before or immediately after the First World War will allow the reader to see signatures such as "Sa'd Zaghlul Effendi," "Mahmud al-Nuqrashi Effendi," and similar. In 1935, *Kull shay' wa-l-dunya* magazine published an article called "What Were Our Leaders Doing a Quarter Century Ago?" The answer lies in a two-page image juxtaposing business cards of various personalities between 1914 and 1935. We read there: Mustafa al-Nahhas Bey: Judge at the Tanta Primary Tribunal (1914), Mustafa al-Nahhas Pasha: Leader of the Egyptian Wafd [Party] (1935); William Makram 'Ubayd [Effendi]: Employee at the Ministry of Justice (1914), William Makram 'Ubayd: General Secretary of the Egyptian Wafd (1935); Hasan Fahmi Rif'at [Effendi]: Assistant Inspector, Public Security, Ministry of Interior (1914), Hasan Fahmi Rif'at Bey: Vice Minister of Justice (1935); *Kull shay' wa-l-dunya* 491, 3. 4. 1935, 8–9.

38 Beinin, "Egypt," 314.

39 See the chapter by Barak Salmoni in this volume. See also Tignor; Reid, *Cairo University*, and Gregory Starrett, *Putting Islam to Work: Education, Politics and Religious Transformation in Egypt* (Berkeley: University of California Press, 1998).

40 Expenditure on education rose from 1 percent under Cromer to 13 percent at the eve of World War II. Roger Owen and Sevket Pamuk, *A History of Middle East Economies in the Twentieth Century* (London: I.B. Tauris, 1998), 33. See also Charles Issawi, *Egypt at Mid-Century* (Oxford: Oxford University Press, 1954), 43, and Robert Mabro, *The Egyptian Economy 1952–72*, (Oxford: Clarendon Press, 1974), 12, 16.

41 Beinin, "Egypt," 314.

42 Jankowski, *Rebels*, 2–3.

43 See the analysis of Avriel Butovski, "Languages of the Egyptian Monarchy," in *The Languages of History: Selected Writings on the Middle East*, essays by Avriel Butovski in memoriam (Cambridge: Harvard University Press, 1995).

44 See again the chapter by Barak Salmoni in this volume, and Jankowski, *Rebels*, 3. Safran is another who describes the ethos of political liberalism in Egyptian schools; Nadav Safran, *Egypt in Search for Political Community* (Cambridge: Harvard University Press, 1961), 148–50. We should, however, understand the 'liberalism' of this period in its context. For instance, one of the great proponents of Egyptian liberalism, the thinker and writer Ahmad Amin, narrates in his memoirs how he struggled for access to education and the knowledge of foreign languages, and became a great admirer of western thought. Then he decided to marry; and went to his mother to choose him a suitable bride, who he saw for the first time on his wedding night. Ahmad Amin, *My Life* (Leiden: E.J. Brill, 1978).

45 The cartoon personality al-Misri Effendi was most probably created by Rakha, Egypt's most celebrated cartoonist of the interwar period. Al-Misri Effendi can be translated as "Mr. Egyptian," though with a specific meaning of the title effendi, as discussed through this chapter. The cartoon first appeared regularly on the pages of *al-Ithnayn* magazine (*Dar al-Hilal* publisher) in the mid-1930s. It became very famous during the Second World War. After the

war ended, al-Misri Effendi cartoons mushroomed in many other magazines, and were also no longer exclusively the work of Rakha, its original author. In the late 1930s and throughout the 1940s, we can see him appearing on the pages of *al-Sabah, Ruz al-Yusuf, al-Mukhbir, al-Shu'la, Akhir sa'a*, and others. The al-Misri Effendi character was most often used to comment on political events, but not exclusively: sometimes it was used for commercial advertising—an indisputable sign of his popularity. He also gave the name to at least one magazine—called simply *al-Misri Effendi*—published in Alexandria between the early 1940s and through the early 1950s. For a description and analysis of al-Misri Effendi see also Gershoni and Jankowski, 7.

46 For the discourse of the liberal intellectuals see, for instance, Smith, *Haykal*, and William Shepard, "The Dilemma of a Liberal. Some Political Implications in the Writings of the Egyptian Scholar, Ahmad Amin (1886–1954)," in *Modern Egypt: Studies in Politics and Society*, ed. Elie Kedourie and Sylvia Haim (London: Frank Cass, 1980). For critical assessments of the liberals' discourses, see Walid Kazziha, "The Jarida-Umma Group," in *Middle East Studies* 13 (1977), Roel Meijer, *Quest for Modernity: Secular Liberal and Left-Wing Political Thought in Egypt, 1945–58* (Amsterdam: University of Amsterdam Press, 1995), and Alain Roussilon et al., *Entre réforme sociale et mouvement national: identité et modernisation en Égypte (1882–1962)* (Cairo: Centre de recherche et de documentation économique, juridique et sociale/CEDEJ, 1995).

47 In economic terms—though not discursively—the Egyptian elite was fully congruent with the interests and capital of local foreign communities. See Vitalis, *When Capitalists Collide*.

48 See Israel Gershoni and James Jankowski, *Egypt, Islam and the Arabs: The Search for Egyptian Nationhood, 1900–1930* (New York: Oxford University Press, 1986) for an exhaustive discussion of the ethos of Pharaonism, and see their second volume, *Redefining the Egyptian Nation*, for an analysis of the changes that occurred to perceptions of Egyptian identity in the 1930s.

49 Between 1917 and 1937 Cairo's population almost doubled, and the population of Egypt's 20 largest cities rose by 54 percent. By 1947, Cairo's population was over two million, compared with 790,939 in 1917. Gershoni and Jankowski, *Redefining*, 12.

50 Ibid., 12 and 13. The percentage of literate Egyptians increased from 13.8 percent in 1927 to 22.8 percent in 1947. See also Issawi, *Egypt at Mid-Century*, 67.

51 Gershoni and Jankowski, *Redefining*, 12; they also contend that another crucial factor behind the students' involvement in politics was their growing disillusionment with the 1923 political generation, a fact supported by a number of novels and memoirs. For Egyptian students in politics see also Ahmad Abdalla, *The Student Movement and National Politics in Egypt, 1923–73* (London: Saqi Books, 1985), H. Erlich, *Students and University in Twentieth-Century Egyptian Politics* (London: Frank Cass, 1989).

52 R. Mabro, 12–13, 18–22; Issawi, 69, 85; Owen and Pamuk, 34–35. For a contemporaneous account, see Doreen Warriner, *Land and Poverty in the Middle East* (London: Royal Institute of International Affairs, 1948), 26–51.

53 Owen and Pamuk, 34–35.

54 Economic and social historians often mention the "chronic instability of middle classes." See, for instance, Mabro, 11, and Issawi, 29–30. What did this mean in practice? Chronic instability of middle-class households can be seen in narratives, such as, for instance, Naguib Mahfouz's *al-Bidaya wa-l-nihaya* ("The Beginning and the End," Cairo: Nadi al-Qissa, 1956), when the father—the sole wage-owner of the whole household—dies in what was certainly a critical moment: before the sons could finish their education. In this novel, the oldest son has to abandon his hopes for a higher degree, and has to search for employment. Another illustration of such a situation appears in many films, in scenes of *muzayadat*, or public auctions. Auctions were common whenever a family's income fell under a certain level, and a public auction was announced to sell their belongings. Not only does the oldest son in *The Beginning and the End* leave for an unattractive teaching job in a small provincial city,

but the mother starts selling her furniture piece by piece. In *al-'Azima* ("Determination," or "Resolution," 1939, Kamal Selim—a classic of the Egyptian pre-revolution cinema, often written-about), the father of Muhammad Effendi Hanafi is compelled to sell his barber shop in a public auction. He has used it in a mortgage to finance his son's education, but Muhammad Effendi can't find a job immediately after graduation, with disastrous effects for his family. *Bint al-basha al-mudir* ("Daughter of His Excellency the Governor," 1938, Ahmad Galal) starts with a scene of a public auction, after the heroine's brother had a car accident, again, with serious effects on the family's material standing. To save the situation, she puts on male apparel and takes up her brother's job. Another public auction scene is used in Muhammad 'Abd al-Wahhab's classic, *Rushasha fi-l-qalb* ("A Bullet in the Heart," 1944, Muhammad Karim). Such situations must have been common, because it was often single-person's wage (the father's, less often the oldest brother's) which determined the social and material situation of the whole family. Several popular magazines featured a regular page or two at the end of each issue with lists of public auctions in both Cairo and provincial towns, see any issue of *Ruz al-Yusuf* or *Akhir sa'a* magazines in 1935.

55   For excellent accounts of the transformation of commercial practices and the development of commercial establishments in urban centers, see recent works by Reynolds, Russell, and Shechter. Mona Russell, "Creating al-Sayyida al-Istihlakiyya: Advertising in Turn-of-the-Century Egypt," *Arab Studies Journal* VIII/IX (Fall 2000/Spring 2001): 61–96; Nancy Reynolds, "Sharikat al-Bayt al-Misri: Domesticating Commerce in Egypt, 1931–56," *Arab Studies Journal* VII/VIII (Fall 1999/Spring 2000): 75–118; Relli Shechter, "Press Advertising in Egypt: Business Realities and Local Meaning, 1882–1956," *Arab Studies Journal* X/XI (Fall 2002/Spring 2003): 44–66. In some cases, however, we tend to take the practice of shopping too much taken for granted, assuming that once there are new products and new commercial venues, the consumer is automatically there (actually, that the act of commercial exchange in the conventional sense is there). Perhaps that new products—and, even more importantly, new sites for marketing and display, such as popular illustrated magazines, the cinema, or even shop windows—had even more impact on those who could *not* buy the commodities they displayed, rather than those who could, and who already in one way or another counted among consumers. How 'seductive' and life-transforming commodities could be for those who could only consume them visually (and thus experienced a new dimension to their deprivation). See, for instance, the story of Hamida in Mahfouz's *Midaq Alley*.

56   For how the cinema, for instance, functions as a zone of construction of such a 'cultural middle' in which modern national bourgeois culture and identity are articulated, see Armbrust, *Mass Culture and Modernity in Egypt* (Cambridge: Cambridge University Press, 1996), and his "Golden Age Before the Golden Age," in *Mass Mediations. Approaches to Popular Culture in the Middle East and Beyond*, ed. Walter Armbrust (Berkeley: University of California Press, 2000).

57   PRO files explicitly devoted to the "effendi problem" are FO 371/52365 (Relations between Great Britain and Middle East Effendis, 1946), FO 371/61538 (The "effendi" problem in the Middle East, 1947) and FO 141/1223 (Propaganda: British: The Effendi Class, 1947). Many other files discuss the effendis in relation to other issues, for instance FO 371/61542 (Youth Movements in the Middle East, 1947), FO141/892 (Education and student employment, 1943) as well as some files dating to the previous decade: FO 141/543 and FO141/618 (Students: political activities and strikes, 1936 and 1935). Another careful observer who devoted much attention to the effendis was writer and traveler Freya Stark. She seems to have aimed the proselytizing activities of her "Brotherhood of Freedom" (a pro-Allied propaganda club she has set up while in Cairo) at the effendis.

58   Walter Smart, 3 December 1946, FO 371/ 52365.

59   Bevin's circular dated 15. 1. 1947, 371/52365.

60 P.G.D. Adams memorandum, FO 141/1223.

61 Bird to Bevin, Baghdad, 10. 3. 1947, FO 141/1223.

62 W.E. Houston-Boswall to Bevin, Beirut 15. 5. 1947, FO 141/1223.

63 W. Smart, 3. 12. 1946, 371/52365.

64 W.F. Crawford to Bevin, 9. 6. 1947, FO 141/1223. The question of reading, especially changing reading habits among the effendis, but also among the urban population generally, is an important issue that unfortunately cannot be developed in this chapter. Popular (and mostly illustrated) magazines mushroomed in Egypt from the 1920s, and they were the print material most commonly read by urban Egyptians. However, there was also a parallel and growing market for non-periodical cheap prints, such as romantic stories and serialized fiction (including police and erotic fiction), which in many ways resembled western pulp fiction. However, I do not think that this is what Crawford and the British officials in Egypt and the Middle East had in mind. In my opinion his comment about "more cheap books" is as irrelevant to the core of the effendi problem as his suggestion about "more tennis parties." For more on the development of illustrated magazines and serialized fiction in Egypt, see Lucie Ryzova, "I Am a Whore But I Will Be a Good Mother: On the Production and Consumption of the Female Body in Egypt's Magazine Culture," *Arab Studies Journal*, Spring 2005 (forthcoming). For the spread of literacy and the democratization of reading, understood as a pleasurable activity rather than one generated from above, see Walter Armbrust, "Ramadan, Marketing, and Heritage: Visualization and Commodification," Paper presented at the Fifth Mediterranean Social and Political Research Meeting, Florence, Montecatini Terme, 2004.

65 Sports represented an important part of effendi culture, whether it was playing sports, or watching and reading about them. Most popular magazines—ranging from the most expensive titles such as *al-Musawwar* to the cheaper black and white ones—featured regular sport pages since at least the 1920s. Playing sports had long been available to the elites in their clubs; now—in the years between the two world wars—it was also becoming increasingly accessible to the less privileged middle-income urban youths. Local communal football clubs were current in the 1930s, and according to some sources at least, there were boxing facilities in popular neighborhoods after the Second World War. See for instance, films *Shalom al-riyadi* ("Shalom, the Sportsman," 1937, Togo Mizrahi) and *al-Mazahir* ("Outward Appearances," 1945, Kamal Salim). As to cinema in the 1930s and 1940s, cheap theaters were common in both less-privileged urban areas and in provincial cities. See Jacob Landau, *Studies in Arab Theater and Cinema* (Philadelphia: University of Pennsylvania Press, 1958), see also Flibbert chapter in this volume. For a first-hand account of what cinema-going was like for teenagers in around 1940, see Saleh Mursi, *Layla Murad* (Cairo: Kitab al-Hilal, n.d.).

66 Compare this mocking of the *shaykh* with rivalry between the 'turban' and the 'tarboosh,' mentioned in note 27. This song might have been common, since there is a very similar one mentioned in Malika Zeghal, *Gardiens de l'Islam* (Paris: Presse de la fondation nationale des sciences politiques, 1996), 17.

67 Yahya Haqqi, *Qindil Umm Hashim* (Cairo: Dar al-Ma'arif, 2001), 6–7. We note that there are two different cultures among the schoolchildren: one is the "awlad al-effendiya" (children of the *effendiya*) whose Arabic is poor. Was it due to their previous education in foreign missionary schools or English at primary school? Because they spoke French at home? We can only guess, but the perception of the turn-of-the-century effendi who is excessively westernized is there. The other culture is that of Yahya Haqqi, son of a merchant from the very traditional neighborhood of Sayyida Zaynab. He is undergoing his 'effendification' only now. We might also speculate that the hero was more articulate in Arabic because he had been to the *kuttab*, the Qur'anic school, before, which was most probably not the case for the *awlad al-effendiya*.

68   A number of issues are of interest, but they remain beyond the scope of this paper. They are developed in my dissertation. Becoming an effendi, or making one's son an effendi, is an interesting social practice, involving various educational strategies, economic practices, and justifying narratives. These are, for instance: sending the male child first to *kuttab*, then to governmental school; diversifying options among male siblings, of which the oldest would often receive only the rudiments of formal education and would be kept in the shop or on the land to take over family affairs, while subsequent sons might be sent to complete the effendi track; in some cases, the son could be sent to Europe to obtain a prestigious diploma, like in the case of Yahya Haqqi's narrative here, on either a government grant or at his own expense (this practice seems to have been available even to relatively modest families due to Egypt's currency being tied to the sterling); what families generally sought the 'effendi track' for their sons, from what backgrounds and regions did they originate; last, but not least, what were the avenues of 'effendification' other than formal schooling, especially the role of the media and popular press in diffusing notions of "new lifestyles." Becoming an effendi was not always a parent-programmed strategy, rather one increasingly sought by young unprivileged men, such as in the memoirs of Sayyid 'Uways. 'Uways, after a brief period in governmental school, suffered a relapse into the world of the 'turban' (in his case actually the *gallabiya*) when his father suddenly died. He could only accomplish his higher education many years later, when he was well in his thirties, already married with children. 'Uways actually spoke about his struggle for education is messianistic terms—as a kind of civilizing mission back in his popular neighborhood—not dissimilar to words in which Yahya Haqqi described his neighborhood upon his return from England. Unless otherwise stated, all translations are the author's.

69   Haqqi, 8.

70   Ibid., 18–19.

71   For the representational economy of various social categories in modern Egypt, see Armbrust, *Mass Culture and Modernism*, Booth, *Bairam al-Tunsi's Egypt*, Messiri, *Ibn al-balad*, and Lucie Ryzova, *L'effendiya ou la modernité contestée* (Cairo: Centre de recherche et de documentation économique, juridique et sociale/CEDEJ, 2004).

72   The same expression "*saraft 'alayhi damm qalbi*" is used in another film discussed below *(Ibn al-haddad)*: "I have spent on you the blood of my heart, to enable you to work as *miri* (higher government official), to see you, Taha Effendi, son of Mu'allim Salah, walking in and out of the *diwan* (government offices, ministry)," says the father, this time a town craftsman, to his son. I shall return to the *miri* ideal below.

73   While Dr. Hilmi is of course an effendi, he does not bear the title in his name, because it is superseded by his identification as 'doctor.' Effendi means just any secondary school graduate, and—in the interwar period—it can increasingly also be usurped by people who have not even completed a degree, but are literate and dress in 'the western manner.' Because of the general drop in the social standing of the title, as discussed through this chapter, whoever actually has a higher diploma, tends to invariably use that instead of the too 'general' title of effendi. We thus see, when perusing popular magazines for instance, how journalists or readers in their readers letters pages, identify themselves as '*al-muhami*' (lawyer), or '*licensié fi-l-adab*' (B.A. in literature), rather than simply effendi. It should be remembered that these titles are derivative from being, essentially, technically an effendi, but in the 1930s and 1940s, they sound much better.

74   The backgrounds of Egyptian leaders are commonly known, and have been discussed in earlier parts of this chapter. For the best reference, see Arthur Goldschmidt, *Biographical Dictionary of Modern Egypt* (Boulder: Lynne Rienner Publishers, 2000). See also notes 15, 19, and 20.

75   Egyptian illustrated magazines, as a genre, have a specific approach to portraying the Egyptian countryside. Through the 1920s and 1930s, there is virtually *no* mention of the

countryside. However, there is *lots* of talk in the form of reportages in word and image from foreign lands and European capitals. I mean specifically magazines published by *Dar al-Hilal*, which were a vanguard of the industry, with best print quality, largest numbers of images, and largest circulation numbers: *al-Musawwar, al-Dunya al-musawwara, Kull shay' wa-l-dunya, al-Ithnayn*; but others were no exception. This attitude changed only after the Second World War, with the rise of popular sensibilities within the Egyptian mainstream media as well as political discourses: concepts such as workers, peasants, social reform, the land, the countryside, and its problems, were looming.

76 Precisely this ethos is also expressed by a statue made by Egypt's foremost modernist sculptor Mahmud Mukhtar, called "Knowledge." It shows a boy reading in a book and his mother, a *fallaha* (peasant woman), is standing above him and supervises him. Photograph of the statue was published in *IMAGES* (French-language Egyptian magazine published by Dar al-Hilal), issue 1287, 8 May 1954. See Caroline Williams' chapter in this volume.

77 A further indication of his social status is his wife, Sitt Amina, a prototype of the 'traditional' woman. She has never left the house of her husband, whom she calls her "master" (Sayyid), on her own; and when she does so—in order to visit the neighboring mosque of al-Husayn—she is severely punished by him. She serves as the antidote to ongoing calls for female emancipation on the part of Egypt's *male* intellectuals, who feel an acute shortage of women: to be precise, of modern middle class women, who—with basic education and elementary foreign languages, with rearing in modern house-care and child-care—would be their appropriate social counterparts. See Lucie Ryzova, "Laila the Bourgeoise: Mass Media and the New Woman in Egypt," paper presented at the MESA annual conference in San Francisco, California, 2004. See also Omnia Shakry, "Schooled Mothers and Structured Play: Child Rearing in Turn-of-the-Century Egypt," in *Remaking Women. Feminism and Modernity in the Middle East*, ed. Lila Abu Lughod (Princeton: Princeton University Press, 1998).

78 A very similar situation was used by Mahfouz again in his *Midaq Alley*: the merchant had three sons, all of them effendis, and none of them was willing to continue the father's job. Naguib Mahfouz, *Midaq Alley*, 63.

79 There are many examples that testify how wrong it is to imagine that one can simply change his clothes and become a different person. There are a number of 'traditional' characters in films or cartoons who attempt to dress in a modern suit, but end as mere travesties: funny and mocked by all. A popular cartoon character by Rakha, the author of *al-Misri Effendi*, was called War Profiteer *(Thari al-harb)*. He dressed in modern suit and smoked a cigar, yet he remained a mere yahoo. The film *Law kuntu ghani* ("If I Were Rich," 1942, Henry Barakat) narrates a similar story. A barber inherits wealth, and subsequently does what the rich do: buys a car and moves to a villa in a posh neighborhood. He ends up ridiculed—as just a barber—and abandoned by all, including his immediate family. In *Layla, bint al-rif* ("Layla, Daughter of the Countryside," 1942, Togo Mizrahi) Layla's transition from a peasant girl into an urban lady of society can only be successful because Layla has already been a lady once, she was educated in an elite establishment for girls, but too many years have past since her return to the farm. Her transformation is thus not really a transformation from one cultural category to another—from a peasant *(fallaha)* to a lady *(hanim)* but it is a process of remembering what she already used to be. The *only* social category that can successfully straddle the boundary separating social identities is the effendi.

80 Messiri, 48. Al-Misri Effendi disappeared from the pages of *al-Ithnayn* magazine, but it continued being used in other magazines with unchanged vigor. *Al-Ithnayn* has replaced al-Misri Effendi with another character, called simply Ibn al-balad, and who dressed actually more like a *fallah*. This change in front-page iconography most probably corresponds to what has been said about the rise of popular sensibilities in note 76 above.

81 See note 51 for the rise in the numbers of graduates. But the status of diplomas was also changing. One now had to have a higher diploma, or be a graduate of a European university, in order to access to the sort of jobs that were almost automatic for secondary school graduates two decades earlier.

82 Quoted in Hasan Darwish, *Min ajli abi Sayyid Darwish* (Cairo: General Egyptian Book Organization, 1990), 416–17.

83 'Aziza 'Abd al-Gawwad Mustafa, interview Cairo April and May 2003. 'Aziza was born in 1923 into the family of a rich merchant in Benha. Her family belonged to the upper echelons of the local hierarchy, but different from the local pasha, whose family spent most of their time in Cairo. 'Aziza went to school for a few years, but did not finish her formal schooling because her father considered her "too pretty" and thus feared for her going to public places. In her mid-teens she was asked for marriage by a police officer—originally from a different province—stationed in the city. This was in 1938 or 1939, and her family accepted the offer as suitable, because of the young man's rank. She later saw to it that all her children would complete at least an undergraduate degree.

84 The importance of the army grew together with the development of the "National Question," or negotiations about British withdrawal from Egypt (expansion of the strongly circumscribed Egyptian army was made possible after the 1936 treaty, when a Military Academy was established to train Egyptian officers, see Aclimandos chapter in this volume), as well as with new challenges and demands posed by both the Second World War and the Palestine War.

85 Despite the lasting myth about the 1936 Military Academy reforms among historians and the general public alike, inscription fees and conditions for the Academy remain high and each candidate has to pass through the *kashf al-hay'a* exam, set up to assess his family origin and income (see Aclimandos article in this volume). Narratives such as Mahfouz's *The Beginning and the End* offer a glimpse into the theoretical possibility, but practical difficulty, of this route for lower middle class youths. Incidentally, both later presidents 'Abd al-Nasser and Sadat were such "exceptional" cases: they were singled out among their officer colleagues by their comparatively low origin. Both were sons of effendis employed in government service, while most other top-command Free Officers came from old notable families, though subsequent accounts sponsored by the Egyptian state stated otherwise. I thank Tewfiq Aclimandos for this information.

86 From a larger historical perspective, the avenues of social ascent have thus developed from the Azhari track to the *miri* and *muwazzaf* track, and then to the officer track. With respect to the symbolic value of the uniform, see films featuring Anwar Wagdi, a star actor and director, prolific in the 1940s. Wagdi was a great uniform fan. He often wore them on the screen, including in situations where the story did not in any way require a uniform. The purpose of the uniform clearly was to make him more sexy to both male and female publics. See *Layla bint al-fuqara'* ("Layla, Daughter of the Poor," 1945, Anwar Wagdi), *Qalbi dalili* ("My Heart Is My Proof," 1947, Anwar Wagdi), *'Anbar* ("Anbar," 1948, Anwar Wagdi), *Ghazal al-banat* ("The Flirtation of Girls," 1949, Anwar Wagdi), *4 Banat wa dhabit* ("4 Girls and an Officer," 1954, Anwar Wagdi); all were also produced by Wagdi's production company Sharikat al-Aflam al-Muttahida. The charm of the uniform—its impact on both the neighbors in general and women in particular—is again well-pictured in Mahfouz's *The Beginning and the End*.

87 'Abd al-Latif Baghdadi in Lutfi Hamdi, *Thawrat yulyu: al-wajh al-akhar* (Cairo: Kitab al-Hilal, 1977), 59.

88 *Mu'allim* is a title of address associated with the realm of the *awlad al-balad*; it means boss, chief. In this line it is made specifically to contrast with the earlier title of effendi after Taha's name, to signify the progression from one generation to another and from one status to another, in the same manner as the advertisement for al-Rashidi al-Halawani pastry did.

89 Note the ambivalence of the word *'amil*, worker. Taha is certainly no worker. i nis ambivalence resonates with Taha's corporatist ethos. He refers to his workers as "brothers" and stresses the fact that he grew up among them to assert his social justice, based on communal or actually "family" ties. This ethos has yet another dimension: the film was shot in a moment of intensifying trade unions struggle for workers rights. See Beinin and Lockman, *Workers on the Nile*, and Ellis Goldberg, *Tinker, Tailor, Textile Worker: Class Politics in Egypt, 1930–54* (Berkeley: University of California Press, 1986).

90 *"Hatefdal nusf aynaya al-amana wa ikhlas fi-l-'amal."* The choice of words, *amana* and *ikhlas*, evoke a pious ethos of local authenticity, and are made to contrast with the language of the *dhawat* characters, who use foreign words extensively. Taha's wife blames him for talking to their son in Arabic (she talks to their son in French).

91 The cinematic techniques used here, such as shots of modern boulevards and new machinery, reinforce this reading.

92 There was a growing negative representation of the *dhawat*, the Egyptian upper class, in the cinema after 1945. It was subtle—not least because of the censorship—but overwhelming. It was not expressed in political terms, but in cultural and generational terms, such as, for instance, narratives in which the parents are wrong while the children are right, and suffering from their parents' heavy hand (like in *al-Duktur* discussed here; also in many films with Layla Murad, in which plots usually evolve around the right of the young couple to their free choice of the partner, clashing with parents who have already chosen a partner on the basis of economic interests). Many comedies explore the stratagem of class corruption—expressed by tropes such as the cabaret, dancers, and alcohol—to describe the whole class, while a single character from this class could be presented as utterly positive. Other films use subtle symbols or situations, again pointing to class corruption of the *dhawat*, but not necessarily as individuals. To give just one example, in an utterly non-political comedy such as *Ghazal al-banat* ("The Flirtation of Girls," 1949, Anwar Wagdi; see Armbrust, "Golden Age" for a thorough analysis of this film) there would be a scene in which a wretched effendi (played by the great comedian Nagib al-Rihani) who has just lost his job as a school teacher, first enters the villa of the pasha, searching for employment. The first person he runs into is a secretary whose job is to take care of the pasha's pet dog, and for which he takes a salary five times as much as Rihani used to get as a schoolteacher. The pasha himself is portrayed as a kind and harmless old man; but the message of implicit class criticism was passed through the above situation, which was otherwise marginal to the main line of the narrative.

93 Muslim ethics, understood as social justice, the quest for knowledge, and local authenticity is a message reiterated in *al-Duktur*, discussed above, and stated in even more explicit terms in *al-Misri Effendi* ("Mr. Egyptian," 1949, Husayn Sidqi). *Ibn al-haddad*, *al-Duktur*, *al-Misri Effendi*, and *al-Muzahir*, are films with much more pronounced class criticism than was the case in films described in the previous note.

94 Yusuf Wahbi was a leading actor, founder and owner of the Ramsis Theater, one of the most famous theater troupes of the time. Aristocrat by birth, he opted for the acting profession early in his life—temporarily losing all his family fortune in it—and his relations with his family were severely strained. Early in the film era, he made a successful transition onto the screen, where he appeared as both actor and, in some cases, as director (he directed *Ibn al-haddad* for instance). Some of his films were versions of his earlier theater plays. His films can be said to have had a moralizing agenda: he often sought to articulate his views through using opposing concepts such as "the virtuous" versus the "corrupt." His films discussed such issues as "proper" behavior, a married woman's obligations toward her husband, the value of work, and even of art, see his *al-Fannan al-'Azim* ("The Great Artist," 1945, Yusuf Wahbi), *al-Tariq al-mustaqim* ("The Straight Path," 1943, Togo Mizrahi), or *Habib al-ruh* ("Beloved of the Heart," 1951, Anwar Wagdi). In his own—markedly aristocratic—ways, he was often socially critical,

especially in assigning value judgment to modernity, as either "good" or "bad" modernity (see *Layla, Daughter of the Countryside*, mentioned above, or *Layla, Daughter of the Schools*, 1941, Togo Mizrahi). He was peered under the monarchy (became Yusuf Wahbi Bey) as recognition of his lifelong work in the Egyptian theater. See his memoirs: Yusuf Wahbi, *'Ishtu alf 'amm*, 3 vols. (Cairo: Dar al-Ma'arif, 1973). See also Armbrust, *Mass Culture and Modernity*, 77, 201–203, and Armbrust, "Golden Age," 313.

95 These themes indeed echo the discourse of the radical movements, whose main line of argument was the moral corruption brought to the country by the west and articulated either in religious (Muslim Brotherhood) or secular (Young Egypt Party) terms. Far from suggesting any tangible link between the filmmakers (clearly impossible due to the persona of Wahbi) and the radical movements, these films simply targeted the sensibilities of their audiences.

96 Both *Kull shay' wa-l-dunya* and *al-Hilal* were published by Dar al-Hilal, the largest and most powerful publishing house in Egypt (in terms of its latest technology, greatest number of publications and of staff, and largest share of the market). Both periodicals were quite 'mainstream' and reflective of a cultural elite. Other press organs—small-circulation magazines often published by one individual—had already discovered the 'youth' long ago. Large number of popular magazines was in circulation therough the 1930s, specifically geared to a youth public, and an effendi public. Those who wrote the articles in the Dar al-Hilal "youth issues" were not themselves youths, and certainly did not risk their lives in the 1935 clashes with British soldiers. What was happening was that the youth asserted themselves— as a social category and a political force—during the 1935–36 events, and the mainstream politicians and cultural producers acknowledged them by giving them an important place in their own discourse, thereby attempting to co-opt the youth movement.

97 'Abd al-Latif Baghdadi in Hamdi, 59.

98 Muhi al-Din, 11. His memoirs are, however, presumably the work of his friend and colleague Rif'at al-Sa'id, a known communist activist, writer, and co-founder of the contemporary *al-Tagammu'* political party (together with Khaled Muhi al-Din). It might not be harmful since Rif'at was only slightly younger then Muhi al-Din.

99 Another good example of this point is that a year later, while the older generation of politicians celebrate the 1936 Treaty as a victory, the youth movements denounced it as treachery.

100 Naguib Mahfouz, *Sugar Street*, trans, William Maynard Hutchins and Angele Botros Samaan (Cairo: The American University in Cairo Press, 1992), 187.

101 This trope is often suggested in narratives. In Mahfouz's *Midaq Alley*, for instance, the decision of the young man, Hussein Kirsha, to leave his native *hara* and search for what he understands as "better life" is specifically expressed in terms of his "right" to do so. Mahfouz, *Midaq Alley*, 116–17. I understand the notion of "right to make one's own rules" also in the fact that many members of the effendi clandestine groups who attempted assassinations in the mid-to-late 1940s were law school students.

102 "*Ma na'ilu matalibu bi-l-tamanni wa-lakin tukhadhu al-dunya ghilaban.*" Virginia Danielson, *A Voice Like Egypt*, documentary film on Umm Kulthum (Seattle: Arab Film Distribution, 1996).

103 Beinin's expression, Beinin, "Egypt," 314.

104 It was Beinin, Smith, Gershoni, and Jankowski who claimed that the new *effendiya* was "traditional" because of its mostly rural origin. Strictly speaking, the previous generation of effendis (those who became pashas and beys in the interwar period) was probably much more rural—many of them being actually born in the *rif*—than the generation of new effendis, who often came from recently urbanized migrant families. This hypothesis can only be ascertained after more research, but certainly it is not useful to think about one generation as "rural" and the other not. The crucial difference lay in their identity and structural relationship to the State.

•

6 Historical Consciousness for Modern Citizenship

Egyptian Schooling and the Lessons of History during the Constitutional Monarchy

Barak A. Salmoni

To paraphrase the great Alsatian sociologist Maurice Halbwachs, history is a present-oriented resource.[1] Rather than objective truth or fact, it is a group's consciousness of history that interprets current circumstances and frames future needs. Society's concerns about the present elicit a collective memory of the past, which helps people to process contemporary circumstances. Politically engaged ideologues seek more proactively to disseminate within their societies understandings of the past which can direct present action. In the Middle East during the twentieth-century process of nation formation, state elites and nationalist leaders considered it a priority to create present-oriented collective memories, and then communicate them to new citizens as a narrative providing a road map to contemporary conduct. These groups "sought to win over as many . . . as possible to the project of creating a future nation" possessing a fully modern sociopolitical structure.[2] In so doing, social engineers throughout the Middle East fastened upon national education systems, exhibiting a faith in schooling as "the secular equivalent of the church," with a curricular gospel of nationalism.[3]

Egypt exemplifies this process. Rifa'a Rafi' al-Tahtawi (1801–73), one of the first bureaucrat-historians of modern Egypt, thought that state-run education was essential to crafting a sense of patriotic community based on loyalty to the ruling dynasty and a conviction of Egyptian grandeur going back to pharaonic accomplishments.[4] Later, during the first phase of independent statehood between 1923 and 1952, Egyptian state educators transcended the prescriptive for the concrete and practical, using curricula to cultivate among students particular understandings of their own history. Such understandings could ingrain lasting assumptions regarding Egypt's motive forces, and communicate the proper traits necessary for Egyptian citizens emerging into the newly established constitutional monarchy. Much more than simply academic, Egyptian history was deployed as a socializing, even programming tool for modern citizenship.

The intense concern to access history's sociopolitical potential was no coincidence: several indigenous contributors to Egyptian historiography during the first half of the twentieth century worked in state education at some point. Ya'qub Artin, undersecretary in the Ministry of Education from 1884 to 1906, also wrote history books on public education and Egyptian finances. Amin Sami, whose six-volume history of Egypt began with the arrival of Islam and culminated with the era of Khedive Isma'il (r. 1863–79), headed the Dar al-'Ulum Arabic teachers college from 1895–1911, after which he directed the Mubtadayan school for a quarter century. Involvement with education was no less the case for the "founding fathers" of independent Egypt's historiography. Muhammad Rif'at whose *Political History of Egypt in Modern Times* will be explored in detail below, first taught history at the Higher Teachers College, then went on to several posts in the Ministry of Education, becoming general director for secondary education in 1946, undersecretary for the ministry by the late 1940s, and then education minister in 1952. Likewise, Egypt's first solidly academic historian, Muhammad Shafiq Ghurbal (1894–1961), began professional life as a secondary school history teacher before obtaining advanced degrees in Britain. From 1940 he was closely involved in state schooling, serving as assistant deputy director in the ministry from 1940–42. In 1945, he worked as technical adviser to the ministry, becoming undersecretary during Rif'at's tenure as minister, and remaining employed in state education until 1954. Likewise, the nationalist-inclined historian Muhammad Sabri (1890–1978) also worked in the 1920s at the teachers college and in the 1930s represented the Ministry of Education abroad in Geneva.[5] To quote Ghurbal, educator-historians concerned with "the construction of public opinion" and the fulfillment of "political duties" sought to create a school history able to "propagate a connection—real or fictitious did not matter—between the Egypt of the Pharaohs and the Egypt of today."[6]

Present-oriented aspirations thus naturally dictated the goals of Egyptian schooling throughout the 1920s to the late 1940s. Even at the declaratory level, when reading official state guidelines issued to schools, teachers saw that, through highlighting personages exemplifying the best ethics, historical study could achieve one of its most important tasks, the direct teaching of morality. More fundamentally, education officials urged teachers to teach history in order to "lay the basis for true patriotism . . . and proper judgment."[7] According to the Egyptian curriculum, history's explicit goal became the provision of a program for students' future life as citizens, where historical consciousness furnished the overarching ambience of a moral and civic life. By the mid-1930s secondary schooling even intermingled history, civics, and ethics in the course schedule.

Though educational substance encountered by youth in school has not been seriously examined in modern Egypt, it is essential to do so. Through investigating educational discourse and school curricula one may gain unique insight into how professional and semi-professional historians, educational policy makers, and teachers crafted a collective memory to motivate the current actions and future aspirations of rising generations. Students of 1919–52 Egypt can then grasp what a particularly influential, ideologically engaged stratum of society wanted emerging citizens to believe. Likewise, by evaluating materials actually encountered by Egyptian students, one better understands ideas influencing, consciously or unconsciously, large numbers of Egyptian citizens during the constitutional monarchy years—including makers of the 1952 coup and those who welcomed it. Finally, this type of examination opens the way to assessing the relationship between school history and the over-arching trends in Egyptian history writing during the 1922–52 years, when the country's first professional and widely-read semi-professional historians emerged.

Egypt's educators injected the lessons of history for modern Egyptian life into nearly every curricular subject, including language, religion, civics, and ethics. History curricula, however, brought all these lessons together on primary and secondary education levels, through government syllabi and teachers' guides, and history texts approved or commissioned by the Ministry of Education. Pedagogical literature and school magazines also complemented this process, through teachers' and students' own voices. In these important sources crafted by officials-cum-nationalist academicians and ideologues, teachers at various levels, and even students, certain themes proved quite durable between the early 1920s and late 1940s, resonating with notions taught as proper comportment in civics, morality, and even literature.

Two periods in Egypt's long history provide the sharpest indication of history's use as a present-oriented ideological resource: the 4000-year-long pharaonic era, and the forty-five-year-long rule of Muhammad 'Ali (r. 1805–48), who arrived in Egypt as an Albanian Ottoman officer in the wake of the 1798 French invasion, and proceeded to conquer large parts of Ottoman Syria and Anatolia, ultimately establishing a hereditary dynasty in an autonomous Egypt. Though the other periods in Egypt's history were indeed taught, the pharaonic era, from 3500 BCE down through the Ptolemies, as well as the Muhammad 'Ali period from 1801–48, received the greatest narrative intensity in syllabi and texts composed between 1919 and the late 1940s. In secondary schooling Egypt's antiquity was regularly accorded a whole year of history. This was also the case for the 180 years after 1750. Here, the mere four decades of Muhammad 'Ali's rule dominated, taking up over 30 percent of the assigned text. Primary schooling likewise highlighted these two eras. Curricula written in 1930 and 1935 prescribed a jump in the first year of study from pharaonic history to Muhammad 'Ali, eliding the Roman, Islamic, and Ottoman eras, while primary school texts for the post-1517 years privileged the Muhammad 'Ali era, according it between two and four times more space than its nearest competitor.[8]

The Character of Egyptian History in Constitutional Era-Schools

Between 1919 and 1952, Egyptian syllabi were revised and reissued several times, exhibiting gradually increasing nationalist intentionality. Unlike other Middle Eastern countries, initial post-independence efforts were not explicitly ideological in inspiration. The 1924 primary syllabus was nearly identical to that of 1921, which was based on directives from 1907 and 1913. Significantly, the course schedule included no civics or ethics classes (*tarbiya wataniya; akhlaq*), while the Arabic language curriculum was nearly apolitical in prescriptions.[9] Likewise, the 1924 secondary curriculum was quite similar to that of 1913, though it brought history class forward into the first two years of study. The 1930 primary syllabus espoused socializing goals somewhat more forthrightly, affirming a direct relationship between moral lessons in school and conduct in daily national life. Now, curricula stipulated that teachers would introduce youth to bygone eras in order to cultivate reverence for the past (*'atifat al-ihtiram li-l-madi*) and inculcate a sense of duty for the future (*wajib li-l-mustaqbal*).[10]

By 1935, primary schooling educational planners had moved far beyond the apolitical syllabus guidelines of the early 1920s, emphasizing the task of education as inspiring youth with a sense of nationalist greatness and virtue *(ruh al-'uzma wa-l-fadila)* by focusing on the accomplishments of the mightiest people *(a'zam al-ashkhass)* in Egypt's past—implicitly casting a star role for history classes.[11] In the same year, after a major review of secondary education under Minister Nagib al-Hilali, officials instructed educators at this level to live up to their duty of being spiritual leaders *(ru'asa ruhiyun)* by "forming an ethical and national consciousness" among students, and by focusing on historical dynamics in the context of contemporary realities.[12] One history teacher and text writer commented that anything else "held the student back from being a proper member of Egyptian society."[13] Though topic apportionments changed in the 1948–49 syllabi, these sentiments remained fixtures.[14] And, particularly as secondary and primary schooling did not include civics as its own class until the 1930s and 1940s respectively, history class would fulfill the lion's share of political socialization in Egyptian schools. Furthermore, since Egyptian school history consciously espoused a "history of great personalities" approach, memorable pharaohs and their latter-day successor Muhammad 'Ali emerged with the most to offer to Egyptian youth in terms of lessons for contemporary life. At the same time, studying the progenitor of Egypt's ruling dynasty in such laudatory detail could challenge anti-Muhammad 'Ali views propagated by previous European writers, while rendering the pharaonic era more firmly the patrimony of young Egyptians rather than European archeologists.[15]

Perhaps the most fundamental of history's lessons for young Egyptians of the 1920s–40s was that Egypt was one of the earliest, most solidly civilized realms *(aqdam al-mamalik tahadduran)*.[16] As the prescribed primary level history text put it in 1928, "almost none of the countries that we see today can match [Egypt] in the antiquity of its history; even in ages long past there dwelled in it a nation *[qawm]* advanced in their lifestyle and knowledge, and they maintained control over their territory, preceding by thousands of years other nations in the domain of progress and civilization *[taqaddum wa hadara]*."[17] In the same fashion, secondary guidelines for teachers indicated that the first goal was to "make students grasp that Egypt—even if dynasties of non-Egyptian origin successively ruled her since the sixth century BCE—was an independent state *[dawla mustaqilla]* under the Ptolemies, Tulunids, Ikhshidids, Fatimids, Ayyubids, and Mamluks, just as she enjoyed a tremendous amount of autonomous [internal: *dhati*] independence until the days that governors ruled her from the Eastern Roman state, the Islamic caliphate, and the Ottoman state."[18]

On this basis, the historical narrative linked the pharaohs, Muhammad 'Ali, and Egypt's twentieth-century destiny by presenting eternal truths and thematic lessons that explicitly suggested values and societal guidelines for students. Chief among them included the relationship among between unity, strong central rule, and national sovereignty. As such, obedience to political and social superiors would prevent chaos. Students also learned of the metahistorical endurance of a national Egyptianness, which always attained independence and regional dominance when directed by strong rulers. This was balanced by the repeatedly demonstrated ability of Egyptians themselves to form their own political destiny. Further, history informed young citizens of the civilizational, even ethnic distinctiveness of Egyptians in relation to neighbors both near and far, and warned them of the pitfalls of intermingling with other peoples. Finally, Egypt's students during the constitutional monarchy encountered the overarching truth of post-1750 Egypt as its continued, orderly march toward democracy, and decorous popular participation in government. This orderly progression included a lasting bond of emotional reverence and loyalty to a dynasty which fundamentally identified with the betterment of Egypt, to the point of effacing its foreign roots. As the curriculum informed students, with the exception of the Romans and Ottomans, since the Hyksos, all who ruled Egypt possessed "the Egyptian character [al-taba' al-misri]."[19]

History in Primary Schooling, 1924–48

Students encountered these lessons from the start of pharaonic history study in primary school. As early as 3200 BCE, King Mina (Menes) — "a courageous man of good policies" — guaranteed continuous Egyptian national unity through control of the Nile and establishing a government, thus binding disparate regions of Egypt to its riverine core. Students saw that powerful rule and unity with the Nilotic heartland set Egypt up for consequent progress (taqaddum al-bilad al-Misri),[20] just as the history text itself indicated that throughout the life of the succeeding four dynasties, "Egypt continued to proceed on the path of advancement [tariqat al-taqaddum]," as manifested in regional trade and technological prowess. In particular, the building of the pyramids provided contemporaries and later Egyptians "a brilliant symbol of the uplift of the Egyptian civilization . . . and a measure of the government order [nizam] and the welfare of the country,"[21] while conquests beyond the Nile Valley proved essential to Egypt's great national wealth. The first period of national flourishing ended when petty rulers undermined the central government during the sixth dynasty, illustrating one of the meta-historical dichotomies in Egyptian life, that between chaos *(fawda)* and order *(nizam)*.

In the Middle Kingdom, Amunmahut III in particular deserved modern Egyptians' praise and emulation, since he "realized that the salvation of Egypt rests upon the improvement of its irrigation."[22] The syllabus thus prescribed strong focus on the building of dams, reservoirs, and the 'Murius' lakes during his tenure.[23] Also demonstrating Egyptians' preternatural technological prowess was the Labrant palace, "famous in ancient times for its innovation." Here, it was important for text writers to remind students that such accomplishments were remarked upon by the Greek historian Herodotus, since they established Egypt's civilizational credentials at the highest literary level, and in the words of a foreign, ostensibly unbiased source. The invading Hyksos also demonstrated important Egyptian truths, as they too "were stamped with much of the Egyptian character," indicating that even in this early age, dynasties *in* Egypt could not help but become *of* Egypt.[24] Here, curriculum recalled the discourse of early twentieth-century nationalist leaders who then served as education ministers in the late 1920s and 1930s.[25]

As for the Late Kingdom, the basic textbook celebrated the accomplishments of particular rulers. Ahtamose, founder of the Eighteenth Dynasty, was "one of the greatest kings of Egypt; for beyond rescuing his nation [*inqadh watanihi*] from the yoke of the foreigner, he unified authority in the hand of one leader." Thutmose III was "the greatest of the Late Kingdom kings," due chiefly to conquests in the Levant and his building program. Finally, in a literary method becoming a pattern, Egyptian text writers wrote that Ramesses II was "without doubt the greatest king of the Nineteenth Dynasty, because he is due the greatest credit for rescuing the state . . . and reclaiming most of the Asian possessions of Egypt." By the 1930s and 1940s, Arabic language class reinforced these lessons. Texts referred to Ramesses as "that youngster" and "that courageous youth loving his nation" *(watan)*, in order to cultivate a direct and concrete student-pharaonic era bond.[26]

The themes of pharaonic history already emerged early on for Egyptian students. When united under a single ruler and militarily strong, Egypt preserved independence *(istiqlal)* from foreigners, and dominated the region as the center of trade, agriculture, and science. Military capability proved essential to independence, and after Ramesses II, the loss of martial prowess led to Egypt's conquest and seizure *(istila')* by foreign Assyrians. In this case too, the curriculum provided lessons with contemporary value. Responding to Assyrian occupation, Psamtik's governmental centralization made him "one of the most powerful paraohs of Egypt and the most awesome of them, for in his day Egypt reawakened [*nahadat*] from its repose and began to regain its ancient glory," especially due to increased attention to the military.

In an Egypt of the 1920s still emerging from the shadow of a foreign occupier, such lessons were of particular importance to new citizens. Rather than solely as a source of pride, in a very concrete sense pharaonic history set out the cycles of Egypt's subsequent national history and established criteria to judge later Egyptian rulers: to the extent rulers demonstrated commitment to independence, technological advancement, and cultural uplift, the new state's contemporary leaders from Muhammad 'Ali forward would fulfill the nation's ancient destiny.[27]

On the individual level, the glory of ancient Egypt possessed moral content able to influence youth conduct. Ancient Egypt's heroes were courageous, strong-willed, and emotionally committed to an orderly life. Proper Egyptians in earlier times had also been active, resolute, and "protective of personal dignity without haughtiness or presumption." That ancient Egypt was indeed intended as a model for contemporary Egyptian school youth emerges from the advice parents gave children in antiquity: "Devote yourself to knowledge and love it as you love your mother. Do not expend your day in pleasure and laziness, lest you be struck by the lash. . . . Do not forget to revere those older than you or of greater status, and do not sit while they stand."[28] New Egyptians as well would thus learn from history to be industrious, self-reliant, and committed to modernization, while respecting society's leaders and honoring their nation's glorious past. Significantly, such qualities of pharaonic Egyptians paralleled closely the traits that modern Egyptian educators called for in teachers and students in the pedagogical press of the 1920s and 1930s, while Arabic language readers communicated similar concepts.[29] Likewise, as seen below, descriptions of Muhammad 'Ali were not entirely dissimilar.

The very end of the pharaonic era also illuminated Egypt's historical cycles, while providing lessons about enduring national dangers. The Ptolemaic kingdom was "Egyptian in form," maintaining several Egyptian customs. In particular Ptolemy I "followed the manner of Alexander in his good treatment of Egyptians, and his veneration of their religion. They thus loved him and the country proceeded in the path of uplift" *(ruqi)*. By contrast, the Roman period began with protection *(himaya)*, which was soon "turned into control [*saytara*] through the increasing weakness of the

Ptolemies. The matter then ended with total Roman conquest [istila'] of Egypt." And, while Egypt had previously been a cultural and political center in its own right, after 31 BCE, it became "merely a Roman province."[30]

Secondary Level Pharaonic History

As Misako Ikeda's chapter in this volume makes clear, for most of the constitutional monarchy era Egyptian educational officials retained the guiding logic of British occupation schooling policies regarding the rungs of the educational ladder. On the one hand, primary school (madrasa ibtida'iya) was intended as a preparatory track for secondary school (madrasa thanawiya). On the other hand, the frequent testing as a condition of promotion between ibtida'i grades, and the requirement of a diploma for entry into madrasa thanawiya meant that there were several exit-points which could prevent an Egyptian youth from ever entering secondary school. Attrition was high for other reasons as well, be they financial or related to migration. For many youngsters, therefore, primary school was their sole educational experience.[31]

Still, the school logic did presume continuation of study, and in many ways, those who completed both ibtida'i and thanawi education were considered the foot soldiers of nationalist modernity. Students proceeding to secondary school in the 1920s–40s thus encountered ideas similar to what they had found in madrasa ibtida'iya's coverage of the pharaonic era, yet with some different morally didactic emphases which educators judged more appropriate to an adolescent and young adult. Syllabi began by reinforcing primary school messages that "the basic factor in the existence of Egypt is the Nile, without which Egypt would have been a barren desert." Officials directed teachers to devote sufficient attention to the early and Middle Kingdoms to communicate the unity of Egypt (ittihad Misr).[32] Yet, receiving greater attention, particularly in the 1935–48 curriculum, was the New Kingdom (1580–1075 BCE) beginning with the era of post-Hyksos independence. According to a Ministry of Education-approved text written by teachers, under Ahmose "Egypt was saved from the occupation [ihtilal] of the loathsome Asian, that heavy nightmare." Likewise, curriculum writers directed teachers to focus on the militarization of society and subsequent foreign conquests. While primary school students had learned to see Egypt as naturally regionally dominant, the explicitly positive evaluation of militarism, and an ethnically-suggestive narrative, had not been part of their school book fare.

In another divergence from the ibtida'i approach, secondary history emphasized certain aspects of the "religious revolution" of Amenhetop and Nefertiti, who introduced (temporarily) a sort of monotheistic worship to Egypt. According to text writers, this religious experimentation, both in terms of its impetuses and consequences, caused the decline of the Egyptian empire of that era. Though the worship of Amon had been "a purely Egyptian creed" unifying the nation, subjects in newly acquired territories began to "migrate into Egypt and intermingle with the people." This intermingling (ikhtilat) elicited the new religion as something of a political expedient. The excessive political influence of the priests of Amon, who "departed . . . from their primary, religious duty" also motivated the cultic change.[33] By the same token, according to some secondary school texts, Nefertiti's half-Asian background and overweening power were also partially to blame for a politically unwise decision that led to internal dissent and successful revolts.[34] Further, because the "pharaoh of Egypt had become a religious teacher and not a man of war," the country lost most of its Asian possessions, leaving it open to foreign invaders.[35]

By relating in detail these events with particular explanations, curricularists and text writers communicated to students the need to preserve national customs in the face of foreign importations. Further, they continued to emphasize the great importance of regional dominance to Egyptian welfare, especially as the syllabus placed "the fall of the Egyptian empire" shortly after this episode.[36] Also, by criticizing priestly political influence and monarchical meddling in religious affairs, text writers likely sought to stress to emerging citizens the importance of the secular state's control of temporal affairs, a theme espoused by several pedagogical experts in the realm of educational administration.[37] Finally, reference to odious (baghid) Persians and Nefertiti's foreign roots may have been intended to provide secondary students with an ethnic perspective on history, warning against intermingling (ikhtilat) with other peoples. It also communicated the pseudo-biological conception of the nation echoed in 1930s–40s ibtida'i and thanawi civics descriptions of Egypt as a family writ large.[38] This extended the primary level approach without contradicting it. The overall consequences of diluted Egyptianness, decreased regional dominance, and the confusion of religion and politics were disunity and chaos, decline and subjugation.

When studying Egyptian civilization (hadara), students found a fully formed society possessing all aspects of agriculture, commerce, crafts, and the arts. And, like their Turkish and Iranian counterparts,[39] Egyptian educators portrayed their own ancient society as the one contributing a series of civilizational firsts to posterity, thus implying that Egypt in the 1920s–40s would regain its earlier status if its young citizens studied diligently and worked hard. Texts with a plethora of illustrations depicting artifacts from all aspects of daily Egyptian life in the commercial and domestic spheres served to connect students concretely to a past they would see as their own. Even more than in *ibtida'i* schooling, curricular guidelines promoted construction of historical dioramas and drawing pictures about daily Egyptian antiquity, such that Egyptian youth recreated their heritage with their hands. At the same time, focus on the socioeconomic and intellectual history of these years also worked to convince Egyptians of their superiority as a people. Not only had Egypt always been a farming country, but it was "the first great agricultural nation in the world." As regards industry, students also saw that "ancient Egyptians were the first in the world to produce paper," and led the peoples of antiquity in textiles as well as manufacturing. In trade, "Egyptians used rings of gold and copper at fixed weights, which was the first currency that history knew."[40]

Ancient Egypt made its greatest contribution to world civilization in intellectual terms. In particular, Egyptians of the pharaonic age "were the first to know writing." After hieroglyphics and herotica, Egyptians invented the demotica script, and eventually Coptic. Before that, however, the Phoenicians adopted demotica. "From them the Greeks took it, and the Romans learned it from the Greeks. Thus, ancient Egyptian writing became the basis of writing in all civilized nations of modern times." Finally, even the ancient Egyptian calendar was "the current calendar which the world inherited after six thousand years, with minor modification." Through it all, Egyptians had remained "firm in the belief in a deity that supervises actions and thoughts and calls one to account for them." For this reason, youth learned, Herodotus had said of Egyptians that they were "a god-fearing nation [*qawm*]."[41] Based on such past accomplishments, Egyptian youth could indeed feel pride, and understand even better the cautionary lessons of the past regarding the need for unity, order, loyalty to leaders, and keeping religion out of politics.

Secondary schooling materials used from 1935 into the late 1940s reproduced the primary level's negative view of "the entry of Egypt under Roman rule," as the new rulers saw the country only as a "field through which to provision the people of Rome" from its agricultural riches. Older students, however, encountered their forebears' own historical agency even during the pharaonic twilight, as "the Egyptians tried from time to time to lift the yoke of foreign rule." This would prepare young Egyptians to view events during the Muhammad 'Ali era as a continuation or reawakening of the indomitable national spirit.

Finally, Christianity's entry into the land provided another opportunity to review the present-relevant patterns of Egypt's history. The new religion found eager acceptance due to a readiness for monotheism. More important, as the first to espouse monasticism, Egyptians made an essential contribution to Christian history by providing the world with one of the fundamentals of medieval civilization.[42] In this respect, secondary schooling matched quite closely the *ibtida'i* narrative regarding Christianity. Rather than a discussion of it as an autonomous religio-civilizational phenomenon, students in both levels of schooling encountered it solely in its (Egyptian national) Coptic manifestation, as a component of Roman instability in Egypt. According to a primary schooling text, since Christianity acquired many adherents in Egypt, when Diocletian "wanted the subjects to make him a deity, the Christians of Egypt would not submit . . . , so he oppressed, tortured, and massacred a great number . . . the period of Diocletian left a great imprint on the souls of the Copts." Such a presentation united a negative Egyptian historical view of the Roman period with the Coptic struggle itself, thereby demonstrating a nationhood continuing from the pharaonic period. Subsequent emperors supported a variant of Christianity "which did not represent the nation [*umma*] in the way that the native Copts [*al-qibt al-wataniyin*] did." Naturally, then, Egyptians "welcomed the Arabs when they conquered Egypt, spreading justice and freedom, under the leadership of the great hero 'Umar ibn al-'As.[43]

The Egyptian Muhammad 'Ali and the Egyptian People in Primary Curricula

Before reaching the towering figure of Muhammad 'Ali, the renewer of Egypt, students did learn something of the intervening 1,300 years. In pre-Ottoman Islamic Egypt, curricula recalled pharaonic patterns, by focusing on the continual return to Egyptian independence, as a sort of genetic predisposition not to be ruled by others. Here, the history of Egypt after "gaining independence [*istiqlal*] from the 'Abbasid state" was prominent in *ibtida'i* and *thanawi* levels, showing that Egypt recouped her ancient prestige and regional dominance.[44] Coverage of the Tulunid, Fatimid, and Ayyubid years also demonstrated a tendency to present successive dynasties *in* Egypt as becoming *of* Egypt, as had been the case with pharaohs, and would again be the case for Muhammad 'Ali. As for the post-1517 years, across the board, Ottoman Egypt was the dark "Turkish era." Whereas previous periods represented independence as a sovereign state (*dawla mustaqilla*), the Ottoman years recalled Roman occupation (*istila*) and domination by a foreign race. Egypt was constantly seized with rebellion and disturbance *(fitna wa idtirab)*,[45] the polar opposite of *nizam*. Curriculum and text writers from the 1920s to the 1940s could thus assert that poverty, urban-rural gaps, ignorance, and improper observance of Islam—all observable in contemporary Egypt—were a consequence not of inherent, insurmountable Egyptian character defects, but of Ottoman neglect.[46] More broadly, civilizational backwardness was not innately Egyptian, but could be blamed on (foreign) others.

In the Egyptian curricular presentation, the era of Muhammad 'Ali began with the arrival of the French, when Egypt's true character reemerged. The first, and perhaps the most important lesson young students learned was that even from the arrival of Napoleon, Egypt and her people were never the canvas upon which others acted. Rather, Egyptians themselves launched the country on a post-Ottoman trajectory. In the opening stages of the French campaign, the country's own notables interceded with Napoleon to elicit guarantees of safety for the people. In one text, a page of illustrations featured *shaykh*s prominently.[47] Later, indigenous Egyptian notables joined a representative council *(majlis niyabi)* initiated by Napoleon, through which they ensured "reliance of the Egyptians on themselves, and their participation in administration of the country." Later French "insensitivity to Egyptian religious feeling" elicited further manifestations of Egyptian self-reliance, as "the flame of revolution [*thawra*] flared up in Cairo, and the residents of Cairo rose, struggling for their freedom."[48] In the review section of his text, one author summed up the significance of Egyptian actions for political development:

> The Egyptians . . . felt the responsibility placed upon their
> shoulders—the responsibility of expelling the French from their
> country—and undertook the revolution against Napoleon. . . .
> And this was the first time the Egyptians stood up in the face of the
> Europeans and the conquerors since the loss of their independence.
> And they began to feel their power, just as from that time they
> began to be quite impressed by European methods. . . . And in such
> a manner, they [Egyptians] laid the basis for the modern awakening
> which Muhammad 'Ali undertook.

The Egyptian people reemerged onto the stage of history as self-conscious actors, and their "exercise in representative rule [*hukm niyabi*] during the time of Napoleon rendered them unsatisfied by anything else."[49] For Egyptian educators then, the liminal Napoleon episode signaled a revitalization of Egypt's character, establishing its course as well as cultural associations for the future. Most importantly, by viewing developments in this manner, Egyptian students could espouse a conviction in the capacity of Egyptians for self-reliance and agency; their commitment to independence; and the long pedigree of parliamentarism in Egypt. Indeed, Egyptian students found that their forebears prepared themselves for Muhammad 'Ali's arrival by claiming their destiny of their own accord, just as some might believe that Egyptian parliamentary life in the 1920s and 1930s was a necessary outgrowth of Egyptians' own actions and predilections.

Turning to Muhammad 'Ali himself, text writers portrayed the founder of Egypt's ruling dynasty in unabashedly effusive terms. In what became an enduring formula of Egyptian curricular orthodoxy from the 1920s on, texts indicated that "Muhammad 'Ali is considered the creator [founder; *munshi*] of modern Egypt, for he is the inventor of the basis of Egypt's current awakening, and it is he who exalted the status of Egypt during his period such that it attained the rank of the most developed European states."[50] Students thus encountered a world-class leader whose personal characteristics set him apart, and were worth emulating by individual Egyptian students. In Muhammad 'Ali's dealings with Europeans, Ottomans, and local grandees, curricularists pointed to the pasha's nobility (*basala*), far-sightedness (*bu'd al-nazar*), perceptiveness (*basara*), sharp wit and mental discernment (*thaqib al-fikr wa-l-daha'*), and good fortune (*hasan al-tali'*) in turning events to Egypt's advantage.[51]

Even more important to state curriculum writers was the nature of the relationship between the Egyptian people and their new, foreign-born leader. Rather than a subordinate relationship to a foreign adventurer, students found a concrete *link* between Muhammad 'Ali and the Egyptian people. Already in the precarious months just after the French departure, Muhammad 'Ali earned the acceptance of Egyptians, as they grasped that "he was their only defender against the injustice of the [Ottoman] governor and the oppression of the Mamluks."[52] Likewise, Muhammad 'Ali had felt an affinity toward the people (*al-sha'b al-misri*), who "felt within themselves the power which had appeared during their revolt against Napoleon, savored the taste of victory and the taste of rule as well, . . . and who desired the independence of their country." The new Egyptian leader grasped that "the power of the Egyptian people is eternal, so he worked from the very beginning for the victory of it [the people's power], and [sought] to shelter in it and rely on it." Rather than selfish ambition, Muhammad 'Ali only undertook to rule in response to popular Egyptian acclaim. Just as a group of *'ulama'* and notables asserted their new-found social leadership status by proclaiming Muhammad 'Ali governor, the masses *(al-ahali)* "encouraged him and supported him with all their strength." Thus, rather than a victory solely for an Albanian interloper, through Muhammad 'Ali's ascent "the power of the Egyptian people was victorious yet again in history, and its prestige rose," while the founder of Egypt's ruling dynasty proved the "only man who could salvage the country from this chaos" of Ottoman-Mamluk conflict.[53]

As such, the curricular portrayal of the 1920s–30s contradicts the general direction of western contemporary scholarly historiography regarding Muhammad 'Ali, according to which Egypt was nothing more for him that an asset or property *(mulk)* to exploit for his own selfish political and material goals. This excessive curricular hagiography served a purpose. In a new political order whose foundations were ostensibly parliamentary democracy and popular political participation, state educators sought to cultivate in emerging citizens acceptance of a monarchy descending from foreign roots. By casting Muhammad 'Ali as truly concerned for the Egyptian masses, wedded to Egyptian nationalist causes, and as having come to power through the nation's will, curriculum writers countered the potential view of Muhammad 'Ali dynasty as just one more set of foreign interlopers—at the same time as they implicitly communicated a sense of cohesive Egyptian nationhood projected back to the beginning of the nineteenth century.

Primary school history then proceeded to a detailed description of Muhammad 'Ali's military campaigns into Arabia, the Sudan, Morea, and ultimately against the Ottoman sultanate itself. Nearly all of these activities were portrayed as undertaken either with the interests of Egyptians in mind, or in order to exalt the global status of the Egyptian nation, in spite of the material and physical hardships such adventures imposed upon the students' forebears. Thus, while modern scholarship has shown us that most of Muhammad 'Ali's initiatives for centralization and expansion caused dislocation, hardship, and opposition at home in Egypt,[54] according to curriculum writers in the 1920s and early 1930s, some of the most onerous intrusions into Egyptians' lives were even welcomed. Muhammad 'Ali's military—which entailed conscription, separation from families, and often death—received quite favorable coverage: "from the formation of the army Egypt reaped inestimable cultural and national benefits, for the army was the emblem of its [Egypt's] unity, and the spirit of its order."[55] In the same way, though the Egyptian government's veritable nationalization of agriculture restricted land ownership, commodity production choices, and prices, text writers chose to emphasize the ruler's attention to irrigation, transportation and agricultural training. "And he extended the hand of help to the *fallah* as well by giving him tools and livestock."

Ultimately, students were to come away from study of these years with a conception of Muhammad 'Ali as a flawless leader who cared for the people, and whose reforms were stymied only by European intrusion and interference. Both primary and secondary schooling thus portrayed the struggle against and effects of foreign intrusion *(tadakhkhul ajnabi)* as a major dynamic of Egypt since the end of the Mamluk era. This resonated with contemporary affairs visible to students, such as continual Egyptian attempts to renegotiate its relationship with Britain from the 1920s to 1950s. In this sense students encountered the dominant theme of post-1750 Egyptian history as a cycle whereby foreign penetration was followed by indigenous response, empowerment, and acquisition of growing freedom of action, which was then halted just short of its ultimate goals by imperialistic interests. This theme did not, however, obscure the fact that by the end of Muhammad 'Ali's tenure, "Egypt won the corner-stone of its independence, for Muhammad 'Ali was able to found a ruling dynasty whose members devoted care to exalting Egypt and elevating it culturally and materially."[56] All responsible, patriotic Egyptian rulers had done the same since Menes. Broadly speaking, then, the glorification of Egypt's rulers from Menes to Muhammad 'Ali was aimed at teaching acceptance of strong rulers, hence Fu'ad and Faruq by extension.

Deepening the Muhammad 'Ali Portrayal in Secondary Schooling

By 1930s, secondary students had a common canonical text for study of the Muhammad 'Ali years. Entitled *The Political History of Egypt in Modern Times (Ta'rikh Misr al-siyasi fi-l-azmina al-haditha)*, it had been composed in its first edition in 1920 by Muhammad Rif'at under commission from the Ministry of Education. Seven years later, it became required reading in the Higher Teachers College on whose faculty Rif'at served, and remained so until 1952. By 1932, Rif'at had revised his text to extend into the post-British era of Egyptian history, after which the book became the standard secondary school text for fourth-year modern Egyptian history. Rif'at was among that first generation of Egyptian historians-cum-educationists described above: after obtaining a Masters degree in history from the

University of Liverpool, he combined teaching and academic research with off-and-on service in the Ministry of Education, before assuming senior posts in the ministry from the 1940s, becoming minister in 1952. At several points in his career he contributed to school texts,[57] and represented the Ministry of Education in teachers conferences during the 1940s.[58] His *Political History of Egypt in Modern Times* directly communicated the state educational vision of history's contemporary nationalist significance.

Rif'at introduced his readers to the founder of the ruling dynasty as possessing the "genius, determination, and courage" to succeed where Mamluks, French, and Ottomans had failed: "and one man succeeded . . . because he realized in his sagacity and sharp-wittedness the manifestations of emergent Egyptian patriotism [*wataniya misriya*], and worked with and for it." Throughout his first years in Egypt, Muhammad 'Ali's conduct toward other competitors for power "proved to the Egyptian people that he did not have personal goals, . . . and that he undertook to serve the Egyptian interest." In this standard secondary history text, an almost emotional bond of affection then resulted between ruler and people: on their own initiative, Cairene notables had approached Muhammad 'Ali to become the Egyptian leader, just as in the ensuing years, an identity of interest emerged between Muhammad 'Ali and their forebears. Students learned that contrary to any selfish motives, Muhammad 'Ali wished "to build *for Egypt and himself* an exalted position and deep-rooted glory."

Rif'at's analysis of Muhammad 'Ali's outmaneuvering of the British during their short-lived campaign in 1807–1808 highlighted these themes: "Muhammad 'Ali overcame the greatest danger threatening him until that time in his new life, and love for him multiplied in the hearts of the Egyptians, such that he became in their eyes the hero of Egypt and the protector of its cherished honor." Moving farther beyond the *ibtida'i* approach, the author emphasized that Muhammad 'Ali also restored Egypt to its rightful global status, as "the name of Muhammad 'Ali reached the ears of Europe."[59]

An important analytical device employed by Rif'at involved discussing motives and results for Muhammad 'Ali's initiatives. Broadly, students needed to grasp that a desire for reform (*islah*) and increase of Egyptian welfare underpinned all Muhammad 'Ali's actions, especially as regards unpopular or costly initiatives. For example, though learning that the campaign against the Wahhabis was undertaken at great cost for Egypt in material and human terms, secondary school students were encouraged to

focus on the resultant elimination of the Mamluks and Albanian mercenaries, "whose effect in Egypt had been only ruin, destruction, wars, and
famine . . . [and] who stood as a stumbling-block in front of Muhammad
'Ali in the path of reform."

The campaign in the Sudan was even more costly for Egyptians. By
focusing on intentions, however, Rif'at evoked a positive evaluation of
the Muhammad 'Ali dynasty. The primary reason for the campaign was,
as with the Wahhabi adventure, to remove the Albanian forces from
Egypt so they could not "distract him from his reforms." Further, Rif'at
cautioned students to "not forget the interest and concern of Muhammad
'Ali for the Nile . . . upon which rests the irrigation of the country, . . . and
its people." As for the campaign's results, Rif'at did indicate that it failed
to acquire gold, new markets, or new soldiers, but chose to balanced this
with benefits: "the Red Sea became an Egyptian lake, and Muhammad
'Ali ensured for Egypt control of the sources of the water of the Nile, and
opened up a broad arena for Egyptians in commerce and exploitation."[60]

Recounting certain reforms' drawbacks and then overshadowing
them through discussion of the benefits also characterized exploration of
Muhammad 'Ali's entire approach, presented to students as a coherent program worthy of praise and emulation in individual citizens' lives between
the 1920s and 1940s. The hardship and dislocation for great numbers of
Egyptians of forming of a large army paled in comparison to its benefits
for the national collective:

Egypt derived from the army inestimable cultural and national benefits
[fawa'id adabiya wataniya]. The army was the symbol of its [Egypt's]
unity, since Copt and Muslim were equal in it, and it established
within the country an orderly nationalist spirit [ruh nizami qawmi]
that had been lost for centuries, while the country was secured from
the afflictions of the oppressive and chaotic groups. And we must
not forget the patriotic spirit that was born following the army's
formation, for Egyptians would compete in the arena of [martial]
faculties, and the spirit of confidence and pride pervaded their hearts.

Students might thus understand that it was Muhammad 'Ali they
could thank for a unified nation, a reinvigorated martial spirit, and inter-
confessional harmony guaranteeing social orderliness. Just as important,
and none-too-implicitly, students would see that such traits were actually
primordial Egyptian qualities developed in antiquity and then renewed

by the founder of the current monarchy. Likewise, they—or curriculum writers—could claim that such accomplishments could be taken as a given as far back as the 1820s.

In the same vein, discussion of the constraints put on peasants by agricultural reforms was balanced by details on the tremendous increase in national wealth and economic autonomy. Rif'at was also prepared to criticize educational efforts, though more important in this regard was Muhammad 'Ali's desire that "indigenous Egyptians [*al-wataniyin*] possess all the privileges of the foreigners" culturally and intellectually. Likewise, in spite of the government now being more intrusive and demanding, "it does not escape us that the credit goes to Muhammad 'Ali for dividing up actions of the government, and working with good intent and faithful determination for progress and uplift [*taqaddum wa irtiqa'*]." The ultimate assessment of the Muhammad 'Ali years appeared as unbiased analysis, yet exonerated and celebrated him while focusing on his intent to help the Egyptian people in the context of particularly Egyptian circumstances:

> It is unjust to judge Muhammad 'Ali according to the criteria
> of the West, . . . for the system of monopolies and conscription
> was—unfortunately—necessary . . . and there was no other way
> to protect Egypt and prevent it from falling under Turkish rule
> again. . . . Ultimately, we see that if we take into account the special
> circumstances in which Muhammad 'Ali appeared, and if we know the
> magnitude of the duty which he undertook to perform in the midst
> of that chaos [*fawda*], ignorance [*jahl*], oppressions, and intrigues
> prevalent in Egypt and Turkey, we must consider as an indication of
> his brilliance his success in ruling Egypt, as well as those influences
> and reforms that immortalized, and the role he played in the
> European diplomatic world.[61]

Taken together, students were to view Muhammad 'Ali as an Egyptian ruler of unrivaled power, farsightedness, and concern for his people. At the same time, they encountered a highly positive evaluation of military service. Though celebration of martial attributes and military service is not an approach associated with Egyptian thinking of this era, both language texts and articles in student-compiled magazines featured it, as covered below. They could also see that Egypt's not entirely European nature, or its particular route into modernity, was not abnormal, but uniquely proper to Egypt—at the same time as they saw an Egypt much more European, and much more important to the larger world, than their neighbors to the south or east. Finally, students might view their history and contemporary world in terms of key dichotomies—such as chaos and order, ignorance and uplift—resonating with lessons encountered in primary and secondary school civics.

Even more than in primary school, however, the secondary curriculum cast students' recent forebears as active partners in determining the national destiny, from the very beginning of Egypt's modern period. In this respect, Rif'at accorded great importance to the French period, during which Napoleon set up a National Council (*diwan watani*) to "join indigenous elements in government for the first time in modern Egyptian history." Later, however, harsh French measures elicited a national-religious revolt (*thawra*) on the part of Cairene masses, who "took matters into their own hands . . . for the sake of the nation." A major result of the French campaign was thus to show Egyptians "the possibility of relying on themselves instead of the Mamluks. . . . And the principle of election rather than appointment to positions. . . . In such manner the Egyptians acquired practice during the French presence in undertaking their share in ruling the country, and this training had its impact on future events."[62] Egyptians themselves had gone on to choose Muhammad 'Ali as leader. In this respect they proved unique in the region for advocating their own political causes, just as Rif'at could portray Egyptian history from this period as a linear, natural progression culminating with the events of 1919 and the resultant parliamentary order. This too could make Egyptians consider themselves distinct from their neighbors in North Africa and the Arab world, who could not point to nineteenth-century progress to independence and representative government during the twentieth century.

As seen here in discussion of the army and other matters during the Muhammad 'Ali years, Rif'at emphasized equal Coptic contribution to Egyptian uplift. Likewise, discussing the French period, he indicated that "people from all [confessional] groups were enthusiastic and helped each other to seize the opportunity to rise up in the face of the French. . . . And the Copts were not at all less nationalist than the Muslims." The message here appears clear, but was implicitly ambiguous. Students could on the one hand see that regardless of religious difference Egyptians had (and could) unite behind common nationalist causes. On the other hand, by singling out the Copts to assure readers of their nationalist loyalty, curriculum may have inadvertently (or purposefully?) suggested that such loyalty could not be assumed, and that even in the era between the 1919 and 1952 Revolutions, the Copts might remain a special case in an otherwise Muslim Egypt. Curriculum writers alerting students to the need for national unity could not avoid Coptic particularity.

Conclusion

The pharaonic epoch and the era of Muhammad 'Ali were not only separated by a gap of three millennia, but they were both temporally distant from the constitutional monarchy as experienced by adolescents and young citizens. To the extent that these two periods represent the zenith of national accomplishment, the overall school narrative thus inferred that young Egyptians of the 1920s–40s were living through the coda of national glory. This approach differs from Egypt's neighbors in the same years, such as Republican Turkey, Zionist Palestine, and Pahlavi Iran, where students were encouraged to perceive themselves as living through and contributing to the most dynamic eras of their nation.[63] Still, notwithstanding the distance in time separating the pharaohs and Muhammad 'Ali from young Egyptians, and even though curriculum inferred that the latter were emerging in the afterglow of national accomplishments, state education used both earlier eras to communicate important present-oriented lessons regarding the motive forces of Egyptian history meant to condition citizen conduct.

To be sure, state educational curricula do not 'prove' what students believed. Messages in educational discourse, state syllabi, and textbooks most accurately convey convictions held by pedagogical experts, educational planners, academic and semi-academic writers, and teachers animating the nationalist educational project in constitutional monarchy Egypt. By contrast, evaluating student reception of the pedagogical message remains a precarious enterprise. Student diaries composed at the time remain beyond our reach; likewise, rather than illuminating contemporary experiences and attitudes, interviewing Egyptians who were students in between 1919 and 1952, or probing their memoirs for references to their schooling experiences, runs the risk of highlighting how intervening decades have colored memory.[64]

A relatively unstudied source, however, consists of student magazines from these years, which provide a certain insight to student views. From the 1920s into the 1950s, Egyptian primary and secondary school students composed several magazines. The initiative either of school-based literary clubs or administrations, such magazines were published on a semesterly or yearly basis. Their reliability as indicators of student attitudes is debatable: teachers edited them, and school administrations vetted submissions, which often originated as essays in language, history, or civics classes. Still, though covering a broad gamut of topics, material from these magazines proves remarkable in the extent to which it echoes ideas presented above. Cover illustrations of magazines routinely included pharaonic imagery, often combined with pictures of Muhammad 'Ali and representatives of the ruling dynasty.[65] Likewise, students frequently wrote about ancient Egyptian civilization and its physical remains, often based on school field trips.[66] Such essays often appeared along with patriotic poems,[67] historical articles on the Muhammad 'Ali era, and extended discourses on the meaning of the nation and Egypt's civilizational destiny—reinforcing the association among pharaohs, the ruling dynasty, nationalism, and modernity.[68] Additionally, articles about the Egyptian army were a much more prominent feature of these magazines than current scholarly understandings of the constitutional era would suggest.[69] In this sense, students from the 1920s through the 1940s demonstrated an amplified attraction to particular aspects of their nationalist curriculum.

Perhaps the clearest indication that Egyptian students absorbed the curricular message during these years is a poem enumerating Egypt's heroes and their qualities, published in the May 1939 edition of the Helwan secondary school magazine. Along with 'Umar bin al-'As and Salah al-Din—generals who facilitated Egypt's rise as an Islamic land and then guaranteed its "independent" hegemony in the Arab Islamic world—the student included Mina, Thutmose, and Muhammad 'Ali. Mina's greatness sprung from his direction of the Nile waters to "make fertile the Valley as you see it / for it is indeed a majestic act / from which we benefit every year." As for Thutmose, though his reign was long ago, "in every era his mention is [as] new," due to his conquest of vast areas for national glory. "Egypt became the finest of great capitals [ghurrat al-amsar], and in that era the master of the seas." Muhammad 'Ali, however, was the greatest of Egyptians:

The master of grandeur and determined resoluteness and [clear] vision / and the creator of the Nile barrages / he who drove the Mamluks to destruction / when he saw them as the reason for the malady of confusion / And he battled [in] the Levant and Greece / and made the Hijaz and the Sudan submit.[70]

Like the pharaohs, the progenitor of Egypt's ruling dynasty up to 1952 had ordered the country's internal politics, contributed to material and industrial uplift, and restored Egypt's regional dominance, due to laudable ethical qualities worthy of emulation. In literary form, students thus appropriated for themselves Egyptian education's themes. As these few comments imply, more analysis of this large body of material is vital, as it is likely to further corroborate the lessons of history for modern Egyptian citizenship during the constitutional era.

As seen here through curriculum, perhaps the central lesson involved the correlation of strong central government rule—be it pharaonic, monarchical, or parliamentary—with national sovereignty. Obedience to political, social, and familial superiors would ensure such strength through maintenance of order and prevention of chaos. Just as important, students encountered a post-1798 Egyptian reality of orderly progress toward democratic government, so what they were witnessing in Egypt during their lifetime was not a foreign, European import, but something at which Egyptians had long shown themselves proficient. Curriculum thus reflected quite well the convictions of educational experts and policy makers.[71] This democratic progress, however, could only be furthered by adherence to order (*nizam*) as opposed to chaos (*fawda*). Though beyond the Muhammad 'Ali years, this requirement emerged in particular in secondary school discussions of Colonel Ahmad 'Urabi, who in *ibtida'i* curricula was presented as no less than the unproblematic hero of the 1882 anti-British revolution. Likewise, according to Rif'at, because the 'Urabi movement (*haraka*) emerged partially to establish "constitutional rule in the country and to guarantee the principles of liberty, justice, and equality for all," it paralleled "the constitutional revolutions [*thawra*] which transpired in Europe and by which the history of the nineteenth century was distinguished." It thus reaffirmed that Egypt had rejoined western civilization.

Yet, the ordered working of people and ruler for national independence thus also became the criterion to judge Urabi. Here, the revolution failed as it publicly aggressed against the khedive. History class thus sought to communicate a sense that a central characteristic of modern Egyptian history—and the proper state of affairs—was the ordered, peaceful march of people and ruler toward ever greater participatory government and nationalist independence. Indeed, nationalism properly interpreted included democratic, popular, yet decorous rule. More broadly, ever since a stable dynasty had established itself on the banks of the Nile, Egypt had distinguished itself from other Eastern countries (such as the Ottomans and Arabs) where dynastic strife was the rule. This divergence from a politically decrepit East continued throughout the nineteenth century, as a conscious Egyptian political community with a common will had begun to act in concert. Egyptians were thus indeed equal to Europeans, and merited a politics similar to that found in Europe. This entailed standing up for freedom, democratic political participation, and national sovereignty. Yet, rather than military coups subverting legitimate leadership, young Egyptian citizens needed to remember that truly effective politics encapsulated all social groups while remaining respectful of order, the monarchy, and those social elites endowed with political prowess.

A second frequently reiterated historical lesson for young Egyptian's modern lives involved the need to continue the lasting bond of reverence and loyalty begun by their ancestors to the Muhammad 'Ali dynasty, the inheritor of the pharaonic legacy, which fundamentally identified with Egyptian national goals and the betterment of the Egyptian people. Again, students in both *ibtida'i* and *thanawi* schooling learned this lesson in connection with Muhammad 'Ali's descendants as well. These lessons recurred on the primary and secondary level synergistically with curricular subjects beyond history.

Third, by reaching back all the way in to the mists of pharaonic time, curriculum writers sought to communicate to new citizens a conviction in an enduring Egyptianness, which always could achieve regional dominance. This national character permitted common Egyptians themselves to form their own destiny, while the Egyptian national essence also distinguished them from neighbors. It is important to bear this in mind in relation to Arabs, since existing scholarship emphasizes the turn away from pharaonism and a territorial nationalism celebrating the Muhammad 'Ali dynasty in favor of a more Arabist and Islamist attitude among Egyptian intellectuals in the 1930s and 1940s.[72] Yet, school materials continued to focus on the pharaonic-territorial Egyptian nationalism up until the 1950s, communicating an antiquity — Muhammad 'Ali dynasty linkage with implications for young students' conduct. As regards Arabs, state curricula from the 1920s up until the July 1952 coup did not conceive of them as kin to Egyptians. From the 1920s on, primary curricula portrayed Arabs as "an exalted nation, ancient of lineage, mighty, of strong intellect, and inclined to freedom and self-respect." Still, pre-Islamic Arabs were distinct from Egyptians, with discussion of them in separate sections of texts not at all integrated with the Egyptian narrative. Here, students encountered Arabs as different from Egyptians, yet possessing laudable qualities rendering them worthy of affinity.

Secondary school texts set out an even more nuanced relationship between Arabs and Egypt. Texts during these years approached pre- and early Islamic Arabs in quite positive terms. Yet, by juxtaposing "the establishment of the Arab state and a description of Islamic civilization," and by asserting that through Islam, "the Arabs became one nation [*umma*] . . . conforming in ethnicity, language, and emotions," Egyptian curricula cast early Islam and the Umayyad dynasty as a firmly Arab phenomenon. In a sense, just as pharaonic religion had been for ancient Egyptians, Islam in its pristine form became the Arabs' national experience. Leaving aside instructors' presentation, an important curricular message was that Arabs were noble, alike in linguistic, religious, and historical terms; at the same time, Egyptians comprised a distinct people. Though kindred, Arabs were not yet kin in the curricula of these years. For nationalist pedagogues, teachers, and school curriculum, therefore, themes focusing on pharaonism, Egyptian distinctiveness, Islam, modernism, and mild affinity for Arabs coexisted more than has been assumed in contemporary scholarship.

Fourth, as seen here, curriculum assured students that rather than passive objects, their forebears had been active participants in Egypt's history, particularly in the modern era. The discussion here thus revises recent ventures into curricular analysis.[73] As a conclusion to the present inquiry, it is equally important to note that the school history narrative highlighting common Egyptians' contributions to Egyptian history also contradicted the approach of prominent Egyptian academic historians from the 1920s to the 1940s. Muhammad Shafiq Ghurbal's *The Beginnings of the Egyptian Question* provides just one example. On several matters he agreed with the curricular presentation. The latter had proclaimed "Muhammad 'Ali is considered the creator [*munshi'*] of modern Egypt"; Ghurbal declared forthrightly that "Mehemet Ali made modern Egypt." Likewise, just as curricula covering both the Muhammad 'Ali era and the pharaonic years had valued order and a strong central government, *The Beginnings of the Egyptian Question* praised Muhammad 'Ali's "orderly system of government" and "a highly centralized authority" able to "create a healthier moral tone." Similarly, both school history and Ghurbal's academic narrative portrayed the pre-Muhammad 'Ali years as one long dark age after Fatimid and Ayyubid greatness.[74]

Regarding the Egyptian people themselves, however, school children and adolescents saw a very different history from that which Ghurbal's readers encountered. Whereas curriculum promoted the idea of societally- and politically-engaged residents of the Nile Valley conscious of being Egyptians at least as early as 1798, these same Egyptians were nearly absent from Ghurbal's text, or were visible only as an undifferentiated, apathetic, and atavistic mass inhibiting Muhammad 'Ali and Egypt's progress. The Egyptians' "dull apathy, . . . the trait of the oriental" was entirely unequal to the circumstances presented by the French arrival, and even the local notables and religious leaders—praised in school texts for leadership and acclamation of Muhammad 'Ali—were consumed with "accumulation of wealth and the cultivation of the powers that be."[75] In the face of such "miserable natives," the new dynasty "spared no effort in forcing the Egyptians to become a regimented nation," in spite of their seemingly genetic disposition toward inaction.[76] In short, while academicians and educational planners both sought to praise the ruling dynasty and affirm Egypt's progress toward modernity, Ghurbal dismissed the role of Egyptians themselves. By contrast, school history, and its echoes in civics and language class, strove to incorporate students' forebears into the recent national past as subjects and not merely objects, while it communicated a guide for present and future requirements of citizenship. Several coexisting, even conflicting understandings of national history in Egypt during this period thus had different audiences, and in the case of students, the national history they encountered was deliberately crafted into a programmatic narrative. More than historical accuracy, this narrative was concerned with teaching sociopolitical traits suitable to a modernizing state stewarded by a monarch deserving loyalty and an emotional bond, as well as a parliamentary system animated by participation and order.

Notes

1   Maurice Halbwachs, *On Collective Memory*, ed., trans., and intro. Lewis A. Coser (Chicago: University of Chicago Press, 1992).

2   Miroslav Hroch, "From National Movement to Fully-Formed Nation: The Nation-Building Process in Europe," *New Left Review* 198, 1993, 4–6.

3   Eric Hobsbawm, "Mass-Producing Traditions: Europe, 1870–1914," in E. Hobsbawm & T. Ranger, eds., *The Invention of Tradition* (Cambridge: Cambridge University Press, 1983), 264–65. Also see Hobsbawm's *Nations and Nationalism since 1780* (2nd ed.; Cambridge: Cambridge University Press, 1992); David Miller, *On Nationality* (Oxford: Clarendon Press, 1995), 141–44; Etienne Balibar, "The Nation Form: History and Ideology," in E. Balibar and Immanuel Wallerstein, *Race, Nation, Class: Ambiguous Identities* (London: Verso, 1991), 90–96.

4   See Anthony Gorman, *Historians, State and Politics in Twentieth-Century Egypt: Contesting the Nation* (London: RoutledgeCurzon, 2003), 13; Albert Hourani, *Arabic Thought in the Liberal Age, 1798–1939* (London: Cambridge University Press, 1983), 67–82.

5   Anthony Gorman, *Historians, State and Politics in Twentieth-Century Egypt* 22–27; Barak A. Salmoni, "Pedagogies of Patriotism: Teaching Socio-Political Community in Twentieth-

Century Turkish and Egyptian Education" (Ph.D. diss., Harvard University, 2002), 125–47; also, see the chapter by Arthur Goldschmidt in this volume.

6 Shafiq Ghurbal, *Tarikh al-mufawadat al-misriya al-britaniya, al-juz' al-awwal* (Cairo: Maktabat al-Nahda al-Misriya, 1952), i–ii; Shafik Ghorbal, *The Beginnings of the Egyptian Question and the Rise of Mehemet Ali: A Study in the Diplomacy of the Napoleonic Era* (London: G. Routledge, 1928), 210.

7 Wizarat al-Ma'arif al-'Umumiya, *Manhaj al-ta'lim al-ibtida'i li-l-banin wa-l-banjat, mu'aqqat* (Cairo: al-Matba'a al-Amiriya, 1930), 47–49.

8 See Barak A. Salmoni, "Pedagogies of Patriotism," 842, 999–1001, 1011.

9 Wizarat al-Ma'arif al-'Umumiya, *Madaris al-hukuma al-misriya: manhaj al-ta'lim al-ibtida'i li-l-banin wa-l-banat* (Cairo: al-Matba'a al-Amiriya, 1924).

10 Wizarat al-Ma'arif al-'Umumiya, *Manhaj al-ta'lim al-ibtida'i li-l-banin wa-l-banjat, mu'aqqat* (Cairo: al-Matba'a al-Amiriya, 1935), 47.

11 Wizarat al-Ma'arif, *Madaris al-hukuma al-misriya: manhaj al-ta'lim al-ibtida'i li-l-banin wa-l-banat* (Cairo: al-Matba'a al-Amiriya, 1935), 52. Henceforth *Ibtida'i li-l-banin wa-l-banat '35.*

12 *Taqrir wazir al-ma'arif 'an ta'lim al-thanawi: 'uyubuhu wa wasa'il islahihi* (Cairo: al-Matba'a al-Amiriya, 1935), 25.

13 Muhammad Amin Hasuna, "Taqrir hamm," *Majallat al-tarbiya al-haditha* 9: 1 (October 1935), 4.

14 See Wizarat al-Ma'arif al-'Umumiya, *Manahij al-madaris al-ibtida'iya li-l-banin wa-l-banat* (Cairo: al-Matba'a al-Amiriya, 1949); idem., *Manhaj al-ta'lim al-thanawi li-l-banin* (Cairo: al-Matba'a al-Amiriya, 1947); idem., *Manahij al-dirasa li-l-marhala al-mutawassita li-l-banin wa-l-banat* (Cairo: al-Matba'a al-Amiriya, 1949).

15 See Donald M. Reid, *Whose Pharaohs? Archeology, Museums, and Egyptian National Identity from Napoleon to World War One* (Berkeley: University of California Press, 2002); idem., "Indigenous Egyptology: the Decolonization of a Profession?" *Journal of the American Oriental Society* 105: 2 (1985), 233–46.

16 Wizarat al-Ma'arif al-'Umumiya, *Madaris al-hukuma al-misriya: manhaj al-ta'lim al-ibtida'i li-l-banin wa-l-banat*, 7, 14. Henceforth *Ibtida'i '24.*

17 Major Savage, Salim Hasan Effendi, Shaykh Ahmad al-Iskandari, 'Umar al-Iskandari Effendi, *Safwat ta'rikh Misr wa-l-duwal al-'arabiya, al-juz' al-awwal* (Cairo: Matba'at al-Ma'arif, 1928), 5. Henceforth *STM1*. This was the eleventh printing of the text, reaching back to 1919.

18 Wizarat al-Ma'arif al-'Umumiya, *Manhaj al-ta'lim al-thanawi li-l-banin* (Cairo: al-Matba'a al-Amiriya, 1935), 155. Henceforth *Thanawi '35.*

19 *STM1*, 24, 27.

20 *Ibtida'i '24*, 14.

21 *STM1*, 13–14, 15–16.

22 Ibid., 23, 24.

23 *Ibtida'i '24*, 14, 15.

24 *STM1*, 24, 27.

25 These include Ahmad Lutfi al-Sayyid and Muhammad Husayn Haykal. See Israel Gershoni and James Jankowski. *Egypt, Islam, and the Arabs* (Oxford: Oxford University Press, 1986), 11–15, 33–39.

26 Ahmad al-'Awamiri, Ahmad 'Ali 'Abbas, 'Awad Lutfi Ahmad, 'Abbas Hasan, *al-Mutala'a al-mukhtara li-l-madaris al-ibtida'iya, juz' III, Sana III* (Cairo: al-Matba'a al-Amiriya, 1946), 152–154, 335; also see I. Mustafa, M.A. al-Ibrashi, M.S. 'Abd al-Latif, A.M. al-Shafi'i, 'Abd al-'Azzam, H. 'Abd al-Qadir, compiler, *al-Mutala'a al-'arabiya li-l-madaris al-ibtida'iya, al-juz' III, al-Sana III* (Cairo: Matba'at al-Ma'arif, 1945), 39.

27 *STM1*, 29, 36–37, 46–47.

28 Ibid., 63.

29 For educators' discourse, see Amir Buqtur, "Ahamm mabadi' al-tarbiya," *Majallat al-tarbiya al-haditha* 7: 1 (September 1933), 37; Husni al-Naggar Ahmad, "Kayfa nurabbi al-tifl 'ala al-hurriya," *Sahifat al-ta'lim al-ilzami* 1:6 (February 1934), 19; Girgis Mikha'il, "al-Nizam fi madarisina,"

Majallat al-tarbiya al-haditha 22: 2 (December 1948), 127–29. For state guidelines and language texts communicating the very same values, both in reference to the pharaonic era, as well as the contemporary duties of Egyptians, see *Ibtida'i li-l-banin wa-l-banat '35*, 24–27; al-'Awamiri et al., *al-Mutala'a al-mukhtara li-l-madaris al-ibtida'iya, juz' III, Sana III*, 39–40, 65, 75–76, 140; Ahmad al-'Awamiri, Ahmad 'Ali 'Abbas, 'Awad Lutfi Ahmad, 'Abbas Hasan, *al-Mutala'a al-mukhtara li-l-madaris al-ibtida'iya, juz' II, sana II* (Cairo: Maktabat al-Hilal, n.d.), 95–96.

30 Ibid., 83, 87, 90, 91.

31 As Misako Ikeda discusses in her chapter, an entirely different "elementary" *(awwali / ilzami)* track of education existed. For free, it was meant for the lower urban and rural economic classes as a terminal track. Graduates were able to proceed on to *thanawi* schooling only with the greatest difficulty. For British-era educational policies, see David C. Kinsey, "Egyptian Education Under Cromer: A Study in East-West Encounter in Educational Administration and Policy, 1883–1907" (Ph.D. diss., Harvard University, 1965); M. Richard Van Vleck, "British Educational Policy in Egypt Relative to British Imperialism in Egypt, 1882–1922" (Ph.D. diss., University of Wisconsin, Madison, 1990).

32 *Thanawi '35*, 158.

33 Ibrahim Numayr Sayf al-Din, Zaki 'Ali, Ahmad Nagib Hashim, *Misr fi al-usur al-qadima* (Cairo: Matba'at al-Ma'arif, 1939–40), 9, 3, 73, 87, 88.

34 See G. Idgar, M. Shafiq Ghurbal, *Kitab al-ta'rikh al-qadim, li-talamidh al-sana al-ula al-thanawiya* (Cairo: Matba'at al-Ma'arif, 1931), 45–48.

35 Sayf al-Din, 'Ali, Hashim, *Misr fi al-usur al-qadima*, 91.

36 *Thanawi '35*, 159.

37 See "Hadith 'an al-najjah ma'a rajul najih: Wisa Wasif," *al-Hilal* 36: 4 (February 1928), 397; Muhammad 'Ali 'Alluba, *Mabadi' fi-l-siyasa al-misriya* (Cairo: Matba'at Dar al-Kutub al-Misriya, 1942), 202–205; Muhammad Husayn Haykal, *Mudhakkirat fi-l-siyasa al-misriya, al-juz' al-thani: 'abd al-faruq* (Cairo: Matba'at al-Nahda al-Misriya, 1953), 106–104,

38 See 'Abd al-'Aziz al-Bishri, *al-Tarbiya al-wataniya* (Cairo: Matba'at Dar al-Kutub, 1928), 2–6; Muhammad Rif'at and 'Abd al-'Aziz al-Bishri, *al-Tarbiya al-wataniya li-l-madaris al-thanawiya* (Cairo: al-Matba'a al-Amiriya, 1937/1949), 2–3.

39 See Barak A. Salmoni, "Pedagogies of Patriotism," 780–819, 940–61, 974–82; Firoozeh Kashani-Sabet, *Frontier Fictions: Shaping the Iranian Nation, 1804–1946* (Princeton: Princeton University Press, 1999).

40 Sayf al-Din, 'Ali, Hashim, *Misr fi al-usur al-qadima*, 138, 143, 145.

41 Ibid., 155, 158, 174.

42 Ibid., 159, 223, 225, 227.

43 *STM1*, 83, 87, 90, 91.

44 Major Savage, Salim Hasan Effendi, Shaykh Ahmad al-Iskandari, 'Umar al-Iskandari Effendi, *Safwat ta'rikh Misr wa-l-duwal al-'arabiya, al-juz' al-thani* (Cairo: Matba'at al-Ma'arif, 1930), 44, 45, 48. Henceforth, *STM2*.

45 *STM2*, 81; 'Umran Faraj al-Jumal, *Ta'rikh Misr al-hadith, li-l-sana al-rabi'a al-ibtida'iya* (Cairo: Matba'at Misr, 1930), 11. Henceforth *TMH*.

46 *TMH*, 13; 'Abd al-Rahim Muhammad 'Uthman and Shahata 'Isa Ibrahim, *Ta'rikh Misr al-ibtida'i, al-juz' al-thalith li-l-sana al-rabi'a al-ibtida'iya* (Cairo: Maktabat al-Matba'a al-Haditha, 1928–29), 14, 15. Henceforth *TMI*.

47 *TMI*, 28.

48 *TMH*, 30, 25

49 *TMI*, 37

50 *TMI*, 70

51 *TMI*, 40, 42, 46.

52 *TMH*, 35.

53 *TMI*, 41, 45.

54 See Khaled Fahmy, *All the Pasha's Men: Mehmed Ali, His Army, and the Making of Modern Egypt* (Cambridge: Cambridge University Press, 1997); F. Robert Hunter, *Egypt Under the Khedives, 1805–1879: From Household Government to Modern Bureaucracy* (Pittsburgh: University of Pittsburgh Press, 1984); Kenneth Cuno, *The Pasha's Peasants: Land, Society, and Economy in Lower Egypt, 1740–1858* (Cambridge: Cambridge University Press, 1992); Judith Tucker, "Decline of the Family Economy in Mid-Nineteenth Century Egypt," *Arab Studies Quarterly* 1, 1980, 245–71.

55 *TMH*, 43.

56 *TMI*, 67.

57 See, for example, Muhammad Rif'at and Muhammad Ahmad Hasuna, *Ma'alim ta'rikh al-usur al-wusta* (Cairo: al-Matba'a al-Amiriya, 1951); Muhammad Rif'at and 'Abd al-'Aziz al-Bishri, *al-Tarbiya al-wataniya li-l-madaris al-thanawiya*.

58 See Anthony Gorman, *Historians, State and Politics in Twentieth-Century Egypt*, 22–23; Khayr al-Din al-Zirikli, *al-A'lam* (Beirut: Dar al-'Ilm al-Malayin, 1986), 128.

59 Muhammad Rif'at, *Ta'rikh Misr al-siyasi fi al-azmina al-haditha, li-l-madaris al-thanawiya* (Cairo: al-Matba'a al-Rahmaniya, 1934), 50–51, 55, 53, 59. Italics added.

60 Ibid., 65, 69, 70, 73.

61 Ibid., 78, 86, 88, 128–29.

62 Ibid., 27, 29–31, 37, 43.

63 For Republican Turkey, see Barak A. Salmoni, "Turkish Knowledge for a Modern Life: Innovative Pedagogy and Nationalist Substance in Primary Schooling, 1927–1950," *Turkish Studies* 4: 3 (2003), 103–44; for Zionist Palestine, see Yael Zerubavel, *Recovered Roots: Collective Memory and the Making of Israeli National Tradition* (Chicago: University of Chicago Press, 1995), 39–144; Rachel Elboim-Dror, "Israeli Education: Changing Perspectives," *Israel Studies* 6: 1 (2001), 76–100; for Iran, see Rudi Mathee, "Transforming Dangerous Nomads into Useful Artisans, Technicians, Agriculturalists: Education in the Riza Shah Period," in Stephanie Cronin, ed., *The Making of Modern Iran: State and Society under Riza Shah* (London: Routledge, 2003).

64 For a well-conceived use of memoirs for this purpose, see Benjamin C. Fortna, *Imperial Classroom: Islam, the State, and Education in the Late Ottoman Empire* (London: Oxford University Press, 2002).

65 For examples, see *Majallat madrasat al-mahalla al-kubra al-thanawiya*; *Majallat madaris al-nahda al-misriya bi-l-Qahira*; *Majallat al-madrasa al-khudaywiya*.

66 Salah al-Din Mahmud Hamri, "Hisab al-Qabr 'ind Qudama' al-Misriyyin," *al-Mansura: mir'at al-bi'a al-madrasiya wa-l-iqlimiya, madrasat al-Mansura al-thanawiya* 13 (1938), 60–62; Girgis Farag, "Adab al-Fara'ina," *Majallat madrasat al-aqbat al-kubra* 10 (1946), 96–100; Ahmad Safwat, "Qadish . . . ," *Sahifat madaris al-Ahram* 1 (1932), 44–46; Gibran Nasif Mahrus, "al-Tarikh: Qudama' al-Misriyyun," *Majallat madrasat al-Fayyum al-thanawiya* (1933), 74–76; 'Abd al-Majid 'Ammar, "Misr wa majduha al-khalid bi-athariha," *Majallat al-madrasa al-ibrahimiya al-thanawiya* 1: 2 (1927), 16–17; 'A'isha Qandil, "Waqfa amam al-Nil," *Majallat madrasat al-Amira Fa'iza al-thanawiya li-l-banat bi-l-Iskandariya* 1: 1 (1935), 32–33; Hasan 'Abd al-Halim al-Yamani, "Misr al-Qadima," *Majallat al-madrasa al-khudaywiya* 5: 1 (1925), 22–24; Nagib Sulayman, "Qudama' al-misriyyin: akhlaquhum, 'aqa'iduhum, 'inayatuhum bi-mawtihim," *Majallat Shubra al-thanawiya al-amiriya li-l-banin* 3 (1929), 61–63.

67 See, for example, 'Ali 'Ali Shahin, "Ya Misr nahnu laki al-fada," *Majallat al-madrasa al-khudaywiya* 5: 3 (1925).

68 See Helwan M., "al-Wataniya;" Muhammad Wahid al-Din al-Rali, "al-Tadrib al-'askari;" idem., "Jawla fi madinat Ramsis," all in *Majallat madrasat Helwan al-thanawiya* (May 1939), 49, 60–61, 70–73.

69 Gamal al-Din Sayyid, "al-Jaysh al-misri," *al-Mansura: mir'at al-bi'a al-madrasiya wa-l-iqlimiya, madrasat al-Mansura al-thanawiya* 13 (1938), 82–83; "al-Tadrib al-'askari," Mustafa Samir Haydar,

"Hayatuna al-ijtima'iya: al-hafl al-'askari," Muhammad 'Abd al-Rahman, "al-Jundi ahaqq bi-l-'inaya min al-fallah," idem., "Ma'a jaysh Ibrahim," all in *Sahifat madrasat khudaywi Isma'il* 3 (1939), 7–10, 11–12, 31–32, 52–54; Muhammad 'Arifa al-Bishri, "al-Harb," *Sahifat madrasat Qibba al-thanawiya* 1 (May 1934), 73–75; Muhammad 'Adli Abaza, "Limadha ahibbtu an akun jundiyan," *Majallat madrasat al-Mahalla al-Kubra al-thanawiya* (1939), 15–16; Hanri Ibrahim Rizq, "al-Jundi al-Majhul," *Majallat al-madrasa al-'Ubaydiya, al-qism al-misri* 1 (1936–37), 70–71; Riyad Tawfiq, "Dim'a 'ala qubur al-shuhada'," *Majallat al-madrasa al-ibrahimiya al-thanawiya al-amiriya* 1: 1 (1926), 15–16.

70 'Abd al-Hamid Abu Sammara, "'Uzama' al-Rijal," *Majallat madrasat Helwan al-thanawiya* (May 1939), 36–37.

71 See Amir Buqtur, "al-Hurriya: ma laha wa ma 'alayha," *al-Hilal* 45: 1 (December 1936), 77–81; Muhammad Husayn Haykal, "al-Hurriya wa madluluha al-insani," *al-Hilal* 45: 1 (December 1936), 12–13; idem., "al-Dimuqratiya fi Misr," *al-Hilal* 34: 3 (December 1925), 241–46.

72 See Israel Gershoni and James Jankowski. *Egypt, Islam, and the Arabs*, and *Redefining the Egyptian Nation* (Cambridge: Cambridge University Press, 1995). For an earlier approach, see Nadav Safran, *Egypt in Search of Political Community: An Analysis of the Intellectual and Political Evolution of Egypt, 1804–1952* (Cambridge: Harvard University Press, 1961).

73 For the notion of Egyptian passivity in curricula, see Gabriel Piterberg, "The Tropes of Stagnation and Awakening in Nationalist Historical Consciousness," in Gershoni and Jankowski, eds., *Rethinking Nationalism in the Arab Middle East* (New York: Columbia University Press, 1997), 58–60.

74 Shafik Ghorbal, *The Beginnings of the Egyptian Question and the Rise of Mehemet Ali: A Study in the Diplomacy of the Napoleonic Era*, 284, 73, 209.

75 Ibid., 207–209.

76 Youssef M. Choueiri, *Modern Arab Historiography: Historical Discourse and the Nation-State* (London: RoutledgeCurzon, 2003), 87, 93

7 The Cairo Fire of 26 January 1952 and the Interpretations of History

Anne-Claire Kerbœuf

That day had been a real nightmare, for sure the most dreadful day in the modern history of Cairo. (R.T., *Almanach du Progrès Égyptien*, 1953)

As a dominant event in the historiography of modern Egypt, the Cairo Fire on 26 January 1952 has been passionately discussed by historians and journalists. Until today, the main question has been who set fire to Cairo and which political leader is to be blamed. From the very beginning, the Cairo Fire has been regarded as a political plot. Yet, the idea of rioters as *ordinary people* being the main actors and initiators of such a tragedy has always been denied by Egyptian historiography, thus highlighting the absence of historical studies on social demonstration in modern Egypt. Therefore the national mobilization on 26 January is still regarded the Egyptian nation marching as "one single person." On the contrary, this chapter emphasizes how different actors' interests and actions can be during a single mobilization. Likewise, interactions exist between rioters and politics,[1] such that 26 January 1952 was a decisive blow to the whole structure of the state. More than a British plot, the Cairo Fire was the denunciation, in a symbolic way, of the Egyptian liberal elite's failure to bring Egypt to independence (figs. 7.1–7.2).

This chapter begins by introducing the Isma'iliya district through the recollections of local people prior to the Cairo Fire itself. It then delineates the people targeted by the riot and the rioters, after which the political and social stakes underlying the 26 January crisis receive attention. By looking also at the various interpretations given to the fire under the regimes of Gamal 'Abd al-Nasser, Anwar al-Sadat, and Husni Mubarak, this chapter will show how ideologies influence the writing of history. Since the latest 'instrumentalization' of the Cairo Fire legitimates a restoration project of the City Center, this notion remains particularly meaningful.

Isma'iliya: The Urban Target

Until 26 January 1952, Isma'iliya represented the "finery of Cairo," a "piece of Paris": a flourishing place of wealth and insouciance for the Cairo elite. The Khedive Isma'il (1863–79), who gave his name to this district, wanted to build a new "town" reflecting the path to modernization undertaken by his country. Contrasting with the urban structures of the capital historical center, the new neighborhood was equipped with large avenues, traffic circles, European-style buildings, and aspects of affluent urban culture (unknown in the old city) such as the opera, coffee shops, hostels, the hippodrome, and public gardens.[2] With this modern town, the Khedive intended to welcome in a proper western way the international personalities he invited to the opening of the Suez Canal in 1869.

From the beginning Isma'iliya was an answer to the local elite's aspiration to modernity. Its development, however, was stopped by the country's bankruptcy and the installation of the French and British dual control of the Treasury and the Ministry of Civil Engineering (1878). Isma'iliya resumed its extension and modernization with the British occupation (1882) and the following influx of Levantine and European migrants to the Egyptian capital. Between 1866 and 1882, the population increased from 282,000 to 375,000, including 19,000 foreigners.[3] During the first decades of the twentieth century, Isma'iliya became the modern business district center of Cairo. It was at the same time the political center including 'Abdin palace, British barracks and the residency, the fashionable commercial center with prestigious shops and clubs, and the financial as well as administrative center, featuring banks, state administration, and companies' head offices. This elitist new neighborhood soon became a social enclave, complete with sartorial and linguistic markers. It became assumed that to enter one of the center's shops or coffee shops, one had to have an effendi look (shoes, a suit, and a tarboosh) and speak a foreign language. Financial means were consequently required. As one department store worker recalled, "Groppi! L'Américaine! They were unique places! . . . Everybody, if he had money, could enter it. Without, no way . . . You had to wear a tie. The tarboosh was not required. But you had to be well-shaved."[4]

As such, Isma'iliya was actually a European micro-society few Egyptians could frequent. "You could not see Egyptian people, they were not living here, they were somewhere else. You could walk in the whole of Cairo and you would only find European people. Even for the well-dressed Egyptians, you could not say they were real Egyptian people. Arabs did not exist!"[5] Ordinary people would only stroll up and down the streets and look into windows on days off. The urban shop window of the upper class was the object of admiration, envy, frustration, and hate. Above all, for members of the middle class: "When we learned that the City Center was burning, we were enthusiastic! Only my mother could go there because she spoke French. Then it was like a celebration. She would wear the smartest clothes she had."[6]

This idyllic image of the City Center described by a member of the bourgeoisie (who longs for the streets' and buildings' former cleanliness) was not shared by everybody. A different, negative perception existed, which is well-represented in contemporary realistic literature. For instance, Naguib Mahfouz, born in old Cairo, described the "European City" in his novels as a place of corruption for true men and values.[7] Albert Cossery, who used to live in the European city, saw it as the "citadel of the oppression," a cruel and voracious town fed by the misery of the poor. In 1946 Cossery published a collection of short stories entitled *Les Hommes Oubliés de Dieu* ("The Men Forgotten by God") in which the 1952 riot is suggested several times. For example, in the story "Le coiffeur a tué sa femme" ("The Hairdresser Killed his Wife), a humble man of the old city is meditating on an unusual strike of the road sweepers in Fu'ad I street. He then realizes that anger is spreading around him, that people will soon be overwhelmed by it, and horrible acts will be committed. At the end of the "Danger de la fantaisie" ("The Threat of Fantasia"), in the same collection, the teacher of the school of the beggars in the old city, looking in the direction of the European town, sees "the future written in blood stains at the center of this town."[8]

The Premises of the Revolt

According to interviewees living or working downtown, the country's political affairs were far from their mind, even shortly before the Cairo Fire. People have retained the memory of the advantages of the district's "Golden Age," rather than the large and repeated demonstrations. Yet, between January 1950 and January 1952, numerous demonstrations had been organized against the British occupier.[9] The return of the Wafd

Party to government in January 1950 brought immense hopes of social and political change. Political formations and media exploited the larger freedom of expression granted to them. Nevertheless, the Wafd Party was in an awkward position given its own electoral promises, such as the repeal of the 1936 Treaty,[10] the right for civilians to bear arms, and amnesty for political prisoners. Wafd popularity decreased very soon with press accusations of corruption, lukewarm nationalism, and collaboration with the palace. Inside the Wafd Party itself, the young militants influenced by socialist ideas forced the old conservative leaders to lead a fierce nationalist campaign. By the fall of 1951, mounting pressure inside and outside the party forced the government's hand, and on 8 October Prime Minister al-Nahhas Pasha unilaterally repealed the treaty he had signed fifteen years earlier with the British government. This historical and unique act in the history of Egyptian nationalism opened a guerilla war for the control of the British-garrisoned Canal Zone.

In Cairo, demonstrations became all the more violent with the British killing of Egyptian "martyrs" in the Canal Zone. Other actions, like the boycott of British products and institutions, were largely supported by the opposition press, especially the Muslim Brotherhood and the Socialist Party newspapers. The latter's mouthpiece published in November 1951 a "black list" of the British companies and the "unpatriotic" Egyptian companies.[11] The closing of bars and places of entertainment was also demanded in solidarity with the *fida'iyin* (those who sacrifice themselves for their country). In a message addressed to the government on 15 December 1951, Brotherhood Supreme Guide Hasan al-Hudaybi claimed "it is unfair that supporters of the Muslim Brotherhood should fight and sacrifice their lives for the sake of their country while others spend their time in places of amusement."[12] As the government did not take any measures, the Socialist Party encouraged people to act: "Cairo continues to flourish and the cinemas also. This shows that people's nerves are not ready yet. This is why the people with political consciousness must react. Patrols of the alert and organized people must awaken the people sitting at cafés, the drunkards in the bars and cabarets, and those in the cinemas. As for the gentlemen who do not contribute their money, we have a score to settle with them."[13] As merchants and customers disobeyed these verbal recommendations and threats, "patrols" of young people started to walk the streets, particularly in the City Center where British institutions and places of amusement were concentrated. Peaceful actions like human walls were organized. The troops of the Socialist Party created a human wall barring the entrance to the cinema Rivoli.[14] Doria Shafik's Bint al-Nil barred the entrance to Barclays Bank.[15] English license plates were concealed, and French or English signs were changed into Arabic. Egyptian radio stopped its musical programs and started to broadcast Qur'anic verses commemorating the martyrs in the Canal Zone—yet only after one hundred young militants violently attacked one of its studios at the Royal Opera on Ibrahim Street. The same group almost destroyed the Auberge du Turf on 'Imad al-Din street later in the day.[16] These actions convinced cabarets and bars located in the same street to close for the day.[17]

While violence was increasing in the capital, the Socialist Party leader Ahmad Husayn presciently threatened the government with its forthcoming fate: "Will you continue, O you ministers, will you continue, O you Mustafa al-Nahhas, to live in scandal, wealth, joy, and illuminations? Will our cinemas and theaters and our cabarets stay open? . . . The anger that stirs up now the people has neither started nor ended. It looks for an exit to express itself. . . . If the government continues for a week the method it has adopted until now, the explosion will be directed against the government itself and will overthrow it. Does the government hear me? I say one week left and not a month or two. I say a week of seven days."[18] Finally, on 24 January 1952, during a press conference at the party headquarters, Ahmad Husayn announced that he would "unleash the crowds" against the government and that "terrifying crimes" would be committed. Two days later the "crowds" were indeed unleashed.

'Black Saturday'

Black Saturday actually started on 25 January 1952, in the Canal Zone city of Isma'iliya where the British troops were besieged for four months. Unorganized though it was at the beginning, the guerilla war launched after the abolition of the 1936 Treaty became a real problem for the British army, which was losing an increasing number of soldiers in the battle. The British were further isolated in the Canal Zone as the roads were blocked, and the railroads were sabotaged. Moreover, several hundred Egyptian workers went on strike and left. Consequently, the British were ready to seize the first opportunity to brutally stop the guerilla fighters. They chose the city of Isma'iliya where the Egyptian police had rallied the *fida'iyin*. On 25 January, at dawn, the police auxiliaries *(buluk nizam)* woke up to find themselves surrounded by British tanks. The unequal balance of power was evident and the British demanded unconditional surrender. Minister of the Interior Fu'ad Sirag al-Din, however, ordered the *buluk nizam* to fight up to the last bullet: around fifty policemen were then killed, almost eighty wounded, and 1,000 taken prisoner. The news triggered anger in Cairo. A huge national protest for the following day was planned, organized during the night in universities, firms, and barracks. Meanwhile, at Faruq Airport, the employees and the immigration police decided to go on strike at once. From two to seven o'clock in the morning, they grounded four planes of the British Overseas Airlines Company until the intervention of an army detachment.[19]

The demonstration in Cairo on 26 January started in an unusual way: the police joined the students at Fu'ad I University. Then the infuriated demonstrators walked downtown where they met other demonstrations of workers and the ones of al-Azhar students. Next, the protesters gathered in front of the courtyard of the presidency where Minister of Social Affairs and War 'Abd al-Fattah Hassan made a speech that incited them further. Then the crowd dispersed in the heart of Isma'iliya. The riot itself started with an altercation between demonstrators and people sitting at the terrace of the Casino Badi'a in the Opera Square. The opportunity was seized by a group of thirty young people, who invaded the casino, threw out furniture, splashed it with petrol, and set it alight. At one o'clock, the Casino Badi'a was ablaze. But nobody moved: neither the demonstrators nor the policemen or the firemen. A few minutes later, the Cinema Rivoli in Fu'ad I Street too disappeared into flames. During the following hours cinemas, bars, cabarets, hostels, restaurants, coffee shops, and shops were looted and set on fire. This arson spread to Bulaq, Shubra, 'Abbasiya, and the Pyramids Road. In the midst of this anarchy, murder took the lives of ten foreigners inside the Turf Club.[20] During that long day, several policemen either took active part in the arson or turned a blind eye on it. When the state of emergency was finally proclaimed in the evening, the army too showed little enthusiasm: it deployed slowly and refused to fire at the rioters.

Between Plotters and the Rabble

After he had declared martial law, Premier al-Nahhas Pasha addressed a message to the nation in which he expressed sadness and accused "disruptive elements" and "traitors" of infiltrating the ranks of the nation and committing a horrific act. The riot was immediately discredited and qualified as a political "crime" and "plot." The political consequences of 26 January were particularly serious for the Wafd, since this party was held responsible for the disorder. On the following day, the king dismissed the Wafdist government for failure to maintain public security. The independent 'Ali Mahir, appointed to form a new government favorable to the king, stopped the national struggle in the Canal Zone. Liberation battalions had to withdraw from the Delta or were jailed.[21] Nevertheless, the Wafd leaders refused responsibility for the affair. Fu'ad Sirag al-Din, held responsible for the anarchy, denied all charges. On 10 February 1952, he pleaded not guilty in the party press organ *al-Misri*. He stated that his orders had been bypassed; that he had been prevented from contacting the king directly despite all his efforts (he phoned, then came to the palace); and that the army had been very slow to deploy.

These accusations outraged the palace and especially the army. They resulted in the quick opening of an inquiry into "administrative responsibility for the events of January 26." In his report, the prosecutor-general refuted allegations that the army had not done its duty and declared that the responsibility fell upon the minister of the interior and the authorities responsible for public security.[22] Consequently Fu'ad Sirag al-Din (the minister of the interior and treasury), 'Abd al-Fattah Hassan (the minister of social affairs and war), the Cairo governor and several police officers were accused of administrative responsibility for the Cairo Fire.

Other political personalities were also charged for the Cairo Fire. Ahmad Husayn and five other Socialist Party members were tried for "instigating the burning of Cairo," by using their press organs. They were also suspected of participating in the riot because some witnesses saw them supporting the rioters in the City Center on 26 January. In addition to this confusing aspect of the affair, politicians blaming each other fed rumors and nourished various interpretations. Thus, the hypothesis of a British plot emerged. During his deposition at Ahmad Husayn's trial in July 1952, 'Ali Mahir Pasha declared: "Authentic patriotism does not know egoism or anarchy but freedom in the framework of the law." He asserted that the riot, far from being spontaneous, had been planned by a "foreign hand," the British one.[23]

This affirmation was taken up by a panic-stricken "cultural" elite, eager to find a foreign explanation of the tragedy. The setting of the city ablaze was to them intolerable and incomprehensible, insofar as it was completely opposed to the image they had of the "Egyptian people." To both the Egyptians and the foreign elite, the "Egyptian people" were docile and welcoming to foreigners, as King Faruq recalled it in his royal message on 5 February 1952. Thus, when the trial of the rioters opened, one could read in the press such contradictory speeches: "We proclaim to the world that those who have committed these crimes are not ours. However they are here, among us, until we catch them and deliver them to the judges. . . . Egypt, on that day, has been dropped form the slate of civilized nations. The Egyptian people who ask for their liberty have burned with their own hands the capital of the country. We want to let the world know that the Egyptian people did not do anything. It was the work of criminals."[24]

A few months later, the picture had changed: civilized Egypt was falling into the hands of torturers, and criminals were on the path of becoming heroes. After six months of political vacuum following the Cairo Fire during which none of the three governments appointed restored order and stability, the 'Free Officers' took power on 23 July. Consequently, the ongoing trials were reviewed. "Instigating the burning of Cairo" was termed a political crime and the Socialist Party was acquitted. The judges accepted the defense of Ahmad Husayn who argued that "the events on 26 January 1952 were entirely political and were caused by the violent action of the British Occupation against the Egyptian police in the Canal Zone the day before. This event [the Cairo Fire] flared up emotions and inflamed the feelings of the people, who lost control and started to destroy and sack on a large scale. In the meantime, enemies and partisans of the accused could not be distinguished."[25] The sentences of the mutinous policemen were also reduced: of 181 *buluk nizam* accused, one-hundred were acquitted, thirty-four received a three-month imprisonment, and forty-seven were sent to prison with hard labor for two years.[26] The accused police officers were relieved of any administrative responsibility.[27] As for the rioters, they were collectively amnestied in February 1959.[28]

This judgment was important inasmuch as it allowed the commemoration of the Cairo Fire, overshadowed until that date. Hence, *al-Ahram* published a front-page article in memory of the Cairo Fire on the tenth anniversary of the event. The anger of "the great people" *(al-sha'b al-'azim)* was described as a horrible show. Yet, it "symbolized in many aspects the repression that the people suffered" under the reign of "feudalism and occupation."[29] The newspaper echoed President Gamal 'Abd al-Nasser's statement to the parliament in 1960: "The Cairo Fire was the first sign of the social revolution against the corrupt institutions. The Cairo Fire expressed the people's anger, when Egypt was bending beneath the yoke of feudalism, speculation, and capitalism."[30]

Censorship and the socialist ideology did not, however, eradicate the notion of a plot. At the end of 'Abd al-Nasser's regime, the journalist and leftist militant Sa'd Zahran wrote an article on the nationalist struggle in the Canal Zone.[31] Despite the lack of evidence, he doubted that the

Egyptians had sabotaged the national mobilization on their own initiative, and suggested that the British Intelligence Service and the palace had plotted together. Under Anwar al-Sadat's regime, Muhammad Anis emphasized this idea in a 1972 short study based on censored reports of the BBC correspondent in Cairo and on ministerial records.[32] Despite the relevance of his thesis, and in particular the role ascribed to the Socialist Party, his analysis remains superficial.

Gamal al-Sharqawi commenced study during these years as well. His first publication was based on the judicial records of "the instigating of the burning of Cairo" trial and on almost forty interviews with political personalities and intellectuals.[33] Al-Sharqawi, as many other specialists, could not bear the idea of the Egyptian people burning their own capital. He criticized fiercely the historian 'Abd al-Rahman al-Rafi'i who defended this point of view in a book published in 1957.[34] Like Muhammad Anis, al-Sharqawi supported the theory that the British and the palace had planned the Cairo Fire. The author reached this conclusion after confronting the existing interpretations of the role of political players (the Socialist Party, the Muslim Brotherhood, the Communists, the Free Officers, the palace, and the British). Nonetheless, he totally refuted Muhammad Anis' opinion that Ahmad Husayn had participated in the Cairo Fire, by arguing that the Socialist Party was a peaceful one.[35] The author completed his research in the 1980s. He published a second book based on the British public records,[36] which reinforced the British conspiracy hypothesis. The impressive and convincing work of al-Sharqawi was warmly welcomed in the press, though rather than resolving the Cairo Fire question his work revived debate. During the 1990s, the Cairo Fire was still an event cherished by journalists. As for the question "who set the fire," articles concluded with the same answer: the Cairo Fire is an "enigma." The insistence on this approach is itself enigmatic, suggesting that over time, the Cairo Fire became a date to commemorate the former parliamentary monarchy and the "Golden Age" of Egyptian economic and political liberalism.

When the Elite Inspires Violence

Historians and journalists have always been interested in one single aspect of the Cairo Fire trial. They have focused on the "instigating the burning of Cairo" trial, which involved the Socialist Party, and have therefore considered the Cairo Fire a "political crime." By contrast, they have never paid sufficient attention to the "the events of the 26 January 1952" trial of the rioters themselves. This can be explained by Egyptians' self-censorship when it comes to subjects viewed as "shameful" and contrary to the idyllic and elitist image of Egypt. The fact that rioters still have no place in Egyptian history is confirmed by the absence of social studies on demonstrations in the Egyptian historiography. The neglect of the social background of the Cairo Fire gives way to Manichean analysis and conspiracy theories, which separate the 'good' actors from the 'bad' ones, and ignore interactions between them. Yet, daily relationships sometimes existed between the victims of the Cairo Fire and the rioters, a fact that traumatized the bourgeoisie.

In the aftermath of the Cairo Fire, the police searched for the goods looted during that day. The press regularly reported the results of the searches in the surroundings of Isma'iliya district. The rioters' and thieves' identities were progressively revealed through arrests, and then with the opening of the rioters' trial in March 1952. Examination of the press articles on this trial[37] reveals that of the arrested rioters, 25 percent were policemen, 30 percent were students and minors, and 30 percent were skilled workers, craftsmen (shoe repairers, tailors), small shopkeepers, service employees (coffee waiters, sales clerks, petrol station attendants) or domestic employees (bawwab, sufragi, farrash).[38] The press was very interested in this last group. For instance, Le Journal d'Alexandrie et la Bourse Égyptienne reported the complicity between the cook and the bawwab of the same building in an article entitled, "Arrest of a cook and a doorman of Cairo and seizure of boxes of whisky looted on the twenty-sixth." According to the piece, "'Abd al-Salam Ali, cook in a family living on 8 Tal'at Harb Street was hiding objects looted on January 26 in a safe place. . . . The cook placed responsibility on the doorman, but the latter argued that the cook carried the stolen goods on the evening of January 26, and that his hands were bleeding."[39] Other press articles claimed that employees of damaged buildings participated in looting and arson themselves. An employee of the Cinema Metro was arrested at the railway station while carrying the cinema curtains.[40] The owner of the Doll Cabaret on 'Adli Pasha Street claimed that he recognized one of his former employees among the rioters who attacked his bar.[41]

These stories reported in the press terrorized the local elite because they showed how the relationships between employers and employees had deteriorated and how much the employers had lost their legitimacy. After the Cairo Fire, awareness of this relationship's deterioration appeared in editorials. For instance, in al-Akhbar, Mustafa Amin, concerned with servants' living conditions, accused the ruling elite of ignoring them:

Those who took advantage of the profits of the [world] war represented a minority while the majority did not get any benefit from it. . . . Although the masses did not enjoy good fortune as the rich and the rulers did, they would not bear any other charges unless they [these privileged groups] join the people to face adversity. The gamblers circles, where the rich used to play every night, losing thousands of pounds in one hour, should be definitely closed. . . . It is not enough to ask the press not to speak about it. The *suffragi* and the waiters are very much more talkative and gossipy than the newspapers.[42]

Other members of the elite, however, seemed still not to realize how deep the social and political crisis was. Their "capitalist consciousness" appeared to have replaced their political consciousness:

The events of January 26 are so serious that we cannot ignore the consequences for our economic life. . . . Several big merchant houses have been ruined. . . . Is there someone who doubts that commerce is still one of the main levels of civilization? Certainly, stopping both imports and exports will reduce our standard of living, when we are doing whatever we can to increase for the purposes of ranking among great nations. . . . Cairo cinemas and theaters have been destroyed. How shall we relax without our innocent entertainment after our daily efforts? We won't follow whomever wants to damage the capital and to prevent from being renewed. Otherwise we would be responsible for our own suicide. How could we ignore that our economic force is the first source of our political independence?[43]

After 26 January 1952, members of the elite knew they were about to be delegitimized. The City Center attack was not directed exclusively against the British but against the Europeans, the Levantines, and the Egyptians as well. It was against the whole elite who made profits from capitalism. By attacking the Isma'iliya district, the rioters attacked and rejected the westernized identity of Egypt in a symbolic way. Capitalism, modernism, and cosmopolitanism benefited only a minority of Egyptian people. More importantly, the liberal economy hindered the access of Egypt to independence.

Egyptian citizens tolerated capitalism as long as they believed it would lead the country to political independence. They were confident in the promising nationalist project of Tal'at Harb, who created the first national bank and national firms (the Misr companies) in the 1920s.[44] However, the

Egyptian elite, who invested in the national economy and who aroused hopes of bringing Egypt out of a sociopolitical and social deadlock, quickly proved to care exclusively for their own social and financial interests. This elite comprised a group of landowners who decided to diversify their investments on the outbreak of World War II, inasmuch as the cotton revenues were no longer secure. They invested in financial, commercial, and industrial sectors, which were monopolized by British and Levantines. In doing so, they were supported by the state, which had implemented an import-substitution policy in order to promote local industries and prevent the shortage of goods resulting from the war.

Consequently, between 1946 and 1948, Egyptians founded 84 percent of the companies, while greatly expanding joint stock companies.[45] In an interesting study, Robert Tignor underlines the major transformations in the board of directors of the companies: of 351 joint stock companies listed in *The Stock Exchange Yearbook of Egypt* in 1946, 163 had a mixed nationality directorates, which included the most prominent Egyptian businessmen (among them political leaders). By contrast, in 1923, the economic and financial sectors counted only thirty companies with mixed nationality directorate in eighty-five companies.[46] This change resulted from 1920s governmental decisions requesting predominantly foreign-ruled joint stock companies to appoint at least two Egyptian directors.[47] A 1947 law reinforced the "Egyptianization" of the economy: 40 percent of the directors, 75 percent of the employees, and 90 percent of the workers had to be Egyptians.[48]

Paradoxically, these protective measures did not promote an autarkic national economic sector, but resulted in acute dependence on foreign capital. On the one hand the "mixed" phenomenon observed in the economic sector was mainly superficial: the few Egyptian directors were recruited mostly for their political influence and were granted high salaries. On the other hand, this phenomenon had social repercussions. More than the company boards, foreign and Egyptian elite shared a common cultural identity and social outlook.[49] They met in clubs like the Royal Automobile Club or the Gezira Sporting Club, which opened its doors more easily to Egyptian pashas after 1936.[50]

The Egyptian members of this coalescing "mixed" elite were educated abroad or were the products of the new Egyptian educational system.[51] As they climbed the social ladder, they competed dangerously with landowners. This is an important point to stress insofar as Egyptian society was still ruled by the very conservative and anti-reformist landowner class. Nevertheless, the urban elite did not present an opposition force to the rural elite. Even as influential a politician and advocate of economic nationalism as Isma'il Sidqi did not succeed in gathering the necessary political support.[52] Other prominent political and industrial figures were too unpopular, too close to the British, and too preoccupied by their own interests to promote a national economic policy.[53] Most of these politicians were Wafdist dissidents who entered minor opposition parties close to the palace and/or the British.[54] Sharing the same social and economic interests as the British, this urban elite disregarded nationalist priorities.

Political Rivalries, Intrigues, and 'Skids'

In the context of increasing nationalist fervor and popular discontent, the British viewed sidelining the Wafd as a necessity. For that purpose they used their pro-British intermediaries in the palace to put pressure on King Faruq, who was obviously reluctant: he shared some landowning interests with Fu'ad Sirag al-Din and did not want to be even more unpopular. However, he gave in under British pressure, appointing to his royal cabinet the pro-British and very unpopular Hafiz 'Afifi and 'Abd al-Fattah 'Amr Pashas in December 1951.[55] The British also played on the widening fracture the nationalist campaign had created between Wafdists and royalists. The royalists had more economic interests in common with the British (particularly through the joint venture companies established after the war) than with the Wafdists. Therefore they had much to lose in the crisis and desired, like the British, the fall of the Wafd government. The royalists voiced their critiques through an anti-government campaign in the newspapers such as *Akhbar al-Yawm*, *Akhir Lahza*, and *al-Assas*. That campaign was, consequently, countered by Wafdists' vain call for national unity in *al-Misri*. As for the Socialist Party press, it criticized fiercely both the palace and the Wafdists. The Party leader Ahmad Husayn, particularly conscious of the current political stakes, was also manipulating intra-elite rivalries.[56]

Founded in 1933, Ahmad Husayn's Party, called at that time Young Egypt *(Misr al-Fatat)*, was one of those extra-parliamentarian forces used by the traditional parties to divide the student nationalist movement. The 'Green Shirts' (Young Egypt phalange) were manipulated by the palace whereas the 'Blue Shirts' were used by the Wafd.[57] After the dissolution of these paramilitary groups in 1938, Ahmad Husayn's party continued to sell its services to traditional parties. In 1950, although the party had won its first parliamentary seat in the person of Ibrahim Shukri, Ahmad Husayn appeared totally disillusioned by the parliamentary regime and by the possibility of independence while the ruling elite—royalists or Wafdists—

remained in control. On 26 January, therefore, Ahmad Husayn may have taken the deliberate decision to foil the plans of King Faruq and Minister of the Interior and Treasury Fu'ad Sirag al-Din, by double-crossing both through creating a conflagration.

Following the repeal of the 1936 Treaty, the Wafdist government assumed control of the Liberation Battalions (kata'ib al-tahrir), which they armed. In this context the minister of interior and treasury met the Socialist Party leader to make a deal with him. Both Fu'ad Sirag al-Din and Ahmad Husayn would provoke trouble in order to dissuade the king from dismissing the Wafd. On January 26, Fu'ad Sirag al-Din very likely wanted a riot to frighten King Faruq and to counter the increasing British pressure. Indeed, according to a British Foreign Office report based on a conversation with an agent close to the Muslim Brothers, "He [the agent] says that the [Socialist] party had received so much help from Sirag al-Din in the form of funding, weapons, incendiary equipment, and police protection that the preparation for 26 January was not too difficult. Until the end, Sirag al-Din was stupid enough to believe that this would be used in the Canal Zone. Of course, he hoped for and wanted a riot in Cairo on the 26 January, but only an 'ordinary riot.'"[58] The same source also confirmed participation of the radical branch of the Muslim Brotherhood in the riot despite the opposition of the Supreme Guide al-Hudaybi: "Some of the gangs that operated in Cairo on 26 January were formed by Muslim Brothers. They attacked bars and cafés but not cinemas. Al-Hudaybi let go and was unable to control some members, although he had hoped in the current situation he would be able to regain control over them."[59]

King Faruq also might have turned once again to Ahmad Husayn, yet to counteract the Wafdists. If the Socialist Party started rioting, to be blamed on the Wafdist government, the king could dismiss it. On Black Saturday, he kept 800 police and army chiefs in his palace during the riot for a banquet to celebrate the birth of his son. This banquet was organized for lunch when it was usually for dinner and was maintained despite the circumstances. Furthermore, the persuasiveness of the king's counselors to permit Fu'ad Sirag al-Din to speak directly to him, as well as the numerous conversations whispered between King Faruq and Commandant of the Armed Forces Haydar Pasha during the lunch,[60] suggest that the king was aware of developments, but delayed the army's intervention on purpose.

In any case, British Intelligence Service certainly knew what was in train. In a Foreign Office report dated 1 February 1952, a Cairo-based diplomat wrote that "Mr. Fay," the head of the Brothers of Liberty, "has confirmed to me most of today's events. Although he [the so-called Mr. Fay] left Cairo before the riots, he had a number of reports that indicated the probable course of events."[61] In Cairo, despite the dissolution of this obscure organization by the parliament on 14 January 1952, some of its British agent members might have helped Ahmad Husayn to organize the arson.[62] Meanwhile, in the Canal Zone, the British army was ready to maneuver in the direction of the capital: this threat provided the king with the necessary excuse to order the army to intervene.[63]

Although the British Intelligence Service did assist in organizing the riot to serve their short-term interests, the Egyptian rulers still bore an important if not decisive responsibility. Because of their rivalries and their continuous resort to political intrigue as common practice, the ruling elite not only undermined national mobilization, but also weakened the whole state apparatus. Indeed, on 26 January 1952, high officials inside the Interior Ministry and the palace harmed the state by blindly using political intrigue, thus surrendering control over sectors "strategic" to the functioning of the state, including the police and the army.[64] This was the result of a good part of the incoherent policy the Wafd had implemented by the fall of 1951.

After the abrogation of the 1936 Treaty, the government faced the crucial dilemma of fighting the British without using the army.[65] The police could not face the British army, so the Wafd decided to transfer most of the security forces' capabilities to the civilian sector. On 10 December 1951, the Wafdist government legalized the guerilla war by giving the right to bear arms to civilians. Weapons could now circulate in the country and the government could supply arms to civilians through political parties and organizations. Finally, citizens were mobilized to fight while the army was kept on the sidelines of the conflict. This inactive posture humiliated the army. In early 1952, signs of insubordination and outright mutiny became manifest. As covered in much greater detail by Tewfik Aclimandos in chapter three of this volume, on 6 January, army candidates won a landslide victory over King Faruq's men in the Officer's Club board elections. Twenty days later, when the government sent the army at dawn to break up an airport employees' strike, an officer warned the representatives of the British airline company that it was the last time they would help them.[66]

The auxiliary police were also mistreated. The minister of the interior decided to sacrifice his forces, by neither paying nor providing them with sufficient weapons. "Occupation means murder to us and if we are to die, we must do so with our heads high and not in an attitude of surrender. When we abrogated the Treaty, we were fully alive to its serious consequences and the sacrifice it would involve," declared Fu'ad Sirag al-Din in December 1951, to justify his contradictory policy.[67] Anger thus rose among the police, especially as the auxiliaries who surrendered to the vastly superior British forces were subsequently tried for treason.[68] In Cairo, policemen were also abused, this time by fellow citizens. Clashes with demonstrators were increasingly violent, and in January 1952 the police found themselves dodging bullets as well as rocks. "The government's action in the last few months has made it unavoidable that the police had, sooner or later, to dodge bullets of such demonstration. It remains to be seen how long its morale will bear the situation," wrote British Ambassador Ralph Stevenson in his report to the Foreign Office following the 20 January clash.[69]

By 26 January, the government's political intrigue had promoted mutiny among the ranks of both the police and army. The police, overwhelmed by anger, largely participated in the demonstration, riots, and arson. In spite of the army's limited insubordination compared to that of the *buluk nizam*, the signs of rebellion were clear. The army showed little enthusiasm in intervening: they deployed slowly, refused to fire at the rioters, and even watched them.[70]

Mobilizations

Besides the police and the army, the societal mobilization on January 26 encompassed multiple social and professional sectors. Although students and industrial workers had been demonstrating especially since the 1940s, craftsmen, shopkeepers, menial employees, peddlers, and servants had usually not. Indeed, the ideological, economic, and social context emerging from World War II had changed the organization of urban collective actions. As Guislain Denoeux explains,

> Such processes led to the marginalization or disappearance of some
> of the actors who had played a prominent role in urban uprisings until
> the nineteenth century (notables, guild leaders, sufi shaykhs, lower-
> ranking ulama, religious students, lutis, and urban gangs, to name just
> a few). They promoted however the emergence of new social strata
> (professionals, civil servants, Westernized intellectuals, and industrial
> workers) that often became attracted to new, forward-looking
> ideologies (socialism, communism, Ba'athism, nationalism, and
> pan-Arabism) and adopted new forms of collective action, including
> mass demonstrations, strikes and boycotts. More importantly,

these groups, whose lives revolved around universities, high school, factories, and modern offices, did not usually engage in politics through the old networks built around mosques, quarters, and the crafts and trades. Instead, they were attracted to better organized, more recently established, and modern-looking entities, such as political parties, trade unions, and syndicates. . . . As a result, the first half of the twentieth century saw the unmistakable tendency toward the formation of broadly based movements of political protest.[71]

Although students and industrial workers were recruited in political parties or trade unions, the political affiliation of craftsmen and service employees in the early twentieth century is usually ignored. Their violent action during the January 26 riot thus surprised the elite, but highlights how extra-parliamentary forces such as the Muslim Brotherhood and Young Egypt (the Socialist Party) recruited their members among those neglected by the traditional political parties.

After 1936 and particularly 1938, Ahmad Husayn's party, which used to recruit students, turned its policy toward workers, peasants, urban laborers, craftsmen, civil servants, and unemployed people.[72] A few days before the Cairo Fire, Ahmad Husayn encouraged party members to organize peaceful anti-British actions among "young people, who are not members of parties or organized groups, [and who] will take illegal actions."[73] Moreover, the arson commandos described in the British inquiry report were dressed quite diversely: in middle class apparel, overalls, *gallabiya*s, or in uniforms (one may have worn a Misr Air uniform).[74] Ahmad Husayn's party had thus incited neglected and diverse segments of the population to mobilization and violent actions.

The conflagration of Black Saturday served only the short-term interests of the British government. Unlike other political actors, Ahmad Husayn had understood the fragility of the regime, and that one blow could topple it. In twenty years, the political ideology of Ahmad Husayn's party shifted several times: he was royalist, Islamic, democratic, or socialist. Nevertheless, from the "Piaster Plan" in 1931 to the 1950 socialist program,[75] Ahmad Husayn continuously maintained a political line advocating promotion of national industry as a way to reach political independence. The economic elite, whose attachment to the British was even stronger after World War II, did not agree. The 'autonomization' of the national economy had failed, and foreigners still dominated. The 1947 law came too late and was not implemented before 1956. The two-year debate around this law revealed that few Egyptians had benefited from industrial and business activities. For Ahmad Husayn and his partisans, setting fire to the Cairo business district meant denying legitimacy to this same liberal elite, and condemning the capitalism that preserved elite privilege.

Ahmad Husayn's party had never been a peaceful organization as argued by Mohamed al-Sharqawi. It had always been a paramilitary organization, although the violent actions were especially prominent at the outbreak of World War II and were resumed after wartime government repression ceased.[76] Ahmad Husayn took advantage of a large societal appeal that provided him with a kind of immunity and allowed his party to stage violent actions. Young Egypt's leader built numerous networks within the political class, the police, and the army (Anwar al-Sadat for instance had been a member of Young Egypt). Ahmad Husayn used these networks to obtain funds, arms, and protection. In the aftermath of the Cairo Fire, he was arrested and condemned to eighteen months' imprisonment.[77] The July Revolution interrupted his trial and he was acquitted a few months later. Indeed, the Socialist Party leader had prepared the revolution and paved the road for the army.

A Selective Memory

The fiftieth anniversary of the Cairo Fire was celebrated on January 2002, evoking several different opinions. For the first time in thirty years, several intellectuals analyzed the political context, seeking to explain why people could have set fire to Cairo.[78] Yet, they did not provide any further insight into the identity of the people except that some thieves and firemen exploited the situation. A one-day conference organized by the Egyptian Society of Historical Studies on 26 January 2002 followed the same tack,[79] with historians opining that the king, the British, or the Zionists were responsible.[80]

Still, a new urban-oriented perspective on the Cairo Fire was presented during the second part of the conference. A team of architects, historians, and intellectuals seized the opportunity of the fiftieth anniversary to contemplate a restoration project of the City Center. In their opinion, the Cairo Fire was a dramatic breakdown in the history of Isma'iliya. Since 26 January 1952, the Cairo City Center has lost its prestigious places and monuments, and has become a blighted area. As Egypt is considered by these cultural elites a modern country and the meeting place of world civilizations, its glorious center and its function as the regime's shop window need to be restored.

This last interpretation and instrumentalization of the Cairo Fire signifies the enduring influence of ideologies on history and collective memory. This instrumentalization suggests that the enigmatic treatment of the Cairo Fire during the 1990s represents the commemoration of the parliamentary monarchy and Egypt's economic and political liberalism.[81] Indeed, as economic liberalization has dominated the rhetoric of Mubarak's Egypt, the former and new liberal elite has been progressively allowed to express nostalgia for the monarchy. Through their 2002 speeches, architects, historians, and politicians made it clear that restoring the City Center entailed "re-investing" in the former elitist district, which came to be a popular, mass area after the 1952 Revolution. This restoration project might spatialize the bourgeoisie's collective memory and inscribe it in the long-term. In chapter six, Barak Salmoni begins with an important reference to Maurice Halbwachs. His thinking merits consideration here as well. As Halbwachs writes that "collective memory cannot be without a spatial frame,"[82] the contribution of the Egyptian government to this project hints at the liberal bourgeoisie's official entry into national history and collective memory. This recovered legitimacy is confirmed by the new cultural policy the government undertook, which included the opening of several national historical museums in newly restored European-style villas.[83]

On the fiftieth anniversary of the Cairo Fire, some intellectuals expressed their new interest in the rioters while others expressed their solidarity with the victims. These different opinions are voiced when Egypt is facing a terrible economic and social conjuncture. Current difficulties may remind a few people of the 1952 crisis. We may place in this light the claim made by a sociologist during the 2002 conference: he declared that the informal areas surrounding Cairo endanger the capital, which might well burn once again.

Conclusion

Considering the Cairo Fire a "political plot" or an "enigma" means passing silently over the failure of the democratic experience and therefore refusing to draw lessons from it. Yet, deep social and political crises preceded and resulted in Black Saturday. The latter was thus the real blow to the whole state apparatus, providing the crucial moment of de-legitimization of the urban Egyptian liberal elite. Through the attack of the City Center, the rioters denied the legitimacy of this urban liberal elite, who failed to raise itself as an alternative to the traditional agrarian and monarchical elite. Indeed, they did not implement the necessary social and agrarian reforms, thus proving to be as conservative as the rural elite. Moreover the urban elite did not make the national economy autonomous, because of their shared interests with the British. Still, no other political force could govern the country. The Socialist Party and the Communist organizations were not mass parties and the Muslim Brothers were weakened by the government's repression. It would thus be the army, which took power on 23 July—and, as Aclimandos shows, it would be an army autonomous from other social formations. In the 1990s, then, the Cairo Fire became the "commemorative date" of the end of the parliamentary monarchy, permitting the bourgeoisie to mourn the dramatic breakdown of their history. As well, the recent City Center restoration project implies government recognition of the bourgeoisie's collective memory. The contemporary liberal elite intends to re-appropriate the Cairo Fire area, and to reconcile Egypt with its former liberal "Golden Age." However, when speaking of the City Center's prestigious past, this elite risks ignoring the socioeconomic as well as political reasons for the 26 January events.

Notes

1   I base this study on the theory of Michel Dobry, *Sociologie des crises politiques* (Paris: Presses de la Fondation Nationale des Sciences Politiques, 1992); for political and social analysis of demonstrations see also Olivier Fillieule, *Stratégies de la rue: les manifestations en France* (Paris: Presse de Sciences Politiques, 1997) and Pierre Favre, ed., *La Manifestation* (Paris: Presses de la Fondation Nationale des Sciences Politiques, 1990).

2   The urban work of the baron Haussmann inspired the khedive when visiting Paris in 1867.

3   André Raymond, "Le Caire," in *L'Égypte d'Aujourd'hui* (Paris: Éditions du Centre National de la Recherche Scientifique, 1977), 221–41. See as well André Raymond, *Cairo* (London: Hardcover, 2001); and Jean-Luc Arnaud, *Le Caire. Mise en place d'une ville moderne 1867–1907* (Paris: Acte Sud, 1998).

4   Interview with Salon Vert merchant (Cairo, 2000).

5   Interview with an Italian classical singer (Cairo, 2001).

6   Interview with the son of a former civil servant (Cairo, 2001).

7   See for instance Naguib Mahfouz, *Midaq Alley* (Washington: Three Continents Press, 1977); *The Beginning and the End* (Cairo: The American University in Cairo Press, 1985).

8   Albert Cossery, *Les hommes oubliés de Dieu* (Paris: Joelle Losfeld, 1994).

9 · Those demonstrations were not only organized by the traditional parties (Wafd, Liberal Constitutionalist, Nationalists) but as well by new parties such as the Bint al-Nil, and the Socialist Party and organizations such as the Muslim Brothers, the Young Muslim Men's Association, the Partisans of the Peace, the Communists, etc.

10   According to the 1936 Treaty signed for twenty years, the British troops had to decrease their number and the army had to be under Egyptian control.

11   *Misr al-Fatat*, 11/11/51; 25/11/51.

12   *The Egyptian Gazette*, 16/12/51.

13 *Al-Sharq al-Jadid*, 22/11/51, quoted in *Accusation*, "instigating the burning of Cairo" trial, microfilm 10001, National Center for Judicial Studies (Cairo).

14 *Al-Sharq Al-Jadid*, 22/11/51; 19/11/51.

15 *Al-Misri*, 24/01/52.

16 *Al-Misri*, 14/01/52.

17 The same kind of actions were organized in the city center of Alexandria; Metro and Rivoli cinemas were blown up (*al-Misri*, 20/01/52; 21/01/52).

18 *Misr al-Fatat*, 09/12/51, quoted in *Accusation*.

19 *Report of the British Embassy Committee of Enquiry into the Riots in Cairo on the 26th January 1952*, 11/02/1952, Cairo, PRO, FO 371/96873, JE 1018/86.

20 Ralph Stevenson to FO, 30/01/1952, Cairo, PRO, FO 371/96871, JE 1018/34.

21 The government seized this opportunity to repress, in particular, the Communists.

22 *The Egyptian Mail*, 08/03/52.

23 *Al-Ahram*, 23/07/52.

24 *Al-Ithnayn*, quoted in the press review of *Journal d'Alexandrie et La Bourse Égyptienne*, 07/02/52.

25 *Al-Misri*, 17/05/53.

26 *Al-Ahram*, 20/10/52.

27 *Al-Ahram*, 14/05/53.

28 *Al-Ahram*, 09/02/59.

29 *Al-Ahram*, 26/01/62.

30 Gamal al-Sharqawi, *Hariq al-Qahira: "qarar ittiham jadid"* (Cairo: Dar al-Jil li-l-Taba'a, 1976), 278.

31 *Al-Tali'a*, June 1965, 69–79

32 Muhammad Anis, *Hariq al-Qahira* (Beirut: Mu'assasa al-'Arabiya li-l-Dirasat wa-l-Nashr, 1972).

33 Al-Sharqawi, *Hariq al-Qahira*.

34 'Abd al-Rahman al-Rafi'i, *Muqaddimat thawra 23 yuliyu* (Cairo: Maktabat al-Nahda al-Misriya, 1957); the author might have infuriated al-Sharqawi because he used pejorative vocabulary to qualify the people ("rabble," "ill elements"). He was the son of a bourgeois family who witnessed the events on January 26.

35 Al-Sharqawi acquits as well the Wafd Party. The author's study re-legitimizes the Wafd Party, which was re-emerging in the mid-seventies.

36 Gamal al-Sharqawi, *Asrar hariq al-Qahira fi al-watha'iq a-siriya al-britaniya* (Cairo: Dar al-Shuhdi li-l-Nashr, 1985).

37 I gathered information on the rioters from the Egyptian press (*al-Misri, The Egyptian Gazette, Journal d'Alexandrie et La Bourse Égyptienne*).

38 A *bawwab* is, strictly speaking, a doorman; a *sufragi* is a butler; and a *farrash* a manservant.

39 *Le Journal d'Alexandrie et La Bourse Égyptienne*, 28/02/1952: my translation from the French.

40 *The Egyptian Gazette*, 14/03/52.

41 *The Egyptian Gazette*, 17/03/52.

42 *Al-Akhbar*, quoted in the press review of the *Journal d'Alexandrie et La Bourse Égyptienne*, 17/06/52.

43 *Al-Ahram*, quoted in the *Journal d'Alexandrie et La Bourse Égyptienne*, 08/02/52.

44 See Robert L. Tignor, "Bank Misr and Foreign Capitalism," *International Journal of Middle Eastern Studies* 8: 1 (1977), 161–81.

45 See Malak Zaalouk, *Power, Class and Foreign Capital in Egypt: The Rise of the New Bourgeoisie* (London and New Jersey: Zed Books, 1989), 18.

46 Robert L. Tignor, "The Economic Activities of Foreigners in Egypt, 1920–1950: From Millet to Haute Bourgeoisie," *Comparative Studies in Society and History* 22: 3 (July 1980), 431–34.

47 Ghislaine Alleaume, "La production d'une économie 'nationale': remarques sur l'histoire des sociétés anonymes par actions en Égypte de 1856 à 1956," *Les Annales Islamologiques*, T.XXXI

(1997), Cairo, IFAO, 1–16. Ninety percent of the workers and 50 percent of the employees had also to be Egyptians.

48   Alleaume, ibid.

49   Tignor, "The Economic Activities of Foreigners in Egypt," 441–44.

50   Magda Baraka, *The Egyptian Upper Class between Revolutions, 1919–1952* (Oxford: Ithaca Press, 1998), 192–93.

51   Tignor calls this mixed elite "haute bourgeoisie."

52   Isma'il Sidqi had been successively minister of the treasury, minister of the interior, prime minister, vice president then president of the Egyptian Federation of Industries.

53   I would mention for instance: Hafiz 'Afifi Pasha, doctor, chairman of Misr Bank in 1939, company director, influential counselor of the King Faruq, and British agent; Ahmad Abbud Pasha, engineer educated in Scotland, senator, industrial and company director, and British agent.

54   Until the late thirties, representatives of the "urban wing" (Makram 'Ubayd, Mahmud Fahmi al-Nuqrashi) led by al-Nahhas Pasha were ruling the Wafd Party; but in the forties, they were supplanted by the "rural wing" led by Fu'ad Sirag al-Din Pasha.

55   These appointments outraged the public opinion since these personalities were famous pro-British agents.

56   *Al-Ishtirakiya*, quoted in *The Egyptian Gazette*, 09/11/51; Ahmad Husayn declared: "We do not need to state that we have inside information if we tell the people that intrigues have begun for the downfall of the Egyptian Government . . . we must therefore keep this in mind while following the intrigues now taking place to divert the attention of the people away from the great Battle now under way to internal and petty disputes. But should the government remain passive or hesitate, its fate will be the worse. The enemies of the people will cause its downfall and the people will be unable to protect it. Even if the enemies of the people do not cause its downfall, the people itself will pull it down from power."

57   About the palace and 'Ali Mahir's support to Young Egypt, see James Jankowski, *Egypt's Young Rebels. "Young Egypt": 1933–1952* (Stanford, California: Hoover Institution Press, 1975), chapter 3. For 'Blue Shirts,' see Haggai Erlich, *Students and University in 20th-Century Egyptian Politics* (London: Frank Cass, 1989), 15–23.

58   Chancellery to FO, 18/02/52, Cairo, PRO, FO 376/ 96872, JE 1018/78.

59   Chancellery to FO, ibid.: In the aftermath of the murder (February 1949) of the Muslim Brotherhood Supreme Guide Hasan al-Banna (in retaliation for the Prime Minister al-Nuqrashi's murder by a Muslim Brother), the new Supreme Guide implemented a prudent policy. This way he aimed at returning the Brotherhood to legality.

60   See for instance the testimony of Mohamed Naguib, *Egypt's Destiny: a Personal Statement* (London: Doubleday, 1955), 92.

61   Minute, London, 01/02/52, PRO, FO 371/ 96871, JE 1018/36.

62   *Al-Misri*, 15/01/52.

63   Stevenson to FO, 27/01/52, Cairo, PRO, FO371/96870, JE1018/21: The threat of the British army infuriated the king who complained to the American ambassador he convened at four o'clock in the afternoon; he warned that he would not be a "collaborator" if the British army was moving in the Delta. He nevertheless gave up under the British pressure as he convinced al-Nahhas Pasha to proclaim himself the state of emergency.

64   Dobry, *Sociologie des crises politiques*: the author considers the state security forces as "strategic sectors," which have to remain isolated from the others social and professional sectors of the society, especially during large social mobilizations. On the contrary, the state apparatus is endangered.

65   Neither the Wafd nor the palace wanted to use the army. They could not anyway as the 1948 defeat by Israel revealed how under-equipped and under-trained the Egyptian army was.

66 *Report of the British Embassy Committee of Enquiry into the Riots in Cairo on the 26th January 1952.*

67 *The Egyptian Gazette*, 18/12/51.

68 *Report of the British Embassy Committee of Enquiry into the Riots in Cairo on the 26th January 1952*; 130 policemen and their superiors were tried by the minister of the interior for surrendering to the British army at al-Hamada.

69 Stevenson to FO, Cairo, 21/01/1952, PRO, FO 371/ 9873, JE1018/5

70 *Report of the British Embassy, Committee of Enquiry into the Riots in Cairo on the 26th January 1952.*

71 Guilain Denoeux, *Urban Unrest in the Middle East. A Comparative Study of Informal Networks in Egypt, Iran and Lebanon* (New York: State University of New York Press, 1993).

72 Jankowski, *Egypt's Young Rebels*, chapter 3.

73 Accusation, "instigating the burning of Cairo" trial; following an incident that occurred during the organization of a human wall in front of the Rivoli cinema, Ahmad Husayn wrote in *Misr al-Fatat*, 23/12/51: "What we fear the most is that the police stay. If the police lose control and popular anger takes over, then young people who are not members of parties or organized groups will take illegal actions. This is the last time that we deal with this question. After this, we will abstain from taking part in this comedy, leaving the Rivoli Cinema to the people's and young extremists' anger."

74 *Report of the British Embassy Committee of Enquiry into the Riots in Cairo on the 26th January 1952.*

75 See Jankowski, *Egypt's Young Rebels*, 11–12. In late 1931 a committee of Egyptian university students headed by Ahmad Husayn organized a national collection to develop Egyptian industry. The success and the funds gathered in this campaign enabled them to construct a tarboosh factory.

76 See Jankowski, ibid., 38–39: "The first specific object of the party's intensified militancy was the Western and 'un-Islamic' social practices prevailing in Egypt's cities. . . . In January and February 1939, there were more than a dozen attacks on bars in Cairo, Alexandria and provincial cities, ranging from youths entering a café and destroying its stock of liquor to actual arson against taverns. At the same time bar owners began to receive anonymous letters promising similar destruction if they did not cease selling alcoholic beverages."

77 Stevenson to FO, Cairo, 18/03/52, PRO, FO371/96873, JE1018/114.

78 See for example the article of Latifa Muhammad Salim (historian) in *Wijhat nazar*, issue 37, February 2002; and 'Asim al-Tahar (writer) articles in *al-Wafd*, 25–26–27/01/02; his point of view is quite interesting as he insists on the fact that the Cairo Fire victims never spoke, and he criticizes the immoderate use of conspiracy theories.

79 "Fifty years after the Cairo Fire. Glance into the Architecture and the Cultural life of Cairo in the Middle of the Twentieth Century," 26/01/02, The Egyptian Society of Historical Studies, Cairo. For a detailed report on this conference see *Akhir sa'a*, 06/02/02.

80 The sociologist 'Ali Fahmi made an interesting testimony asserting that Egyptian common people participated in the riot; but he concluded by saying that Zionists set the city ablaze because Jews were working in the shops that burned.

81 This last interpretation differs a lot from the Nasserist interpretation, which considered the Cairo Fire a "revolutionary" day.

82 Maurice Halbwachs, *La Mémoire Collective* (Paris: Presses Universitaires de France, 1950), 146.

83 For some more details on this subject see Anne-Claire Kerbœuf, "La restauration du centre-ville: enjeux sociaux et historiques d'un projet urbain," *La Lettre d'information* 4, April 2003, Observatoire Urbain du Caire Contemporain (OUCC), CEDEJ.

Part III

Social Action,
Social Discourse

8 Toward the Democratization of Public Education

The Debate in Late Parliamentary Egypt, 1943–52

Misako Ikeda

Public education in Egypt in the aftermath of World War I was a crucial part of the Egyptian nationalist movement, and the expansion of
public education was one of the most important goals of the Egyptian
government. The British policy of keeping Egyptian public education
at a minimal level during the military occupation from 1882 to 1922 had
a deeply impeding effect on the development of a modern educational
system in Egypt. To remedy this shortage of opportunity, foreign schools
and Egyptian private schools provided some primary and secondary education, and al-Azhar offered Islamic education at all levels.[1] Egypt's recovery
from this hindrance and the establishment of the national educational
system, therefore, were primary concerns for the Egyptian government
and the general public from the twenties onward.

When the British unilaterally declared Egypt independent in 1922,
they handed over the administration of public education entirely to the
Egyptian government while retaining some control over other key areas.
Consequently, the new Egyptian government confronted the task of
creating a new national educational system after nearly a half-century
of interruption. The task included reorganizing public schools at the
elementary and secondary levels, creating new schools and expanding
existing schools to meet the ever-increasing demand from students who
wanted to attend public schools, organizing various types of schools—

private, foreign, and religious—under state control, and establishing a national university. Another serious issue the government faced was the eradication of illiteracy, which required special attention at the elementary level. According to official statistics from 1917, 92.1 percent of Egyptians were illiterate; illiteracy for males was 86.4 percent, and for females 97.9 percent.[2] The Constitution promulgated in 1923 guaranteed free education to all Egyptians based on the principle of democracy, and Article 19 of the Constitution declared that elementary education was compulsory and free for all Egyptian boys and girls.

Numbers and Ideas

Statistics on education in Egypt from the twenties to the fifties testify to the efforts of the Ministry of Education and to the enthusiasm of the Egyptian public for expanding educational opportunities. The portion of the state budget assigned to education steadily increased, from about 1 percent in the early years of the British occupation to 6.4 percent in 1925/26 and to 10.1 percent in 1935/36. From the mid-thirties onward, it stayed between roughly 10 percent and 13 percent. In the fiscal year 1951/52, for example, the education budget was 12.1 percent of the total.[3] The increase in the number of students at all educational levels is also impressive. The total number of enrolled students increased nearly six-fold over forty years, from 324,000 in 1913 to 1,900,000 in 1951.[4] Enrollment in mass-oriented public *elementary* and *compulsory* schools rose from 232,458 (26,514 of whom were girls) in 1913/14 to 895,089 (418,254 girls) in 1944/45, while the enrollment in the elite-oriented public *primary* schools (including kindergartens) rose from 13,978 (2,168 girls) in 1913/14 to 59,939 (11,620 girls) in 1944/45.[5] The increase of students in secondary and higher education was even more dramatic. The number of public secondary students rose from 2,500 (all boys) in 1913 to 37,000 (3,000 girls) in 1944/45. By 1951, after the complete abolition of secondary school tuition in 1950, the number reached 122,000 (19,000 girls).[6] The number of students in higher education, 1,554 in 1913/14, rose to 13,927 (5 percent female) in 1945 and finally to 42,494 (8 percent female) in 1952.[7] The population as a whole was growing in Egypt; there was a 65 percent increase between 1917 and 1952, from 12,750,000 to 21,000,000. Even taking this population increase into account, the relative increase in the number of students between 1913 and the early fifties of 500 percent is still pronounced (see Table 1).

Number of Enrolled Students	1913/14	1933	1944/45	1951
All Schools	324,000	942,000	–	1,900,000
per 1000	27	62	–	91
Public Elementary and Compulsory Schools	232,458 (26,514)	–	895,089 (418,254)	–
per 1000	19 (2)	–	49 (23)	–
Public Primary Schools	13,978 (2,168)	–	59,939 (11,620)	–
per 1000	1 (0.2)	–	3 (0.6)	–
Public Secondary Schools	2,500 (boys only)	15,000 (1,500)	37,000 (3,000)	122,000 (19,000)
per 1000	0.2	1 (0.1)	2 (0.2)	6 (1)
Higher Education	1,554	4,247[*] (0.5%)	13972 (5%)	42,494[**] (8%)
per 1000	0.1	0.3	0.8	2
Total Population	12,186,000[#]	15,275,000	18,134,000[##]	20,872,000

Table 1: Student Enrollment in Schools and Ratios to the Population

Note: The numbers and percentages in parentheses are those of girls.
[*] year 1930   [**] year 1952   [#] year 1913   [##] year 1944

(Sources: Ahmad Abdalla, *The Student Movement and National Politics in Egypt 1923–1973* (London: Al Saqi Books, 1985), 26; Charles Issawi, *Egypt at Mid-Century: An Economic Survey* (London: Oxford University Press, 1954), 67; Roderic D. Matthews and Matta Akrawi, *Education in Arab Countries of the Near East* (Washington, D.C.: American Council of Education, 1950), 34; The Egyptian Government, The Ministry of Finance, Annuaire Statistique de L'Égypte 1956, 11).

This proven achievement of the Ministry of Education, however, should not obscure the critical problems in public education during the parliamentary era. Rapid expansion inevitably created various unresolved questions at all levels. Despite the nominal adoption of the democratic principle in education in the Constitution of 1923, it was not implemented at the foundational level of education. The attempt to restructure this level in the forties and the early fifties involved the Ministry of Education in a long, uneven process. Difficulties arose as a result of several factors: the illiteracy of the great majority of the people, the absence before World War I of the concept of modern public education for the masses, the lack of serious commitment on the part of the government and the ruling elite to general socioeconomic issues relating to the Egyptian masses, and, consequently, insufficient funding for mass education.

Even after the transfer of the administration of public education to the Egyptian government, the elementary level of public education was divided into two systems: elite education in primary schools (*al-madrasa al-ibtida'iya*), which included kindergarten, restore mass education in elementary schools (*al-madrasa al-awwaliya*), and compulsory schools (*al-madrasa al-ilzamiya*). Only graduates of primary elite schools were permitted to receive secondary and higher education. Primary schools charged tuition until 1943 and produced a small group of upper- and middle-class youth who became government officials and professionals. In contrast, the great majority of Egyptian children went to elementary or compulsory schools, which were free. Graduates of these schools, however, were not qualified to pursue secondary and higher education. In addition to other barriers, youths needed to pass an examination in order to receive the primary certificate enabling progression to secondary school.

The basic difference between elementary schools and compulsory schools is that the former provided full-time schooling, while the latter provided schooling on a half-day basis. The compulsory schools were designed to offer a minimum of education to children in rural areas. But the distinction between elementary schools and compulsory schools was often blurred. Only about 45 percent of the eligible children were attending these schools in 1943.[8]

The neglect of elementary and compulsory schools was reflected in the allocation of the education budget. For example, in 1942, elementary and compulsory schools received 23 percent of the education budget, and primary schools 16 percent,[9] although there were about fifteen times more elementary and compulsory students than primary students.[10] The low proportion allotted to elementary and compulsory education in the Egyptian budget becomes clearer when compared to the spending of European countries on elementary education. The figure reached 60 to 70 percent in these European countries after initial spending on buildings and equipment.[11]

From the early 1940s on, experts on education began to talk about the failure of elementary education and to offer possible solutions. Among the proposed solutions, the most comprehensive was to unify the two primary and elementary-compulsory tracks. This solution was expected to produce sweeping effects throughout the Egyptian educational system. The first official proposal for unification was drawn up by the Ministry of Education as early as 1941, but it was not enacted in parliament until 1949 and 1951. Progress during this span of ten years was by no means easy. Lack of a clear national educational policy, internal rivalries in the Ministry of Education, and frequent changes of government all complicated the process. During the forties, every time the government changed, new educational policies replaced old ones.

But the most critical factor was the conservative nature of the ruling circle during this period. Since unification implied the complete overhaul of education at the elementary level and, in the long run, structural changes in Egyptian society, conservative elements took a cautious approach to the issue. Despite all these obstacles, however, the law of unification was finally enacted in 1951. It was a notable achievement in the history of modern education in Egypt. After the military takeover in 1952, the revolutionary government was able to take this policy and implement it in a more complete form.

The second important topic debated during the forties and fifties was free education. The government decided to abolish tuition in primary schools in 1943 and in secondary schools in 1950. The problem of free primary schooling was by nature closely related to the issue of unifying elementary education. Theoretically, it was impossible to achieve unification without abolishing fees, and free primary education inevitably blurred the distinction between the two systems. But in reality, despite the fact that both issues arose at almost the same time during the early forties, the Ministry of Education treated each one independently. More precisely, these goals were considered mutually exclusive. Even after the government decision of 1943, free primary education was not assured during the second half of the forties due to changes of government. At one point, in fact, the decision was virtually revoked, although in a disguised form. Yet this backward step encountered vigorous public opposition, and the issue of free education at the elementary level was finally settled at the end of the forties.

The third important problem in education was the issue of quantity versus quality. In the debate it was called *kamm* (quantity) versus *kayf* (quality), each of which constituted its own school of thought. The school of thought that supported *kamm* held that every child had a right to receive an education at all levels. The school of thought supporting *kayf*, on the other hand, believed that financial and logistical preparations must be made instead of allowing the unplanned and uncontrolled expansion of education, chaos in instruction and administration, and a decline in educational standards. Of course, the issue of quantity versus quality often appeared during debates on unification and free education in primary and secondary schools, as it was so closely connected to the these two issues.

The Beginning of Debates on Free Education and Unification: Nagib al-Hilali's 1943 Report

By the mid-1930s, sociopolitically engaged Egyptians became increasingly concerned with internal social problems. The educational issue was one of the major topics discussed during this period. Debates on education at the time particularly centered on the expansion of elementary education as well as the unemployment of secondary school graduates.[12] This debate on education was, however, temporarily disrupted by the outbreak of World War II. Then, in February 1942, the British forced the palace to replace the anti-British government with the Wafd government headed by Mustafa al-Nahhas. The education policies that had been under consideration in the previous government were abandoned.

The minister of education under the Wafd government, Nagib al-Hilali, formed his own education policy, the first comprehensive one since the Constitution of 1923.[13] In 1943, he wrote *Report on Educational Reform in Egypt*, which drew on international, particularly British and American, models for postwar reform according to the principles of democracy. In the report al-Hilali proposed that Egypt should follow these examples in order to become a member of the international democratic community. Equality of opportunity *(takafu' al-furas)* furnished the key concept of this new educational policy, and al-Hilali announced the government's decision to abolish fees for primary schools.

In the section entitled "New Orientation in Educational Policy—Equality of Opportunity," after discussing at length how this concept had been applied in the United States and Britain, al-Hilali proposed free education for Egypt's primary and secondary school students. He implied that the educational reform he proposed was necessary in order to prevent social schism, which was incongruous with the larger national educational scheme laid out in 1930s and 1940s. As Barak Salmoni discussed in depth in chapter six, the state held a clear educational vision of inculcating in Egyptian youth a sense of unity and national consciousness.

Al-Hilali cited the common problem of impoverished parents unable to pay school fees and expressed concern about the consequences: "These distressing conditions are bound to engender class hatred and breed animosity."[14]

> A feeling of bitterness towards his wealthier schoolmates is inevitably bred and fostered, resulting in the severing of the sacred spiritual ties. Thus, the citizens of one motherland, far from being bound together by unity of sentiment, mind and way of thinking are driven to form hostile factions.[15]

Al-Hilali tried to justify abolishing school fees and providing free primary and secondary education on the grounds that the fees collected from students constitute only a small portion of the entire education budget. He further asserted that the imposition of school fees contradicted "social justice" and "democratic principles," because generous state funds were expended only on children who could afford the fee-charging schools.

Another issue al-Hilali discussed in his education reform plan was compulsory education. Completely discrediting the existing policy, he proposed extending the length of compulsory education to six years, and whole days, "with the utmost expeditiousness that our budget and our resources permit."[16] He also suggested giving compulsory education a practical orientation in conformity with the children's home environments; that is, to train children in "agriculture in agricultural communities, commerce and industry in big cities, and navigation and nautical studies in seaside towns." By treating primary education and mass elementary and compulsory education separately, al-Hilali denied any possibility of the unification of the two systems and even reinforced the special character of compulsory education by tying it to local environments.

Al-Hilali's *Report on Educational Reform in Egypt* was printed in December 1943 and soon submitted to parliament. Al-Hilali opened the session on 3 January 1944 with a detailed explanation of his report to the Chamber of Deputies. Some deputies pointed out crucial issues that were missing in al-Hilali's report, such as equality of opportunity in compulsory education and the unification of primary education and elementary-compulsory education.

In a speech responding to the report, Muhammad Farid Za'luk, a deputy and former Wafdist student leader,[17] pointed out al-Hilali's partiality to applying the principle of equality of opportunity. He argued:

His Excellency the Minister decided to apply this principle to primary and secondary education to the letter, especially by designing free education in all the schools at these two stages of education. On the other hand, he neglected to apply this principle to students in compulsory education, though students in primary and secondary education are less numerous than those in compulsory education.[18]

Deputy Za'luk further pointed to the contrast in his attitude toward primary and secondary education and toward mass education. The minister was highly enthusiastic in applying equality of opportunity to primary and secondary education; yet, when the topic of compulsory education was brought up, his attitude changed and he became much more cautious and reluctant. Za'luk believed that "students in compulsory education are poor, deserve more attention than any other, and are the first ones to whom the principle should be applied"[19] and therefore he considered al-Hilali's treatment of compulsory education inadequate.

Before replying to Za'luk's specific comments on compulsory education, al-Hilali observed that Za'luk's opinion was similar to that expressed by an official in the Ministry of Education who had recently given a lecture under al-Hilali's sponsorship.[20] The Ministry of Education was pressured by two opposing sides, al-Hilali remarked, as if "between a hammer and an anvil." Those like the official and Za'luk claimed that "the Ministry of Education is unfair because primary schools are limited to a small group of Egyptians, when primary schools have to be expanded to villages and small communities in order for Egyptians to have equal opportunities." On the other hand, many others held that "agricultural fields will be ruined if primary schools are extended to the countryside."[21] Al-Hilali leaned toward the latter position. As he explained in his report, he preferred to reform elementary-compulsory education itself, instead of introducing primary schools to villages and towns.

The Committee on Educational Affairs had prepared a statement on al-Hilali's report for the Chamber of Deputies. In the statement, Ibrahim Takla, the chairman and reporter of the Committee, urged the minister of education to examine whether primary and compulsory education should remain as they are or be unified. A little later, another deputy, 'Abd al-'Aziz al-Sufani (Watanist), also raised the issue of the unification of primary and compulsory education, particularly in relation to the abolition of fees in primary schools. After expressing his support for unification, he asked al-Hilali to clarify his opinion about it.[22]

In his reply, al-Hilali finally made it clear that he wanted to keep rural schools and primary schools separate; he opposed the idea of integration of the two different systems:

This important subject did not escape my attention. It is not accurate to say that the report did not indicate this question that is the matrix of the issues. When the report described the policy for the future, differentiating two kinds of education, one called rural education and another primary education, this meant that there will be no integration of rural and primary education.

Al-Hilali defended his position by citing a newly emerging school of thought that supported diversity in elementary education and refuted the once predominant old school position that advocated one type of elementary education "in order to educate sons and daughters of one nation uniformly in thinking, customs, inclination, and predilection." He believed that strict uniformity in elementary education did not bring good results.[23]

Al-Qabbani's Response

Soon after the appearance of al-Hilali's report, an influential expert on education, Isma'il Mahmud al-Qabbani,[24] gave two lectures, on 26 December 1943 and 5 January 1944, under the auspices of the Alumni Association of the Institute of Education. The lectures, which are most likely the ones al-Hilali referred to in the Chamber of Deputies, were subsequently published in a book, *Siyasat al-ta'lim fi Misr* ("The Policy of Education in Egypt").[25] Al-Qabbani had long worked for the Ministry of Education, but when his book was published in 1944 he was the dean of the Institute of Education. When the Wafd government stepped down and the coalition government took office about a year later, al-Qabbani became a technical advisor at the Ministry of Education. Al-Qabbani was one of the most prominent educational experts during this period and represented a school of thought in education, which will be discussed later. He was a main architect of educational policy in non-Wafd governments, thus often at variance with Wafd educational experts, including al-Hilali and the litterateur Taha Husayn.

Al-Qabbani's response to al-Hilali's report was concentrated in the third chapter of his book, "Education of the Common People." Here he agreed with al-Hilali's emphasis on equality of opportunity and free education in primary schools but criticized his approach to compulsory (elementary) education. In order to truly implement equality of opportunity, al-Qabbani stressed the importance of unifying primary and elementary education.[26]

At the outset of the chapter, al-Qabbani defined "equality of opportunity" as the expansion of education to all classes of people to the greatest extent possible. He said, "it is necessary to pay attention to the expansion of general education among the people, before turning to special [elite] education which affects only a limited group."[27] Here, al-Qabbani clarified his usage of "general education." To him it denoted "common education" or what was usually called "compulsory education." The customary usage indicating primary and secondary school, he claimed, was wrong.[28]

Looking back at the development of compulsory education over the past twenty years, he asserted the effort had failed completely in terms of quality and quantity. Thus, he defined the same problem as al-Hilali, but al-Qabbani's solution was radically different. He cast doubts about the existing system:

Where is this equality of opportunities?
What is the justification for this obvious separation among
the sons of one nation? Do all of the students of special [elite]
education have excellent qualities which are not found in general
elementary schools?[29]

To the last question, he asserted that many students in special elite education were of only average or below-average intelligence. Al-Qabbani, known as the only Egyptian child to receive a government scholarship during the British occupation,[30] argued that "many poor children possess an extraordinary level of intelligence and great talents." After listing several great figures from poor families, he asked "how many geniuses are buried and wasted in compulsory schools in villages and towns in Egypt?"[31]

Because compulsory education was a terminal track from which graduates could not proceed to secondary and higher education, al-Qabbani stressed the importance of integrating primary and compulsory education. Keeping the two systems separate produced harmful effects at both individual and national levels. At the national level, it created "a bottomless chasm" between the privileged and the popular classes and "prevents the nation from benefiting from the talents of many of its gifted sons."[32]

Al-Qabbani thus established the importance of unification without directly criticizing al-Hilali, never referring to him by name or quoting passages from his report. Nonetheless, his lectures revealed implicit but strong disagreement with al-Hilali, particularly on elementary education policy. Al-Qabbani's objections were clear: "if we do not achieve the unification, the phrase 'equality of opportunity' will remain a name without substance," and "the decision for free primary education cannot be implemented without this unification."[33]

Unification Under the Coalition Government in 1945: A Long-Term Project

A little over a year later, in May 1945, al-Qabbani submitted a memorandum called *General Policy for Expanding Education in Egypt* to the minister of education. By this time, the Wafd government had stepped down, and after the assassination of Prime Minister Ahmad Mahir, who headed the succeeding government for a few months, Mahmud Fahmi al-Nuqrashi formed a new coalition government in February 1945. Al-Hilali was no longer the minister of education, and the official who received al-Qabbani's memorandum was 'Abd al-Razzaq al-Sanhuri. The content of the memorandum overlapped quite significantly with that of his lectures the year before. Noticeable differences, however, were on two points: freer criticism of al-Hilali's objection to unification and his revised view of free primary education.

After explaining the failure of compulsory education and the need to unify the two elementary systems, al-Qabbani criticized al-Hilali's proposal.

> Last year, the Ministry of Education took one step further to speed up this development [of unification], for it decided to abolish school fees for primary education, as an application of the principle of equality of opportunity in education. In this situation, logic requires the unification of compulsory and primary schools, since equality of opportunity demands that all children receive education in one system. . . . However, the ministry, instead of working toward eliminating this difference, moved to increase it. It decided to make the education of compulsory schools a "vocational" education.[34]

Al-Qabbani asserted that the ministry's decision "destroyed the principle of equality of opportunity from its foundation and increased the barrier which severely impedes the students of compulsory schools from pursuing education and improving their lives."[35]

The second change in his opinion involved reluctance to support al-Hilali's decision on free primary education. Theoretically, if al-Qabbani wanted to achieve unification, he could not oppose the idea of free education, yet if unification was a long-term plan requiring several steps, primary schools could continue to charge fees until the last stage. This was very likely what al-Qabbani had in mind. In 1945, with al-Hilali gone and al-Qabbani back at the ministry as a technical adviser, he voiced open criticism of al-Hilali's policy. His main objection was that a sudden increase in applicants would intensify pressure on primary schools. The pressure on primary schools was already so great, he said, that it was not possible to teach and supervise students correctly. "We assume that the decision for any type of free education is predicated only on the availability of space for all those who want to enroll." Yet, he concluded, "the current situation in primary education is impossible."[36]

Al-Qabbani's objections reveal his cautious attitude toward educational expansion. These issues are also at the heart of important debates that were to unfold later: the first on free primary education, which was hardly settled in 1943 and would preoccupy many critics until 1948; and the second, on quantity versus quality in education. Al-Qabbani gave quality priority over quantity in order to avoid disorder in the schools and a decline in the standard of education, but this position was to be challenged by a majority of people considering education.

Unifying primary and elementary-compulsory schools, which al-Qabbani so forcefully advocated, was not a new issue in the Ministry of Education. In 1940, the ministry had already started to investigate the possibility and had drawn up a preliminary plan.[37] The plan was shelved when the Wafd government came into power in 1942. As discussed earlier, al-Hilali, the Wafdist minister of education, wrote a report in 1943 that was significantly different from the report of 1941. The story was repeated in 1945 when the coalition government took over the ministry.

In an interview given to *al-Ahram* in June 1945, 'Abd al-Razzaq al-Sanhuri[38] explained his long-term educational policies.[39] Their main focus was the rapid expansion of education and its unification at the elementary level. Al-Sanhuri's policies in 1945 were similar to the ideas in al-Qabbani's lecture of 1944 and memorandum of 1945, which indicates al-Qabbani's close collaboration with al-Sanhuri. *Al-Ahram* quoted al-Sanhuri as saying that "there is no justification for having different kinds of education such as compulsory, elementary, and primary." The separate system, he said, was "outmoded and incompatible with democracy" and the advanced countries had abandoned it.

His more reserved attitude toward unification itself, however, emerged a month later when he discussed three reform projects in elementary education at the Chamber of Deputies.

> [T]his third duty [unification] will be secondary in importance to the first two duties, which are the expansion of elementary education and the change of compulsory schools into elementary schools. These two are the duties which will require a larger portion of the effort and money of the ministry. The remaining effort and money will be spent for converting elementary schools into primary schools.[40]

Whether it was derived from his hope of avoiding the chaos of hasty implementation or from a lack of determination and enthusiasm, his reluctance epitomized the attitude of the Ministry of Education toward unification over the next four years. Despite its vow to implement the principle of democracy in education, this slowness confused and frustrated the Egyptian public. This was exacerbated by the ministry's ambivalent attitude toward abolishing primary school fees, a measure that had been introduced by the Wafd government. In contrast, many of the experts and a majority of the people enthusiastically supported the unification project, including the abolition of primary and secondary school fees, and expected the government to fully implement these projects.

Debates on Primary Education Fees 1945–48

In December 1945, the Ministry of Education submitted a proposal on general education, particularly the unification of education at the elementary level, to the Higher Council of Education for consultation.[41] The Ministry of Education proposed that both elementary and compulsory schooling should last six years on a full-day basis and have identical curricula except for instruction in foreign languages. Until this change was accomplished, current primary education would remain as it was. Upon the completion of the elementary level, all students in both school systems would take the same examination and those who passed would qualify for secondary education.[42] Thus, the proposed project was not designed to merge these two different systems but to standardize their duration and curriculum in expectation of a future merging.

The Higher Council for Education delegated the examination of the plan to the Committee on General Education. After two months of investigation,

the Committee agreed on the principles of the plan, but wanted to introduce some modifications. One was to resume the fees for lunch and books
charged to the students in primary schools, except for outstanding students
who had transferred from elementary schools and could not afford them.

At first glance changing fees seems a trivial modification, but in fact it
had significant implications and reflected the major issues and problems
involving education during this period. It not only had effect on the issues
of free public education and unification at the elementary level, but it also
demonstrated the inconsistency of the Ministry of Education's policies.
In addition, the debate over fees reflected the conflict over quantity and
quality and revealed serious rivalries among education experts. Finally, the
government's subsequent compliance with the public's demand to cancel
these primary school fees proved the growing power of the public to
influence government policy.

As al-Qabbani's memorandum of 1945 suggested, the new government
was concerned about congestion in primary schools, which worsened each
year. In his note on educational policies in 1945–47, al-Qabbani used this
congestion as a reason to justify the Committee's decision to modify fees
for lunch and books.

> The pressure exerted on them [primary schools] will increase year
> after year, which inevitably results in a decline in the standard of
> primary education. The Committee decided to request the restriction
> of the number [of students] by limiting free meals to outstanding
> pupils from elementary schools who transferred to the third year of
> primary school.[43]

The Committee's modification of the ministry's proposal regarding
these fees was further extended during the discussion in the Higher
Council and the final decision in the Ministry of Education. Having examined the report of the Committee over three sessions, the Higher Council
announced its own decision in June 1946, consenting to the principle of
unification but imposing further restrictions: students exempted from the
fees had to be not simply "outstanding" (mutafawwiqin) but "excellent"
(mumtazin) in examination performance.

Under the new minister, Muhammad Hasan al-'Ashmawi, the Ministry
of Education further restricted free primary education.[44] In the memorandum it submitted to the Council of Ministers in the same month, fees
were charged not only for meals and books, but also for stationery, health

care, social activities, sports, and the examination for the certificate. The Council of Ministers approved the decision of the Ministry of Education.[45] Al-Qabbani admitted in his memorandum, "A Note on the Projects of the General Educational System from 1945 to 1947," that the decision of the Higher Council for Education to impose fees was "the return of education fees in disguise."

When the news of the new primary education fees reached the general public, the government faced enormous pressure from experts, parents, and others. As early as June 1945, the public criticized the Ministry of Education's ambivalent attitude toward free primary education. One such critic was Taha Husayn who wrote an article submitted to the daily newspaper *al-Balagh*. He perceived the ministry's real intention and strongly condemned its attempt to reverse the decision on free primary education. He states: "The truth of the matter is that people have already gained free primary education. It is a crime against the people and a denial of their rights to cancel this free education, whether this nullification would be an open confrontation or a twisted trick."[46] The issue of modifying the policy of free primary education was brought up in the Chamber of Deputies in December 1945, in the annual "Speech from the Throne" session. Muhammad Hanafi al-Sharif, a Wafdist deputy, criticized the government's policy change, revealing that the amount of new fees was almost equal to the earlier formal tuition.[47]

In September 1946, a few months after the Higher Council decision to charge extra fees for primary education, three articles discussing free primary education appeared consecutively in the journal *al-Thaqafa*. The articles were written by three prominent figures in education, Muhammad Farid Abu Hadid, Ahmad 'Abd al-Salam al-Kirdani, and Muhammad Hasan al-'Ashmawi. The first, by Muhammad Farid Abu Hadid, the dean of the Institute of Education, was entitled "By Special Mail: To His Excellency the Minister of Education." It was addressed to al-'Ashmawi, the minister.[48] While highly praising the achievements of the previous two ministers, Abu Hadid was critical of 'Ashmawi's new policy:

It is not beneficial for us to take a new direction again. It is not in the interest of the country to stop the natural course to which the circumstances of our practical life lead us.

It is doubtful that al-'Ashmawi was the only one who tried to bring about change; as Taha Husayn pointed out, the ministry under al-Sanhuri had already begun this process. However, it is true that al-'Ashmawi took a further step toward reversing the policy.

In the following issue of *al-Thaqafa*, in an article entitled "By Regular Mail: To Professor Farid Bey Abu Hadid," Ahmad 'Abd al-Salam al-Kirdani responded.[49] Al-Kirdani clearly favored the ministry approach to changing fees, and his tone was highly confrontational.[50] In response to Abu Hadid's suggestion to continue on the original course set by the Wafd government, al-Kirdani claimed that this position would discourage innovative ideas in education and impede freedom of thought.

Minister al-'Ashmawi responded to these two articles the following week.[51] In "The Statement of His Excellency the Minister of Education," he denied Abu Hadid's accusation that he was attempting to revoke the policy of free education, instead claiming that he had implemented the principle of equality of opportunity in "its true sense." But al-'Ashmawi soon made it clear that the imposition of fees was intended to keep the present system of primary schools intact, at least for the time being. "It is extremely wrong to think that the present primary education is a [kind of] elementary education which has to open its door to every student." He compared the number of students in primary schools and in other elementary schools: no more than 50,000 attend primary schools, whereas attendance at other schools was approximately one million out of more than three million eligible students. He stated frankly what he thought of the whole issue.

> The fact is that this level of primary education is a "special" level
> of education in which only certain classes of people are accepted.
> It is not reasonable to accept every son and daughter of the common
> people in primary schools in order that they may continue their paths
> through the following levels of education to obtain university degrees.

Al-'Ashmawi's position was, in fact, a highly conservative one, especially in its use of social class as the sole measure for admitting students into primary schools. He makes no mention of giving poor but promising students a chance to enter the primary schools, only children from "certain classes." This position sets him apart from other educational leaders, such as al-Qabbani, who advocated high primary school standards, but also wanted to make it possible for bright students from poor families to attend. Thus, although al-Sanhuri's Ministry initiated the new fee policy in primary schools, al-'Ashmawi carried it a step further, even though it proved incongruous with an effort to democratize education.

Despite his defense of his position in the article, al-ʿAshmawi was forced to modify the fee policy in the face of strong public pressure. In August 1946, a pro-Wafd daily newspaper, *al-Misri*, expressed its objection to the policy in an editorial entitled "The New System of Free Education Returned Primary Education to The System of Charging Tuition."[52] The editorial described the fluctuations in tuition policy since 1945 and expresses a strong objection to the latest decision to limit the number of students exempted from certain fees and urged the ministry to reexamine this system "so as to realize that the issue must be returned to the place where it was." In the face of such opposition, the Ministry of Education modified the policy by exempting those students who could not afford the fees for books, stationery, and the examination—which had previously been charged to all students—without limiting the number of eligible students.[53]

Public pressure on the government continued until, under the new al-Nuqrashi government, al-Sanhuri was again appointed minister of education.[54] In December 1947, the Chamber of Deputies summoned al-Sanhuri to be questioned once again by Muhammad Hanafi al-Sharif, a deputy. Among other issues, al-Sharif addressed free primary education and spoke about the ministry's "dangerous behavior," that is, "vacillating between making primary education free and charging tuition." In support of his allegation, al-Sharif related that when he attended primary school, tuition was £E 6, whereas students were now charged about £E 5 altogether to cover a number of different fees. Al-Sanhuri in reply attempted to frame the fee for meals as a minor adjustment of the original policy.[55]

Despite the ongoing pubic criticism of primary schooling fee, the government managed to retain some of the fees in primary schools. The charge was even stipulated in the proposal for the primary school law submitted by the Ministry of Education to parliament in 1948. In the draft, primary school students were still charged fees for books, stationery, meals, and other fees.[56] While this law was being drafted, however, the Committee for Education Affairs removed all of the fees and presented it to the Chamber for approval. The minister of education, al-Sanhuri, eventually supported the modification, and the Chamber approved the bill at the end of the session.[57] In the final version of the bill, passed by the Senate early in 1949, the fees were dropped altogether, except for an optional ten piasters a month for study activities or extracurricular activities that students joined.[58]

Public pressure was a major factor in the parliament's decision to remove virtually all fees for primary education; at least, the government decided it would be wise to please the people on this matter. The anger directed at the government following the defeat in the Palestine War seems to have been the most urgent reason urging parliament, as well as al-Sanhuri's Ministry, to amend the ruling and appease the people. An atmosphere of extreme political violence prevailed in 1948, which culminated in the assassination of Prime Minister al-Nuqrashi in December. These circumstances were important factors behind the people's victory.

The Primary Education Law of 1949

The primary school law passed in early 1949 ended four years of public debate on the issue of primary school fees. The law was the result of ongoing research and discussion in the Ministry of Education starting in 1945, primarily under the supervision of al-Sanhuri. Shortly before the 1948 parliament session discussing the bill, al-Sanhuri wrote an article explaining the new system stipulated in the bill.[59] In the article, which appeared in *Sahifat al-tarbiya*, a journal sponsored by the Ministry of Education, he expounded the importance of the Egyptian people's support in establishing the project. He asked not only that they understand the extent and the goal of the reform but also that they fully support it. This emphasis on public support was partially derived from the democratic nature of the project, but it was most probably the result of his calculation of the power of public opinion in influencing the course of educational policy. At one point, he said, "the Ministry of Education anticipates the support of the people for this reform with trust and belief in government" and again in his conclusion, "The Ministry fully depends on the support of the people. With these projects, it only aims at their welfare and benefit."

The law was the first comprehensive general education law enacted since the Egyptians took over responsibility for public education three decades earlier. Another article in *Sahifat al-tarbiya* announced the enactment of this law, as well as a law dealing with secondary education, calling the occasion "a critical event in the history of education in Egypt. . . . For the first time in the modern history of Egypt, a comprehensive national system of education was established."[60] The law marked a legal milestone by setting a definite course for unifying primary and elementary education; unification was later completed at least on paper by the Wafd government in 1951, though the real task of implementing the project fell to the post-1952 revolutionary government.

Still the Primary Education Law of 1949 clearly embodied the cautious approach of the old ministry. To preserve the current academic standards in primary education and eventually, to raise the level of elementary education to that of primary education, the two systems were to remain separate for the time being. In both systems, the law stipulated six years of study from the age of six and the use of the same curriculum except foreign languages. At that point, in 1949, the ministry expected unification to take place in twenty or twenty-five years.[61] Despite such cautious measures, the law was based on the principle of democracy, particularly equality of opportunity, and reflected the people's wish to receive education regardless of economic condition.

"The Crisis of Education" in 1949: The Kamm Camp Versus the Kayf Camp

With the enactment of the primary and secondary education laws of 1949, the public became even more eager for state educational provision and demanded expanded educational opportunities. The general political atmosphere in Egypt in the late 1940s also contributed to the public's increasing boldness. After Egypt's miserable defeat in the Palestine War, the authority of the political establishment, including the palace, started to crumble in the eyes of many Egyptians. Public pressure on the government to provide expanded educational opportunities should be understood within this larger sociopolitical context. Thus, just as Fred Lawson showed in chapter two that foreign policies were influenced by domestic political events, this public pressure for more educational opportunity indicates the parallel extent to which domestic policy expectations could be affected by foreign policy performance.

The public gained further strength from the support of such popular figures as Taha Husayn. A new slogan, "water and air," conceived of education as an indispensable part of human life. In an article entitled "The Story of Water and Air" in *al-Thaqafa*, Muhammad Farid Abu Hadid discussed the current public mood,[62] explaining the power of this vivid slogan to attract people and describing the tense beginning of the academic year.

> I have been devoted to my responsibility in the field of education,
> spending day and night in apprehension of the academic year, to the
> extent that my work has cost me my family and my health. Then
> the beginning of this year came. Clamor arose from every corner,
> rebuking the Ministry of Education for not accommodating everyone
> who sought education.

He explained the domination of the popular phrase "water and air" in the public debate.

Some of my respected friends introduced a wonderful innovation about education in their writing and then in their speech: as with water and air, one should not deprive one who seeks education or shut the door in his face. If the Ministry of Education prevents one student, it would be just like depriving him of water and leaving his stomach burned or keeping him from air and letting his breath stop. I truly believe that this invention is novel, witty, amiable, and pleasant. One is pleased to listen to it and is delighted to speak about it. No sooner did people read what these respected friends wrote than they snatched it, reproduced it and repeated it over and over. It has become like a popular song or a beautiful story, or like a well-known proverb about which people do not ask where it is from or who is credited with creating it.

The discourse of "water and air" was so powerful that Abu Hadid confesses, "the fervor almost overtook my heart. I wanted to soothe my soul with these words. Therefore, I joined those who claim: education is a right just like water and air."

Thus, the public debate in 1949 was instigated by the intensified public demand that primary and secondary schools accept as many applicants as possible. In essence, it boiled down to the familiar issues of quantity and quality—*kamm* versus *kayf* in contemporary usage. Each had its own prominent spokesman: the *kamm* camp represented by Taha Husayn, and the *kayf* camp by Isma'il al-Qabbani. An Egyptian historian of education, Sa'id Isma'il 'Ali, refers to the battle between the school of Taha Husayn, or the school of "water and air," and the school of al-Qabbani fought in the 1940s and 1950s. Public opinion at the beginning of the 1949 school year was overwhelmingly in favor of the school of "water and air."[63]

Indeed, in November 1949 *al-Ahram* reported al-Qabbani's comment at a conference for teachers on the government's plight.[64] According to *al-Ahram*, al-Qabbani said: "The ministry, more precisely the ministries, have not been able to direct the attention of public opinion to reality and facts. Rather, in the face of strong public pressure and the discussion in parliament, they were forced to open schools and institutes without arranging everything these schools needed." Taha Husayn, the popularly perceived leader of the school of "water and air," also presented his view in *al-Ahram*. In the summer of 1949, he wrote an article entitled "The Story of Education," in which he criticized the government's inability to respond to the people's desire for education and its excuse that the education budget was limited.[65] Despite the outcry of the people every year, he says, the governments either listened to criticism but did little, or "put their fingers into their ears at other times for fear of listening."

The public debate between the "school of al-Qabbani" and the "school of water and air" was printed in a series of three articles in *al-Ahram* in October 1949. Al-Qabbani represented the current ministry and his own school, and Muhammad Mandur spoke for the school of "water and air." In the first article, entitled "On the Crisis of Education," published 14 October, al-Qabbani defended the position of the ministry.[66] He tried to prove that the government had indeed achieved remarkable progress in expanding public schools and that public demands were not based on a rational assessment of possibilities. Al-Qabbani asserted that much writing on "the crisis of education," over the past ten years had been based on emotion and harmed the progress of education.

He moved on to address the unreasonable request for a sufficient number of schools and teachers for all students. Achieving this goal in secondary education in five years, he estimated, would require 400 new schools to provide sufficient space for 250,000 students, and currently only sixty-two public and fifty-three private secondary schools accommodate 84,000 students. He asked again, more sarcastically:

> With which magic wand can the Ministry of Education and its senior officials . . . double this number of students and classes in five years? Do the respected writers think that it is enough for the ministry and its officials to say to the schools, "come out," and will they appear?

Applying the same logic to the need for teachers, al-Qabbani then warned the public against pressing too hard in this direction. It would only result in a decline in standards, particularly in secondary education, and would endanger the future of the country. To describe this situation, he cited a *hadith*: "we are like a horseman who neither reached his destination nor kept his horse."[67]

Three days later on 17 October, Muhammad Mandur's reply to al-Qabbani appeared in *al-Ahram*.[68] In an article called "The Crisis and Policy of Education,"[69] repeatedly calling al-Qabbani an "honorable educator," Mandur tried to show that al-Qabbani's policy contradicted the general rights to receive an education. Mandur emphasized the Constitution's statement that "every Egyptian has a right to education at all levels as long as one fulfills the conditions stipulated by the law." He regretted that these internationally accepted "self-evident facts" were not recognized by someone like al-Qabbani.

Mandur refused to accept al-Qabbani's explanation for not expanding education because of the short supply of new schools and teachers, stressing the capacity of the ministry to exercise its power and find solutions. He believed, for example, that the ministry possessed the right to take over buildings and to construct new buildings. As for teachers, Mandur affirmed that there are other sources of teachers, for example, graduates of religious schools, but claimed the ministry was reluctant to employ them and saved certain positions only for graduates of its institute. He also suggested making teaching more attractive as a profession by raising teachers' salaries to the level of those of government officials.

Al-Qabbani returned to the debate two weeks later, on 30 October.[70] Despite Mandur's direct attack, al-Qabbani did not respond to Mandur's article at all, nor did he argue about any of the particular points Mandur raised. As the title of his article, "The Crisis of School Space and the Policy of 1944," suggests, al-Qabbani focused on al-Hilali's statements in parliament immediately following the decision on free primary education in 1944. His basic premise was that all the current problems collectively called the "crisis of education" stemmed from that decision. According to al-Qabbani, he simply followed al-Hilali's definition of equality of opportunity and the basic policy al-Hilali had laid. He quoted al-Hilali's definition of equality of opportunity that represented the core of al-Qabbani's argument.[71]

The principle of the equality of opportunity is not meant to create opportunity for every human being to such an extent that the costs and responsibility required exceed the capacity of the nation, whose capacity is restricted by its finance, wealth, ability, and the supply of teachers.

Having quoted al-Hilali's other statements, al-Qabbani added a final remark: "this is what the minister of education responsible [for the current crisis] stated in 1944. By reporting it, I wanted to clear the air and to enlighten those who search for truth." Thus, al-Qabbani adroitly defined the origins of the current dispute and of his position.

Taha Husayn's Leadership
under the Wafd Government 1950–52

The Wafd government, which returned to power in January 1950 after a
five-year absence, brought with it new educational policies under the leadership of Minister of Education Taha Husayn. As mentioned earlier, Taha
Husayn represented the popular school of "water and air" as opposed to
the "school of al-Qabbani," which had provided the basic principles for
the previous Ministry of Education. Taha Husayn introduced the popular
wish for the rapid expansion of educational opportunities. These expectations were soon realized with the new government's announcement of
completely free secondary and vocational education in the Speech from
the Throne in January 1950.

Taha Husayn made his first speech in parliament on January 30,
expressing his frank opinion of the educational policy of the previous
coalition governments. He explained the failed attempts by the previous
governments to revoke the policy of free education enacted by the previous Wafd government.

> Those who came after al-Hilali Pasha in the Ministry of Education
> were concerned about this free education. They circled around it as
> an army circles around a citadel and wanted to penetrate it from any
> possible back door. But they finally realized that there was no way
> to take back what the people had gained. No one could say that free
> education had to be abolished.[72]

He also discussed the blame laid on the Wafd government for the previous
year's crisis. It is likely that the "advocate" mentioned is al-Qabbani, who
criticized al-Hilali's decision in *al-Ahram*.

> Then the advocate of the previous governments said last
> summer, when the crisis of education occurred, that those who
> established free primary education are responsible for this crisis.
> Responsible for this crisis after five years since their departure
> from power?![73]

This first speech by a reputed free thinker and outspoken advocate for
democracy and justice was accusatory toward the previous governments
and defensive of his own. However, such a statement would have pleased

many people and contributed to his ever increasing popularity and the popularity of his educational policy.

In addition to his already-established reputation, Taha Husayn's popularity can also be attributed to the simple and vivid expressions with which he described his principles. Through his style as well as the content of educational policy, Taha Husayn had an insurmountable advantage over al-Qabbani, whose writing and speaking style was that of a competent technocrat: concise, rational, and well-argued, but decidedly lacking in charm and emotion. His analyses, which often forced his audience to see hard facts, did not help him with the public.

Education as "water and air" was already one of the most well-known expressions. Another typical example of his style is "ignorance and fire" analogy. In an interview given to *al-Ahram* prior to the announcement, Husayn encapsulated his view of education while talking about the urgent need to increase the number of teachers.[74]

> I consider ignorance in Egypt as a demolishing fire. A demolishing
> fire has to be extinguished with every sensible means available. It is
> quite foolish to say that the fire should not be put out except with
> clear water supplied by systematic pumps. The fire will be put out
> with clear water or unclear water, with a pump or without a pump,
> anything carrying water.

Taha Husayn coined other memorable expressions as well. An interview in *al-Ahram* in May 1950 was called "We Are in an Age in Which Education is Not Sold."[75] Another expression, "education as a spiritual defense," was used as a subcaption in the article. He explained:

> The state does not bargain with citizens in matters related to the
> defense of the nation. Likewise, it should not bargain with them in
> matters related to the defense of the "spirit of the nation." Ignorance,
> particularly in a country like Egypt, is considered a threat of no less
> importance than a foreign enemy.

The common theme of these expressions was clear: education is the natural right of all citizens. Taha Husayn recognized the obligation of the government to make every effort to provide educational opportunities.

In the same interview, Taha Husayn claimed that those concerned with the progress of education in Egypt shared common goals despite apparent differences of opinion. In answer to a question about the delay in discussing the free education bill in the Senate, he stated:

It is believed that the opposition agreed to free education, but it in fact wants to oppose the government. This is customary behavior for the opposition and the government. The important thing is that the bill won approval. There is no doubt that the opposition and the government agreed particularly on the necessity to put educational issues in Egypt above political differences among the parties and above any bargaining between the government and students or students' fathers.[76]

At first glance, this statement seems to contradict his January speech in parliament, which revealed fierce rivalries. It can also be taken as political rhetoric intended to undermine the power of the opposition. Taha Husayn's statement, however, expressed the true nature of educational debate during this period. Rivalries, mistrust, and animosity among individuals and various groups inside and outside of the Ministry of Education caused delay, complication, and confusion in educational development.[77] Each official and expert had different priorities and methods. The debate on quantity and quality, for example, touched upon the fundamental issue of how to approach education, especially when aggravated by frequent changes in government. With all these differences and difficulties, however, most of those involved in public education in Egypt shared a few fundamental goals. Among these goals was the democratization of education. Factionalism, differing priorities, and common goals were intertwined, giving rise to a complicated development process. Yet overall, public education moved toward democratization.

In addition to its decision on free secondary and vocational education, the new Wafd government passed a law unifying education at the elementary level in 1951. The law of 1949 had marked a major step toward unification, but the previous government considered the final merging of elementary schools and primary schools premature and did not expect to complete the merging for another twenty years. The Wafd government sped up the process.

The new law stipulated complete unification and termed all the schools at the elementary level "primary schools." Certainly, this did not mean that all the schools became primary schools overnight. The implementation of this legislation was expected to take a long time. Nevertheless, the

1951 law was a significant achievement for the Wafd government, one that went beyond the 1949 law of the previous government. As the minister of education, Taha Husayn also considered free university education. He encountered strong opposition, however, and the idea was not carried out until 1962 under 'Abd al-Nasser.[78]

Conclusion

During the final ten years of parliamentary rule in Egypt, the system of public schools underwent fundamental changes. A new direction based on the principles of democracy and nationalization was mapped out, and the task of implementing the new system undertaken. Both primary and secondary education were made free, and the elementary level of education was unified. In the new system, all children in the nation attending public primary schools were to receive the same education, and all children regardless of financial or social background could continue their studies in secondary schools, if they were qualified.

However, implementing these new policies was far from easy. Frequent changes of government during this period produced serious repercussions in educational policy. Every time a new government took over, another faction of educational experts gained control of the Ministry of Education and implicitly or explicitly modified the policies of previous governments. Fierce rivalries among factions and individuals caused delays and complications in policy development. Moreover, the underlying tendency to neglect mass education in comparison with elite education, despite mass illiteracy, made the implementation of the new policies difficult. This was clearly reflected in the uneven allocation of the state budget.

At the same time, however, common aspirations for public education were held by educational experts as well as the Egyptian public. Many Egyptian educators hoped to achieve equality of opportunity in public education, while the Egyptian public wanted access to public primary and secondary education regardless of their financial and social background. The aspirations of the common people often became such a powerful force that when they gained the backing of influential educators, they were able to change government policies. For example, in the late 1940s, powerful public pressure forced the government to remove the fees it charged primary school students.

The division into two educational camps also became clear with time: the *kamm* camp, which advocated rapid implementation of the right of all people to receive education, and the *kayf* camp, which emphasized the quality of education and order in educational operations. Though the former appeared to win over, the divergence between the two points of view was evident in almost all debates on public education, and no easy settlement was reached. When Egypt entered a new era in 1952, the approach committed to quantitative educational expansion was finally enshrined in law and nationalist educational policy.

Finally, it is necessary to see the debate on education in the larger sociopolitical public discourse during this time, particularly with regard to the generally accepted idea of equality of opportunity. In the 1930s but even more so in the post-World War II era, internal social problems became the agenda for public discussion. Poverty, class cleavage, living standards of the people, mass education, and public health were among the major topics, tackled by social critics, politicians, journalists and scholars. The concepts of "social justice" and "social reform" were frequently employed as bases of their arguments. The issue of education was one of the three central concerns of the day, as epitomized in the oft-used phrase, "poverty, ignorance, and disease."

The Egyptian regime was eventually taken over by the military in 1952, despite the warnings voiced within the establishment against radical political change. The government of Free Officers under the leadership of 'Abd al-Nasser implemented many social policies that could not have been carried out in the monarchical regime, the first of which was the agrarian reform. The close examination of these policies, however, reveals that the roots of the policies and the public debate on these issues can be traced to the previous era.

Educational policy was not an exception. Free public education and the unification of the elementary level of education, for example, had made a steady progress in the ten years prior to the revolution of 1952. The new regime simply took over and completed the efforts, embodied first in the new educational law of 1953, enacted without rivalries among political parties or educational experts, as the former were outlawed and the latter were widely supportive of Nasserist populism. The educational policy in the new regime, along with other social policies, owed much to public debate in the parliamentary era and represents a continuity between the two seemingly separate eras.

Author's note: This is a revised version of the article entitled "The Debate on Public Education in Late Parliamentary Egypt 1943–1952" published in *Annals of Japan Association for Middle East Studies (AJAMES)* 16, 2001, 265–307. The author was granted permission from *AJAMES* for this publication.

Notes

1   The role of foreign schools for primary and secondary education cannot be ignored. But the number of students in these schools was still limited, and the students were disproportionally foreign citizens and non-Muslim Egyptians. Equally important, but often overlooked, was the role of Egyptian private schools at primary and secondary levels during the occupation. Run by individuals and charitable and religious societies, these schools adopted a similar system and curriculum to public schools and continued to play a significant role after World War I as an alternative to public schools. Since public schools accepted only a small number of students, private schools educated more students than public schools. But in general the quality of private education was lower than that of public education. See H.M. Ammar, "An Enquiry into Inequalities of Educational Opportunities in Egypt" (M.A. thesis, Institute of Education, University of London, 1949), 183–84. Later, Egyptian private schools were greatly affected by new policies for free education and unification. A comprehensive study of Egyptian schools in the nineteenth and twentieth centuries has yet to be done. For the Egyptian schools during the occupation, see Sa'id Isma'il 'Ali, *Dawr al-ta'lim al-misri fi-l-nidal al-watani* (Cairo: General Egyptian Book Organization, 1995).

2   Egyptian Government, Ministry of Finance, *The Census of Egypt Taken in 1917*, vol. II, 1921, 565.

3   Ahmad Abdalla, *The Student Movement and National Politics in Egypt 1923–1973* (London: Al Saqi Books, 1985), 25.

4   Charles Issawi, *Egypt at Mid-Century: An Economic Survey* (London: Oxford University Press, 1954), 67.

5   Roderic D. Matthews and Matta Akrawi, *Education in Arab Countries of the Near East* (Washington, D.C.: American Council of Education, 1950), 34. The differences between elementary, compulsory, and primary schools are explained below.

6   Issawi, *Egypt at Mid-Century*, 67; Matthews and Akrawi, *Education in Arab Countries*, 34.

7   Ibid.; Abdalla, *The Student Movement*, 26.

8   H.M. Ammar, *An Enquiry*, 128–29. The figure of the enrollment perhaps includes the number of children attending private and foreign schools.

9   Ibid., 141.

10 This figure was calculated from the student numbers in 1944/45, in Matthews and Akrawi, *Education in Arab Countries*, 34.

11 Ammar, *An Enquiry*, 143–44.

12 Among the notable publications on education and other social issues in the late 1930s, see Taha Husayn, *Mustaqbal al-thaqafa fi Misr* (Cairo: Matba'at al-Ma'arif, 1938); Mirrit Ghali, *Siyasat al-ghad* (Cairo: Matba'at al-Risala, 1938); and Hafiz 'Afifi, *'Ala hamish al-siyasa* (Cairo: Matba'at Dar al-Kutub al-Misriya, 1938).

13 He graduated from the Khedivial Law School in 1912. He was the minister of education in Tawfiq Nasim's government in 1934–36. After joining the Wafd party in 1938, he again became the minister of education under al-Nahhas's government in 1938–39 and 1942–44. He headed cabinets twice in 1952 prior to the Free Officers' coup.

14 he concept of class began to make an appearance in public discourse in Egypt in this period. The liberals often used it to warn of the danger of class conflict and social upheaval and prevent the breakdown of the liberal democratic system.

15 H.E. Naguib El-Hilali, *Report on Educational Reform in Egypt* (Cairo: Government Press, 1943), 23.

16 Ibid., 31.

17 He was the Wafdist student leader during the student uprising in the mid-thirties. See Abdalla, *The Student Movement*, 86.

18 *Madabit* (Parliamentary Records), the Chamber of Deputies, 3 January 1944, 329.

19 Ibid., 330.

20 The lecturer that al-Hilali mentioned is most likely Isma'il al-Qabbani, who was the principal promoter of the unification of elementary education at the Ministry of Education. Al-Hilali said the lecture was given at the Royal Geographical Society (Ibid., 332), where al-Qabbani had given lectures on the unification of elementary education on 26 December 1943 as well as 5 January 1944 (*al-Ahram*, 27 December 1943). It seems that al-Hilali tried to belittle Za'luk by implying that he merely copied the opinions of the lecturer. When Za'luk said that he had not heard about the lecture, al-Hilali sarcastically said that "whatever the matter may be, it is well-known—especially among important people." This induced laughter from the audience.

21 *Madabit*, the Chamber of Deputies, 3 January 1944, 332.

22 Ibid., 337, 338. Za'luk asked Takla his opinion, but Takla's answer was cut off by the president of the Chamber, who warned him not to deviate from his role as the reporter of the committee.

23 Ibid., 338, 339.

24 He was involved in creating the Institute of Education in 1929 and taught there. He also worked for the minister of education as a technical adviser and a secretary of state. Later he became the minister of education in the military government in 1952–54.

25 sma'il Mahmud al-Qabbani, *Siyasat al-ta'lim fi Misr* (Cairo: Lajnat al-Ta'lif wa-l-Tarjama wa-l-Nashr, 1944).

26 Al-Qabbani had already expressed his conviction regarding the unification of elementary education much previously. In 1925, he gave a lecture entitled "The Unification of Primary and Elementary Education" at the invitation of the Syndicate of Teachers and quotes from it in his lecture of 1943/44. The full text of the lecture given in 1925 is in Isma'il Mahmud al-Qabbani, *Dirasat fi masa'il al-ta'lim* (Cairo: Maktabat al-Nahda al-Misriya, 1951), 118–41.

27 Al-Qabbani, *Siyasat*, 32.

28 Ibid.

29 Al-Qabbani, *Siyasat*, 35.

30 When Sa'd Zaghlul was the minister of education, he visited a village school in Asyut in 1908 and found a gifted child, Isma'il al-Qabbani, from a poor family. Zaghlul, against the British policy on education, provided a scholarship to the child to study at government schools. See Sa'id Isma'il 'Ali, *Wijhat nazar fi fikr Isma'il al-Qabbani al-tarbawi* (Cairo: Dar al-Thaqafa li-l-Tiba'a wa-l-Nashr, 1974), 8.

31 Al-Qabbani, *Siyasat*, 35.

32 Ibid., 36, 38–39.

33 Al-Qabbani refuted two arguments opposing the unification scheme. The first, that compulsory education should not be separated from the environment in which children live, and that it should include practical training in agriculture and industry in the countryside, he firmly rejected, saying that educational experts agree that vocational training should not begin at the elementary level. The second argument, the discrepancy in teaching foreign languages, al-Qabbani answered by arguing that teaching foreign languages in primary schools was no more than the remnant of foreign occupation. He also asserted that educational experts in other countries generally agreed that learning a foreign language should not begin until the age of ten or eleven.

34 Al-Qabbani, *Dirasat*, 188–89.

35 Ibid.

36 Ibid., 192, 193.

37 Ibid., 238.

38 He was a prominent jurist. Born in 1895, he received a doctorate in law from the University of Paris. He was a prosecutor, judge, and dean of the Faculty of Law (1936). He became secretary

of state in the Ministry of Education in 1939 and in the Ministry of Justice in 1944. He was anti-Wafd.

39   *Al-Ahram*, 5 June 1945.

40   *Madabit*, the Chamber of Deputies, 9 July 1945, 1162.

41   The Higher Council for Education was reactivated after three years of suspension in December 1945. With the minister of education as the chairman, the other members were all former ministers of education, permanent secretaries of education, technical advisers and their assistants, the chancellors of the two government universities, officials of other ministries, and some members of parliament. See Matthews and Akrawi, *Education in Arab Countries*, 5.

42   Al-Qabbani, *Dirasat*, 238–39.

43   Ibid., 242–43.

44   Al-'Ashmawi was the minister of education in the Sidqi government, which was in office from February to December 1946.

45   Ibid., 246.

46   "Free Primary Education: A Right which Egyptian People have Gained," *al-Fajr al-jadid*, 16 June 1945, 14. The quotations of Taha Husayn's 10 June article in *al-Balagh* are from this article.

47   *Madabit*, the Chamber of Deputies, 24 December 1945, 356.

48   Muhammad Farid Abu Hadid, "By Special Mail: To His Excellency the Minister of Education," *al-Thaqafa* 402, 10 September 1946, 1011–13. Abu Hadid was an educationist, novelist, and social critic. He became a undersecretary of state at the Ministry of Education in 1950.

49   Ahmad 'Abd al-Salam al-Kirdani "By Regular Mail: To Professor Farid Bey Abu Hadid," *al-Thaqafa* 403, 17 September 1946, 1040–42. Al-Kirdani was the dean of the Institute of Education in 1937 and the general secretary of Fu'ad I University in 1945–47. He became a secretary of state at the Ministry of Education in 1949.

50   Both Abu Hadid and al-Kirdani were original founding members of the Committee of Composition, Translation, and Publication. They were supposed to have known each other for a long time.

51   Muhammad al-'Ashmawi, "A Statement from His Excellency the Minister of Education," *al-Thaqafa* 404, 24 September 1946, 1068–70.

52   *Al-Misri*, 28 August 1946.

53   Al-Qabbani, *Dirasat*, 247.

54   The new al-Nuqrashi government, which succeeded the Sidqi government in December 1946, lasted until the assassination of al-Nuqrashi in December 1948. Al-Sanhuri was the minister of education in al-Nuqrashi's government and kept this position until July 1949 under the government headed by Ibrahim 'Abd al-Hadi.

55   *Madabit*, the Chamber of Deputies, 15 December 1947, 165.

56 ' Awad Tawfiq 'Awad, "'Alaqat majjaniyyat ta'lim al-marhala al-ula fi Misr bi-l-'adala al-ijtima'iya bayna al-talamidh: dirasa ta'rikhiya min 1923 ila 1981" (M.A. thesis, Ain Shams University, 1992), 205.

57   *Al-Ahram*, 7 July 1948.

58   'Awad, "'Alaqat majjaniyyat al-ta'lim," 206.

59   'Abd al-Razzaq al-Sanhuri, "The Reform of the System of General Education," *Sahifat al-tarbiya*, June 1948, 4–7.

60   "The New System for Education," *Sahifat al-tarbiya*, February 1949, 4.

61   *Al-Ahram*, 27 October 1948.

62   Muhammad Farid Abu Hadid, "The Story of Water and Air," *al-Thaqafa*, 569, 21 November 1949, 5–6.

63 Sa'id Isma'il 'Ali, *Wijhat nazarin fi fikr Isma'il al-Qabbani*, 4–5. Isma'il 'Ali cited al-Qabbani's assessment in 1945 that *kamm* had always had the upper hand over *kayf* except for the period 1935–41. Al-Qabbani's assessment may also be true of the period following 1945. (Ibid., 13.)

64 *Al-Ahram*, 4 November 1949.

65 *Al-Ahram*, 11 July 1949. Taha Husayn wrote another article with a similar argument under the same title a month later, 2 August in *al-Ahram*.

66 *Al-Ahram*, 14 October 1949.

67 The horseman pushed his horse too far, because he was in a hurry.

68 Muhammad Mandur (1907–65) was a literary critic, lawyer, professor, and journalist. He was the editor of *al-Wafd al-misri*, the Wafd Party's daily newspaper, and the leader of the Wafdist Vanguard, the left-wing faction of the party, which had close tie with Marxists. He was elected to parliament in 1949. In the twenties he studied with Taha Husayn at Cairo University.

69 *Al-Ahram*, 17 October 1949.

70 *Al-Ahram*, 30 October 1949.

71 He cites it from the report of the Financial Committee in the Chamber of Deputies in 1944.

72 *Madabit*, The Chamber of Deputies, 31 January 1950, 38.

73 Ibid., 39.

74 *Al-Ahram*, 23 January 1950.

75 *Al-Ahram*, 8 May 1950.

76 Ibid.

77 Taha Husayn pointed out as early as the mid-thirties, based on his twenty years of observation, that no other ministry in the country was so plagued by competition, hatred, deception, and distrust at all levels as the Ministry of Education. Taha Husayn, *Mustaqbal al-thaqafa fi Misr* (Cairo: Dar al-Ma'arif, 1993), 109–10.

78 However, by 1955, 71 percent of university students were exempted from tuition either because of financial need or because they achieved the exam score set by the university for exemption. Malcolm Donald Reid, *Cairo University and the Making of Modern Egypt* (Cambridge: Cambridge University Press, 1990), 110.

9 Empowering Women, Engendering Change

Aziza Hussein and Social Reform in Egypt[1]

Amy J. Johnson and Scott David McIntosh

It is something of an axiom today that development projects work best when the people who will benefit from them are active participants in the organization, planning, implementation, and evaluation stages of the projects. It is also generally acknowledged that reforms cannot be forced; in order to succeed, the people for whom they are designed must want them to work. Likewise, it is widely accepted that both men and women have a role to play in national development—women, as men, must be the agents as well as the beneficiaries of reform if it is to be successful.

This was not always the case. In Egypt, the early twentieth century marks the first time that women began to mobilize and become politically active on a large scale. Although there are examples of prominent female activists in earlier periods of Egyptian history, it is not until this period that women became increasingly involved in writing and publishing, in demanding political rights, in debating their own roles in the family and in public life, and in forming charitable associations on a wider scale. Likewise, the concept of aided self-help as a governing methodology of social reform and development initiatives did not gain favor in Egypt until the mid-1930s. Prior to this time, "reform" projects tended to be small-scale charity projects geared toward the short-term, ignoring the need for large-scale programs that would involve the people of a particular area as active participants and seek to achieve development or change over the long term.

Born in 1919, Aziza Hussein grew up in this changing environment, a time when women were becoming more vocal, more active, and more politically oriented. She was educated at a time when new ideas of social reform were being taught, debates about reform were commonplace, and innovative strategies for national development were being devised. In 1950, Hussein began building on these two trends in Egyptian political life and created what was at that time a new mode of social activism: aided self-help projects designed by and for the benefit of women. Her pioneering work with the Cairo Women's Club and the Rural Social Centers project resulted in the founding of the nation's first rural day-care center in the village of Sindiyun—a center that became the foundation of women's activism throughout the countryside.

This chapter begins by reviewing the patterns of women's activism in the earlier twentieth century and locating Hussein within that context. It then analyzes the Sindiyun project, arguing that it was a unique and new form of women's social reform activism. The chapter concludes by arguing that in merging the two trends or women's activism and aided self-help for social reform, Hussein created a new philosophy of development, forged an ideology that would guide her throughout her career, and set the pattern that later NGO, IGO, and governmental efforts would follow. She thus stands out as a unique figure in the history of Egyptian development, and her projects provide examples that can be used to refute the notion that social reform efforts in pre-1952 Egypt were simply confined to private, small-scale, charity-oriented endeavors.

Women's Activism and Social Reformist Initiatives

At the turn of the twentieth century, Egyptian women were becoming increasingly active in the public sphere.[2] They began publishing magazines, journals, and newspapers, became active writers, and joined the nationalist struggle for complete independence from Britain. Simultaneously they were both the objects of and participants in the debates over veiling and gender segregation. Women also founded organizations to lobby for increased political rights for women, changes in family law, and more liberal interpretations of religious law.[3]

From the 1890s until the World War I era, women were becoming more and more engaged in journalism; as Beth Baron has documented, the rise of the women's press in Egypt served as one of the foundations upon which later women's activism was built. This emerging "female literary culture" allowed women a new forum in which to "debate issues such as marriage and divorce, veiling and seclusion, and education and work."[4] The period, Baron asserts, also witnessed an "expansion in education, the rise of associations, and greater mobility for women." All the while, "newspapers and periodicals proved key instruments for transmitting new ideas in Egypt."[5] Interestingly, she notes that 1919, the year Hussein was born, was the year that

> the narrative of Egyptian women's history and the story of the women's movement often begins. Yet women's participation in the 1919 Revolution must be seen as a continuation of actions undertaken in earlier decades. Moreover, the seeds that bore fruit in the 1920s and 1930s — notably the formation of women's organizations, educational and legislative reform, and greater integration in society — were planted from the 1890s. The Egyptian women's press stood at the center of this process, documenting and defending a widening range of activities in certain urban circles.[6]

Building upon their involvement in the literary revolution, then, women also became involved in political revolution. In 1919, after Wafd party demands for Egypt's complete independence from Britain were denied and its leaders were exiled,[7] many of the wives of Wafd revolutionaries continued what their husbands had started. They created a women's committee of the Wafd and "paraded in the streets shouting slogans for independence and freedom from foreign occupation. They organized strikes and demonstrations, they organized boycotts of British goods . . . in brief they agitated side by side with their men."[8] Women thus were active participants in the revolution of 1919.

Their involvement in this political revolution soon spread to the social sphere, where women became vocal advocates of social change. Many of the most notable Egyptian women of the century were key figures in such protests. Huda Sha'rawi joined with women like Mary Kahil and Nabawiya Musa to found the League of Women in 1923. Sha'rawi and the League of Women began fighting not only for independence from Britain, but for the political rights of women. In other words, they not only took up the male-dominated cause of political independence, but they also began fighting for social independence — for increased roles for women in politics and public life. They were "fighting the political establishment — which comprised their husbands and relatives — to gain recognition of their right to education and to political equality."[9]

With groups such as the League of Women to build upon, exclusively women's parties began to form within twenty years. The new women's parties, going a step further than their predecessors, "embraced more radical ideas and were prepared to engage in more aggressive strategies for change. Their tactics were populist, their goals comprehensive, and their tone forceful."[10] Political reform was fundamental to the platforms of parties like the Egyptian Feminist Party, established in 1944 by Fatma Ni'mat Rashid, which advocated the legalization of birth control and abortion. In 1948, Doria Shafik's Bint al-Nil organization began a campaign for gender equality in the political sphere.[11]

In other words, the early twentieth century was a time of vibrant women's political activism. It was also a time of vibrant social activism. By the early twentieth century, there were a wide variety of groups and organizations active in providing various types of aid and charity to those in need. Such groups were by no means new in this period; indeed, governments, individuals, and religious organizations had provided such aid throughout Egypt's history.[12] In the early twentieth century, however, there were also a growing number of bodies dedicated to alleviating both urban and rural poverty, expanding access to education, and combating endemic and epidemic diseases. These groups were formulated to respond to what were deemed the three most fundamental problems of the nation: "poverty, ignorance, and disease."[13] Many of them were operated by women.

Groups which attempted to address the problem of poverty included the traditional *awqaf* (charitable endowments; singular: *waqf*). Wealthy women with substantial resources at their command had often been leaders in charitable activity, using their money to set up *awqaf*.[14] By the mid-twentieth century, this practice had become routine, and charitable activity in a broad sense had become a standard part of aristocratic life, adding a new dimension to reform efforts.[15] The charities administered vaccinations and distributed medicine to both urban and rural populations and provided emergency relief in cases of natural disaster. In short, they attempted to improve the general standard of living for the *fallahin* and for the urban poor.

The year 1944 saw the establishment of the formidably-titled League of Women Students and Graduates from the University and Egyptian Institutes, which called on the government to establish nurseries for working class women,[16] thus making it easier for these women to work outside the home and contribute to family income. Yet, as Botman notes, this group was like many others of the period in that it was primarily concerned with debating the issues rather than in implementing actual reformist programs. It "conceived of itself essentially as a gathering place for young women who were interested in both the gender-oriented problems of women and the larger difficulties challenging Egypt as a nation," a place for exchanging ideas rather than carrying them out.[17]

While urban issues were the focus of most such endeavors, by the 1940s problems in rural areas were significant enough to merit substantial attention from a number of charities. One such group, the Oeuvre des Écoles Gratuites des Villages de Haute-Égypte, visited villages periodically to give basic health and literacy instruction and to distribute food, clothing, and cleaning supplies to the rural poor.[18] They also assisted in times of crisis, providing aid during epidemics and natural disasters.

Groups that focused their activities on the second problem, "ignorance," were largely non-governmental, and many of the groups mentioned previously that were engaged in poverty alleviation efforts were also attempting to spread education and literacy.[19] In the period of British control of Egypt that began in 1882 and lasted until independence in 1922, education was not vigorously promoted by the government. Until the British occupation, education had been free, yet with British control came substantial changes in education, including the mandate that education was henceforth to be fee-based. In part, this was based on British financial concerns—one of their primary objectives was to stabilize the economy to ensure the repayment of Egypt's European debts. But part of the rationale was political—in the view of British Agent and Consul General Lord Cromer, education was dangerous and would create a group of educated young men who could endanger British control.[20] Indeed, only three state secondary schools were allowed under the Cromer administration, and, although "in the decade before World War I, state spending on education increased," "at its peak it only reached 3.4 percent of the national budget."[21] Thus, until 1922, activities to combat "ignorance" were largely informal, outgrowths of societies engaged in poor relief, or often based in the existing framework of religious schools (kuttabs).[22]

The Mabarrat Muhammad 'Ali, founded in the nineteenth century, was primarily concerned with issues of public health and disaster relief—the third "great problem" of rural Egypt. While this organization established some permanent health clinics in rural Egypt,[23] it was mainly engaged in responding to immediate health threats by mobilizing its members, moving into an area of crisis, administering aid, and moving on.[24] For all the good work done by the Mabarra, its programs were by nature short-lived, and its methods held some inherent problems. As discussed by several scholars reviewed in chapter twelve by Nancy Gallagher, the Mabarra took a top-down approach: its members would plan a project and find a willing donor of a plot of land on which they could build a clinic or dispensary. They would then talk to the 'umda (village leader) and convince him of the importance of their project to the village. The 'umda, in turn, would go to the village and convince the people. In other words, "the villagers, following the suggestions of their hierarchical superior, would cooperate in building the dispensary, which thus lost a little of its 'charitable' aspect and became a cooperative village venture."[25] The picture arising from such charitable projects is one of the villagers not as active participants in the programs, but as passive recipients of aid, "following the suggestions of their hierarchical superior," and being "wheedled into accepting hospitalization."[26]

While the intentions of such charitable organizations may be applauded, the groups did not succeed in bringing any type of lasting, practical reform to the areas in which they operated—nor was this even their goal. Likewise, they did not involve the people of the areas in which they operated in their programs as anything other than objects of aid. Reform agendas were thus dictated and imposed, with positive intentions and with some positive short-term results, but without creating opportunities for self-help among the people themselves. Rather than listening to the priorities of the people and involving them as agents of social change, the organizations imposed their own reform agendas upon the people and delivered aid to them. Indeed, even the women's groups engaged in some of the more development-oriented initiatives were still ones where rural or urban poor women were the objects of reform by their wealthy, urban counterparts.

Nevertheless, reform efforts grew in number, strength, and importance in the 1930s and 1940s as Egypt underwent a series of economic, social, and political crises as a quasi-independent state.[27] Against the backdrop of a worldwide economic depression, increased British influence and occupation with the beginning of World War II, the instability of the government due to frequent cabinet changes and the 'Abdin incident of 1942 (see Malak Badrawi's chapter in the present volume), and military defeat in Palestine in 1948, the debates about Egypt's internal problems were gaining momentum. A number of parties born during this era had platforms based in part on social reform. The Young Egypt party of Ahmad

Husayn[28] and its continuously evolving philosophy of fascism, religious activism, and socialism was attracting adherents. Likewise, the recently established Muslim Brotherhood was becoming a significant political and social activist group with rapidly growing membership, and though it was not a numerically significant political party, the communist movement was also gaining ground.

Intellectuals were also becoming increasingly aware of the need to address Egypt's internal problems, particularly the living conditions of the *fallahin*. Beginning in the 1930s, more books dealing with the plight of the peasantry were published in Cairo, agricultural economics became a popular field of study, and statistics on rural populations, land rents, size of land holdings, and types of crops were increasingly collected.[29]

Soon enough, government officials joined the public debate. Debates on land reform and social service provision in rural areas began in parliament; newspapers ran frequent articles urging reform and blaming various groups for the government's failure to act, and the cholera and malaria epidemics sweeping through rural Egypt in the early 1940s brought exposure to the harsh conditions of life in the countryside.[30] Politicians, recognizing the need to identify themselves and their parties with the rural population, were quick to praise the *fallahin* as the true backbone of Egypt. By the mid-1940s, it was rare to find any politician who was openly anti-reform, and prominent politicians even began referring to King Faruq as an "honorary *fallah*."

Yet while virtually every stratum of Egyptian society was engaged in the debates on these issues and while both religious and secular groups were providing some social services in both urban and rural areas,[31] it was not until the 1939 founding of the Ministry of Social Affairs[32] that the government became actively involved in social service provision. The Fallah Department of the new ministry, under the leadership of its first director, Ahmed Hussein, Aziza Hussein's future husband, designed a program of integrated village reform that was to serve as the cornerstone of an ambitious plan of rural development and political and social change on a national level.[33]

The idea for the new plan, called the Rural Social Centers (RSC) program,[34] came from a pilot project introduced in 1936 by the Egyptian Association for Social Studies (EASS), which had been supervised by Ahmed Hussein.[35] Although its goals were similar to the charitable groups already discussed (to respond to and combat the three primary woes of rural Egypt, "poverty, ignorance, and disease"), the RSCs adopted a new philosophy. Its reforms relied on the concept of aided self-help, in which the *fallahin* were encouraged to set their own reform agendas. As a result, they would become active participants in every stage of development in their villages, while gaining access to the means to improve their standard of living. The RSCs stressed two central ideas: the involvement of villagers in every aspect of reform, and the importance of integrating reform efforts by addressing health, medical, economic, social, agricultural, and cultural issues in the village at the same time. Ahmed Hussein explained the philosophy of the project in this way:

> Above all, the strategy is based on the doctrine that people must learn to help themselves if they are to be helped at all. And the central notion behind the great forward push [for reform] is that it must be made on all fronts at once. For it is useless to attack the health problems of families who must remain hungry, or to preach sanitation and cleanliness to those who lack the means of purchasing such simple things as soap and adequate clothing.[36]

The EASS had established two rural social centers for its pilot project; in 1942, six additional centers were founded by the Fallah Department of the Ministry of Social Affairs. The program expanded at a modest rate, and in 1949 the village of Sindiyun, located near Cairo, was one of the sites chosen for the establishment of a new RSC. As was the case with all RSCs, the primary focus of the Sindiyun center was to improve village welfare through aided self-help. At Sindiyun, all social reform efforts were integrated, coordinated, and unified. Just as high a priority was to instill in the villagers a sense of ownership of and responsibility for those efforts by actively involving them in the planning, implementation, financial obligations, administration, and evaluation of the projects, all while minimizing the involvement of the government.

The center in Sindiyun had been established with the help of the Ministry of Social Affairs in response to the desire and commitment of the villagers to this new type of rural development program. Indeed, this was the method for creating all new centers; the impetus for each RSC, after the initial six were established in 1942, had to come from the people themselves. A required financial contribution of the people ensured that their request for a center was genuine and, more importantly, made the people partners in the center. This way, the center was truly theirs, not a project imposed upon them by the government. The centers were designed to ensure that its reforms would be simple and affordable to maintain, so that the people of the village would be able to continue the projects after their initial implementation.

Like all RSCs, the center in Sindiyun had two permanent staff members: a male agricultural-social specialist and a female health visitor.[37] The agricultural-social specialist established five committees (health, social and cultural, agricultural and economic, charity and public assistance, and conciliation), all of whose members served voluntarily and were elected from the adult population of the village. These committees were in charge of planning, implementing, and evaluating new projects in Sindiyun with the aid of the social center staff, who also served as liaisons between the villagers and the Ministry of Social Affairs in Cairo.

These inequalities notwithstanding, the RSC program was considered to be a highly innovative one with a strong potential for success.[38] It was embraced by the burgeoning young intellectual population in Egypt, international organizations, and diplomatic sources.[39] Yet like the charitable organizations discussed previously, the RSCs also had their problems. While the RSCs and the programs run by the women's charities both benefited women indirectly, neither provided rural women the opportunity to pursue their own economic or educational interests, and neither afforded rural women the chance to set their own reform priorities.

The women of Sindiyun benefited indirectly from the program and its general improvement of the standard of living in the village. Yet, the only direct benefit to women came from the health services provided by the center's maternity and child welfare clinic. The design of the program was partly to blame for the imbalance; while the planning committees allowed female participation, they participated in these representative institutions at much lower rates than did men.[40] The predictable result of this was that the development projects designed and implemented by the center were designed and implemented primarily by and for the men of the village. Most of the center's programs, then, were geared toward purchasing modern farming equipment, teaching new agricultural techniques, and developing small-scale rural industries. As the female staff member of the center had an extremely broad range of responsibilities that centered on maternal and child health,[41] she was functionally prevented from taking a more proactive role in the expansion of non-health related services explicitly designed to benefit village women. Moreover, she was not trained to take a more active role in social service work outside of the scope of her medical duties.

A New Type of Activism: The Sindiyun Project

By the 1940s, with more political and charitable groups paying attention to the living conditions of the *fallahin* and with more women debating the issue, the political landscape of Egypt had begun to shift. It was at this point that Aziza Hussein, who recognized the gender inequalities inherent in even the most progressive of these reform efforts, began forging her own path. Building on the established tradition of women's activism and drawing on her own experience and training, Aziza Hussein began working toward a new goal—aided self-help by and for women. Her programs and their lasting success would soon set the standard for social reform projects worldwide.

Aziza Shukri Hussein was born in 1919 in the village of Zifta to a rather atypical family.[42] Her father, Sa'id Shukri, was something of a political revolutionary, known for his opposition to the British occupation of Egypt and his military exploits in Libya.[43] Perhaps more significantly to the life of his daughter, however, Shukri was also a something of social revolutionary. Although his family was wealthy and owned a fair amount of land in the countryside, Shukri's concerns lay not in his status or wealth, but in other issues. After financing his own medical education in Ireland and France, [44] Shukri returned to Egypt—not to Cairo, where he might reasonably expect to establish a lucrative medical practice catering to the urban elite, but to his village to establish a modern medical clinic for the benefit of the *fallahin*. Throughout his career, Shukri established a number of clinics in rural Egyptian villages, the first of which was eventually renamed the Shukri Clinic in honor of its benefactor. Although these clinics did not bring the doctor great wealth, they did bring Shukri a great deal of respect and a reputation as an active, engaged, socially conscious reformer.

Due to the chronic illness of his wife, Shukri played the main role in raising Aziza and her four siblings.[45] Perhaps contrary to what one might expect of an Egyptian man of rural origins in the early twentieth century, Shukri was a firm believer in gender equality—and he sometimes went to the other extreme, even arguing that women were intellectually superior to men.[46] Shukri's own political and social convictions had a tremendous influence on all his children, perhaps most profoundly on young Aziza.[47] She came of age in a family that was actively engaged in reform, where one's actions were seen as more important than one's wealth, and at a time when reformist ideas were widespread among the intellectual, educated elite; her own course of study testifies to the impact her upbringing and the reformist atmosphere of the day had. In accordance with her father's conviction that girls and boys should receive equal education, Aziza Hussein was educated at French and

American schools in Cairo.[48] She continued her education at the American University in Cairo, graduating in 1942 with a degree in social science.

As an educated and attractive girl from a wealthy family of good reputation, Aziza Hussein fielded many offers of marriage. However, Shukri had taught his daughters not to be hasty in choosing a husband; he argued that a woman should first be educated and capable of supporting herself economically before marrying. Once this was accomplished, she should not accept a proposal of marriage unless she was completely satisfied with her potential husband in every regard. Thus, although many young men sought her hand, none were a good match for the educated, modern, liberal Aziza—until Ahmed Hussein presented himself. Already well-respected and with a reputation as a brilliant young reformer in the Ministry of Social Affairs, Ahmed Hussein's personal and career goals matched Aziza's.[49] The couple married in 1945, a few years before the RSC was established in the village of Sindiyun. Agreeing to the marriage meant that Aziza gained a husband and a professional partner; after the marriage, Aziza and Ahmed began collaborating together on social reform projects, and Aziza Hussein quickly made a name for herself as a leader in the Egyptian social reform community.[50]

As was expected of a woman of her education and class, Aziza Hussein became active in a number of organizations and charitable groups, including the Cairo Women's Club[51] shortly after her marriage. Here the adherence to tradition ends; Hussein's family background, her educational training, and her personal inclinations drove her to seek out new opportunities for action and innovation.[52] As Hussein noted in 2003, she has "always believed in the non-governmental sector as the appropriate channel for [serving] country and humanity."[53] In her view, "voluntary associations are interested in the human person on the level of his basic needs," and therefore, they serve as the most effective vehicles for social change.[54]

By 1949, deeply engaged in developing the RSC program, Ahmed Hussein fully recognized the program's inability to cater to the needs and desires of rural women. As he often would throughout his career, Ahmed Hussein sought the advice of his wife on how to improve the program and address this shortcoming. Both agreed that something needed to be done to increase the involvement of women in the development projects of the villages. At the time, the CWC had been discussing ways in which the club might be able to get involved in rural development and women's issues in the villages, yet it had not been able to determine any potentially effective means of doing so. As Aziza Hussein noted, "It had been inconceivable that women who lived away from a village and were too busy to make daily trips to it could have been expected to do any worthwhile work along any social welfare lines."[55] The Husseins decided that one way of allowing the CWC to serve as an instrument of social reform in the villages would be to link it with the existing RSC program. Since the village of Sindiyun was located near Cairo and its RSC was new, the Husseins believed this village offered the ideal opportunity for their experiment.

Given the historically charity-oriented nature of women's social reform activism and the CWC's lack of experience in rural reform projects, it is likely that had Aziza Hussein and her husband not insisted the group follow the aided self-help principles of the RSC program, its efforts would have followed tradition and been oriented toward simple charity—the provision of aid by wealthy, urban, elite women for their poor, rural, underprivileged sisters. Instead, as the CWC project developed, it strictly adhered to the ideology of aided self-help embodied in the RSC program. It thus formed the first link between the emerging trend of aided self-help with Egypt's by then longstanding tradition of women's activism, creating a new trend of aided self-help projects designed, implemented, and evaluated primarily by and for rural women.

The experiment began in 1950 with visits to the village by the CWC three times a week for three months. During this time the Cairo women only engaged socially with the village women; they were not to suggest projects nor were they to say they had come to help the village. This approach was designed to demonstrate to the village women that the members of the CWC were serious in their friendship and goodwill. Aziza Hussein described the process as follows:

> We started working slowly and carefully. We followed conscientiously all the instructions of the social experts concerning the democratic approach, and the patience and time to be taken in establishing friendships with the village women before involving them in any project. We would pay weekly visits to several homes, visit socially with the women, and listen to what they had to say without trying to project our own ideas. Most of them, especially those whose husbands were active in committees in the [rural social] center, expressed their enthusiasm and gratitude for what the social center had enabled them to do for their community in the short period of three years. Then they talked of what they, as women could also do for themselves. At that point, we immediately offered our services to help them in whatever projects they would like to undertake.[56]

The work of establishing friendships with and gaining the trust of the village women proved worthwhile, and the village women became comfortable expressing their own development priorities:

> It was discovered that the women were most interested in learning embroidery, knitting and sewing. Sewing was a task the village women had previously not done; even those with little money had given their sewing to a seamstress. Classes to teach these sewing skills were soon opened with the help of some club members. The knitting class was for the youngest girls, from 7–10, and the embroidery class for girls from 10–14.[57]

Aziza Hussein recalled that, "at the end of one year, Sindiyun had its first Village Women's Committee which took up various organized activities such as sewing and knitting, the preparation of jams and preserves, etc."[58] Though these types of activities may not appear to be revolutionary, the methodology that brought them about was. The success of the first projects taught the women of Sindiyun that they could set up, organize, and succeed in running their own ventures. The CWC and the women of Sindiyun worked as partners in the pursuit of the village women's goals, whatever they might be; in the process, the CWC members came to be seen as resources for the village women, rather than as outsiders come to impose an upper class, urban agenda upon them.

As a result, the activities of the newly established Sindiyun Women's Committee did not long remain limited to small-scale rural industries. The committee began working with the CWC to plan additional, larger scale projects for Sindiyun. The committee soon decided that what would most benefit the women of the village would be a nursery school or daycare center for preschool children that would provide a safe place for their children to learn and play, and, perhaps more significantly, would free the village women from child care responsibilities for several hours a day and allow them to pursue other activities of their own choice. As a result, Aziza Hussein and her colleagues in the club, in coordination with the Ministry of Social Affairs, worked with the women of Sindiyun to establish Egypt's first rural nursery school.[59]

Because the school could not accommodate the initial demand for enrollment, difficult choices had to be made. The first twenty-five children admitted to the new school, based on socioeconomic surveys carried out by the RSC staff, were chosen from poorer village families in which both parents spent the majority of the day in the fields. Initially the Sindiyun nursery school simply provided a place where children from the ages of three to six could play in a clean environment, eat healthy food, and receive educational instruction. In later years, the school extended its activities by providing a library for children ages six to fourteen, founding a *kilim-* and rug-making workshop, opening its own healthcare and family-planning clinic, and enlarging its handicrafts workshop. The center later expanded its activities to serve some thirty-five neighboring villages. Today, the school continues to operate, has greatly expanded its library and handicrafts activities, and has added computer classes for both children and adults.[60]

A follow-up study conducted in 1956 by a researcher at the American University in Cairo showed that children who attended the nursery school in Sindiyun had higher grades, lower absenteeism in primary schools, were more involved in extracurricular activities, and had better health than children in the village who had not attended the nursery school. The study attributed their success to the nutritional, health, and social services of the nursery school.[61]

In addition to the direct benefits accruing to the attending children and their families, the nursery school also became a staging ground for the expansion of women's activities within the village. Handiwork classes and participation in the nursery school's programs gave women an opportunity to get out of their homes and into the RSC twice a week, which soon became socially accepted in the village as part of women's regular activity. By making women's activities outside the home acceptable to both village women and men, the nursery project opened the window for women to participate in other village activities. As Aziza Hussein explained, "This nursery school soon became the center of gravity for women's participation. It proved to be an effective means of reaching the mother and the family through the child. It became very easy through it to organize the mothers into groups to participate in adult education classes, in childcare and in hygienic habits."[62] Village women began to envision new roles for themselves in the village as a result of the nursery school. Some began attending literacy and handiwork classes, while others began to work for salaries in the nursery.

The quiet revolution begun by the day-care center had succeeded—and a new tradition of women's activism had been born. Perhaps one of the most remarkable aspects of the day-care center and its results is that these innovations in the life of Sindiyun were accepted and even welcomed by both men and women. Women in nearby villages began asking for advice in setting up day-care centers in their own villages—centers that included not only childcare but also handicrafts, expanded healthcare, and literacy classes. The school soon began recruiting and training paid female supervisors from the village, and the neighboring villages began recruiting the women of Sindiyun to assist in forming and training the staff in their own nursery schools.[63]

The project's ability to economically fill a real need in many areas brought it praise as a model project. Hussein remembered how "Sindiyun's name rapidly rose to fame in the surrounding villages. One after the other representatives from different villages came pleading with us to start a project in their respective communities. We seemed to have hit on the practical approach to meet an acute basic need."[64] A second project was established in the village of Tirsa, ten miles from Sindiyun. Like its predecessor, it was set up with the help of the CWC and administered in conjunction with the local RSC. Soon after the Tirsa project was established, the Egyptian government began establishing day-care centers at all government RSCs, using the Sindiyun school as a model. By June 1954, six new centers had been established, some by groups of women within a village, and some in cooperation with the health visitor of the village's RSC.[65]

The Egyptian and the international reform communities praised the philosophy embodied in the Sindiyun project. The success of the nursery school project attracted the attention of the United Nations, which adopted it as a model project for rural reform in the 1950s.[66] After the 1952 Revolution, Gamal 'Abd al-Nasser praised the program as well, committing his government in 1954 to providing two hundred additional rural nursery schools.[67] When 'Abd al-Nasser introduced his new rural social service program, the Combined Units, he made the inclusion of nursery schools a prominent feature.[68] By 1970, the number of nursery schools run by the Ministry of Social Affairs had skyrocketed. There were 601 nursery schools in rural areas, 351 in urban areas, and 26 in desert areas. The total number of children attending these schools was 46,998. The Ministry of Education also began a nursery school program, and by the same year, the total number of children attending those nursery schools was 12,469.[69]

The Acceptance and Expansion of the Sindiyun Model
The success of the day-care center project in Sindiyun is a good example of the overall success of Aziza Hussein's aided self-help projects in pre-revolutionary Egypt. In the Sindiyun nursery project, Hussein merged two existing traditions—the longstanding tradition of women's activism and

the emerging tradition of aided self-help for rural development—into a third direction: aided self-help projects designed and implemented by and for the benefit of rural women. In doing so, Hussein became a pioneer in the Egyptian women's movement. As Hussein noted in a 2002 speech, the project taught her a valuable lesson in social reform:

> One of the first lessons learned in the village was the prime importance of listening to the people before action, learning from all of them, the young and the old. We learned a great deal from the grandmother, the midwife, the village girl, the village caller, the nurse, the teacher, and the village preacher. . . . We were . . . playing the role of facilitators and agents of social change. Our success in helping with these pioneer projects seems to have stemmed from the trust gained through persuasion, perseverance, altruism, and love.[70]

The philosophy of aided self-help and the lessons learned in the Sindiyun project served as a model for Hussein's subsequent reform projects, most notably in the arena of family planning. Here too, the government followed her lead. Although the problem of Egypt's rapidly increasing population was recognized by the revolutionary government, 'Abd al-Nasser did not begin calling for family planning until the mid-1960s, and even then his government took few concrete steps. In 1963, in keeping with her reformist commitment and building on her experiences in the Sindiyun project, Hussein worked with the CWC to hold weekly forums on family planning. These forums included as speakers demographers, health professionals, and religious authorities like Shaykh Ahmad Sharabasi. Soon thereafter, Hussein organized the Joint Committee on Family Planning (JCFP), a collection of twenty-two women's organizations that subsequently opened and maintained family planning clinics that incorporated an integrated approach including local participation and planning.[71] It was not until 1966 that the Egyptian government became actively involved in the family planning efforts, with its decision to open 2,200 family planning clinics to distribute birth control.[72]

Still believing more needed to be done via the proper methodology, Hussein established the Cairo Family Planning Association (CFPA), and outgrowth of the JCFP, in 1967. The guidelines of the organization and the resulting structure of the CFPA's rural clinics again gave the *fallahat* a significant voice and position of influence within their villages. Realizing that the clinics would be ineffective if they were not at least partially staffed by village women themselves, the CFPA began a program to select a village girl to staff each clinic. The duties of these pioneers *(ra'idat)* covered the entire range of community development needs, from cooperation with other projects to communication with village leaders. Hussein argued that the use of the *ra'idat*, who were the most basic agents of social change at the clinics, "Could well be considered revolutionary in view of the traditional male-dominance characteristic of rural society."[73] In other words, the clinics of the CFPA, like the rural nursery school in Sindiyun, were programs run by and for village women.[74]

Once considered a revolutionary, Hussein is today one of her country's most prominent reformers and is regarded as something of an institution in her own right. Her initial approach and more than fifty years of successful subsequent reform projects has brought her recognition and respect in the international community, and as a leader of national and regional social reform in the last half century, Hussein's contributions and awards are too numerous to recount here. Among other things, Hussein helped establish the Arab Women's Commission, an organization of the League of Arab States, and represented the League in seminars on the status of women and family planning. She also represented Egypt in the United Nations General Assembly, becoming the first woman to do so. Further, Hussein served numerous U.N. agencies and commissions, including the commission on the status of women, the committee on fertility studies, an expert group on women in development, the convention on the elimination of discrimination against women, the commission on international humanitarian issues, and the international institute for training and research for the advancement of women. As an outgrowth of her work on reproductive health, Hussein became involved in Egypt's first attempts to eradicate the practice of female genital mutilation, or FGM.[75] As a result of her family planning efforts, she became the president of the International Planned Parenthood Federation from 1977–83. She was chairperson and organizer of Egypt's national NGO steering committee for the International Conference on Population and Development (ICPD) in 1993–94 and subsequently became the head of the national NGO commission on Population and Development, an Egyptian NGO umbrella group that emerged from the ICPD. Today, she continues to champion the cause of development, reform, and better lives for Egyptian women.[76]

Like Hussein herself, aided self-help was once considered revolutionary, and like Hussein, it too has gained international and national acceptance. Although charitable agencies are still active worldwide, such agencies are no longer deemed sufficient to engender lasting change. Rather, current development thinking has incorporated the idea of aided self-help, recognizing that the only way to ensure lasting change is for the people themselves to be agents of that change. Indeed, international organizations like the United Nations now emphasize the participation of the people themselves as key to the effectiveness of reform programs, as statements by the UNDP indicate: "Developing countries are working to create their own national poverty eradication strategies based on local needs and priorities. UNDP advocates for these nationally-owned solutions and helps to make them effective through ensuring a greater voice for poor people. . . ."[77] As another report states, this is common in international aid thinking today: "Policies aimed at the plight of the poor . . . cannot be effective unless they combine sound technical analysis with the political support and legitimacy that emanates from the poor themselves. This is another way of expressing the idea of 'popular participation and national ownership' so often used in development aid strategies."[78]

Conclusion

Aziza Hussein once argued that "the crucial problem is that Egyptian women do not think for themselves; it is always men who think and act on their behalf. This attitude deprives women of intellectual progress. . . ."[79] The methods of many women's social programs prior to the 1952 Revolution perpetuated this problem by using the men of the village as vehicles for reform ideas rather than the women, and similar problems arose when urban women's groups attempted to set reform priorities for rural women.

Hussein broke from this tradition when she established the Sindiyun nursery school at the request and with the active participation of the women of the village. Most importantly, the ideas were theirs—village women set their own priorities and guided their own projects. Hussein and her colleagues in the CWC simply facilitated the implementation of a project that otherwise would have remained a remote and perhaps unexpressed goal. Since the 1950 Sindiyun project, Aziza Hussein has continued with her commitment to create vehicles for rural and lower class women to express their own reform priorities. Through five decades and multiple governments with diverse orientations, her programs have remained. The same holds true for her philosophy: while theories about social reform were constantly changing, her commitment to the philosophy of aided self-help was a rare constant, bringing longevity and success to a diverse body of social programs.

In successfully merging these two trends, Aziza Hussein has made a major contribution to both women's activism and the course of development programs in Egypt. She is thus a uniquely important figure in history of the Egyptian women's movement and in history of development, and her ideology, principles, and methodology are in part products of the vibrant, reformist environment of pre-revolutionary Egypt. The post-1952 regime would have a complicated relationship to Aziza Hussein and her development pattern. 'Abd al-Nasser himself admired Hussein greatly. As one journalist noted, "Nasser, as the oft-repeated story goes, used to say that he wanted his daughters to grow up to be 'like Aziza Hussein.'"[80] Likewise, 'Abd al-Nasser's government would go on to emphasize "modern" ideas like the nuclear family, family planning, the expansion of education for women, women's political rights, and employment opportunities for women, and although it was active in development projects. Still, the new regime failed to emphasize women as actors and priority setters of development projects. In keeping with the overall philosophy of the revolution, social services were presented as the offerings of the new government to its people who had suffered under the corruption of the previous regime. As time progressed, international development thinking and later governmental, NGO, and IGO activities in Egypt built not on 'Abd al-Nasser's directed development approach of government as donor and people as recipients of aid, but on the aided self-help approach of government as facilitator and people as agents of change.[81] Women's groups built on Aziza Hussein's new approach, worked to allow women to choose their own priorities, and worked with them to enable them to fulfill their own goals, rather than simply dictating priorities.

Even as Hussein's efforts have extended and evolved, her methodology has remained the same; each of her programs has been based and dependent on the concept of aided self-help by and for women. When governments and other reform groups tried to force change, Hussein asked what change was needed. Whether she was setting up a clinic in Sindiyun or setting the agenda for an international social reform NGO, Hussein allowed the women to speak, and she listened to their voices.

Notes

1   The authors would like to thank Berry College, Harvard University, the National Endowment for the Humanities, and the American Research Center in Egypt for funding portions of the research upon which this chapter is based. Some portions of this chapter were presented within the context of related research papers at the 1999 Middle East Studies Association annual conference in San Francisco, CA, the 1999 Australasian Middle East Studies Association annual conference in Sydney, Australia, the 2001 Association of Third World Studies annual conference in Savannah, GA, and the 2001 Third World Studies Conference in Omaha, NE. The authors also gratefully acknowledge the assistance of Mme. Aziza Hussein in allowing Johnson to access her family archives and for acceding to a lengthy series of interviews.

2   The most prominent of these early activists, women like Huda Sha'rawi, Nabawiya Musa, and Doria Shafik, were skillful organizers and strategists who fought to gain political equality for Egyptian women.

3   It has been argued that the first female Egyptian activists arose as a response to French occupation in the early nineteenth century, when some Egyptian women, seeing the unveiled French women in the streets of Cairo, began unveiling themselves and keeping the company of Frenchmen. If this was a social revolution, it was short-lived. Upon Napoleon's exit (and the exit of the French settlers with him), a backlash against the women began and the revolution ceased. See Ghada Hashem Talhami, *The Mobilization of Muslim Women in Egypt* (Gainesville: University of Florida Press, 1996).

4   Beth Baron, *The Women's Awakening in Egypt: Culture, Society, and the Press* (New Haven: Yale University Press), 2.

5   Baron, 2.

6   Baron, 3–4.

7   The Wafd was a political party organized by Sa'd Zaghlul that demanded complete independence from Britain. The group was originally formed to represent Egyptian nationalists at the Paris Peace Conference after World War I; it became a political party in 1923. The party won 90 percent of the seats in the first post-independence parliamentary elections in 1924. Zaghlul's wife, Safia Zaghlul, also became a prominent political activist.

8   Afaf Lutfi al-Sayyid Marsot, "The Revolutionary Gentlewomen in Egypt," *Women in the Muslim World*, Lois Beck and Nikki Keddie, eds. (Cambridge: Harvard University Press, 1978), 269.

9   Ibid. Although Aziza Hussein appears to be the opposite of this trend (in that she worked with her husband, himself a member of the socioeconomic elite and a member of the government), in fact this is not the case. Ahmed Hussein can be viewed as a sort of "establishment rebel" in that he refused to join any political party, he was fiercely independent while in the government, and in contrast to many of the extremely conservative politicians of the day, Hussein himself was almost radical in his ideology. Ahmed Hussein's views on gender issues developed to be very similar to those of Sa'id Shukri. In this too, he was unusual. For details, see Amy J. Johnson, *Reconstructing Rural Egypt: Ahmed Hussein and the History of Egyptian Development* (Syracuse: Syracuse University Press, 2004).

10 Selma Botman, *Engendering Citizenship in Egypt* (New York: Columbia University Press, 1999), 42.

11 Bint al-Nil did not officially become a party until 1953. Botman relates how Shafiq filed a suit with the Egyptian State Council just before the revolution of 1952, "asking that the election law be amended. While she was not successful, Shafiq made the point that citizenship should grant to men and women equal participation in the political system." Botman, 43. See also Cynthia Nelson, *Doria Shafik, Egyptian Feminist: A Woman Apart* (Gainesville: University of Florida Press, 1996).

12 Both men and women had become more engaged by this time. This is not to suggest that women and women's groups were utterly unconcerned with social issues prior to the 1940s; however, this time period witnessed a significant increase in women's activities and groups that were specifically geared toward charity, social service provision, and relief efforts.

13 A popular catch phrase since the early 1930s, "poverty, ignorance, and disease" had been used to describe the problems of rural life by numerous reformers, including American sociologist Wendell Cleland in his discussion of Egypt's population problem in 1937. It gradually became the term used by all those involved in discussing proposed rural reforms. See Johnson for details.

14 These resources were generally obtained by women through inheritances or dowry (*mahr*), after which point even a woman's husband had to ask permission to access her property. Not surprisingly, this stipulation could only be taken advantage of by upper-class women with property to control. See al-Sayyid-Marsot, 262. While men set up *awqaf* as well, many of the most important *awqaf* were controlled by women. Both men and women also founded charities in the broader sense. Some of the notable female-organized and run charities include the Mabarrat Muhammad 'Ali, the Coptic Ladies' Society for the Education of Children, and the Oeuvre des Ecoles Gratuites des Villages de Haute-Égypte.

15 Al-Sayyid-Marsot, 264.

16 Botman, 46.

17 Botman, 46.

18 Margot Badran, *Feminists, Islam, and Nation: Gender and the Making of Modern Egypt* (Princeton: Princeton University Press, 1995), 121. Valuable though these projects were, even they were not viable long-term efforts, as the projects were simply organized and left in the village without any permanent or trained staff to oversee them.

19 One such example was the Oeuvre, which was dedicated in part to set up literacy lessons for local village women, and the Jam'iyyat al-Sayyidat al-Qibtiya li-Tarbiyat al-Tufula (Coptic Ladies Society for the Education of Children). The Egyptian Feminist Union, led by Huda Sha'rawi, also was involved in setting up schools for both boys and girls, as Badran notes, 120–21.

20 Johnson, 4. Sir Evelyn Baring, Lord Cromer, was British Agent and Consul-General from 1883–1907. For an elegantly crafted academic biography, see Roger Owen, *Lord Cromer: Victorian Imperialist, Edwardian Proconsul* (London: Oxford University Press, 2004).

21 Johnson, 4.

22 See Amy J. Johnson, "Encouraging Education, Increasing Income: The al-Manayil Village School as a Model for Rural Education in Egypt," in *Education and the Great Depression*, Tom Ewing and David Hicks, eds. (New York: Peter Lang, 2005) for more details on the development of the Egyptian educational system. See also Barak A. Salmoni, "Pedagogies of Patriotism: Teaching Socio-Political Community in Twentieth-Century Turkish and Egyptian Education" (Ph.D. diss., Harvard University, 2002).

23 The Muslim Brotherhood and Ministry of Health were also involved in healthcare in rural areas, but the Brotherhood's units were mobile and the Ministry's efforts minuscule. See Gallagher and Richard P. Mitchell, *The Society of the Muslim Brothers* (London: Oxford University Press, 1969).

24 Al-Sayyid-Marsot, 273.

25 Al-Sayyid-Marsot, 273.

26 Al-Sayyid-Marsot, 274.

27 This is contrary to the views of some historians who tend to see the beginning of real interest in social reform as something that occurred primarily under government direction after 1952.

28 There were two men of note with the same name active in roughly the same time period: Ahmed Hussein, Aziza Hussein's husband, who has already been mentioned, and Ahmad Husayn, the leader of Misr al-Fatat (Young Egypt). We use two different spellings of their names for the sake of differentiating between them.

29 See Misako Ikeda, "Sociopolitical Debates in Late Parliamentary Egypt" (Ph.D. diss., Harvard University, 1998). She lists the following books as indications of increased interest in rural life: *Siyasat al-ghad* ("The Policy of Tomorrow," 1938) by Mirrit Ghali; *Mustaqbal al-thaqafa fi Misr* ("The Future of Culture in Egypt," 1938) by Taha Husayn; *'Ala hamish al-siyasa* ("On the Margin of Politics," 1938) by Hafiz 'Afifi; *al-Rif al-Misri* ("The Egyptian Countryside") (Cairo: Maktaba wa Matba'at al-Wafd, 1936) and *Qadayat al-fallah* ("The Issue of the Peasant") (Cairo: Maktabat al-Nahda al-Misriya, 1938) by Ibnat al-Shati' (the pen name of Aisha 'Abd al-Rahman). See also Jacques Berque, *Egypt: Imperialism and Revolution* (New York: Praeger Publishers, 1972), chapter 7, "Emergent Groups and Latent Classes," for more details.

30 For more details on the political attention paid to such problems, see Ikeda, and Nancy Elizabeth Gallagher, *Egypt's Other Wars: Epidemics and the Politics of Public Health* (Syracuse: Syracuse University Press, 1990). The appeal to the impoverished rural majority and the attempts of government officials to present themselves as the spokespersons of that group continued after the 1952 Revolution. See Johnson for details.

31 An oft-cited example of a religious group that provided social services in the pre-revolutionary period is the Muslim Brotherhood. The Brotherhood was initially focused on social issues; not until the 1936 strikes in Palestine did it become involved in political affairs, and not until 1939 did it define itself as, among other things, an explicitly political organization. In 1945, as result of the passage of Law no. 49 (dealing with the organization of social work and charity), the Brotherhood was split into two sections, one of which dealt with social services. The Brotherhood provided services like education, encouragement of small industries, health care clinics, charity for the poor, and a blueprint for rural reform which, though it was never put into action, was remarkably similar in structure to the RSC program. For further details, see Mitchell.

32 By the late 1930s, the EASS was an active participant in the debate on social reform, yet its members were increasingly aware that while their own projects might be useful on a limited scale, the government needed to take a hand in addressing the social problems of its people. In 1936, while prime minister, 'Ali Mahir Pasha founded a formal governmental body, the Higher Council for Social Reform, as a first step in governmental reform efforts. Mahir, who was also the first president of the EASS, was a conservative and a royalist but was also concerned with the growing social problems in Egypt. Ahmed Hussein and his colleagues in the EASS envisioned the government taking an active role in social service provision, thus moving away from the trend of social services being provided as charitable services by non-governmental organizations. They believed that the government not only should become involved in the social sphere but also that it should be the leader in the development of the country. Accordingly, this group drew up a plan to establish a larger governmental body whose purpose would be to address all social and labor issues in both urban and rural Egypt. This governmental body was the Ministry of Social Affairs. 'Ali Fu'ad Ahmad. *'Ilm al-ijtima' al-rifi* (Cairo: Dar al-Thaqafa wa-l-'Ulum li-l-Tiba' wa-l-Nashr, 1960). Robert Bianchi and others have argued that the primary reason for the foundation of the Ministry of Social Affairs was the government's desire for control. While this may be true of people like 'Ali Mahir, others involved, like Ahmed Hussein, sincerely believed in the Ministry's mission.

33 These centers were to accustom the peasants to participating in governance, in setting priorities and making decisions, and in implementing their own projects, but they were

not to operate in a vacuum. In addition to the RSCs, Hussein planned a widespread network of agricultural cooperatives, limited land reform, the establishment of a minimum agricultural wage, and the regulation of the landowner-tenant relationship. Hussein saw all of these elements as essential steps in the reform of the Egyptian countryside. The results of the RSC project were extremely positive. General health levels increased in villages where centers were located, sanitary conditions improved, illiteracy decreased, education levels increased, agricultural yields and farmers' income rose, and handicrafts practiced by the centers' members generated added income. Hussein summarized the results of the centers in a 1955 speech in Washington, D.C., saying: "The success of the social center as an institution most suited to serve the civic, economic, cultural, and social needs of the Egyptian village is now fully recognized. It is living proof that sincere cooperation between government and people can do much to bring about a real uplift in the social standards of rural areas. The enthusiasm of the people in some of these centers is very gratifying. With a little financial help and technical guidance from the Government, they were able to fill swamps, construct roads, build schools, introduce playgrounds and public parks. In a democratic fashion, they discuss their needs and plan their course of action. They volunteer their varied abilities to serve their communities. They have been able to improve agricultural production and to introduce certain cottage industries. They formed drama groups and sports teams. In one village I visited . . . the people's center had organized 18 evening classes to combat illiteracy." Ahmed Hussein, *Some Aspects of Agricultural and Rural Life in Egypt* (Washington, D.C.: United States Department of Agriculture, 1955), 9. For a summary of independent evaluations of the project, see Johnson. As the improvements in the RSC villages became increasingly apparent, the demand for new centers skyrocketed. Villages strove to raise the necessary funds and locate suitable plots of land so that they would be able to participate in the program as well. Hussein, writing in 1950, remarked that: "They [the villagers] are now all anxious for the establishment of centres in their areas. They all take their share; some contributing funds, others contributing land; while others give building materials and finally the labour required; they all believe that they have an interest in this scheme and hence no canvassing is necessary." Ahmed Hussein, *Rural Social Welfare Centers in Egypt* (Cairo: Ministry of Social Affairs, 1951), 14. The Rural Social Centers program began in 1942, with six centers serving only 50,000 people. By 1950 there were Centers in 126 villages across Egypt, serving 1.5 million people; by 1951, there were 141 centers. While the number served by the social centers represented only about one-tenth of the rural population (a fraction of those in need of services) the program's benefits, its popularity with the people, its constant expansion, and its adoption by the United Nations as a model to be emulated by other developing nations are testimony to the effectiveness of the program and its revolutionary methodology. Ahmed Hussein's German training influenced his development philosophy; however, all indications are that Hussein was no blind imitator of western ways. Rather, he adapted what he saw as useful to Egyptian conditions. This issue of the foreign origins of Ahmed Hussein's reform ideas is discussed at length in Johnson.

34 See Johnson, *Reconstructing Rural Egypt.*

35 The EASS was a private, voluntary organization in Cairo that had as its goal the formulation of model reform projects for both urban and rural areas. For more information on the EASS, see al-Jam'iya al-misriya li-l-dirasat al-ijtima'iya, *al-jam'iya al-misriya li-l-dirasat al-ijtima'iya: madiha–hadaruha–mustaqbaluha, 1938–1994* (Cairo: al-Jam'iya al-Misriya li-l-Dirasat al-Ijtima'iya, 1994).

36 Ahmed Hussein, "Egypt's War on Poverty," *United Nations World,* (March 1951), 69.

37 The department also required that the villagers choose a doctor and make arrangements for him to visit the village a minimum of three times per week.

38 The two main limitations of the program were considered to be ones that the program could not realistically change: the inequity in land distribution and the problem of the country's rapidly growing population. Hussein, however, pushed for solutions to both of these.

39 See Johnson, chapter 3.

40 As women were excluded from politics until the 1952 Revolution, this is not surprising. Many involved with the RSC program, including Ahmed Hussein himself, advocated an expanded role for rural women in development. The RSCs were criticized by Abbas Ammar, one of Hussein's protégés, in 1954 for not doing enough for village women. As part of his plan to reorganize the Egyptian village, Ammar advocated that each village have a village center, and that there be a female and male social worker in each center. Ammar, commenting on the activities for women, said that they were largely confined to health matters and that "social-work aspects are relegated to the background, and performed with amateurism and intermittent improvisation." Abbas M. Ammar, *Reorganization of the Egyptian Village on the Basis of Regional Decentralization*. (Sirs el-Layyan: Arab States Fundamental Education Center, 1954), 20. He did cite the Sindiyun experiment as a successful model for future social work with village women. For details on some of 'Abd al-Nasser's training programs for female leaders in rural areas, see "Training for Social Welfare" (Cairo: U.A.R. Ministry of Social Affairs, 1967).

41 As Johnson notes, "The health visitor's duties centered on the women and children in the village. Her main duty was to take care of pregnant women and newborns. Her other duties included visiting each home regularly and teaching the village women proper housekeeping methods, general cleanliness, and ways to supplement their families' incomes through needlepoint, dressmaking, and other cottage industries, overseeing the cleanliness of the children, visiting the village school and teaching the children basic hygiene, cutting the boys' hair, brushing the girls' hair, trimming the children's nails, sending sick children to the doctor, giving health lectures to village women, training several young village women in nursing in midwifery, and organizing groups of village girls for courses in needlework, knitting, and first aid." Johnson, 81.

42 Zifta is in the governate of Gharbiya. Information regarding Hussein's family, personal life, background, and philosophy comes from a series of interviews by Johnson with Hussein in Cairo from 1995–2003.

43 Egypt was occupied in 1882 by British forces; it remained a veiled protectorate until the formal declaration of the protectorate at the outbreak of World War I. Libya was also struggling with European colonialism in the early twentieth century. In 1911, while formally part of the Ottoman Empire, Libya was invaded by Italy; the Ottomans sought peace in 1912, but local resistance to Italian colonization continued throughout World War I.

44 Shukri specialized in gynecology.

45 Aziza Hussein had four siblings—brothers Muhammad and Hussein and sisters Esmat and Leila. Muhammad followed in his father's footsteps and became a gynecologist. Hussein was born deaf and mute and did not pursue a career. Esmat married and raised a family. Leila became a professor of anthropology.

46 While rural women often were accorded more freedom of movement than urban women and many worked in agriculture-related fields, the idea espoused by Shukri that women were intellectually superior to men was rarely voiced.

47 As is a common theme in the lives of many prominent feminists, Hussein's father was clearly influential in her life; he was her adviser, mentor, and hero.

48 Hussein attended the Mère de Dieu School until her penultimate year of secondary school,

when she transferred to the American College for Girls upon the recommendation of family friends and because she and her father thought the teaching methods at Mère de Dieu were antiquated and ineffective. However, as Gallagher notes in her chapter in this volume, the school is frequently cited as one which inculcated into its students the belief in social work and social service.

49 Ahmed Hussein earned his Ph.D. in agricultural economics in 1927 from the Landwirtschaftliche Hochschule in Berlin. He joined the Ministry of Agriculture as an inspector in 1928, and at the same time he taught agricultural economics at Fu'ad I (later Cairo) University. In 1936 he helped found the Egyptian Association for Social Studies (EASS) and was involved with its numerous reform programs. In 1939, he helped found the Ministry of Social Affairs and he served in a variety of posts in that ministry (including his brief tenure as minister from 1950–51) until his resignation in 1951. He also served as Egyptian ambassador to the United States from 1953–58. See Johnson for details of his career.

50 Although in Egypt it is not customary for a wife to take her husband's last name, Aziza came to use Hussein as her last name. Foreign press reports referred to her as Mrs. Hussein and as Mme. Ahmed Hussein, and she became accustomed to this. Her father was unhappy with this development even though Aziza told him that since his own father's first name was Hussein, she could (even sticking to custom) legitimately use Hussein as her third name. Aziza's father, interestingly, had also changed his name. The family name had been Dahroug, and while in school, her father was called Sa'id Dahroug. However, his teachers told him that Dahroug sounded too "peasant-like" and suggested he change his name to Sa'id Shukri (a more Turkish-sounding, and hence more upper-class sounding, name). He agreed; a brother also changed his second name to Hilmi for the same reasons. Though Shukri's teachers apparently believed the family name to reveal a lack of upper class origins, the family was of the economic elite and had relatively substantial land holdings.

51 The first women's club in Egypt, the CWC was founded in 1934 as a social and cultural organization. It was an international organization, in that the first lady of each embassy in Cairo was invited to become an honorary member, and other women affiliated with foreign embassies were invited to join as well. In addition, the club was affiliated with the U.S.-based General Federation of Women's Clubs. While this club has a significant foreign membership, and while its members were from the upper classes, the methodology used in the Sindiyun project comes from the RSC project, an Egyptian program.

52 Aziza Hussein did not begin a paid career, though she was equipped by education and training to do so. Her father's view had been that women must be able to support themselves, though he did not believe that they should be required to do so. Rather, his insistence on the ability to support oneself stemmed from his aversion to women being entirely subject to male authority or having to stay in a disagreeable marriage solely for economic reasons. It was unusual at the time for a woman of Aziza's class to work, and she thus did what most upper class women did—began a career as a volunteer. Her husband, who came from a more traditional upbringing, encouraged her to remain a volunteer, rather than being a paid worker, throughout their life together. In his view, women should not subject themselves to the authority of male bosses, because that could result in undesirable moral consequences.

53 "Aziza Hussein bio-data," unpublished document, written by Hussein and provided to Johnson, 2003.

54 Aziza Hussein,"'The Population Question and NGOs," unpublished speech presented at the General Federation of NGOs, Cairo, December 16, 2002.

55 Aziza Hussein, *Women in the Moslem World*. (Washington, D.C.: Egyptian Embassy Press Department, n.d.), 23.

56   *Women in the Moslem World*, 24–25.

57   Cairo Women's Club, *A New Life for Rural Children in Egypt*, n.p., n.d.

58   *Women in the Moslem World*, 24–25. See also Jessie Ashe Arndt, "Women Around the World Build Better Communities," (*Christian Science Monitor*, 16 May 1956).

59   *Women in the Moslem World*, 25–26.

60   Visits by Johnson to the day-care center in 2000 and 2001.

61   Aziza Hussein, interview with Johnson, Cairo, Egypt, 13 November 1996. The study was conducted by Samia Sidky in 1956. It is summarized in *A New Life for Rural Children in Egypt*. Written records of the villagers' reactions to the project are difficult to come by. However, the rapidly increasing demands for such schools in nearby villages is evidence of their acceptance and success.

62   *Women in the Moslem World*, 25–26. The nursery school project won first prize in the General Federation of Women's Clubs' Community Achievement Contest in 1956. Favorable reports on the project's success are numerous in the Egyptian media, and in the U.S. media especially after 1953 when Ahmed Hussein was appointed Egyptian ambassador to the United States and the Husseins moved to Washington, D.C.

63   Aziza Hussein, unpublished, undated papers provided to Johnson, "Dar al-hadana bi-qaryat Sindiyun" and "Tajribat dar al-hudna al-ula fi qaryat Sindiyun bi-mudiriyat al-Qalyubiya— 'am 1950."

64   *Women in the Moslem World*, 25.

65   In a 1954 speech in Washington, D.C., Aziza Hussein reported on the progress of the project started by the CWC in Sindiyun, saying: "More promising still is the fact that in a conference recently organized by the Health Administration of the Fallah Department, the Cairo Women's Club, as well as the other agencies which subsequently worked on nursery schools in villages were called upon to pool all the information they had gained in their respective experiences, with a view to formulating a basic program for the rapid spread of nursery schools all over Egypt. The United Nations World Health Organization's regional office was so favorably impressed that they decided to adopt this movement, and assumed the initial responsibility for establishing, as a first installment in Egypt, thirteen nursery schools in one province." Aziza Hussein, interview with the author, 24 October 1996 and *Women in the Moslem World*, 26–27. The World Health Organization (WHO) became interested in the day-care centers established at Sindiyun and Tirsa because of the ability of the centers to reduce the incidence of bilharzia, a parasitic disease endemic to Egypt. Speaking in 1954, Aziza Hussein recalled asking WHO officials about the reason for their commitment to the day-care project: "They found out, they explained, that the village youngsters who were 3 to 6 years old were the most vulnerable group to the Bilharzia worm, and that the nursery schools, by caring for them and teaching them and their mothers hygienic habits, have reduced the incidence considerably. In other words, unintentionally, and as a by-product of our nursery schools, we furnished the WHO and the country with a positive program that may finally check and eliminate a grave public health problem that has damaged the peasants' productivity and cost us incalculable sums of money for many, many years." *Women in the Moslem World*, 27. Day-care centers in urban areas did not develop at the same time, however; in a 1974 speech Hussein criticized the lack of day-care centers in urban areas, saying that it was a major obstacle to employment for women. See Barbro Blomberg, "I Egypten Finns Kvinnans Rättigheter Bara på Papperet" (*Arbetet* 14 August 1974).

66   The centers were endorsed by the United Nations as an integral part of its endorsement of the RSC program. This was done in Resolution 390D (XIII), "Use of Community Welfare Centers as Effective Instruments to Promote Economic and Social Progress Throughout

the World," passed by the Economic and Social Council of the United Nations on 9 August 1951. The text of the resolution may be found in Official Records of the Economic and Social Council, Thirteenth Session, Supplement #12. Ahmed Hussein stressed the importance of this resolution, noting that "Egypt became for the first time a country that offered technical expertise on a wide scale, whereas it had previously been only a recipient country." He also noted that the United Nations offered positions to many staffers of the RSC project, and that various RSC personnel went on UN missions or took UN positions in countries such as Jordan, Iraq, Pakistan, Saudi Arabia, and Paraguay. Ahmed Hussein, *Summary of Qualifications and Positions Held*. (Unpublished document, in Arabic, from the Hussein family archives).

67 The government's commitment to expanding the program of rural day-care centers culminated in the 1954 decision to provide "200 more nursery-equipped rural social centers." *Women in the Moslem World.*

68 The Combined Units program did not have the same measure of success as the RSCs, however. Rather than involving villagers in the process, services were provided to the villagers without their input or participation. Considering the dramatic success of Hussein's Sindiyun nursery school project, the subsequent ineffectiveness of the Combined Units and their nursery schools is a testament to the importance of Hussein's philosophical approach. See Johnson for details. In 1954 the Permanent Council on Public Welfare Services decided to establish a new program of social service units in rural Egypt called the Combined Units. Each Combined Unit was to include a rural nursery school. See Information Administration, *The Permanent Council for Public Welfare Services* (Cairo: Société Orientale de Publicité, 1955).

69 Aziza Hussein and Nagiba Abdel Hamid, "Report on Egypt" (prepared for the regional conference on "Education, Vocational Training and Work Opportunities for Girls and Women in African Countries," May 17, 1971, 15–16). Although this is evidence of the success of the idea, it is simultaneously evidence of the failure of the government to adhere to the principles of aided self-help. The Combined Units replaced the RSCs, and both they and the government nursery schools were simply provided to villages by the government. In other words, 'Abd al-Nasser's changes to the Husseins' successful programs had the effect of both expanding the programs and ensuring their failure by repudiating their methodology. Aided self-help was replaced by directed development, and villagers were relegated to the status of recipients of government charity. See Johnson, *Reconstructing Rural Egypt*; James B. Mayfield, *Rural Politics in Nasser's Egypt* (Austin: University of Texas Press, 1971); and Keith Wheelock, *Nasser's New Egypt* (New York: Praeger Publishers, 1960).

70 "The Population Question and NGOs."

71 Other NGOs were formed and got involved in the campaign as well—e.g. the Egyptian Association for Population Studies, an organization for all voluntary societies concerned with family planning in Egypt.

72 The government again failed to integrate and incorporate community involvement, and its efforts were again largely unsuccessful. An integrated approach would have included not only providing contraceptives but also providing education and counseling, as well as addressing issues related to fertility like maternal and child health, women's education, illiteracy, and general social and economic development.

73 Aziza Hussein, "The Role of the Village Girl Leaders in Family Planning." Unpublished speech given at the International Planned Parenthood Federation (IPPF) Regional Seminar, 1 May 1973.

74 Speaking in 2002, Hussein noted that the government initially focused solely on providing contraceptive technologies, and "meantime advocacy was neglected and no effort was made to learn from past experiences of NGOs, particularly in the field of local participation or

the collaborative efforts between official and unofficial leadership—women, youth, elderly, teachers, religious leaders, etc. . . . nor did they pay attention to the concept of social marketing." "The Population Question and NGOs."

75 Hussein founded the Egyptian Society for the Prevention of Harmful Practices to Woman and Child (ESPHP), the nation's first anti-FGM NGO. Though not formed until 1992, the group has its roots in a seminar held in 1979 by the CFPA entitled "The Bodily Mutilation of Young Females." See Aziza Hussein, "Legal Tools for the Prevention of FGM," unpublished paper, 2003.

76 Hussein remains the Chairperson of the NCPD and is an active board member of numerous other organizations, including the CFPA and the ESPHP.

77 United Nations Development Programme, "Promoting National Initiatives to Help the Poor," available at http://www.undp.org/poverty, accessed 25 January 2004.

78 Conference Report, "Poverty Reduction Strategies: What Have We Learned" held in Bergen, Norway, 15–17 March 2001 (New York: UNDP, 2001), available at http://www.undp.org/poverty/publications/docs/Poverty_Bergen%20Report.pdf, accessed 25 January 2004.

79 Botman, 17.

80 Aziza Sami, "Hot line to Washington," *Al-Ahram Weekly*, 13–19 June 2002.

81 In Aziza Sami, "Hot line to Washington," *Al-Ahram Weekly*, 13–19 June 2002, Aziza Hussein is quoted as saying "One of Nasser's great achievements was the rights he extended to women, expanding the scope of these to an extent that was unprecedented in Egypt. Women now have the right to vote, but how many do? The top-down approach has permeated all aspects of our life. The door has yet to be opened to allow individuals who are not a part of the power structure to have an impact on society. When this occurs the 23 July revolution will have corrected its course from within."

10 *Fallahin*: The 'Mud Bearers' of Egypt's 'Liberal Age'

Samia Kholoussi

The true duty of society is to liberate the fallah's spirit from the stifling envelope of mud; to free him from the defects of the soil, while leaving him its good qualities.

—*Henry Habib Ayrout*

Ground as he was into the mud, he derived from that mud a strength that sustained him and on occasion rewarded him bountifully, and for that rich mud he developed a love that surpassed all other and to which he devoted his life. To a fallah, a plot of land was the ultimate boon, and to acquire it he would do anything. And yet the supreme irony of fate was that the fallah who loved and tilled the land was denied its possession, and the legal owners of the land were frequently those who lived away from it and who regarded it simply as a source of income.

—*Afaf Lutfi al-Sayyid Marsot*

Throughout Egypt's history, the bulk of population has consisted of the masses of its rural inhabitants—*fallahin*. They live in Upper Egypt and the Delta along the narrow ribbon of the Nile Valley where rich soil and water are available. The *fallah* emerges as both a microcosm of the nation and the principal component of its cultural heritage. Ni'mat Fu'ad's statement is a case in point, "Egypt is the gift of the Nile and its common people: the peasant being one of its main pillars of well-being and the other is the river Nile." The truest representation of the Egyptian character emanates from its peasantry. Marsot explains, "In order to grasp the essence and logic of Egyptians one has to understand the *fallah* and his society, to trace his values and beliefs in the political pattern of the land; for Egypt's political configuration is the outcome of the interaction among the *fallahin*, the native Egyptians, and the rulers, whoever they might be."[1] Shielded from the foreign influences of centuries of non-native rule, they represent the most indigenous and unadulterated segment of the population. In fact, Mustafa Kamil identified the Egyptian *umma* and the antiquity and continuity of the history of the Egyptian people in the union of the blood brethren, the Copts and Muslim Egyptians who are racially and culturally one, and a proud vaunting of *fallah* descent.[2]

This chapter focuses on representations of peasantry from 1919 until the military revolution of 1952. Selma Botman describes these years as "Egypt's liberal age" which "have not been replicated" since.[3] The uprising of 1919 is unique—as a grass-roots movement, it drew people from every sector of the population engaging both the mainstream and the marginalized alike. "Every group and community considered itself to have been the first to act, the first to feel the fiery new emotion. Yet no one understood that that sensation had arisen in all their hearts at the same time because they are all the children of Egypt [*abna' Misr*] and they all have one heart."[4] Except for the 'Urabi Revolution of 1881–82, prior uprisings in the eighteenth and nineteenth centuries mobilized only certain categories of the society and were limited in locale. Taha Husayn, one of the literary spokesmen of the period, reflected a widespread attitude at the time: "In the course of the War [World War I], a revolution has occurred for which history has no parallel, other than the American and French revolutions in the eighteenth century. It was a revolution aiming to bring about an order of things which people read about in books but considered to be unrealizable ideals of life."[5] The 1919 nationalist effort to rid the country of foreign occupation and the oppressive government it brought to power ultimately resulted in a state of semi-autonomy, through treaties in 1922, 1923, and 1936.

Egypt's 'Liberal Age': Historical Overview

The decades following the 1919 Revolution witnessed a sense of euphoria generated by the belief in imminent independence. In spite of the rapid rise and fall of governments and incessant internal unrest, the *Zeitgeist* of the new nationalist momentum suggested ground-breaking transformations in the basic structure of the society. Once an official form of independence emerged through the mist of British suzerainty, Egyptian politicians launched an unprecedented experiment in a liberal regime. For the first time in the entire history of Egypt, the constitution of 1923 and an elective parliamentary assembly introduced democratic features into a milieu overpowered by royal autocracy and a lingering foreign supremacy. The formation of parties in the political arena laid ideological and institutional foundations for a pluralistic order which provided channels for the popular masses and the non-elite humble classes *(tabaqat al ru'a)* to participate in the politics of decision-making.

In the domain of agrarian policies, it was only after the 1919 Revolution that programs of public works allowed a place for radical discussions of problems of rural Egypt, namely: the question of private property in the countryside, the increasing hardships caused by large scale landownership, and the adverse effects of the British economic policy which had turned Egypt into a one crop country in order to feed the insatiable cotton mills of Lancashire. Discourses of rurality emerged and several statesmen started to work out detailed plans for an agrarian reform.[6]

The *Fallah* in the Eye of the Storm

Due to centuries of foreign domination and long years of exploitation by despotic governments, the ruling body had always been an alien entity in the minds of the rural population. "The fact that no native Egyptian had ruled Egypt for more than a millennium was to give Egyptian political life a characteristic trait, that of the nonidentity of the population with the government."[7] Mistrust and suspicion of authority estranged the *fallah* from his own country and extracted ambivalent reactions that alternated between the need to placate and outwit it, and the urge to defy and resent it.

At this historical juncture, the *fallah* came to the center of ideological conflicts, nationalist fervor, and patriotic upheavals. Uplifting the peasantry for the betterment of the nation was bound up with nationalistic ideas such as highlighting the role of peasantry in enhancing society's cohesion and endowing it with stability and character. "The growth of the democratic and national spirit in Egypt after the war made the nation aware that helping the peasant is not only a duty but also an insurance against social unrest."[8] Leading nationalists were of *fallah* background. They were products of villages who spent formative years in a rural environment, attended the *kuttab* (village school), possessed *fallah* traits, used rural dialects, and maintained their emotional ties with the peasantry in some degree or another throughout their lives.[9] In one of his speeches, Sa'd Zaghlul identified the peasant cause as pivotal to the goals of liberation. He declared,

The most important results of the revolution have been the Egyptianization of the Egyptian economy, the abandonment of the veil by women, their participation in the national movement, the destruction of the class of pashas, the seizure of power by the *fallahin*, the disappearance of the Turkish element from Egyptian politics — and independence comes from all this because external independence has no value unless there is also internal liberation.[10]

For the peasants, Zaghlul was the epitome of *fallah* reality, who talked like a *fallah*, understood the *fallah*, and was therefore accessible and comprehensible to the masses who were able to identify with him. With Zaghlul in the government, the *fallah* felt that the ruling men in the capital were sympathetic to him.[11] Though one of the major causes of peasant participation in the 1919 Revolution stemmed from the hardships which *fallahin* underwent during World War I when thousands were recruited into labor corps, it was in fact Zaghlul's arrest in 1919 that prompted demonstrations in many provincial capitals. Peasants attacked railroad stations, cut telegraph lines, and in their resentment of foreign oppression, beat several Europeans and burned property.[12]

With the founding of a constitutional system, the *fallahin* played a prominent role in political life. They participated in national elections. Candidates counted on them as voters. The Wafd sustained itself through a network of village committees extending through Upper and Lower Egypt, and derived its power from a massive rural backing. It formed a grass-roots organization based on a thorough understanding of the village order. The *fallahin* population was briefly empowered by appealing to the Wafd Party.

A Beleaguered Peasant in a Euphoric Period

The country's ephemeral prosperity in the period between 1919 and 1952 was for the common working peasants a time of dire hardship and deprivation which grew progressively worse during the 1930s and 1940s. They bore the brunt of all political, economic, and social crises. The economic enterprises and social transformations which followed the 1919 uprising did not include drastic measures to overhaul the living conditions among the peasants who constituted the overwhelming majority of the Egyptian population. The flourishing new urban middle class in which hope for agrarian reform resided, had its interests bound up with landholding magnates and was not inclined to side with the *fallahin*. Hard-pressed national leaders were too embattled to think about intractable local problems or risk changes in the social order.

Factors responsible for the peasant's continual trials and tribulations were partly human and partly natural. Marsot points out that the peasant society is characterized by "centuries of exploitation and abuse by alien rulers and native superiors alike. He has been at the mercy of the elements, which were capable of devastating him equally with drought and flood, trailing in their wake epidemics and starvation. . . . Everything and everyone seemed to conspire against him to render his life miserable and condition pitiful, yet not one of his rulers had pity on him."[13] Peasants suffered the downside of the wave of industrialization manifested in the increasing rapacity of the rich and the disregard for the welfare of the masses.

The two World Wars had an adverse effect on the vast majority; and the *fallah* condition reached a nadir point. During World War I, "numerous peasants and their livestock were conscripted for service with the Allied forces. . . . The world demand for cotton made some fortunes but caused too much land to be given to the production of cotton, too little to the growing of food and in the later year of the war, food grew scarce."[14] In some cases, *fallah* possessions, whether cattle or jewelry, were sent to the Hashemites in the Arabian Peninsula to procure their loyalty to the British.[15] Upon their return to their villages, peasants were faced with the problem of overpopulation and the resultant scarcity of cultivable land, the rising rents, and the decline in wages. The *fallah* family sank deeper into misery.[16] Though some peasants shared in the evanescent prosperity of the World War I cotton boom, with the violent economic fluctuations of 1921, 1926, and 1931, cotton prices dropped sharply, debts of the farmers rose dramatically, and they faced one of the worst challenges to their livelihood.

During and after World War II, social tensions mounted due to unfulfilled promises of land reforms and economic amelioration. The dismal state of the *fallah* reached tragic heights in the shadow of the terror exercised by the governments of Muhammad Mahmud (1877–1941), "The Man with the Iron Fist," in 1928–29, and of Isma'il Sidqi (1875–1950), which lasted from 1930 to 1933. Members of the parliament were limited to a coterie of elite who turned a deaf ear to the question of social justice and the peasants' paltry existence. In order to implement their ideas of social reform, liberal nationalists had no alternative but to turn to the despotic figures in the political system, who often reacted with smug heedlessness to the deepening socioeconomic fissures. While poor peasants wallowed in starvation and bankruptcy, the government preached to the *fallahin* about the alleged effectiveness of their economic policies. Large landowners were granted absolute power over tenants, elections were forged, the tax-imposing state was more abusive than ever, the economy was in shambles, and the peasants bore the brunt, becoming more destitute than before.[17]

With no tangible rewards for the rural masses' endurance, frustration flared and the government resorted to suppression. Cudgels were used to subjugate the peasants and demonstrations were curbed violently by the British rifles. In the postwar years, violent uprisings occurred on several large estates. Peasants attacked guards, set fire to offices, squatted on the land, took up arms, and demanded that the government sell it to peasants.[18]

Peasants fought another more ferocious battle which claimed enormous casualties. There were two epidemics: one was malaria from 1942 until 1945 and the other was cholera in 1947. During the malaria attack, they stood defenseless in the face of invaders descending to the Nile valley from Sudan.[19] The number of deaths was so high that "there weren't enough healthy men left alive even to carry the dead. People were hauled to their graves on the back of a camel."[20] Local defenses were weak; poverty, malnourishment, and unsanitary living conditions in villages were favorable for parasites, which killed peasants at the rate of hundreds a day.

Inimical forces inherent in peasant conditions conspired to intensify the austerity and affliction. Bilharzia was exacerbated by the change from basin to perennial irrigation; subsistence on a meager diet deficient in essential nutrients; washing and drinking directly from unpurified Nile water; and living in unsanitary mud-brick dwellings shared with livestock. These chronic diseases had a debilitating effect on the energies and lowered the work capacity. Moreover, illiteracy, which reached 90 percent at the time, disqualified the rural population from engaging in public affairs and expressing its rights. The *fallah* class was incapable of making itself publicly recognizable or rendering visible the grave miscarriages of justice. It possessed strong will and moral courage but lacked the means of effective communication. It remained for long inarticulate, pining for the need to present its concerns and galvanize public opinion. *Fallah* grievances have thus been routinely forgotten and often swept under the rug.

For centuries, the tyrannous exactions of the system of landownership in Egypt constituted the core of peasant impoverishment. A mere 11 percent of the total number of landowners owned about 70 percent of the land of Egypt. Few peasants could afford plots of land, which in any case barely permitted subsistence.[21] The majority was condemned to landlessness and dispossession where lands were owned by the state or governor, and the peasant could only till the land for a meager reward. Ahmad Lutfi al-Sayyid described the ruthlessness in collecting taxes and the mortification to which the peasants were subjected, "I was a witness to the thrashings of the village head ('umda) when the rents were overdue. As a schoolboy, I used to go on Fridays to the house of one of my father's friends who was an overseer. I saw him seated in the foremost part of his courtyard with two of his guards ready with their whips to carry out the beatings."[22]

Rural Discourses in the Inter-Revolution Years

After the Anglo-Egyptian treaty of 1936, thinkers of both secular and religious political currents faced a dilapidated socioeconomic structure.[23] Reorganizing Egyptian society had to include rectifying the agrarian situation due to the important role it played in stabilizing the social and economic systems. The villages were the key to bring Egypt "more in accordance with the spirit of the age and its demands" and achieve any progress.[24] Reconstruction programs could not be undertaken in isolation from agrarian reform propositions. As an Egyptian political economist wrote, "The creation of a ministry of health in 1936 and of an independent section in the ministry of interior devoted to the planning and execution of rural reforms, is a welcome sign of increased public interest in the fallah."[25] The educated Cairene elite considered the wretched conditions of the rural population a national problem. Learning and writing about the common people had a revolutionary potential and works of art become works of reform, raising the awareness of the nation regarding peasant malaise and thereby propagating measures to improve them.

Between 1919 and 1952, rural discourses assumed two directions: one was elicited by the official parliamentary proposals, and the other developed beyond the pale of parliamentary life. Whenever debated in the parliament, the ruling party, which expressed the interest of the large landowners, sought to diffuse the threat to their material interests. Any interest in remedying the condition of *fallah* landlessness or censuring the concentration of wealth in the hands of large landowners was restricted to a small circle of politicians. In point of fact, a striking feature of the attitude of the political parties was their reluctance to dispute landowners' supremacy or undertake any rectification in the rural status quo. Those who dominated the parliament and influenced representative bodies were themselves those whose power in political life depended on land-ownership. They sought to reconcile a maze of conflicting principles. With vested interests they needed to protect, they faced the chronic disjunction between power and morality. For the most part, they intended to make sure that things went unchanged and unchallenged. Accordingly, it was impossible for any legislation limiting the size of the great estates or encouraging the formation of rural labor unions to succeed, and it was very long before any legislation that set a minimum wage for agricultural workers could ever succeed.[26]

Outside the parliamentary parameters, politicians, social scientists, and activists of various affiliations appropriated the rural discourse to the purposes of their agenda and ideological orientations. Full-length books appeared generating a language of and about rural entities. Mirrit Boutros Ghali's (1908–91) *The Policy of Tomorrow* (1938) and Hafiz 'Afifi's *On the Margin of Politics* (1938) focus on the patriotic spirit *(al-ruh al-wataniya)* and the national consciousness *(al-shu'ur al-qawmi)*. As Misako Ikeda has also demonstrated in her chapter on educational debate, these authors cautioned that the rural population was "dead as regards healthy nationalistic life," and needed a sociopolitical education to instill national consciousness which could nourish mature public opinion. Writing about the marginalization of peasants in the national life of the country, Ghali stated, "These people miss all the advantages of the stir and enthusiasm of nationalistic feelings . . . they are dead as regards healthy nationalistic life. The right to vote has not educated them."[27] He advocated government involvement in the minute details of villagers' daily life, with persistent supervision to maintain control of social life, all with the intention of drawing villagers out into the open and integrating them into national life. Similarly, 'Afifi explained how peasants had been banned from modern society through utter backwardness, while also proposing transformation of the rural community to encourage social and political integration. Poor public services in the areas of health, housing, and education contributed to the backwardness of the peasants, prevented enlightenment regarding public welfare, discouraged participation in the national life and undermined a strong society. Clean and well-ordered villages promoted a feeling of pride, national consciousness, and social responsibility. Political independence would thus be coupled with social change and an improvement in the quality of the life.[28]

The colonial context framing early peasantry research in Egypt promoted a schema fusing functionalist social anthropology and orientalism. Henry Ayrout's *The Egyptian Peasant* (1938) situated his vision of *fallah* and progress in the context of orientalist images recurrent in the writings of European travelers. Emerging from earlier representations of Egyptian peasantry dating back to the French *Description de l'Égypte*, Ayrout perceived peasant character and lifestyle as categorically deficient, so that elite intervention would need to revive the rural population. "The initiative can never come from his own community, which is completely numb and powerless, but only from the classes which overshadow him, from the elite, who with their riches of minds and money can vitalize him. In this dough must work the leaven of intelligence and sympathy."[29] Diagnosing peasant conditions through an environmental outlook attributed dynamics of rural Egypt more to the timeless peasant mentality and less to changing political and economic forces.

Communist and socialist movements, and the Muslim Brotherhood, took up the cause of social justice and freedom from want, which surfaced in the 1930s, and focused on peasant property rights and land reform.[30] Blandishments of the class institution and proposals for land reform—including radical measures such as sequestration—courted the rural population to enlist its support for their different ideological orientations. The agrarian discourse of the communist current was geared toward socialism,[31] examining problems of the agricultural economy, social and material conditions of farmers, feudal agrarian socioeconomic relations, and the system of monopoly. Ahmad Sadiq Sa'd's (1919–88) *The Problem of the Fallah* (1945) proposed new constructs within the context of the capitalist and imperialist intervention in Egypt. Seeking to free agrarian production from exploitation, he maintained that "the main source of retardation is the monopoly of the large landowners . . . [they] are a parasitic class which is allowed to increase its income without contributing to the economic development of the country."[32] Programs for agrarian change attacked large landlords' monopolization of Egyptian politics—they were the greatest enemy of the nationalist movement and the source of economic retardation.

Though both the Communists and the Muslim Brotherhood had concrete programs to eliminating large estates and alleviating burdens of exploitative agrarian systems, it was the Brotherhood more than the imported western ideology of the Communist groups that developed roots in the villages, and gained the sympathy and support of the afflicted peasantry. For example, Brotherhood leaflets called on the government to observe the teachings of the Prophet as the only way to ensure rural justice. In 1948, it proposed a land law advocating redistribution of agricultural land among landless peasants at a reasonable price; enabling them to buy the surplus and reclaimed lands on easy terms; setting an acreage limitation on individual landholding; ensuring landlords and tenants equal shares in the produce of the land and establishing rural rent control.[33]

In spite of the limitations of agrarian policies developed by different reform groups, the search for alternative development models seriously challenged the socioeconomic and political power of the landed aristocracies. Rather than using political power, politicians and social scientists generated intellectually brilliant, systematic studies of multi-dimensional rural reality. Interpretative approaches alternated between both empirical studies grasping the varied historical experiences and contemporary realities, and conceptual analysis and theoretical debates.

Representations of the *Fallah*: 'A Multiplicity of Imaginary Captures'

Though concerned with a faithful reflection of concrete reality, peasant representation bore a blatant political agenda. Portrayals sought to combine truthfulness and historical concreteness with the ideological remolding and education of toiling people in the spirit of socialism. In the period between 1919 and 1952, Egyptian peasantry continued to be reinterpreted. As an early example, Yusuf al-Shirbini's *The Shaking of Skullcaps in the Poem of Abu Sahduf* (1857) was a landmark for its poignant portrayal of peasant poverty. It promulgated the designation of the "bearer of mud" which accompanied the peasant for a long time. Shirbini, himself a former country boy who went to Cairo to study at al-Azhar to become a *shaykh*, viciously mocked the rural people with whom he grew up. The tract is a combination of invective and satire in which derogatory epithets denounced peasant character. It diminished the subject through ridicule, contempt, scorn, amusement, and indignation. The author pronounced the peasants obsequious: "if you do them a favor they disavow it; if you are gentle with them they hate you; if they are not oppressed, they oppress others."[34] *Shaking of Skullcaps* is significant as a compilation of themes recurring in peasant narratives for centuries: everyday forms of peasant resistance to exploitation; abject fear of the tax collector which turned the peasant into a cowering creature; vilification and ridicule of the rural population as uncouth and churlish; the hopelessness of ever trying to improve the peasant—"a *fallah* remains a *fallah* and there's no chance he'll ever change"—and the conflict between the economic, social, and cultural environments of the countryside *fallah* and townspeople.

With the appearance of embryonic fiction in 1881, the narrative discourse responded to a new sensibility informed by the need to reach the public through tackling social problems. It combined didacticism with concern for the daily life of ordinary people. It aimed at raising the consciousness of readers and changing attitudes. 'Abdallah al-Nadim's (1845–96) portrayal of the peasant predicament took a clearly reformative twist, evoking a new perception of the writer as a social reformer. Deploying dialogue and the oral tradition helped to connect his writing to reality, and elicited a forcefully authentic evocation of intimate scenes and experience. Al-Nadim identified with the peasants, and demonstrated great concern for their suffering. He described his pieces as "passionate sighs to provoke an emotional response."[35] Seeking to appeal to the masses in order to enlist support for social justice, he addressed the common uneducated country people. His humorous journal *al-Tankit wa-l-tabkit* ("Raillery and Reproof," 1881) used colloquial Egyptian Arabic as a way to raise consciousness. Most of the literary vignettes in his periodical *al-Ustadh* ("The Professor") were dedicated to provocative issues on the derelict peasant reality.[36] Denunciatory reproach and mordant criticism exposed the brutality and exploitation as well as the humiliation to which rural dwellers were subjected. Al-Nadim also dauntlessly castigated the Khedive Isma'il and his coterie of foreigners as unjust oppressors of the masses, attributing oppression and corruption in the countryside to their tyranny, greed, and criminality.

The Dinshaway tragedy generated passionate depictions of the incident in fictional narratives by Egyptian authors. Mahmud Tahir Haqqi's (1884–1964) novella, *The Maiden of Dinshaway* (1906) achieved best-seller status when it was first published because of the actuality of its horrific topic. The intensity of the horror was evoked by the indictment of innocent and helpless *fallahin* by an Egyptian attorney and the brutal force of the British authorities who used the *fallahin* to discipline all Egyptians.[37] To avert the retribution of the colonial government, Haqqi incorporated a fictitious tale of love and intrigue into the historical incident of the tragic clash between the *fallahin* and the British officers. As one of the most powerful Egyptian causes, the incident effectively transformed *fallahin* into a catalyst for nationalist aspirations.

The *Fallah* as the Essence of Egyptian Nationalism

Following the 1919 Revolution, the evolution of the Egyptian national image and the concept of a local Egyptian nationhood (*al-umma al-misriya*) embraced an identity anchored in the Nile Valley and with rural roots. Egypt's rebirth was closely associated with the peasantry—the primordial nation. The stalwart and close-to-nature peasant became an image dear to the hearts of many nationalists. The unsullied goodness of the peasant ideal was aligned with true nationalist sentiments. National slogans such as "Egypt for the Egyptians" *(Misr li-l-misriyin)* and fiery debates over Egypt's unique and distinct personality *(al-shakhsiya al-misriya)* gathered strength through the new configuration of the peasant as an embodiment of the authentic national character.

The cultural climate of the 1920s and 1930s responded to the new awareness of the role of identity in reinforcing the movement toward nationalist awakening and political independence. An Egyptian national literature *(adab misri)* embraced the village *(al-rif)* and its inhabitants as the true reflection of a distinctive national identity. Activists in the political, social, and literary fields embarked upon an unprecedented celebration of peasantry virtues, commending their character and acclaiming their heroic struggle for survival throughout centuries of oppression and exploitation. The peasants stood for everything authentically Egyptian: their worldview, beliefs, rituals, and patterns of thought and behavior were all perceived as typically Egyptian. Polemical literature and creative writing drew their inspiration from folkways of peasants to portray the spirit of the nation, "the essence of which was exemplified most completely in country life."[38] To be Egyptian was to be aware of the eternal and unchanging peasantry.

The peasant was also depicted as a paragon of qualities Egypt needed to revive to regain its past dignified status. Hence, there was an urge to recast the image of the *fallah* which had been debased in the normative discourse. The peasant was rehabilitated as his negative traits were explained away, endowing them with positive overtones or even inverting them into strengths. The peasant apathetic attitude was interpreted as steadfastness and a moral strength to deal with hardship. It was a mechanism of defense against the ravages of time. Primitiveness was viewed as spontaneously intuitive living, and an unchanging lifestyle preserving the essence of ancient Egypt. Peasants also excelled in their fortitude: "When I looked at a European peasant and compared him to the Egyptian peasant, I saw in this comparison that the Egyptian *fallah* is stronger and more patient in his work."[39] In fact, Egyptian nationalism was particularly popular precisely because of this focus on the peasants. For Salama Musa (1887–1958), the *fallah* personified ancient and civilized Egypt: "the Egypt of the pharaohs is still alive among the *fallahin*" who cling intimately to the land. They were the genuine heirs to ancient Egyptian perfection.[40]

Appeals to intellectuals to convey and capture their Egyptianness materialized in The Association of National Literature (1929–31). The failure of earlier literature to render a true picture of rural life was attributed to detachment from, and neglect of, the rural masses who constituted the heart of the country. For writers to produce genuinely Egyptian national literature, they needed to understand the nature and character of the peasant. The driving force of the Association, Muhammad Zaki 'Abd al-Qadir, promoted 'rural literature' (al-adab al-rifi) as a new genre considering the countryside an imaginative resource. Writers of the period supported the culture of the rural masses. Ahmad Mahmud Sulayman espoused the integration of peasant oral tradition into the dominant discourse and the official written literature. This was declared to be an ideal way to initiate a campaign for the advancement of peasantry. For 'Abbas Mahmud al-'Aqqad, the "Egyptianization" of poetry was achieved by using the popular songs of the fallahin, the oral traditions of the masses which retain the features of genuine Egyptian temperament and humor.[41] The features of the arche-typal Egyptian are preserved in the villagers. Salama Musa went further, to advocate a "language of the people" that would create a "literature of the people" with ideas relevant to their lives and times. Ibrahim al-Misri set a program for urban writers to remedy deficiencies in their knowledge about rural life, starting with renouncing urban arrogance, creating a protagonist out of the common people, and locating the peasant at center-stage as the site of different ideological forces. He entreated city-dwellers to "go to the countryside. Drop your arrogance toward the fallah."[42] In order to achieve a deeper comprehension of peasant character, sufferings, and struggles, the writer ought to come close to peasant reality and mingle with them.

National interest in depicting the constituent elements of a distinc-tive Egyptian identity culminated in Tawfiq al-Hakim's Return of the Spirit (1933). It loomed large as a prime example of the "Egyptianist" perspective with its glorification of the potential of Egyptian peasantry. The image sublimated the power hidden in the peasants' souls, the perpetual and mys-terious spirit prodding them into action manifested in the 1919 Revolution. The narrative marked the culmination of a vision of an Egyptian national fiction. Al-Hakim captured the spirit of that generation and its urge to create a uniquely Egyptian self-awareness and image. Muhsin, the artist protagonist, was driven by the desire to become the eloquent tongue of the Egyptian people and forge the national conscience. The narrative based the recovery of the nation's authentic culture on magnifying the genuinely and distinctively Egyptian, as contrasted with negative traits in the Arab char-acter. Muhsin was convinced of the superiority of the honorable and noble fallah who is extolled for "his goodness, calm, [and] love of peace, which are the hallmark of civilization and stability."[43] During a short vacation on a farm near Damanhour, he empathized with the "simple" *fallah* tilling his family's lands. Unlike his parents—the pernicious and oppressive masters devoid of compassion or humility—he identified with rural lifestyle, admires the farm laborers' modes of expression, lighthearted joy for life, and envies their permanent ties to the land and their love for it.

The elevation of the peasant to a nationalist icon emerged most effectively in monumental visual representations. As Caroline Williams has described so well in her chapter, Mahmud Mukhtar's (1891–1934) "Reawakening of Egypt" *(Nahdat Misr)* typified the spirit of the time. Henry Ayrout describes its first location, "In the great square in front of Cairo station stands a massive group of statuary hewn from Aswan granite. It represents the Sphinx rising on its forefeet, with a woman standing beside it, her hand on the nape of its neck, and her veil raised."[44] The pharaonic inspired bust with the several times life-size figure of an Egyptian peasant woman towering over it and gazing into the distance, epitomized the back-to-roots trend. It was a tangible reflection of a firm belief that "the *fallah* is the crown of Egypt and the secret of its strength, and that the one truth which had not changed in the world in six thousand years is that he is the one thing that has kept Egypt vibrant and strong until today."[45] Mukhtar worked on the sculpture in an atmosphere saturated with the spirit of revolution and revival. The statue was a genuine artistic expression of the re-awakening of the nation in the post-1919 era. It was created to commemorate a national renaissance combining past glory and the contemporary character represented in the *fallahin*.

The Pitfalls of 'Romanticized' Nationalism

The exclusive focus on the rural idyllic theme was politically and nationally expedient. Muhammad Husayn Haykal's (1888–1956) *Zaynab: Scenes and Manners of Egyptian Country-life* (1913) emerges as a tour de force of idyllic representations of village life. The compassionate country romance of a poor but beautiful peasant girl who emerges as the perfect child of nature was depicted against an elegantly painted backcloth of an Eden-like country life. Haykal admits, "I am infatuated with a countryside that my imagination conjured up."[46] Rurality emerged as an imaginary cultural geography with emotional connotations and an overbearing nostalgia attached to it. After reading *Zaynab*, the protagonist of al-Sharqawi's *The Egyptian Earth* sees through the gloss of sentimentality and observes pertinently,

How I wish my village could be . . . without troubles like the village in which Zaynab lived . . . the farmers there had no troubles with their irrigation water, the government did not take their land away, nor send men in khaki to flog them with whips. The children's eyes were not consumed with flies. In Zaynab's village men did not pass blood and pus in their urine, nor were they convulsed with pains which did not leave them till they passed away . . . Zaynab's village had never tasted the whip . . . had never known the threats of fate in the form of the foreigner, the omda, the government, nor the thrill of defying and winning, at times.[47]

The social order was mapped across a picturesque terrain. Haykal comments on what prompted the choice of the alternate title for this novel, *An Egyptian Peasant*: "I wanted to show [that] . . . the Egyptian peasant feels deep in his heart a sense of value and worth that deserves all due respect, that he takes pride in upholding Egyptianism and *fallahism* as a banner and slogan to brandish before the public, exacting from others esteem and honor."[48] The pride in identification with the peasantry however dealt a blow to the presumption and arrogance of Turks toward the peasants. In line with the liberal nationalist discourse, Haykal's narrative of pastoral life romanticized peasant hardships, and glorifies their simplicity.

Peasant idealization is further accentuated by the language used. Haykal addressed the readers in village vernacular. All the conversation is conducted in the dialect of Lower Egypt regardless of the status of the speaker. Phrasing village life in plain peasant dialogue made it necessary for the author to apologize to his readers for this departure from classical norms. Haykal grappled with the cherished legacy of the florid classical language which constituted the bedrock of Arab literary creativity.[49]

To link to a topic ably explored by Andrew Flibbert in chapter sixteen of this volume, cinematic representation of peasantry drew a veil of illusion over the realities of the villages. In the popular imagination, rustic life was valued as an idyll of bucolic communion with nature, and the image was taken for the whole reality. The appeal of the imaginary for the urban dwellers remained strongly magnetic. The rural was regarded as a place to retreat from the ever-quickening pace of urban life, and its restorative powers acted as a cure for the problems of urban disease. *Zaynab* (1930), a landmark in the history of Egyptian cinema, conjured up a construct of the countryside derived from western pastoral romances. The film presented a view from above, not from within. Its creators oscillated between a film recreating the world in its own image and making an ideal world in the likeness of the real world. After paying a visit to the village, the director pondered core issues,

> I was . . . shocked at what I learnt about the peasant's life; this was one of my worst disappointments and disillusionments in my life.
> I have come out of these visits with a great deal of painful facts about peasant life. I have visited in person the homes of these wretched peasants . . . in which I would be ashamed to keep animals . . .
> I have seen a repulsive display of ignorance, injustice, poverty, and naiveté . . . I was a little disgusted when dinner was served to us.
> A sumptuous feast . . . offered by undernourished hosts. The horror of human injustice! Impossible, I can't bring myself to present my country in this way. What good is realism if it damages my country's reputation? A peasant's life has to be portrayed as it should be and not as it is.[50]

The conventional city dweller's reaction to the delights of nature in the countryside is adulterated by the obvious dirt and poverty of the toiling peasants. The director consciously refrained from addressing the peasant's misery. He admitted to not only his unfamiliarity with rural life in Egypt, but also to self-deception, an intentional rejection of the truth, and a deliberate misrepresentation of village life. He took upon himself the task of improving on reality by camouflaging its dreadful afflictions.

Similarly, in *Romance and Revenge* (1944), a famous singer of the day, Asmahan, like Muhammad 'Abd al-Wahhab before her, dwelt lovingly on countryside sceneries chanting eulogies of the industrious and diligent peasant who though poverty-stricken was nevertheless content and peaceful. The peasants emerged as naïve and pure, knowing nothing but fresh-air freedom and songs chanted to the field. On another plane, *Layla* (1927), a pioneering production filmed in a rural setting of natural beauty, received negative reviews when it appeared in theaters. The producer and the director were criticized for their preoccupation with the backward rural population instead of scenes from the life of the more educated classes in Cairo. Accordingly, the film was censored to eliminate scenes blemishing the reputation of Egyptians as civilized people. Scenes in which the low round table used by peasants for their meals appeared were considered signs of shameful barbarity. An embellished natural and human landscape was more in keeping with the *Zeitgeist* and more appealing to the blooming nationalist sensibilities.[51]

Although other movie titles like *Storm over the Countryside* or *Layla, Daughter of the Village* promised true-to-life vignettes of rural predicaments, the content betrayed an indulgence in romantic nationalism. The image of the peasant as an embodiment of the social and economic malaise is displaced by a repertoire of stereotypical scenes: the pretty impoverished village girl caught in the throes of change from rural to urban life after the landlord fell for her and transferred her to the city; the *fallah* figure being almost always either the funny and stupid servant or the wicked thief or murderer; scenes where the rich profligate *'umda* (village headman) wasted his money on gambling and fell victim to the ploys of city swindlers; and visits of wealthy landlords to their manors celebrated by the rejoicing and cheering of servile peasants.

The 1920s witnessed the burgeoning popularity of Egyptian caricatures in magazines and newspapers. The predominance of illiteracy resulted in the image being more potent and effective than the word, and gave it precedence. As James Whidden demonstrates in chapter one of this volume, cartoons became a continuation of the political platform and an important medium for social critique. Sarokhan, a famous cartoonist of the day, helped unmask the falsification of peasant reality. His emaciated and sickly peasant surrounded by dry and cracked lands and singing the beauty and charm of peasant life is a poignant parody of the common romantic idealizations. In fact, in the fanciful renditions of the *fallah*, the aristocrat patronized the underprivileged and the saw the peasant as a romanticized object arousing sympathy and pathos.

'Realism': a Streak of Deliverance

With the rise of 'realistic fiction' and the focus on real people in plausible situations, the representation of the peasant evolved through creative writing containing a minute analysis of every aspect of life and character. The interest in realism reached an acme with the New School (*jama'at al-madrasa al-haditha*) (1920) which sought to reformulate the relationship between literature and social reality in order to "interrelate literature and society in such a manner that literature becomes the true reflection and the creative mirror of society."[52] It endeavored to root narrative discourse in readers' daily concerns, and to use fiction to alter perceptions of society and change preconceived ideas. Creating an indigenous Egyptian literature required the trend of realism. Peasant reality was subjected to novelistic conventions whereby the precision and vividness of artistic rendering of details convinced the reader of a story's truthfulness and its relevance to real life. The village was accepted on its own merits rather than on the terms of its urbanized or cosmopolitan sons.

For its proponents, realism required vivid contact with the mental structures and collective consciousness of villagers. Fictional incidents should become a direct reflection of their world- view. Mahmud Tahir Lashin's (1894–1954) short story *Village Small Talk* (1929) reflected the world view of a particular social group with whom he had little relation. Lashin's text refrains from specifying the name of the village concerned. Its social powerlessness typified Egyptian villages. The villager's experience of the visit of two urban dwellers is a "comprehensive textual strategy."[53] Their encroachment on the peasants' evening gathering formed the core of the story. The *shaykh* at the center of the general chat was the potential catalyst of village polemics. The narrator arriving for a day's refreshment in his friend's native village hoped to benefit the misguided peasants.

> Determined to disprove the sheikh's lies and destroy his empty debating points, I noticed him wavering in his argument and jumped in, seizing the opportunity to discuss the peasant's living conditions ... then I elaborated on the subject of free will combined with action, explaining that they could accomplish miracles if they became conscious of their existence and resolved to justify it. . . . However each time I paused to see what effect I was having, I found them open-mouthed in dumb amazement, looking from me to their mentor.[54]

The peasants acted as a chorus, picking up and echoing the *shaykh*'s sentiments. He orchestrated their responses with his oratory. They recognized modes of development but are unable or unwilling to embrace it. The inability to reconcile new and old, or divine arbitrariness with human yearning, condemned any attempts at change. In fact, the response of the peasant audience around the *shaykh* illuminated the warring discourses. The narrative developed into an arena of contradictory views: the clash between conventions and traditional values and modernist attitudes; the confrontation of progress and backwardness, and knowledge and ignorance; as well as conflicts between the urban-secular and the rural-religious, individual freedom and the oppressive pressures of peasant religion, and between resignation to fate and exercising free will.

On another plane, Muhammad Taymur's (1892–1921) *In the Train* (1917), considered by critics to be the first indigenous Egyptian short story, reiterated al-Nadim's complaints about the peasant's crushing poverty and torments.[55] The narrative now integrated the internal perspective in presentating various dimensions of the theme. In conversation among passengers on a train heading toward the countryside, a question about the best methods of maximizing peasant productivity evoked a variety of responses. The contributors to the conversation were stereotypical Egyptian characters, including an effendi—a category ably problematized by Lucie Ryzova in this volume—a *'umda*, a Circassian pasha, and an Azhari *shaykh*. Proposals for peasant reformation alternated between education and the whip. The majority favored the latter as the least costly means to overhaul peasant conditions: "Don't forget that lashing has been the means of subjugating the peasant for centuries. He's accustomed to it from the cradle to the grave."[56] Ironically, the proposition elicited a passive reaction from the author representing cultured intellectuals. He withdrew from the gathering, compliant and resigned, without suggesting a more constructive and humane solution.

This narrative reflected the then-common laissez faire attitude toward the peasants. The romanticized view of the beautiful countryside with its distant horizon and the notion of pure rural naïveté was often countered by a scorn for sentimentality and a cynicism mocking romanticism and seeing only the vices of peasants. This cynicism—that the peasant's deplorable state suited him well as he was oblivious to the misery in his life—reverberated with views that the peasant in such natural ambience was better off in spite of illiteracy and ignorance. The peasant was made to express acceptance of his impoverishment and the surrounding misery.

An amalgam of naturalism and realism formulated a mature understanding of description and illustration *(wasf taswir)* as the means for the true depiction of life and human behavior devoid of exaggerated romantic sentiment or excessive imagination.

> Description of the setting from which characters emerge is one of the most important requirements of fictional art, because it has a tremendous effect on forming their characteristics and feelings. Furthermore, the vivid narrative and use of accurate realistic description have a strong impact on the reader, for they convince him of the truthfulness of the story and of its relevance to real life.[57]

Based on such an understanding of realism, Mahmud Taymur (1894–1973) strove to recreate Egyptian life. His realism appears mainly in the portrayal of the effect of human sentiments on the behavior of the characters, with slight attention to the impact of society on such behavior. *Al-Shaykh Jum'a* (1925) described countryside malaise. It dwelt on illiterate laymen who became blessed and venerable *shaykh*s by accident. The theme of corruption of *shaykh*s reflected a struggle between the new enlightened generation of Arab intellectuals and the older generation with their conservatism and traditional leanings.[58] The attack against *shaykh*s typified a common stance of the younger generation. Graduates of the modern educational system opposed *shaykh*s taught in old theological institutes. They could no longer tolerate the exaggerated respect and great reputation *shaykh*s enjoyed among the general public, considering this status unjustified.

> For . . . whereas the *'ulama'* make abundant discourses on every field
> of learning unattended by anyone save their pupils in Cairo, the
> rural ulama . . . come and go surrounded by reverence and the aura of
> prestige. When they preach people listen attentively to what they say,
> full of awe and rapt admiration . . . this attitude places the ulama on
> a pedestal, and almost believing that they were made of superior and
> purer metal than anyone else.[59]

Al-Shaykh Jum'a revealed the falsity of this social class in the village. Taymour employed his stories to subvert and deconstruct meanings attached to this position. The supposedly learned religious figures behaved in a ridiculous manner. The narrative is pitiless toward the *shaykh*s, who loomed large as the villagers' spokesmen and negotiators with the outside world. The *fallah* "has been comforted and beguiled by his religious mentors."[60] The attire of piety, devoutness and learning was a mere mask disguising charlatans. The *shaykh*s offer false advice, misconstrue words with sophistry, twist the sacred texts to suit their purposes, and use the ignorant mob to their advantage. In Taymour's story, they do not elicit any sympathy or appreciation from the readers.

The ethic of national belonging celebrating the peasant as society's backbone worked to minimize tensions about class divisions and social differences. Both were added to national independence as political issues and became integrated in the country's cultural consciousness. With the widespread realization of the fundamental dysfunctionality of a society where a handful enjoyed tremendous wealth while a helpless majority worked for starvation wages, an emerging intellectual elite created a highly critical climate. They attached great importance to the question of class struggle and the demand for social justice. With the appropriation of the realism formula, the social and political state of affairs was subjected to analysis and revision.[61]

From 1939, novels and short stories explicitly divulged concern with social justice. Though written in a political tract-like manner, 'Isam al-Din Hifni Nasif's *A Storm over Egypt: A Societal Story* was the first work of fiction in which the *fallah*-landowner relationship was the main subject matter. It focused on a large landowner's exploitation of the *fallah*, with a strong sociopolitical content. A moderately rich landowner gets richer at the expense of the *fallahin* by resorting to ruthlessness and lack of integrity. On his deathbed, the greedy landlord confesses to a group of peasants surrounding him:

> I know you'll never forget that you were not part of the wealth that
> I enjoyed all my life . . . from your sweat. Your housing conditions
> were not improved and the magnificence of my palace has only made
> your huts look more hideous. Regardless of the bountiful harvest, I
> never added a single penny to your wages in spite of the rising costs of
> living. . . . When you demanded some of your rights, I ignored you and
> declared war on you. . . . I did not put in account the storm that would
> rage so strongly.[62]

In a poignant and censorious vein, the quasi-polemic portrait captured the hopeless lives of the desperately poor with great compassion. The work addressed the privileged classes, urging them to open their eyes to greed and poverty around them. It reflected a frustration at the complacency of the wealthy upper classes blinded to the misery of the poverty-stricken Egyptian majority.

For some writers, a strong sense of belonging to the village urged them to explore the rural world with a true-to-life descriptive intent. Autobiographers of peasant stock thus emerged as the product of the rhythm and culture of their environment. Autobiographies of childhood described and analyzed peasant experience as it was lived at the most mundane levels. Hamed 'Ammar indicates the significance of such autobiographies by observing that historians have been interested in the ruling powers whereas "it is the habits and traditions of the common ruling folks that have, in fact, been the ultimate determining force."[63]

One of the keynotes of village autobiographical narrative was an anthropological perspective leading to critical judgment of rural social conditions. In *A Child from the Village* (1946), Sayyid Qutb (1906–66) presented one of the earliest attempts at depicting a portrait of the Egyptian village from the perspective of a villager. He wrote, "many of these portraits of village life date back to the time of my childhood, a quarter of century old. I have not embellished or fabricated them, just transferred them from the page of my memory to the page of the paper." As a native of the village, the author-narrator posed as an authority on the ethnographic details he provides about the locale; its institutions, practices, landscape, and living conditions as well as its religious-medical-magical complex and the signs of awareness of Egypt as a nation in the consciousness of the *fallahin*. In its depiction of the villagers' contacts with their external environment, the narrative contrasted deep compassion toward the servitude of the peasants with the unsympathetic attitude of urban officials appointed to inspect, discipline, or administer the villagers. Strangers like the physician, the district attorney, the police officer, and the commissioner become through the narrative consciousness of the child the laughing stock of the reader. Exposing the life-style gap between the urban and the rural constituted a common feature of Qutb's discourse. The degenerate state of affairs in the countryside was captured on many occasions. Describing the primitive means to put out fires in the time of harvest, he wrote, "some of the city dwellers may ask: but why don't they resort to fire-extinguishers or hoses or call the fire-brigade? A fire-brigade? My dear sir, these things are only found in the city. The one closest to this village is situated at a great distance." The prefatory conveyed reformist ideas about the author's motive for portraying village life of his childhood,

> Many of these portraits are still a living reality. But people in the city who are used to a life of luxury can hardly believe they exist, neither in the real world nor in the world of fantasy. The recording of them here will show the young generation pictures from the popular countryside that has both good and bad sides. Hopefully they have an opinion about what must remain and what must disappear.[64]

The episodes in the child's life unraveled the general backwardness of poor education, lack of sanitary and medical facilities, corruption of authorities, cruelty of rigid moral customs, exploitation of the landless, and unfair distribution of land and goods. The work heralded the social changes of revolutionary Egypt. Village liberation from ignorance and superstition of popular beliefs developed into an important theme of the autobiography.

Another critical image emerged in Taha Husayn's (1889–1973) *The Days*, depicting the life of a blind child with his poor family in a small Egyptian village. Social injustice and rural backwardness had direct bearing on his personal experience of the poverty, ignorance, and disease in Upper Egypt. A much-loved younger sister dies for lack of medical care and he was a victim of the destructive effect of ignorance when a simple eye infection was maltreated by an unskilled local practitioner and caused the loss of his eyesight. *Al-Ayyam* stands out for both its espousal of justice and equality as Islamic principles, for its delineation of practical measures for change. Husayn seized on ignorance and illiteracy as the root cause of peasant malaise which overshadowed the good qualities of the *fallah*'s character and cramped any strides of progress. When his sister died, he condemned the ignorance of his people as responsible for her death and the loss of his eyesight. "For the women of the villages . . . have a criminal philosophy and a knowledge that is no less criminal. The child complains and the mother seldom takes any notice . . . and if the mother does take any notice, she either despises the doctor or else is ignorant of him. And so she relies upon this criminal knowledge of women and those like them."[65]

Husayn's solution involved the democratization of education through a free government-sponsored schooling. As Misako Ikeda's chapter in this volume shows, both as a litterateur and education minister, he fought fiercely for literacy which he declared to be a necessary and natural right of all human beings "like water and air."[66] Only justice and literacy could prevent an existence rife with wretchedness, hunger, sickness, and degradation.

In autobiographical records of professionals serving in the villages, rural reality was examined from the perspective of visiting outsiders of urban background. Such personal narratives are characterized by the non-identity of the narrator with represented reality. The narrator is outside peasant life, a distanced witness, or a non-involved observer. Hence, the credibility of the narrated statements becomes an issue. In Tawfiq al-Hakim's *Maze of Justice* (1947), the peasants—for an attorney attempting to administer justice in rural areas—are a closed mystery. They remain as impenetrable as the intricacies of the case he investigates. Realizing the futility of his inquiries, the disenchanted prosecutor suspends the investigation and shelves the case. Unlike *Child from the Village*, the clash between the representatives of the authorities and the rural inhabitants is presented through a detached and biased official, and the village population is ordered about in an authoritarian way.

Like *The Tale of the Eloquent Peasant*, the work depicts the two traditional groups in the Egyptian provincial society: the governing and the governed. Yet it emerges as a foil to *The Maze of Justice*. The court sessions in al-Hakim's autobiography reveal the unscrupulousness of the magistrates and the lack of integrity of the officials who are prone to make hasty decisions based on superficial evidence. They deal with the cases of the peasant community without listening to the defendant's pleas. Taha Husayn's yearning for justice turns into the maze of justice in al-Hakim's work. The district attorney was constantly frustrated at his failure to bring order and discipline to village life. Subjected to laws and procedures made for another society, imported without alteration from Europe, and imposed without regard to background or tradition, the district attorney was confronted with the perplexity of the rural citizens who are unable to fathom judicial procedures and baseless punishment. One of the court sessions featured the following interchange:

"You are charged with having washed your clothes in the canal!"
"Your honor, may God exalt your station, are you going to fine [me] just because I washed my clothes?" "It's for washing them in the canal." "Well, where else could I wash them?" The judge hesitated deep in thought and gave no answer. He knew very well that these poor wretches had no washbasins in their villages, filled with fresh flowing water from the tap. They were left to live like cattle all their lives, and were yet required to submit to a modern legal system imported from abroad. The judge turned to me and said: "The Legal Officer! Opinion, please." The State is not concerned to inquire where this man should wash his clothes. Its only interest is the application of the law.[67]

The account is deficient in offering an insider's insight into chronic peasant problems and silent struggles. The author lacks sympathetic identification and fellow-feeling, which could have engaged him with the state of mind and emotions of the peasant.

Despite their stoicism, Egyptian peasants have been responsive to political mobilization. The stereotype of the defeated and obedient villager hid turbulent currents of resentment of exploitation and by oppressive authorities. In the period between 1919 and 1952, crime in rural Egypt had a social and political dimension reflecting rejection of the political structure rulers wished to impose, as well as retaliation against arbitrary authority. In *Crime in Egypt: its Causes and Methods of Treatment*, the legal authority Muhammad al-Babli presented a personal perspective of crime in rural Egypt which at the time became a national issue stirring fear in the rulers. It reflected the local defiance of exhortation of taxes, land or crop confiscation, eviction of tenants, and landowners raising "or even refusing to lower rents which had been agreed upon or postponing payment of debts."[68] Repeated rural aggression against landowners and their agents among local officials revealed everyday forms of peasant resistance, as well as peasant ingenuity and resourcefulness in dealing with repressive measures.

In fact, what was branded by the authorities as a disruptive force of criminality was applauded by the villagers as heroism and individual initiatives to redress grievances. Peasant rebellion constituted an indispensable component of the populist literature (adab sha'bi), described by Ahmad Shawqi 'Abd al-Hakim as "the mirror of the existential condition of the masses and a true reflection of peasant outlook on life."[69] Folk culture reveals how peasants experienced politics. The narrative ballad named after Adham al-Sharqawi evoked a tradition in Egyptian peasantry of social and political "acts by individuals or small groups involving little coordination . . . to defeat or attack immediate enemies."[70] Such acts targeted the prevailing order's injustices. The passive support they received from the peasant community; the consensus that encouraged vengeance; and the unanimous refusal to cooperate with state agents all transformed such activity into dramatic and revolutionary moments in peasant history. More than any other sector of the society, they awaited the emergence of a savior.[71]

The story of the rural anarchic figure of Adham al-Sharqawi left an indelible mark on the Egyptian consciousness. He erupted into the lives of villagers existing in a seething cauldron. His activism loomed large over peasant-state relations. "Then came the 1919 revolution, Adham and Badran (his partner) turned into princely robbers à la Robin Hood, as they and their men waged war against both the British occupying forces and Egyptian feudal landowners. Instead of just stealing for the sake of stealing, they began to take from the rich and give to the poor."[72] Motivated by a rebellion against authority and spurred by resentment of fallahin afflictions at the turn of the twentieth century, his raiding of rich landowner homes went beyond individual self-interest to encompass social and political concerns. He was driven by the sheer force of a quest to achieve lost justice and a fair distribution of wealth. He emerged as the revolutionary ideal of nobility conferred by merit rather than by birth. As such, popular action and mobilization moved from socially disruptive processes to become learning experiences in self-organization and self-development.

Rewriting or reinventing the *fallah* was an enterprise in which writers in the period under study invested immense imaginative effort. It generated a wide variety of constructions of rural reality incorporating the four archetypal generic plots in literature which Northrop Frye identifies as the comic, the romantic, the tragic, and the ironic or satiric.[73] For many intellectuals village reality gave rise to a mixture of critical images and nostalgic impressions in which subjective yet abstract reality is juxtaposed with dynamic reality.

Ibnat al-Shati':
A Female Intellectual Framing the Margins of Society

In Arab critical theory, intellectuals do not operate in a sociopolitical vacuum. Their most common role has been revolutionary figures agitating for a revolutionary consciousness against domination. Intellectuals have been symbols of public causes and fathers of national movements. There is hardly a major revolution or counter-revolution without its intellectual figurehead and spokesman. They are perceived as the agents of social transformation and progress. They undertake to define and change the political, social and moral tone of their era, often at the risk of imprisonment, ostracism, or exile.

'A'isha 'Abd al-Rahman (Ibnat al-Shati'; 1913–98) embodied the intellectual as subversive of the status quo, who refuses to placate the opinion of others.[74] She enjoyed a sixty-year career as a columnist writing for *al-Ahram* beginning as a twenty-four-year-old, broaching controversial issues of her times, including attacks on government oversight and critiques of reactionary views. Although her appeal and popularity rest on her contributions to Qur'anic exegesis and scholarship in Islamic culture, her solicitude concerning the ordeals of the peasant marked the debut of her intellectual vocation.

Al-Rif al-Misri:
A View from Within

With the publication of *The Egyptian Countryside* (*al-Rif al-misri*, 1936) and *The Problem of the Peasant* (1938), Ibnat al-Shati' emerged as the first Egyptian woman to espouse the cause of the peasant in full-length works. The texts are a collection of essays appearing originally in *al-Ahram* in 1935. They contributed to the press debate of rural reform and agricultural conditions in the late 1930s and 1940s. She commented on the impact of her activism in this field,

I started my second year of college with all the bookstores in town selling my book *al-Rif al-misri*, the literary circles deliberating on my winning the first prize in a contest carried out by the government on the subject of the reform of the village and the peasant, and the village community applauding the news of electing me a member of the first conference on agriculture organized in Cairo in 1936 which included leading personalities in the field.[75]

With roots in the countryside, Ibnat al-Shati' presents a view from within. *The Egyptian Countryside* and *The Problem of the Peasant* combine empirical observation and an appeal for a sympathetic understanding. The preamble of her work foregrounded two dichotomous portraits: the overpowering king and the downtrodden peasant. She began with a dedication that gives precedence to the protagonist of her work. She wrote, "To the Egyptian peasant, who would be the first to perceive the truth in my words and capture the anxiety embodied in this cry which comes from the depth of the soul of one who witnessed sufferings she would never forget." With the dependence of the intellectuals on the state to realize their agenda, it was imperative to acknowledge the position of the authorities vis-à-vis the subject of research. She follows her pledge to the peasant with a tribute to King Faruq (r. 1936–52), for his unremitting efforts to support the peasantry.[76] Writing about the peasant at that time was circumscribed by the authorities. Unraveling the horror of their suffering meant the indictment of the regime. Thus, it had to be done indirectly to avert any retribution. By placating the authority, Ibnat al-Shati' averted censure.

In a period in Egyptian history marked by a heightened awareness of self and nation, and at a time when the nation was in the process of finding its own direction for development and progress, Ibnat al-Shati' gave voice to disempowered groups in society and seized on the peasants as a segment outside the mainstream. It was high time that those who sought to provide help attempted to achieve a deeper level of understanding of those to whom they intended to give assistance. Her work examined the politics of social marginality; mainly the "processes of differentiation, pauperization and marginalization."[77]

The Egyptian Countryside and *The Problem of the Peasant* expounded experiences of social marginality as connected to poverty and social injustice. They developed a strategy of reading rural space that speaks to the historically muted native subject. She expressed with much chagrin,

What have we done to the peasantry, what services have we rendered it? Ironically, both the government and the citizens collaborated in persecuting it. We subject it to our sarcasm and disdain, forgetting that the mud-bearer—as we dubbed it—has made it possible for us to enjoy the best of life's blessings. What has the government offered it? Has it supplied it with clean drinking water? Has it provided hospitals to help peasants stay healthy or schools to educate their children or built hygienic abodes? None of these duties were performed.

Ibnat al-Shati' argued for those without agency and for those issues routinely swept under the rug: "it is time we disinter the graves of the living in rural Egypt," to unravel the consciousness of the repressed and subordinated groups. She remarked in disappointment,

How ungrateful we are . . . we glorify the immortal Nile, value and appreciate its bounty, and we forgot the hands which tended the lands and yielded the bounty, the people who made it possible for us to enjoy the blessings of the Nile, we neglect the peasants on whose diligence and devotion to the land any prosperity and advancement depend . . . the people who materialized the miracle of the Nile and transformed its banks into a paradise on earth.[78]

Amidst the discrepancy between the ruling powers and the peasantry, Ibnat al-Shati' "listen[ed] to the unarticulated yearnings of those in society unable to express their aspirations,"[79] and highlighted the conditions rendering their voice unheard. Her graphic portrayal captured the rhythm of life in the village, chastised all sectors in society for failing to appreciate peasant sacrifices, and for turning a blind eye to their desolation.

The representation of the reality of the peasant had been profoundly influenced by the appearance of the female intellectual on the cultural scene. Ibnat al-Shati''s speculations signaled a significant stage in Egypt's developing consciousness of peasantry. Her critique pursued three tracks: 'The Distress of the *Fallah*,' 'When Will We Wake up?' and 'Reforming the Village,' which diagnosed the malaise, indicated the urgency, and made suggestions for reform projects concerning agriculture, health, and education. She vehemently argued for a solution to the wretchedness of the *fallah*:

I can't afford to remain tongue-tied and passive when I witness a surge of misery and desolation overcoming the peasant stifling all signs of liveliness and hope. I cudgel my brain to descry more words to convey his ordeal but can hardly find anything more to say. Heed my jeremiad! I entreat you to salvage our peasantry.

Ibnat al-Shati' thus emerged as one of Egypt's most consciously reflective social analysts.

Acting on the advice of her physician to retire to one of the villages to reduce mental and emotional anxiety and overcome the exhaustion of city life, Ibnat al-Shati''s experience in the countryside turned out to be even more stressful:

> I arrived in the countryside feeling weary and drained, and departed feeling downcast and disheartened. . . . The beauty of countryside nature cast its spell on me yet promptly I shed my enchantment and looked around to inspect a horrid scene: Next to blooming vegetation loaded with flowers and fruits, I see frail disease-ridden bodies, agony and fatigue, and amidst thriving fields, life-threatening swamps sprawl out infesting the fresh air with obnoxious odors.[80]

The discrepancy between her pre-conceived idyllic notion and the gruesome reality of village life proved eye-opening. She set out to rehabilitate peasant conditions by exposing the afflictions and adversities. At times oscillating between romanticism and socialist realism, her texts adopted a studied approach to peasant problems. She opined that "the best of all sunrises dawns on the most miserable of all people. . . . Instead of connoting inexhaustible wealth, treasures, and resources, the word peasant has become synonymous with all the implications and associations of destitution, humiliation, degradation, impoverishment, and disease." Different aspects of the larger power structure were described analytically, while the text's dynamic lifelikeness enabled the readers to absorb peasant experience into their personal world.

Ibnat al-Shati' also sought to create in her audience a guilty conscience to initiate change. The first spectacle of peasant suffering appalled her: "The horror! The horror! I have to do something. I can't just overlook what I saw." Her exhortations recurred throughout the works: "Mercy on the peasant! No, mercy on us, on the coming generations who would face a gruesome future if peasantry remains as it is a mortified and derelict entity. . . . We guarantee a better future for our children and grandchildren by observing our duties toward the peasant." She assumed an antagonistic stance toward the conservative unsympathetic forces,

> Most of the rich and powerful have a personal interest in the peasant who cultivates their land and thus maintains the flow of riches into their bank accounts . . . yet one wonders why wouldn't such a relationship incite the landowners to rectify peasant conditions, to care for the health and well-being of the peasant, the progenitor of their wealth.[81]

Continually questioning preconceived ideas, intellectuals serve as mirrors for the society. Ibnat al-Shati' depicted sharply the paternalism and hypocrisy of the wealthy,

> We have to understand that rectifying peasant conditions would never be efficient or beneficial because those who plan it are dissociated from peasant reality. They discuss peasant starvation and privation as they gather around lavish dinner tables relishing the best food or as they recline relaxed in the comfort of their armchairs and the luxury of their elegant homes.

The upper class with its life of leisure was shown idling away its time at the expense of the poor: "We have taken our fill of the harvest without a thought for the man who made it grow." The overriding social malaise of injustice exacerbated poverty, disease, and ignorance. The developmental process needed to ensure the dynamic balance among order, change, and social justice. Ignoring this balance would cause social disintegration. She affirmed that "the bulk of the population of frail and exhausted peasants is drudging and slaving in the scorching heat of the day to cater for the few. . . . If we don't attend to its misery, if it withers and collapses under the weight of its hardships, we would all perish."[82]

Written with the purpose of rectifying the neglected rural geographies, the texts sought to influence decisions of powerful policy-makers for more effective and just interventions, and to persuade nonchalant authorities to direct their attention to the needs of the peasant. She reminded her audience,

> How many of us realize that digging the Mahmudiya Canal in 1819 cost twelve thousand peasant lives, due to the widespread use of corvée labor for public works and agriculture? . . . it is an honest bloody truth.

Nevertheless, life goes on as usual . . . we got used to reading about the costs of projects but never about the losses in peasant lives and the damages which the corvée incurs on the families whose only bread winner is forced to labor at no recompense whatsoever.[83]

Al-Rif al-misri and *Qadiyat al-fallah* were dedicated to representing the suffering of country people, and testifying to their travails. They illustrated peasants striving to hold out against heavy odds, yet the ultimate goal was to redress the measures manipulating the peasant powerlessness. The author struggled to bring to the attention of authorities on all levels the condition of peasants as a neglected and ignored sector of the society.

The Egyptian Countryside juxtaposed the portrait of horrible peasant squalor with heartening and promising prospects, drawing on both domestic and western examples. Ibnat al-Shati' envisioned a solution for many of the problems in the regeneration of the Egyptian countryside through rebuilding its villages. Thus the model hamlet of Bahtim, built by the Royal Agricultural Society in 1933, became the idyllic countryside of her imagination. It was a pilot project in which the dark, dirty mud houses lacking windows, latrines, and clean water, with cattle virtually sharing space with inhabitants, were all replaced by a well-ventilated, sanitary, and attractive housing complex. The planning of this prototype village

puts into accounts the problems the rural dwellings suffer. It all began with a person who is closely connected to rural reality, who comes originally from the countryside, who experienced as a child all the horror of peasant misery. It was such empathy that sowed the seeds of a practical project which evolved as the child grew up.[84]

Rather than emerging as the state's incursion into peasant internal structures and affairs, demolishing an inveterate lifestyle and tradition, the designs evolved from within village life, to suit village needs, with the participation of the villagers themselves. For Ibnat al-Shati', launching a national program for rural reconstruction led to the regeneration of peasants and self-esteem.

The Egyptian Countryside accounted for the relationship between text and public consciousness. At one point, gender status is an issue, "I fear that some would accuse me of exaggerating, claiming that girls possess a fertile imagination and are prone to fantasizing."[85] She recognized the centrality of readers in her discourse and the significance of their entanglement in the text's questions. Ibnat al-Shati' included the reader's responses to and experiences of the work when it was first published as an integral part. In "Rectifying Rural Egypt," one of the readers responded:

> In her visit to the village, Ibnat al-Shati' has grasped the tragedy of the peasant's life, nevertheless what she conveys is only a fraction of the truth of the calamity which we the inhabitants of rural Egypt endure.... As a physician who grew up in the village and undertook a study of health conditions there, I would like to complete the picture with my findings.

The multiple dimensions of the subject matter crystallized through reactions conveying shifting perspectives, understandings, and recollections, as well as judgments and criticisms. An orientation toward the text-reader nexus captured the original reception of the work. A sudden flare into revelation encouraged one of the readers to ponder: "I join forces with Ibnat al-Shati' and invoke public conscience, isn't it time to rise and act before it is too late?" The text made demands upon readers to renounce the shelter of familiar pre-conceptions. The section entitled "The Voice of the Peasant" conveys a congruence of the intent of the work and the expectation of the social group. One of the village dwellers maintained,

> In the past, I have perused the articles in *al-Ahram* tackling the problems of peasantry and unfortunately none offered practical solutions or even convinced the readers of genuine concern for peasant woes. I came to the conclusion that all such writings were mere rhetoric seeking merely to conciliate and placate public opinion until I came across the works of Ibnat al-Shati' and only then I detected any glimmer of hope in effecting change.[86]

The intellectual's achievement and fame could then be mobilized on behalf of the ongoing struggle to reform the community. A spirit of contestation drove both *al-Rif al-misri* and *Qadiyat al-fallah*. Such literature performed a political function in relation to the hegemonic culture, struggling on behalf of underrepresented and disadvantaged groups.

Conclusion

Between 1919 and 1952, rural reality in Egypt emerged as a site of opposition rather than accommodation. The wind of reform and revival accentuated the isolation and dependence of the peasant, and widened the gap between the status quo powers of the national state and the disadvantaged populations suppressed by it. Strategies for empowerment involved two widely divergent methodologies of the oppressed. They alternated between rural populations' violent upheavals against injustice and economic straits, and the passive resistance of peasant persistence, endurance, asceticism, and resignation. A constant grappling with helplessness in the face of ravages and powerlessness with regards to the successive oppressive governments engendered several forms of survival skills. "It would seem that [the peasant] epitomized all the travails that the fall from paradise entailed, and yet he was also granted a divine gift, that of survival."[87] Continually exposed to threats, Egyptian peasants were bent on transgressing boundaries. "They remain as calm and unmoved as the depths of the sea beneath a storm . . . they are as impervious and enduring as the granite of their temples."[88] In fact, actual political activity unraveled peasant nature as acquiescent but resistant, patient yet unyielding.

The development of rural discourse is commonly attributed to Egypt's liberal age. Faced with the dearth of critical examination of rural societies, there was a pressing demand for studies which would help in grasping peasants well enough to render change productive, and achieve effective communication with the *fallah* as the direct beneficiary of agrarian reform proposals. The peasantry needed intellectuals with expertise in the art of representing to pose as advocates and act as its intermediary with the ruling powers. A stream of studies tackling village milieu as an analytic category influenced a generation of Egyptian scholars in the field. It benefited a great deal from the role the press played in disseminating ideas and experience during the period between the two revolutions.

Professionals from all walks of life developed an interest in peasantry as the key to understanding and developing Egypt. Reforming society meant including excluded classes in the political system, and the road to modernity necessitated integration of rural lower classes into the country's advancement along modernist lines. The engagement with provincial reality as a "field of expertise" and "object of a distinct body of theory and description"[89] subsumed, under the liberal agenda of parliamentary politics and the multi-party system (*hizbiya*), organizing people around common principles, the growing scope of drastic reform (*islah*), the exigencies of renaissance (*nahda*), and the evolution of nationalism. It was undertaken amid vigorous movements to revitalize the nation. A proliferation of proposals for the amelioration of the peasants' plight was inspired by the discourse of modernity and its ideals of political, economic, and social justice with which the mood of this era was imbued.

Attempts at reform were for the most part ineffective. On the reformers' side, loyalty was more to party than to country. Reformers of landowning stock felt a particular attachment to the property-owning establishment, which hampered their ability to make the *fallah* a subject rather than object. Luwis 'Awad wrote, "to regard the proletariat merely as a set of material interests tends to make thinkers forget that the most important thing about a worker or a peasant is that he is a human being."[90] Moreover, official measures were formulated far from the life and thought of the peasant and in accordance with a preconceived ideal. Ayrout observed, "Whether they are concerned with health or education, agriculture or justice, they spring more from theory or imitation of other countries than from a practical knowledge of the true state of affairs."[91] In fact, efforts to institute land-holding peasantry were initiated by state policy rather than by peasant initiative. The most constricting reason for the implementation of projects of agrarian reform was "the elite-based politics in the country" and "the system of personality politics" which challenged constitutionalism.[92] Despite the liberal appearance, decision-making was undertaken by a few powerful individuals and with minimal interaction between the disparate groups.

The fondness of literati for exploring the rural world manifests the strong collective identity which the village provides for the intellectual. As a textual repertoire, the peasant world order lends itself to a variety of representations. Each image is issued and constructed in the shadow of earlier images. Representations of peasantry in narrative discourse constitute a broad arena that seeks to unravel a multi-dimensional reality. They reveal attempts at a comprehensive grasp of the changing perceptions of peasantry on the social, cultural, and political levels. Filtered through the consciousness of a narrator standing between the reader and the peasant, each representation carries partial truth and reflects a segment of the characterized phenomenon. None permits the original reality to subsist in its entirety. Peasant reality has always been richer and more complex than any one single representation.

Representations of the neglected rural geographies were often replete with devices of exclusion. They segregated the *fallah*, as a social and economic class, from the rest of the society. The range of images construed the peasant as an object with fixed meanings and designed rural reality as a construct made up of a complex of abstractions. The swinging pendulum between peasant idealization and depreciation produced both romantic images of idyllic rurality and satirical portraits treating peasants with condescension and arrogance as an ignorant mob *(ra'a')*. On another plane, the peasant was appropriated by the master narrative of national emancipation. He was presented as the authentic and true Egyptian when this seemed politically and nationally expedient. Eliding the different interests of peasants and overlooking the existence of their multiple burdens, the nationalist rhetoric of a new collective personality elevated the peasant as a national icon and depicted peasantry as the one authentic class. It glorified *peasant* culture as the source of *national* culture.

As a member of the burgeoning female intelligentsia of humble provincial origin, Ibnat al-Shati' took on the responsibility of lifting the peasantry from misery and backwardness. This helped her to gain access to the narrative of marginalized others. The reception of her work on provincial Egypt testified to the need of village communities for intellectuals to assist rural development. Ibnat al-Shati' undertook a quest for a transformed social order. An ideal of service as well as the articulation of the peasant cause prodded her mission to help society choose meaningful courses of action. Her intellectual endeavors acted as a synthesizing force of collective action. Nevertheless, one of the immediate issues in Egypt's liberal age remained—how to bring engaged and unremittingly devoted intellectuals to the point of decision-making, and how to bring their rational investigation and moral judgments to fruition.

Notes

1   Ni'mat Ahmad Fu'ad, *Shakhsiyyat Misr* (Cairo: al Hay'a al Misriya al 'Amma li-l-Kitab, 1972), 19; 'Afaf Lutfi al-Sayyid-Marsot, *Egypt's Liberal Experiment: 1922–1939* (Los Angeles: University of California, 1977), 10.

2   'Abd al-Rahman al-Rafi'i, *Mustafa Kamil*, 4th ed. (Cairo: Maktabat al-Nahda al-Misriya, 1962), 113.

3   Selma Botman, *Egypt from Independence to Revolution, 1919–1952* (New York: Syracuse University Press, 1991), 136, 3.

4   Tawfiq al-Hakim, *'Awdat al ruh*, vol. II (Cairo: Matba'at al Ragha'ib, 1933), 214.

5   Taha Hussein, *The Days*, trans. E.H. Paxton et al. (Cairo: The American University Press, 1997), 398.

6   'Abd al-Rahman al-Rafi'i, *Fi a'qab al-thawra al misriya*, vol. II (Cairo: Maktabat al-Nahdha al-Misriya, 1949), 269–71, 283–87, 290–91, 334–35, 352–57, 360–64.

7   Afaf Lutfi al-Sayyid-Marsot, *Egypt's Liberal Experiment*, 2.

8   Hussein Kamel Selim, *Twenty Years of Agricultural Development in Egypt* (Cairo: Ministry of Finance, Egypt, 1940), 66–67

9   Muhammad 'Abd al-Jawad, *Fi kuttab al qarya* (Cairo: Dar al-Ma'arif, 1939); al-Rafi'i, *Fi a'qab al-*

thawra al misriya thawrat 1919, vol. I. (Cairo: Kitab al Sha'b, 1969), 217; Marsot, *Egypt's Liberal Experiment*, 111.

10   Qadri Qal'aji, *Sa'd Zaghlul* (Beirut: n.p., 1948), 96.

11   Sayyid al-'Ashmawi, *al-Fallahun wa-l-sulta fi du' al-harakat al-fallahiya al-misriya* (Cairo: Merit li-l-Nashr wa-l-Ma'lumat, 2001), 69–70.

12   Ali Barakat, *al-Mulkiya al-zira'iya bayn al-thawratayn 1919–1952* (Cairo: Markaz al-Dirasat al-Siyasiya wa-l-Istratijiya, 1987), 89.

13   Al-Sayyid-Marsot, *Egypt's Liberal Experiment*, 10–11.

14   Albert Hourani, *Arabic Thought in the Liberal Age 1798–1939* (London: Oxford University Press, 1962), 209.

15   Hassan Muhassab, *Qadiyat al-fallah fi-l-qissa al misriya* (Cairo: General Egyptian Book Organization, 1971), 50.

16   'Ali Barakat, *al-Mulkiya al-zira'iya bayn al-thawratayn*, 88–89.

17   Hassan Muhassab, *Qadiyat al-fallah fi-l-qissa al misriya*, 61; 'Abd al-Rahman al-Rafi'i, *Fi a'qab al-thawra al-misriya* II, 72.

18   Al-Rafi'i, II, 120, 177–78; James Mayfield, *Rural Politics in Nasser's Egypt: A Quest for Legitimacy*. (Austin: University of Texas Press, 1971); 52; 'Ali Barakat, *al-Mulkiya al-zira'iya*, 94–95; Fathi 'Abd al-Fattah, *al-Qarya al-misriya* (Cairo: al Hay'a al-Misriya al -'Amma li-l-Kitab, 1991), 187; Timothy Mitchell, *Rule of Experts: Egypt, Techno-Politics, Modernity* (Los Angeles: University of California Press, 2002), 127–28.

19   'Abd al-Rahman al-Rafi'i, *Fi a'qab al-thawra al-misriya thawrat 1919*, vol. III (Cairo: Dar al-Ma'arif, 1989), 118–19, 242.

20   Timothy Mitchell, *Rule of Experts: Egypt, Techno-Politics, Modernity*, 20.

21   Fathi 'Abd al-Fattah, *al-Qarya al-misriya*, 161.

22   Ahmad Lutfi al-Sayyid, *Qissat hayati* (Cairo: Dar al Hilal, 1982).

23   Hafiz 'Afifi, *'Ala hamish al-siyasa* (Cairo: Matba'at Dar al-Kutub al-Misriya, 1938), 3, 5, 7.

24   Mirrit Butrus Ghali, *al-Islah al-zira'i: al-mulkiya, al-ijar, al'amal* (Cairo: Dar al-Fusul, 1945), 3.

25   Hussein Kamel Selim, *Twenty Years of Agricultural Development in Egypt* (Cairo: Ministry of Finance, Egypt, 1940), 66–67.

26   For a detailed analysis and statistical surveys of landownership and views on land reform by members of parties represented in the parliament, see Gabriel Baer, *A History of Landownership in Modern Egypt 1800–1950* (London: Oxford University Press, 1962), 201–15.

27   Mirrit Butrus Ghali, *The Policy of Tomorrow*, trans. Isma'il R. el Faruqi (Washington, D.C.: American Council of Learned Societies, 1953), 99–100, 102.

28   Hafiz 'Afifi, *'Ala hamish al-siyasa*, 10.

29   Henry Ayrout, *The Fallaheen* (1938), trans. Hilary Wayment (Cairo: R. Schindler, Hyperion Press, 1945), 23.

30   Nathan Brown, *Peasant Politics in Modern Egypt: The Struggle Against the State* (New Haven: Yale University Press, 1990), 159, 161–62; Fathi 'Abd al-Fattah, *al-Qarya al-misriya*, 188–90.

31   The embryo of the Communist and Socialist Workers' Party started in 1920 and had better success in recruiting the support of the urban workers. In fact, the cause of the *fallahin* was brought to attention in post World War I years when industrial labor movement in 1922 called for the first time in Egypt for agrarian reform and the improvement of the *fallah*'s lot. The industrial workers' struggle for rights and achievements underlined the injustices of agricultural laborers. Their organizations formulated explicit and practicable plans in which moral outrage about injustices played a central role.

32   Ahmad Sadiq Sa'd, *Mushkilat al-fallah* (Cairo: Dar al-Qarn al-'Ishrin, 1945), 27–28.

33   James Mayfield, *Rural Politics in Nasser's Egypt*, 53; Christina Phelps Harris, *Nationalism and Revolution in Egypt: The Role of the Muslim Brotherhood* (London: Mouton & Co., 1964), 201.

34   Yusuf al-Shirbini, *Hazz al quhuf fi qasidat Abi Shaduf* (Cairo: Dar al-Nahda al-'Arabiya, 1963), 5: 26–29, 6: 2.

35   Quoted in Sabry Hafez, *The Genesis of Arabic Narrative Discourse: A Study in the Sociology of Modern Arabic Literature* (London: Saqi Books, 1993), 116.

36   As just a few examples, themes of concern to al-Nadim included peasants falling prey to imposters and the exploitation of swindlers; inattention to rural people by courts; the effects on peasant women of migration to cities, including problems of social and cultural transition. Often the peasant was identified in the title as the focus, as in "The Crafty Swindler and the Peasant," "The Stupid Usurer and the Cunning Peasant" in *al-Tankit wa-l-tabkit* VI, 17 July 1881; "Ignorant Lawyer and Foolish Peasant" in *al-Tankit wa-l-tabkit* VIII, 31 July 1881.

37   Saad Elkhadem, *History of the Egyptian Novel: Its Rise and Early Beginnings* (Frederickton, NB: York Press, 1985), 23.

38   Yusuf Hanna, "al-Da'wa ila al-adab al-qawmi," *al-Siyasa al-usbu'iya*, 9 August 1930, 10

39   Quoted in Israel Gershoni and James Jankowski, *Redefining the Egyptian Nation, 1930–1945* (New York: Cambridge University Press, 1995), 107.

40   Salama Musa, *Mukhtarat Salama Musa* (Cairo: 1926), 195; Tawfiq Mikha'il Tuwayj, "Tatawwur al-adab al-misri wa aghraduhu," *al-Siyasa al-usbu'iya*, 25 May 1929, 118.

41   Israel Gershoni and James Jankowski, *Egypt, Islam, and the Arabs: The Search for Egyptian Nationhood, 1900–1930* (London: Oxford University Press, 1987), 206; 'Abbas 'Aqqad, *Sa'a bayna al-kutub* (Cairo: n.p., 1929), 106–107, 112–13.

42   Ibrahim al-Misri, *Wahy al'asr* (Cairo: n.p., 1935), 61

43   Tawfiq al-Hakim, '*Awdat al-ruh*, vol. II (Cairo: Matba'at al Ragha'ib, 1933), 23–24.

44   Henry Ayrout, *The Fallaheen*, 141.

45   *Al-Sakhra* 21 October 1933, 5.

46   Hussein Haykal, *Zaynab, manazir wa akhlaq rifiya* (Cairo: Maktabat al-Nahdha al-Misriya, 1967), 11.

47   Abd al-Rahman al-Sharqawi, *The Egyptian Earth*, trans. Desmond Stewart (Delhi: Hind Pocket Books), 1972, 224–25.

48   Hussein Haykal, *Zaynab*, 8.

49   Ibid., 206–208.

50   Rida al-Tayyar, *al-Fallah fi-l-sinama al-misriya* (al-Mu'assasa al-'Arabiya li-l-Dirasat wa-l-Nashr, 1980), 20.

51   Ibid., 18.

52   Mahmoud Amin al-'Alim,, and 'Abd al-Azim Anis, *Fi al-thaqafa al-misriya* (Cairo: Dar al-Fikr al-Jadid, 1955), 27.

53   Sabry Hafez, *The Genesis of Arabic Narrative Discourse*, 235.

54   Ibid., 264.

55   'Abbas Khadr, *Muhammad Taymur: hayatuhu wa adabuhu* (Cairo: al-Dar al-Qawmiya, 1966), 71–85; Muhammad Yusuf Najm, *al-Qissa fi-l-adab al-'arabi al hadith* (Beirut: al-Maktaba al-Ahliya, 1966), 271–84.

56   Hassan Muhassab, *Qadiyat al-fallah fi-l-qissa al-misriya*, 50.

57   'Isa 'Ubaid, *Ihsan Hanim* (Cairo: 1921), 6.

58   Muhammad Jibril, *Dirasat fi al-qissa wa-l-masrah* (Cairo: n.p., n.d.), 146; Sabry Hafez, *The Genesis of Arabic Narrative Discourse*, 202–203.

59   Louis Awad, *The Literature of Ideas in Modern Egypt, Part I* (Atlanta: Scholars Press, 1986), 136.

60   Al-Sayyid-Marsot, *Egypt's Liberal Experiment*, 10–11.

61   In this regard, see Raymond Williams, "Realism and the Contemporary Novel," in David Lodge, ed., *Twentieth Century Literary Criticism: A Reader* (London: Longman, 1971), 582.

62   'Isam al-Din Hifni Nasif, '*Asifa fawq Misr: qissa ijtima'iya* (Cairo: Dar al -'Alam al-Jadid, 1939), 142.

63 Hamed 'Ammar, *Growing up in an Egyptian Village: Silwa, Province of Aswan* (London: Routledge and Kegan Paul, 1954), 70–71.

64 Sayyid Qutb, *Tifl min al-qarya* (Cairo: Dar al-Shuruq, 1973 [1946]), 5, 80.

65 Taha Hussein, *The Days*, 71.

66 Louis Awad, *The Literature of Ideas in Modern Egypt*, 134.

67 Tawfiq al-Hakim, *The Maze of Justice* trans. A.S. Eban (London: The Harvill Press, 1947), 20–21.

68 Nathan Brown, "The Conspiracy of Silence and the Atomistic Political Activity of the Egyptian Peasantry, 1882–1952," in Forrest D. Colburn, ed., *Everyday Forms of Peasant Resistance* (New York: M.E. Sharpe, 1989), 96.

69 Ahmad Shawqi 'Abd al-Hakim, *Adab al-fallahin* (Cairo: n.p., n.d.), 13.

70 Nathan Brown, *Peasant Politics in Modern Egypt: The Struggle Against the State* (New Haven and London: Yale University Press, 1990), 83. Adham al-Sharqawi belongs to a long folkloric tradition, resulting from economic depression and social and political corruption, when what was not granted by law and order was obtained through violence. In the eye of the populace such figures were heroes (Shaheen 83).

71 Sayyid al-'Ashmawi, *al-Fallahun wa-l-sulta*, 41.

72 Saeed Okasha, "Friends for Life," *Cairo Times* 4: 29 (28 September–4 October 2000), 6.

73 Northrop Frye, *Anatomy of Criticism* (New Jersey: Princeton University Press, 1957), 162.

74 Her pen name means Child of the Shore / Daughter of the Riverbank. It relates to her birthplace, the shore of Damietta, where the eastern branch of the Nile opens onto the Mediterranean.

75 Ibnat al-Shati' ('A'isha 'Abd al-Rahman), *'Ala al-jisr: usturat al-zaman* (Cairo: Dar al-Hilal, 1967), 93.

76 Ibnat al-Shati', *al-Rif al-misri* (Cairo: Maktaba wa Matba'at al-Wafd, 1936), 3.

77 Teodor Shanin, "Defining Peasants: Conceptualization and De-conceptualization: Old and New in a Marxist Debate," in Joan Mencher, ed., *Social Anthropology of Peasantry* (Bombay: Smaiya Publications LTD, 1983), 69.

78 Ibnat al-Shati', *al-Rif al-misri*, 14, 46, 8.

79 Ibid., 77.

80 Ibid., 47, 15, 30.

81 Ibid., 28, 46, 77, 44, 33.

82 Ibid., 120, 8–9, 47.

83 Ibid., 54.

84 Ibid., 101–102.

85 Ibid., 48.

86 Ibid., 194, 230, 205.

87 Marsot, *Egypt's Liberal Experiment*, 10–11.

88 Henry Ayrout, *The Fallaheen*, 19–20.

89 Timothy Mitchell, *Rule of Experts*, 124.

90 M.M. Badawi, "Commitment in Contemporary Arabic Literature," in Issa J. Boullata, ed., *Critical Perspectives on Modern Arabic Literature 1945–1980* (Washington, D.C.: Three Continents Press, 1980), 35.

91 Henry Ayrout, *The Fallaheen*, 154.

92 Selma Botman, *Egypt from Independence to Revolution, 1919–1952*, 20.

Part IV

Engendering
a Modern Nation

11 The Nationalization of Marriage in Monarchical Egypt[1]

Hanan Kholoussy

While scholars of nationalism in monarchical Egypt and beyond have come to recognize that "the nation has invariably been imagined via metaphors of family,"[2] they nevertheless continue to ignore the role of the state in the production and promotion of modern, nuclear families.[3] Even scholars, who have written women into traditional nationalist narratives, focus almost exclusively on women, reinforcing a rigid binary opposition between Egyptian feminism and nationalism.[4] For example, Beth Baron, who argues that women's political participation from the 1920s onward must be seen as a continuation of actions taken in the women's press in earlier decades, claims that the male nationalist press focused on politics as its central preoccupation, while women's journals dealt with topics pertaining to the home.[5] While these scholars have drawn attention to the 'separate' contributions of women writers, they have done so in a vacuum, inadvertently reifying a somewhat rigid dichotomy between the 'public' domain of the state and male nationalists and the 'private' cultural sphere of women and the family.

By upholding this public/private divide, scholars on early twentieth-century Egypt echo Partha Chatterjee's argument about the inner/outer domain of nationalism in colonial contexts, which sought to situate 'woman' in an inner domain of spirituality, localized within the home.[6] Such a dichotomy suggests that the so-called "inner domain" of women and the family was far removed from the nationalist arena of state politics. This approach does not reveal the intrinsic role Egyptian nationalists and state officials wanted the family to play in the formation of a modern nation. In contrast to scholarly notions, the family was one of the most important tenets on nationalist and state agendas, not just feminist agendas. Even the few scholars who recently have researched the divide between the 'public' political domain of men and the 'private' cultural sphere of women and the family do not consider the state's legal campaigns to discipline its subjects into forming modern, nuclear families as the foundation for the emerging nation.[7]

Etienne Balibar insightfully notes that one of the critical questions yet to be addressed by scholars of nationalism and the family is the state's intervention in family relations—the "nationalization of the family."[8] Yet, Balibar neglects an even more vital matter: the fundamental ties that make and break the family; that is, the institutions of marriage and divorce. In the case of modern Egypt, the state's unparalleled intervention into the family focused largely on marriage and divorce laws. Scholars cannot begin to talk about the family or the nation without first examining marriage and divorce, as many Egyptians during the monarchical era viewed the institution of marriage as the foundation stone of the emerging nation. The public debates that emerged during this period led to a series of drafts and laws governing marriage and divorce through the next three decades. The laws passed in monarchical Egypt were the last such pieces of legislation until Law no. 44 of 1979, which offered women increased divorce rights and curtailed polygamy.[9]

Although a number of legal and women's scholars have described the laws of marriage and divorce in modern Egypt, few, if any, explain how and why these laws were proposed, how the larger public reacted to them, and where they fit into articulations of Egyptian nationalism. Rather, they have tended to focus on the effects these laws had on the status of women.[10] James N.D. Anderson and John L. Esposito, for example, assert respectively that it was "the miserable lot of Muslim wives" and the elevation of their position in Egyptian society that served as the primary motive behind this new legislation.[11] Amira El Azhary Sonbol, on the other hand, views these laws as propping up a new patriarchal order that is the cause for the present subjugation of Egyptian women,[12] whereas Margot Badran argues that this legislation preserved the legal structure of the old patriarchal culture.[13] Mervat Hatem and Selma Botman, by contrast, claim that these laws represented minimal interference by the state in the patriarchal household.[14] State legislators did not necessarily intend to improve the lot of women or intentionally seek to oppress women. Nor did they adopt a minimalist approach.

In contrast with the above-mentioned studies, this chapter argues that the Egyptian government sought to pass marital laws in order to take a more active role in creating a nationalist, nuclear, and 'modern' family. To rephrase Balibar's term, the intention of Egyptian legislators was the "nationalization of marriage," that is, the creation of married subjects who would form adult, permanent, preferably monogamous families that, in turn, would serve as the foundation for a modern nation free of social ills. State officials made attempts to abolish or limit Islamic marriage and divorce laws that it deemed unfit for a modern nation. This chapter demonstrates how, in those same vital years covered by James Whidden in chapter one, notions of marriage emerged in monarchical Egypt as a hotly contested ideological terrain where different factions held competing formulations about the purposes and meanings of marriage and the family for the emerging Egyptian nation.

Despite the notion of a prevailing state-sponsored model of adult, permanent, and monogamous marriage, it is important to note that neither the state nor its models were hegemonic or monolithic. Not only did individual members of the state propose multiple and often conflicting legislation, but also their inability to pass a number of proposals to limit the marriage of minors, to curtail the ability of males to obtain divorce easily, and to restrict polygamy suggests that its model was highly contested, particularly in a society where such practices had been sanctioned religiously. As B.F. Musallam points out, Islamic marriage, historically and legally, is not a monogamous and permanent institution because polygamy is permissible and because the ease with which men can initiate divorce theoretically can end it at any time.[15] During the monarchical period, however, Egyptian officials increasingly attempted to pass laws that would curtail the marriage of minors, divorce, and polygamy. It is only by examining these state-sponsored legal campaigns, and the reactions from within the state, the monarchy, feminists, and press writers to these proposals, that we can begin to understand competing articulations of modern Egyptian nationalism. An analysis of legislative and press debates during this era not only elucidates various challenges to state-sponsored, hegemonic models of the family, but also reveals how different Egyptian writers used marriage to construct multiple visions of modern husbands and wives. Because a variety of nationalists viewed marital identity as an essential component of national identity, this chapter examines not only how state officials, religious legislators, nationalist authors, and feminist writers attempted to mold Egyptian men and women into husbands and wives, but also how the state attempted to make both into modern national subjects. 'Marriage' was thus deployed in a fashion similar to 'peasants,' those 'mud bearers' Samia Kholoussi in chapter ten shows to be so critical to Egyptian literary imaginings during the 1920s to 1940s.

Curtailing the Marriage of Minors

By the turn of the twentieth century, the jurisdiction of Islamic law *(sharī'a)* and its courts in Egypt had been restricted mostly to issues of personal status laws *(al-ahwal al-shakhsiya)*, namely, marriage, divorce, child custody, inheritance, and religious endowments.[16] In 1915 and 1916, the Ministry of Justice attempted to draft legislation to further reform personal status laws, but no provisions resulted from these recommendations.[17] In spite of legal reforms undertaken in other parts of the Ottoman Empire, such as the Ottoman Law of Family Rights in 1917,[18] state-sponsored *sharī'a* legislation was not passed in Egypt until 1920.[19] Attempts at personal status reform elicited strong opposition because many considered the *sharī'a* to be valid "for every time and clime" in which no new interpretation *(ijtihad)* was to be undertaken.[20] Nonetheless, in 1923, the Egyptian government for the first time established legal minimum ages for marriage. That members of the state felt compelled to regulate the marriage of minors at this time is particularly significant because such unions appear to have been in decline by the early twentieth century.[21] This suggests that some Egyptians wanted the government to establish a new means of monitoring the marital habits of the population to ensure that only adult Egyptians would marry and reproduce, regardless of whether such unions were prevalent.

The debates leading up to this unprecedented regulation of the marriage of minors also are noteworthy, as an earlier attempt to legally abolish this practice had failed. In March 1914, assembly member Zakariya Bey Namiq presented a bill on marital issues to the Legislative Assembly,[22] including a proposal to establish the legal female age of marriage at sixteen. The bill sparked widespread controversy and led to several months of public debate in the press where reporters and readers alike argued over a variety of issues, including the marriage of minors, the aversion of youth to marriage, the duty of government employees to marry, and the purposes and meanings of marriage.[23] The age of marriage, in particular, generated heated reaction as readers debated the appropriate age for marriage in front-page articles and letters to the editor, offering personal opinions as well as their own legal proposals.

Although male writers largely initiated the 1914 debates, discussions about the proper age for marriage also were common among women writers in the years leading up to Namiq's bill. Many women writers, for example, argued that girls who married at a young age were prone to difficult and fatal pregnancies, and to diseases such as hysteria.[24] Namiq similarly believed that females risked their health when they married young and consulted several doctors to determine the "moderate" age of sixteen, even though he realized that this proposed age would be highly unpopular among Muslims.[25] As Baron notes, Muslim authorities could find no basis in Islamic law to justify the establishment of minimum age limits for marriage because the Prophet Muhammad had married his youngest wife before she reached puberty.[26] Indeed, many Muslim doctors attempted to refute medical findings that concluded premature marriage was dangerous.[27]

Nationalists who supported Namiq's bill, however, wrote a number of letters to the editor arguing that the mature age of a married mother indicated her higher reproductive capacity to raise future citizens for a "healthy" and "strong" postcolonial nation. As the editors of al-Ahram wrote, "a strong nation can only be built from a large, well-raised, educated offspring and such offspring can only be formed by mature mothers. The nation needs mature women, not girls."[28] Indeed, the role many wanted the Egyptian state to assume in determining and legally establishing the proper age of marriage, substantiated by the medical findings of doctors, confirm Michel Foucault's assertion that the formation of the modern family was largely the result of medico-legal state intervention that sought to consolidate and control the nuclear family as an apparatus to create "the healthy, clean, fit body, a purified, cleansed, aerated domestic space."[29]

Namiq's bill was subjected to such harsh criticism from Muslim jurists, doctors, and laypersons that he was forced to retract it.[30] The withdrawal of Namiq's bill, however, did not end debates over the proper female age of marriage, evidenced by the passage of Law no. 56 of 1923. This law set the legal marriage age for women at sixteen and for men at eighteen. It also required the registration of all marriage contracts and directed the courts not to hear claims if the bride was under sixteen and the groom under eighteen.[31] As Mrinalini Sinha points out in the case of colonial India, attempts to regulate the marriage of minors were more concerned with a commitment to nationalist modernity than an interest in improving the social and health status of young females, marking a crucial turning point between the de-legitimization of colonialism as the agent of modernity and the advent of a new nationalist 'Indian' modernity.[32] The debates over the 1914 proposal, and the eventual passage of the 1923 law, suggest similar tensions about anticolonial nationalist modernity in the Egyptian context.

Paul Rabinow has argued that it is fruitless to define modernity; rather, it is more productive to explore how its self-proclaimed practitioners have used and understood the term.[33] Egyptian claims to being modern can be likewise traced. The debates on the marriage of minors provide convincing evidence of the political and cultural anxieties that many Egyptians held about anticolonial modernity. Indeed, the institution of marriage often served as an arena where various Egyptians in and outside the state produced and reproduced notions of nationalist modernity as a condition for the "enlightenment" and "progress" of the burgeoning Egyptian nation and its subjects. The aforementioned press debates reveal how different writers used the topic of the marriage of minors to critique Egyptian society and to construct multiple visions of "modern" husbands, wives, and national subjects.

The state's success in establishing minimum age limits to ensure healthy and productive married national subjects did not go uncontested by many Egyptians, although it was supported by members of the Egyptian Feminist Union (EFU).[34] Badran notes that the 1923 law was "a relatively easy starting victory for the feminists" because establishing the minimum marriage age for females at sixteen was one of the first demands the EFU presented to the Egyptian government in June 1923.[35] The EFU had made reform of personal status laws one of its central tenets, although it never called for adopting secular laws, but rather insisted upon reforming them within an Islamic framework.[36] It sought "reform of the operating laws of the marital relationship and conforming them completely to the spirit of the religious *sharïa* with respect to the administration of justice among families and the regulation of marital bonds."[37] The fact that a similar law had been proposed nearly a decade before, however, indicates that it was not only the EFU that had campaigned for marriage age limits.

EFU members still criticized the loopholes that existed in the 1923 law.[38] The cabinet of Prime Minister Sa'd Zaghlul, assuming power in March 1924, permitted the testimony of the bride's male guardian *(wali)* to be considered as a substitute for the required documents verifying her age.[39] Likewise, the state permitted the government official who issued marriage licenses *(ma'dhun)* to accept the verbal testimony of two witnesses to determine the age of a minor in lieu of a birth certificate.[40] The EFU, outraged by these loopholes, insisted that birth certificates be presented as proof of age.[41] If impossible to produce a birth certificate, the prospective bride's age should be determined by a medical examination by two government doctors.[42] It is interesting to note that Egyptian feminists in monarchical Egypt, at least initially, viewed the state as a mechanism to institute and enforce social change, and by appealing to it, they evidently believed, or at least hoped, that it would. Yet, while representing themselves as championing women's liberation by insisting on legislation to control the age of marriage, they in fact were encouraging medico-legal state intervention and control.

The Egyptian government eventually addressed these concerns, evidenced by the passage, eight years later, of Law no. 78 of 1931, which consolidated the 1923 provisions with the directive that courts were prohibited from hearing claims of disputed marriages unless these marriages first had been verified by an official certificate. The courts also were prohibited from hearing any claims in cases where the wife and husband had not reached the legal minimum age of marriage at the time of the claim.[43] While welcoming these changes, Egyptian feminists complained that doctors often falsified a female's age. They therefore demanded that the state make it a criminal offense for the *ma'dhun* to authorize marriages of minors.[44] Minor couples could circumvent the government's regulations by asking a doctor, or two witnesses to the marriage contract, to certify a false age in order to secure registration. Law no. 44 of 1933 sought to curtail such attempts by prosecuting doctors, witnesses, and the *ma'dhun* if it could be proven that these parties had "acted in bad faith."[45] While such regulations did not necessarily void marriage of minors, they did tend to discourage it.[46]

These laws were an indirect attempt to severely restrict the marriage of minors by refusing to register such unions or grant them judicial recognition, because few would agree to marry without the future protection of the law.[47] As Judith E. Tucker explains, "The advantages of such registration included the establishment of a permanent written record of the marriage agreement. To register your marriage in court was to place marriage and its consequent rights and obligations squarely under the jurisdiction of the Islamic court, in anticipation of the court's playing a role in any later disputes. . . ."[48] A direct declaration of the marriage of minors as invalid would have been considered an act of interpretation (*ijtihad*), which by departing from the *sharia* would have made passage of these laws virtually impossible.[49]

Indeed, even after the various marital age laws were passed, many Egyptians continued to voice their opposition. Shaykh Muhammad Bakhit, the former mufti of Egypt, severely attacked the 1923 law on the grounds that the jurisdiction of the *sharia* court could only be restricted for a stated public interest.[50] Religious leaders were not the only ones to voice their opposition. Two members of the Chamber of Deputies, for example, proposed to abolish the minimum marriage age law altogether. In the 1930s, 'Uthman Sawi Bey and 'Abduh Mahmud al-Burtuqali each made separate proposals to abolish the laws.[51] Thus, even within the state, members held disparate notions about state policy regarding marriage. These proposals to abolish the prohibition of the marriage of minors, coupled with the legal loopholes and failed passage of the 1914 bill, indicate that certain state-sponsored visions of the family were not linear and hegemonic, and that the model of mature and 'modern' marriage did not go unchallenged.

The contentious debates over personal status laws during this period in no way detract from the unprecedented state intervention in the so-called 'private' realm of the family. Not only had the Egyptian legislators found a way in 1923, 1931, and again in 1933 to circumvent Islamic law sanctioning the marriage of minors, it also had managed to mandate the registration of marriage in its legal system. Marriage contracts were not required to be registered in Egypt until 1923.[52] Whereas the Islamic marriage contract theoretically can take place anywhere, and before 1923 had typically taken place in the homes of Muslims, the government had now begun to involve itself in a domain that was considered private by many Egyptians. By declaring that the courts would not hear any marital disputes unless an *official* marriage certificate was furnished by the government, state legislators were making it increasingly perilous for couples to marry outside of the government's legal system. They also were attempting to make it more difficult for Egyptian men and women to divorce.

Deterring Divorce

As part of its ongoing effort to 'modernize' the emerging Egyptian nation, the Ministry of Justice, under the supervision of a committee of state-appointed *shaykh*s, introduced two new personal status laws in 1920 and 1929 that sought to discourage divorce. While a number of scholars have either commended this legislation as expanding women's rights or castigated it as restricting female access to divorce, a closer investigation reveals that these laws neither provided wives nor husbands with many increased rights. Rather, the state's intervention in this marital realm further complicated and restricted both male and female access to divorce. This unprecedented involvement by the Egyptian government was motivated largely by efforts to make marriage a more permanent, but still hierarchical, bond to buttress the family. State officials were attempting to reduce what westerners and Egyptians alike portrayed as an excessively high divorce rate. Divorce statistics for the early twentieth century ranged from 30 percent to as high as 90 percent.[53] Although these statistics are problematic and some are undocumented, they are worth noting as they reflect the observers' perception of social reality.[54] Furthermore, Kenneth M. Cuno notes that Egypt had the highest divorce rate of any "independent" state reporting data during the first half of the twentieth century.[55] According to the drafters of Law no. 25 of 1929, Egyptian men, contrary to the spirit of Islam, were frivolously exercising their unilateral right to divorce instead of using it solely as a last resort. They further explained that in order to protect the stability and welfare of the family and society as a whole, it was necessary to restrict and "cure [such] social diseases" as easy male divorce.[56]

In his treatise *The Liberation of Women*, Qasim Amin, one of the most prominent legal and nationalist thinkers in late nineteenth and early twentieth-century Egypt, raised a number of similar concerns. Although published in 1898, his suggestions to reform divorce served as the basis for divorce legislation passed in monarchical Egypt. It is important to bear in mind, however, that Amin was not the first Egyptian to suggest a reform of the practices and laws of divorce.[57] While he lamented the frequency of divorce and advocated more permanent marriage as "the hope for a healthy society," he recognized the necessity for divorce.[58] Amin thus offered a model in which a wife could initiate divorce. He recommended departing from the Hanafi legal school which only permitted a wife to initiate divorce if her husband were impotent, an apostate from Islam, or if a minor wife, upon reaching majority age, claimed that a guardian other than her father or grandfather had married her to a suitor without her consent.[59] Amin proposed that the government adopt the Maliki view that a woman could sue for a judicial divorce *(tatliq)*, "in any case in which a man may harm her."[60]

Although Amin often is acclaimed as "the father of Arab feminism," and his treatise traditionally is hailed as the founding feminist text in Egypt because of its call for reforms for women,[61] several scholars have criticized the overemphasis on his ideas, noting that he was not a feminist who believed in full equality between the sexes.[62] However, Amin's views on marriage, divorce, and the family[63] are worth exploring precisely because they were adopted by nationalists, feminists, and state legislators more than two decades later. Amin's views on female-initiated divorce reveal that he did not believe men and women should enjoy equal legal rights. While he believed a man could divorce his wife for any reason, he advocated female divorce only if the woman were married to "an evil, criminal, or godless husband with whom she is unable to live," or "in any case in which a man may harm her."[64] Furthermore, while he recommended that Muslim women stipulate the right to divorce in their marriage contracts, which the Hanafi majority permits,[65] he urged that they first appeal to a judge to ask for a divorce "because if divorce is controlled by the judge, its incidence can be minimized and the institution of marriage strengthened."[66] Thus, Amin's motive was not to strengthen a woman's right to divorce, but rather to preserve the institution of marriage.

Egyptian legislators in the 1920s adopted Amin's suggestion to depart from the Hanafi legal school and draw on the Maliki and Shafi'i legal schools in order to provide women with more legal grounds for divorce.[67] Divorce laws in monarchical Egypt deviated from Hanafi doctrine by adopting elements from the other three schools of Islamic law in an eclectic manner *(takhayyur)* and by combining different elements from various schools *(talfiq)*.[68] Law no. 25 of 1920, for example, recognized three grounds on which a wife could be granted a judicial divorce: (1) the husband's failure to provide financial support (article four); (2) the husband's failure to provide financial support because of his absence or disappearance (articles five and seven); and (3) the husband's contraction of an incurable or chronic defect such as leprosy or insanity unknown to the wife at the time of marriage or that developed after the marriage contract was signed (article nine).[69] The first two grounds addressed the customary Islamic obligation placed on husbands to provide financial support for their wives, whereas the third grounds introduced a novel innovation, that of disease. Indeed, the only health condition under which Hanafi law permitted a wife to seek divorce was if her husband were impotent. If unhealthy men married, Egyptian legislators now deemed that their wives had a right to divorce them.

As in the discussions on the marriage of minors, unhealthy and diseased bodies were seen as unfit for the emerging Egyptian nation. This discourse not only was part and parcel of the larger international movement of eugenics and reformers' debates that engaged with European discussions on colonized bodies;[70] it also had its roots in the early nineteenth century. Under Muhammad 'Ali's reign (1805–48), public health campaigns were conducted for state building and military projects that required industrious, physically fit bodies that could be mobilized to provide corvée labor and signified strength for the state.[71] Discussions about the need for strong, healthy bodies for the nation only continued to grow in monarchical

Egypt.[72] In 1923, for example, a women's periodical advised young people to contemplate their suitor's health when considering marriage, arguing that poor health "will affect the health of the children and marriage will be a felony to the self, offspring, and the nation."[73] Others called for the state to assume a central role to ensure that only healthy Egyptians be given the right to marry. One writer, who condemned families that married off their "disease-ridden," sons and daughters, proposed that the state adopt a law that required brides and grooms to submit a health certificate from a certified doctor testifying that they are not afflicted with disease, for it was "essential for the sake of healthy offspring."[74] Because a strong family was seen as the cornerstone of the nation, many nationalists wanted only the physically fit to have the right to marry and reproduce.

Discourses about healthy families were not only linked to disease and reproduction, but also to financial health. If a husband could not, or refused to, support his wife financially, then his wife also had legal grounds for a divorce. However, before the divorce was actually granted, the government instructed the courts to closely examine the financial circumstances of the husband.[75] In a society where many did not favor female-initiated divorce, the legislators deemed judicial divorce appropriate if its intention were to preserve the financial welfare of the family. As one writer put it, women whose husbands refused to divorce them ended up living as fugitives, without the legal possibilities of alimony or remarriage, and that the Egyptian nation only would benefit by allowing these desperate women to divorce and remarry.[76]

Although legislators ultimately responded to these calls for reform, it was not until nearly a decade later that another factor was recognized as grounds for divorce, that of spousal abuse. Whereas the 1920 law did not address Amin's proposal for a wife's right to divorce "in any case in which a man may harm her," the 1929 law did.[77] Article six of Law no. 25 of 1929 stipulated that an Islamic judge (qadi) could grant a wife an irrevocable divorce if she substantiated her claim of maltreatment (darar) and if reconciliation between the husband and wife were impossible.[78] The concept of maltreatment was not defined explicitly, only stating that it contributes to marital discord (shiqaq) and makes smooth marital relations impossible, thus leaving the determination of whether or not harm occurred to individual (male) judges.[79] While it is difficult to ascertain how individual judges interpreted these new laws, it is likely that the greater autonomy judges enjoyed in Ottoman Egypt where the four legal schools of Islam were available to them no longer existed after the nationwide codification of personal status laws.[80] Furthermore, judges in twentieth-century Egypt most likely felt the pressure to apply these new laws since they had become government employees, paid, promoted, transferred, and retired by a largely secular state.[81]

Given the encroaching role the legal system assumed in monitoring marriage and divorce in the lives of Egyptian women (and men) and the complicated nature of female initiated divorce, it is difficult to claim that these divorce laws constituted major new gains for women. For example, with regards to the second grounds for judicial divorce, a wife whose husband was absent or missing could file for divorce only on the basis of his failure to provide financial support (nafaqa), that is, she had to prove that he was not sending her money or had not left her with a sufficient amount to sustain herself.[82] If the husband did not send or personally provide payment by the judge's deadline, then the judge could issue the wife a divorce.[83] The divorce, however, was revocable, meaning it could be reversed if the husband returned, willing to provide for her financially.[84] If the husband were missing and there was no information on his whereabouts, then the wife had to wait four years from the date she filed the case until she could begin her 'idda (the waiting period a wife must observe before she is permitted to remarry), which the law set at four months and ten days after which the judge theoretically was able to issue a divorce.[85] After the wife completed her 'idda, she was free to marry another, but if the ex-husband reappeared before her marriage was consummated, she was forced to return to him.[86]

The Ministry of Justice also used personal status legislation to create another avenue by which the government could monitor its male subjects and intervene in their marital lives. Both the 1920 and 1929 divorce laws also addressed the plight of prisoners' wives, in conjunction with Amin's proposals that a wife married to a criminal should be granted a divorce. Indeed, many Egyptians wrote about the injustice of the legal system in which "we deny the woman to divorce her husband even if he is sentenced to life imprisonment, so her life is destroyed and her reputation is smeared with the shame of a deed which she did not commit."[87] Whereas article five of the 1920 law stated that even if the whereabouts of an absent, imprisoned husband were known divorce proceedings could not be initiated by his wife as long as he continued to support her,[88] article 14 of the 1929 law decreed that a woman whose husband was imprisoned for not less than three years could, after a separation of at least one year, petition the court for divorce.[89]

Some Egyptians were outraged by the introduction of this article. The prominent Egyptian nationalist lawyer, Muhammad Husayn Haykal, who served as minister of education and Senate president in the 1940s, published an article in *al-Ahram* lambasting this law that "presents a danger which threatens the morals with corruption on one hand and the extermination of the existence of the family on the other," because it would compel wives to claim potential infidelity if they remained married to their imprisoned husbands in order to convince judges to grant them a divorce.[90] For Haykal, an intellectual described as "a proponent of the extensive Westernization of Egyptian society" in the 1920s,[91] a woman could not be trusted with the right to divorce because it would threaten both public morality and the family unit.[92] It is worth noting that he did not consider that male-initiated divorce endangered the nation's morality or foundation.

'Abd al-Hamid Hamdi, the editor of *al-Sufur*, responded to Haykal's comments by arguing that marriage should not be a forced bond, which only the husband had the right to dissolve. He commended the Ministry of Justice for attempting to modernize personal status laws that were, "ridiculous," and, "irrelevant to our times."[93] While Hamdi was critical of *sharia* laws that he presumed did not give women grounds for divorce, he was careful not to directly criticize Islam. Rather, he believed that state legislators could find elements in Islam to support the reform of marital life in order to recover the true, original purpose of marriage, and not its contemporary meaning as "a contract in which the husband owned his wife."[94] Hamdi's explicit situation of his calls for reform within an Islamic discursive tradition confirms Omnia Shakry's argument: "Even Westernized modernizing reformers . . . situated their own projects as a defense of Islam and a critique of *taqlid* [blind imitation]. Their projects were often conceptualized as an illustration that 'true Islam' was entirely compatible with modernity."[95]

Another writer agreed with Hamdi, arguing that the high rates of suicide and spousal murder committed by miserable wives, well-publicized in the press — along with homicides committed by women in general, as shown by Shaun Lopez in chapter thirteen — would continue to rise if women were not permitted legal recourse to end unbearable marriages.[96] Although many of these male writers advocated female rights to divorce not in the name of gender equality, but rather as a means to improve the social welfare of the nation, some were more adamant in their calls for marital reform than others. For example, one writer, 'Abduh al-Barquqi, called on the government to create a unified law that permitted women and men, as well as Copts and Muslims, equal rights to divorce. He argued that if marriage were not coupled with the right to divorce, then it was equivalent to bondage and slavery, and that a nation that forbids divorce leads its youth to fear marriage as they fear prison.[97] Voices such as al-Barquqi's, however, were rare even among feminists.

While the 1920 law did intervene in the 'private' lives of men, especially those of missing, criminal, or unhealthy husbands, male-initiated divorce was not regulated until Law no. 25 of 1929. This law departed from the 1920 law, not only because it expanded the grounds on which a wife could seek divorce, but also because it attempted to curtail slightly a man's unilateral right to divorce. Law no. 25 of 1929 sought to restrict the male declaration of divorce in the following ways: oaths uttered under intoxication or compulsion are invalid (article one); pledges uttered as a threat to force the wife or a third party into a particular action are null (article two); even if repeated several times in one sitting, the divorce oath was to be considered a single instance of the husband's intent (three oaths must be uttered on three separate occasions for the divorce to be realized) (article three); and implicit, metaphorical expressions, unless divorce was actually intended, were void (article four).[98] In a particularly radical departure, legislators formulated articles two and three, which lacked any basis in the majority views of the four Sunni schools.[99] Instead, they cited individual jurists to depart from the Hanafi school, which considered male divorce binding in all instances, even if the husband uttered the divorce oath indirectly, or under duress, negligence, jest, or intoxication.

Many women writers in monarchical Egypt welcomed the committee's legal restriction of unilateral male divorce. Like the male writers discussed above, EFU members publicized male abuses of divorce in the pages of its newspapers.[100] Other women writers also bemoaned the divorce oath that enabled men to hastily divorce their wives without serious contemplation. One went as far as to suggest that the triple divorce oath should be outlawed completely: "If the rash husband realizes that the door to divorce is closed and that it is not easy for him to get rid of his life companion, he will be forced to abide by the law . . . but if the door of divorce is left wide open for every rash, irrational man . . . then the number of divorced women will increase, chaos in families will spread, and the situation of the children who do not find someone to tend to their upbringing will worsen and, thus, they will grow up as ignorant vagabonds."[101]

Nationalist legislators also diverged from the legal schools' interpretation that divorce is considered irrevocable (talaq ba'in) when it is pronounced on three separate occasions during the waiting period. An irrevocable divorce, for instance, meant that the husband would have to remarry his wife and pay her a new dower in order to resume marital life with her. A revocable divorce *(talaq raj'i)*, on the other hand, meant that the husband retained the right to return to his wife during her waiting period against her will and without having to conclude a new marriage contract or pay a new dower.[102] Although such attempts to curtail irrevocable divorce would at first appear favorable for women, a closer examination reveals that the intentions of nationalist legislators were not necessarily to protect wives from their husbands' hasty, but permanent, utterances of divorce. In fact, it can be argued that a revocable divorce preserves the institution of marriage more than an irrevocable divorce does. Thus, the drafters of the 1929 law attempted to make marriage more permanent by introducing article five, which stated that every divorce would be considered revocable except a third divorce, a divorce that occurred before the consummation of a marriage, or a divorce over money *(talaq 'ala mal)*.[103]

Interestingly, the drafters of Law no. 1929 did not adopt Amin's system for male divorce in which the husband must declare his intent to divorce before an Islamic judge or an authorized official, who would then appoint arbitrators. Under Amin's system, if the arbitrators did not succeed in reconciling the couple, they would present a report to the judge or official, who would then permit the husband to divorce his wife. Divorce would thus only be considered legal if it occurred before a judge or an authorized official, if there were two witnesses, and if a formal document was signed.[104] Amin apparently did not view his proposal as a deprivation of a man's right to divorce, because a husband did not have to explain his desire to divorce. Rather, Amin envisioned this system as protecting the family and Egyptian women from husbands who acted in the heat of anger, or without genuine intentions for divorce.

The fact that the state legislators did not legalize such a model, which would have severely curtailed unilateral male divorce, suggests that they were not prepared to completely limit a husband's right to divorce. Indeed, in 1943 and again in 1945, the Ministry of Social Affairs drafted a bill that made unilateral male divorce conditional upon a court's permission and only after the *qadi* had investigated the cause for divorce and unsuccessfully attempted to reconcile the parties. Under this bill, any husband who divorced his wife without the court's permission would be subjected to a fine, imprisonment, or both, but this controversial proposal was never passed into law due to widespread opposition.[105] The failure of its passage reveals that such a blatant attempt to make marriage more permanent for men was unacceptable for many.

It appears that the state officials' aim to deter divorce through legal intervention was achieved. As several scholars have noted, divorce rates in Egypt steadily decreased over the course of the twentieth century, from 26.9 percent in 1935 to 16.0 percent in 1991.[106] Although the divorce rate dropped from 26.2 percent in the 1930s to 22.25 percent in the 1940s, Egyptians paradoxically continued to lament what they perceived as escalating divorce rates throughout this period.[107] In 1933, for example, the prominent social reformer Muhammad Farid Junaydi criticized high divorce rates that he claimed resulted from men who abused their right to divorce.[108] He viewed the divorce problem as "one of the most vital social problems disturbing society's spirit, since it is the basic reason for the corruption of morals, especially the morals of children."[109] Similarly, in 1949, Egyptian feminist Doria Shafik argued that Egypt suffered from one of the highest divorce rates in the world: "Out of the homes created at the beginning of the year, one third are destroyed by the end of the year. Accordingly, our lives are constantly threatened by a word that could be spoken by an idiot or a drunkard or someone who is ignorant of social and religious manners."[110] Although Shafiq lamented the divorce rate, she advocated for female divorce rights. When Queen Farida sought a divorce from King Faruq (r. 1936–52) in 1948, Shafiq extolled the actions of this queen, who suffered from his public extramarital affairs. "In exchange for her liberty, Farida gave up a throne, one of the supreme gestures in the history of the Egyptian woman. A queen descending from the stairs of the palace of her own free will, leaving behind the honors, grandeur and even her three daughters, to go and find, under her paternal roof, the most beautiful of all thrones: that of liberty."[111] Shafiq not only called for increased female rights to divorce, but also for the outright abolition of polygamy, a practice that certain Egyptian state officials themselves would attempt to restrict.

Mainstreaming Monogamy

In 1926, the Council of Ministers formed a committee, headed by Minister of Justice Zaki Abu al-Sa'ud and Shaykh Muhammad Mustafa al-Maraghi, to recommend a draft proposal for a revised personal status code. Most of the committee's suggestions sought to limit polygamy,[112] including the bride's right to insert a clause in her marriage contract stipulating that she could be granted a divorce if her husband sought a second wife and/ or that her husband was required to divorce any wives he already might have before he married her.[113] Furthermore, the committee proposed that officials should be prohibited from registering a second marriage contract to a man who was already married without the permission of the local *qadi* who, in turn, would determine whether the man was capable of treating his wives equally and providing support for a second wife.[114] Although these proposals to restrict polygamy were not passed, the proposed legislation and the wider social debates surrounding them represent the first time in Egyptian history that the state attempted to prohibit polygamy, and point to the importance of emerging nationalist discourses in the press that sought to mainstream monogamy for a modern nation.

Legislative attempts to limit polygamy also assume a greater significance given that polygamy was not a common practice and appears to have been on the decline in late nineteenth- and early twentieth-century Egypt. Statistics based on census registers appear to substantiate the low occurrence of polygamy. The 1907 census reported a 6 percent rate of polygamy,[115] and a decade later, in 1917, up to 4.8 percent of Egyptian husbands may have been polygamous.[116] Relying on *sharia* court records and census registers, respectively, Tucker and Cuno maintain that polygamy was by no means widespread in the nineteenth century. Tucker suggests that such a low occurrence of polygamy among the peasantry may have been a product of material conditions, since their scarce resources did not allow for the financial maintenance of a second wife.[117] Similarly, Cuno notes that most non-elite families in the countryside were non-polygamous.[118] When polygamy did occur, it served as both a function and a product of wealth for the landowning rural elite, since a polygamous man presumably had "a way of increasing the family labour force and of increasing the possibility of having male heirs."[119]

In the early twentieth century, several Europeans noted the further decline in polygamy. British social anthropologist Winifred S. Blackman, who conducted fieldwork in Upper Egypt in the mid-1920s, observed that "monogamy is becoming much more common in Egypt, and to have more than one wife is looked upon as rather barbarous even among the peasants."[120] American traveler Elizabeth Cooper asserted that the "great social evil, judged by Western standards, polygamy, is dying out."[121] Interestingly, Blackman, as well as E.L. Butcher, insinuated that Egyptian men preferred to divorce their wives in order to remarry, rather than engage in polygamy.[122] Although problematic as sources,[123] these observations perhaps reveal why some Egyptians advocated polygamy as a practice that would deter husbands from divorcing their first wives in order to marry another. Indeed, an Egyptian academic noted in the 1930s that male-initiated divorce "substitutes for polygamy among the poor."[124]

Although some Egyptians defended polygamy, many nationalists had begun to deploy monogamy as a nationalist ideal. Clarissa Lee Pollard notes that monogamy had become the showpiece of Egyptian modernity beginning in the late nineteenth century. She argues that by marrying only one wife, Khedive Tawfiq (r. 1883–92), brought a new form of the royal familial relationship into the "public" sphere and that the public display of Tawfiq's monogamous household very literally connected the shape and practices of his domicile to the building of the nation-state. According to Pollard, the affairs of the public realm required the display of monogamous marital relations.[125] Likewise, even before Lord Cromer wrote of the "baneful" effects of polygamy on Egyptian life,[126] Egyptian reformers had begun to publicly denounce it, demonstrating the similarities of colonial and anticolonial nationalist discourses. In 1898, Muhammad 'Abduh, who served as the grand mufti of Egypt from 1899 to 1905, and in 1899, Qasim Amin, respectively, called for the restriction of polygamy and extolled the benefits of monogamy as the Islamic ideal, arguing that the Qur'anic verses that legitimized polygamy only did so under extreme cases and simultaneously warned men against it.[127]

Nor were denunciations of polygamy limited solely to prominent legal reformers. In chapter fourteen, Mervet Hatem explores the nationalist memory of Malak Hifni Nasif. In 1911, this well-known women's rights advocate, who spoke publicly and wrote a weekly column addressing a variety of women's issues in *al-Jarida*, presented a list of demands to the Egyptian Congress through a male proxy, one of which demanded severe limits on polygamy. This demand, however, generated such heated debate that the motion was suppressed.[128] In 1917, when the Ministry of Justice was considering personal status reform, Ahmad Safwat called for the legal restriction of polygamy so that monogamy could prevail.[129] Following in his footsteps, in 1922, 'Abd al-Fattah al-Sayyid, a law professor who later became president of the Court of Cassation, advocated limiting polygamy to those cases in which the first wife was sick, old, or barren, and only if the husband successfully could maintain a second wife.[130] Perhaps because these earlier attempts elicited strong resistance, state legislators did not make a concerted effort to limit polygamy directly until 1926.

Once again, the government-sponsored committee to limit polygamy was influenced by 'Abduh and Amin.[131] With regards to polygamy, both 'Abduh and Amin proposed that a man who already had one wife should be forbidden to marry another unless the courts were satisfied that he would be able to distribute his favors equally and attained the competence to meet all his financial obligations. Like 'Abduh and Amin, the committee sought to limit polygamy for the sake of the offspring, that is, the future citizens of the nation. The explanatory memorandum that accompanied the draft articles to limit polygamy argued that it should be curtailed since the vast majority of neglected children in Egypt were the result of polygamous marriages contracted by men who were incapable of supporting even one family.[132] Once again, nationalist legislators did not seek to better women's marital lives. Rather, under the rhetoric of improving the social fabric of Egyptian society and the quality of upbringing for its future citizens, they sought legal intervention as a means to represent and control the population along newly national lines.

Egyptian feminists and women writers also continued in the tradition of their predecessors by publicizing the negative effects of polygamy on women.[133] Among the demands the EFU repeatedly presented to the government was one for legal restrictions on polygamy, insisting that a man be permitted to take a second wife only if his first wife were sterile or had an incurable illness.[134] Throughout the 1920s and 1930s, in the pages of the official journals of the EFU, the Daughter of the Nile Union, and other women's journals, writers launched vibrant press campaigns for the restriction of polygamy.[135] As Badran notes, these women writers viewed polygamy as a patriarchal tool, which subjugated women.[136] Yet, even more significantly, like the nationalist legislators, they portrayed polygamy as a threat to the Egyptian family and, by extension, the nation. Perhaps in efforts to win support from the government and the larger public, women writers were often more direct in their linking of marriage to the nation.

From the 1920s onward, women activists began to frame their criticisms of polygamy much more explicitly within a discourse of modernity and nationalism. These press debates reveal that for many nationalist writers and political activists in monarchical Egypt, monogamy increasingly was becoming viewed as a path to modernity for the semi-independent nation. For example, Huda Sha'rawi told *al-Ahram* that polygamy "is an obstacle to [creating] a harmonious home generating the moral force able to form and guide the good citizen."[137] Her disciple, Sa'iza Nabarawi, declared that if Egypt considered itself a progressive nation it should follow other, more advanced Muslim countries where polygamy had already been abolished or severely limited.[138] She wrote, "This resistance to modern currents in a nation priding itself on being at the head of all progressive movements amazes me."[139]

Scholars similarly have noted the links that were drawn between modernity and marriage in debates over polygamy. Baron, for example, argues that a new notion of companionate marriage, one based on choice and affection as opposed to the "traditional" form of arranged unions, surfaced in early twentieth century Egypt at a time when concubinage and polygamy had come to be seen as the main obstacles to the new marital ideal.[140] For Baron, the abolition of concubinage and slavery by the 1877 Anglo-Egyptian Convention strengthened the institution of marriage and served as a necessary first step toward the ideal of monogamy.[141] She argues the marriage and divorce laws passed in modern Egypt "sought to terminate unions that did not conform to the emerging ideal of companionate marriage."[142] While notions of companionate marriage may have served as one justification for the mainstreaming of monogamy, this was not the committee's purported goal for limiting polygamy. As noted above, Egyptian legislators explained that polygamy should be restricted in order to safeguard the welfare of children and the nation. While feminists, nationalists, and writers utilized a variety of explanations to denounce polygamy, the committee's particular objective was to subordinate the reproductive and conjugal capacities of its subjects within a monogamous, adult, and nuclear space.

Marilyn Booth likewise echoes Baron's claims that the women's press, as well as women's biographies, began to privilege the notion of companionate marriage in modern Egypt. For Booth, this representation of marriage helped to construct the image of the nuclear family as the building block of the nation. She argues that this ideal of marriage and the family was part of the middle-class elite's attempt to define itself against other socioeconomic strata, as well as a means to assert its authority as the group that would lead the nation to independence.[143] Drawing on Deniz Kandiyoti, she suggests that the dominant nationalist program for social organization was the portrayal of the nuclear family as the primary, productive unit of the nation. Such a program not only attenuated other kin-based identities, but also, idealized women's management of the nuclear family in women's biographies and the women's press as a site of nationalist strength that could potentially reorient the loyalties of subnational groups.[144] Other scholars also have offered a number of different reasons for the shifts in discourses promoting, and practices reflecting, the emergence of an independent, single nuclear household over the nineteenth-century ideal of multiple households, such as the end of the harem system, the use of 'western' architecture, the coeval development of socialized production under capitalism, and the development of private property and urbanization.[145] Yet, none account for how Egyptian state officials actively sought to support the ideal of a single household and none, with the exception of Booth, explain why this discourse on the modern, nuclear family emerged when it did.

As with the perceptions of high rates of marriage among minors, the occurrence of polygamy was imagined to be much higher than statistics reveal it to be. This leads to the question as to why certain state officials and press writers sought to curtail polygamy if it was not a common practice. During the monarchical period, at least, it appears that attempts to restrict polygamy were motivated by the state's desire to promote and solidify single, nuclear households that would not be able to constitute a threat to its political and socioeconomic power. By promoting a nuclear family based on a vision of monogamy as modern, nationalist writers and state officials indirectly denounced large familial networks that could potentially encourage subversive activities against the authority of the state. As in its attempts to legally restrict the marriage of minors and divorce, certain state officials, as well as many Egyptian nationalists and feminists, sought to discourage polygamy as yet another means to control, represent, and subordinate the marital habits of the population to the ordered supervision of the national state. By portraying the nuclear family as the most fruitful reproductive unit for the burgeoning nation, the Egyptian state could secure its hold over the population.

It also is important to bear in mind that while certain legislative reformers and press writers promoted monogamy as a path to Egyptian modernity and national independence, it was not the only one. For example, although the Cabinet approved the 1926 proposals to restrict polygamy in 1927, King Fu'ad (r. 1917–36) rejected them and they never were passed into law. Anderson claims that the king was forced to reject these proposals because polygamy was still viewed by many as a source of reproduction for labor and an economically conducive institution for the destitute, peasant population.[146] Yet, this explanation contradicts both discussions in the Egyptian public at the time, and the historical findings of Tucker and Cuno that polygamy was practiced by the wealthy, not the poor.[147] Furthermore, as several scholars have noted, Egypt's rapid population increase began to attract public scrutiny around this time, resulting in calls for limitations on the escalating birth rate.[148]

A better explanation of the king's rejection of these proposals appears to lie in the fact that King Fu'ad, who was not a popular king and reportedly harbored aspirations to become the Islamic caliph, was more concerned about public support and could not justify restricting such a religiously mandated male prerogative.[149] Muslim opponents decried both state-sponsored innovations that were designed to forbid what God had permitted, and the government's intervention in a matter considered binding before God rather than enforceable by courts.[150] Similar recommendations to limit polygamy were proposed again by the Ministry of Social Affairs in 1943 and 1945, but to no avail.[151] It also should be noted, however, that the Maliki principle of maltreatment, introduced by article six of Law no. 25 of 1929 as discussed above, had been interpreted broadly enough by some judges to allow an insistent wife a judicial divorce if her husband took on a second wife and if she could prove that he was not treating her financially, or emotionally as well as the co-wife.[152] Although it appears that the introduction of the broad and vaguely defined concept of maltreatment may have been an indirect attempt and legal circumvention by the Egyptian government to deter polygamy, neither the article, nor the explanatory memorandum that accompanied this law, make any direct mention of polygamy.[153]

This, however, did not deter some Egyptian feminists from pressing the government to take a firmer legal stance against polygamy. Perhaps more directly than her EFU predecessors, Doria Shafik actively advocated for the complete abolition of polygamy and called on Egyptian parliamentarians to do so, which resulted in vicious attacks from Azhari *shaykh*s and members of the Muslim Brotherhood.[154] Her campaign against polygamy resulted in an increased defensiveness and protection of an institution that was already on the decline, and perhaps worked against similar appeals by later feminists. Even al-Maraghi, who headed the original 1926 committee that sought to curtail polygamy, later wrote in support of polygamy in the Egyptian press, after he had become *shaykh* of al-Azhar.[155] Thus, not only were there diverse opinions over personal status issues within the state itself, but some state officials themselves held contradictory stances. His successor advanced the familiar socioeconomic argument that polygamy was conducive for peasants who counted their productive labor by the number of wives and children they had.[156] The heated reactions to the state's attempts to restrict polygamy not only led to an increased defensiveness of this practice, but also confirm that notions of marriage in monarchical Egypt constituted a hotly contested ideological terrain.

Conclusion

When the unprecedented promulgation of state legislation on marriage and divorce in monarchical Egypt is situated in a larger context, it becomes clear that government legislators attempted to consolidate their control over the population by nationalizing the institution of marriage and by integrating the family into the sturdy bulwark of the burgeoning nation. Even more significantly perhaps, the government introduced legislation mandating marital habits that appear to have already been widely practiced. As western observers and census registers indicate, the marriage of minors and polygamy were on the decline long before state officials attempted to restrict these practices. In this respect, Egypt resembles late nineteenth- and early twentieth-century Istanbul, where marriage occurred later in life for both men and women, families were primarily nuclear, and polygamy was negligible. In light of demographic evidence pointing to the prevalence of the idealized family model in Istanbul, Alan Duben and Cem Behar puzzle over the modernist press' concern about polygamy, the marriage of minors, and joint families, which could be construed only as a misconception of prevailing practices.[157] Yet, as Kandiyoti points out, to understand such concerns one must look for explanations in the urge to articulate a new nationalist morality. She has asked why it was that press reformers staked their claims to modernity and political independence on this "new" form of the family.[158] In the case of Egypt, a multiplicity of reasons account for the attempts of the state's various religious and nationalist legislators, feminists, and writers to advocate their respective visions of monogamous, adult, and/or permanent marriage as a basis for the emerging Egyptian nation.

While western officials and travelers in Egypt often condemned high divorce rates and backward practices of the marriage of minors and polygamy, it is important to bear in mind that Egyptian proposals for reforming marriage laws were not simply a reaction to, or inspired by, western critiques. Egyptian calls for reform of conjugal practices through authentically religious and anticolonial rhetoric represented their assertion of an indigenous identity, which was essential to the nation-building project to counter the colonial project. At the same time, however, efforts to reform marital practices by the state, religious officials, nationalist reformers, feminists, and press writers also evolved from a number of complex processes embedded in the growth of the legal and medical establishment, urbanization, and calls for modernization. In short, the marriage of minors, unilateral male-initiated divorce, and polygamy, increasingly became viewed as incompatible with a strong and 'modern' Egyptian nation. In its attempts to restrict these practices, the state aimed to make marriage more healthy and permanent so that it could serve as a solid foundation for an independent Egyptian nation free of social ills.

Although the government assumed an unprecedented role in the so-called 'private' sphere of the family, many Egyptians actively encouraged the state to do so. Many members in the state, as well as a wide variety of social reformers, nationalist commentators, and feminists clearly perceived adult, monogamous, permanent marriage as a key path to an independent, modern Egyptian nation. Yet, marriage in monarchical Egypt remained a contested site of national identity formation that was being defined and redefined by these actors to an unprecedented extent. Legislative and press debates on the purposes, goals, and meanings of marriage during this period likewise provide convincing evidence of the political and cultural anxieties that often underwrote experiments in anticolonial nationalism.

Marriage served as a critical arena where notions of nationalism were produced and reproduced by the state, and where citizens criticized Egyptian society and offered multiple visions of the role of the state, marriage, and the family in the emerging nation. While certain secular nationalists and nationalist feminists promoted adult, monogamous, permanent marriage as the road to national independence, this view-point was by no means a unanimous one, as different factions, particularly religious ones, held competing views. The sociocultural assumptions embedded in debates over marriage not only demonstrate the divergent articulations of Egyptian nationalism that existed among the state, press, and literate upper-class elites, but also, the unparalleled nationalization of marriage. More research needs to be conducted to understand the range and impact of the state's unprecedented national legislation on Egyptian society. An extensive survey of the *sharīʿa* court records of monarchical Egypt, for example, may reveal how Egyptian men and women who used the courts perceived the state's intervention in their marital conflicts, as well as individual judges' interpretation and implementation of the new marriage and divorce laws. These records need to be closely examined in order to gauge whether or not the state's laws influenced understandings of what it meant to be a husband, wife, and Egyptian national subject in a semi-colonial nation still fighting for full independence.

Notes

1   I would like to thank Bernard Haykel, Liat Kozma, Zachary Lockman, Mary Nolan, Mario R. Ruiz, Katayoun Shafiee, and Shareah Taleghani for their invaluable comments and insights on this chapter.

2   Geoff Eley and Ronald Grigor Suny, "Introduction: From the Moment of Social History to the Work of Cultural Representation," in idem, *Becoming National: A Reader* (New York: Oxford University Press, 1996), 26.

3   See, for example, Joel Beinin and Zachary Lockman, *Workers on the Nile: Nationalism, Communism, Islam, and the Egyptian Working Class, 1882–1954* (Princeton: Princeton University Press, 1987); Ralph M. Coury, "Who 'Invented' Egyptian Arab Nationalism?" *International Journal of Middle Eastern Studies* 14 (1982): 249–81 and 459–79; Israel Gershoni and James P. Jankowski, *Egypt, Islam, and the Arabs: The Search for Egyptian Nationhood, 1900–1930* (New York: Oxford University Press, 1986); idem, *Redefining the Egyptian Nation, 1930–1945* (New York: Cambridge University Press, 1995).

4   See, for example, Leila Ahmed, *Women and Gender in Islam: Historical Roots of a Modern in Debate* (New Haven: Yale University Press, 1992); Margot Badran, *Feminists, Islam, and Nation: Gender and the Making of Modern Egypt* (Princeton: Princeton University Press, 1995); Beth Baron, *The Women's Awakening in Egypt: Culture, Society, and the Press* (New Haven: Yale University Press, 1994); Selma Botman, *Engendering Citizenship in Egypt* (New York: Columbia University Press, 1999); Juan Cole, "Feminism, Class, and Islam in Turn-of-the-Century Egypt," *International Journal of Middle Eastern Studies* 13 (1981): 387–407; Thomas Philipp, "Feminism and Nationalist Politics," in *Women in the Muslim World*, ed. Lois Beck and Nikki R. Keddie (Cambridge: Harvard University Press, 1978), 277–94.

5   Baron, *The Women's Awakening*, 13–14.

6   Partha Chatterjee, *The Nation and Its Fragments: Colonial and Postcolonial Histories* (Princeton: Princeton University Press, 1993), 116–34.

7   Focusing on constructions of Egyptian women as mothers of the nation, Timothy Mitchell and Omnia Shakry demonstrate how Egyptian nationalists attempted to advance and develop women as *both* an inner domain of culture and an outer domain of progress. See Timothy Mitchell, *Colonising Egypt* (Berkeley: University of California Press, 1991), 113; Omnia Shakry, "Schooled Mothers and Structured Play: Child Rearing Turn-of-the-Century Egypt," in *Remaking Women: Feminism and Modernity in the Middle East*, ed. Lila Abu-Lughod (Princeton: Princeton University Press, 1998), 126–70. See also, Beth Baron, "Mothers, Morality, and Nationalism in Pre-1919 Egypt," in *The Origins of Arab Nationalism*, ed. Rashid Khalidi, Lisa Anderson, Muhammad Muslih, and Reeva S. Simon (New York: Columbia University Press, 1991), 271–88; Marilyn Booth, *May Her Likes Be Multiplied: Biography and Gender Politics in Egypt* (Berkeley: University of California Press, 2001); Rebecca Joubin, "Creating the Modern Professional Housewife: Scientifically-Based Advice Extended to Middle- and Upper-Class Egyptian Women, 1920–1930s," *Arab Studies Journal* 4, 2 (Fall 1996): 19–45; Clarissa Lee Pollard, "Nurturing the Nation: The Family Politics of the 1919 Egyptian Revolution" (Ph.D. diss., University of California, Berkeley, 1997).

8   Etienne Balibar, "The Nation Form: History and Ideology," in idem and Immanuel Wallerstein, *Race, Nation, Class: Ambiguous Identities* (Verso, London, 1991), 101, 102.

9   See Abdullahi A. An-Na'im, ed., *Islamic Family Law in a Changing World: A Global Resource Book* (London: Zed Books, 2002), 169–70; John L. Esposito, *Women in Muslim Family Law*, 2nd ed. (Syracuse: Syracuse University Press, 2001), 59–60; Mervat Hatem, "The Enduring Alliance of Nationalism and Patriarchy in Muslim Personal Status Laws: The Case of Modern Egypt," *Feminist Issues* 6, 1 (1986), 19.

10   James N.D. Anderson, *Islamic Law in the Modern World* (New York: New York University Press, 1959); idem, "Law Reform in Egypt: 1850–1950," in *Political and Social Change in Modern Egypt*, ed. P.M. Holt (London: Oxford University Press, 1968), 209–30; idem, "The Problem of Divorce in the Shari'a Law of Islam: Measures of Reform in Modern Egypt," *Royal Central Asian Society Journal* 37 (1950): 169–85; idem, "Recent Developments in Shari'a Law II: Matters of Competence, Organization and Procedure," *The Muslim World* 40, 1 (January 1950): 34–48; idem, "Recent Developments in Shari'a Law III: The Contract of Marriage," *The Muslim World* 41, 2 (April 1951): 113–26; idem, "Recent Developments in Shari'a Law IV: Further Points Concerning Marriage," *The Muslim World* 41, 3 (July 1951): 186–98; idem, "Recent Developments in Shari'a Law V: The Dissolution of Marriage," *The Muslim World* 41, 4 (October 1951): 271–88; idem, "The Role of Personal Status in Social Development in Islamic Countries," *Comparative Studies in Society and History* 13, 1 (1971): 16–31; Badran, *Feminists*, chapter 7; Beth Baron, "The Making and Breaking of Marital Bonds in Modern Egypt," in Nikki R. Keddie and Beth Baron, ed., *Women in Middle Eastern History: Shifting Boundaries in Sex and Gender* (New Haven: Yale University Press), 275–91; Noel J. Coulson, *A History of Islamic Law* (Edinburgh: Edinburgh University Press, 1964), chapter 12–14; Esposito, *Women*, chapter 3; Hatem, "The Enduring Alliance," 19–43; Amira El Azhary Sonbol, "Introduction," in idem, *Women, the Family, and Divorce Laws in Islamic History* (Syracuse: Syracuse University Press, 1996), 1–20.

11   Anderson, *Islamic Law*, 26; Esposito, *Women*, 50.

12   Sonbol, "Introduction," 11.

13   Badran, *Feminists*, 135.

14   Botman, *Engendering Citizenship*, 23, 49; Hatem, "The Enduring Alliance," 26.

15   B.F. Musallam, *Sex and Society in Islam: Birth Control Before the Nineteenth Century* (Cambridge: Cambridge University Press, 1983), 11.

16   For brief accounts of the efforts to limit the jurisdiction of the *shari'a* courts to personal status matters, see Anderson, "Shari'a Law II," 35; Nathan Brown, *The Rule of Law in the Arab World: Courts in Egypt and the Gulf* (Cambridge: Cambridge University Press, 1997), 38–39; P.J. Vatikiotis, *The Modern History of Egypt: From Muhammad Ali to Mubarak*, 4th ed. (Baltimore: Johns Hopkins University Press, 1991), 119, 299. In 1897, the Law of the Organization and Procedure for *Shari'a* Courts, further amended in 1910 and 1913, reorganized the *shari'a* courts, whose jurisdiction lasted until 1955 when President Gamal 'Abd al-Nasser abolished the courts and transferred their jurisdiction to civil courts. See Anderson, "Law Reform," 222; Ron Shaham, *Family and the Courts in Modern Egypt: A Study Based on Decisions by the Shari'a Courts, 1900–1955* (Leiden: E.J. Brill, 1997), 10–12.

17   Anderson, "Shari'a Law V," 272, 281.

18   For a detailed analysis of the 1917 Ottoman Law of Family Rights, see Judith E. Tucker, "Revisiting Reform: Women and the Ottoman Law of Family Rights, 1917," *Arab Studies Journal* 4, 2 (1996): 4–17.

19   The committee which devised and passed the first major marital legislation included the *shaykh* of al-Azhar, the *shaykh* of the Maliki school of Islamic law, the head of the Supreme Shari'a Court, the mufti of Egypt, the minister of justice, Ahmad Dhul-Fiqar, the president of the Cabinet of Ministers, Muhammad Tawfiq Nassim, and the sultan of Egypt, Ahmed Fu'ad, who ascended the throne in 1917 and became king of Egypt in 1922. See "Qanun nimrat 25 li-sannat 1920" (Law Number 25 of 1920) in *Majmu'at al-qawanin wa-l-marasim al-mutalaqa bi-l-shu'un al-'amma li-l-thalathat al-ashhur al-ula min sannat 1920* ("Collection of the Laws and Regulations Regarding Public Affairs for the First Three Months of 1920") (Cairo: al-Matba'a al-Amiriya, 1921), 36. Located in Dar al-Watha'iq al-Qawmiya al-Misriya (The Egyptian National Archives) (DWQ). All translations from Arabic into English are my own, unless otherwise indicated. Later marriage and divorce laws were signed only in the king's name with

explanatory memorandums signed by the Cabinet of Ministers. See, for example, "Marsum bi-qanun raqam 25 li-sannat 1929" (Statute Number 25 of 1929) in *Majmu'at al-qawanin wa-l-marasim wa-l-awamir al-malakiya li-l-thalathat al-ashhur al-ula min sannat 1929* ("Collection of the Laws, Regulations, and Royal Decrees for the First Three Months of 1929") (Cairo: Matba'a al-Amiriya, 1930), 203, 208. Located in DWQ.

20   Farhat J. Ziadeh, *Lawyers, the Rule of Law and Liberalism in Modern Egypt* (Stanford: Hoover Institution, 1968), 116.

21   The census registers of 1907 and 1917, for example, indicate that most females married between the ages of twenty and twenty-nine, and the number of females who married at an earlier age was less than ten percent of the female population. See Baron, *The Women's Awakening*, 164. For historical studies on the marriage of minors, see Amira El Azhary Sonbol, "Adults and Minors in Ottoman *Shari'a* Courts and Modern Law," in idem, *Women*, 236–56; Judith E. Tucker, *Women in Nineteenth-Century Egypt* (Cambridge: Cambridge University Press, 1985), 53. For European travelers' accounts on the decline in the marriage of minors in Egypt, see E.L Butcher, *Things Seen in Egypt* (London: Seeley, Service & Co. Limited, 1931), 38; Elizabeth Cooper, *The Women of Egypt* (New York: F.A. Stokes, 1914), 201–202; Edward William Lane, *An Account of the Manners and Customs of the Modern Egyptians* (London: East-West Publications, 1978 [1836]), 160; William Nassau Senior, *Conversations and Journals in Egypt and Malta*, 2 vols. (London: S. Low, Marston, Searle and Rivington, 1882), 2: 169.

22   The Legislative Assembly was created by a 1913 law, promulgated by Lord Kitchener, British consul-general of Egypt from 1911 to 1914, which provided for the merger of the General Assembly and Legislative Council. It was comprised of nationalist reformers, lawyers, and landowners who sought internal reform as the path to Egyptian independence. Although it was short-lived (1913–15), many of leaders of the 1919 Revolution emerged from it, including 'Abd al-'Aziz Fahmi, Sa'd Zaghlul, and 'Ali Pasha Sha'rawi, who would found the Wafd party in 1919. See Baron, *The Women's Awakening*, 33; Afaf Lutfi al-Sayyid Marsot, *Egypt's Liberal Experiment: 1922–1936* (Berkeley: University of California Press, 1977), 45–48; Vatikiotis, *The Modern History*, 213.

23   There are too many articles to cite, but in *al-Ahram*, for example, they ran almost daily throughout March 1914.

24   See, for example, Malak Hifni Nasif, "Sinn al-zawaj" (Marital Age) in *al-Nisa'iyyat: majmu'at maqallat nushirat fi-l-jarida fi mawdu' al-mar'a al-misriya* ("Women's Affairs: A Collection of Articles Published in *al-Jarida* on the Subject of the Egyptian Woman"), 3rd ed. (Cairo: Multaqi al-Mar'a wa-l-Thakira, 1998 [1910]), 79–82.

25   "Iqtirah mashru' qanun li-zawj al-qasirat" (A Draft Law Proposal for Minor Wives), *al-Ahram* 39 (3 March 1914), 7.

26   Baron, "The Making," 281.

27   See, for example, Muhammad Tawfiq Sidqi, "Sinn al-Zawaj li-l-Banat: Dirasa 'Ilmiya, Diniya, wa Qanuniya" (The Marital Age of Girls: A Scientific, Religious, and Legal Study), *al-Ahram* 39 (12 March 1914), 1.

28   "Zawaj al-Banat al-Saghirat" (The Marriage of Young Girls), *al-Ahram* 39 (18 March 1914), 1.

29   Michel Foucault, "The Politics of Health in the Eighteenth Century," in *Power/Knowledge: Selected Interviews and Other Writings, 1972–1977* (Brighton: Harvester, 1980), 173–76. See also, idem, *The History of Sexuality: An Introduction*, vol. I, trans. Robert Hurley (New York: Pantheon Books, 1978 [1976]).

30   "Mashru' Tazwij al-Banat" (The Legislative Proposal for Marrying Girls), *al-Ahram* 39 (18 March 1914), 5.

31   Anderson, "Shari'a Law III," 113–15. It should be noted that an 1897 law already had required written marriage contracts in order to hear divorce and certain inheritance claims. The 1923 law differed from the 1897 law in that it explicitly directed the courts not to register marriage

contracts between brides and grooms who had not reached the minimum age of maturity. See Anderson, "Law Reform," 225.

32 Mrinalini Sinha, "The Lineage of the 'Indian' Modern: Rhetoric, Agency, and the Sarda Act in Late Colonial India," in *Gender, Sexuality, and Colonial Modernity*, ed. Antoinette Burton (New York: Routledge, 1999), 207.

33 Paul Rabinow, *French Modern: Norms and Forms of the Social Environment* (Cambridge: Massachusetts Institute of Technology Press, 1989), 9.

34 Huda Sha'rawi founded the EFU in 1923. For a detailed study of the EFU, see Badran, *Feminists*.

35 Badran, *Feminists*, 128, 127.

36 Ibid., 126.

37 "Jam'iyyat al-ittihad al-nisa'i al-misri" (The Egyptian Feminist Union), *Fatat al-sharq* (Young Woman of the East) 24, 4 (February 1930), 247.

38 Badran, *Feminists*, 128.

39 Hatem, "The Enduring Alliance," 27, quoting Huda Sha'rawi, *Mudhakirat ra'idat al-mar'a al-'arabiya al-haditha* ("Memoirs of a Modern Arab Female Pioneer") (Cairo: Dar al-Hilal, 1981), 253.

40 Badran, *Feminists*, 128.

41 Ibid., 128.

42 See, for example, "Une victoire féministe" (A Feminist Victory), *L'Égyptienne* (The Egyptian Woman) (December 1928): 37; Saiza Nabarawi, "Une loi n'a de valeur que par son application" (A Law That Only Has Value in Its Application), *L'Égyptienne* (January 1931): 5–8.

43 Anderson, "Shari'a Law III," 115; Ziadeh, *Lawyers*, 123.

44 See, for example, "Zawaj al-qasirat" (Marriage of Minor Girls), *al-Misriya* (The Egyptian Woman) (15 October 1939), 28–29; "Zawaj al-qasirat, ittijar bi-l-raqiq al-abyad" (Marriage of Minor Girls: The Trade in White Slaves), *al-Misriya* (1 August 1938), 21–22.

45 Anderson, "Shari'a Law III," 115.

46 Ibid., 113–15; Baron, "The Making," 282; Esposito, *Women*, 50. It should be noted that although the average female age of marriage has increased from 18.7 to 21.9 years old between the 1930s and 1990s, the marriage of female minors continues in Egypt, especially in rural areas, where recent reports note rates of 20 percent to over 30 percent in Upper Egypt. See Philippe Farguès, "Terminating Marriage," in *The New Arab Family*, ed. Nicholas S. Hopkins (Cairo: The American University in Cairo Press, 2003), 263.

47 Anderson, "Shari'a Law III," 114–16; Esposito, *Women*, 50; Ziadeh, *Lawyers*, 124.

48 Judith E. Tucker, *In the House of Law: Gender and Islamic Law in Ottoman Syria and Palestine* (Berkeley: University of California Press, 1998), 72.

49 Anderson, "Shari'a Law III," 114–16; Esposito, *Women*, 50.

50 Shaykh Muhammad Bakhit, "Tahdid sinn al-zawaj" (Limiting the Age of Marriage), *al-Muhamah* (Lawyers) 4, 4 (January 1924): 399–411.

51 See "Barlamaniyat" (Parliament), *al-Misriya* (15 February 1937), 29.

52 Under Islamic law, all that is needed to unite a male and female in matrimony is their agreement before two male witnesses (or, alternatively, one male witness and two female witnesses) to a marriage contract, whether oral or written, in which the names and lineages of the bride and groom are given and the amount of the dower paid by the groom to the bride is stated. See Tucker, *In the House*, 38.

53 In the early twentieth century, American traveler Elizabeth Cooper reported, "the percentage of divorce is very large, some say as high as 90 per cent." See Cooper, *The Women*, 214, 219. According to the statistics of Qasim Amin, a Muslim judge and nationalist leader, derived from the *shari'a* court registers, three out of every four women in Cairo were divorced between 1880 and 1898, while one out of every four marriages throughout

Egypt ended in divorce. See Qasim Amin, *The Liberation of Women and the New Woman: Two Documents in the History of Egyptian Feminism*, intro. and trans. Samiha Sidhom Peterson (Cairo: The American University in Cairo Press, 2000 [1899, 1900]), 98. At the same time, however, in 1903, *shari'a* registers of marriages and divorces reported by Lord Cromer revealed a divorce rate of 30 percent, but as Beth Baron points out, these figures do not record marriages and divorces that occurred outside of the courts. See Baron, "The Making," 286, fn. 54. Indeed, as Judith E. Tucker points out, the most prevalent form of divorce was the unilateral repudiation of a wife by her husband *(talaq)*, pronounced outside the courtroom. See Tucker, *Women*, 53–55. French scholar Philippe Farguès argues that divorce represented almost 50 percent of marriages at the beginning of the twentieth century. See Fargues, "Terminating," 258. It should be noted that complaints about the high divorce rate in Egypt were not new. In the 1830s, Edward Lane observed the facility of divorce that enabled many Egyptians, both men and women, to marry and divorce several times in a lifetime. See Lane, *An Account*, 183. Lord Cromer, the British consul-general in Egypt from 1882 to 1907, also discussed the "great facility given to divorce [which] necessarily weakens the strength of the family tie" in Egypt where "the Moslem, when his passion is sated, can if he likes throw off his wife like an old glove." See Evelyn Baring Cromer, Modern Egypt, 2 vols. (London: Macmillan and Co., 1908), 2: 159, 157.

54 As Kenneth M. Cuno points out, Amin's statistics are not necessarily accurate because, among other reasons, they include revocable divorces *(talaq raj'i)*, which can be considered legal separations because they often resulted in marital reconciliation. See Kenneth M. Cuno, "Divorce and the Fate of the Family in Modern Egypt," paper presented at the conference, "Institutions, Ideologies, and Agency: Family Change in the Arab Middle East and Diaspora," the University of North Carolina at Chapel Hill, April 11, 2003, 4–5. With regards to western observations, Cuno notes that norms in the West—where divorce was legally difficult to obtain until the twentieth century—served as the standard in determining whether a divorce rate was high or low. See Cuno, "Divorce," 14–15.

55 Cuno, "Divorce," 5, 15. See also, Shaham, *Family*, 103.

56 "Marsum," 208–11.

57 In 1892, jurist Ahmad Muhammad Shakir suggested that young wives whose husbands were sentenced to long imprisonments should be granted divorce on the grounds of loneliness and fear of unfaithfulness. In 1899, he submitted a memorandum to Grand Mufti Muhammad 'Abduh, advocating the adoption of Maliki principles regarding a wife's right to claim judicial divorce, but it was rejected by the *shaykh* of al-Azhar. See Ahmad Muhammad Shakir, *Nizam al-talaq fi-l-Islam* ("The System of Divorce in Islam"), 2nd ed. (Cairo: Dar al-Tab'a al-Qawmiya, 1389 H. [1969–1970]), 9–11. For 'Abduh's support for female-initiated divorce, see Muhammad 'Imara, *al-Islam wa-l-mar'a fi rayy al-imam Muhammad 'Abduh* ("Islam and Woman in the Opinion of Imam Muhammad 'Abduh") (Cairo: Dar al-Hilal, 1979), 25–31, 78–95.

58 Amin, *The Liberation*, 87.

59 The Hanafi school, one of four Sunni schools of legal thought, was the authoritative school espoused by the Ottoman Empire and was, therefore, the official school of the Egyptian administrative and commercial elite. As Amira Sonbol notes, however, the Maliki and Shafi'i schools were preferred in the *shari'a* courts of Upper and Lower Egypt, respectively. See Sonbol, "Adults," 238.

60 Amin, *The Liberation*, 99. See also Anderson, "The Problem of Divorce," 169–70; Muhammad Qadri Pasha, *al-Ahkam al-shar'iya fi-l-ahwal al-shakhsiya* ("Shari'a Rulings on Personal Status") (Cairo: al-Hindiya Press, 1917 [1875]), 50–51; Sonbol, "Adults," 239–46.

61 See, for example, Soha Abdel Kader, *Egyptian Women in a Changing Society, 1899–1987* (London: Lynne Rienner Publishers, 1987), 8; Cole, "Feminism," 401; Yvonne Y. Haddad, "Islam, Women and Revolution in Twentieth-Century Arab Thought," *The Muslim World* 74

(1984), 160; Robert Tignor, *Modernization and the British Rule in Egypt, 1882–1914* (Princeton: Princeton University Press, 1966), 341.

62 See, for example, Lila Abu-Lughod, "The Marriage of Feminism and Islamism in Egypt: Selective Repudiation as a Dynamic of Postcolonial Cultural Politics," in idem, *Remaking Women*, 255–69; Ahmed, *Women*, 162–63; Badran, *Feminists*, 18–19; Baron, *The Women's Awakening*, 4–6; Mitchell, *Colonising Egypt*, 111–13.

63 With the exception of Cuno, "Divorce," 3, scholars have overlooked these issues in favoring his views advocating women's education and the abolition of the veil and female seclusion,

64 Amin, *The Liberation*, 99.

65 Because an Islamic marriage is a contract, both parties can stipulate certain conditions provided that they are not in opposition to the essence of marriage, as defined by the jurists. For instance, a woman can be given the right to divorce, but a contract that takes away the husband's right to divorce is void. See Ziba Mir-Hosseini, *Marriage on Trial: A Study of Islamic Family Law* (London: I.B. Tauris, 1991), 32.

66 Amin, *The Liberation*, 100.

67 Anderson, "Shari'a Law V," 278–88; Baron, "The Making," 285; Esposito, *Women*, 51.

68 Shaham, *Family*, 14.

69 "Qanun," 37–38.

70 Mitchell: *Colonising Egypt*, chapter 4–5; Omnia S. El-Shakry: "The Great Social Laboratory: Reformers and Utopians in Twentieth Century Egypt" (Ph.D. diss., Princeton University, 2002), part 1.

71 Kamran Asdar Ali, *Planning the Family in Egypt: New Bodies, New Selves* (Austin: University of Texas Press, 2003), 25; Laura Bier, "From Birth Control to Family Planning: Population, Gender and the Politics of Reproduction in Egypt," paper presented at the conference, "Institutions, Ideologies, and Agency: Family Change in the Arab Middle East and Diaspora," the University of North Carolina at Chapel Hill, April 11, 2003, 4, fn. 2. For a detailed study of the disciplinary methods of 'Ali's regime, see Khaled Fahmy, *All the Pasha's Men: Mehmed Ali, His Army and the Making of Modern Egypt* (Cambridge: Cambridge University Press, 1997).

72 For an extensive study of Egyptian concerns over the health, hygiene, and vitality of the population during the monarchical period, see Shakry, "The Great Social Laboratory," part 3.

73 "Tadbir al-Manzil: al-Zawaj" (Household Management: Marriage), *Fatat al-sharq* 18, 1 (15 October 1923), 23.

74 Iliyas al-Ghadban, "Zawaj al-mu'aliyin wa hal min al-amkan mana'hu" (The Marriage of the Sick: Is it Possible to Prevent), *al-Ahram* 39 (31 March 1914), 2.

75 See article four as cited in "Qanun," 37. Likewise, if a husband were missing, the judge was obligated to report his absence to the Ministry of Justice, which would conduct a search for him that could last up to four years. See article seven as cited in "Qanun," 37. Although it is difficult to determine whether this actually occurred, absent husbands theoretically could not easily escape the vigilance of the modern state, as it would create a team to search for his whereabouts.

76 Jalal Husayn, "Qanun al-ahwal al-shakhsiya" (The Personal Status Law), *al-Ahram* 46 (29 June 1920), 2.

77 Amin, *The Liberation*, 99.

78 "Marsum," 204.

79 Ibid.; Hatem, "The Enduring Alliance," 27, 29.

80 Although the Hanafi school was the official legal school of Ottoman Egypt, as Amira Sonbol notes, other schools were implemented: "The fact that the different *madhahib* [schools] were honored by the system shows that there was greater legal and social elasticity than would later be the case following Egypt's legal reforms (beginning in 1897) when the Hanafi code was established as the main source of *shari'a* law. It also shows the greater independence enjoyed by

court judges before the reforms in determining legal findings." See Sonbol, "Adults," 238.

81 Sonbol, "Reforming," 97.

82 It was not until article 12 of Law no. 25 of 1929, however, that desertion in and of itself was presented as a wife's ground for divorce. It used the Maliki opinion to decree that if a husband is absent for one year or more without sufficient reason, such as study or business, his wife has the right to sue for an irrevocable divorce on the grounds of harm resulting from his unwarranted absence. It departed from the 1920 law in that it stated that a petition based on desertion can be initiated even if the husband has property from which the wife's maintenance can be obtained. If the husband can be reached, the *qadi* must inform him of the pending suit. The husband's failure to return or make arrangements for his wife to join him results in a decree of divorce. If contact with the husband proves impossible, the court must then grant the wife a divorce immediately (article 13). See "Marsum," 204–205.

83 Articles five and seven of Law no. 25 of 1920. See "Qanun," 37.

84 Article six of Law no. 25 of 1929. See "Qanun," 37.

85 Ibid. The divorce only would be issued if no information about the whereabouts of the missing husband surfaced during the four-year period. The judge also was obliged to report the missing husband to the Ministry of Justice, which would conduct a search for him.

86 Ibid.

87 'Abduh al-Barquqi, "al-Talaq" (Divorce), *Majallat al-mar'a al-misriya* ("The Egyptian Woman Magazine") 6 (June 1920), 193.

88 Ibid.

89 "Marsum," 205.

90 Muhammad Husayn Haykal, "Qanun al-talaq al-jadid: wa wajh al-khatr fihi" ("The New Divorce Law: And the Aspect of Danger Within It"), *al-Ahram* 46 (24 June 1920), 2.

91 Gershoni and Jankowski, *Redefining*, 41.

92 Haykal, 2.

93 'Abd al-Hamid Hamdi, "Qanun al-ahwal al-shakhsiya" (The Personal Status Law), *al-Ahram* 46 (29 June 1920), 2.

94 Ibid.

95 Shakry, "Schooled Mothers," 148.

96 Husayn, "Qanun," 2.

97 Al-Barquqi, "al-Talaq," 192–95.

98 "Marsum," 203.

99 Ibid., 208–10.

100 Badran, *Feminists*, 127.

101 A.F., "al-Firaq," *Majallat al-Mar'a al-Misriya* 5 (May 1920), 183–84.

102 Amin, *The Liberation*, 92.

103 "Marsum," 203.

104 Amin, *The Liberation*, 97.

105 Anderson, "Shari'a Law V," 287–88; Ziadeh, *Lawyers*, 126, fn. 52.

106 Fargues, "Terminating," 271–73. See also, Hamed Ammar, *Growing up in an Egyptian Village*, 2nd ed. (London: Routledge & Kegan Paul Ltd., 1966 [1954]), 199–200; Cuno, "Divorce," 1, 18–19; Hani Fakhouri, *Kafr El-Elow: An Egyptian Village in Transition* (New York: Holt, Rinehart and Winston, Inc., 1972), 72–73; Enid Hill, *Mahkama! Studies in the Egyptian Legal System* (London: Ithaca Press, 1979), 86; Andrea B. Rugh, *Family in Contemporary Egypt* (Syracuse: Syracuse University Press, 1984), 177; Shaham, *Family*, 101.

107 Cuno, "Divorce," 18; Fargues, "Terminating," 271.

108 Muhammad Farid Junaydi, ed., *Azmat al-zawaj fi Misr* ("The Marriage Crisis in Egypt") (Cairo: Hijazi, 1933), 56.

109 Ibid.

110 Doria Shafik, "Let Our Enemies Listen," *Bint al-Nil* (Daughter of the Nile) (June 1949) as cited in Cynthia Nelson, *Doria Shafik, Egyptian Feminist: A Woman Apart* (Gainesville: University Press of Florida, 1996), 153.

111 Nelson, *Doria Shafik*, 143–14.

112 A Muslim man's license to have up to four wives comes from two Qur'anic verses (4: 3 and 4: 129).

113 The idea that a bride could stipulate in her contract that she be granted a divorce if her husband married another woman was not an invention of these committee members. In his survey of marriage contracts in Ottoman Egypt, Abdal-Rehim Abdal-Rehim located contracts which stipulated the wife's right to an automatic divorce should the husband take another wife or a concubine. See Abdal-Rehim Abdal-Rahman Abdal-Rehim, "The Family and Gender Laws in Egypt During the Ottoman Period," in Sonbol, *Women*, 98–110. It should be noted, however, that because the majority of marriage contracts were not registered in colonial Egypt since they were not legally required, it is difficult to determine whether these cases served as the norm. In my own sample survey of 100 marriage contracts, I found none that included such stipulations. See *Qawa'im sijillat al-zawaj li-mahkamat al-Iskandiriya al-shar'iya* (Marriage Register of the Shari'a Court of Alexandria), no. 22, Serial no. 1–100 (2/2/1297–19/2/1321 H, 14/01/1880–17/05/1903 AD). Located in DWQ.

114 Anderson, "Shari'a Law III," 124; Badran, *Feminists*, 129–30; Esposito, *Women*, 57.

115 Fargues, "Terminating," 253. Both William J. Goode and Beth Baron, however, suggest that this statistic may not be accurate because they are based on the number of married women reported in the census as against the number of married men. See Baron, *The Women's Awakening*, 165; William J. Goode, *World Revolution and Family Patterns* (New York: The Free Press, 1963), 104.

116 Kenneth M. Cuno, "Joint Family Households and Rural Notables," *International Journal of Middle East Studies* 27, 4 (1995), 499, fn. 9.

117 Tucker, *Women*, 53.

118 Kenneth M. Cuno and Michael J. Reimer, "The Census Registers of Nineteenth-Century Egypt: A New Source for Social Historians," *British Journal of Middle Eastern Studies* 24, 2 (1997), 208.

119 Idem, "A Tale of Two Villages: Family, Property, and Economic Activity in Rural Egypt in the 1840s," in *Agriculture in Egypt From Pharaonic to Modern Times*, ed. Alan K. Bowman and Eugene Rogan (Oxford: Oxford University Press, 1999), 321.

120 Winifred S. Blackman, *The Fellahin of Upper Egypt: Their Religious, Social and Industrial Life with Special Reference to Survivals from Ancient Times* (London: Frank Cass & Co. Ltd., 1968 [1927]), 38.

121 Cooper, *The Women*, 220, 221.

122 Butcher, *Things Seen*, 37–38.

123 While travelers' accounts are problematic sources that can be used to highlight the different ways in which westerners represented the Other, they also contain rich, descriptive detail that can be extracted from the authoritarian and moralizing voice of the writer. For perspectives on using travel accounts as historical sources, see Edward Said, *Orientalism* (New York: Pantheon Books, 1978); Billie Melman, *Woman's Orients: English Women in the Middle East, 1718–1918: Sexuality, Religion and Work* (Ann Arbor: University of Michigan Press, 1992).

124 Fargues, "Terminating," 256.

125 Pollard, "Nurturing," 127–28.

126 Cromer, *Modern Egypt*, 2: 158.

127 Muhammad 'Abduh, "Hukum al-shari'iya fi ta'addud al-zawjat" (The Shari'a Rule on Polygamy), "Ta'addud al-zawjat" (Polygamy), "Fatwa fi ta'addud al-zawjat" (Religious Ruling on Polygamy) in *al-A'mal al-kamila li-Muhammad 'Abduh: al-kitabat al-ijtima'iya* (The Complete

Works of Muhammad 'Abduh: Social Writings), 3rd ed., ed. Muhammad 'Imara (Beirut: al-Mu'assasa al-'Arabiya li-l-Dirasat wa-l-Nashr, 1980 [1974]), 78–83; 84–89; 90–95, respectively; Amin, *The Liberation*, 82–87.

128 Baron, *The Women's Awakening*, 183–84.

129 Ahmad Safwat, *Bahth fi qa'idat islah qanun al-ahwal al-shakhsiya li-l-mahakim al-shar'iya: surat al-muhadara allati alqaha Ahmad Effendi Safwat* (A Study of Cases of Reform of the Personal Status Law in the Islamic Courts: A Copy of the Lectures Presented by Ahmad Effendi Safwat) (Alexandria: Matba'at Jurji Gharzuzi, 1917). According to Margot Badran and Farhat J. Ziadeh, Safwat's book elicited strong opposition. See Badran, *Feminists*, 129; Ziadeh, *Lawyers*, 118–22.

130 Ziadeh, *Lawyers*, 122–23.

131 Anderson, "Shari'a Law III," 124; Esposito, *Women*, 57.

132 Anderson, "Shari'a Law III," 125; Esposito, *Women*, 57–58.

133 During the first two decades of the twentieth century, women writers had begun to gently critique the institution of polygamy in the pages of the women's press. Rather than call for its direct abolition, however, these writers depicted the hardships women experienced as victims of polygamy. See, for example, Shajarat al-Durr, "al-Talaq wa ta'addud al-zawjat," (Divorce and Polygamy), *Anis al-jalis* (The Intimate Companion) 1, 7 (1898): 203–206; Zakiya al-Kafrawiya, "Ma wara' al-khudur" (What Lies Behind Women's Quarters), *al-'Afaf* (Virtue) 1, 19 (17 March 1911): 2; Malak Hifni Nasif, "Ta'addud al-zawjat" (Polygamy), in *al-Nisa'iyyat*, 76–79. Beth Baron also discusses the critiques of polygamy among writers during the 1910s. See Baron, *The Women's Awakening*, 113.

134 Badran, *Feminists*, 127.

135 See, for example, "Hors-texte" (Beyond the Text), *L'Égyptienne* (October 1931): 2; "La nouvelle loi sur le statut personnel musulman" (The New Law of the Muslim Personal Status), *L'Égyptienne* (March 1929): 22–37; "Ray al-ustadh al-akbar: radd muqtarahat al-sayyida al-fadila Munira Thabit" (The Opinion of Shaykh al-Azhar: The Reply Suggested by the Distinguished Munira Thabit), *al-Misriya* (1 January 1940): 7–9, "Ta'addud al-zawjat wa ray fadilat al-anisa Munira Thabit" (Polygamy and the Opinion of the Distinguished Munira Thabit) *al-Misriya* (1 March 1940): 5–7; Saiza Nabarawi, "Examen du nouveau projet du statut personnel musulman" (An Examination of the New Project on the Muslim Personal Status), *L'Égyptienne* (April 1927): 2–7; idem, "La polygamie trouve encore des défenseurs en Égypte!" (Polygamy Still Finds Defenders in Egypt!), *L'Égyptienne* (November 1935): 9–14; idem, "La situation juridique de la femme égyptienne: Conférence de Mademoiselle Ceza Nabarouy," (The Legal Situation of the Egyptian Woman: Ms. Saiza Nabarawi's Lecture) *L'Égyptienne* (February 1931), 6; Doria Shafik, "Hizb Bint al-Nil," (The Daughter of the Nile Party) *Bint al-Nil* (February 1949), as cited in Nelson, *Doria Shafiq*, 154, fn. 22

136 Badran, *Feminists*, 130.

137 "Une interview de Madame Hoda Charaoui" (An Interview with Madame Huda Sha'rawi), *L'Égyptienne* (April 1927), 11–14, as cited in Badran, *Feminists*, 128. For the original interview, see, "Rayy al-sayyida Huda Sha'rawi fi mashru' qanun al-zawaj wa al-talaq al-jadid" (The Opinion of Madame Huda Sha'rawi on the New Marriage and Divorce Draft Law," *al-Ahram* 53 (9 April 1927), 1.

138 Turkey had abolished polygamy in 1926 and Iran had restricted it in 1932. In Afghanistan after 1928, a government employee who took a second wife would lose his job. See Badran, *Feminists*, 129.

139 Nabarawi, "La polygamie," 10.

140 Baron, "The Making," 282.

141 Ibid., 283.

142 Ibid., 285.

143 Booth, *May Her Likes*, 207.

144 Ibid., xxix–xxx. As Marilyn Booth points out, Deniz Kandiyoti notes that the reformist Committee for Union and Progress in Turkey defined the monogamous nuclear family as the "National Family." See Deniz Kandiyoti, "Introduction," in idem, *Women, Islam, and the State* (Philadelphia: Temple University Press, 1991), 11.

145 Baron, "The Making," 287; Cuno, "Joint Family," 486; Shakry, "Schooled Mothers," 137, 164, fn. 59.

146 Anderson, "Shari'a Law III," 126.

147 It is worth noting that European observers, in contrast, claimed that when polygamy did occur, it was practiced among the lower classes in nineteenth- and early twentieth-century Egypt. See Cooper, *The Women*, 220, 221; Cromer, *Modern Egypt*, 2: 158; Lane, *An Account*, 184, 138, 180.

148 Ali, *Planning*, 24–28; Badran, *Feminists*, 129; Bier, "From Birth Control," 2–7; Nadav Safran, *Egypt in Search of a Political Community* (Cambridge: Harvard University Press, 1961), 196.

149 On King Fu'ad's ambitions to assume the Islamic caliphate, see Elie Kedourie, "Egypt and the Caliphate, 1915–52," in *The Chatham House Version and Other Middle Eastern Studies* (London: Weidenfeld and Nicolson, 1970), 177–212. For an alternative view of the king's aspirations, see Ralph M. Coury, "Who 'Invented' Egyptian Arab Nationalism?," 249–81 and 459–79.

150 Anderson, "Shari'a Law III," 125. Esposito also ties the king's refusal to support these proposals to the widespread acrimonious response in the press. See Esposito, *Women*, 58.

151 Anderson, "Shari'a Law III, 126; Esposito, *Women*, 58.

152 Coulson, *A History*, 207, 187–88; Hill, *Mahkama!*, 89.

153 Coulson, *A History*, 187–88.

154 Nelson, *Doria Shafik*, 147–49, 162.

155 In 1935, the *shaykh* of al-Azhar, Muhammad Mustafa al-Maraghi, wrote an article defending polygamy in one of Egypt's most popular social magazines, *Majallati* (My Review). See Nabarawi, "La polygamie," 10.

156 See "Rayy al-ustadh al-akbar," 7–9.

157 Alan Duben and Cem Behar, *Istanbul Households: Marriage, Family and Fertility, 1880–1940* (Cambridge: Cambridge University Press, 1991), 139–40.

158 Deniz Kandiyoti, "Gendering the Modern: On Missing Dimensions in the Study of Turkish Modernity," in *Rethinking Modernity and National Identity in Turkey*, ed. Sibel Bozdogan and Resat Kasaba (Seattle: University of Washington Press, 1997), 116–17.

Fig 1.1: The satirical journal *Kashkul* depicts the parliament as a classroom, with Zaghlul dressed in the effendi attire of suit and tarboosh lecturing an unruly 'class' of rural notables dressed in *gallabiya* and turban.

Fig. 5.1: "Muhammad 'Ali the Great cigarettes . . . With them, young people revive the memory of glory and greatness." One of many advertisements representing, as well as catering to, the effendis. Lotus advertising agency for Mahmud Fahmi cigarettes. *Al-Sarih* magazine, 18 May 1933.

Fig. 5.3: "Al-Rashidi al-Halawani family."
Advertising for sweet manufacturers,
representing three generations.
Al-Ithnayn magazine, issue 562,
19 March 1945.

Fig. 5.2: "And finally . . . !"
Al-Misri Effendi kicking the British
ambassador, Sir Miles Lampson,
in the rear. *Ruz al-Yusuf* magazine,
issue 852, 12 October 1944.

Fig: 5.4: Students embracing
each other on the occasion
of the restoration of the
Constitution. *Kull shay'
wa-l-dunya* magazine, issue
528, 'Students' special issue,
18 December 1935.

Fig. 5.5: "The most fabulous nationalist theft" *(Arwa' al-sariqat al-wataniya)*. Poster encapsulating the emerging cult of student martyrs following the 1935 wave of demonstrations. It represents students stealing the body of their dead fellow activist, shot on the previous day in a clash with the British, from the Qasr al-'Ayni Hospital mortuary for a 'national' burial. This event actually happened in November 1935. Poster distributed to the readers of *al-Musawwar* magazine soon afterward (n.d.).

IMPRESSIONS OF EGYPT, COLLECTION MAGED FARAG

Fig. 7.1: Vandalized vehicles in Downtown Cairo in the aftermath of the 26 January 1952 Cairo fire.

IMPRESSIONS OF EGYPT, COLLECTION MAGED FARAG

Fig. 7.2: Storefront devastation in al-Azhar in the aftermath of the 26 January 1952 Cairo fire.

AL-AHRAM ARCHIVES

Fig. 13.1: Raya and Sakina

Fig 13.2: "The Alexandria Crime (Raya and Sakina)." Raya, depicted as a beast, tells her victim, "There is no escape for you from my talons." *Al-Rashid* magazine, 9 December 1920, 291.

Fig. 15.1: Mahmud Mukhtar, *Egypt's Awakening*, 1928.

CAROLINE WILLIAMS

Fig. 15.2: Yusuf Kamil, *Darb al-Labana*, 1919.

Fig. 15.3: Raghib Ayad, *Waterwheel*, 1960.

Fig. 15.4: Raghib Ayad,
Mother and Son, 1962.

Fig. 15.5: Raghib Ayad, *Coffeehouse in
Aswan* (detail), 1933.

Fig. 15.6: Raghib Ayad,
The Monastery, 1936.

CAROLINE WILLIAMS

Fig. 15.7: Muhammad Naghi, *Karnak Temple*, 1914.

Fig. 15.9: Muhammad Naghi,
Shepherd Holding Sheep, 1925.

Fig. 15.8: Muhammad Naghi,
Self-Portrait, 1922.

COURTESY ESMAT DAOUSTASHI

Fig. 15.10: Muhammad Naghi, *The Pledge of Allegiance
to Muhammad 'Ali*, 1941.

SOBHI AL SHAROUNI

Fig. 15.11: Mahmud Said, *Self-Portrait*, 1919.

BOULOS ISHAK

Fig. 15.12: Mahmud Said, *Prayer*, 1934.

CAROLINE WILLIAMS

Fig. 15.13: Mahmud Said, *Life of the City*, 1937.

CAROLINE WILLIAMS

Fig. 15.14: Mahmud Said, *Expectant Maid*, n.d.

Fig. 15.15: 'Abd al-Hadi al-Gazzar, *Destiny*, 1949.

LILIANE KARNOUK

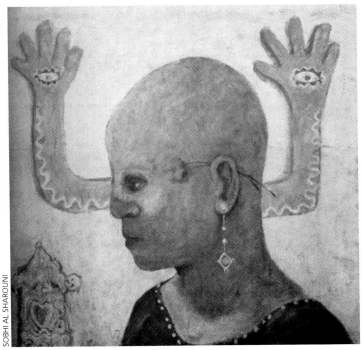

SOBHI AL SHAROUNI

Fig. 15.16: 'Abd al-Hadi al-Gazzar, *The Green Fool*, 1951.

Fig. 15.17: Hamid Nada, *Lamp of Gloom*, 1946.

LILIANE KARNOUK

CAROLINE WILLIAMS

Fig. 15.18: Hamid Nada, *Lady with Fish*, 1970s.

Fig. 15.19: Mahmud Said, *The Opening of the Suez Canal*, 1946.

Fig. 15.20: 'Abd al-Hadi al-Gazzar, *The Digging of the Suez Canal*, 1965.

12 Writing Women Medical Practitioners into the History of Modern Egypt

Nancy Gallagher

Women in Egypt entered the modern medical arena at a relatively early date when compared with women in other regions of the Middle East or North Africa—or for that matter in France or Britain. In the 1830s, women gained access to western-style medical education and graduates became *hakimat*, or women physicians, while the military ran Muhammad 'Ali's fledgling public health system. In the early twentieth century, elite women left their homes and utilized their educational and organizational skills to found clinics, hospitals, and vaccination and public relief programs. As Amy Johnson and Scott McIntosh show in chapter nine through the experiences of Aziza Hussein, women had come to spearhead such initiatives by the 1940s. These remarkable developments have fascinated scholars interested in gender in the history of Egypt. Scholars have, however, varied widely in their evaluations of the women's roles. This chapter discusses the many ways in which the women health workers have been and might be 'written' into a social history of modern Egypt.

The *Hakimat*

In 1832, Muhammad 'Ali established a school to train women health workers, or *hakimat*. When families proved reluctant to send their daughters to the school, the first class was recruited from among the lowest classes of women, who had little family protection. The students received four to six years of training in reading, obstetrics, postpartum hygiene, first aid skills, vaccination, and administration. Upon graduation, the women became officers in the military and were married to men of similar station. The *hakimat* worked in government sponsored immunization programs, gave primary medical care to women and children, registered births and deaths, examined rape victims, and gave testimony at court.

For many years, historians of contemporary Egypt relied on Naguib Bey Mahfouz's 1935 publication, *The History of Medical Education in Egypt*.[1] Mahfouz, who consulted government documents and interviewed government personnel for the book, described the first class:

> When Clot Bey founded the School of Medicine at Abou Zaabal in 1827, he realized the importance of having a maternity block attached to the hospital, as well as a school for midwives. He, however, soon discovered that the prejudices he had to overcome were immense. It was not possible to get pupil midwives to enter this school. To solve this difficulty the Government resorted to a measure that appears to us now as very queer. Ten Abyssinian and Sudanese girls were bought from the slave market and attached to the school, as well as two eunuchs from the Viceroy's palace at the Citadel. These formed the first batch of pupils. In 1835 ten more slaves were bought to bring the number up to twenty-two. The number was further increased by the addition of ten young orphan girls who were inmates of the Bimaristan and were sent to hospital for treatment. When cured they were not claimed by their relatives and the Government took them on as pupil midwives.[2]

Because of the difficulty in recruiting students, the Board of Schools would write to the authorities to ask the police to seize a girl twelve to thirteen years of age to complete the number of pupils. In 1845, the Board of Schools informed the police that a girl they seized was found on examination "not virgin" and too young, and was released. The board then demanded that the police seize another more suitable girl, who was a virgin.[3] According to Mahfouz, once the graduates of the Hakimat School began to work in private homes and found employment with aristocratic families, it became easier for the authorities to find prospective students. Most of the students were thereafter daughters of soldiers or orphans.[4] Mahfouz notes that the *hakimat* did not wear the veil. This could have reflected their low status or their newfound professional status

Mahfouz described the types of midwives:

A) The '*Dayah*' or ordinary midwife, who up till recently was an illiterate extremely ignorant woman who learned her profession from any practising midwife in her district. The government, after giving the candidates 2 weeks theoretical instruction followed by an absurd examination, used to give them permission to practise their profession. These formed the main bulk of the profession.
B) The *hakeema*, or graduate of the training school attached to Kasr el Ainy Hospital, who usually attends the middle class of the population.
C) Graduates of the Faculty of Medicine. These have little to do with normal labour but usually conduct difficult labour entailing the use of instruments when no specialists are available.[5]

Regarding Class B, he wrote, "This class comprises the graduates of the school of Midwives attached to the Faculty of Medicine. The curriculum of this school has been revised on more than one occasion with view of raising the standard of the pupils. Graduates for the School are now chosen from amongst the graduates of the Nursing School."[6] Little research has been done on the *hakimat* in the twentieth century, but the record suggests that by the 1930s they had become licensed midwives.

Mahfouz's narrative concerned medical education and did not attempt a feminist analysis of the *hakimat* or other women medical workers. In a 1974 article, LaVerne Kuhnke, a medical historian and professor emeritus, began what was to become a major discussion of women's roles in Egyptian history.[7] Scholars took note because the *hakimat* were among the few women professionals mentioned by name in the archival record of the nineteenth century. Kuhnke wrote that the school for *hakimat* marked an impressive early start for women's education in Egypt. She consulted the documents in the Egyptian state archives relating to the Hakimat School, Clot Bey's *Mémoires*, a historical article published in the *Egyptian Gazette*, and various secondary sources including Mahfouz.[8] Kuhnke argued, "[The school for *hakimat*] was the first government educational institution for women in the Middle East, and it was an unprecedented experiment in drawing into social service women who appeared to be more secluded from public activity than women in any other part of the world."[9] In contrast to the British and French medical systems where registration and licensing of educated male medical practitioners led to the discrediting of uneducated female midwives in Egypt, Kuhnke argued that Muhammad 'Ali's sponsorship of the school for *hakimat* elevated the long-time female profession of midwifery. While she stressed Muhammad 'Ali's initiative, Kuhnke is quite clear that the French physician, Clot Bey, introduced the idea of training women health officers to him. She noted that Muhammad 'Ali "could not escape the logic of Dr. Clot's (his French director of health services) argument that concern for future manpower resources required active promotion of maternal and infant health care by female personnel."[10]

Trained midwives would presumably avoid many of the medical mishaps that were limiting population growth in Egypt. Kuhnke stressed that the six years of medical school required for the *hakimat* would have been impressive anywhere in the world at that time. She also noted that the students were called *hakimat* or "female doctors" rather than the more customary term, *qabila* or *daya*, midwife, to indicate their elevated educational status. Kuhnke believed that the *hakimat* brought "trained and rational practice" to midwifery. She acknowledged, however, that although Clot wanted the *hakimat* to replace the "old-wives medicine" of the untrained *daya*s, few women sought the obstetric services of the *hakimat*, "as long as their school was located near the military hospital, the radius of their operations was limited to the few army-related women who might come to its small maternity care center."[11] When the school was transferred to the Civil Hospital, she argued that the *hakimat* made up both the budding public health establishment and the municipal smallpox immunization service. In the new immunization service the *hakimat* went into the private homes of the elite to vaccinate children against smallpox and in urban and rural areas vaccinated tens of thousands women and children. The *hakimat* were also posted to the quarantine service to examine women, to register births, and determine the cause of death of women in Cairo and then all of Egypt, and in general to facilitate the collection of vital statistics. For Kuhnke, collection of the mortality statistics was "a requisite for identifying endemic health problems and planning any program of preventive medicine."[12] She regretted that the school was unable to attract more than sixty students at a time. The students, often slaves, orphans, and the illegitimate, were drawn from the very lowest classes, but were given a military rank and married to military spouses.

According to Kuhnke, Suzanne Voilquin, a St. Simonian, was head of the Hakimat School.[13] In the nineteenth century, a series of utopian socialist movements gave women a platform for improving women's rights. The movement soon disintegrated in France but was partially reconstituted in Egypt where Muhammad 'Ali was thought to be building a new industrialized society. One of the Saint Simonians in Egypt was Suzanne Voilquin (1794–1876/77). Voilquin was separated from her husband and France offered little to a separated, but legally married woman. Voilquin joined the Saint Simonians in 1830 when she was thirty-four. She wrote in the Owenist journal, "The complete emancipation of women must be the fundamental principle . . . of the new social system we are laboring to establish."[14] Citing Guémard's *Réformes en Égypte*,[15] Kuhnke wrote that Voilquin died in the plague epidemic in 1835. Clot then recruited Palmyre Gault, a graduate of the midwifery program and the maternity hospital in Paris.

Guémard, however, actually stated that Clot Bey founded a maternity school under the direction of the "energetic and devoted Mme. Gault," who had arrived in Egypt in 1836 with her certificate and ten years of experience. Gault taught midwifery to many young women who were Abyssinian slaves. It was Gault who died of plague in old Cairo in 1840. In a footnote Guémard states that Voilquin had been her predecessor.[16] He referenced the 1866 edition of her memoirs, but apparently misread it.

In the 1866 edition of her memoirs, Suzanne Voilquin, who worked as a medical assistant to French physicians in Egyptian hospitals, described the school in one paragraph at the end of a section on women's lives:

Schools of medicine and veterinary medicine are established at Abu Zabel, a type of citadel situated four leagues from Cairo. There one instructs in a special section some young Abyssinian women in the art of accouchement. It is there that the young students pass exams in each school. Every year members of the council of health doctors of Cairo, and a dozen Muslim leaders are delegated to attend and check the improvement in studies. Finally to make the affair most solemn a number of guests are invited. After the ceremony of exams, a great meal is offered to the attendees by the general Clot-Bey, president of the Council of Health.[17]

Voilquin added that in July 1836, Clot Bey informed her that the construction of the hospital in which she had hoped to work had been postponed indefinitely.[18] He added that the aged director of the school for midwives in Abu Zabel, Mme. Féry, was retiring, but that Voilquin was not eligible for her position due to her lack of credentials. Instead, Mme. Gault had been hired. Disappointed, Voilquin resolved to return to France to continue her medical training there. She got letters of recommendation from Dr. Delong and Clot Bey that certified that she had followed a year of midwifery instruction in Egypt and proved to have much intelligence and aptitude.[19] She returned to France and was certified in Paris in 1837.[20] Voilquin was never director of the Hakimat School and the Saint Simonians, despite their great interest in women's health and medicine and their presence in Egypt, they had no direct influence on the school. In 1844, a Coptic male physician, Issawi al-Nahrawi, became director, followed by two graduates of the school, Tamruhan in 1858, and Arifa 'Umar in 1863.

Kuhnke was writing in a time when scholars sympathetic to Middle Eastern peoples attempted to demonstrate that the negative stereotypes of Muslim women were mistaken and that Muslim women were not the secluded and repressed figures widely portrayed in the popular press. She implied that Muhammad 'Ali was a skilled and brilliant modernizer whose reforms would have resulted in rapid political, social, economic, and military development had not the European powers intervened.

Kuhnke's article has been widely cited to demonstrate women's agency in early nineteenth-century Egypt. Women were not all ensconced in harems and some were playing a responsible role in the modern medical sector decades before their counterparts elsewhere. This interpretation has helped counter negative stereotypes common in the 1970s and has encouraged scholars anxious to demonstrate women's agency in Muslim societies to look further in the medical sphere.

Judith Tucker considered the institution of the *hakimat* a happy exception to a dismal state of affairs. Writing in 1985, she lamented Muhammad 'Ali's lack of interest in social welfare, but observed, "A notable exception [to limited state intervention in health care] lay in repeated official attempts to control and professionalize the occupation of midwife, a central activity in the community life of women."[21] After briefly describing the school, she commented that medical teams sent out during epidemics routinely included *hakimat*, and in the 1880s, of 142 physicians listed in state service, forty-three were women.[22] Graduates of the school, she argued, slowly lost professional status after the establishment of the Sanitary Service in 1884. Tucker took no position on the benefits of the introduction of rational "Western-style" medicine, but did consider the school and institution itself a "notable exception" to governmental shortcomings in the general area of social and public health services. Tucker relied primarily on French accounts and the British Public Record Office. She did not cite Kuhnke in her 1985 study.

In 1998, Tucker elaborated further on the Hakimat School: "the history of the government school for health officers *(hakimas)* illustrates the ambitions, and the limits of these forays into female education."[23] Now citing Kuhnke but adding her own interpretation, she argued that the state had taken the initiative in developing health care and education to improve maternal and child health with the long-term goal of combating under-population. Only women could gain admittance to the interior quarters of private homes in both urban and rural areas so the *hakimat* alone could introduce modern medical practices. For Tucker, the women were not agents of change. The state was the agent of change, the principal historical actor in nineteenth-century Egypt. To achieve its program of social reform the state had to train and mobilize women. Neither Muhammad 'Ali nor his successors carried out their reforms to benefit ordinary women, but rather to expand state power. For Tucker, the expansion of capitalist economic relations in Egypt undermined the existing socioeconomic structure to the disadvantage of ordinary women and men. In both of her accounts, she stressed the role of British colonial authorities in causing the decline of the Hakimat School: "Western disdain for paramedical personnel and the pro-motion of hospital-based curative medicine led to the devaluation of the *hakima* and the stillbirth of female professional training."[24] While Kuhnke emphasized women's unprecedented access to western medical training, Tucker focused on the role of western intervention in undermining it.

In a 1991 publication, Amira Sonbol argued that the medical needs of the army were being met even before Muhammad 'Ali's medical reforms and that he wanted to provide "missing services to the country as a whole."[25] She added, "when Clot Bey arrived in Egypt from Marseilles in 1825, the health services consisted of one army hospital located at Abu Zabal; the Maristan al-Mansuri, which had fallen into ruins."[26] The British discon-tinued the "School of Maternity" and encouraged the provinces to open schools for midwives and "the title 'hakima' gave way to 'daya' (midwife)."[27] In an endnote she lauded Kuhnke for "calling these ladies *hakimas*, which in Arabic is roughly equivalent to 'doctoresses.'" Kuhnke considered the name more fitting than 'midwives' because they not only were trained to perform the very particular task of childbirth on the most modern basis but were sent out to the villages to perform a large number of other med-ical tasks.[28] Citing Heyworth Dunne's 1938 *An Introduction to the History of Education in Modern Egypt*, Sonbol stated that four eunuchs became stu-dents in 1835. Heyworth Dunne actually stated that Muhammad 'Ali sent two eunuchs from the palace to accompany the first batch of girls to the Madrasat al-Wilada and added that the eunuchs were "also made to follow the course."[29] Heyworth Dunne cited Naguib Mahfouz.

The fact that eunuchs were included indicates the difficulty of finding recruits and their place in the gendered hierarchy of nineteenth century

Egypt. Like the Abyssinian and Sudanese slaves purchased for the project, the eunuchs were slaves and were entirely dependent on the state. They were considered un-gendered and, with access to women's quarters, were suitable candidates for the school.

Sonbol believed that "the School made the selection [of spouse] but it was up to the two concerned to agree or refuse."[30] The archival record, however, suggests that little agency in marriage selection was accorded to the *hakimat*. In general, Sonbol argued that the *hakimat* should be understood as one aspect of the professionalization of medicine in Egypt, her basic theme. For many decades, the *hakimat* were an integral part of the public health establishment.

Leila Ahmed, in her 1992 book, relied on Kuhnke's article and concluded that Muhammad 'Ali opened the School for "women doctors" to train medical practitioners who would have access to women. His motives were to control epidemic and endemic diseases to strengthen Egypt's labor force. For Ahmed, the important point was that the school's training, which stressed obstetrics, took the same length of time as the training at the School of Medicine, which was for men. She noted that the school had trouble recruiting enough students at first but that it was filled to capacity by 1846 and remained that way until the end of the century. She then emphasized Cromer's restrictions on women's education. Not only did he raise fees for public schools, but he also curtailed the purview of the Hakimat School. "Under the British, the School for Hakimas, which had given women as many years of medical training as the men received in the School of Medicine, was restricted to midwifery," because Cromer believed that "throughout the civilized world, attendance by medical men is still the rule."[31] Again following Kuhnke, she noted that Suzanne Voilquin was principal of the women's college for doctors.[32] For Leila Ahmed, who relied on Kuhnke's article and the Cromer papers cited in Tucker, the key point was that the British reversed the advances instituted by Muhammad 'Ali.

In contrast, Soheir Morsy, a medical anthropologist, argued in 1993 that Muhammad 'Ali's industrial development was underwritten by the labor of women and men and that the *hakimat* were trained to protect women's capacity to work.[33] Morsy's analysis centered on the role of women's labor in Muhammad 'Ali's industries and argued that the purpose of the *hakimat* school was to protect the health of adult women workers. She emphasized that while the state had intruded in women's lives long before the reign of Muhammad 'Ali it was now more direct.[34] Morsy focused on the development of a new wage labor working class and the central role played by women workers rather than on women's agency or on the role of western imperial interests. She relied exclusively on Kuhnke's study for her source material, but differed fundamentally in her interpretation.

In 1997, Mervat Hatem criticized the "canonized view" that the introduction of western medicine and public health institutions improved the status of women.[35] She argued that Muhammad 'Ali's medical and public health reforms were not only a means of expanding state control, but also a new way of controlling women. Hatem argued, "The modern medical discourse taught at the [*hakimat*] school was preoccupied with the inscription of new forms of power on women's bodies. The state was to play a new and important role in determining the uses of women's reproductive skills. . . . The result was domesticated femininity that glorified women's mothering functions at the same time that it denied them autonomy. In contrast, that same discourse glorified the sanctity of male bodies and their autonomy and used it to distinguish masculinity from femininity"[36] Employing a Foucauldian analysis, Hatem argued that the graduates of the school became agents of the state and were subject to "new relations of power, forms of consciousness, and types of authority that became the bases of the government of the self and of others."[37] The delivery of health care services revolved around the state's interest in surveillance, control, and discipline. Citing Basim Musallam's 1983 study,[38] she argued that the pre-modern indigenous medical discourse and practice gave women and men considerable individual freedom in matters of contraception and reproduction. Clot Bey, the French founder of the school, however, wanted to curtail this freedom. He complained that the *daya*s or midwives were highly skilled in giving "quick and effective abortions," and that they were "committed on a daily basis."[39] Neither the *daya*s nor the pregnant women thought abortion was a crime and there was no law against abortion, which was traditionally tolerated until the fourth month of pregnancy. Men and women made reproductive choices based on individual and family rather than state needs.

Hatem noted that the *daya*s, or traditional midwives, had contradictory functions, since they also carried out surgeries such as female circumcision that were intended to control women's reproductive capacities. The *hakimat* did not perform female circumcision but were to register births and deaths, which extended state control into new areas. Hatem developed an argument launched by Tim Mitchell in 1988.[40] Mitchell argued that in the late nineteenth century the British authorities had greatly expanded the registration of births in urban and rural areas of Egypt in order to facilitate recruitment into the army and to supervise and control local affairs. A common aspect of modern public health and medicine, the collection of birth and death statistics, became an important means of social control. It was also an important tool of public health workers who could track outbreaks of disease, epidemics, and morbidity and mortality rates. Hatem pointed out that well before the British instituted their reforms, Muhammad 'Ali and his successors had relied on the *hakimat* to report on abortions, which had recently been made illegal, enabling the state to prosecute the *daya*s for murder. In doing so, the state consciously "created" a new domesticated femininity based on the sanctity of motherhood.[41] Hatem showed that Clot Bey thought that abortion was a crime and a sin and that humanity would come to an end should women be allowed access to it. According to Hatem, Clot accordingly established the school for *hakimat*, mainly to educate midwives who would not perform abortions.

Clot Bey considered female circumcision to be a misguided but harmless pre-Islamic custom that had survived to the present, but thought that castration was violation of the laws of nature and morality and lowered a man's social standing and autonomy. The thrust of Hatem's argument is that women lost rather than gained control over their lives through the introduction of the *hakimat*'s services. Women lost their informal access to abortion, they found their familiar medical practices devalued, and they found their failure to register births and deaths penalized and their reliance on *daya*s, rather than *hakimat*, criminalized. Hatem argued that "the new midwives," her term for the *hakimat*, were to spread the new western style morality, which enabled the state to govern the bodies and souls of other women. Middle-class professional women were given the task of policing working-class *daya*s and their middle-and working-class women clients.[42] The modern health profession considered the indigenous medical practice to be inferior. Relying on *daya*s and other indigenous practitioners accordingly became for many women a means of rebellion against the oppressive modern nation-state. Hatem relied on Kuhnke, but reinterpreted the role of the *hakimat*. She did not address the vaccination or other public health programs carried out by the *hakimat*, but focused on their role in policing abortion. Hatem did not consider the *hakimat* to be positive examples of women's agency, the negative role of western interests in women's lives, or of the importance of women in the working class. They were examples of Muhammad 'Ali's government intruding into women's private lives in new and harmful ways.

In 1998, Khalid Fahmy argued that Muhammad ʿAli was neither trying to spread modern education to Egyptian women, to increase the population through better maternity care, nor to expand state control over women's bodies.[43] Fahmy argued instead that the spread of syphilis and smallpox in the military motivated Muhammad ʿAli to establish the school. Syphilis was running rampant in the standing army, and he wanted trained women to report on prostitutes who might have the disease. He needed women to vaccinate the masses against smallpox because men did not have access to private homes. Smallpox was not only decimating his army but also causing high infant mortality thereby limiting the size of the future army. In addition, Muhammad ʿAli, on the advice of Clot Bey, believed that untrained *dayas* were causing stillbirths. Hence, the *hakimat* were trained to report on the *dayas* who were outside government control. They also were trained to perform postmortem exams of female corpses, and to examine women in rape cases. The *hakimat* were investigators for the police and state agents. When they had to examine women in rape cases and testify at court they were serving the state, which was "beginning to police female 'decency' and sexuality, taking over these functions from fathers, brothers, and families."[44] Thus the state was expanding its role in controlling women's sexuality through the *hakimat* institution. This of course may have been beneficial for at least some women whose lives had been controlled by the male members of their families. Fahmy concluded that despite the rigid control of the state, which forced the *hakimat* to marry fellow officers selected for them, the women were able to gain some agency of their own by maneuvering within the system. The school enabled its students to leave behind their very low status and to become educated and employed. He emphasized that the *hakimat* occupied a controversial social position. Like Kuhnke, Fahmy focused on women's agency, finding that women could take steps to improve their lives in a society that gave them limited options.

Writing in 2002, Kamran Asdar ʿAli relied on Morsy to report that the *hakimat* were recruited and trained from the times of Muhammad ʿAli Pasha in the basics of public health, surgical skills, gynecology, and obstetrics to serve the female population of Egypt. He stresses that by the end of the nineteenth century, the *hakimat* were allowed only to practice midwifery and were being rapidly replaced by European nurses and male medical doctors. For Asdar ʿAli, and Leila Ahmed, the key point is that the British authorities marginalized the *hakimat* to monopolize the medical profession themselves.[45]

Terminology

The terminology used by our series of scholars is of course significant. Kuhnke titled her influential article, "doctoress on a donkey." In her book, this became "women health officers." Tucker considered the term *hakimat* their "professional title," but preferred the term "official midwives" thereby stressing their role in midwifery and downplaying their role in immunization programs, the quarantine service, and police work. Morsy used the term *hakimat* and also called them "middle-class professionals," which served to elevate their status. Hatem avoided the term *hakimat* altogether. To her they were the "new midwives" or "professional midwives," which left them with diminished social status. Fahmy used the term *hakimat*, a respectful term which not only preserved the Arabic used in the Egyptian state archival sources, but also fit with his argument that their education gave them a degree of agency. Whether they were doctors, midwives, or public health nurses, it depends on the interpretation of the historian, the sources, and the translation of terms. If the historian is impressed with the women, she or he uses the term, *hakimat*, or "women health officers." If not, "midwives" is used. Our second group of women agents in the field of public health and medicine were, unlike the *hakimat*, volunteers from the most elite levels of society.

Women Volunteers

In a 1978 article, Afaf Lutfi al-Sayyid Marsot stated that "the history of the Middle East abounds in stereotypes and clichés nowhere more abundantly than in the realm of women's studies."[46] To counter the stereotypes and clichés, she focused on the royal princesses and elite women who established the Muhammad 'Ali the Great Philanthropic Association (Mabarrat Muhammad 'Ali al-Kabir) in 1908. The women began by sponsoring a small clinic in 'Abdin and within decades maintained twelve hospitals and eighteen dispensaries that served millions of patients. They held massive fundraisers and encouraged both elite and ordinary people to support their efforts. They did not work as doctors or nurses, but rather as fundraisers, founders, and hospital administrators. In the 1940s, during epidemics of malaria and cholera, the women left their homes to bring emergency relief services to the poor. For Marsot,

> The [Association] was successful as an organization because it was efficient. The members gave not only of their money, but also of their time. A committee of members who daily inspected the wards and

the kitchen and heard any complaints from the patients supervised every hospital and clinic. Yet these women were under no compulsion to volunteer their time, except an inner one. Perhaps they were sublimating their energies into constructive work when they were unable to join in other public activities; perhaps they had more of a social conscience and felt that it was not enough to give money. . . .[47]

Thus, the Association women exemplified the admirable qualities of dedication, initiative, organizational ability, and leadership skills. Muslim women had long contributed to charitable causes and had through their representatives endowed religious and other organizations, but now the women themselves were working in public. This would have been unlikely in the early nineteenth century, but in the early twentieth century, customs had changed. Women were educated at home or in foreign, often missionary run schools, and were finding more choices in life.

In contrast, in 1980 Nawal El Saadawi, the physician, writer, and activist, denounced the charitable nature of and the close involvement of the palace in the women's activities. She wrote,

The movement was not representative of the overwhelming majority of toiling women, and its leadership ended, just as the political leadership did, by seeking accommodations with the British, the palace and the reactionary forces in the country. The women's movement therefore became a pawn utilized to serve the interests of the palace and the reactionary parties. It kept away from active involvement in national and political life of the country and limited its activities to charitable and social welfare work.[48]

For El Saadawi, the Mabarra women were dispensing charity rather than working to reform the political and economic injustices of Egypt. They were seeking to maintain the system and to reinforce their privileged status. As such, they were not positive examples of women's agency in the Muslim world. El Saadawi did not make an extended study of the volunteer women but her views were influential.

Another important factor was the political impact of the volunteer women. Because the women were closely associated with the palace, the anti-palace Wafd's newspapers scarcely covered their activities; they were seen as "ladies playing." Journalist Ishan 'Abd al-Quddus complained that not epidemics but the elite class was the real scourge of Egypt, and that the number of women volunteers was very small compared with the need. In reality, he thought, society had to be remade from its foundations up. The pro-palace and foreign newspapers lauded the women volunteers, which served to underscore the deficiencies of the Wafd government in dealing with its public health emergencies. It was argued,

> The missions were unprecedented because, while neither visiting nurses nor women philanthropists were a new phenomenon in Egypt, neither customarily traveled long distances to establish and administer large-scale relief programs by themselves. The *hakimas* had worked for the government health service under the direction of government officials. Women philanthropists before the twentieth century had usually carried out their charitable work from within their homes with the assistance of male intermediaries, who represented them in official arrangements. . . . During the malaria epidemic, the women of the Mabarra and the Red Crescent traveled independently of their families to organize their own large-scale relief programs and sought to draw attention to their efforts to gain public support.[49]

Yet, while the women demonstrated considerable agency, they were primarily interested in charitable service and not in social reforms that might have curtailed their privileged status. The volunteers were modern women who advocated medical care in the clinic, rather than at home, and who supported the new forms of social control and wanted to play a role in public life. Scholars have yet to apply a Foucauldian or post-colonial analysis to the volunteer women and their activities.

Relying on Marsot, Leila Ahmed (1992) stated, "Among the organizations that upper class women instituted and ran were some that played a critical role of the medical services of the nation. The Mabarrat [Association of] Muhammad 'Ali, for example, launched by two princesses in 1908, provided clinics, hospitals, and dispensaries."[50] Ahmed was impressed that the Mabarra institutions treated over 13 million patients over a twenty-one year period, before the nationalization of its hospitals in 1964.

In 1995, Margot Badran focused on the motivations and educational backgrounds of the elite women activists. She argued that the women of Mabarrat Muhammad 'Ali were motivated by the Muslim practice of caring for the poor, and by their exposure to European notions of charitable service through study at the Mère de Dieu School or private lessons with

European women tutors. While Marsot had emphasized the major role of the princesses in founding Mabarrat Muhammad 'Ali, Badran emphasized the role of feminist women.

> It was women who extricated social service from the exclusive hold of religious [or religious affiliated] institutions in Egypt when they created the first secular philanthropic societies and other non-religiously connected social service projects. Huda Sha'rawi, the founder of the Egyptian Feminist Union, and other Egyptian women formed the Mabarra Muhammad 'Ali, creating a dispensary for poor women and children. The immediate impetus was the alarming infant mortality rate reported the year before, but there was also a nationalist impetus. Earlier, British women had created the Lady Cromer Society, which operated a foundling home and dispensary for poor women and children. Several upper-class Egyptian women had joined the society including Iqbal Hanim, Huda Sha'rawi's mother, but Sha'rawi herself consciously refused for nationalist reasons to affiliate herself with colonial philanthropy.[51]

Badran argued that the secular philanthropic organization removed social assistance from a religious context and brought it into the civic and national sphere. While some volunteers focused only on providing charitable services, others hoped their work would assist lower-class women in gaining their rights. Many working class women found employment in the Mabarra hospitals and clinics, and over time voluntary work in the hospitals and clinics became an accepted activity for women of the upper class.[52] The Mabarra hospitals and clinics may well have employed *hakimat*, but the hospital records remain unexplored. For Badran, the women were agents of Egyptian change. Their activities in the medical and public health sphere encouraged the government to form a Ministry of Social Affairs.[53] Their hospitals and clinics came under the supervision of the new ministry, but remained without government funding. This lack of funding both forced and enabled women to continue to run the facilities as before.[54]

As primary sources, historians of the women's voluntary associations used newspaper articles, brochures put out by the associations, diaries, personal papers and photographs, memoirs, interviews with the women themselves and with their acquaintances and relatives, and to a limited extent parliamentary records and Ministry of Health archives. Once again, terminology is telling. In discussions centering on the Mabarra volunteers,

Marsot referred to the organizations as "so-called charitable organizations" which, she suggested, were really "large-scale social services." The volunteers themselves were "revolutionary gentlewomen." While some were of the dreaded "lady bountiful" sort, others were "social activists."[55] Marsot focused on one central figure, Hidiya Hanim Barakat, to demonstrate the strong and selfless commitment of at least some of the women. By contrast, Saadawi dismissed the women's activities as "charity" and fundamentally reactionary. For Badran, the volunteers were part of the women's movement and in some cases active feminists. However, the volunteer women may have been motivated primarily by their desire to serve. Perhaps it would be better to state that they defined their motives as service, but served the interests of the palace—and therefore those of their families and themselves. Because of their social position, they had access to the highest levels of government and garnered considerable publicity. A few of the women, unlike any of the *hakimat*, became prominent feminist activists.[56]

Conclusion

How should we sort out the conflicting historical assessments of the *hakimat* and Mabarra volunteers? In the 1970s, when the international women's movement was gaining ground, many scholars looked for indigenous and women's agency and for progressive social movements in Muslim societies. For scholars writing in the 1970s, the *hakimat* school was primarily an example of a genuine advance for Egyptian women. Nothing like it was to be found in other Muslim or European societies. The *hakimat* school was therefore of great importance in the history of Egyptian educational and public health services. In the late 1970s and into the 1980s, many scholars took a political economy approach and focused on the impact of the expanding world market on non-western societies. Its proponents were disenchanted with the modernization theorists who stressed the benefits of westernization and argued instead that the political and economic changes of the nineteenth century were generally harmful to ordinary women and men. The *hakimat* school was at best a partial exception to the rule. Still others, aware of the importance of the working class in social reforms, were interested to highlight the importance of the *hakimat* in strengthening the women workers though their medical and public health services. In the later 1980s, Foucauldian theories became influential and Muhammad 'Ali's medical reforms in general and the *hakimat* school in particular became a means of expanding state control. The expansion of state control was harmful to women's interests because it resulted in limiting their customary reproductive choice. The *hakimat* were agents of state control, not individuals furthering their own interests. Most recently scholars have focused on Muhammad 'Ali's motivations in controlling epidemic disease and have argued that though occupying a low social position, *hakimat* managed to benefit from their education by maneuvering into a space for themselves within the system.

Scholars have generally taken the Mabarra women volunteers to be proof that Egyptian women, when given the opportunity, had the initiative and skills to make a significant contribution to public life. Others have argued that they were giving charity to avoid confronting the kind of fundamental social and political reform that might curtail their families' wealth and power. Still others have focused on the women as influential agents of social change who, by leaving their homes to carry out large-scale public health campaigns and projects, became the standard for other women to follow. They have been seen as princesses and other royal or pro-palace women demonstrating the largesse of the palace in contrast to the secular Wafd government. They have been seen as feminists engaging in social services, a key part of the women's movement. A Foucauldian analysis could also be extended to the Mabarra volunteers who were used as agents of state control by the palace and its allies.

It appears that scholars have moved from positivist, to political economic, feminist, postmodern and postcolonial explanations, and now back to positivist interpretations. Quite importantly, then, scholars need to reflect more carefully on the contexts in which they write, their analytical frameworks, their choices of terms, and their purposes. Can scholars move from demonstrating women's agency to incorporating a gendered analysis of the role of women medical and public health workers in the 'mainstream' history of modern Egypt? Do historians engage with these actors for their own pedagogical and ideological needs? To borrow a contemporary quip, do scholars 'just add women and stir,' or can they fit them into a gendered history of the modern Middle East? If so, are scholars celebrating women's agency; working class struggles; Muhammad 'Ali's reforms; Muhammad 'Ali's, the British authorities', or the Free Officers' expansion of state control; or the detrimental effects of the centralizing state in general? Are scholars constructing an imagined community of women medical workers with little historical importance? If women's agency is the issue, were the reforms an advance for women?

A social history of the women medical practitioners before and during the constitutional monarchy era will have to begin with a careful comparison of both the primary and secondary historical source materials, taking into consideration who wrote them, for whom, and to what ends. Clearly both the *hakimat* and the Mabarra women could maneuver some space to expand their choices and opportunities in public and perhaps private life, though in very different historical contexts. Yet the *hakimat* and the Mabarra women were indeed furthering state interests or the interests of factions within government. The *hakimat* were recruited from the lowest classes of nineteenth-century Egyptian society, while the Mabarra women were self-selected and from the elite classes of twentieth-century Egypt. The *hakimat* were manumitted Abyssinian and Sudanese slaves, lower class daughters of the Egyptian military, orphans, and even eunuchs. The women volunteers were from wealthy families, mostly Muslim, but also Christian and Jewish, with access to education and often travel to Europe. The *hakimat* or their daughters were all birthright or converted Muslims from poor families or without families. They did not become feminists or write memoirs. They remained at the lower ranks of society and there are no photographs or portraits, newspaper articles, memoirs, diaries, personal papers, or oral histories to consult. No descendants have come to the attention of scholars. Because the school and its graduates were under the direct control of the state and testified at court, the archives and court records are far richer than for the volunteers. The women volunteers or their daughters and granddaughters, however, had access to the media and to scholars. Social class was far more important than either religion or state in determining the agency of both groups of women in their public health activities and in their ability to shape the historical record.

Notes

1   Naguib Bey Mahfouz, *The History of Medical Education in Egypt* (Cairo: Government Press, Bulaq, 1935).
2   Mahfouz, 71.
3   Ibid., 72. Mahfouz cites government document #2081.
4   Ibid. In one instance, a place was sought for an orphan French girl whose parents were killed in the plague epidemic. See Suzanne Voilquin, *Souvenirs d'une fille du peuple: ou, La saint-simonienne en Égypte* (Paris: F. Maspero, 1978).
5   Mahfouz, 85.
6   Ibid., 36.
7   LaVerne Kuhnke, "The 'Doctoress' on a Donkey: Women Health Officers in Nineteenth Century Egypt," *Clio Medica*, 1: 3, 193–205. The revised article became a chapter in her book, "Women Health Officers," *Lives at Risk: Public Health in Nineteenth-Century Egypt* (Berkeley: University of California Press, 1990), 122–33.

8   Ibid., 121.

9   Ibid., 122.

10 Ibid.

11 Ibid., 130.

12 Ibid., 132.

13 Ibid., 219, n. 23.

14 Linda Anne Kelly Alkana, "Suzanne Voilquin, Feminist and Saint-Simonian" (Ph.D. diss., University of California at Irvine, 1985), 152.

15 Gabriel Guémard. *Les réformes en Égypte d'Ali-bey el kébir à Méhémet-Ali, 1760–1848* (Cairo: P. Barbey, 1936), 233.

16 Ibid.

17 Voilquin, 355.

18 Ibid., 378.

19 Ibid., 378–79

20 Ibid., 395.

21 Judith E. Tucker, *Women in Nineteenth-Century Egypt* (New York: Cambridge University Press, 1985), 120.

22 Ibid., 121.

23 Guity Nashat and Judith E. Tucker, *Women in the Middle East and North Africa: Restoring Women to History* (Bloomington: Indiana University Press, 1998), 82.

24 Ibid.

25 Amira El Azhary Sonbol, *The Creation of a Medical Profession in Egypt, 1800–1922* (Syracuse: Syracuse University Press, 1991), 34.

26 Sonbol, 35.

27 Sonbol, 129–30.

28 Sonbol, 156, n7.

29 J. Heyworth-Dunne, *An Introduction to the History of Education in Modern Egypt* (London: Luzac, 1939), 132.

30 Sonbol, 47.

31 Leila Ahmed, *Women and Gender in Islam: Historical Roots of a Modern Debate* (New Haven: Yale University Press, 1992), 134, 143, 153.

32 Ibid., 123.

33 Soheir Morsy, *Gender, Sickness, and Healing in Rural Egypt: Ethnography in Historical Context (Conflict and Social Change)* (Boulder: Westview Press, 1993).

34 Ibid., 16.

35 Mervat Hatem, "The Professionalization of Health and the Control of Women's Bodies as Modern Governmentalities in Nineteenth-Century Egypt," in Madeleine Zilfi, ed., *Women in the Ottoman Empire: Middle Eastern Women in the Early Modern Era* (Leiden: E.J. Brill, 1997), 66–80.

36 Ibid., 67.

37 Ibid., 69.

38 B.F. Musallam, *Sex and Society in Islam* (New York: Cambridge University Press, 1983).

39 Hatem, 70.

40 Timothy Mitchell, *Colonising Egypt* (New York; Cambridge University Press, 1988).

41 Hatem, 75.

42 Ibid., 79.

43 Khalid Fahmy, "Women, Medicine, and Power in Nineteenth-Century Egypt," in Lila Abu-Lughod, ed., *Remaking Women: Feminism and Modernity in the Middle East* Princeton: Princeton University Press), 35–72.

44 Ibid., 61.

45 Kamran Asdar Ali, "Creating Bodies, Organizing Selves," in Cynthia Nelson and Shanhaz Rouse, eds., *Situating Globalization* (Bielefeld: Transcript Verlag, 2001), 241.

46 Afaf Lutfi al-Sayyid Marsot, "The Revolutionary Gentlewomen in Egypt," in Lois Beck and Nikki Keddie, eds., *Women in the Muslim World* (Cambridge: Harvard University Press, 1978), 261.

47 Ibid., 274.

48 Nawal El Saadawi, *The Hidden Face of Eve* (London: Zed Press, 1980), 176.

49 Nancy Gallagher, *Egypt's Other Wars: Epidemics and the Politics of Public Health* (Syracuse: Syracuse University Press, 1990), 53.

50 Leila Ahmed, *Women and Gender in Islam*, 173.

51 Margot Badran, *Islam, and the Nation: Gender and the Making of Modern Egypt* (Princeton: Princeton University Press, 1995), 50.

52 Ibid., 116–17.

53 For the emergence of the Ministry of Social Affairs, see Amy J. Johnson, *Reconstructing Rural Egypt: Ahmed Hussein and the History of Egyptian Development* (Syracuse: Syracuse University Press, 2004).

54 Margot Badran, *Islam, and the Nation*, 122–23.

55 Afaf Lutfi al-Sayyid-Marsot, "The Revolutionary Gentlewomen in Egypt," 261.

56 Gallagher, 54.

13   Madams, Murders, and the Media

Akhbar al-Hawadith and the Emergence of a Mass Culture in 1920s Egypt[1]

Shaun T. Lopez

It is nearly impossible to find an Egyptian who has never heard of Raya and Sakina. Any taxi driver, businessman, or schoolchild above the age of twelve can recall at least something about these two sisters, executed in December of 1921 for the murder of seventeen women in Alexandria. Mothers who want their children to return home at a decent hour warn them to come home "before Raya and Sakina get you." Others who suspect shady dealings in their neighborhood might describe those dealings as "doing Raya and Sakina" *(bi-ya'milu Raya wa Sakina)*.[2] Thanks largely to the infamy of the sisters, the very names themselves have fallen out of favor with Egyptian parents. Thanks in part to at least three motion pictures and a theatrical version that millions of Egyptians have seen on television or video, Raya and Sakina remain the most infamous criminals in modern Egyptian history, and a ubiquitous part of Egyptian popular culture (fig. 13.1).

This chapter tells the story of the 1920 Alexandria serial murders, known to most as the 'Raya and Sakina' murders, and argues that they played an important role in constructing the notion of an Egyptian national culture in 1920s. The discovery of seventeen bodies buried under the floors of houses in Alexandria's al-Liban neighborhood engendered the first major media sensation in modern Egyptian history, and literally hundreds, if not thousands, of articles related to the case appeared in the press in the months after the discovery of the first bodies. Commentators

371

writing in the wake of the murders characterized Egypt as being in the throes of a "moral crisis" and offered both blame and possible solutions to stem the erosion of so-called "Egyptian values." The primacy of the "woman question" in both British colonial discourse and Egyptian nationalist formulations made a case involving women as both perpetrators and victims of a heinous crime relevant not only on a local level, but on a national level as well. After the murders, commentators thus formulated an Egyptian cultural identity based on a unitary, national notion of moral behavior. Examples of immorality, drawn from the lives of those involved in the murders, thus became symbolic of the negative impact of Europe on Egyptian society, and of the need to formulate a modernity that respected the cultural practices of the Egyptian nation.

As for the myriad articles linking the Raya and Sakina murders with the political and cultural agendas of the Egyptian nation, whom did they influence? This chapter will demonstrate that the exponential expansion of the Egyptian press after 1918, and changes in the form and content of these publications, had important implications for the development of something resembling a mass culture in modern Egypt. Most previous studies of the period between 1919 and 1952 have assumed that the ideas and actions of Egypt's subaltern masses are neither recoverable nor relevant to the construction of identity, the production of gender, or the other currents that have dominated historiography of the period. Important works about the period, such as Margot Badran's *Feminism, Islam and Nation* or Israel Gershoni and James Jankowski's *Egypt, Islam and the Arabs* concentrate almost exclusively on discourses drawn from Egypt's small elite class. Although elite and middle class Egyptians were the intended consumers of Egypt's daily, weekly, and monthly press, crime coverage *(akhbar al-hawadith)* transformed local matters involving Egyptians from all classes, religions, and genders into matters of public or national concern. Individual tales of immoral lives made public by this new mass medium thus became *shared experiences* among those who consumed the press. Commentators and politicians thus often referenced the lives of Raya, Sakina, and their victims as they constructed their versions of what Egyptian identity should be, and thus played an important part in the formation of elite discourses about Egyptian identity and gender.

More importantly, however, this chapter will demonstrate that the *experiencing* of these events through the press was not limited to Egypt's literate elite. Lower-class Egyptians were not only the objects of articles written in the wake of the most sensational *hawadith*, but in certain cases also consumed them. Through public readings, channels of gossip, and photographic evidence, the Egyptian masses were both aware of and influenced by stories written in the wake of the Raya and Sakina murders. These stories also engendered concerns about a moral crisis among lower-class Egyptians. The latters' reactions to the case suggest that ideas about a national moral order helped form the basis for a truly mass culture in modern Egypt.

This chapter begins with a brief history of the development of the press in Egypt, its role in imagining a politically and culturally distinct notion of Egypt into being, and the role of women in the elite discourses of Egyptian politicians and intellectuals. It then moves to the Raya and Sakina murders and considers how the case both contributed to and was representative of a new mass culture in modern Egypt based on notions of acceptable public behavior.

The Press and the Nation

Despite the case's sensational nature, it was not a foregone conclusion that the 1920 Alexandria murders would receive widespread media attention. Although the first modern newspapers appeared in Egypt in the 1870s, crime coverage did not generally occupy a significant portion of the newspaper prior to World War I. For example, from its inception in 1876, Egypt's first and most important privately owned newspaper, *al-Ahram*, generally focused its coverage on matters of national and international importance. Crime appears to have been considered a local rather than national concern, and as such was simply not deemed important enough to warrant much attention in the nascent press. Prioritizing matters of national or international importance over local matters was perhaps in part due to Egypt's low literacy rates during the nineteenth century, as newspapers targeted those Egyptians mostly drawn from the upper class who could read. Although literacy rates went up from 1–2 percent in 1800 to 7 percent by 1897, readers were still drawn almost exclusively from the upper classes and were overwhelmingly urban. Cole estimates readership of Egyptian newspapers at 75,000 nationwide in 1880, not counting the considerable coffeehouse audience whose reception of the newspaper was through its public, rather than individual, reading.[3] While this is not an insignificant number, the limited dissemination of the newspaper necessarily limited its utility in creating something resembling a mass culture based on matters of common concern.

The 1882 arrival of British troops in Egypt hastened the beginning of forty years of outright occupation.[4] Although the British colonial administration in Egypt did monitor and at times censor articles from the Egyptian press critical of their rule, the number of newspapers and magazines published in Egypt continued to grow during the colonial period.[5] By the turn of the century, large daily publications such as *al-Ahram* had been joined by weekly and monthly publications of varying types and perspectives. Legal, religious, and economic journals were increasingly available to Egypt's literate population, hastening the development of what Benedict Anderson has called a print culture.[6] Very little has been written about Egyptian print culture at the turn of the century, with the notable exceptions of Ami Ayalon's *The Press in the Arab Middle East*, Beth Baron's *The Women's Awakening in Egypt: Culture, Society, and the Press*, and Marilyn Booth's *May Her Likes Be Multiplied: Biography and Gender Politics in Egypt*. Ayalon, for example, notes that the 1890s saw the publication of upwards of ninety newspapers and magazines in Cairo alone, although most of them disappeared as quickly as they began. He also notes that cultural, scientific, and religious journals joined the political press in this period.[7] Baron and Booth both focus on women's journals as conduct literature—writings designed to educate their small, elite, and middle-class female readership about how to properly perform their roles as good wives and mothers. Both argue that these journals were central to the creation of a community of elite women, and as such formed the basis for the feminist movement that emerged in the 1920s and 1930s.[8]

Rising resentment against the British occupation in the early years of the twentieth century manifested itself in a number of ways, not least in the political re-orientation of many newspapers and magazines. Mustafa Kamil's Nationalist Party, al-Hizb al-Watani, and Ahmad Lutfi al-Sayyid's Party of the Nation, Hizb al-Umma, were two of several new political groupings committed to pursuing Egyptian independence, either within the framework of Egyptian territorial nationalism or as part of the Ottoman Empire. During the years between 1906 and 1914, Egypt's newspapers and magazines were joined by a lively partisan press, with the two most prominent examples being *al-Jarida*, published by al-Sayyid's party, and *al-Liwa'*, the official paper of Kamil's party.[9] The press clearly played an important part in the dissemination of early nationalists' conceptualization of Egypt's future. A culturally distinct and politically viable Egypt thus was, by World War I, a topic of great discussion and imagination in the press every day.[10]

On the eve of the war, the press still had its limitations. It remained primarily the domain of urban Egyptian elites and intellectuals by virtue of the fact that they alone possessed the literacy to read it. Moreover, the

Egyptian press continued to focus on matters of national and international concern, or related to elite life in Egypt, at the expense of the local matters that were more likely to impact the lives of 'ordinary' Egyptians. The growth of Egyptian newspapers in terms of both number and circulation may have created the beginnings of what might be called a 'print culture,' but it excluded both the vast majority of Egyptians and the day-to-day concerns that were likely to have dominated their lives.

World War I and the Rise of a Mass Medium

World War I had important implications for Egyptians on a number of fronts. First and foremost, Egypt's status as a British possession, and its use as a base point for British troops during the war meant severe hardships for most of Egypt's population. Egyptians of all classes experienced shortages of one kind or another, and those who owned the presses were no exception.[11] Many newspapers and magazines, unable to secure adequate amounts of paper or to sell their newspapers during difficult times, simply disappeared. Most of those that did survive drastically reduced the frequency, size, or number of pages in each issue.[12] There were important new press developments as well. Egypt's first illustrated journals appeared during the war years. *Al-Lata'if al-musawwara*, for example, appeared in 1915 and supplied its readers with a steady diet of hand drawn illustrations and photographs. The war in Europe and parts of the Middle East provided the subject for the lion's share of these illustrations, and a steady supply of battle scenes and war maps regularly graced the pages of *al-Lata'if* until the conclusion of the war in 1918. The reduced size of publications, combined with the sensational events provided by the war, also meant that coverage about Egyptian crime and other local matters remained of marginal concern to editors. Such coverage was usually limited to the occasional article buried deep within the newspaper.

The marginality of local reporting began to change at the conclusion of the war. As Egyptian newspapers and magazines began to flourish, and new publications joined those that had survived the war, editors struggled to fill space previously occupied by war coverage. Many publications, especially illustrated journals like *al-Lata'if al-musawwara*, turned to crime reporting, although prior to 1920 much of the coverage focused on European, rather than Egyptian, crime. Major dailies like *al-Ahram* also increased the attention they devoted to *akhbar al-hawadith*, although coverage prior to 1920 tended to consist of crime summaries from various neighborhoods, cities, and provinces, rather than on specific events.

The war also had major implications for the nationalist aspirations of Egypt's most influential elites. Egyptian delegations attended the postwar conferences and lobbied aggressively for an end to British occupation based on the principles of self-determination outlined by U.S. President Woodrow Wilson. The end of the war also allowed for the renewed growth of Egypt's newspapers and magazines, whose most important story focused on the increased efforts of the Egyptians lobbying for the country's independence from British rule. Certainly, hardships felt during the war by Egypt's masses, as well as the visible presence of British troops stationed throughout the country, hastened popular support for the *wafd* that aggressively pursued Egypt's nationalist aspirations. By 1919, press coverage also no doubt played an important role in nationalist imaginings that extended well beyond Egypt's small but growing literate population. Through public readings of the newspaper in Egypt's ubiquitous coffee shops, and word of mouth more generally, news about the negotiations likely filtered down to a more broadly national audience. As Samia Kholoussi indicates in her chapter on *fallahin*, a 1919 uprising that included peasants, factory workers, and women alongside Egypt's landowning elite may have been organized and manipulated by members of the powerful Wafd Party, but it nonetheless also affirmed the beginnings of a mass culture whose shared concerns were at least partly a result of the growing influence of the mass media in Egypt, after the conclusion of the war.[13]

Women in the Nationalist Imagination

Although the political notion of an independent, culturally distinct Egypt had achieved widespread acceptance among Egyptians by 1919, discussions about the basis of that identity remained the exclusive province of elites. The so-called "woman question," i.e., debates about the appropriate status or role for women in Egyptian society, was an important part of both British colonial discourse and constructions of Egyptian national identity, and as such was a topic of much contestation both between British officials and Egyptians, and among Egyptians. This discursive contestation was largely the result of western notions of modernity and Islamic gender conceptions, meeting in nationalist discourse of the time. Calls for the liberation of women by progressives such as Qasim Amin and early feminists such as Bahithat al-Badiya and Huda Sha'rawi occurred mainly within the framework of Egypt's nationalist project both before and after 1919. For example, female writers almost unanimously called for the education of women, but also, agreed that their primary responsibility was to be good wives and mothers.[14] Appeals for women's rights in Egypt before 1919 were therefore regularly subsumed by the needs of Egypt's nationalist project. On the eve of the Raya and Sakina case in 1920, the role and status of women was contested, but remained secondary to the needs of the nascent nation-state.

As central as women were to nationalist discourse, these ideas were limited in their influence, and probably not part of the broader Egyptian public's notions of feminine or masculine behavior. The woman question was not the motivating factor behind the 1919 popular uprising, nor was it something most Egyptians were likely to have spent much time thinking about. The idea of an "Egyptian nation" certainly had permeated society across class and literacy divisions, but notions of a unitary culture were primarily constructed by elites for elite consumption. It would take a sensational murder investigation and trial in 1920, and perceptions of a "moral crisis," to transform local concerns about moral propriety into a matter of national importance, and a foundational moment in the formation of a gendered mass culture in Egypt.[15]

Murder in al-Liban

The discovery of bodies buried under houses in Alexandria's al-Liban district in November of 1920 transformed an otherwise marginal neighborhood into the focus of hundreds, if not thousands, of newspaper and magazine articles. Al-Liban's reputation as a haven for crime and deviance may have placed it on the margins of society, but in the wake of the discovery of the bodies, it became a symbol for a nation characterized as being in the throes of a moral crisis. The rise of a diverse and potentially national press, the emergence of a strong nationalist movement, and the centering of women in that nationalist movement's political discourse created unique conditions within which a sensational series of murders might engender national interest. Editors no doubt understood the enormous financial potential of a sensational case on Egyptian soil. As mentioned previously, newspapers and magazines had already begun reporting *akhbar al-hawadith* from European contexts, and local crimes in a similar vein might reasonably have been expected to garner an even wider audience.

Even given all of these factors, al-Liban's four missing women might well have become just another statistic in the crime summaries that regularly appeared in *al-Ahram* and other newspapers. After all, Alexandrian police certainly did not make finding the missing women a priority, and the results of their search corresponded with the level of effort. All that changed when on a mid-November morning in 1920 workmen digging a ditch in al-Liban discovered the remains of a female body under a house directly adjacent to the work site. The police were immediately notified and upon their arrival searched the home in question. Until recently, the dwelling had been rented by one Sakina Bint 'Ali Hamam and her husband, Muhammad 'Abdul-'Al Marzuq, and police searching the rooms immediately found a number of suspicious items, including clothes belonging to one of the women missing from al-Liban. Upon these discoveries, Sakina and Muhammad were immediately arrested, and Cairo's chief coroner, Dr. Sydney Smith, was called in to supervise the search for more bodies under the house.[16]

Meanwhile, police received another break when residents in another section of al-Liban reported a horrible stench emanating from a local apartment. Authorities discovered that Sakina's older sister Raya Bint 'Ali Hamam lived in the home with her husband Hasaballah Sa'id. Suspecting a connection between the two cases, police arrested this couple as well, and began excavating the floors of their residence. Over the next two weeks, police would find multiple victims buried under the floor of the two apartments, as well as under other houses formerly occupied by the two sisters and their husbands. The connection between the four missing women and the discoveries was by now obvious to the police, but far more than four corpses were unearthed by investigators.

Just who were these unidentified victims? Initial investigations revealed that both Raya and Sakina worked as prostitutes in the neighborhood, and that the houses under which the bodies were discovered were often used as brothels. Their husbands, as well as several other men seen frequenting these houses, were also known criminal types, and were purportedly the muscle behind al-Liban's lucrative prostitution business. Through interviews with neighbors, the police also learned that Raya had recently befriended one of the four missing women, and police therefore aggressively interrogated the older of the sisters. This interrogation yielded quick results, and Raya confessed to killing the four women, implicating her younger sister in the process. According to Raya's initial confession, robbery was their primary motive, thus implying that the murders were pre-meditated. Upon meeting a potential victim on the streets of al-Liban, the two sisters would invite her back to their home and ply her with drugs and alcohol until she was weak. At that point, Hasaballah, Sakina's husband Muhammad 'Abdul-'Al Marzuq, and at least two other men would suffocate the victims, strip them of their clothes, jewelry, money, and anything else of value, and bury them under the floors of the house. The sisters would then attempt to mask the crime scene, burning incense in an attempt to cover the stench of the rotting bodies.[17]

Over the next several days, the Egyptian authorities were shocked by the discovery of yet more bodies buried under the floors of several houses in al-Liban that had been rented either by Raya and Hasaballah, or Sakina and Muhammad. The Egyptian press immediately seized upon the sensational story, and within days of the publication of the first articles, virtually everyone who could read, or who knew somebody that could read, was aware of the murders. While public interest in the case was initially the result of the exceptional nature of the murders, commentators writing in the wake of the crimes linked it to Egypt's struggle for independence and the intrinsic character of the Egyptian nation. The exceptional murders would thus be transformed into an example and a lesson for Egyptians of all social classes.

The Investigation and Pre-Trial

Regardless of whether its orientation was political, social, cultural, or religious, virtually every publication in Egypt—well over a hundred in 1920—was likely to have covered the case or published some commentary on it.[18] That the story was able to transcend differences in form and content and was deemed suitable for such varied publications underscores the story's perceived marketability and relevance for Egyptian readers. Editors of the most widely circulated daily newspapers, such as *al-Ahram*, *al-Balagh*, *Misr*, *Wadi al-Nil*, and *al-Basir*, did not initially accord the story the same importance that they gave political affairs. Page one, for example, remained the almost exclusive domain of affairs of state. Yet, the Raya and Sakina murders were not 'buried' in these daily newspapers; the stories occupied center stage on the *akhbar al-hawadith* pages of *al-Ahram* and other publications. Moreover, when *al-Ahram* published photos of the suspects in November 1920, it was very likely the first time Egyptian newspapers and magazines had published photos of criminals.[19] Illustrated journals such as *al-Lata'if al-musawwara* also published multiple photos of the suspects, the bodies, the crime scene, and the police investigating the murders.[20] To the casual reader of the newspaper, articles about the murders undoubtedly stood out. The publication of photos also suggests that consumption of the press was no longer limited to those who could read or hear the newspapers read aloud in coffeehouses or other public places. Rather, any Egyptian who could get his hands on a newspaper could at least understand the potential magnitude of the murders.

Centering the Women

The importance of the 'woman question' in nationalist discourse virtually guaranteed that gender norms would play a role in the way articles about the murders were written—as well as received. Despite considerable evidence to suggest that the male suspects, Hasaballah Sa'id, Muhammad 'Abdul-'Al Marzuq, and several others, were intimately involved in the planning and murder of the approximately seventeen women found buried in al-Liban, most newspapers quickly focused their attention on the two sisters. The Alexandrian daily *al-Basir's* headline during the month following the discovery of the first bodies illustrates the typical pattern of press accounts. As the story broke, headlines in *al-Basir*, such as "The Disappearance of the Women," or "The Murder of the Women," concentrated on the nature of the crime. By 27 November, only ten days after the story broke in the Egyptian press, *al-Basir's* headlines clearly indicated a particular focus on the two sisters. Articles entitled, "Raya and Sakina," and featuring pictures of only the two women made it patently clear whom the press wanted to write about, and about whom they believed the public was most curious.[21] Cairo weekly, *al-Haqa'iq*, followed a similar pattern, with early headlines such as "The Slaughter of Women" and "The Horrible Crimes in Alexandria." By late December, *al-Haqa'iq* stories, like those in *al-Basir*, usually appeared under the simple headline, "Raya and Sakina."[22] Despite evidence that the male suspects were equally culpable in the commission of the murders, almost every newspaper in Egypt followed a similar pattern in both headlines and article content. The women involved were highlighted, while the male suspects were either marginalized or in many cases completely ignored.

This development appears perplexing at first. Little conclusive evidence exists that the two sisters were the ringleaders of the gang of thieves that perpetrated the murders. Likewise, little difference could be discerned between the male and female suspects with regard to either motives or methods. Both the sisters and their husbands were originally from Upper Egypt, had migrated to various cities while still young, and were engaged in the business of prostitution long before they ever arrived in Alexandria. In Alexandria, the two couples proved able entrepreneurs, operating a chain of "houses of depravity" throughout the city's poorer neighborhoods.[23] Murdering prostitutes and stealing the jewelry they carried with them appears simply to have been an extension of their entrepreneurial aspirations. Finally, little differentiated the two sisters from their husbands with regard to how the loot was spent. According to several accounts, both the male and female suspects sent a significant portion of their ill-gotten wealth to their families in Upper Egypt. If there is little to discern either the motives of the women, or their role in the commission of the crimes, how can their centrality in news reports be explained? The centering of Raya and Sakina in these stories likely occurred for a number of related reasons. In particular, the behavior of the women both engendered and facilitated concerns about a moral crisis in modern Egypt, and as a result, the construction of a national moral order in a country where local practices varied from one neighborhood, village, town, or province to the next.

Imagining a Virtuous Egypt

To be sure, the sensational nature of the murders helps to explain why it received such immediate and widespread attention from Egypt's newspapers and magazines, but how did a seemingly isolated and exceptional event help to foster the beginnings of a mass culture in modern Egypt? The answer lies in media discussions of morality in the wake of the case. As elsewhere globally, morality, honor, and shame were important to Egyptians from all social classes prior to 1920. Notions of moral or sexual propriety were based on religious tenets or long-held cultural traditions, but exactly what these were and how they were practiced varied depending upon gender, class, and place of residence. At the end of the nineteenth century, for example, upper class urban women generally donned the veil and kept to the confines of their homes. Rural women whose labor was utilized in farming were, on the other hand, much more likely to work alongside, and interact with, men on a daily basis. Whether or not certain modes of dress or behavior were deemed appropriate was, in reality, then, localized and situational, rather than national.[24]

In the wake of the Alexandria murders a unitary vision of a morally "virtuous Egypt" that existed before the arrival of the corrupting influence of Europe and the West assumed a more central place in the nationalist narrative. Concerned about European cultural influence in Egypt, the newspaper commentaries that followed the 1920 murders first imagined into being a pre-colonial era in which all members of the nation followed the same moral compass. This event-related discursive approach developed in parallel with the trend described by Samia Kholoussi in chapter ten, whereby the rural *fallah* and his society became the locus of a superior, more authentic Egyptian morality stretching back to the pharaonic era, now under siege by foreign influences and urbanization. As a slight shift of emphasis, in the aftermath of the Raya and Sakina murders, these imaginings were more specifically based on the notion of Egypt as, first and foremost, a society of like-minded Muslims. As an editorial in the Cairo daily *al-Umma* asserted immediately following the murders,

> We are an Eastern Muslim society. Muslim because our religion forbids Muslim women from being visible outside the home unless she is with a close family member strong enough to protect her if an assailant attacked her, to keep away from her suspicion and the suspicious, to order her to stay in her house and to not display her beauty out of ignorance, order her to veil or seclude herself for fear of *fitna*, sin, and the forbidden, and we are Eastern because she has traditions and a disposition greatly different from her western sister.[25]

Others also recalled an earlier time when Egypt was more virtuous, and decried the erosion of that virtue. One commentator, for example, wrote that, "In Egypt there is a system to protect morality [*adab*] but [today] it is disregarded completely."[26] Egyptian writers like the one responsible for the above passage thus imagined Egypt's moral order as unitary and in opposition to the West. Egyptian women were different from western women because of cultural and religious conventions that protected both themselves and society from the more dangerous characteristics of feminine sexuality. Moreover, in a climate of national unity in opposition to British occupation, any religious differences between Egypt's Muslim population and sizable Christian minority were downplayed. In nationalist demonstrations, for example, Egyptians of both religious groups carried flags containing both the crescent and cross, effectively marginalizing any cultural differences that might be detrimental to the idea of a "virtuous Egypt."[27] The press thus wrote about the virtuous moral tendencies of Egyptian society as a whole, at a time when cultural differences actually varied tremendously depending upon class or regional differences. Most Egyptians prior to 1920 had neither cared nor considered the possibility of a national moral standard, but the making of a national moral outrage would begin to change that.

The Making of a National Moral Outrage

Once writers had constructed the virtuous Egypt, the Raya and Sakina murders could be understood as a violation of Egypt's moral compass, and commentators generally displayed outrage at the implications of the murders for Egyptian society. Their most familiar target was the increased presence of women in public spaces that had traditionally been all-male domains. Certainly, most Egyptians in 1920 believed that interaction between men and women not related to each other could result in sexual acts resulting in *fitna*, or moral chaos. As Beth Baron notes, since the turn of the century many women believed that the veil and women's seclusion were essential to the maintenance of modesty—which they believed to be a cornerstone of Islamic practice. Baron, for example, cites Sarah al-Mihiya, who in 1910 derided women who adopted a more public presence in Egyptian society. Al-Mihiya asked, "Where are these women who are sauntering in the streets come from? Did they fall from the sky or emerge from under the earth? Have they no family?"[28] The shifting social terrain of post-World War I Egypt left notions of public and private porous and undefined. As chapters in this volume by Kholoussy, Ikeda, and Johnson and McIntosh show, discussions about gender equality or the salience of domestic confinement for women occurred against a backdrop in which the state itself entered into the realm of gender relations through education and law; upper- and middle-class women like al-Mihiya wrote in and published journals; activists called for greater women's participation in the nationalist movement; and lower class women worked in the streets as vendors, entertainers, or prostitutes.

The Alexandria murders, and the subsequent media blitz surrounding them, were in fact a moment when the rhetoric of separate spheres engaged with the realities of everyday Egyptian life. Neither the female murderers nor their victims were confined to their homes, and like thousands of other women of similar means they lived and worked on the streets of Egypt's poorest urban neighborhoods. Many of those involved in the murderers were prostitutes, but at least a few of the victims made their living by other means. Zanuba, for example, was described by *al-Ahram* as a poultry saleswomen and another victim, the "one-eyed Fatima," was described as a servant broker.[29] Descriptions of al-Liban during the investigation into the murders clearly demonstrated that non-elite women were already a part of the public fabric of 1920s urban Egypt. In the wake of the murders, however, the press associated women who left the confines of the home and who met men on a daily basis with both the female suspects and their victims. In this formulation, violent crime was due at least in part to the supposedly new presence of women in public spaces. Thus while life in al-Liban may never have reflected the imagined virtuous Egypt that writers constructed in the wake of the murders, the neighborhood's women were nonetheless viewed as a threat to Egypt's moral order, and manipulated as evidence to question the supposedly 'foreign' practice of allowing women to move freely in urban public spaces. Nationalist constructions of appropriate feminine behavior were, thanks to mass media coverage of the murders, rapidly interconnecting with the new, nationwide popular concern with moral order.

As the central figures in news accounts about the murders, commentators focused their concerns about public women first and foremost on Raya and Sakina. As entrepreneurs who traded on sex for profit, they were not the kind of women whose presence was welcome in the virtuous Egypt imagined by some writers. Writers in the press immediately focused on the incongruity between what they deemed acceptable feminine morality and the violence and callousness with which the murders were committed. Both news reports and editorials commented on the shocking brutality of the two sisters. According to an editorial in *al-Haqa'iq*, "Egypt has never heard the like [of this crime] over the course of its history, and never before had this level of infamy been achieved by two women, with the amount of sin that they have committed."[30]

For most writers in both the secular and religious press, Raya and Sakina's greed and pursuit of pleasure were uniquely female traits that had grown out of control in the absence of male supervision. Thus both men and women could be held responsible for the commission of violent crimes in which women were involved, such as the 1920 murders. The result was the transformation of feminine weakness into feats of inhumanity. An editorial in *Wadi al-Nil*, for example, described the two women as so evil that they were no longer people, but rather fully possessed by the devil. Editorials and literary pieces dedicated to the case and published in *al-Rashid* repeatedly referred to Raya in non-human terms. "Raya, you are not human . . . you are a beast in the desert, a fox that embraces deception, a treacherous wolf." Countless articles described the two sisters as any number of non-human forms, including tigers, vipers, and monsters. Through editorials like these, Raya and Sakina became symbols for many opposed to calls for the integration of women into more public walks of Egyptian life, on the grounds that women were powerless to control their own sexual natures (fig. 13.2).[31]

The victims of the murders as well factored heavily into concerns about the appropriateness of women in public spaces. In the press, the murdered women were in fact described not so much as victims, but rather as violators of Egypt's moral order. Editorial after editorial placed at least part of the blame for the murders on the murdered prostitutes and street women—or at least on the presence of these victims in spaces where their presence was potentially disruptive. An editorial in *al-Haqa'iq*, for example, attributed the murders directly to the behavior of those killed. "Raya didn't go find just any women, but rather she found those with weak souls and little honor or morality. And God knows that these women would not have died had they been sheltered, well-protected, and virtuous. So the matter facing society is moral before it is criminal."[32] *Al-Umma* was even more explicit in blaming the murders on the victims as well. "What is the force that compelled these women to enter these whorehouses and bring about their own destruction at the hands of the murderers? The answer is easily comprehensible from their comments, and it is the loss of decency on the part of men and women."[33]

In these and most other press accounts the victims were as much to blame for their deaths as the killers themselves. By transcending the boundaries that were seen to separate male spaces from female ones, these women were flirting with disaster. That these boundaries had long been porous, undefined, and situational was not part of the discussion. The "virtuous Egypt" of many commentators, which imagined a unitary and clearly delineated gender separation for all Egyptians prior to the arrival of European modernity, had become a historical truism.

Media coverage of the murders blamed them on the actions of women who transgressed the intrinsic social and spatial boundaries preventing *fitna*. As exceptional as the serial killings may have been, they became a key moment in discussions about the gendering of public space in modern Egypt, the impact of foreign notions of modernity and gender equality on Egyptian society, and in the founding of a national notion of moral behavior. Reports that Raya and Sakina preyed mostly on women they met in al-Liban's public market, coffeehouses, and streets became emblematic of the dangers of allowing any woman into these spaces. As a result, in late 1920, defining appropriate boundaries to prevent male-female inter-action was done largely in response to the murders. Brothels, the streets, coffeehouses, markets, and schools were among public spaces where the presence of women was new and potentially threatening. Editorial after editorial accused women of inciting moral indecency by "wander[ing] around public places and coffeehouses."[34]

Many writers criticized not only the presence of women in public as potentially disastrous, but also, the relaxing of the cultural tradition of veiling. As previously noted, veiling and the strict segregation of the sexes was practiced primarily by urban elites, as it was neither practical nor common among poorer Egyptians, especially those who lived in rural areas. By the 1920s, whether women should continue to wear the full veil had become an increasingly contentious issue in some Egyptian circles. Leading feminist Huda Sha'rawi, for example, would write in 1925 that the veil had become "the greatest obstacle to women's participation in public life."[35] In the wake of the Alexandria murders commentators generally blamed the relaxation of female dress restrictions as a factor in the murders. *Al-Umma*, for example, asked its readers, "Where are the proponents of unveiling in situations such as this disgraceful event?"[36]

Given the central role of women in both colonial and Egyptian nationalist discourse, female behavior considered dangerous or deviant was bound to interest those who wrote newspaper articles, as well as their normal audience of educated middle and upper class Egyptians. What was new was the inclusion of lower-class men and women's lives in discussions about appropriate gendered behavior. Also new, was the way in which *hawadith* involving non-elites played a role in the elevation of morality to an issue of national concern. A moral crisis had been born, and press commentators did not hesitate in proposing ways to recover Egypt's lost moral compass.

(Re)Creating a Moral Egypt

Those who commented on the implications of the murders for Egyptian society did not merely point out what had gone awry. Many also proposed the ways in which Egypt might regain its misplaced moral foundation. Editorials called for a number of reforms, and urged the monarchy, colonial regime, or most importantly, individual males, to act on behalf of Egypt's moral well-being. An editorial in *Wadi al-Nil*, for example, recalled a time when Egypt was more virtuous, and decried the erosion of that virtue. "In Egypt there is a system to protect morality *(adab)*, but [today] it is disregarded completely."[37]

However, what were the seductive temptations that were steering Egypt's women in particular, and men more generally, away from Egypt's imagined virtuousness? For most commentators, the influence of Europe in particular and modernity in general were the targets. *Al-Umma*, for example, blamed the erosion of Egyptian moral values on the "ingesting of all that is pleasant and evil that comes to us, crossing the sea like all new arrivals. It is the temptation of western civilization that contains depravity and deficiency that our social system and morality are not accustomed to."[38] In the face of the West's undermining of Egyptian values, virtually every other Egyptian newspaper called for immediate action to reinvigorate cultural practices deemed Egyptian and, by extension, moral. Significantly, appeals to indigenous authenticity and negative cultural perspectives on the West emerged when Egypt's political and social elite described in chapters one and five by James Whidden and Lucie Ryzova cultivated a pro-western cultural stance, at times with legislative ramifications, as Kholoussy demonstrated in her chapter. An editorial in the illustrated weekly *al-Lata'if al-musawwara* cited the need for Egypt's moral restrictions to keep up with Egypt's modern nationalist movement. "The time has arrived for the activation within the community of a moral renaissance to correspond with its political renaissance and to mesh with modern progress."[39] Belief in the need that something had to be done was nearly unanimous. What that was exactly was a matter of much debate in the winter of 1920 and throughout 1921.

In this climate of charged debate about the place of women in Egyptian society, the fact that Raya and Sakina and many of their victims were prostitutes gave particular resonance to popular cultural narratives about the dangers of unleashed feminine sexuality. Many editorials published in the wake of the murders called for the abolition of prostitution in Egypt. Under the British colonial regime, Egyptian prostitution had remained legal, as sexual outlets were deemed necessary to ensure the psychological well-being of British soldiers stationed on Egyptian soil. At the same time, the colonial administration vehemently opposed European prostitution in Egypt, based on fears of the so-called "white slave trade" in Egypt and elsewhere.[40] Prostitution was, then, a political issue for nationalists, albeit one on the back burner to be dealt with after Egyptian sovereignty was achieved. The Raya and Sakina murders temporarily altered the priorities of the press, the public, and ultimately, government officials. Many commentators noted that several of the suspects and victims were linked to prostitution and called for the immediate and complete abolishment of the practice on Egyptian soil. *Wadi al-Nil*, for example, wrote that, "these crimes occurred in the evil light of these houses [of sin] and they brought one evil on top of another, and due to this it is warranted for us to also call the houses of moral depravity houses of eternal damnation."[41] Many writers believed that stemming the tide of prostitution would in turn stem the erosion of the Egyptian moral order in general. In the wake of the murders, the abolition of prostitution thus became a moral issue in addition to a political one.

Editorials also directly linked the occurrence of crime and immorality to the nationalist cause. Fikri Abaza, a prominent journalist of the period, attributed the murders in particular and lawlessness in general to the colonial administration's preoccupation with security against popular uprisings. In a 25 November 1920 article in *al-Ahram*, Abaza asked,

Where are the police? Where is the sword of government that should fall on the necks of bloodthirsty criminals? Where is the vigilant eye of justice that should never wink? Where is the mighty hand of authority? Indeed, the government has been too intent upon training the hordes of its secret political police to concern itself with training forces necessary to safeguard our internal security or personal safety. It is time for us to ask it to address the dangers posed by that negligence. The recent murders are a great calamity, the horrors of which have blackened the forehead of the twentieth century.[42]

If Egyptians were in agreement that Egypt was suffering from a moral crisis, one induced in part by the influence of modernity on Egyptian society, there was clearly a diversity of opinions about what to do about it. Calls for an end to prostitution, for educating the poor and destitute, and for an increase in government security were all exponentially amplified in the wake of the Alexandria murders and the extensive media coverage they received.

Moral Outrage for the Masses

The Alexandria murders of 1920 clearly were a catalyst for the creation of the idea that moral behavior was something that could be defined not just for separate local communities, but also for the nation as a whole. Perhaps most strikingly about the discussions of morality directly following the murders, interest in these formulations was not limited to a small group of upper-class intellectuals and politicians. There is evidence to suggest that Egypt's popular masses also experienced moral outrage and a concern about the maintenance of moral order in modern Egypt. This is an important observation, for the traditional historiography of twentieth-century Egypt has emphasized low literacy rates as mitigating the impact of the press on popular opinion. Certainly, the majority of city-dwellers (probably somewhere around 70 percent of the men and 90 percent of the women in Cairo and Alexandria[43]) were functionally illiterate, and Ami Ayalon's assessment that low literacy rates "signified limits on the impact, political and otherwise, of the press on society,"[44] indicates how researchers have accepted the distinction between a press culture and popular culture in modern Egypt. A closer examination of the media blitz surrounding the Alexandria murders suggests that the biggest sensations affected the lives and opinions of non-literate Egyptians every bit as much it did those who could read. The vast majority of urban Egyptians clearly read the articles about the case. The tradition of reading important articles aloud in crowded coffeehouses and the recent introduction of illustrated journals exposed both literate and non-literate Egyptians to the most sensational stories, and it is clear from accounts of the Alexandria murders that Egyptians of all social classes were interested in, and to some extent, involved in the crime and the negotiation of its greater meaning.

The Cairo weekly *al-Haqa'iq*, like other newspapers that covered the murders, often mentioned the widespread interest in and physical reaction to the murders. "Who is worthier of their reputation than Raya and Sakina, whose names are on every tongue and in every newspaper?" A comment in the same newspaper is indicative of the public reaction newspapers regularly noted in their stories:

> newspaper boys on every street cry out "Raya and Sakina, Raya and
> Sakina for a piaster." And thus their evil was transported everywhere,
> to the houses and to the kids in the schools and to the factory workers
> and in every neighborhood they took notice of this crime. And the
> hearts in people's chests sensed it and its echo has reached even the
> dead in their tombs.[45]

Writers in the press certainly claimed that the case affected Egyptians across class and literacy lines, and while it is perhaps possible that these claims were exaggerated to elevate the importance of a story and sell more newspapers, there is considerable evidence that demonstrates the reach of press coverage beyond literacy and class lines. *Wadi al-Nil*, for example, noted that following the murders, large numbers of Egyptians regularly trekked to see the houses where Raya and Sakina had murdered and buried their victims. "The people are repelled by passing the tombs, and they shake and get goose bumps due to what they see."[46] Another report in *Wadi al-Nil* noted that, in the weeks following the discovery of the bodies, any female arrested by the police in Alexandria was jeered and cursed by angry citizens who saw them as symbolic of Raya and Sakina and the decay of moral decency in Egyptian society.[47]

The most notable expression of public feeling about the murders occurred in late December 1920, when newspapers were full of stories describing Raya and Sakina as snakes, wolves, and myriad other beasts. According to stories in both *al-Ahram* and *al-Basir*, rumors spread among ordinary citizens that the sisters were on display at the zoo, rather than at the prison. Thousands of Egyptians are reported to have flocked to see them, only to find that the rumors were unfounded.[48] While there is no direct evidence linking press descriptions of the two sisters as animals to the run on the zoo, it strongly suggests that the lower class, largely illiterate Egyptians who visited the zoo were reacting to gossip based on those press accounts. Through public readings, illustrations, and channels of gossip, Egyptians therefore consumed press coverage of the murders, whether literate or not. Thanks to the popular appeal of *akhbar al-hawadith*, and to the sensational nature of the press coverage, Raya and Sakina became a moment when a localized event became a *shared experience* for Egyptians of all social classes. As such, concerns about gender roles within the newly imagined Egyptian moral order no longer remained the exclusive domain of elite intellectuals. Thus, while those who publicly debated and wrote about gender roles necessarily remained elites (by virtue of their literacy and access to both politics and the press), the Alexandria murders and their protagonists were both utilized in, and incorporated into, these debates. The case, therefore, was transformed into a shared concern of the imagined Egyptian nation and, as a result, ideas about proper moral behavior were described as an Egyptian cultural trait rather than local or religion specific.

Making Sense of Murder and Immorality: The Trial

While the trial of Raya, Sakina, their husbands, and two other men charged with the murders was primarily a formality, public interest in the case remained high throughout. Egyptian readers were once again bombarded with a stream of articles about the murders immediately preceding, during, and following the trial, which took place from 11 May to 17 May 1921. *Al-Ahram*, for example, published the trial transcripts of each day in full, using up large swaths of the paper usually designated for other stories. Other newspapers, such as *Wadi al-Nil*, *al-Muqattam*, *al-Rashid*, *Misr*, and *al-Basir*, also printed at least part, if not all, of the proceedings.[49] These published transcripts of the trial are clearly mediated, for quotes attributed to members of the gang and other residents of al-Liban are rendered in Modern Standard Arabic, rather than the colloquial Egyptian dialect in which they no doubt spoke.[50] They nonetheless demonstrate that the voices of Egypt's non-elite population were present in the press, and that non-elites played a role in how Egyptians came to understand their own gendered identities.

Given the intense media attention the case had received over the previous six months, it is not surprising that the press and the public was acutely interested in the trial. *Wadi al-Nil* once again noted the public's interest in the murders at the beginning of the trial, as evidenced by the crowds that surrounded the Alexandria courthouse. "The masses present at the criminal courts yesterday were huge, despite the fact that no one was admitted to the courtroom except those who carried a ticket from among the special tickets issued by the governorate. A strong force of police was sent to maintain order."[51]

The pro-British daily *al-Muqattam* also noted the huge public interest in the beginning of the trial, noting that the outside hall of the courtroom was packed with people, while the courtroom itself was, "completely crowded with the entry ticket holders who were present."[52] The daily newspapers, all of which covered the case, continued to mention the crowds present for the duration of the trial, indicating that interest in the case had not waned in the six months since the murders were first reported.

Press accounts also suggested that readers of the press had already formed keen opinions about the case in general, and the suspects in particular. *Al-Ahram*, for example, noted that

> It is rare for the court to face a criminal case in which the masses
> agree with the request for a harsh punishment such as in the current
> case. There are many people who in normal circumstances feel
> pity for women if they commit a crime and thus there is a request
> for mercy if she committed even the crime of murder. In this case,
> however, there is not one person asking for a drop of mercy for Raya
> and Sakina and the rest of the individuals in the gang.[53]

After several months of press coverage about Egypt's "moral crisis" and depictions of the case as a violation of Egypt's intrinsic morality, it seemed that the masses had all come to the same conclusion that the sisters and their accomplices had to die for the crimes they committed. A guilty verdict on 17 May 1921 was followed in December by the execution of Raya, Sakina, their husbands, and two other men. Their deaths were noted in the newspapers of the day, but with little immediate fanfare. It would seem that, once the verdict was decided, the Egyptian reading public was perhaps more interested in stories explicitly about Egypt's nationalist struggle or other timely political events. More lasting, however, would be the legacy of the two sisters, for in the course of Egypt's first modern media sensation, the beginnings of a mass culture, based on shared notions of moral behavior, were emerging.

Conclusion

Explicit references to Raya and Sakina died down after their execution in December 1921. With the murderers dead and the victims long forgotten, al-Liban again faded into the background of Egyptian affairs. The legacy of the case endured long after the conclusion of the legal proceedings and the end of the media frenzy. Raya and Sakina, for example, had a lasting impact on what kind of news the press reported, and how they reported it. No case before Raya and Sakina had received similar attention, but from the 1920s onward, sensational *hawadith* cases appeared regularly in the press. This can, in part be attributed to the business of selling newspapers. Raya and Sakina were national villains, across class and gender lines. As such, the demand for coverage of such stories greatly expanded the audience and the potential circulation of Egypt's largest newspapers. The 1920s were, in fact, a booming period for the press, with greater circulations for established newspapers and new publications sprouting up regularly. Thus, while newspapers continued to report crime statistics in daily, weekly, or monthly columns, editors no doubt realized the interest in, and power of, stories that were more sensational and that focused more closely on the lives of those involved. While *hawadith* columns, photos, and sensational prose all became a regular and important feature of the press, the influence of *hawadith* would not stop there. New developments in media technology, such as radio and film, would soon create even more space for sensational coverage of everyday events. Through at least the mid-1950s, a number of sensational stories would, like the 1920 Alexandria murders, serve as media flashpoints for discussions of morality and national identity in Egypt.

Raya and Sakina also had an impact far beyond just how and when certain news was covered in Egypt. Rather, the timing of the murders played a pivotal role in elevating the importance of morality to the identity of the Egyptian nation. Although concerns about moral behavior in Egypt obviously pre-dated the modern period, earlier conceptions of it were based on local understandings of Islam or Christianity. The media firestorm after the 1920 murders, however, made concerns about moral behavior a national issue and transformed the issue of determining moral behavior from a strictly religious concern to a secular one as well. To be sure, others have noted the secularity of official discourse related to issues of morality such as marriage and the family. For example, in chapter eleven of this volume, Hanan Kholoussy details the political and legislative debates around marriage and divorce law in early twentieth-century

Egypt. What the Alexandria murders demonstrate, however, is that alongside these debates among the secular and religious elite there also existed a more popular forum for discussion that both engendered and represented concerns about the negative impacts of secular modernity on the moral foundations of the Egyptian nation. The details of the case, most importantly the presence of female suspects and victims, led to re-formulations in the press of just what was appropriate behavior for both men and women, and commentators, as well as at least some of their readers, clearly saw the murder case as a cautionary tale for both sexes. The victims had died because they transgressed the new/old traditional Egyptian moral boundaries, and Raya and Sakina were extreme examples of what might befall society if men failed to closely monitor the movements and behavior of women. Our understanding of the "woman question" in Egypt, then, needs to take into consideration not only the writings of a relatively small community of intellectuals, political leaders, and religious officials, but also the impact of sensational moments like the 1920 murders on the very discursive environment within which their ideas were formulated.

The post-1920 murder press in Egypt certainly realized the power of sensational *hawadith*, not only on their circulation numbers, but also on the public's conception of gender and moral order in modern Egypt. Sensational *hawadith* reports and the moral crises they seemed to suggest were certainly factored into heated debates about the moral imperatives of Egypt's nationalist movement through the 1950s, and scandalous sexual or criminal behavior was often characterized as a negative impact of European modernity on Egyptian values. It should be noted, then, that these media sensations played an important role in creating a climate for debates about moral order that existed alongside (and at times, in relation to) the kinds of social reform described by Amy Johnson and Scott David McIntosh in chapter nine of this volume. Moreover, it seems likely that, on occasion, the public persona afforded to women who advocated for social reform or engaged in other seemingly charitable pursuits may have been at odds with an emerging moral discourse that worried about the interaction of men and women in public spaces.[54]

Perhaps even more striking about the moral concerns raised in the wake of media sensations like the 1920 murders is that they seemed remarkably free of overt class implications. For perhaps the first time, the press had taken a case involving subaltern Egyptians and made it relevant in the minds of the upper classes to their own lives. There is little doubt that the educated elite and middle class who wrote about the murders sometimes deployed the case in support of pre-existing upper-class definitions of morality. At the same time, however, this deployment also signaled an important development in the formulation of gender discourse in modern Egypt: the inclusion of real-life stories taken from the lives of subaltern Egyptians, and their extrapolation into a concern for a more broadly defined Egyptian public that included both elites and the uneducated masses. Thanks in part to one widely publicized series of murders, notions of a national moral order thus provided an important basis for a truly mass culture in modern Egypt. Throughout the period from 1919–52, the ever-increasing proliferation of newspapers, magazines, radio, and film would continue to provide a foundation for the notion of Egypt as a moral community as well as a political one, and other media sensations would play a role in linking national agendas with cultural practices.

Notes

1   The research for this article was made possible by a fellowship from the American Research Center in Egypt. I would also like to thank Mario Ruiz for his comments on an earlier draft.
2   These observations and quotations are a result of my own conversations with Egyptians in Cairo about the case in 2001 and 2002.
3   Juan Cole, "Printing and Urban Islam in the Mediterranean World, 1890–1920," in Leila Tarazi Fawaz and C.A. Bayly, eds., *Modernity and Culture: From the Mediterranean to the Indian Ocean* (New York: Columbia University Press, 2002), 344–51.
4   An uprising led by Ahmad 'Urabi against Egypt's foreign-born monarchy in 1881 hastened the British occupation. British officials were concerned about the repayment of debts owed them by Egypt, access to the Suez Canal, and the extraterritorial rights they had gained in Egypt during the nineteenth century.
5   A number of writers have addressed the issue of British censorship of the Egyptian press during the colonial period. See for example Israel Gershoni and James Jankowski, *Egypt, Islam and the Arabs: The Search for Egyptian Nationhood, 1900–1930* (New York: Oxford University Press, 1991), 26, 32.
6   Benedict Anderson, *Imagined Communities: Reflections on the Origin and Spread of Nationalism* (London: Verso, 1995), 37–46.
7   According to Ami Ayalon, the 1897 Egyptian census showed male literacy in Cairo and Alexandria at around 20 percent. My figure of 30 percent is an estimation based on the rising availability of education in urban areas throughout the ensuing twenty years. Ayalon, *The Press in the Arab Middle East* (New York: Oxford University Press, 1995), 54–55.
8   For more on this, see Beth Baron, *The Women's Awakening in Egypt: Culture, Society, and the Press* (New Haven: Yale University Press, 1994), and Marilyn Booth, *May Her Likes Be Multiplied: Biography and Gender Politics in Egypt* (Berkeley: University of California Press, 2001).
9   Gershoni and Jankowski, *Egypt, Islam, and the Arabs*, 6–8.
10   For more on the Egyptian press and its relationship to nationalism, and on its role in the 1919 Revolution, see Ramzi Mikhail, *al-Sihafa al-misriya wa-l-haraka al-wataniya, 1882–1922* (Cairo: General Egyptian Book Organization, 1996).

11 Selma Botman, *Egypt from Independence to Revolution, 1919–1952* (Syracuse: Syracuse University Press, 1991), 26.

12 This statement is based on my own observations while researching at Dar al-Kutub (The Egyptian National Library in Cairo) in 2001 and 2002.

13 For more on the press in Egypt during the 1919 uprising, see Ramzi Mikhail, *al-Sihafa al-misriya wa al-thawra 1919* (Cairo: General Egyptian Book Organization, 1993).

14 For more on this emphasis on education in line with the requirements of female domesticity, see Baron, *The Women's Awakening*, 155–58, and Omnia Shakry, "Schooled Mothers and Structured Play: Child Rearing in Turn of the Century Egypt," in Lila Abu-Lughod. ed., *Remaking Women: Feminism and Modernity in the Middle East* (Princeton: Princeton University Press, 1998), 126–70. For a comparative Middle Eastern perspective, see Barak A. Salmoni, "Women in the Nationalist-Educational Prism: Turkish and Egyptian Pedagogues and Their Gendered Agenda, 1920–1952," *History of Education Quarterly* 43: 4 (2003).

15 Gershoni and Jankowski argue that discussions about Egyptian nationalism did not overtake Islam as the central focus in the daily life of most Egyptians. Rather, these discussions only had major influence on the customs and ideas of the heavily westernized elite. See Israel Gershoni and James Jankowski, *Redefining the Egyptian Nation, 1930–1945* (Cambridge: Cambridge University Press, 1995), 54.

16 Egypt in 1920 had a mixed police force and coroner's office consisting of both British and Egyptian officers. The Egyptian press of the time never mentioned Dr. Sydney Smith by name, perhaps because of the uncertain political climate created by the nationalist struggle. For more on the role of Smith in the Raya and Sakina investigation, see Sydney Smith, *Mostly Murder* (London: George Harrap and Co., Ltd, 1959), 71–73.

17 This version of events, taken primarily from a series of articles published in *al-Ahram* in November and December of 1920, was but one of several that appeared in various Egyptian newspapers at the time. The story appears somewhat differently in each; for example, in some versions, police searched Raya's dwelling before searching Sakina's former residence. Louis Awad also examined a number of different accounts in building his own narrative of the investigation. For example, see Awad, *Awraq al-'amr: sanawat al-takwin* ("Papers of a Lifetime: The Formative Years") (Cairo: Maktabat Madbuli, 1989), 161–207.

18 Although listed in the Dar al-Kutub (Egyptian National Library) index, many of the newspapers being published in Egypt in 1920 could not be found. In addition to those I did actually see, however, there is evidence (such as regular press review articles in the major daily newspapers) to demonstrate that most newspapers actually did cover the story in one form or another.

19 "The Women Killers," *Al-Ahram Weekly*, 434 (17–23 June 1999).

20 For an example of photojournalism related to the case, see "Twenty Photos of the Horrible Alexandria Crime," *al-Lata'if al-musawwara*, 2 December 1920, 5.

21 See, for example, "The Disappearance of Women," *al-Basir*, 20 November 1920, and "Raya and Sakina," *al-Basir*, 27 November 1920.

22 For an example, "The Slaughter of Women," *al-Haqa'iq*, 28 November 1920, 1 and "Raya and Sakina," *al-Haqa'iq*, 26 December 1920, 1.

23 According to *Al-Ahram Weekly*, the sisters and their husbands opened and operated at least five brothels in the Alexandria area with the help of Orabi Hassan. Hassan provided the muscle needed to collect payment from unruly customers, and was the key suspect in the murder investigation along with the two couples. "The Women Killers," *Al-Ahram Weekly*, 434 (17–23 June 1999).

24 For more on the diffences between urban and rural women in early twentieth-century Egypt, see Afaf Lutfi al-Sayyid-Marsot, *Egypt's Liberal Experiment, 1922–1936* (Berkeley: University of California Press, 1977), 22.

25 *Al-Umma*, 21 November 1920, 1.

26 "After the Recent Crimes," *Wadi al-Nil*, 25 November 1920, 3.

27 For more on this, see J.D. Pennington. "The Copts in Modern Egypt," *Middle Eastern Studies* 18, no. 2 (April 1992), 161.

28 Al-Mihiya's quotation is from an article she published in the journal *al-'Afaf*. See Baron, *The Women's Awakening*, 114–15.

29 Those victims who were identified in the press usually appeared only under their first names. See "The Women Killers," *Al-Ahram Weekly*, 434 (17–23 June 1999).

30 "Raya and Sakina," *al-Haqa'iq*, 26 December 1920, 1–2.

31 Interestingly, very little was written as to the sex lives of Raya and Sakina themselves. They were reported to be madams and thus implicated in the commission of sexual immorality, but the press focused far more on linking this implication to the potentially immoral consequences of public women more generally.

32 *Al-Haqa'iq*, 20 December 1920 (the page numbers were unreadable on the archive copy of the journal).

33 *Al-Umma*, 21 November 1920, 1.

34 "Oh, What an Indignation to Morality," *Misr*, 11 December 1920, 2.

35 This quotation can be found in Margot Badran, *Feminists, Islam, and Nation: Gender and the Making of Modern Egypt* (Princeton: Princeton University Press, 1995), 93. For more on the debate over veiling, see Badran, 91–96.

36 "Some of our Leaders," *al-Umma*, 21 Novemer 1920, 1.

37 "After the Recent Crimes," *Wadi al-Nil*, 25 November 1920, 3.

38 "Some of our Leaders."

39 "Twenty Photos of the Horrible Alexandria Crime," *al-Lata'if al-musawwara*, 2 December 1920, 5.

40 European prostitutes were of particular concern to both colonial officials and also to officials back in Europe. The so-called "White Slave Trade" was an issue with international implications at the turn of the century. For more on these concerns as they related to Egypt, and on prostitution on Egyptian soil more generally, see Badran, *Feminists, Islam, and Nation*, 192–94. See also Bruce Dunn, "Sexuality and the Civilizing Process in Modern Egypt" (Ph.D. diss., Georgetown University, 1996), 154–70.

41 *Wadi al-Nil*, 9 December 1920 (the page numbers were unreadable on the archive copy).

42 The quote from Abaza is taken from Yunan Labib Rizk, "The Women Killers," *Al-Ahram Weekly*, 434 (17–23 June 1999).

43 For more on this, see Ayalon, 144.

44 Ibid., 143.

45 *Al-Haqa'iq*, 21 November 1920 (the page numbers were unreadable on the archive copy).

46 *Wadi al-Nil*, 1 December 1920, 3.

47 "A Series of Crimes in the Licensed Houses," *Wadi al-Nil*, 28 November 1920 (unreadable page number).

48 The story of the zoo incident is re-told in a 1999 article that appeared in *Al-Ahram Weekly*, the English language version of *al-Ahram*. The article relies on the original articles published in *al-Ahram* at the time of the murders. See "The Women Killers," *Al-Ahram Weekly*, no. 434 (17–23 June 1999). The Egyptian national library's microfilm copies of *al-Basir* are, regrettably, blurry, rendering the recovery of some article texts impossible. I was thus able to make out a headline referencing the zoo story, but not the text itself.

49 The most complete coverage appeared in *al-Ahram*, and it is possible that some of the reports that appeared in the other newspapers (especially those outside of Cairo and Alexandria) simply reprinted *al-Ahram's* coverage. It is not clear whether each newspaper had a correspondent in the courtroom taking notes as the trial went along, or whether they were given access to, or copies of, the official courtroom transcript.

50 Modern Standard Arabic is a formal language based on classical Arabic, used primarily in literature or in newspapers, radio, and television. It was not, and is not today, spoken on the streets and villages of Egypt or any other Arab country. Rather, people speak a colloquial form of the language, which is in some cases markedly different from standard Arabic. Everything published in Egyptian newspapers and magazines in 1920 and 1921 appeared in Modern Standard Arabic, and in the case of this trial, was converted by either courtroom scribes or newspaper editors.

51 "The Case of the Murdered Women: In Front of the Criminal Court," *Wadi al-Nil* 11 May 1921, 2.

52 "The Trial of Raya and Sakina and Their Accomplices," *al-Muqattam* 11 May 1921, 3.

53 Ibid.

54 Badran, for example, talks of widespread concerns about female nurses whose profession would bring them into close proximity with male doctors and thus create a climate for sexual impropriety. See Badran, 181.

14 The 1919 Revolution and Nationalist Constructions of the Lives and Works of Pioneering Women Writers

Mervat F. Hatem

Historians who have discussed the roles of Egyptian women in the 1919 Revolution directed their attention to the participation of elite women in different nationalist activities like demonstrations, the boycott of foreign goods, and articulating their political views on the pages of Egyptian and British newspapers.[1] The Wafd's Committee for Women, headed by Huda Sha'rawi who was the wife of one of the original members of the Wafd, organized these activities. Some historians added to this elitist narrative a discussion of the spontaneous roles played by urban and rural working class women in support of the revolution.[2]

Until now, there has been no discussion of Mayy Ziyada's biographies of Malak Hifni Nasif and 'A'isha Taymur, which were delivered in public forums in 1919 and 1922 respectively and then published by *al-Muqtataf* in 1920 and 1923 as examples of nationalist intellectual production.[3] Ziyada, who had emerged as a leading writer and speaker, with a weekly salon attended by all the leading male public figures of this period from 1913 on,[4] was well suited for the task of putting Egyptian women's history in the service of the dominant modernist nationalist discourse articulated by members of her salon and reinforced by the revolution. More specifically, for the purpose of this chapter, the biographies of Nasif and Taymur, which were written at the beginning and toward the end of the 1919 Revolution, allow us to examine the effect that the nationalist movement had on Egyptian women in general and on Ziyada's discourse in particular though her construction of the lives and views of these writers. Ziyada listed her love of nature, her appreciation of the eloquence of the Arabic language found in the Qur'an and the nationalist movement, which developed in response to the 1919 Revolution, in that order as having influenced her writings. She said that without the nationalist movement her writings would not have developed as fast as they did.[5]

This chapter will begin by examining Ziyada's description of the national context, which inspired her interest in writing these biographies of pioneering Egyptian women. Next, it will examine how her embrace of the different narratives produced by the modernist nationalist discourse influenced her constructions of the lives and works of Nasif and Taymur. It also will show how Ziyada's discussion of the national identities of pioneering women writers underwent significant discursive changes reflecting the evolution of the national and the women's movements. In the conclusion, this chapter will discuss how Ziyada's nationalist and feminists constructions failed to appreciate the very distinct discourses and agendas that Nasif and Taymur contributed to the national debates of their time.

The 1919 Revolution and the Incorporation of Women in National History

When Malak Hifni Nasif died on 17 October 1918 at the age of 32, Ziyada reported the generalized public grief that engulfed many ordinary men and women, Muslims and Christians, writers and the advocates of women's rights. As Hanan Kholoussy has shown in chapter eleven, Nasif was a well-known and highly respected champion of women's rights in the nationalist press of the first decade of the twentieth century, both among males and females. Commentaries thus filled the columns of different newspapers, acknowledging her contributions to public debate. In addition, prominent men and women discussed holding public memorials for the author. Men quickly took the initiative holding their memorial on the occasion of the forty-day anniversary of her death leaving women to mark the first year anniversary of that event.[6] The minister of education at the time, 'Adli Yakan,[7] formally headed the memorial organized in recognition of Nasif's educational accomplishments. She was one of the first graduates of al-Saniya public school, the only public school for girls at the time, who also completed its teachers' diploma in 1903 and worked as a teacher until she married 'Abd al-Sattar Bey al-Basil in 1907.[8]

Ziyada, who did not attend the memorial held by the men because it was a segregated affair, gave more attention to the details of that event than she did to the women's memorial in which she took part. She reported that the former was attended by every knowledgeable, well-known and respected public figure, but that the majority did not belong to the younger generation that supported the unveiling of women *(sufur al-mar'at)*, but rather were conservatives who wore *'amam* and tarbooshes (the headdresses worn by traditional men as well as those who belonged to the new middle class). One of them offered what she considered to be a significant statement, "O man, inform women that we honor knowledgeable women just as we honor great men."[9] In her attempt to interpret this statement, Ziyada reminded the readers that the death of brilliant figures made people pay attention to and take pride in the causes for which they struggled. She also argued that the different histories of the women's movements in the Occident and the Orient explained the interest that men took in Nasif:

> When Western women began their movement, very few men supported them with the majority mocking them. These painful years of struggle were gone; and women have successfully gained the support of the most prominent men in America and in Europe. In our case, the mention of the women's movement reminds us that it was men who founded it, gave it support and continue to infuse it with dynamism. The memorial held by men for Bahithat al-Badiya [the pen name used by Nasif after she was married] provided complete support for this view.[10]

According to this reading of western and Egyptian women's histories, western women had to struggle to build a movement and to gain the support of men, but Oriental Egyptian women faced no such hardship because the men created a movement for them and provided it with public support. Ziyada suggested that this explained why men were quicker in holding a memorial for Nasif and why they showed up in large numbers to mourn her passing. This view must have had personal resonance for Ziyada who became a prominent author because of the support she received from the leading male figures of her time. It did not successfully explain why many conservative men who did not support women's rights attended Nasif's memorial.

Why did such a majority of conservative men show up to pay their respects to the memory of this woman writer? The very fact that both conservative and liberal men attended her memorial would suggest that the author had achieved national status. Nasif was a critic of the way modernist men sought to impose their social views on women at the same time that she sought to expand women's participation in public debate, which the conservatives did not support. While she was not clearly allied with either camp, each could find something to support in her work. The fact that she developed a relatively independent agenda that reflected the views of women, not those of men, helped her claim an autonomous discursive space where the two polarized segments of the general public could meet on women's rights and entitled her to a distinct national status and support.

The date of Nasif's memorial, 26 November 1918, provided another explanation of the rare show of unity among liberal and conservative men. It came three days after Egyptian nationalists completed the process of selecting members of the Wafd that represented different classes and ethnic groups in Egyptian society whose goal was to begin negotiation of Egyptian independence from Great Britain. Not only was 'Adli Yakan, the minister of education, a member of the delegation, but the Wafd had just added Hamad al-Basil Pasha, a member of the same Bedouin tribe to whom Nasif's husband belonged, to its ranks.[11] Because the British continued to restrict public meetings during the last days of the First World War, the appearance of a large number of conservative men along with the supporters of women's rights in Nasif's memorial represented a show of national unity in support of Nasif and the Wafd.

What about the significant quote, "O man, inform women that we honor knowledgeable women just as we honor great men"? In asking men to inform women of the honor men bestowed on Nasif, the speaker acknowledged the segregated character of this important public event and sought to make sure that women learned of it. This seemed to be part of an attempt to appeal to women at a critical historical juncture as members of the nation. The statement also revealed the unequal status of women within the nation. It acknowledged the new status that Nasif had acquired for women in modern society, promising to honor the acquisition of knowledge in women and greatness in men. Whereas the greatness in men went beyond the acquisition of education, the women that men honored deserved a comparable status through education and/or knowledge. The combined roles of teacher and writer entitled Nasif to the status of a knowledgeable woman.

Finally, it was not clear from Ziyada's reporting whether the source of the above quote was a conservative or a liberal man; the quote scored points against the dead Nasif who had claimed that men continued to have an overbearing attitude toward women. She had questioned the leading men of *al-Jarida* newspaper, who claimed to be the voice of liberalism in Egypt because they gave her a column. She pointed out that *al-Jarida* and its male writers presumed to tell women what views to hold, what to wear, what kind of education they should have, what role they should play in the reform process and what kinds of relations they should have with their husbands in the family! This, she argued was a clear attempt to continue male tutelage over women in the name of liberation.[12] In honoring her, the men who attended her memorial tried to exonerate themselves from these charges and to prove her wrong.

In response to this national/public embrace of Nasif, Ya'qub Sarruf, the owner of the Syrian magazine *al-Muqtataf* published in Egypt, asked Mayy Ziyada to write an article summarizing Nasif's views on various issues.[13] By capitalizing on this interest, Sarruf was operating as the enterprising owner of a magazine who selected topics that appealed to the readers and increased his magazine's circulation. At this historical moment, the male reading public was interested in Nasif and her views. Ziyada's articles, which first appeared in a serialized form, satisfied this demand. Sarruf's decision to put these articles together in the form of a book anticipated a second round of interest in Nasif when the second memorial organized by women took place a year later.

Benedict Anderson has discussed the important role that print capitalism played in the imagining of modern national communities, which were conceptualized and operated as horizontal fraternities.[14] How could one reconcile the fraternal character of national communities with interest in the rights of women in the Egyptian case? The history of the first two decades of the twentieth century offered interesting insight into this question. During this period, mainstream newspapers and magazines, like the Egyptian *al-Jarida* and the Syrian *al-Muqtataf*, along with the few women's journals that existed at the time, used the issue of women's roles and rights to mobilize the community in the discussion of what distinguished the modern national community from the pre-modern one. While the women's journals relied on female writers and female readers, who constituted a very small percentage of the reading public, to influence the discussion of the changes taking place in the roles that women played in family and public life.[15] *Al-Jarida* and *al-Muqtataf*, which were mainstream newspapers and magazines that did not ordinarily have women writers, addressed themselves to male readers engaging them in the broader debates about modernity and nationalism, using women's rights as a measure of the development of both phenomena. Until Nasif joined *al-Jarida* and its writers, gender was a topic of fraternal debates in mainstream newspapers—a discussion undertaken exclusively by men, privileging male views of women and their roles. In the pre-modern community, men did not publicly discuss women, who were considered to be private beings that belonged to their families. By making women the topic of public debate, men reasserted the rights they had over women, not by virtue of kinship relations, but by virtue of being men and members of a fraternity. One of the earliest rights men exercised in a colonial modern community was the right to control the discussion of the minute details in women's lives (their relations with children and husbands, and the way they managed their households). Their views of the gender roles of women also began to be treated as important markers of the larger ideological divisions that characterized the new modern Islamic society.

When Nasif began to write in *al-Jarida*, she used her privileged position as a graduate of al-Saniya School and a trained teacher to challenge the exclusively fraternal character of this debate, which assumed that women were still not fit to speak for themselves and/or to articulate positions that challenged the exercise of this modern form of male power. From this modernist forum, she began the thorough critique of modernity and the way modernist views advocated by Egyptian men devalued women and blamed them for the woes of Egyptian society.[16] Equally important, she argued that this largely fraternal debate on women's liberation revealed the lack of difference between pre-modern and modern communities. The following is one of her most eloquent statements on this subject,

> Men should let leave us alone so that we can investigate their
> opinions and choose those that are the most rational. Man should
> not assume a despotic attitude toward our liberation just as he did
> toward our enslavement. We are sick of his despotism. We do not
> fear the air or the sun as much as we fear his eyes and his tongue.
> If he promises to lower his gaze, as he is ordered to do by his religion
> and to hold his tongue as good manners require, then we will look
> into his concerns and ours.[17]

The new fraternal debates contributed to an overwhelming number of opinions offered by men about women. Nasif suggested that women needed to sort them out and pick those that they deemed most rational. She saw these new debates as part of the same old despotic attitude toward women. In advising men to avert their eyes and to hold their tongues, she wanted to secure women some degree of freedom in discussing these important concerns.

Bahithat al-Badiya and Ziyada's Views of the Modernist Nationalist Discourse of Men

In obliging Ya'qub Sarruf by writing a series of articles on Malak Hifni Nasif in *al-Muqtataf*, Ziyada used the project to add interest in women rights to her reputation as an essayist. This explained why Ziyada's biography of Nasif, titled *Bahithat al-Badiya* (the pen name that Nasif took when she married a prominent member of a Bedouin family and moved to live with him in the Fayyum desert) devoted as much space to Ziyada's views about women's rights as it did to Nasif's. As a Syrian immigrant woman who wanted to fit in the Egyptian literary and public milieu, Ziyada critiqued Nasif's independent views very harshly and in the process reestablished the power of male/fraternal tutelage and discourse.

The first literary critic to try to make sense of this confusing biography was Huda al-Sadda who noted that in Ziyada's biography of Malak Hifni Nasif the line between the author and that of her subject was blurred, which made it very difficult to classify. The following quote explains the problem:

> It is a biography of Malak, but it is also an autobiographical work about Mayy. . . . The reader recognizes that there is a strong connection between the two writers and their ideas. When Mayy describes Malak or discusses her ideas, she is dealing with someone or something close to her, *yet there was no identity between them.* We find that when Mayy argues about Malak's ideas, criticizes them and offers alternative suggestions that lead to different doors, she does it in such a way that it feels like she is looking for an opportunity to express her own views either by agreeing or disagreeing with [Nasif]. As I mentioned before, Mayy confesses that she was not very objective in her book about Malak. For every paragraph she writes about Nasif, there is a paragraph about Mayy.[18]

The above description indicated that Ziyada used a complex narrative strategy in her book about Nasif, whose life and work were just one part of the discussion. Al-Sadda suggested that even though the biographer and her subject were friends and women writers, there was no identity in their views. Ziyada's feminine voice turned out to be that of the Levantine-Egyptian Christian woman who felt threatened by Nasif's Islamic/Egyptian voice and preferred the dominant (masculine) nationalist discourse on gender issues with its orientalist overtones. The readers of Ziyada's biography of Nasif in 1919 and at present assume feminine, if not feminist, solidarity and a shared modernist nationalist discourse. Upon closer examination, one discovers two very distinct discourses on the gender concerns of women at the time and their relations to men.

Ziyada divided her biography of Nasif into six chapters with each chapter exploring one aspect of the complex identity of the author shaped by being a woman, a Muslim, an Egyptian, a writer, a critic, and a reformer. The first chapter focused its attention on Nasif as a charismatic woman who possessed characteristics that were shared by other members of her gender as well as some that set her apart. For example, she had a certain magnetism that distinguished her from others, but like other women, she paid attention to details, empathized with others, was emotional, adaptable, and tactful. Ziyada also hypothesized that Nasif had a depressive personality that felt things deeply and was inclined to sadness.[19]

In this chapter, Ziyada gave ample space to Nasif's view of the problem of polygamy. While in the present volume Hanan Kholoussy examines Nasif's views on polygamy in the broader context of evolving Egyptian state approaches to marriage, we should note here that Ziyada adopted a position of Christian privilege in order to sympathize with the woes of Muslim women who were part of polygamous marriages. "We [Christian women] who were used to see our mother as the permanent mistress of the house and its absolute goddess could not comprehend the conditions of a large group of our sisters who live in misery under constant threat and could not understand their humiliation . . . or low self esteem."[20] In other words, the devaluation of women in Islamic and/or Arab societies was a problem faced by Muslim women, but not Christian ones. The resulting silence on the problems facing Christian women supported her belief in their privileged position vis-à-vis Muslim women.

Next, Ziyada directed her attention to Nasif's Islamic identity. According to Ziyada, Nasif was enamored with her religion, loving and taking pride in it, making her "Muslim before anything else." As evidence, she cited the fact that Nasif was known for her piety among her Muslim sisters. Islam influenced her approach and discussion of all issues whether they were political, social, or ethical and occupied an important position in her reform agenda: she advocated teaching Muslim women the principles of their religion, which included understanding the Qur'an and Islamic traditions as well as permitting them to pray in mosques so that they could listen to religious sermons and be part of the religious life and festivities of the community.[21]

Ziyada thought Nasif's religiosity explained her stern and unjust view of missionary schools, especially those run by nuns. As the graduate of missionary schools herself, Ziyada defended them against Nasif's criticisms, which included their emphasis on rote learning and not the ability to think; teaching them the history of other countries, but not their own; emphasizing the learning of foreign languages at the expense of Arabic; and developing a very limited definition of femininity that included learning to play the piano and speaking a foreign language. They were thought to look down on others, which meant that they were not well-behaved and they tended to be spendthrifts who had an ostentatious demeanor.[22]

In response, Ziyada suggested that these problems were not specific to missionary schools and that they might reflect the failings of the students, not the schools. As a graduate of these schools, she vouched for the emphasis they put on high principles and religiosity. As for not teaching the students Islamic and oriental history, this was the duty of the family! The learning of other languages was a weapon that gave Orientals the ability to live in both worlds.[23]

Immediately following this discussion, Ziyada accused Nasif of being a fanatic: "One group will see *Bahithat al-Badiya* as a fanatic. Of this, there is no doubt, but how could one expect her not to be a fanatic? Is not fanaticism the closest emotion to the self?"[24] This was a disingenuous interpretation of Nasif's views of missionary schools. Nasif did not criticize them because of their religious orientation, but for nationalist reasons: they neglected teaching the language and history of the society within which they operated and imposed on its women culturally specific roles.[25] Yet, Ziyada considered Nasif's critique of these schools as well as her pride in her own religion as expressions of fanaticism. It would be difficult to imagine other Muslims considering Nasif's views about valuing their religion as fanatic. Only members of minority religions were likely to see this it as such. Ziyada did not frankly state this was a Christian perspective, but chose to make fanaticism an instinctive human emotion felt by everyone. The use of blunt and pointed attacks on Nasif that are then somewhat softened developed as a consistent strategy that Ziyada used in the different chapters of this biography. While Ziyada fostered the impression that she and Nasif were friends and allies in the same struggle, her biography of Nasif was not a sympathetic one. The subtitle of the biography, *Bahithat al-Badiya: dirasa naqdiya*, described the work as a critical study of the author, but it was in fact a *severely* critical study of the author.

In the chapter that Ziyada devoted to Nasif as an Egyptian, she underlined her sense of humor, courteousness, facility with beautiful expressions and national pride as components of that identity. Whether she was discussing Islam or the Orient, Nasif's Egyptian nationalism was always latent and close to the surface. She called on all writers to develop a civilization that was "particular to the Orient which suited its instincts, and customs without undermining its ability to take advantage of the contributions of modernity."[26] When she turned to the discussion of women, Nasif dismissed the Orient and Islamic countries as frames of reference and only focused on Egyptian women and their problems. Finally, she unapologetically declared her love for everything Egyptian including the attractive dark skin color of most Egyptians, and their ancient history.

In concluding this chapter, Ziyada identified herself as a naturalized member of the Egyptian national community—implicitly agreeing with the concept of the eternally "Egyptianizing" capacity of the Nile Valley as mooted by Muhammad Husayn Haykal and others in the first decades of the twentieth century.[27] This was how she described the abstract category of homeland and how it defined her relationship to Egypt,

> Among different social categories, there was nothing that inspired more enthusiasm than the mention of the name of one's homeland because it represented the sum total of one's existence: it represented one's family and loved ones, the place where one laughed and shed tears, where the graves [of one's ancestors] were located. . . . It stood for the collective archeological, historical, ethical, scientific and practical heritage. It consisted of one's daily experience of beautiful dawns and dignified sunsets.

> We who love Egypt single out her natural beauty, historical greatness, archeological glory and the sweetness of its young men and women. We recognized that the true and authentic Egypt was the one that marched proudly behind the flying flags. It is those young men aspiring to develop and a nation that smartly remembers that the path of progress is not that of disturbance, destruction, and ruin, but that of calmness, labor, and thought.

Egypt is the Egyptian woman who has shown us these days that she has what we had hoped for. . . . How fine it was to see the smiles of these women behind the white veil during the days of the demonstration. How joyous it was to see the Egyptian flag that united the cross and the crescent and how lovely it was to hear the low melodious voices that chanted the national anthem.

Let the Bahitha rest safely and peacefully for her sisters have the same national aptitude. I salute her Egyptianess and I salute every Egyptian woman and I do not fear ending this chapter with one cheer: Long live Egypt![28]

In addition to the emotional/personal dimension that identified the homeland with family, loved ones, and ancestors, Ziyada cited the collective memory shared with others shaped by archeology,[29] history, and ethics. There were other important national symbols, like the flag and the national anthem, which also had an emotional content. During the 1919 national revolution, Egypt was well-represented by both its men and women who came out in demonstrations carrying flags that had both the cross and the crescent. Although Ziyada supported these demonstrations, she was wary of the destruction and the ruin that resulted from protests and protestors, preferring order, thought, and labor as means of national expression. This long passage, beginning with Ziyada recognizing Egypt as an adopted home where she lived with her family, ended with her joining in the national cheer for Egypt.

Ziyada then turned to Nasif's writing skills. She began by acknowledging that Nasif was a great writer who was skilled in the use of language as an elegant and graceful tool of expression. Paradoxically, Ziyada criticized her writings for not being able to look inward into the psyche and went further to say that she lacked any spirituality.[30] Both of these claims contradicted her earlier claims about Nasif's ability to empathize with the feelings of others and her religiosity.

While Ziyada recognized Nasif's role as a social critic, she suggested that she was naturally critical and that she was able to polish her critical capacities through education, painful experience, and the access she had to different classes. Through her father and then her husband, she belonged to the upper classes, but as a schoolgirl she had friends from the middle class. After her marriage, she moved to the Fayyum where she gained access to the worlds of Bedouin and peasant women. Through them, she was able to examine the role that class played in distinguishing the experiences of women as well as some sources of social dysfunction, which they shared together.[31] For example, Nasif's opposition to the unveiling of women was based on her recognition that women's education was still inadequate and that men and women were not ready for the social transition to a desegregated society. In documenting the way Egyptian society expressed its devaluation of women from childhood into adulthood, she opened the doors of the family for critical examination, especially the pain inflicted on women through polygamy.

In concluding this chapter, Ziyada stated that she felt helpless because, as a Christian, she was unable to diagnose the strange maladies that resulted from polygamy because they "were not existent in my people and even though my feminine heart could understand them, they remained unreal to me." She also felt sad because the family, which was the reservoir of happiness, became the swamp of disaster and sorrow.[32] She, again, remained silent about any of the problems which Christian women faced in the family.

Finally, Ziyada reserved her harshest criticism for Nasif's role as a reformer. She reminded the reader of what she had said in previous chapters about how Nasif "does not give her reader two wings with which to fly; she does not provide him with much imagination that allows him to soar over the Olympus. . . . She is only interested in the obvious feelings that are widely shared in groups. She remains within the walls of her environment gazing at the manifestations of distress with teary eyes and addressing them in very inflammatory tones. . . ."[33] After reviewing Nasif's legislative agenda, which proposed making all levels of education, including the study of medicine, open to women; advocated women's enhanced religious education; supported veiling according to the Islamic principles; and called for pre-marital engagements and polygamy in exceptional cases, Ziyada commented, "Sorry my lady, but all of these suggestions have already been discussed in Syria."[34] Even though Nasif's suggestions went beyond Qasim Amin's limited reforms that Ziyada considered as the blueprint for the liberation of the Egyptian woman, she was not willing to acknowledge their importance and/or originality. The claim that they were not original because they have already been discussed or tried in Syria ignored the way they expanded the boundaries of the debate in an Egyptian context. It reaffirmed the competitive edge enjoyed by the Syrian community in the Levant and in Egypt in the gender arena without much discussion of what was specifically debated in Syria. As if to reinforce this point, she criticized Nasif's reform agenda.

As I close her book, *al-Nisa'iyyat*, a big question mark materializes. I want to understand how come she did not think of focusing women's attention on poor women and the importance of forming a benevolent society for Muslim women? I have always been shocked to see benevolent societies organized by women of all ethnic and religious groups with Muslim women being the exception even though Muslims represent the wealthiest and most generous groups. Because they represent the majority, the needy among them were also large in numbers.

Welfare activities appeal to a woman's hearts. . . . So, I do not understand why Muslim women have not constituted their own benevolent society. Other than that, does anyone object to the feasibility of the reforms proposed by Nasif? Her minor reform program emphasized two things: first the need to open all doors of education to women and secondly the need to make all reforms compatible with Islamic teachings and national customs. Her fanaticism about the latter point led some to comment that she only needed an *'imma* (a headdress worn by the religious scholars) to become a *shaykh*. I am inclined to see her views positively because they will reassure the strictest conservatives [about the desirability of change].

In the above paragraph, Muslim women were faulted for being behind all other religious groups in organizing their own benevolent societies. This general criticism was also used as a specific criticism of Nasif's reform agenda, which was again described as not only unimaginative, but uncaring. As though this was not enough, Ziyada categorized Nasif's approach to reform as a minor one whose emphasis on education was radical but marked with fanatic stress on Islamic principles. In an attempt to soften the harshness of her criticism, Ziyada concluded that her religious fanaticism had some political usefulness, making conservatives open to the suggested social changes.

In the conclusion of this chapter, Ziyada viewed the veil as a supreme sign of the oppression of the Muslim woman and as a measure of the limited character of Nasif's reform agenda. The veil separated the Muslim woman from the business world and allowed her agent, guardian, and her guards to abuse her economically. Here, she interjected that her thoughts on this subject were not going to matter because this was a Muslim issue.

It was interesting then, that she proceeded to publish her views on that matter in an article titled "Musulmanes d'Aujourd'hui" in the Egyptian *Le Progrès*, which gave an account of an exchange she had with Nasif on this subject. In that article, she persistently challenged Nasif's views on how the veil would eventually be torn away, but that at present was needed to protect the interests of some women who were not ready for the dramatic transition to a desegregated society. For Nasif, the veil was not just a symbol or an article of clothing; it was connected to the development of a new understanding of freedom that mothers could teach their children. In response, Ziyada argued that short-term social chaos was a small price to pay for the abolition of this symbol as a step toward long-term moderation.[35]

Ziyada concluded this biography by devoting chapters eight and nine to the work of Qasim Amin who developed the modernist nationalist discourse of which Nasif was critical. The chapters were titled "the comparison between Qasim Amin and *al-Bahitha*." She began the first of the two chapters with a quote by Dr. Shibli Shumayyil,[36] which underlined the track she was going to take in this comparison. Shumayyil began by stating that Nasif made a contribution equal to that of Qasim Amin in her critique of the problems facing the family and the emphasis she put on the importance of education of women, but concluded that "she did not, however, go far enough in her call for the liberation of women because she did not call for the complete abolition of the veil, which some consider to be a sound opinion."[37]

Like Shumayyil, Ziyada asserted that the works of Amin and Nasif were connected in her mind as well as that of many others. It was for that reason that she decided to devote the last chapters of this biography to Amin's work. Even though Ziyada cited a poem that Nasif wrote strongly denying that she was a follower of Amin and/or his approach, she belittled Nasif's position in the following quote:

[Nasif's denial] indicated that she was not fair to [Amin]. I do not
dare say that she did not understand him. How do I dare make that
claim? I believe that he greatly influenced her. She only courageously
took to the pen because of his inspiration, having paved the way,
preparing people for what she was about to say. She addressed certain
issues and sought to reform them along the same lines he outlined.
How can a sophisticated woman not be influenced by writings that
were the first of their kind from someone who wanted the good of

women and the nation? This is why I would like to publicly declare that she is his intellectual and courageous daughter. She is his student in calling for the reform of the conditions of women. This does not negate the existence of slight differences between them.[38]

Here, Ziyada utilized the same strategy used throughout the book, leveling serious charges against Nasif and then softening them. She claimed that Nasif was not fair to Amin and more seriously did not understand him. She then qualified these offensive claims by saying that his work influenced her and that his ideas made people receptive to her views. She also described her as his follower because she took the path he charted and her views were minimally different.

Ziyada's two chapters that deal with Qasim Amin and his work offered reverent and romantic views of the author who died in 1908. Based on her readings of his work, Ziyada described him as a gentle man with a nervous personality who was preoccupied with justice, truth, fairness, goodness, and reform. His role as a judge made him both thorough, balanced and the best advocate for women.[39] Ziyada was not bothered by the fact that Amin used the ideal of male friendship to highlight the inadequacy of male-female relations in the family. She opined that "he knew women because he knew men and his knowledge of both was rooted in human nature."[40] She quoted him as saying, "whenever I tried to imagine happiness, its representation was in the form of a woman who possessed the beauty of her gender and the mind of a man."[41] While Ziyada accepted that Amin's knowledge of women was based on his knowledge of men and his definition of a feminine ideal as a woman with a mind of a man, Nasif took issue with both. These representations provided new ways of controlling women: they valorized the needs of men and more seriously encouraged women to see themselves through the eyes and the mind of a man.

In the few comparisons that were made between the reforms advocated by Nasif and those offered by Amin, his agenda was consistently given advantage over Nasif's. She defined reform as a woman refusing to let go of the past, whereas he approached reform as a man determined to look forward. She was more conservative, looking back after every step she took forward and emphasizing changes that only fit her cultural environment. He, on the other hand, was confident, able to transcend the shackles of the past and the differences that separate nations. These familiar nationalist tropes gave Amin and his masculine modern nationalist discourse the last word in the discussion of Nasif's views. They represented Ziyada's way of appealing to an Egyptian women's movement that she said was largely made up of men. Whatever her reasons were, this ending of Nasif's biography allowed the grand old man of Egyptian feminism, Qasim Amin, to overshadow her critical perspective and its success in developing a woman-centered agenda. Only recently have scholars challenged this dominant view of Qasim Amin as a feminist allowing for greater appreciation of Nasif's views and perspectives.

'A'isha Taymur and the Nationalization of the Multiple Identities of Women

If Ziyada's biography of Nasif—in 1919 at the onset of the national revolution—presented national identity as one of the many plural identities of the writer, her biography of 'A'isha Taymur—published in *al-Muqtataf* in 1923 toward the end of the revolution—privileged national identity over all others. Even though Taymur's ethnic and linguistic identities set her apart from the majority population, Ziyada nationalized them in the effort to construct the author as an Egyptian national icon. The resulting construction that relied very heavily on the modernist nationalist discourse, which presented Taymur as a product of modernization, not the old society, privileging the role that her father played in her rise to prominence and overlooking the contributions made by other women to her success.

In the introduction to Taymur's biography, Ziyada explained that after receiving an invitation to give a lecture to the members of the Young Woman of a Young Egypt Association in 1922,[42] she promptly began the search for a "complex feminine personality whose study would offer good lessons in ethics, literature, and sociology, another figure in which the women's movement could take pride and a role model that could inspire others,"[43] as her topic. Ziyada did not explain what the above association stood for, but one could safely assume that it was one of the groups that emerged during this period signifying the interest that middle class women had in national and women's history. Ziyada's reference to the desire to study another figure of interest to the women's movement suggested that she saw this new biography as a continuation of the project that she started with Nasif's biography. In the above quote, one observed a significant switch in Ziyada's view of the women's movement. Her previous emphasis that the women's movement was largely made up of men disappeared and greater stress was given to women's activism during the 1919 Revolution manifested in the lecture organized by the Young Woman of a Young Egypt. In response, she tried to appeal to them through the selection of an inspirational feminine figure, which could serve as a role model. While this represented an important shift in the definition of her audience, she continued to use the modernist nationalist discourse, which privileged the masculine voice and viewpoint.

Ziyada offered five reasons that explained her selection of Taymur as a focus of her second biography. First, Taymur served as "the avant garde of the feminist movement in this country." Second, the general public already knew her as a poet without knowing much about her poetry or life. Third, an appreciation of her accomplishments provided a way of studying the general rise of modern Egypt and the position she came to occupy among the literary figures of her time, not only among women writers. Fourth, the content of Taymur's poetry and writings was worthy of further study because it offered glimpses of the past and present. Finally, her life provided a source of entertainment, instructed the reader about conditions contributing to her awakening at when the general public remained dormant, and offered insight into the factors that shaped her agency.[44]

Just as writing about Nasif provided Ziyada with an opportunity to establish her feminist credentials, the study of Taymur's struggles became a vehicle that reinforced Ziyada's new reputation as a modern literary critic. While she declared Taymur to be the pioneering figure of Egyptian feminism, she did not explain what she meant by that. Taymur's literary appearance among the noted figures of the nineteenth century entitled her to that privileged position even though little was known about her life and work. Paradoxically, Ziyada also hinted that her literary accomplishments and rise to prominence were shaped by the rise of a modern Egypt. So, Taymur's life and work became bases for the simultaneous comparison of traditional and modern Egyptian societies. While her accomplishments were credited to modernity, her failings were blamed on tradition.

In constructing the age in which Taymur emerged, Ziyada articulated the dominant modern nationalist perspective on Egyptian history that posited the economic and cultural rise of the West and the decline of the Orient under Ottoman control as important keys for understanding nineteenth-century Egyptian society. She cited the French expedition to Egypt as the starting point for modern Egyptian history. These events had three important consequences: they united Egyptian national resistance against a European threat, started the scientific study of the country that introduced Egyptians to aspects of European civilization, and weakened the political power of the Mamluks. The latter development paved the way for the rise to political power of Muhammad 'Ali, who it was pointed out was born in the same year as Napoleon and Wellington.[45] Among the men who worked with the new ruler were the Kurdish and Turkish paternal grandparents of Taymur's father.

Ziyada argued that 'A'isha Taymur, born in 1840, was a product of the changes that the first seven rulers of this dynasty introduced in Egyptian education, government, economy, and the army. In a linear account of the positive changes these rulers introduced in nineteenth-century Egypt, she underlined the important role played by "the Syrian geniuses who migrated to Egypt as a result of the catastrophes [in their land] and how the clash of their ideas with those of the Egyptians brought mutual benefits to both parties and to Arab thought in general."[46] These Syrian men and women, along with other Egyptians, provided support to the nationalist movement through their attendance of the speeches of the fiery orator, Jamal al-Din al-Afghani.[47] Here, Ziyada continued her effort to underline the contributions of Syrian men and women to the development of a modern national community in Egypt.

She was conspicuously silent on British occupation and clearly did not consider it to be a significant reversal in the dynasty's modernist project. She quoted a passage from Qasim Amin's reply to Duc d'Harcourt published in 1894, in which he claimed that "complete liberty in thought and writing was now allowed, Egyptians enjoyed all the "rights of man" and since the 'Urabi Revolution have continued their national awakening."[48] Ziyada agreed with Amin's whitewashing of the severe economic, social, and political consequences of British colonial rule as an integral part of the desirable march of modernization. She also used the modernist nationalist discourse to argue that women benefited from the general changes that took place in nineteenth-century Egyptian society, such as the establishment of the school of midwives in 1831. Yet she indicated that the education of the average young girl at that time consisted of learning embroidery and needlework at home or through visiting Coptic teachers. A small group of girls learned the Qur'an at home from elderly *shaykh*s.

As the number of Europeans who settled in the country increased, so did the number of religious missions, which had an impact on the education of young boys and girls. The first missionary school for girls, Le Bon Pasteur, was opened in 1844 in Shubra, followed by the American missionary school for girls in Azbakiya in 1856, and finally Italian Franciscan nuns opened their own school for girls in 1859. In 1873, the first public school for girls was established and was followed by another one in 1874.[49] Christian contribution to modern education, through missionary schools, was positively highlighted here as part of the evolution of girls' education.

While the number of schools for boys and girls during Taymur's time reached one thousand, including many traditional elementary schools/ *kuttab*s, the dramatic change regarding girls' education occurred when a minority of enlightened men began to complain among themselves about the ignorance of their wives. This group saw education as a means of making their wives better partners and mothers. They did not dare, however, to confront the conservative public until Qasim Amin courageously led the charge to change the social views of women quietly bearing the brunt of the angry reactions to his writings.[50]

According to the above modernist narrative, the state, the Europeans/ missionaries and a minority of enlightened Egyptian men represented important sources of change in the public's views of girls' education. Ziyada's enlightened men blamed women, not society or men, for their ignorance and for the backwardness of the family. Unlike Nasif, who had criticized these attacks, Ziyada accepted them, seeing women as the consumers of change, not its instigators.

Paradoxically, Taymur's education did not fit into any of the patterns suggested by the above modern nationalist narrative on girls' education. She gained access to education through her rebellion against the conventional education given to young rich girls of her time. In trying to evoke the home life of Taymur's family in nineteenth-century Egypt, Ziyada relied on the work of Eugénie LeBrun, the French wife of the young Husayn Rushdi, who later on became prime minister, to describe the orderly but very hierarchical private world of women (the harem) in wealthy families at a time far later than that of 'A'isha Taymur's childhood at the middle of the nineteenth century. Within this social context, Taymur's mother, who was a freed Circassian slave, began to teach her daughter needlework and embroidery at the age of seven, but the little girl showed very little aptitude or interest. The repeated efforts of the mother to explain that needlework represented an important feminine tool and a form of education fell on the deaf ears of the young Taymur, who preferred to visit the *salamlik* (the segregated space that belonged to men) where her father met with guest writers. These visits alarmed her mother, contributing to more serious confrontations. Her father eventually intervened to abet her rebellion by teaching her to read and write, leaving her mother with the task of supervising the traditional education of his two other daughters.

In this account, the orderly management of the harem emphasized by LeBrun was easily undermined by the rebellion of a young 'A'isha who not only resisted her mother's tutoring, but also had easy access to her father's guests. Taymur's father emerged as a lenient and enlightened patriarch who recognized the importance of a different type of education for young girls. The problem with this interpretation was that he was clearly not concerned about the traditional education of his two other daughters. 'A'isha clearly forced the issue of learning how to read and write on both parents and her father decided to make an exception in her case. If the enlightenment of 'A'isha's father was questionable, her mother's role as the villain who tried to frustrate her daughter's ambitions was exaggerated. Because of the general contempt shown to slave women, Ziyada did not spend any time pondering the possible motives behind the mother's opposition. In the context of the times, encouraging one's daughter to mingle with male writers and prefer reading and writing to the feminine crafts was a recipe for adult disappointment. In discouraging Taymur from both of these activities, her mother was trying to spare her daughter the pain of having unrealistic social expectations. In any case, 'A'isha Taymur's four years of study that made her proficient in Turkish, Persian, and Arabic came to an end when she was married at the age of fourteen and proceeded to spend the next thirteen years like other women of her class: mothering children and managing the affairs of a wealthy household.

In a significant twist in this narrative of struggle to expand the definition of the non-domestic interests and aspirations of nineteenth-century, upper-class women, Taymur turned to her daughter, Tawhida, for support. At the age of twelve, Tawhida took over the domestic responsibilities of her mother, managing the affairs of the household, providing her mother with the spare time to resume her studies, attending some of these lessons and helping her with the study of poetic meter. The death of both her father and husband in the span of three years provided Taymur with greater freedom and resources to hire two more women instructors, Fatima al-Azhariya and Sitata al-Tablawiya, to help her study grammar and poetic meter.[51] In the middle of this triumphant phase, Tawhida fell sick and a preoccupied Taymur missed the early signs of her illness. Tawhida's untimely death at the age of eighteen plunged Taymur into a long mourning that lasted seven years. Taymur's youngest son, Mahmud, persuaded her to end her mourning and encouraged her to publish her Arabic writings.

Despite these social obstacles and personal blows, Taymur emerged as a prominent member of the court of Khedive Isma'il's mother in the 1870s. In 1887, she published a work of fiction titled *Nata'ij al-awal fi-l-aqwal wa-l-afal*. She published *Mir'at al-ta'mul fi-l-umur*, a social commentary on the changes taking place in the Egyptian family, *Hilyat al-tiraz*, her collected Arabic poems, in 1892 and *Shukufa*, her collected Turkish poems, in 1896. She corresponded in the 1880s with Warda al-Yazji in Lebanon and was acquainted with Zaynab Fawwaz, the Lebanese-Egyptian woman author who devoted a chapter to 'A'isha Taymur in her opus *al-Durr al-manthur fi tabaqat rabat al-khudur.*

Ziyada's discussion of Taymur's literary and poetic production privileged her Arabic works even though she published some of her work in Turkish and Persian. Ziyada discounted the importance that Taymur's family gave to the learning of Turkish and Persian over Arabic in the late 1840s and how these languages were part of the old Ottoman literary ideal that located her within that cultural tradition. Since Ziyada associated Ottoman rule with the decline of Arab societies, she could not appreciate that tradition. Instead, Ziyada treated Turkish, Persian, and Arabic as separate languages that had different meanings for the writer. For example, she explained to the reader that Arabic was the language of Taymur's homeland, Turkish was the language of her parents, and Persian was simply a scholastic language that some writers of the old school learned. The imposition of artificial, modernist significances on these languages gave Arabic more social and political weight and personalized and/or depoliticized the importance of Turkish. Unfortunately, Ziyada's presentation sometimes underlined the contradictory character of these characterizations. For example, Ziyada cited how princess Qadriya, the daughter of Sultan Husayn Kamil of Egypt, read Taymur's Turkish poetry because Turkish, not Arabic, was her national tongue. Princess Qadriya, who became a published Islamic author in her own right in the 1920s, wrote in Turkish and the Egyptian public could only read her work after it was translated into Arabic. Ziyada's discounting of Taymur's Ottoman identity and the linguistic and political connections between the Egyptian royal family, the aristocracy, and the Ottoman imperial system in favor of an Egyptian nationalism did injustice to the fact that these identities competed with each other during the last two decades of the nineteenth century, reflecting important ethnic and linguistic divisions.

Because Ziyada knew neither Turkish nor Persian, she informed her reader that she would only address Taymur's Arabic writings. As a result, Taymur emerged as an Arabic writer even though that was only part of her literary persona. Ziyada's attempt to locate Taymur in the Arabic literary tradition suffered from another problem: the modernist assumption that nineteenth-century Arabic and its literary styles were traditional and, therefore, incapable of originality or change, while generally preoccupied with rhyme, clichéd imagery, and endless iterations. As a result, it was not surprising that Ziyada, the literary critic, found Taymur's poetry and fiction wanting. Because she assumed that the traditional literary forms used by Taymur were not capable of change, Ziyada failed to see how Taymur's poetry and fiction became preoccupied with novel political themes like the changing forms of dynastic Islamic government and their new social and political preoccupations. For example, her poems praising Khedive Tawfiq articulated her political views of the 'Urabi revolution and the new political claims made by the returning khedive.

Conclusion

The period between 1918 and 1923 witnessed wide-ranging debates on the positive and negative aspect of the roles that women of different classes were playing in the newly emerging national community.[52] In addition to Ziyada's biographies of Nasif and Taymur, which transformed them into national icons, Shaun Lopez has clearly demonstrated that the newspaper coverage of the exploits of Raya and Sakina in 1920 constructed them as evil characters in a cautionary tale regarding the corrupting effects and the hazards that desegregated working class women faced in a dangerous public arena.[53] Paradoxically, Ziyada's discussion of the lives and works of Malak Hifni Nasif and 'A'isha Taymur stressed the benefits to be derived from ending the seclusion of middle- and upper-class women and their integration into public debate and the literary arena. At the same time, the state weighed in with the formalization of the laws that govern marriage and divorce that were categorized as determining "personal status." In a theme explored by Hanan Kholoussy, the laws clearly demonstrated that the family was no longer a private institution, but had to be subjected to the monitoring of the state as part of its modernizing project.[54]

The discourses that emerged out of these various debates on gender were liberal. Ziyada used the biographies of Nasif and Taymur to provide individual role models for middle and upper-class women who were taking on new political roles in support of the 1919 Revolution. Similarly, newspaper discussions of Raya and Sakina provided individual representatives of working class women who were engaged in occupations and activities that gained the disapproval of middle class readers. While Nasif and Taymur emerged as positive icons, Raya and Sakina were negative ones reinforcing the familiar modernist assumption that working class women were in need of middle class women's guidance to become valued members of the community. In the constructions of the lives of Nasif, Taymur, and Raya and Sakina, there was a new emphasis on their individual experiences that offered a marked contrast to earlier treatments that dealt with them as an undifferentiated mass. They emerged in these new constructions as individuals whose choices made a difference in their lives, that of their social classes and the larger community.

This liberal discourse was reinforced by the legal discourse of the personal status laws, which focused attention on another definition of the individual. Personal status *(al-ahwal al-shakhsiya)* focused attention on the concept of personhood in the family that was gendered and entitled individual men and women to different rights. The concept of rights also preoccupied Egypt's liberal discourses; the fact that rights of men and women were unequal matched interpretations of liberal discourse in other societies and histories.

More narrowly, this chapter has attempted to show that Ziyada's biographies of Malak Nasif and 'A'isha Taymur, long considered to be feminist works, were more nationalist in character. Not only were they part of the intellectual production that marked the onset and the successful conclusion of the 1919 Revolution, but they also sought to integrate the lives and works of Nasif and Taymur into the national history of the community. Furthermore, the role that women played in the 1919 Revolution led Ziyada to abandon her earlier view that men were the founders of the feminist movement in Egypt, which she stated in Nasif's biography, in favor of representing Taymur as the pioneering figure of that awakening.

Ziyada also used the biographies to integrate herself, as a Lebanese Christian woman, into the new national community. She was prominently featured in the biography of Nasif where she represented herself as another pioneering woman writer who had a strong relationship with Nasif, challenged her views and judged her work. In this way, she inserted herself in the history of the community and its pioneering women. Her embrace of the views of Qasim Amin, one of the key male figures of the Egyptian enlightenment, was another device she used to weave herself into the social and historical fabric of her adopted community. Her biography of 'A'isha Taymur represented another serious attempt to represent herself as the chronicler of the community and the contributions that Egyptian women made to its national history.

Her attempt to integrate her Christian background in the discussion of Egyptian society was less successful. Nasif's biography offered ample evidence of Ziyada's belief in the existence of a Christian-Muslim divides in the conception of the community and its gender agenda. She viewed the Christian Syrian community as more organized and forward-looking in taking care of the needs of its less fortunate segments than its Egyptian Muslim counterpart. She viewed Christian women as more fortunate than their Muslim counterparts in escaping polygamy and the uncertainty of divorce. In this, she uncritically accepted the familiar Orientalist views and attitudes of the colonial government regarding the existence of fundamental differences between the status of Muslim and Christian women. She did not consider the difficulty of divorce as the source of a potential problem for some Christian women and families. In fact, she characterized Christian women as enjoying a problem-free existence.

While these biographies offered a view of a community segmented by gender, religion, ethnicity, language, and class, the success of the 1919 Revolution had a negative effect on the serious exploration of these differences. In Nasif's biography, which was written at the outset of the revolution, Ziyada considered Nasif's Egyptianess to be one of the multiple aspects of her identity, shaped by being a woman, a Muslim, a writer, a social critic, and a reformer. In her biography of Taymur written three years later in the wake of the successful conclusion of the revolution, Ziyada nationalized Taymur's complex upper-class, Ottoman/linguistic, and ethnic identities, to transform her into an Arabic writer and an icon of Egyptian modernity. The result was an impoverished construction of her life and the complex makeup of Egyptian society then. In deconstructing the nationalist and feminist narratives that assumed the solidarity of men and women and the homogeneity of women's experiences, this chapter hoped to create a new space for documenting the way gender, religion, ethnic, class, and discursive differences contributed distinct perspectives on the history of different groups and their relations to the national community.

Notes

1 Latifa Muhammad Salim, *al-Mar'at al-misriyat wa-l-taghyir al-ijtima'i* (Cairo: General Egyptian Book Organization, 1984), 26–24; Amal Kamil Bayumi al-Subki, *al-Harakat al-nisa'iya fi Misr mabayn al-thawratayn 1919 wa 1952* (Cairo: General Egyptian Book Organization, 1986), chapter 1; Margot Badran, *Feminists, Islam and the Nation* (Princeton: Princeton University Press, 1995), 80–84.

2 Al-Subki, 25.

3 Marilyn Booth's study of Mayy Ziyada's biographies followed the familiar narrative that treated them as expressions of a developing feminism. See Marilyn Booth, "Biography and Feminist Rhetoric in Early Twentieth-Century Egypt: Mayy Ziyada's Studies of Three Women's Lives," *Journal of Women's History* 3: 1 (Spring 1991), 38–64.

4 The original members of the salon in 1913 were Isma'il Sabri, Salim Sarkis, Dr. Shibli Shumayyil, Nagib Hawawini, al-Mutran Driyyan, Anton al-Jamil, and Khalil Mutran. They were then joined by Ahmad Lutfi al-Sayyid, Wali al-Din Yakkan, al-Shaykh Rashid Rida, Yaqub Sarruf and Idris Raghib Pasha, 'Abbas Mahmud al-'Aqqad, Taha Husayn, Zaki Mubarak, Salim al-Bustani, Salama Musa, and many others. See Salma al-Hafar al-Kuzbari, *Mayy Ziyada wa ma'sat al-nubugh*, vol. 1 (Beirut: Mu'assasat Nawfal, 1987), 290–91.

5 Al-Kuzbari, vol. 1, 182.

6 Mayy Ziyada, *Bahithat al-badiya* (Beirut: Mu'assasat Nawfal, 1983), 148.

7 Arthur Goldschmidt Jr., "Yakan, 'Adli" in *Biographical Dictionary of Modern Egypt* (Boulder: Lynne Rienner Publishers, 2000), 229.

8 Ibid., 15.

9 Ibid.

10 Ibid.

11 Abd al-'Azim Ramadan, *Tatawwur al-haraka al-wataniya fi Misr min sanat 1918–1936* (Cairo: al-Mu'assasat al-Misriya al-'Amma li-l-Ta'lif wa-l-Nashr, n.d), 99.

12 Huda al-Sadda, "Bahithat al-Badiya 1998" in *al-Nisa'iyyat* (Cairo: al-Mar'at wa-l-Zakira, 1998), 10.

13 Ibid., 9.

14 Benedict Anderson, *Imagined Communities* (London: Verso, 1991), 7.

15 Beth Baron, *The Women's Awakening in Egypt, Culture, Society and the Press* (New Haven: Yale University Press, 1994), chapters 1–2.

16 See Huda al-Sadda's insightful analysis of Malak Hifni Nasif's writings which include: Huda al-Sadda, "Malak Hifni Nasif: halaqat mafquda min tarikh al-nahda," *Hagar*, 2 (1994), 109–19; idem., "Women in Egypt: Education and Modernity," in *The Self and the Other, Sustainability and Self Empowerment*, Ismail Serageldin and Afaf Mahfouz, eds. (Washington D.C.: the World Bank, 1996), 18–19; idem, "Notions of Modernity: Representations of the 'Western Woman' by Female Authors in Early Twentieth Century Egypt," in *The Arabs and Britain: Changes and Exchanges*, Proceedings of a Conference (Cairo: the British Council, 1998).

17 Huda al-Sadda, "Malak Hifni Nasif: halaqat mafquda min tarikh al-nahda," 113.

18 Huda al-Sadda, "Tatawwur nazariyyat al-sira al-dhatiya" in *al-Ma'rad al-awal li-kitab al-mar'at: al-mar'at al-'arabiya fi muwajahat al-'asr* (Cairo: Nur Dar al-Mar'at al-'Arabiya li-l-Nashr, 1966), 207. Emphasis added.

19 Ziyada, *Bahithat al-badiya*, 23–34. It was curious that Ziyada's biographers later on used this same personality type to explain why she was institutionalized by her family at al-'Asfuriya hospital in Beirut in the late 1930s.

20 Ibid., 25.

21 Ibid., 39.

22 Ibid., 41.

23 Ibid., 41–43.

24 Ibid., 43.
25 Nasif's criticism of missionary schools on these grounds mirrored a frequently recurring theme in nationalist educational discourse from the 1910s to the 1950s. For more on this see Barak Salmoni, "Pedagogies of Patriotism: Teaching Socio-Political Community in Twentieth-Century Turkish and Egyptian Education" (Ph.D. diss., Harvard University, 2002), 189–234, 281–91.
26 Ziyada, *Bahithat al-badiya*, 50.
27 For the motif of the Nile Valley Egyptianizing those who enter it, see Israel Gershoni and James P. Jankowski, *Egypt, Islam and the Arabs: The Search for Nationhood 1900–1930* (New York: Oxford University Press, 1986).
28 Ziyada, *Bahithat al-badiya*, 54.
29 See Benedict Anderson discussion of the colonial state's use of the census, map, and the museum to define the colonized communities. Anderson, *Imagined Communities*, 163–85.
30 Ziyada, 61.
31 Ibid., 67.
32 Ibid., 77.
33 Ibid., 80.
34 Ibid., 84.
35 Ibid., 89.
36 Dr. Shumayyil was a Syrian physician who settled in Egypt and used Darwinism to argue for the inferiority of women to men. See Zaynab Fawwaz, *al-Durr al-manthur fi tabaqat rabat al-khudur* (Kuwait: Maktabat Ibn Qutayba, n.d.), 498.
37 Ziyada, 93.
38 Ibid., 95–96.
39 Ibid., 93–120.
40 Ibid., 98.
41 Ibid., 102.
42 *Sha'irat al-tali'a, 'A'isha Taymur* (Cairo: Dar al-Hilal, 1956), 8.
43 Ziyada, 19.
44 Ibid., 20–21.
45 Ibid., 32–33.
46 Ibid., 37.
47 Ibid., 39.
48 Ibid., 35.
49 Ibid., 43.
50 Ibid.
51 Ibid., 72–75.
52 See chapters eleven and thirteen in this volume.
53 Shaun T. Lopez, "Madams, Murders and the Media: *Akhbar al-Hawadith* and the Emergence of a Mass Culture in 1920s Egypt," in the present volume.
54 Hanan Kholoussy, "The Nationalization of Marriage in Monarchical Egypt," in the present volume.

Part V

Art, Cinema, Literature
and Historiographical Memory

15   Twentieth-Century Egyptian Art: The Pioneers, 1920–52[1]

Caroline Williams

When people think of Egypt and the visual arts, images from the more than twenty-five hundred years of the pharaonic period usually come to mind. Some might remember that Egypt for nine hundred years was a part of the Hellenistic-Byzantine world, or that for fourteen hundred years it has had an Islamic legacy. Others might include romantic images painted by European artists in the nineteenth century. Very few, however, link Egypt with modern painting or sculpture, the most recent of Egypt's visual offerings. It is small wonder that this is so. The regrettable assumption persists that representational art is alien to Islam in spite of the rich evidence of manuscript illustrations and figural surface ornamentation. Furthermore, painting on canvas as a new Egyptian art form is not well-documented, either in Egypt or the West, and its artists and its creations remain relatively undiscovered and unpublicized. Its beginnings, however, take place in the early decades of the twentieth century and form another creative aspect of this era.[2]

The period of 1919–52 can be divided into two parts. The first part, 1919–36, began with the fervor of the nationalist Wafdist Revolution and ended with the Anglo-Egyptian Treaty of 1936. In these years characterized by revolutionary energy and constructive vitality, emerging artists contributed new themes to the authenticity of the nationalist movement. Among these, the pharaonic theme most readily allied itself with the new emerging nationalism since it emphasized Egypt's own authentic and distinct historical and cultural past. This theme also distinguished Egypt from the European background of its British occupier.[3] Thus, although the images produced in this first period did not entail radically new and different art forms, they nevertheless laid the foundation for a manifestly modern Egyptian art movement. The second part of the period, 1936–52, began with the intellectual turmoil surrounding a Europe at war and ended with the revolution of 'Abd al-Nasser in 1952. In these years the thematic emphasis moved from descriptions of the external, national context to one that was interpretative and individual. As such, the artistic approach now portrayed an understanding of indigenous and internal experiences.

1919–36

Modern Egyptian art began with the Pioneers—*al-Ruwwad* as they are referred to in Arabic—whose best work belonged to the years of the 1920s and 1930s. These were men born just before the turn of the century. They were trained by European artists in Egypt and Europe, and in European styles and techniques. Their manner of painting thus offers little that is different from the work of conventional western artists and sculptors. In depicting their own country and people, however, their views of their own context are more varied and intimate than the ones described by the foreign Orientalists of a century earlier. Individually, these Pioneers developed their own recognizable style and focus. Collectively, these artists depicted the Egypt they were born into during the early twentieth century: a land 80 percent agricultural, a country fighting for its political independence from Britain, and a society in which women were just being emancipated. These Pioneers in the visual arts were also part of a wider cultural expression, a new artistic revival whose object was to shape a national identity and to portray Egypt as enduring, distinct, and resurgent.

The story in its institutionalized form begins in Cairo. An acceptance of European fashions and artifacts had become an increasing part of court thinking and manners of the Muhammad 'Ali dynasty during the nineteenth century. In 1908, the same year in which a national university was founded, Prince Yusuf Kamal[4] established and funded the School of Fine Arts in one of his palaces in the Darb al-Gamamiz district.[5] The school was organized along European lines and the first faculty was appointed from the community of foreign artists. Guillaume Laplagne, a sculptor and one of the French art counselors to the royal family, was its first director, and Gabriel Biessy, an Italian, taught painting. The school provided free instruction to talented Egyptian youths with no prerequisites other than the desire to learn. After graduation the successful students were sent to Europe on a scholarship for further study.[6]

Mahmud Mukhtar, the only sculptor among the Pioneers, owes his development to this school.[7] He was born 10 May 1891 in Tambara, a small village near al-Mahalla al-Kubra in the Delta, where his father was the '*umda*, or headman. A sensitive and creative child, he fashioned village mud into figurines of animals and people. When his father took another wife, he moved with his divorced mother to the Sayyida Zaynab district in Cairo in 1902. Mukhtar was deeply affected by his mother's displacement and subsequent struggle to maintain her dignity, and his attachment to her remained deep and strong. He was seventeen years old when the new School of Fine Arts opened in 1908 and, eager to learn, he walked in and asked Laplagne, the first person he met, if he could study art there. Laplagne, a sculptor himself, encouraged and oversaw young Mukhtar's work. Graduating in 1911 Mukhtar was the first Egyptian admitted to the École des Beaux-Arts in Paris. In 1913 his figure *Aida* became the first work of art by a modern Egyptian artist to be included in an international exhibition in Paris.

The Egyptian revolution of 1919 brought Mukhtar back to Egypt, and to the installation of his best known sculpture: *Egypt's Awakening* (fig. 15.1). Mukhtar had submitted a marble model of this work to the International Exhibition at the Grand Palais in Paris of 1920, where it had won a gold medal. Sa'd Zaghlul, leading the Egyptian delegation to the Paris Peace Conference at the time, visited the exhibition, where he met Mukhtar and was impressed by the statue: a sphinx, rising on outstretched forelegs, and a woman standing next to it, her right hand on its head and her left hand throwing back her veil.[8]

In June 1921 the Egyptian government commissioned Mukhtar to recreate the sculpture in larger form. Work was begun 15 June 1922, and on 20 May 1928 King Fu'ad I unveiled the finished statue in the square in front of the main railroad station. It was later moved to Maydan Giza, where it faces the Nile at the end of a broad esplanade leading toward the main building of Cairo University. The sphinx, Egypt's unique past, and the woman, the country's vital present, face east, to a new dawn and a new future. As a representation it is both historical summary and prophecy of hope; it is Egypt rooted over the centuries beside the gift-giving river— monumental, authentic, and triumphant.

The statue stands also as the icon of the period. It carried a message which all Egyptians, literate and illiterate, aristocrat or peasant, could understand. Molded of pink granite quarried from Aswan, itself an enduring national element, the awakening gestures of both sphinx and woman were an embodiment of Egypt's aspirations for independence and revival through its people rather than through its rulers. Its creator Mukhtar and its patron Zaghlul were themselves evidence of a new social mobility, creative men who had achieved their positions through energy and talent. The statue, from gestation to completion (1918–28), also encapsulated the significant nationalist events of its creative decade. For example, in March 1919 the British exiled Sa'd Zaghlul to Malta for leading a delegation *(wafd)* against British rule and stirring nationalist agitation. The whirlwind of protest that swept the country was the Revolution of 1919. In February 1922, Britain announced they would end the Protectorate and grant Egypt independence. In November 1922, Howard Carter, after long and patient perseverance, discovered the tomb of Tutankhamun, a boy pharaoh buried with spectacular treasures, an event that electrified the world. In 1923 Huda Sha'rawi, returning from an international feminist meeting in Rome, stepped from the train in Cairo and removed her face veil in public for the first time, thus becoming the standard-bearer for the women's liberation movement.[9] Sa'd Zaghlul, hailed as the father of Egypt's political independence, died on August 1927, and was mourned throughout Egypt. His wife Safiya, referred to as *Umm al-Misriyyin* (mother of the Egyptians), a title given to her in 1919,[10] continued to play a symbolic role within the nationalist movement. The statue personified all of these events.

Mukhtar, never in robust health, died on 26 March 1934. He was buried in the Bab al-Wazir cemetery. In 1963 his remains were re-interred in a newly built museum in his honor on the island of Gezira designed by Ramsis Wissa Wassef. The museum displays a range of Mukhtar's work. He sculpted portrait busts of prominent Egyptians and the new Cairene Egyptian elite,[11] such as Dr. 'Ali Ibrahim, 'Abd al-Khaliq Tharwat, 'Adli Yakan, and Sa'd Zaghlul, all cabinet ministers and premiers who backed the 1919 Revolution.[12] His other statues are of peasant men and women, a tribute to those Egyptian inhabitants who had persevered throughout the millennia with little change. Mukhtar used his French training to create statues of idealized personifications or "types." Among the men are the *shaykh al-balad* (the village headman), the *fallah* (peasant) with his hand hoe, and "the guardian of the fields"; among the women are tall, slim figures who carry baskets or jars of water on their heads, or rounded draped shapes hauling water from the river or battling the fierce winds of the *khamsin* (spring storm).[13]

Yusuf Kamil and Raghib Ayad, companions of Mukhtar, were also in the School of Fine Arts' first graduating class in 1911. They were Pioneer artists, of modest backgrounds and means, who later went on to study art in Rome.[14] Yusuf Kamil (1891–1971), of all the Pioneer artists, best fit the mold into which he had been formed by his European teachers. Born in the Bab al-Shar'iya area, a traditional district of Cairo, he maintained a studio in Matariya, in the rural outskirts. He admitted to being an "impressionist by inclination." His paintings of the corners and streets of Islamic Cairo (fig. 15.2), and of scenes set in the Egyptian landscape, are the only Egyptian paintings to come close to the views and vistas of the nineteenth-century European Orientalist painters. His impressionistic palette and soft brush-stroke technique appealed to the rising middle class.

As an artist and as a focus of national artistic development, Raghib Ayad (1892–1982) is stylistically more interesting. He was also born in Cairo, and after his graduation from the School of Fine Arts, he spent the years from 1920–30 in Rome. Ayad's return to Egypt marked his real beginning as an Egyptian artist. By devoting himself to scenes of popular life, he was a painter who gave to his work a certain autochthonal quality. His paintings of the 1930s best express his themes and style which, once established, he continued to favor throughout his life.[15]

Ayad concentrated on Egypt's agricultural scene and people. By drawing the rural peasant going about his unchanged business, Ayad continued the celebration of daily life so marked in ancient Egypt. With rough and warm vitality, Ayad drew the peasant at work in the fields, tending his animals, selling his produce at market, navigating the Nile. He depicted these activities as a continuation of the ancient past, and with reference to pharaonic friezes: in vertical levels of linear horizontal action, in profile, and in two-dimensional volume. This technique is best seen in his *Market* scenes of 1930 and 1938, and in *Workers in the Field*, 1938, all in Cairo's Museum of Modern Egyptian Art.[16] Ayad's cattle and water buffalo have a flattened, linear, gaunt look to them, but the symbiotic relationship between man and animal, as the beast plows the fields, or turns the *saqiya*, the water-wheel (fig. 15.3), is vividly expressed. The past becomes the present, where only the date has changed. Instead of pharaoh hunting in the marshes with a small-scale daughter at his side, Ayad paints the rural mother standing protectively next to her son (fig. 15.4).[17]

In *Coffeehouse in Aswan*, 1933 (fig. 15.5) and *Sudanese Dancing*, 1937, Ayad offers a contemporary view of two age-old activities, and he does so with new insight.[18] In the *Coffeehouse* it is a *baladi* (of the people) woman, with colorful headscarf and long-sleeved flouncy dress, and silver rings on her fingers and tattoos on her hands, who sits in the center of the picture. A narghile is next to her. She is tired. She ignores, and is ignored by, the men around her. In *Sudanese Dancing*, Ayad records movement and happening: the spontaneous combustion of two women dancing to a musician drumming. In these representations there is none of the voyeurism of nineteenth-century European depictions.

In the 1940s he began a new theme. As a Copt, Ayad recorded the life of the Church in Egypt, in parishes and monasteries, and he did so in strongly outlined forms suggestive of old Coptic images and icons. These works reflect his deep religious roots simply but movingly. This new minority theme evoked the ceremonies, architecture, priests, and mysteries of Egypt's Christian rites. In *The Monastery*, 1936 (fig. 15.6) the curtain of the door of the iconostasis (sanctuary screen) is pulled back to show a priest standing at the altar. Monks standing by the screen and seated on benches participate in the service. In an unsigned *Nativity* scene in a private collection, the setting is an Egyptian village. Donkeys and cattle surround the mother and infant child to whom the oriental kings have come in obeisance. Behind the waiting camels is a cream plastered Coptic Church with dome.

In Alexandria, a Mediterranean city which from the outset has offered Cairo lively competition in the visual arts, the beginnings of modern Egyptian painting were with men who were members of the aristocratic elite and were trained as lawyers. Muhammad Naghi (1888–1956), in a career as artist, diplomat, cultural educator, and administrator, was the most cosmopolitan of the Pioneers.[19] As soon as he had finished his four years of studying law at the University of Lyon (1906–10), he turned to art as a career. During the next decade, Naghi alternated between studies in Europe and the discovery of Egypt, between being a European cosmopolite and an Egyptian patriot. From 1910 to 1914 new horizons were opened to him with his exposure to Renaissance artists at the Academy of Fine Arts in Florence, and in 1918 he spent the year at Giverny with Claude Monet. In 1911 he lived with Shaykh 'Ali of the 'Abd al-Rasul family in Gurna/Thebes, saturating himself with the atmosphere of mystery and grandeur of the pharaonic past (fig. 15.7). Between 1914 and 1920, he kept a studio in the Maison des Arts, below the Citadel in Cairo. His 1922 self-portrait in bust form introduces a lively and vigorous man (fig. 15.8). The colors, red and black, give life to the face and suggest the inner fire of an active and curious person.

As a diplomat, from 1925 to 1930, his assignments took him to Rio de Janeiro and Paris, where he became a friend of the French painter André Lhote, who introduced him to the works of Paul Gauguin, and where he was decorated with the Legion of Honor. After Paris, Naghi joined the

Egyptian delegation to the Congress of Popular Arts in Prague headed by Louis Hautecoeur. This distinguished French art historian and curator was in charge of fine arts in Cairo from 1927–30.[20] A lively discussion about the existence of popular art in Egypt led Naghi to disagree with Hautecoeur and as a result Naghi resigned from the diplomatic service.[21]

In 1931 Naghi was sent on an artistic mission to Ethiopia. In many ways this was the richest period of his artistic life. In Addis Ababa he explored the sources of the Nile, which flowed majestically before him, and he was inspired to paint several pictures of this life-giving river (*Blue Nile* and *Red Nile* in 1934). He painted portraits of the Emperor Haile Selassie I and of members of his court, and of churchmen in ceremonial robes. In these paintings he used chromatic harmonies of warm colors contrasted with dark African shadows.

In the mid-1930s Naghi became increasingly engaged with cultural and administrative projects. He was aware of the importance of establishing groups of artists and writers and of their influence on cultural activities. In 1934 he traveled to Greece and Macedonia where he painted the house of Muhammad ʿAli. The following year he established the Atelier in Alexandria. In 1936 he was honored by an exhibition of his Abyssinian works at the Tate Gallery in London. From 1937–39 he was the first Egyptian director of the School of Fine Arts in Cairo,[22] and from 1939–47 he directed the Museum of Modern Art in Cairo. In 1941 he established a student workshop in Luxor, which was to benefit subsequently many young Egyptian artists. He traveled to France, England, and Spain for UNESCO in its cultural mission to save the temple of Abu Simbel during 1945–46. From 1947 to 1950 he was director of the Egyptian Academy in Rome; and in 1952 he founded the Atelier in Cairo, and was its first president. Muhammad Naghi died in his studio in Giza in 1956 after the new revolution. The studio was dedicated as a museum and opened in 1991.

In the legacy that he has left, two groups of paintings stand out: those inspired by the Egyptian countryside and those inspired by Egypt's history. His year in Luxor and frequent visits to the family estate in the Delta gave him the insights into agrarian village life that he transferred to canvas. In *Shepherd Holding Sheep* (fig. 15.9) the brown-skinned man in brown cotton *gallabiya* holds the white-furred animal by its legs around his neck.[23] A white turban and vest add further highlights around his face. This minimal color scheme—whites and browns—gives focus to the man's strong face, while its 'haloing' highlights also hint at a connection with the Christian icon of the Good Shepherd. In *Boy Asleep on Water Buffalo*, the animal cropping clover fills the picture.[24] The young keeper lies across her broad and bony back. A few slashes of green, blue, yellow suggest the field around them. This simple subject graphically conveys the importance this beast has for the Egyptian peasant. In another painting, *Homeward Bound*,[25] a girl in a red dress sits astride the gray haunches of a buffalo. One sees them from the back. Streaks of blues and greens on either side suggest oncoming dusk in a fertile field. Naghi used broad, long strokes of color to give form and movement to his compositions. He also used color to unite the various elements in his composition and to give them perspective. Naghi also painted the men of Qurna in ritualized stick-fighting,[26] women baking bread,[27] and, in an unusual view of Cairo, he painted a river view of earthenware pots on feluccas as seen from the Gala' Bridge in Giza.[28] The main image concentrates on the river traffic, but it includes the tip of the island of Gezira, where feathery palm fronds are enlivened by a brilliant slash of flame trees in blossom.

However sensitive Naghi was to his sturdy Egyptian compatriots, he was not part of their world and did not live their lives. He recognized this graphically in an unusual autobiographical illustration: *The Village*.[29] In it the Naghis have come to visit their agricultural estate at Abu Hummus. Muhammad and his sister or wife stand at the edges of the painting. A chair has been brought for Naghi's father. The village *'umda* sits on the ground beside him. Around these static posed figures of the men in western suits and the lady in dress with handbag, swirl the activities of village life: peasants in *gallabiya*s and cattle pass through on their way to the fields; a naked boy chases a goose; a cat rubs against the chair leg. Naghi is part of the scene, but he stands on the fringe.

It is as a historian, however, that his work is most novel. For thirty years between 1919 to 1950 the theme of freedom preoccupied him. He transformed this theme into epic and historic manifestations at once glorifying Egypt's past achievements and highlighting its future potential. In 1919 he returned from Giverny and painted *Renaissance of Egypt* or the *Cortege of Isis*, which has hung in the Senate Council Chambers since 1922.[30] Like Mukhtar he identifies and glorifies Egypt as pharaonic. The painting is seven meters by three meters, and it is the first epic statement of the new Egypt. It is an allegorical representation of the nation and its people in a march toward their freedom. It exalts Isis, the mother goddess, whose triumphal cortege is accompanied by the sowers and reapers of fertile Egypt marching at its side. In the same year he painted a portrait of Juliette Adam. In itself the picture was a simple image of a woman in a yellow dress seated in a blue chair with a bowl of fruit at her feet. However, she was an important subject. She was the editor of *La nouvelle revue*, an influential monthly, an intellectual who espoused Egyptian nationalism, and the patron of Mustafa Kamil, the founder of the Nationalist party, and an early proponent of the idea that Egypt should be for the Egyptians.

In 1941 Naghi painted the *The Pledge of Allegiance to Muhammad 'Ali* (fig. 15.10).[31] Five meters by three, the canvas shows Muhammad 'Ali at the Citadel receiving a delegation of notables led by 'Umar Makram. They pledge allegiance to the Albanian commander as their governor instead of the unpopular representative appointed by the Ottoman court. The reference is to the crisis of 1804–1805.[32] 'Umar Makram was a highly respected and influential Cairene merchant and notable. In organizing the artisans in rebellions against Napoleon's invasion, he is remembered as an early hero of Egypt's struggle for independence. Naghi records visually that it was the people, as represented by these civilian notables, who legitimized Muhammad 'Ali's seizure of power. Naghi's use of reds, blues, and yellows intensifies the drama.

In Cyprus he supported freedom in two paintings he did in 1950. Naghi's wife was a Greek-Cypriote, and although Naghi was a Muslim, in favoring the Greek cause he put liberty above his allegiance to religion. His *Enosis* supports Cyprus' right to choose political union with Greece. His portrait of the Archbishop Makarios honors a man who was the hero of the battle against British imperialism for the liberties of the Cypriot people.

Along with these historic panels Naghi also created scenes that celebrated Egypt's contributions to world civilization. In 1935 he painted five large panels for the hospital in Alexandria on the theme of the history of medicine, featuring Imhotep, Moses, and Avicenna. In 1937 Naghi was charged with decorating the Egyptian pavilion at the International Exposition in Paris. He contributed a seven-panel mural entitled *The Tears of Isis*. Between 1939–49 he worked on *School of Alexandria*. Its theme exalted the cultural exchanges around the Mediterranean. Classical colonnaded buildings form a background to an assemblage of historical and modern figures, western and Egyptian, who as artists, scientists, and jurists have contributed to this common civilization. In 1954 it was exhibited at the Biennale in Venice, and was thereafter acquired by what is today the governorate of Alexandria where it adorns the main reception room. In renewing the great decorative tradition of painting, Naghi sought to make art instructive. He wanted these works to remind Egyptians of their past grandeur and also wanted art to have a social mission. He aimed at the formulation of a national art, which would integrate the artist with his community. Naghi's emphasis on the pharaonic and Muhammad 'Ali periods gives visual articulation to the "programmatic narrative" deliberately crafted in the school texts as described by Barak Salmoni in chapter six of this volume.

Mahmud Said (1897–1964) was also from Alexandria. A quiet, shy man from a prominent family,[33] his niece Farida Zulfikar married King Faruq. The family residence was in the Anfushi district of Alexandria, near the Mosque of Abu al-'Abbas al-Mursi. Young Mahmud was tutored at home in Arabic, French, and English. Between seventeen and nineteen he took drawing lessons from Mme. Amelia Casonato, while also receiving instruction at the Zananiri studio in Alexandria. In 1918 he had his first exhibition in Alexandria. In the summers between 1920 and 1930 he haunted museums and Gothic churches on trips to Europe. He received no encouragement from his family, who saw no value in art except as something which foreigners seemed to appreciate. At his father's behest, therefore, he was trained for law, and in 1922 he became an assistant magistrate in the Mixed Courts at Mansura. For the next twenty-five years his life was torn between the values of his society, as represented by his career as a respectable counselor in the Court of Appeals, and by his passionate personal desire to paint. In 1919, he identified this struggle in two self-portraits, one as a young lawyer with slicked-back hair,[34] and the other holding his palette, with tousled hair and intense gaze (fig. 15.11). Even after the death of his father he continued in law. It was not until 1947 that he resigned as a counselor in the Court of Appeals. He was thus fifty years of age before he devoted himself full time to painting, though by that time his identity as an artist had been established in a large and consistent body of work.

As such, the multiple conflicts between convention and personal freedom; social obligation and the expression of self; repression and desire; restraint and passion, show in his work. Mahmud Said produced a few canvases from a sojourn at Marsa Matruh and from his travels to Lebanon, but basically his work was firmly anchored in Alexandria. Typical of his class and his city, his cultural affinities were essentially European and his life was far removed from that of the majority of Egyptians. Even so, in a mixture of imagination and reality, his art subjects had a real Egyptian base. Of the early Pioneer artists he is the only one who sees his Muslim faith as a topic of art. In 1934, after an almost fatal illness, he portrayed himself bearded and in a brown *gallabiya* against a village background.[35] It is an interesting composition underlining the verities of life: behind him on the left a woman is engaged in the ordinary task of hanging up the wash; on the right, a funeral procession moves toward the cemetery.

In many paintings thereafter he exhibited a new sensibility, characterized by sensitivity to aspects of his religion that no other Egyptian painter had heretofore depicted. For example, *Prayer*, 1934 (fig. 15.12), is an evocative and moving depiction of worshipers in the collective act of submission in faith. The palette is of Egyptian colors. The ochre, brown, blue, green colors in the *qamariyat* (stained glass) window are echoed in the robes of the bending worshipers. Rays of light bathe the bowed men with a metaphysical dimension. He painted *The Dhikr*,[36] a gathering of Sufi devotees, in which Muslim mystics turn in rhythmic trance, and *The Zar*, where men and women gather in a popular exorcism ceremony.[37] In *Shaykh in Prayer*, 1941, Said registers the direct communication between man and his God. The rounded, enveloped form of the seated man, head bowed in meditation, contrasts with the straight, almost infinite, rows of stone columns and wooden beams of the unadorned mosque stretching behind him. A beam of light slants down diagonally upon the man.

Said painted portraits of his family—mother, father, sister, wife, and of his daughter Nadia as she grew up—and landscapes, of which his views of Alexandria are the most interesting. He visualized the deserted corniche at night in ghostly moonlight and the canal banks during the day (1929), where the curving forms of date palms and shore offset geometric, linear shapes of houses and diagonal tilt of boat masts in vivid juxtapositions.[38] He favored men in blue *gallabiya*s riding on chunky white donkeys.

His most compelling subjects, however, were women, and paintings of women form the largest category of his work. On the surface, Said's intermingling of religious and female subjects might seem contradictory. However, as a Muslim with an interest in its mystical dimension, Said was aware of the view that the whole world is under God's sovereignty, and that He delights in all his creation: "God is beautiful, and He loves beauty,"[39] and "Woman is a ray of God."[40] For Said, both as a Muslim and as a painter, women were a legitimate subject with which to render additional appreciation for aspects of Egyptian beauty. Said's women can be divided into two groups: the imaginary and typological, and the real and authentic. The women he draws in the first group are types, recognizable by their large dark eyes, flattened noses, thick lips and elongated faces. In their features and postures, Said captures the essence of the Egyptian *baladi* woman—earthy, self-assured, savvy, quick-witted.[41] Of this group, his *Life of the City*, 1937 (fig. 15.13) is perhaps his most famous painting. In the center of the composition, three women stand in a monumental triangular arrangement. Their *milaya*s are draped provocatively around them and they fiddle with their transparent face veils. A *shurbagi* (soft drink vendor) frames them on one side; and on the other, a man and a child ride a white donkey. Behind them the Nile and the Mosque of Muhammad 'Ali suggest Cairo as a setting.

Said's nudes also fall into this imaginary/typological category. As an *œuvre*, whether sitting, or standing or reclining in boats, they portray the Egyptian woman as a beautiful brown Venus on the Mediterranean shores.[42] His brush exalts the strong, simple, uncomplicated beauty of the *fallaha*. His interest in her body is an artistic one. He is not a cultural voyeur: he did not use women, as many European Orientalist painters have been accused of doing, to make political, economic, or cultural statements about their situation. In the second category, Said painted women as real individuals. He rendered them with great psychological insight and in a great variety of feminine guises: mothers, peasants, servants, relatives, courtesans, and patricians. In this presentation he personalized the Egyptian woman, and gave her attributes and functions other than those of just an Orientalist harem occupant. For example, one can compare his portrait of the *Lady Yusuf Zulfikar*[43] with that of the *Expectant Maid* (fig. 15.14). Both women were at opposite ends of the social spectrum, but Said dissolves the class distinction when he painted their portraits in the same seated posture, and in similar orange dresses. Said was the first Egyptian artist to be honored with the State Appreciation Award for Art, in 1959.[44]

1935–50

In this phase a second group of artists completed the process of developing a truly Egyptian art. The first group showed that they had achieved mastery of western based formats; the second group transformed that expression into an art that broke free of the influence and forms of western art and European academic styles, and infused their own aesthetic with concerns and styles that were indisputably Egyptian. The first group of Pioneers, motivated and impelled by the independence movement of 1919, derived their inspiration and subject matter from their land, their culture and their history. Like the Pioneers of the first period, the artists of the second period were also stimulated and shaped by political and economic forces—this time by the events of the region and of the world as they affected Egypt in the guise of World War II. To the external, objective, literal depiction of Egypt under the first period Pioneers, those of the second period added visual representations of the subjective, psychological, and unconscious world of the masses.

'Abd al-Hadi al-Gazzar (1925–65) [45] and Hamid Nada (1924–90) are the best known of those artists who pioneered the new outlook. They emerged during the late 1930s and early 1940s, a period that had much to do with the development of their art and the novelty of their points of view. It was a creative and confusing time; politically and economically the 1930s and 1940s were a time of world turmoil. Egypt was unwillingly drawn into World War II as a major base for troops from all parts of the British Empire when the focus of the war shifted to Eastern Europe and North Africa. Egypt also became increasingly involved in the Arab affairs of the region: in Sudan, Egypt sought to end British control, and Egypt gave political and economic aid to Palestine as it became an Arab cause. In the 1930s Egypt's main source of income on the world market derived from the export of cotton, and Egypt was heavily dependent on these revenues. The Great Depression and then the war led to a fall in cotton prices, causing hardship to an increasing population. The Muslim Brotherhood, founded in 1928, developed from a strict Islamic reform movement into a militant mass organization that viewed Islam as religion and ideology. Anxiety and insecurity were felt by all, and this found expression in art.

Al-Gazzar and Nada were close friends, and their lives, training, and artistic expressions ran along parallel lines until the early 1950s. They were born within a year of each other, and they came from families with traditional, conservative values. Their fathers were Muslim *shaykh*s. Al-Gazzar's father taught at al-Azhar, the major center of traditional Islamic curricula. The boys grew up in Islamic Cairene quarters imbued with a traditional outlook. Al-Gazzar lived in the district of Sayyida Zaynab, an area surrounding the mosque named for a granddaughter of the Prophet Muhammad and one of the patron saints of Cairo since the Fatimid period. Nada lived in the Khalifa district below the Citadel where the Mosque of al-Rifa'i, the patron saint of snake charmers, is located. These were districts imbued by Islam in its formal and popular aspects, in which the inhabitants were immersed in a world where everything was explained by the action of spiritual forces.[46] The two men, as students, enrolled in the Hilmiya Secondary School where they were nurtured by a remarkable man and teacher, Husayn Yusuf Amin (1904–84).[47]

Husayn Amin's interest in the arts led him to the academy of Fine Arts in Florence in 1924, and from thence to Brazil, via Spain, where he spent several years teaching drawing. Upon his return to Egypt in 1931, he gave up a successful career as a painter in order to teach at the Hilmiya Secondary School in Cairo. Amin belonged to a group of pioneers in art education begun by Habib Jurji, who was both thinker and sculptor. Jurji, while studying in London, had been exposed to the new art teachings of Herbert Read which emphasized the importance of the "organic" process in learning. Dissatisfied with the fidelity to European norms that was characteristic of Egyptian art teaching, Jurji began his own educational experiment. He believed that there existed a deep-rooted indigenous artistic talent in all children that could be fostered by encouragement and appropriate technique.[48] Amin also worked along these lines. He noticed young talent and encouraged its development. He worked with students who came from backgrounds totally excluded from the established mainstream of art culture and made them create spontaneously. Through self-discovery and self-analysis he helped them penetrate their subconscious and discover their own sensitivities and sensibilities. Their art was thus based on the cultural and social conditions surrounding them.

Amin, however, was more than just teacher and mentor to 'Abd al-Hadi al-Gazzar and Hamid Nada. As an artist, cosmopolite and intellectual, Amin was also part of the intellectual community that characterized Cairo of the late 1930s and early 1940s, a time alive to intellectual discussion and new artistic influences. Amin was a friend of Yusuf Afifi, another educator with a dynamic personality, and close to Habib Jurji. Afifi had been also inspired by the teachings of Herbert Read and John Dewey, and taught art at the Sa'idiya elementary school, likewise aiming to free Egyptian art from western practices. Two of his students were Kamal Tilmissani (1917–67) and Ramsis Yunan (1913–60), who became protégés of Georges Henein, who was also in Husayn Yusuf Amin's circle of acquaintances.[49]

Georges Henein (1914–73),[50] a well-traveled, multi-lingual Sorbonne-educated essayist, was friends with André Breton and other French Surrealist pioneers.[51] Deploring Fascist censorship and the destruction of art works termed "degenerate," Henein founded the Art and Freedom Group in January 1939, an association of artists. It had as its objective the defense of liberty in art and culture, and the need to link local art with international artistic movements. Fu'ad Kamil (1919–73), a secondary school art teacher, artist, writer, and critic who was trained at the School of Fine Arts (1929–33), joined the Group that included Tilmissani and Yunan, and became its spokesman.

Horrified by the realities of World War II, the Art and Freedom Group announced its aims in a series of articles and statements. First, they revolted against classical and academic styles, which they regarded as backward, stagnant, and arbitrary. They ridiculed "the portrayal of blooming flowers and fresh fruits on clean dishes," and made fun of "slender peasant women, with fresh complexions and nice figures."[52] Additionally they felt that the artist, in order to produce real art, had to engage with the "reality" of the human psyche and subconscious mind, a reality based on Freud's theories and analysis. They proclaimed themselves against everything limiting one's freedom, and chose surrealism as the liberating movement. Between 1938 and 1945 surrealism provided an escape from the dominant figurative trend of the earlier period's art. In their first show, in February 1940, the Egyptian surrealists announced their revolt against their society and against classical and academic styles. In this first exhibition most of the paintings revolved around the theme of the human psyche as it was affected by war. The group felt their duty was to open the public's eyes to the horrible realities of cruelty and ruin that were the products of war. They shocked their audiences with images featuring distortion, the absurd, and the unnatural. Their canvases featured strangely shaped tree trunks with breasts, staring hollow-eyed faces, separate and maimed body parts in wasted and empty landscapes.

By challenging both conservatives and nationalists they alienated the public and lost financial and political support. The group and their surrealist art, therefore, did not last long, but their influence was profound.[53] This new art and ways of seeing and expressing reality dug up the artistic soil and planted new seeds. The surrealist moment provided a rupture that opened the door for the expressionist popular art of 'Abd al-Hadi al-Gazzar and Hamid Nada.

Husayn Amin also believed that generating contacts and exchanges among other young artists could encourage young talents, and to this end he created the Group of Contemporary Art. Its professed aim was to foster the emergence of an Egyptian school of painting, free from the influence of western art. Amin's Group of Contemporary Art held its first exhibition in May of 1946.[54] One hundred and ninety pieces were displayed in the Foyer of the Lycée Français in Cairo. The effect was startling and shocking, and both critics and public knew they were witnessing a radical rupture in Egyptian pictorialism. All the works represented subjects from popular life, and the emphasis was on the truth behind this life: its fatalism, its stupor, and its somber, dramatic, and cruel overtones. These young painters depicted visually the world of a people paralyzed by poverty, ignorance, and superstition, a world that they knew and of which they were a part. They expressed this through traditional visual symbolism. They used popular images of magic as symbols to illustrate their social commentary:

the tortoise to represent patience and peace; the rat as the furtive, sinister, subconscious (fig. 15.15);[55] the bull suggesting sex and fertility; and the cat, symbolizing woman, ghosts, and eternity. As painters, these young artists were also united in feeling that the artist had a social role to play in society, and that he should depict the tragedy and loneliness of man.[56]

In the third exhibition in 1949 held at the Young Christian Association, Husayn Yusuf Amin, as promoter, and al-Gazzar, as artist, were arrested because of al-Gazzar's entry, *Hunger*, a name later changed to *The Theater of Life*.[57] Eight women, variously garbed, stand in a row. One of them has a child. They look vacantly at the viewer. Each represents a different face of female Egypt. In front of them are empty tin plates. The message is one of sociopolitical criticism: Egypt is hungry; its women have not achieved the emancipation so eagerly anticipated in 1923. This use of art as social statement and criticism was a new departure. Muhammad Naghi and Mahmud Said intervened with the authorities to free Amin and al-Gazzar from jail.

Between 1948 and 1951 al-Gazzar's output was considerable. He submitted forty oil paintings for a show in his honor at the Museum of Modern Egyptian Art. *The Wedding of Zulayka* (1948)[58] is an indictment of the practice of child marriage. The girl Zulayka stands small beside her mother who, with an enormous hand (of power and authority?), plucks a red flower from an upturned drum, symbol of deflowered hope. The child, with sad eyes and downcast head, stares mutely at a large white rat.

Gazzar's most famous painting is *The Green Fool* of 1951 (fig. 15.16). It is a simple view of a head in profile. He is green in color, and has a red flower behind his ear from which an earring dangles. The earring emasculates him. Outstretched arms frame his head, each bent at the elbows, an 'eye' in the center of each palm. The 'fool' often acted as an exorcist at *mulid*s or religious fairs. Green is a color of fertility; it was used for Osiris, but green stands also for the Prophet Muhammad and his family, whose intercession may be sought. The raised praying hands and the eyes to ward off evil impart a Coptic and popular dimension to the image and thus make of it a condensation of Egyptian folk religion. Al-Gazzar's works give an extraordinary vision of the persistence and power of folklore, and in this lies their originality.[59]

His friend Hamid Nada also explored the strange popular world, full of superstition, astonishment, and human tragedies. His paintings of the early 1940s depicted those who visited tombs of saints, where they slept, ate, and collapsed in hysterical fits. Nada anthropomorphized the dead-end paralysis of these lives by creating solid, chunky figures that made them look as if carved from wood. As such they are indistinguishable from each other; there is nothing that individualizes them. *The Lamp of Gloom* (fig. 15.17)[60] illustrates Nada's style of these years. A disproportionally large lamp illuminates three people—child, mother and father—who stand paralyzed, staring vacantly into its shadowy glare. The Group of Contemporary Art disbanded in 1954, but by then 'Abd al-Hadi al-Gazzar and Hamid Nada had moved away from the districts in which they had grown up. Their styles changed after the revolution of 1952.

Hamid Nada spent the year at Luxor in 1956, painting at the Atelier founded by Muhammad Naghi. His early interest in magic and symbols of popular superstitions led during the 1970s to paintings of a very personal and distinct kind of folk expressionism (fig. 15.18).[61] Vestiges of surrealism surfaced in his late art, and his themes and figures became repetitive. The developments of his later years—the sudden deafness, his erotic desires—provide an insight into the elements that float about his canvases: receptive women wearing garter belts and hose, iron-frame beds, roosters, cats, strange crab-like creatures, stallions, the ever-present musicians on their drums. He died in 1990, still an influential Egyptian painter, but no longer an innovative forger of new directions.

'Abd al-Hadi al-Gazzar enrolled in the School of Fine Arts in 1944, receiving his diploma with honors in 1950. In 1954 he was given a state scholarship to study in Italy, and from 1957–61 he spent another four years of study in Rome. When he returned to Egypt he was appointed an assistant professor at the School of Fine Arts. After 1952 al-Gazzar became an enthusiastic supporter of the revolution. He moved away from the depiction of the soul, and the unknown, to symbolic representations of Egypt, and to the new relationship between man and technology. In 1962 he won first prize in the competition "The Revolution, Ten Years After" with his *al-Mithaq* (The Charter).[62] It is a painting that brilliantly captures the 'new' Egypt and its inclusive political aims. Egypt, her skin the green color of the resurrected Osiris and crowned with the emblem of the republic, stands in the center, like a pharaonic tree goddess, holding in her hand the charter of the revolution. The farmer and the worker kneel before her while behind her, the priest and the imam embrace. The worker holds a wrench and around him are machine parts, symbols of Egypt's industrialized future. The *fallah* looks down at the cotton blossom and the mound of seeds in his hands. Next to him lies a paper headlined "Ownership of the Earth." Draped over his shoulders is a mantle decorated with an inscribed border in which verse 13:11 from the Qur'an, The Thunder, is clearly legible: "Verily never will God change the condition of a people until they change what is in themselves." Al-Gazzar had turned his back on the survivals of the past to embrace the positives of the future.

Al-Gazzar's vision may have changed, but his emphasis on the common man had not. In 1965, before his untimely death, he visualized the Suez Canal quite differently from the way in which Mahmud Said had memorialized it twenty years earlier. The two paintings offer an interesting comparison of the styles and perspectives of the early groups of Egyptian Pioneers. Mahmud Said, of the first phase, in 1946, highlights the pomp and circumstance of the 1869 opening ceremonies (fig. 15.19).[63] The Khedive Isma'il and the European royalty, his guests, are the most prominent actors in this staged world celebration, and the viewer sees them through drawn curtains. Said celebrates the Europeanization of Egypt, and he has signed his name in Latin letters. 'Abd al-Hadi al-Gazzar's signature is in Arabic. In his version (fig. 15.20)[64] it is the forced corvée labor of the peasants on whose backs this great waterway was achieved that dominates the scene, a scene without frames or borders and so immediate that the viewer is almost a part of it. For the first time since the British occupation of Egypt in 1882, 'Abd al-Nasser had regained control of the Suez Canal in 1956, eleven years before the painting, and al-Gazzar pays tribute to the Egyptian exertion that made it the great transportational gateway between East and West. The artist shows the Egyptian *fallah*, with pickaxe and reed basket, toiling to cut through the rock and remove the earth in much the same way as he had toiled to build the pyramids.

Conclusion

Modern Egyptian painting and sculpture, in its institutional sense, is less than a century old. In the years between revolutions, 1919 to 1952, it broke away from its foreign tutor and matured into its own being. The major artists who helped in this development have been singled out. Other important and interesting artists worked during these years, but they did not have the force or the distinction to make the impression of those here:[65] of Mukhtar, who in a land of great sculpture was the first sculptor to emerge since the Arab invasion; of Ayad who became interested in the life of simple folk and was the first to draw attention to the aesthetic value of popular art; of Naghi who painted national epics of grandeur and independence; of Said whose portraits celebrated the warmth and beauty of Egyptian women; of al-Gazzar and Nada, who reached into the subconscious and depicted the state and soul of the Egyptian masses. These

Egyptian artists took up themes native to Egypt and painted them with indigenous insights.

In these inter-revolutionary years the question of identity was broached and tackled. The Pioneer artists freed Egypt from its dependence on western themes, techniques, and styles. These early artists passed from external descriptions to internal motivations; they made the transition from pharaonic grandeur to Muslim prayer and popular spirituality. This opened the way to other themes. After the revolution of 1952, art would become a visual element in state policy. Artists were encouraged to depict the new Egypt. They found new themes in an identification of Arab roots, and in Islamic abstract art and calligraphy. Also during the ʿAbd al-Nasser years, as a result of the preparation of the 1920s, 1930s, 1940s, a wave of very talented female artists emerged, among whom the most outstanding were: Effat Naghi (1905–94), the sister of Muhammad; Tahiya Halim (1919–2003), Injy Aflatoun (1924–89), and Gazbia Sirry (1925–), the only artist still painting. The efflorescence of art during the second half of the twentieth century would not have been possible without the artists of the first part of the century.

Notes

1   A grant by the American Research Center in Egypt, February–May 1998, enabled research on this topic. Mme. Christine Roussillon, Dr. ʿAbd al-Ghaffar Shedid, Dr. Adel Sabet, Khalid Hafez, and Mahmud Menisi, were most generous in sharing their knowledge and insights. So were the many other artists, gallery owners, critics, and collectors with whom I spoke. Transliteration of Arabic names is always a problem. If the artist signs his/her name in Latin letters, that is the name I use; otherwise I transliterate from the Arabic, or use the name by which they are best known.

2   The few general books in western languages on the subject are Aimé Azar, *La Peinture Moderne en Égypte* (Cairo: Les Éditions Nouvelles, 1961); Liliane Karnouk, *Modern Egyptian Art: The Emergence of a Style* (Cairo: The American University in Cairo Press, 1988); and *Contemporary Egyptian Art* (Cairo: The American University in Cairo Press, 1995). The development of Egyptian painting is treated in more schematic form in Wijdan Ali, *Contemporary Art from the Islamic World* (London: Scorpion Publishing, 1989); Ezz El-Din Naguib, *The Dawn of Egyptian Modern Painting*, trans. Morsi Saad Eddin (Cairo: Ministry of Culture, 1992); *Cairo: A Life-Story of 1000 Years 969–1969* (Cairo: Ministry of Culture, Egyptian Publishing Organization, 1970), images #302–372. *Arts & the Islamic World*: "The Arts in Egypt," 2: 2 (1984); "Egyptian Art Scene," 4: 1 (1986); "Egypt: the Arts in View," v.35, 2000. In Arabic, see Amr el-Bilassy, ed., "Pioneers of Modern Egyptian Art: 15 Artists from Muhammad Nagy to Ahmad Abd al-Wahab," *Shell Co. in Egypt* (April–June 1996); and "Modern Art," *Shell Co. in Egypt* (July–December, 1995). The only book that serves as a catalogue to the art in the Museum of Modern Egyptian Art is Fatma Ismaʿil, *29 Artists in the Museum of Egyptian Modern Art* (Cairo: Center Line, 1992).

3   Barak Salmoni in chapter six sheds further light on the development of this new historical consciousness

4   Born in 1887, the son of Ahmad Kamal, grandson of Ahmad Rifaat and great-grandson of Ibrahim Pasha.

5   The School of Fine Arts, established in 1908, over the century changed its location from Gamamiz to Shubra to Giza, finally settling in Zamalek, and its name from School to College to Faculty of Fine Arts when it became part of the University of Helwan in 1972.

6   Yunan Labib Rizk, "Enlightened Royals," *Al-Ahram Weekly*, 6–12 January 2000.

7   For further information on this sculptor see: Ministry of Culture *Museum of Sculptor Mahmoud Mukhtar* (Cairo, n.d.); Yunan Labib Rizk, "Egypt Incarnate," *Al-Ahram Weekly* 21–27 February, 2002; Suhail Bisharat: "Mahmoud Mukhtar: Memories & Modernity," *Arts & The Islamic World* 35 (2000), 32–35; Ingrid Wassmann, "Written in Stone," *Egypt Today*, May 1991.

8   Yunan Labib Rizk: "Egypt Incarnate," *Al-Ahram Weekly* 21–27 February, 2002

9   This event is detailed in Huda Sha'arawi, *Harem Years: The Memoirs of an Egyptian Feminist*, trans. and intro. Margot Badran (New York: Feminist Press, 1986).

10 "Safiya Zaghlul," Arthur Goldschmidt, Jr., *Biographical Dictionary of Modern Egypt* (Lynne Rienner Publishers, 2000). See also Margot Badran, *Feminists, Islam and Nation: Gender and the Making of Modern Egypt* (Princeton: Princeton University Press, 1995).

11 The complexity of Cairo's human scene in the 1930s is well-described by Magdi Wahba: "Cairo Memories," in *Studies in Arab History*, ed. Derek Hopwood, (Oxford: The Antonius Lectures 1978–87, 1990), 103–15.

12 See Goldschmidt, *Biographical Dictionary*. Dr. Ali Ibrahim, a prominent surgeon and intellectual, was also a collector of Islamic art, and his collection was the basis of the Museum of Islamic Art holdings.

13 See Samia Kholoussi's discussion of the *fallahin* in chapter ten.

14 Outstanding graduates were sent to Europe to finish their art studies. At first Kamil and Ayyad alternated expenses: one would teach and work in Egypt while the other studied in Rome. In 1925 Sa'd Zaghlul arranged state scholarships of £E 200 a year.

15 In the late 1930s Ayad took a series of administrative posts: in 1937 director of the Arts Section of the School of Applied Arts (founded 1928–29); in the 1940s he was director of the Coptic Museum for a few years, and until 1949 the director of the Free Section of the School of Fine Arts; from 1949–54 he was director of the Museum of Modern Egyptian Art (founded 1931); in 1952 he founded the Mukhtar Museum. He was a catalyst in the founding of the Egyptian Academy in Rome, where he had individual exhibitions in 1927, 1937, and 1948.

16 Illustrated in *Cairo: The Life Story of 1,000 Years*, #331 and #332, and *Karnouk: Modern Egyptian Art*, 42

17 Samia Kholoussi, in chapter ten, discusses the *fallah* as a literary subject.

18 Both in the Museum of Modern Egyptian Art, Cairo, and illustrated in Shell, *Pioneers*, 70–78.

19 The major monograph on his life in French is Effat Naghi, ed. et al., *Mohamed Naghi (1888–1956), Un impressioniste Égyptien* (Cairo: Cahiers de Chabramant, 1988). His studio, near the pyramids, has been turned into a museum and exhibits many of his works, as does the Museum of Modern Egyptian Art, both in Cairo. The correct transliteration of the Arabic name is Naji, but the artist signed his work as Naghi.

20 He authored *Les Mosquées du Caire* (Paris, 1932).

21 In 1937 Naghi followed through on his interest in popular Egyptian arts by establishing the "House of Arts" for their exhibition.

22 He succeeded Gabriel Biessy, who taught painting when the School was established in 1908.

23 1925, Naghi Museum, Cairo. Shell, ibid., 15.

24 1943, Naghi Museum, Cairo. Shell, ibid., 27.

25 1934, Museum of Modern Egyptian Art, Cairo.

26 *Cairo 1,000 Years*, #322.

27 1929, oil on textile, Museum of Modern Egyptian Art, Cairo; Shell, Modern Art.

28 No date, oil on canvas, Museum of Modern Egyptian Art, Cairo; Shell, Modern Art.

29 1928–42, oil on canvas, Naghi Museum, illustrated in Karnouk, *Modern Egyptian Art* #9. Karnouk gives the date as 1928; Effat Naghi, in "Chronological Index of the most important works of Muhammad Naghi," in *Mohamed Naghi*, 63, dates it to 1937, while the date on the identification card at the Naghi Museum is 1942. Naghi married Lilika Tavernai 1937–39, 57. If the painting is of a later date then the figure on the right is that of his new bride rather than his sister.

30 Karnouk, *Modern Egyptian Art*, 9.

31 Museum of Egyptian Civilization. Shell, *Pioneers of Modern Art*, 16–17.

32 Afaf Lutfi al-Sayyid-Marsot, *Egypt in the Reign of Muhammad Ali* (Cambridge: Cambridge University Press, 1984) 44–45; 47–53, 68–69.

33 Mahmoud al-Nabawi as-Shal, *Mahmud Said* (Cairo: Ministry of Culture, 1984), in English; *Mahmud Said* (Cairo: Cultural Development Fund, 2001).

34 Museum of Modern Egyptian Art.

35 1934, oil on canvas, Mahmud Said Museum, Alexandria.

36 1929, oil on canvas, Shell: Pioneers of Modern Egypt Art, 88

37 Illustrated in Karnouk, *Modern Egyptian Art*, #4.

38 Shell, *Pioneers of Modern Art*, 74, 92.

39 Ibn Hanbal, *Musnad*, Book 4, vol. 133–34

40 Jalal al-Din Rumi: *Mathnawi* in J.A.Williams: *The Word of Islam* (Austin: University of Texas, 1994), 136.

41 For further reference see Evelyn Early, *Baladi Women of Cairo* (Boulder: Lynne Rienner Publishers, 1993) especially 51–84.

42 No date, oil on canvas, Mahmud Said Museum, Alexandria.

43 1934, oil on canvas, Mahmud Said Museum, Alexandria.

44 His mansion on Bacchus St. in Alexandria was opened as a museum in April, 2000.

45 Alain and Christine Roussillon, eds., *Abdel Hadi al-Gazzar: An Egyptian Painter* (Cairo: Elias Modern Press, 1990). See also Anna Boughiguian, "An Enigmatic Presence," *Al-Ahram Weekly*, 20–26 January 2000.

46 An insight into this world is offered by Nayra Atiya, *Khul-Khaal: Five Egyptian Women Tell Their Stories* (Syracuse University Press, 1982).

47 Anna Boughiguian, "A Lost Master," *Al-Ahram Weekly*, 14–20 October 1999. She ends her piece on a sad note: "what remains of the life of Hussein Youssef Amin is practically nothing." For other references to Amin, see Aimé Azar, *La Peinture Moderne en Égypte*, 43–45 and 75–80; Alain and Christine Roussillon, *Abdel Hadi al-Gazzar*, 70–72; and Liliane Karnouk, *Modern Egyptian Art*, 43–50.

48 See figures #299, 300 in *Cairo: 1000 Years*. His son-in-law, Ramsis Wissa Wassef, successfully implemented these spontaneous art principles in his weaving school at Haraniya, begun 1952.

49 In 1936, Tilmissani published *Declaration of the Post-Orientalists*, which dealt with the state of the arts in Egypt. It emphasized the need to cultivate a unique Egyptian artistic identity, and called for a break from the influence of foreign artists. "If I can arrive only to find the first traces of a new local art, only then will I consider myself an artist." Quoted in A. Azar, *La Peinture Moderne en Égypte*, 48. The new approaches to traditional education had parallels elsewhere in Egyptian thinking. See chapters six and eight.

50 Karnouk, *Modern Egyptian Art*, 29–43, is the only source to refer to Henein as Hinayn. For more on the "Art and Liberty" Group see also Azar, 48–70; Roussillon, 66–69; Ezz el-Din Naguib, 99–125; and Samir Gharieb, *Le Surréalisme en Égypte et les Arts Plastiques*.

51 French writer (1896–1966) whose writings on surrealism influenced Egyptian surrealists.

52 Ezz el-Din Naguib, *The Dawn of Egyptian Painting*, 105.

53   After their last exhibition in 1945 the "Art and Liberty" Group was dissolved. Ramsis Yunan went to Paris in 1947 for ten years; Tilmissani turned to movies and went to Beirut, and Fu'ad Kamil took up abstract art.

54   Other artists in the group included Samir Rafi', Kamal Yusuf, Ibrahim Masuda, and al-Habshi.

55   Al-Gazzar, *Destiny*, 1949, india ink on paper.

56   *Woman with Khul-Khaal*, 1948, oil on canvas, private collection, Roussillon, 45; Karnouk, 46.

57   1948, oil on cardboard, Museum of Modern Egyptian Art; illustrated in Roussillon, 50; Karnouk, 31; Shell, *Pioneers*, 208.

58   Oil on cardboard, private collection; Roussillon, 48.

59   See Roussillon for al-Gazzar's many other images on the theme of popular belief and superstition.

60   1946, oil, Karnouk, *Modern Egyptian Art*, 55.

61   1970s, crayon sketch, private collection.

62   1962, oil on wood, Museum of Modern Egyptian Art. See Karnouk, *Modern Egyptian Art*, #18; Roussillon, 137.

63   1946, oil on canvas, Mahmud Said Museum, Alexandria.

64   1965, oil on celotex, Museum of the Sea, Alexandria; Roussillon, 152–53.

65   For example, Saif (1906–79) and Adham (1908–59) Wanly were brothers from Alexandria who painted whimsical beach and circus scenes; Ahmad Sabry (1889–1955), an academic painter noted for his portraits, who taught at the Faculty of Fine Arts; Husny Banany (1912–88) graduated from and taught at the Faculty of Fine Arts, and is remembered for his landscapes; Salah Taher (1912–) who graduated from the Faculty of Fine Arts, after a trip to the United States in the late 1950s became an abstract artist; Husayn Bikar (1913–) who graduated from and taught at the Faculty of Fine Arts is noted for his academic style; Hamid Abdullah (1917–85) was self-taught and left Egypt after the 1952 Revolution and used calligraphy in his art; Munir Canaan (1919–2000) was an independent, and autodidact who became an abstract artist.

16 State and Cinema in Pre-Revolutionary Egypt, 1927–52

Andrew Flibbert

Egypt's film industry was born in the 1920s, prompted by the introduction of sound to the imported American movies that dominated Egyptian screens. While not designed or intended for nationalist purposes, sound filmmaking created new opportunities for the construction and articulation of national identity, and it did so via an increasingly popular medium that blended commercial imperatives with cultural content. Domestic production began on a small-scale basis, but by the 1930s, Egyptian entrepreneurs had laid the foundation for what would become a vibrant and prolific source of national cultural production. Egypt's film industry extended its influence well beyond state boundaries, exporting its products across the Arab world and to such far-flung locales as Venezuela, Hong Kong, Madagascar, Denmark, and Indonesia.[1] By the late 1940s, the industry's reputation was sufficient to induce the famed American director, Orson Welles, to contract with Studio al-Ahram in Giza to shoot two different films on location in Egypt.[2]

The industry's early successes notwithstanding, pre-revolutionary Egyptian filmmaking often is derided as frivolous and insignificant compared to the later efforts of state-sponsored producers in the 'Abd al-Nasser era.[3] Those unfamiliar with the cultural conventions of non-western cinema are inclined to misread the melodrama, comedy, or musicality of early Egyptian film and to conclude that it offers little of enduring value. This conclusion is reinforced by the fact that, from the very outset, the Egyptian industry was unmistakably commercial in orientation. Most

Egyptian movies in this period lacked a self-consciously didactic purpose and were conceived as simple entertainment for the popular and middle classes. They were produced with the profit motive foremost in mind, even if some actors and filmmakers saw themselves as artists and *auteurs*. Toward this end, the industry built its own studios, star system, distribution networks, genre conventions, and other hallmarks of industrial filmmaking. Egypt's "Hollywood on the Nile" sought to emulate its openly commercial American counterpart more than the French, German, or Italian cinemas, which trained some of its early pioneers.

Yet a blanket dismissal of pre-revolutionary Egyptian cinema is both unfounded in substantive terms and ill-considered in misapprehending the significance of the era for later filmmakers' successes. The Golden Age of Egyptian cinema began long before the Nasserist revolution, and it was extraordinarily productive and dynamic. Without its early achievements, later filmmakers probably would not have had the technical skills, infrastructure, or audience support to sustain a viable industry in subsequent years. Nasser-era state officials are not likely to have deemed filmmaking an appropriate area of state intervention and support, since this choice was conditioned by prior institutional developments.[4] Egyptian movies, moreover, were extraordinarily popular in their early heyday, and their popularity speaks to a fundamental human impulse to see recognizable public representations of the self, as manifested in locally made film. For this reason, the industry's initial creative output need not be evaluated solely through the lens of aesthetic merit or even financial success. Egyptian filmmakers' early accomplishments created a means for local cultural production that would not have existed otherwise, even if the industry had difficulty sustaining itself on a permanently competitive basis in a globally integrating market.

This chapter presents a reconsideration of the first twenty-five years of the Egyptian film industry, from its birth in the 1920s to the Free Officers' coup in 1952. Several chapters in this volume have already alerted the reader to the importance of Egyptian movies as entertainment or social commentary in this era. Samia Kholoussi in chapter ten has examined how in the 1930s and beyond, rurality and peasant life became a topic of cinematographic interest, for both ideological and entertainment reasons. In a related fashion, Lucie Ryzova in chapter five reminds us that film served as a medium to consider urban class evolution, and the frictions between as well as continuities from rural *fallahin* to urban *effendiya* in the 1930s and 1940s. In this chapter, I focus more on the related, yet equally important matter of

Egyptian film's political economy, in order to address three primary issues: the birth and expansion of Egyptian production and export; the response of the industry to international competition, primarily from Hollywood; and the nature of state regulation of cultural products like film.

Rather than offering a wholly chronological account, I address each of these issues in turn, highlighting the analytical connections among them. Early filmmakers had ties to both the European and American industries, and international competition defined the conditions under which Egyptian filmmaking was born and state officials operated, sometimes but not always in the industry's defense. Resident foreign national filmmakers, embassy officials, and film company representatives interacted in a richly contested environment to promote their respective interests. Continuity and crisis in the industry were reflected in cinematic success and failure, and despite decades of change in the global and national context, Egypt's early cinema established patterns that remain evident today.

Domestic Production and Regional Exports

Egypt's domestic film production dates to 1923, when German-trained filmmaker Muhammad Bayoumi returned to Cairo to shoot his first fiction film, *Fi ard Tutankhamun*. Bayoumi also made a short film, *al-Bashkateb*, at about the same time, and both pictures preceded what used to be considered the first Egyptian feature: *Layla*, a 1927 silent film (not to be confused with the film *Layla bint al-rif* in Ryzova's chapter), starring a well-known stage actress, 'Aziza Amir. Sound production followed a few years later in 1932, with Muhammad Karim's *Awlad al-dhawat*, written by and starring the wealthy, theatrically trained Yusuf Wahbi (who did go on to star in *Layla bint al-rif*). *Layla*, in fact, was the first entirely Egyptian-financed film, since most of the earlier filmmaking was done by resident foreign nationals, whose ties to Egypt gave them somewhat ambiguous identities.[5] Before then, Italian and other resident Europeans had produced a modest total output of about 150 short films and newsreels.[6] A small number of cinemas had long served resident foreign nationals, the first of them showing French and Italian movies in Cairo and Alexandria just before World War I.[7] When the war cut off foreign imports, an Alexandrian photographer and a group of Italian businessmen formed a local company to make short films, though local production remained minimal for a decade.[8]

Serious industrial development began cautiously in 1925, when prominent industrialist Muhammad Tal'at Harb founded Egypt's first major production company: Misr Company for Theater and Cinema, led by a small but devoted group of local producers and distributors.[9] From the 1920s onward, the film enterprise in Egypt contained a broad array of countervailing tendencies, reflecting the contending interests of its various subsectors, as well as the influence of their foreign partners and rivals. The business was replete with industrial conflict and efforts at cooperation, and these dynamics had significant consequences for the local industry's capacity to achieve its objectives. The three subsectors of filmmaking—production, distribution, and exhibition—grew at different rates, were subject to different financial exigencies, and had inherently conflicting interests by virtue of their distinctive roles in the commercial process. At times, the fragmentation of interests within and among the subsectors prevented their cooperation and led to self-destructive bouts of infighting. Cinema owners, for example, often refused to join producers to press for trade protection from American imports, because many theaters showed at least some foreign films. Producers and distributors, only some of whom also co-produced or distributed foreign films, had similar difficulty cooperating.[10]

Domestically produced Egyptian exports did not develop in earnest until after 1935, when Tal'at Harb built Studio Misr, the first modern film studio in the Middle East and Africa.[11] Egyptian production and export of feature films grew dramatically in the latter half of the 1930s and 1940s, with Cairo emerging as a self-styled "Hollywood of the Arab East," quickly overshadowing Alexandria as the industry's center of gravity.[12] Entrepreneurs, some of whom were resident foreign nationals, constructed four more major studios by 1947, and the number of independent production companies quintupled from twenty-four to 120 by 1950.[13] Investment capital was most readily available during and just after World War II, when investors sought the quick profits of expanded production and diminished foreign competition. This was the Egyptian industry's first Golden Age, at least financially, when moviegoing became the most popular form of urban entertainment in Egypt and much the rest of the region.[14] It was a notably effervescent and high-profile part of economic and social life, leading some contemporary observers to claim that filmmaking was Egypt's second most important industry.[15]

Profitability of film investments in this period had a crucial effect on the rapid commercialization of Egyptian filmmaking. Entrepreneurs drawn to the business placed a very heavy emphasis on expanding production and extending foreign distribution, rather than improving quality.[16] Small production companies rented out studios simply to make single films and distribute them as widely as possible, either by hiring a distribution agent to handle specific foreign markets or by selling limited foreign distribution rights.[17] Most of the producers in this period made only one or two films per year, revealing the disorganized, almost speculative nature of early production and financing.[18] A few of them, such as Togo Mizrahi and Studio Misr, led the way by their consistent efforts to make and distribute several films each year. But much smaller-scale operators made a majority of Egyptian movies, either entering the business as a temporary venture or failing to last more than a few years.[19]

Risk-minimizing strategies predominated in business decision-making, mostly in the development of a rigid "star system," in which an exceedingly small number of actors appeared repeatedly in multiple films, a hint of which we have seen in Ryzova and Kholoussi's chapters. Their individual popularity assured that a loyal audience of fans would be willing to see any picture in which they appeared, thereby stabilizing demand and bringing predictability to the flow of returns on investments.[20] As the business became more competitive throughout the 1930s and most of the 1940s, the number of cinemas expanded substantially to serve the lower and middle class Egyptians then flocking to the movies. The fastest expansion in the period came during World War II, when declining foreign imports and rising wages for workers led to unprecedented growth, only to contract somewhat in the war's aftermath.[21] The number of cinemas grew steadily, even if weak seasonal downturns forced some large movie houses to close for short periods.[22] At the height of the postwar competitive boom in 1947, nearly two-thirds of Egypt's cinemas still showed either all or some foreign films, assuring that most exhibitors were unwilling to support any degree of control over the level of imports.[23]

Significantly, the industry's expansion and the growth of competition translated into political weakness. Without a network of ownership or organizational connections linking producers and distributors to each other and to their exhibition venues, the film sector's organizational weakness might even have spelled its early demise just after World War II. In August 1947, however, the Ministry of Commerce and Industry sanctioned and funded the formation of a Cinema Chamber (*Ghurfat Sina'at al-Sinima*).[24] Established in accordance with the law governing industrial chambers, it had branches for each subsector, as well as for the film studios and laboratories.[25] It was designed to solve the coordination problems among producers, distributors, and theater owners, and the ministry eventually made membership mandatory.[26] While the Cinema Chamber provided only a weak link among subsectors, its oversight activity and corporatist structure did raise the cost of entry into the sector for new firms. Its establishment marked the beginning of a shift in the organization of Egyptian filmmaking, anticipating later Nasser-era movement toward greater monopoly and corporatist control of the sector.[27]

Egyptian film exports continued to expand internationally in the early postwar years, largely sustained by the efforts of war profiteers to find fruitful investment opportunities for hundreds of millions of pounds in newly acquired wealth.[28] Still handled by individual sales agents, the majority of these exports went to markets in the Middle East and North Africa, though some made their way around the world. As a result, Egypt's actors and singers gained great popularity in neighboring Arab states and established a regional presence that echoed American global dominance, even if on a much smaller scale. Egypt's regional dominance in film—later to be enhanced by radio and television exports—contributed to the diffusion of Egyptian Arabic to make its 'ammiya the world's most widely understood form of spoken Arabic. In this sense, even if the film industry's early financial successes were short-lived, the regional diffusion of Egyptian film may have aided later efforts by Egyptian nationalists like Gamal 'Abd al-Nasser to shape Arab politics throughout the Middle East and North Africa.

International Competition and National Response

In Egypt, on the eve of the sound revolution in 1926, the American Trade Commissioner in the cosmopolitan port city of Alexandria reported to Washington that half the motion pictures shown in the country were American, with U.S. films experiencing no trade discrimination or political interference whatsoever.[29] American and European movies were rented to cinemas by the meter for a fixed price, with the Alexandria market covering two-thirds of local distributors' costs and Cairo responsible for the remaining third.[30] As a whole, Egypt at the time was a small but expanding market, second in the continent only to British South Africa.[31] Egypt's large expatriate community of transplanted Europeans did much of the moviegoing, since most Egyptians had yet to incorporate the pastime into their weekly routines.

American competition was a defining characteristic of the Egyptian market early on. By the 1930s, Hollywood already had come to dominate the market, with American imports comprising 76 percent of all films screened in 1936, followed by France's 10 percent.[32] The country's geographic position at the crossroads of Africa and Asia magnified its significance in the film trade, since American distributors shipped films from the United States to Europe and then on to other markets via branch offices in Egypt. Universal Pictures, for example, maintained its Near East regional headquarters in Alexandria, which served as a transit point for film shipments to markets throughout the Middle East, Africa, and beyond.[33] The substantial movement of film between Egypt and the Sudan, recorded in the transit tables of the *Annual Statement of the Foreign Trade of Egypt*, almost certainly was destined for British troops stationed there.[34]

The popularity of American film over European exports to Egypt had risen steadily in conjunction with its growing worldwide dominance after World War I. The war had weakened the European industry sufficiently to provide an extraordinary opportunity for American filmmakers, who began to shift production to a new West-coast locale, where clement weather permitted year-round activity. Just prior to the sound revolution, and in response to the new industry's implication in a series of scandals, Hollywood business leaders formed the Motion Picture Producers and Distributors Association (MPPDA). Also known as the Hays Office, the MPPDA established a Foreign Department to represent its members overseas, opening dozens of offices throughout the world, including in Cairo. In subsequent decades, Hays Office representatives in Egypt worked closely with embassy officials, theater owners, and local distributors to promote Hollywood exports to what was seen as a potentially lucrative emerging market.

In conjunction with this rising profile in Egypt, American cinema inevitably would be drawn into the turbulence of local politics in the 1930s and 1940s. In 1946, twenty years to the day after the above-mentioned Trade Commissioner's report, the Motion Picture Association of America forwarded to the U.S. State Department information regarding a grenade attack on the Cinema Miami in downtown Cairo by anti-British activists.[35] More commonly, pictures like MGM's *Song of Revolt*—a short portrayal of the French Revolution—suffered at the hands of state censors for dealing with sensitive, discomforting political themes that were deemed unsuitable for Egyptian audiences.[36] In time, American pictures even got caught up in regional political rivalries: Egyptian censors delayed the release of Paramount's *Samson and Delilah* in 1951, claiming that the film was pro-Zionist; Israel, for its part, banned the picture as anti-Jewish.[37]

Nonetheless, the occasional political sensitivity aside, Hollywood imports remained popular, welcome, and largely uncontroversial in Egypt. In purely economic terms, Egyptian state officials maintained liberal trade policies in film for much of this period, an orientation that emanated partly from the European-dominated free trade regime in place in Egypt since the nineteenth century. Until 1930, negligible restrictions were placed on film imports, but even after Egypt obtained tariff autonomy in 1930 with the expiration of the last of its longstanding agreements with the European powers, film tariff levels remained relatively low. Exceptions to the liberal tendency did appear in the 1940s, when World War II precipitated an increase in customs duties on film, which doubled to £E 5 per kilo from 1941 to 1945, as well as an augmentation of the ad valorem duty from 3 percent to 7 percent. Still, these were relatively minor developments in the face of a decidedly liberal trend, marked above all by very few direct restrictions on film imports. This course was maintained until the mid 1940s.[38]

Following the growth of monopolistic tendencies in the Egyptian industry after World War II, a slight closure of the Egyptian market began, with the imposition of remittance restrictions, import licensing requirements, and other targeted quotas and duties. Egyptian producers came out of the war in a particularly strong position financially, though structural problems in the economy limited the gains that filmmakers could realize. On the one hand, production costs in the immediate postwar period averaged £E 25,000 for films that would then earn nearly £E 100,000 at home and abroad.[39] On the other hand, hard currency reserves earned during the war began declining rapidly, limiting the import activities of local distributors. Since film imports to Egypt—as in Britain and much of Europe—were not deemed sufficiently important by authorities to warrant the hard currency expenditure, officials put remittance restrictions on imports. In time, additional measures like the imposition of import licensing indicated a further movement toward protectionism, as the state extended its authority into the cultural domain. By the early 1950s, state authorities placed a three-film maximum on the number of pictures that could be dubbed into Arabic each year, and it raised customs duties on foreign films by 25 percent.[40]

From an American standpoint, the most prominent constraint on exports to Egypt after World War II related to currency remittances. Egypt certainly was not alone in the world in prioritizing its domestic allocation of hard currency. But remittance problems were especially acute for American companies, since an inability to repatriate profits deprived distributors of a return on investments already made and undermined any rationale for developing the market further. Remittance restrictions originated in postwar Egypt's withdrawal from the British sterling area when the Anglo-Egyptian Financial Agreement expired in July 1947.[41] Egyptian uncertainty regarding the availability of dollars to cover imports led to a freeze and then simply a reduction in the amount of hard currency that American distributors could return to parent companies each month. Permitted remittance levels declined from 80 percent during the war to 50 percent in May 1947,[42] and finally to 35 percent under an agreement between the MPPDA and the Egyptian government in January 1948.[43] The shortage of foreign exchange strained the Egyptian government's capacity to permit the remittance of even 35 percent of monthly earnings, at least until the global dollar shortage ended a decade later.

Significant remnants of past liberalism nonetheless remained into the early 1950s. For decades, Egyptian filmmakers had lobbied state authorities for strict protectionist policies, but with only limited success. While the Federation of Egyptian Industry's film section, the Cinema Chamber, repeatedly sought direct relief from foreign competition, such relief was not usually granted. This tendency persisted well into the 'Abd al-Nasser era, for the first five years of the 1952 Revolution produced no dramatic shifts in filmmaking or film policy. The Cinema Chamber, for example, submitted a report to the Ministry of Commerce and Industry in early 1955, calling for strongly protectionist measures to combat the local success of American blockbusters like *Quo Vadis*. An influential critic of the report, however, declared that "competition is the heart of commerce" and noted the longstanding importance of foreign production to the local exhibition market, as well as to tax and customs revenues. Indeed, tax rates were relatively high, as state authorities had always looked to the entertainment industry for revenue more than anything else, and this was reflected in the variety of taxes imposed on all segments of the sector. Yet such taxes did little to restrict the flow of foreign pictures into the country; an open orientation toward international cinema, adopted more than two decades earlier, continued well after the end of the monarchy.[44]

State Regulation and Cultural Production

Throughout the first half of the twentieth century, Egyptian state authorities showed only minimal interest in film, either as an economic sector or as a source of cultural production. State regulation was principally in the hands of bureaucrats with concerns about public order, and the most important state institutions regulating film were the Ministry of Finance and the Ministry of Interior, the latter's primary interests relating to neither the economy nor culture. Additional formal authority over cultural policy was divided between the Ministries of Education and Social Affairs, both of which were infused with strong currents of paternalism that saw the Egyptian masses as needing cultural guidance. All these tendencies, and their institutional embodiments, had origins in Britain's colonial concern with security and stability. A regulation on public establishments in 1911, for example, focused principally on maintaining public order and social standards of propriety, as did Egypt's first film censorship law in 1914.[45]

In regulating film, the institutional division of labor was clear in its prioritization of economic and security matters. With overall direction in the hands of the Ministry of Interior, the Ministry of Finance issued decrees regarding acceptable content for film imports and exports. At the same time, the Ministry of Social Affairs sought to improve the quality of cinematic production by sponsoring contests and offering modest prizes to filmmakers. The Ministry of Education, for its part, housed a Department of Culture that saw motion pictures as playing a salutary role in the moral and intellectual development of young people. The latter piece of the bureaucracy would later play an important role in the state's expansion into the cultural domain.[46] For the time being, however, state authorities generally considered filmmaking to be just another business enterprise, requiring oversight only to the extent to which it brought together the public in ways that potentially could threaten political stability.

This essentially laissez-faire attitude toward filmmaking reflected the regime's arm's-length approach to the kind of cultural production traditionally beyond the state's ambit—as contrasted to state education, covered by Salmoni and Ikeda in their chapters. On the one hand, the state throughout the period claimed that motion pictures played an influential and potentially beneficial role in society, even if this was limited to the ethical formation and acculturation of Egyptians. Beginning in 1933, moreover, the Ministry of Education awarded its own cash prizes to individual producers and actors for laudable work.[47] Reflecting the ideological intentionality of educators highlighted by Salmoni in chapter six, the Ministry of Education saw the popular melodramas and musical films of the period as performing a quasi-educational function by adhering to a conservative set of narrative and presentational norms that were agreed upon by consensus and were only occasionally articulated explicitly.[48] On the other hand, few other forms of state intervention were considered necessary to assure compliance with these norms. No screen quota for Egyptian films existed in the 1930s, even when local industrialists demanded one.[49] The state made no systematic effort to use film for broader, nationalist purposes. Foreigners, the wealthy, and the landowning elite sponsored high culture, but the authorities did little to intervene on a national level in film or other forms of cultural production.

This ambivalence about the state's relationship with cultural production also informed the minimal censorship that existed in filmmaking. Some close state regulation was evident early on, especially relating to the three major taboo subjects of the day: religion, politics, and sex.[50] In its treatment of imports, the Ministry of Finance passed a decree in the early 1920s that restricted imports based on their social content. In 1928, it began requiring exports to be reviewed by the Ministry of Interior, which consolidated its own Office of Censorship of the Press and Publishing in 1936.[51] In handling exports, moreover, the Ministry of Interior began requiring prior approval almost immediately after Egypt started producing its own films in the late 1920s, with the stated purpose of protecting the country's prestige and reputation.[52] Still, all of these state activities were confined to the restriction of cultural production deemed either unsuitable for popular consumption, directly threatening to the regime, or deleterious to Egypt's image abroad. Greater involvement was eschewed because the Egyptian state was essentially indifferent to cultural production. It did not yet see a need to intervene, develop, and support an administrative apparatus, or to articulate a coherent national policy in this domain.[53] This final step would be left to the new post-revolutionary regime.

Conclusions: Continuity and Change in Egyptian Cinema

On the night of 22 July 1952, Anwar Sadat went to the movies, all but missing the coup that launched the Egyptian revolution.[54] While a trip to the movies kept Sadat from participating in the opening hours of the coup, the revolution itself was not entirely responsible for subsequent Egyptian accomplishments in film. Rewinding Egyptian history and replaying it without the pre-revolutionary cinema surely would produce dramatically changed results, and Egypt's cultural production in film would look quite different today if the industry had not been created before 1952. The very existence of an Egyptian cinema prior to the revolution had several enduring consequences, just as its specific attributes had a path dependent effect on later developments in this domain. Any sharp historical dichotomization between pre- and post-revolutionary filmmaking is problematic for this reason, since important elements of continuity can be traced to the industry's earliest days.

Early filmmaking in Egypt left at least four consequential legacies. First, pre-revolutionary Egyptian filmmakers established an industrial and cinematic infrastructure upon which the state later could build. This included the physical construction of film studios, laboratories, and movie houses, as well as the less tangible but equally significant creation of distribution networks and "star systems" that would endure for years. Egypt's early material investment in filmmaking was unparalleled in the region, matched only by a dozen or so other countries in the world. This investment, moreover, allowed Nasser-era officials to nationalize existing film companies and facilities like Studio Misr, and to extend the cinematic industrial hub by building a new "Cinema City" in Giza adjacent to existing facilities. The state's appropriation of private distribution networks, and the cultivation of new stars, would have been impossible without the efforts of Egypt's cinema pioneers in the industry's first quarter century.

If the physical legacies of the past were substantial, the long-term consequences of early developments were not entirely positive. Some of Egypt's older facilities eventually became run down and technically obsolete. Filmmakers in other countries had little choice but to build new studios, uninfluenced by a film-industry past that many never had. But those in Egypt relied for decades on what was there, even when it no longer functioned efficiently. In this sense, the physical legacy of a storied cinematic past may have limited the industry's later capacity to re-imagine itself as anything other than a reinvigorated commercial cinema. Since at least 1945, Egyptian filmmakers have sought to overcome a perennial "crisis of the cinema."[55] Yet this crisis is rooted in structural conditions that were beyond easy redress in a globalized market for cultural production, with powerful international competitors vying for market share.

A second and equally important legacy relates to the training and expertise acquired by the first generation of Egyptian filmmakers, technicians, and creative personnel. While Egypt's early filmmakers learned their trade largely in Europe, later directors, technicians, and actors profited from the experience of an indigenous cinema and its pioneers, who passed on their understanding of filmmaking in the local context. Egypt's Higher Institute for Cinema was not created until 1969, but its staff included people whose pre-revolutionary experience shaped all facets of the filmmaking enterprise. This expertise, like its physical counterpart, may not always have profited later generations, since it reinforced a commercial orientation that could succeed only under circumstances that had long since ended.

But it provided continuity in both technical and artistic terms, allowing later observers of the Egyptian cinema to find filmmaking commonalities across several decades.

Third, pre-revolutionary filmmakers helped to "construct" moviegoing audiences by teaching them how to "read" Egyptian film.[56] While not the passive recipients of cultural content, these audiences were created both at home and throughout the Arab world, beginning in the 1930s. Their existence and the cultural specificity of the film texts they encountered cannot be taken for granted. After all, the Egyptian industry modeled itself after its American counterpart, and Hollywood's global dominance emanated partly from its early success in defining the very nature of the film medium, while cultivating consumer tastes for filmmaking in a linear, continuous, classical narrative style.[57] Even if Egyptian cinema grew up in the shadow of Hollywood—a local variation on the dominant common theme—Egyptian filmmakers did develop unique genres, stylistic conventions, and filmmaking norms that persisted long after the commercial decline of "Hollywood on the Nile." Even Egypt's best-known filmmaker today, Yousef Chahine, continues to use music, for example, in ways that only make sense in a decades-old Egyptian context.

Fourth, and finally, the pre-revolutionary cinema opened up cultural spaces in the Egyptian public imagination, creating the very possibility of national cultural production in an area dominated by international competitors. While these cultural spaces atrophied and were reshaped in subsequent years, their early appearance created opportunities for nationalist articulation in a medium that lent itself admirably to public life. The creation of public spaces for cultural production by and for Egyptians was not automatic or inevitable, a reality demonstrated by their utter absence in other countries in the region. But it is a legacy not easily undone. Even if contemporary economic and political pressures have contributed to the waning and impoverishment of Egyptian civil life, or its movement into other kinds of social space, cinematic production in Egypt remains viable in the present precisely because of past efforts.

Notes

1   *Annual Statement of the Foreign Trade of Egypt,* various years. Ten Egyptian films were exported to Brazil in 1948. *Ciné Film,* no. 26, June 1950, 63.

2   Welles never actually filmed in Egypt, probably due to his declining fortunes in Hollywood after directing *Citizen Kane.* But the fact that he came close to doing so says something about Egypt's impressive standing in the industry in the late 1940s. For more on the Welles contract, see "Échos et Nouvelles: Orson Welles va tourner en Égypte," *Ciné Film,* no. 19, 7 November 1949, 7.

3   This negative assessment is shared by some Egyptian and non-Egyptian film scholars. For a similar recent claim, see Walter Armbrust, "The Golden Age before the Golden Age: Commercial Egyptian Cinema before the 1960s," in Armbrust, ed., *Mass Mediations: New Approaches to Popular Culture in the Middle East and Beyond* (Berkeley: University of California Press, 2000), 292–27. 'Ali Abu Shadi describes the films of the 'Abd al-Nasser era as *"al-intaj al-sinima'i al-hadif,"* and Samir Farid notes elsewhere that the term *"al-hadif"* is used to characterize film "with a purpose," i.e., socialist 'propaganda.' See 'Ali Abu Shadi, *Waqa'i' al-sinima al-misriya fi mi'at 'am: 1896–1995* ("100 Years of Developments in the Egyptian Cinema, 1896–1995") (Cairo: al-Hay'at al-'Amma li-l-Shu'un al-Matabi' al-Amiriya, 1997), 185–86; and Samir Farid, "Periodization of Egyptian Cinema," *Screens of Life: Critical Film Writing from the Arab World,* Alia Arasoughly, ed. (Quebec: World Heritage Press, 1996), 12. An example of the stark dichotomization between 'Abd al-Nasser era and earlier filmmaking is found in Galal Sharkawi's account, "History of the U.A.R. Cinema, 1896–1962," which claims that the Nasserist revolution "was a veritable Renaissance which brought about a complete change in a number of political, economic, social and cultural ideas." He then details film-related institutional developments under 'Abd al-Nasser. Sharkawi in George Sadoul, ed., *The Cinema in the Arab Countries* (Beirut: UNESCO and Interarab Centre of Cinema and Television, 1966), 92.

4   For the seminal argument about how a "logic of appropriateness" conditions institutional (and other) choices, see James G. March and Johan P. Olsen, *Rediscovering Institutions: The Organizational Basis of Politics* (New York: Free Press, 1989).

5   When the Egyptian industry itself celebrated its twenty-first anniversary in 1948, it dated its birth to the 1927 production of *Layla.* See *al-Film Ciné-Orient,* no. 8, 16 October 1948. The early history of Egyptian filmmaking is found in Ahmad al-Hadari, *Tarikh al-sinima fi Misr: al-juz' al-awwal min bidayat 1896 ila akhir 1930* ("A History of the Film Industry in Egypt: Part One, from the Beginning of 1896 to the End of 1930") (Cairo: Nadi al-Sinima bi-l-Qahira, 1989).

6   Ahmad al-Hadari, *Tarikh al-sinima fi Misr.* Official Egyptian historiography usually has downplayed the role of foreign nationals in the development of the industry, especially after 1927.

7   *Sina'at al-sinima: haqa'iq w-arqam,* General Egyptian Organization for the Cinema, Radio, and Television, Technical Office for the Cinema, March 1964, 2.

8   Ministry of Culture: Cinema, Theatre and Music Organization, "The Motion Picture Industry in Egypt," May 1979, 2.

9   Early production was led by four women: 'Aziza Amir, Asia Dagher, Fatima Rushdi, and Mary Queeny. The leading distributors of Egyptian films included the Misr Company for Theater and Cinema, Benha Films, Nahas Films, Charles Lifschitz, and Cairo Films; the major locally owned distributors handling foreign films included Alma (originally Prosperi) Film and Josy Film, as well as Ideal Motion Pictures and Dollar Film. *Ciné Film,* no. 26, June 1950, 26.

10 For more on the political economy of industrial conflict and cooperation, see Andrew Flibbert, "Commerce in Culture: Institutions, Markets, and Competition in the World Film Trade" (Ph.D. diss., Columbia University, 2001).

11 On Tal'at Harb and the founding of Studio Misr, see Ilhami Hasan, *Muhammad Tal'at Harb: ra'id sina'at al-sinima al-misriya, 1867–1941* (Cairo: General Egyptian Book Organization, 1986).

12 For a complete list of the names of more than 1,500 feature films produced in Egypt from 1927 to 1973, see 'Abd al-Mun'im Sa'd, *al-Sinima al-misriya fi mawsim 1973*, 218–46.

13 Studio details are found in Jacques Pascal, ed., *The Middle East Motion Picture Almanac, 1946–47*, 1st ed. (Cairo: S.O.P. Press, 1947), 127–32. Names and details on the explosion of production companies are listed in Galal al-Sharqawi, *Risala fi tarikh al-sinima al-'arabiya* (Cairo: Maktbat al-Nahda al-Misriya, 1970), 101–105.

14 The popularity of the cinema is noted by M.M. Mosharrafa, *Cultural Survey of Modern Egypt, Part Two* (London: Longmans, Green and Co., 1948), 59.

15 The film sector's economic contribution to Egyptian development was regularly exaggerated. Jacques Pascal, editor of the trade journal *Ciné Film*, often referred to filmmaking as Egypt's second industry after cotton; see, for example, *Ciné Film*, no. 18 (1 September 1949), 1–2. In retrospect, however, it seems more likely that the industry enjoyed several spectacularly profitable years but was unable to establish itself permanently on such a lucrative basis.

16 Jacob M. Landau, *Studies in the Arab Theater and Cinema* (Philadelphia: University of Pennsylvania Press, 1958), 179–80.

17 Studio rental cost between £E 1,500 and £E 4,000 per month in 1947. Cost breakdowns are found in Pascal, ed. *The Middle East Motion Picture Almanac*, 111. On foreign distribution, see Karen Finlon Dajani, "Egypt's Role as a Major Media Producer, Supplier and Distributor to the Arab World: An Historical-Descriptive Study" (Ph.D. diss., Temple University, 1979), esp. 130–42.

18 A classified advertisement in an industry trade journal in 1948 provides a telling indication of the ad hoc nature of film financing in this period: "On demande capitaliste disposant de £E 1,000 ou 1,500 pour excellente affaire cinématographique. Immobilisation six mois. Affaire assurée. Ecrire à la direction du journal." *Ciné-Orient*, no. 3 (1 July 1948), 6.

19 *The Middle East Motion Picture Almanac of 1946–47* (111) states that there were 140 production companies in Egypt. The vast majority of these could not have been operating actively, since Galal al-Sharkawi's list of films from the period includes only thirty producers who were affiliated with films released that year. The discrepancy is probably not an error but an indication of the sporadic involvement of individual investors in that period, and therefore of a fragmented and competitive market. See Galal al-Sharqawi, *Risala fi tarikh al-sinima al-'arabiya*.

20 For an overview of Egypt's star system, see Christophe Ayad, "Le star-système: de la splendeur au voile," in Magda Wassef, ed. *Égypte: 100 ans de cinéma*. An indication of the utter centrality of Egyptian stars to the industry is their presentation, along with a handful of directors, in Mustapha Darwish's *Dream Makers on the Nile: A Portrait of Egyptian Cinema* (Cairo: The American University in Cairo, 1998). The limited number of Egyptian stars is discussed and quantified by al-Sharqawi, *Risala fi tarikh al-sinima al-'arabiya*, 105–108. On genres, see Ali Abu Shadi, "Genres in Egyptian Cinema," *Screens of Life: Critical Film Writing from the Arab World*, vol. I (Quebec: World Heritage Press, 1996).

21 A contemporary account of the industry's wartime expansion and postwar decline is found in *Ciné Film*, no. 11, 1 (December 1948), 3. The number of spectators reportedly grew by 245 percent during the war. *Ciné Film*, no. 15 (March 1949), 22.

22 Just after World War II, large Cairo cinemas like the Miami, Royal, Kursal, and Diana closed temporarily in the summer of 1948. *Ciné Film*, no. 3 (1 July 1948), 4. On the perceived overabundance of cinemas, see the lead editorial in *Ciné Film*, no. 6 (1 September 1948), 1.

23 As the following figures indicate, the percentage of cinemas showing at least some foreign films rose considerably in the postwar years. This pattern held true throughout the country, with the notable exception of Port Said, where an unusual segregation of cinemas—probably due to the lingering British military presence—left only one of fourteen theaters offering a mixed program in 1954.

Year	Foreign	%	Egyptian	%	Mixed	%	Total
1946	58	30	73	38	62	32	193
1952	64	20	77	25	170	55	311
1954	69	19	21	6	264	75	354

Source: Calculated from cinema descriptions in Pascal, ed., The Middle East Motion Picture Almanac, 1946–47, 19–38; Pascal, ed., Annuaire du Cinéma, 1951–52, 49–88; and Pascal, ed., Annuaire du Cinéma, 1954, 69–119

24 Mohammed el-Qassass, "Theatre and Cinema," in Mustafa Habib, ed., *Cultural Life in the United Arab Republic* (Cairo: U.A.R. National Commission for UNESCO, 1968), 246.

25 Ahmad Kamel Mursi and Magdi Wahba, *Mu'jam al-fann al-sinima'i* (Cairo: General Egyptian Book Organization, 1973), 72. Official recognition was granted by Ministerial Decree no. 458 of September 1947. *Ciné Film*, no. 14 (24 January 1949), 6.

26 *Sina'at al-sinima: haqa'iq w-arqam*, March 1964, 3. Cinema workers were represented by the Filmmakers' Union (Niqabat al-Sinima'iyin al-Muhtarafiyin), which held its first meeting in November 1943. *Mu'jam al-fann al-sinima'i*, 79; Magdi Wahba, *Cultural Policy in Egypt* (Paris: UNESCO, 1972), 60. On the Ministry of Commerce and Industry's forbidding of any industrial activity without membership in the appropriate Chamber of the Federation of Egyptian Industries, see *Ciné Film*, no. 68 (1 January 1954), 12.

27 A plan to create an actual monopoly reportedly was developed by the Misr Company for the Theater and Cinema, which sought to unify postwar Egypt's many small producers into one or two companies, with Studio Misr controlling all production. See *Ciné Film*, no. 1 (1 May 1948), 12. Other mergers among exhibitors and producers were rumored in the trade press, but, more often than not, failed to materialize in this period. See *Ciné Film*, no. 3 (1 June 1948), 4. For more on Egyptian corporatism in other areas, see Robert Bianchi, *Unruly Corporatism: Associational Life in Twentieth-Century Egypt* (New York: Oxford University Press, 1989).

28 Charles Issawi notes that "by the end of the war Egyptian individuals and institutions had accumulated sterling balances of about £E 400 million." Issawi, *Egypt at Mid-Century: An Economic Analysis*, 204. In a 1947 edition of this book written in 1942–43, he estimated annual film industry expenditures at £E 500,000; filmmaking was widely viewed then as a lucrative business, with Egypt having "possibilities as a first-rate international film centre." Issawi, *Egypt: An Economic and Social Analysis* (London: Oxford University Press, 1947), 93. The so-called war profiteers, however, had no interest in filmmaking as anything other than a short-term investment. See Sa'd al-Din Tawfiq, *Qissat al-sinima fi Misr: dirasa naqdiya* (Cairo: Dar al-Hilal, 1969), 83–84.

29 Richard A. May, American Trade Commissioner, to J. Morton Howell, American Minister, March 13, 1926. National Archives, *Records of the Department of State Relating to the Internal Affairs of Egypt, 1910–29*, 883.40 Social Matters. The fact that films were shipped from the United States to Europe, and on to the Middle East and elsewhere via Egypt, indicates that trade statistics need to be handled with caution, since they often refer only to the country of immediate origin. As May noted in the source above, "The official import returns do not show that the United States enjoys [a] large proportion of the business for the reason that many American films are imported into Egypt from France, Italy, and other countries after having been showed there."

30 *Ciné Film*, no. 26, special edition, June 1950, 26. The French company, Gaumont, introduced the idea of a percentage deal, instead of pricing film rentals by their length, and American companies soon followed suit.

31 C.J. North, "Our Foreign Trade in Motion Pictures," in "The Motion Picture in its Social and Economic Aspects," *Annals of the American Academy of Political and Social Science*, vol. CXXVIII, November 1926, 107. North was head of the U.S. Commerce Department's Motion Picture Section.

32 Nathan D. Golden, *Review of Foreign Film Markets during 1936*, United States Department of Commerce, Bureau of Foreign and Domestic Commerce, Motion Picture Section (Washington, D.C., April 1937), 64. In the year 1934 imported sound films came to Egypt in large numbers. This is evident from the rapidly changing balance between sound and silent film imports in the early 1930s:

Year	Silent (%)	Sound (%)
1931	97	3
1932	93	7
1933	77	23
1934	2	98
1935	1	99

Source: Calculated from Annual Statement of the Foreign Trade of Egypt, various years.

33 May to Howell, March 13, 1926.

34 For data on extensive Egyptian re-exports, see the transit trade tables in the *Annual Statement of the Foreign Trade of Egypt*.

35 Carl E. Milliken, manager, International Department, MPAA to George Canty, assistant chief, Telecommunications Division, Department of State. 883.4061 Motion Pictures/3–1346 and enclosed "Confirmation of Cable," RKO Radio Pictures Inc., Export Division. The MPPDA was renamed the Motion Picture Association of America in 1945, and its Foreign Department was restyled the International Department in 1943.

36 The latter film was banned by Egyptian censors in 1938 for depicting the French revolution. John Eugene Harley, *World-Wide Influences of the Cinema: A Study of Official Censorship and the International Cultural Aspects of Motion Pictures* (Los Angeles: University of Southern California Press, 1940), 121.

37 *Ciné Film*, no. 33, 1 February 1951, 15.

38 Bent Hansen and Karim Nashashibi, *Foreign Trade Regimes and Economic Development: Egypt*. Special Conference Series on Foreign Trade Regimes and Economic Development, National Bureau of Economic Research, vol. 4. (New York: Columbia University Press, 1975), 3–5; Ali el-Gritly, *The Structure of Modern Industry in* Egypt (Cairo: Government Press, 1948), 432–45 and 554–69; and "History of the Customs Regime in Egypt," in *Annual Statement of the Foreign Trade*, 1932, Ministry of Finance, Statistical Department (Cairo: Government Press, 1934), 5–13.

39 The cost and earnings figures come from Samir Farid, "Periodization of Egyptian Cinema," *Screens of Life: Critical Film Writing from the Arab World*, Alia Arasoughly, ed. (Quebec: World Heritage Press, 1996), 8. He provides no source, but these figures are consistent with other estimates, such as those found in *Ciné Film*.

40 Martin Quigley, ed., *Motion Picture Almanac*, 1951–52 (New York).

41 For more on Egypt's postwar balance of payments and foreign trade position, see Charles Issawi, *Egypt at Mid-Century: An Economic Survey* (New York: Oxford University Press, 1954); and Bent Hansen and Karim Nashashibi, *Foreign Trade Regimes and Economic Development: Egypt* (New York: National Bureau of Economic Research and Columbia University Press, 1975).

42 See the correspondence between Gerald M. Mayer, Managing Director, International Division, MPAA and George Canty, Assistant Chief, Division of Commercial Policy, U.S. State Department, 883.40061 MP/5–547 and 5–747.

43 Cairo Airgram A–719 dated 28 June 1949 from H.G. Minigerode/American Embassy to SecState, 883.4061 M.P./6–2249.

44 On the Cinema Chamber's report and local reaction, see *Ciné Film*, no. 82 (1 March 1955), 1.

45 *Ciné Film*, no. 26 (June 1950), 10; *Mu'jam al-fann al-sinima'i*, 70.

46 The Ministry of Education's Department of Culture was transferred to the new Ministry of National Guidance in 1956; the Ministry of National Guidance was renamed the Ministry of Culture and National Guidance in 1958.

47 Magda Wassef, ed., *Égypte: 100 ans de cinéma* (Paris: Éditions Plume and Institut du Monde Arabe, 1995), 23.

48 For one such articulation, see the U.S. State Department report on Egypt's early production code in Confidential U.S. State Department Central Files (declassified), *Egypt: Internal Affairs and Foreign Affairs*, Record Group 59, Reel 8, Motion Pictures, 883.4061.

49 Martin Quigley, ed., *Motion Picture Almanac, 1937–38* (New York), 1124.

50 Mustafa Darwish, *Dream Makers on the Nile*, 13. These areas remain largely taboo today.

51 In 1945, censorship authority was moved to the Ministry of Social Affairs, only to be returned in 1948 with the outbreak of the war in Palestine. Wassef, ed., 20; *Mu'jam al-fann al-sinima'i*, 70–71.

52 Decree of 23 August 1928 in the *Journal Officiel*, no. 77, 30 August 1928, reported in *L'Égypte contemporaine*, no. 116–17 (November–December 1929). Egypt's first cinema regulation actually came out in 1911 from the Ministry of Interior. Jacques Pascal, ed., *The Middle East Motion Picture Almanac / al-Dalil al-sinima'i li-l-sharq al-awsat*, 1st ed., (Cairo: S.O.P. Press, 1947).

53 For similar claims regarding cultural production more broadly, see Michael W. Albin, "Official Culture and the Role of the Book," *Journal of the American Research Center in Egypt* XXIV (1987).

54 Stationed out of town at al-Arish airfield, Sadat was unaware of the exact date of the coup but was summoned by 'Abd al-Nasser. On the night of the 22nd, 'Abd al-Nasser went to Sadat's apartment and learned that the latter had gone to the cinema with his wife, Jehan. Sadat returned home at about midnight, found a note from 'Abd al-Nasser, grabbed his pistol, and rushed out to 'Abd al-Hakim Amer's home, and then to the military barracks at 'Abbasiya. Despite being in charge of communications in the coup plot, Sadat could not get past the base guard because he did not know the password. Eventually, he found Amer, who had returned from the taking of army headquarters. Sadat, nonetheless, issued the regime's first communiqué the following morning. See Anwar el-Sadat, *In Search of Identity* (New York: Harper and Row, 1977), 105–107 and Jehan Sadat, *A Woman of Egypt* (New York: Simon and Schuster, 1987), 125–27.

55 References in the media to the crisis of the cinema (*azmat al-sinima*) appeared as early as the 1940s.

56 For more on the general issue, see James Monaco, *How to Read a Film: The World of Movies, Media, and Multimedia*, 3rd ed. (New York: Oxford University Press, 2000).

57 On the nature and development of this style, see David Bordwell, Janet Staiger and Kristin Thompson, *The Classical Hollywood Cinema: Film Style and Mode of Production to 1960* (New York: Columbia University Press, 1985).

17 Egyptian Historiography, 1919–52

Arthur Goldschmidt

The recording of Egypt's history between its two twentieth-century revolutions began as it was unfolding, as both Egyptians and foreign residents felt the need to record the accelerating pace of change in their society and the outside forces that impinged on it. For Egyptians, their overriding concerns were independence from British rule and the reunification of the Nile Valley. The history that they most cared about was that of their country, especially its relationship to Britain and its internal political evolution. Muslim Egyptians also took an interest in the history of Islam. Rarely at first and then more so as events unfolded around them, they came to care about Arab history as well. Foreigners residing in Egypt cared about the countries from which they came or the ethnic groups with which they identified, but they were also interested in the condition of Egypt's economy that had attracted them and sustained them. Interest in one's past is a universal human preoccupation. Writing about it is not limited to professional historians, who were practically nonexistent in Egypt at that time.

The 1919–52 era was a golden age for the written word in Egypt. Events and trends were recorded in the burgeoning periodical press and in diaries or memoirs. Some were published. Many were tucked away for future generations, for Egyptians often felt that their experiences and observations could not be revealed to their contemporaries without repercussions from the British, the palace, the secret police, or their rivals. Historians now rely heavily on newspapers, magazines, and yearbooks of that time to ascertain what happened and how people at the time interpreted events. Ahmad Shafiq (1860–1940), a lawyer who had served 'Abbas II when the latter was khedive and in exile, provided copious documentation of events in his annual

Hawliyat Misr al-siyasiya from 1926 to 1933, preceded by three preparatory volumes that covered the period from 1840 to 1926 in increasing detail.[1] The political history was recorded, with a bias in favor of the National Party and against the Wafd, by Egypt's distinguished lawyer, parliamentary deputy, and minister, 'Abd al-Rahman al-Rafi'i (1889–1966), in *Thawrat sanat 1919*[2] and *Fi a'qab al-thawra al-misriya*.[3] Amin Sami's *Taqwim al-Nil* chronicles many events and prints government documents.[4] The palace opened other official documents to selected historians, but the archives were—and are—poorly organized and extremely challenging to researchers.

Contemporary works about Egypt in languages other than Arabic include a collective publication by French and Egyptian writers with chapters on Egypt's history up to 1923, its governmental structure, the Mecca pilgrimage, Cairo University, archaeology, geology, irrigation and agriculture, commerce and finance, communications (including detailed harbor maps of Alexandria, Port Said, and Suez harbor), social life, and even tourism, but no reference to the 1919 Revolution or the power struggles among the Wafd, King Fu'ad, and the British.[5] We have histories by the British, such as George Young's *Egypt*,[6] which sympathized slightly with the nationalist movement, and P.G. Elgood's *The Transit of Egypt*,[7] which did not. Lord Lloyd, the high commissioner for Egypt and the Sudan from 1925 to 1929, later wrote a two-volume defense of British rule (including his own), *Egypt since Cromer*.[8] Although Lloyd covered political history extensively, he rarely mentioned any ideas and concerns of Egyptians. By contrast, Anglophone readers have recognized Egypt's central role in the modern Islamic revival since the contemporaneous publication of C.C. Adams' *Islam and Modernism in Egypt*.[9] Slightly later was a collective publication of the Groupe d'Études d'Islam, called *Égypte indépendante*,[10] which extensively discussed internal politics, social classes, relations with Britain, young Egyptians, foreign residents (in the wake of the Montreux Conference that ended the Capitulations), the economy, and the press. Arnold T. Wilson's *The Suez Canal: Its Past, Present, and Future* focused on the period before 1914 but provided useful statistics up to the 1930s.[11] A memoir by Sa'd Zaghlul's nephew, Amine Youssef, *Independent Egypt*,[12] was meant to win support for the Wafd. Marcel Colombe's *L'Évolution de l'Égypte, 1924–1950*,[13] which appeared just before the end of the monarchy, is a well-reasoned analysis of Egypt's politics during the constitutional era. Still, however, these books did not constitute a rich hoard, either in quantity or rigorous historical analysis. Up to 1952, a library of books on Egypt's political history since 1919 could not have filled a two-foot shelf.

There was one subset of contemporary Egyptian history that would have crowded that hypothetical shelf: the economy. Egypt had become a major exporter of cotton and a market for the manufactures of Europe, North America, and Japan. Since 1910 bankers and business entrepreneurs with interests in Egypt have relied on a monthly magazine called *l'Égypte Contemporaine*, a treasure trove for economic historians. There was also the *Annuaire statistique* published annually by the Egyptian government.[14] No other Arab country before World War II provided so much statistical information, for none played so central a role in world trade, transport, and communications. Scholarly work included A.E. Crouchley's *The Economic Development of Modern Egypt*,[15] which is a storehouse of statistical data and analysis. H.E. Hurst's *The Nile: A General Account of the River and the Utilization of its Waters* sums up what was known about the Nile and offers a detailed prospectus for the Century Storage Scheme, with only a brief reference to its alternative that became a major project under 'Abd al-Nasser, the Aswan High Dam.[16] Also useful is Charles Issawi's *Egypt: An Economic and Social Analysis*,[17] which was revised after the 1952 Revolution and published as *Egypt at Mid-Century*.[18]

Once the Free Officers had replaced King Faruq, a flood of new publications became available on Egypt under the old regime or on the 1952 Revolution itself. The best work came out first in French. Well-written and perceptive, although not always accurate, was Jean and Simonne Lacouture's *Égypte en mouvement*.[19] *Gamal Abdel Nasser et son équipe*,[20] by Georges Vaucher, was a thorough account of the life and actions of 'Abd al-Nasser, if not necessarily his team. See also Jacques Berque, *Histoire sociale d'un village égyptien au XXᵉ siècle*.[21] Egyptian writers offered instant accounts of the revolution, such as Rashed el Barawy's *The Military Coup*,[22] which focused on the misdeeds of King Faruq, saying little about the revolutionaries. Another background interpretation is Muhammad Mustafa Ata's *Egypt Between Two Revolutions*.[23] First-hand accounts were Gamal 'Abd al-Nasser's *The Philosophy of the Revolution*,[24] Mohammed Neguib's *Egypt's Destiny: A Personal Statement*,[25] and Anwar al-Sadat's *Revolt on the Nile*.[26] An American Fulbright professor, Austin Lee Moore, wrote *Farewell Farouk*,[27] a memoir depicting the rising unrest of the 1951–52 academic year, but silent on the causes of the revolution or the character of the Free Officers. Among the many works that followed was 'Abd al-Rahman al-Rafi'i's *Thawrat 23 yulyu*.[28]

Politics remained the focus of writings about Egypt in the 1950s. A pioneering work that came out soon after the revolution, Jacob M. Landau's *Parliaments and Parties in Egypt*, analyzed the evolution of representative institutions and popular movements, predicting that the country would soon return to parliamentary government.[29] John Marlowe, *A History of Modern Egypt and Anglo-Egyptian Relations, 1800–1953*, relied almost entirely on English language sources, but did provide an honest assessment of Egyptian political leaders.[30] Other general histories included H. Wood Jarvis, *Pharaoh to Farouk*,[31] and Tom Little, *Egypt*,[32] which later was revised and published just after the June 1967 War as *Modern Egypt*.[33] The 1956 Suez War led to a spate of publications, most of which dealt more with the reactions of Britain, France, Israel, and the outside world than with Egypt itself: most foreign writers at this time saw the Suez Canal as international and not Egyptian, or judged the 'Abd al-Nasser government primarily as a threat to European interests or to Israel. One exception was Erskine B. Childers' *The Road to Suez: A Study in Western-Arab Relations*,[34] which argued for Egypt's right to nationalize a company that had been chartered in Egypt, and defended Cairo's administration of the Suez Canal.

Starting in the late fifties, foreign biographies of 'Abd al-Nasser came out. Notably pro-'Abd al-Nasser was Wilton Wynn's *Nasser of Egypt: The Search for Dignity*,[35] which stressed not only the beneficence of the new regime but also the effects of foreign rule on the lives of the Egyptian people. More even-handed is Robert St. John's *The Boss: The Story of Gamal Abdel Nasser*,[36] which hailed his reforms but also criticized his policy toward Israel (the same author, a journalist like Wynn, had also written a biography of Ben Gurion). Hostile biographies include Joachim Joesten, *Nasser: The Rise to Power*,[37] and Ahmed Abul Fath, *L'affaire Nasser*.[38] Joesten accused 'Abd al-Nasser of committing "aggressive acts that sprang from a psychological compulsion." His defiance of authority went with a fear of retribution. The Abu al-Fath brothers published *al-Misri*, the Wafdist daily newspaper with the largest circulation before the 1952 Revolution. They hoped that the revolution would strengthen democracy in Egypt and went into exile when 'Abd al-Nasser pushed Naguib out of power and shut down their paper. For a general study of Egypt's political and economic condition, including some history, see Keith Wheelock, *Nasser's New Egypt*.[39]

By the 1960s Egypt became a field for scholars as well as journalists. The Free Officers were the focus in P.J. Vatikiotis, *The Egyptian Army in Politics: Pattern for New Nations?*[40] and Eliezer Be'eri, *Army Officers in Arab Politics and Society*.[41] The latter work, with its detailed background study of each member of the Revolutionary Command Council, remains useful to scholars, as Tewfik Aclimandos acknowledges in chapter three of the present volume. Apart from political commentary, historians looked at what Egyptians were thinking about their society and values. The pioneering history of pre-revolutionary Egypt's most popular organization, the Muslim Brotherhood, was Ishak Musa Husaini's *The Moslem Brethren*.[42] It was later supplanted by Richard P. Mitchell's *The Society of the Muslim Brothers*,[43] which provides a detailed history of the Brotherhood's growth, organization, and main ideas. Newer works include Olivier Carré and Gérard Michaud's *Les frères musulmans, 1928–1982*,[44] 'Abd al-'Azim Ramadan's *al-Ikhwan al-muslimun wa-l-tanzim al-sirri*,[45] Brynjar Lia's *The Society of Muslim Brothers in Egypt: The Rise of an Islamic Mass Movement, 1928–1942*,[46] and Yusuf al-Qardawi's *al-Ikhwan al-muslimun*.[47] Lia shows how the society developed a modern organization, articulated the interests of the lower middle class, and did not blindly follow Islamic tradition or even the teachings of its founder, Hasan al-Banna. The earliest foreign book on Egypt's best-known political party was by an Indian, Zaheer Masood Quraishi, *Liberal Nationalism in Egypt: Rise and Fall of the Wafd Party*,[48] featuring a laudatory introduction by Boutros Boutros-Ghali, the future United Nations secretary-general. It has been superseded by Janice Joles Terry's *The Wafd, 1919–1952: Cornerstone of Egyptian Political Power*[49] and Muhammad Farid Hashish's *Hizb al-Wafd, 1936–1952*.[50] All tried to explain why the Wafd, initially the spokesman for the Egyptian people as a whole, gradually lost popular support to other movements.

The Wafd was both the instigator and the result of the 1919 Revolution. What inspired this cataclysmic event in Egypt's history? How did it influence the course of Egypt's political life up to 1952? These questions continue to inspire historians. Books that deal with the 1919 Revolution include John D. McIntyre, Jr., *The Boycott of the Milner Mission: A Study in Egyptian Nationalism*,[51] which covers a broader subject than its title implies. Malak Badrawi, *Political Violence in Egypt, 1910–1924: Secret Societies, Plots and Assassinations*,[52] draws heavily on unpublished government documents, memoirs, and recent scholarship to show how terrorism played a part in the actions (though not the principles) of both the National Party and the Wafd. Closely related is an article by Donald M. Reid called "Political Assassination in Egypt, 1910–1954."[53] Egypt's best-known Marxist historian, Muhammad Anis, criticized the 1919 Revolution for not addressing Egypt's economic and social inequality in *Dirasat fi watha'iq thawrat 1919*.[54] A more nationalist approach was taken by 'Abd al-'Aziz al-Rifa'i's *Thawrat Misr sanat 1919*.[55] The fiftieth anniversary of that event was marked by a commemorative volume published in 1969 by *al-Ahram*.[56] The leading historian of Egypt's nationalist movement during and since the 1919 Revolution is 'Abd al-'Azim Ramadan, whose *Tatawwur al-haraka al-wataniya fi Misr min sanat 1918 ila sanat 1936* was published twice[57] and followed up by the two-volume *Tatawwur al-haraka al-wataniya fi Misr min sanat 1937 ila sanat 1948.*[58] Leftist in his orientation, Ramadan is openly unsympathetic to British imperialism, the palace, and the Muslim Brothers.

In the late sixties and seventies several books appeared that summed up the era's politics, starting with Jacques Berque's *L'Égypte: impérialisme et révolution*[59] Raymond Flower's *Napoleon to Nasser, the Story of Modern Egypt,*[60] and P.J. Vatikiotis' *The Modern History of Egypt,*[61] which remains for many the standard textbook of Egyptian political history. To them was added the entertaining account by 'Afaf Lutfi al-Sayyid-Marsot, *Egypt's Liberal Experiment: 1922–1936.*[62] The complex interplay of political parties was treated by Marius Deeb, *Party Politics in Egypt: the Wafd and its Rivals, 1919–1939.*[63] Egyptian historian Yunan Labib Rizq has written several books on party politics, including *al-Ahzab al-siyasiya fi Misr, 1907–1984.*[64] Ra'uf 'Abbas has more recently edited a collection of articles by Egyptian scholars entitled *al-Ahzab al-misriya 1922–1953.*[65] James Whidden's chapter in this volume describes some of the motives for the creation of the Liberal Constitutionalist and Union Parties in the wake of the 1919 Revolution. On Egypt's cabinets, see Yunan Labib Rizq, *Tarikh al-wizarat al-misriya.*[66] Egyptian attitudes and policies toward the Sudan, over which it shared a condominium with Great Britain, are described in Eva Troutt Powell, *A Different Shade of Colonialism: Egypt, Great Britain, and Mastery of the Sudan.*[67]

Egypt's negotiations with the British for independence were the subject of Muhammad Shafiq Ghurbal's *Tarikh al-mufawadat al-misriya al-britaniya,* of which only the first part, dealing with the 1882–1936 negotiations, was published.[68] Ghurbal, trained in London as a professional historian, developed the history program and served as dean of Cairo University's Faculty of Arts. A devoted teacher, he published little. Mahmud Y. Zayid, a Palestinian historian, wrote *Egypt's Struggle for Independence.*[69] This work focused on the 1936 Anglo-Egyptian Treaty, which the Egyptians accepted due to Italy's threat after its occupation of Ethiopia and their belief that an alliance would improve their chances of ending the capitulations, as indeed did happen in the following year. Anglo-Egyptian relations are also covered in Keith M. Wilson's edited volume, *Imperialism and Nationalism in the Middle East: The Anglo-Egyptian Experience, 1882–1982,*[70] Hoda Gamal Abdel Nasser's *Britain and the Egyptian Nationalist Movement, 1936–1952,*[71] and Amani Qandil and Sara Bin Nafisa's *al-'Alaqat al-misriya al-britaniya, 1945–1954.*[72]

The history of ideas, especially during Egypt's intellectual revival, was illuminated by three books published in the early 1960s: J.M. Ahmed's *The Intellectual Origins of Egyptian Nationalism*,[73] mainly about Ahmad Lutfi al-Sayyid; Nadav Safran's *Egypt in Search of Political Community: An Analysis of the Intellectual and Political Evolution of Egypt, 1804–1952*,[74] especially noteworthy on the Egyptian writers' shift from secularism to Islamism in the 1930s; and Albert Hourani's *Arabic Thought in the Liberal Age, 1798–1939*,[75] which includes a chapter on Egyptian nationalism, somewhat critical of the Wafd's tendency to conflate itself with Egypt. Rashid Rida, covered in Hourani's work, is also featured in M.A. Zaki Badawi, *The Reformers of Egypt*,[76] but his role in Egypt's intellectual life, aside from editing *al-Manar*, was marginal.

Partly because this period was noted for its lively and contentious press (reflecting the country's many political parties), one well-covered aspect of Egypt's history is that of Arabic journalism. The two Egyptian giants in journalism history were 'Abd al-Latif Hamza, noted for his eight-volume, newspaper-centered *Adab al-maqala al-suhufiya fi Misr*,[77] and Ibrahim 'Abduh, who wrote a general history,[78] a series of biographical sketches,[79] and histories of the government journal and the "semi-official" *al-Ahram*.[80] Ami Ayalon, *The Press in the Arab Middle East: A History*,[81] treats extensively leading journalists, newspapers, and readers, covering the entire Arab world; only a small part is devoted to Egypt between 1919 and 1952. This is still a fertile field for future historians.

The gradual commitment of the 'Abd al-Nasser government to socialism occasioned some interest in Egypt's economic and social development and especially in class relations. Some of the pioneering work was done by members of Egypt's Communist Party or its local counterpart, Hadeto. These works included Ibrahim 'Amir's *al-Ard wa-l-fallah*,[82] Fawzi Jirjis' *Dirasat fi tarikh Misr al-siyasi*,[83] and Shuhdi 'Atiya al-Shafi'i's *Tatawwur al-haraka al-wataniya al-misriya, 1882–1956*.[84] Al-Shafi'i, who died in one of 'Abd al-Nasser's prisons, was memorialized by an Egyptian Marxist, Anouar Abdel-Malek. He published *L'Égypte société militaire*,[85] which describes Egypt's society from a Marxist perspective and analyzes the failure of both the monarchy and the 'Abd al-Nasser government to solve its economic problems. Another Marxist interpretation is Mahmoud Hussein's *La lutte de classes en Égypte de 1945 à 1968*.[86] A related work is 'Asim al-Dissuqi's *Kibar mullak al-aradi al-zira'iya wa dawruhum fi-l-mujtama' al-misri (1914–1952)*.[87] The comparable non-Marxist work of this era was done by Gabriel Baer in an early article on "Egyptian Attitudes towards Land Reform, 1922–1955"[88] as well as his books, *A History of Landownership in Modern Egypt, 1800–1950*[89] and *Studies in the Social History of Modern Egypt.*[90] A notable study of Egypt's workers was written by Ra'uf 'Abbas Hamid.[91] Later came several American studies of the rise of Egypt's working class and of organized labor: *Workers on the Nile: Nationalism, Communism, Islam, and the Egyptian Working Class, 1882–1954,*[92] coauthored by Joel Beinin and Zachary Lockman; and Ellis Goldberg's *Tinker, Tailor, and Textile Worker: Class and Politics in Egypt, 1930–1952.*[93] See also Joel Beinin's chapter, "Will the Real Egyptian Working Class Please Stand Up?" in Zachary Lockman, ed., *Workers and Working Classes in the Middle East: Struggles, Histories, Historiographies.*[94] Roger Owen and Sevket Pamuk's recent book on twentieth-century Middle Eastern economies provides balanced, broad coverage of Egyptian economic trends in the 1919–52 era, as a basis for further discussion.[95]

Related to the labor movement was the growth of socialism and communism in Egypt. On this see Walter Z. Laqueur, *Communism and Nationalism in the Middle East.*[96] Also notable are Rif'at al-Sa'id's several works, including *Tarikh al-haraka al-ishtirakiya fi Misr, 1900–1925,*[97] *al-Yasar al-misri, 1925–1940,*[98] *Tarikh al-munazzamat al-yasariya al-misriya, 1940–1950,*[99] and, along with Tareq Ismael, *The Communist Movement in Egypt, 1920–1988.*[100] Perhaps due to Cold War politics, interest in this topic has remained steady. See Selma Botman, *The Rise of Egyptian Communism, 1939–1970,*[101] Gilles Perrault, *Un homme à part*, or *A Man Apart: The Life of Henri Curiel,*[102] and Joel Beinin, *Was the Red Flag Flying There? Marxist Politics and the Arab-Israeli Conflict in Egypt and Israel, 1948–1965.*[103] The broader context is supplied by Roel Meijer in *The Quest for Modernity: Secular Liberal and Left-Wing Political Thought in Egypt, 1945–1958.*[104]

The ideal of Egyptian nationality divorced from religion is the subject of *L'Égypte nationaliste et libérale de Moustapha Kamel à Saad Zagloul (1892–1927),*[105] written by Ibrahim Amin Ghali, the uncle of Boutros Boutros-Ghali. Several articles in *Political and Social Change in Modern Egypt* deal with nationalism before and after World War I.[106] On the ultranationalist Green Shirts, see James P. Jankowski, *Egypt's Young Rebels: "Young Egypt," 1933–1952.*[107] University students have been leading actors in Egyptian nationalism, and their role is discussed sympathetically in Ahmed Abdalla, *The Student Movement and National Politics in Egypt, 1923–1973;*[108] for a slightly more critical treatment by Haggai Erlich, see *Students and Society in 20th Century Egyptian Politics.*[109] Nationalist depictions of Egypt appear in Beth Baron, "Nationalist Iconography: Egypt as a Woman."[110]

The death of King Faruq in 1965 led to the publication of several biographies that shed light not only on the life of that tragic figure, but also on the era in which he reigned, notably Barrie St. Clair McBride's *Farouk of Egypt: A Biography*[111] and Hugh McLeave's *The Last Pharaoh: Farouk of Egypt, 1920–1965*.[112] Both relied heavily on the accounts of Faruq's contemporaries; neither writer knew the king personally. Since then Adel Sabet, a cousin, published a rather biased memoir entitled *A King Betrayed: The Ill-Fated Reign of Farouk of Egypt*.[113] William Stadiem wrote a more detailed biography, *Too Rich: The High Life and Tragic Death of King Farouk*,[114] and Latifa Muhammad Salim published the very detailed *Faruq wa suqut al-malikiya fi Misr*.[115] No scholarly biography exists of Faruq's father, Fu'ad I (r. 1917–36), but see Sirdar Ikbal 'Ali Shah's laudatory *Fuad King of Egypt*[116] and Muhammad Anis' critical *Safahat majhula min al-tarikh al-misri aw sanawat al-sira' al-'anif bayna Fu'ad wa 'Abbas*.[117] The palace role in Egyptian politics during this period is covered by Hasan Yusuf's memoir, *al-Qasr wa dawruhu fi al-siyasa al-misriya, 1922–1952*.[118]

Biographies have indeed been central in Egyptian historiography. The towering figure in Egypt's political life during and after the 1919 Revolution was, of course, Sa'd Zaghlul, who was the subject of numerous works of adulation in his lifetime, mourning at the time of his death in 1927, and hagiography in subsequent years. Most significant was the work by 'Abbas Mahmud al-'Aqqad (1889–1964), *Sa'd Zaghlul: sira wa tahiya*,[119] both because of the author's eminence and his own shifting loyalties. When Zaghlul's memoirs, long held by the Barakat family, became available to scholars and the public, it became possible for historians to work them into a more nuanced treatment of his life and career. The first was 'Abd al-Khaliq Muhammad Lashin's *Sa'd Zaghlul wa dawruhu fi al-siyasa al-misriya*,[120] describing how Zaghlul's class background affected his actions. Publication of Zaghlul's memoirs, which are written in a script indecipherable to anyone lacking the training and patience to read them, has been slow, but under the supervision of 'Abd al-'Azim Ramadan, the Documentation Center for the History of Contemporary Egypt has published nine volumes since 1987.[121] Sa'd has been criticized by some foreign writers, most notably Elie Kedourie in "Sa'ad Zaghlul and the British."[122]

Of Sa'd Zaghlul's contemporaries, the one whose life and thought are best known to English-speaking readers is Dr. Muhammad Husayn Haykal, both for his well-written and oft-cited memoirs of Egyptian politics[123] and for the sensitive biography written by Charles D. Smith.[124] The only major Arabic biography of Haykal known to this writer was written shortly after his death by Ahmad Lutfi al-Sayyid.[125] Another politician of the Liberal Age was the ill-fated Nuqrashi Pasha, once accused of plotting to assassinate enemies of the Wafd, only to fall himself at the hand of an assassin. His biography came out long after his death.[126] Now available to readers in English is the life of a rival politician who has not fared well at the hands of nationalist writers, Isma'il Sidqi (1875–1950).[127] Some reviewers suggest its author may have exaggerated Sidqi's achievements and minimized his mistakes. On a more general scope is Vernon Egger, *A Fabian in Egypt: Salama Musa and the Rise of the Professional Classes in Egypt*.[128] This may be read together with Musa's memoirs, which include the 1920s, when he edited *al-Hilal*.[129] Short biographical sketches of Makram 'Ubayd, 'Ali Mahir, and Mustafa al-Nahhas are contained in a volume edited by Charles Tripp honoring P.J. Vatikiotis.[130] The study in this volume by Mervat F. Hatem views the treatment given by Mayy Ziyada to the life of Malak Hifni Nasif, reminding us that biographies shed light on their writers as well as on their subjects.

A major tool used by Egyptian historians is the biographical dictionary. A fine, comprehensive example is Khayr al-Din al-Zirikli's *al-A'lam: qamus tarajim li-ashhar al-rijal wa-l-nisa' min al-'arab wa-l-musta'ribin wa-l-mustashriqin*.[131] More focused on the modern period of Arab, primarily Egyptian, history is Zaki Muhammad Mujahid's *al-A'lam al-sharqiya fi al-mi'a al-rabi'a 'ashara al-hijriya*.[132] Useful for writers, partly for its detailed bibliographies, is Yusuf As'ad Daghir's three-volume *Masadir al-dirasa al-adabiya*.[133] Anwar al-Jindi wrote several collective biographies as part of his work on literary and religious history; one example is *A'lam wa ashab aqlam*.[134] During the 1990s two valuable dictionaries appeared. One was Lam'i al-Muti'i's *Mawsu'at hadha al-rajul min Misr*,[135] a reference work drawn from several earlier books he wrote about men from Egypt. The other, edited by Mustafa Najib and terser in style and content, is called *Mawsu'at a'lam Misr fi al-qarn al-'ishrin*.[136] This writer has compiled a work that tries to extract the essence of these Arabic sources for approximately 370 men and women who have played a major role in Egypt's modern history in *A Biographical Dictionary of Modern Egypt*.[137] Another work by this writer in conjunction with Robert C. Johnston, the third edition of the *Historical Dictionary of Egypt*,[138] includes a detailed chronology and entries on organizations, countries, events, and persons that have affected Egypt's history since 1750, with appropriate stress on the 1919–52 period.

One genre of historiography that has proven a rich trove of information on the experiences of both Egyptians and foreigners has been the personal memoir. These include, for the 1919–52 period, Mabel Caillard's *A Lifetime in Egypt, 1876–1935*;[139] C.S. Jarvis' *Desert and Delta*,[140] which reflects British prejudices against Egyptians and Islam but includes perceptive comments on Sinai life; Thomas Russell Pasha's *Egyptian Service, 1902–1946*,[141] about his experiences in the Cairo Police; Mary Rowlatt's *A Family in Egypt*;[142] Priscilla Napier's *A Late Beginner*;[143] Laurence Grafftey-Smith's *Bright Levant*;[144] Ahmad Amin, *My Life: The Autobiography of an Egyptian Scholar, Writer, and Cultural Leader*,[145] John McPherson and Barry Carmen's *The Man Who Loved Egypt: Bimbashi McPherson*;[146] Jehan Sadat's *A Woman of Egypt*;[147] Penelope Lively's *Oleander, Jacaranda: A Childhood Perceived*;[148] Leila Ahmed's *A Border Passage from Cairo to America: A Woman's Journey*;[149] Gaston Zananiri's *Entre mer et désert: mémoires*;[150] Nawal El Saadawi's *A Daughter of Isis*;[151] and Harry Keown-Boyd's *The Lion and the Sphinx: The Rise and Fall of the British in Egypt, 1882–1956*,[152] a treasury of gossipy anecdotes about wealthy expatriates in Egypt, which is very anti-Nasser.

Political memoirs and autobiographies shed light on events and personalities of their era, but they usually burnish the reputation of their writer and may defame his or her enemies, so they must be used with caution. Some that are not mentioned elsewhere in this essay are *Mudhakkirat Qallini Fahmi Pasha*,[153] and Yunan Labib Rizq's critical editions of *Mudhakkirat 'Abd al-Rahman Fahmi*[154] and *Mudhakkirat Fakhri 'Abd al-Nur: thawrat 1919: dawr Sa'd Zaghlul fi al-haraka al-wataniya*.[155] The purported memoirs of Ahmad Lutfi al-Sayyid[156] and 'Abd al-'Aziz Fahmi[157] were really based on interviews by an editor of *al-Hilal*, Tahir al-Tanahi.

During this period Egypt—especially Cairo, Alexandria, and the Suez Canal cities—contained economically powerful and socially influential foreign communities. General accounts of these communities include Robert Haddad's *Syrian Christians in Muslim Society*;[158] Peter Mansfield's *The British in Egypt*;[159] Jean-Jacques Luthi's *Le français en Égypte: essai d'anthologie*;[160] Anthony Sattin's *Lifting the Veil: British Society in Egypt, 1768–1956*;[161] and Alexander Kitroeff's *The Greeks in Egypt, 1919–1937*.[162] During World War II almost half a million foreign troops occupied Egypt, and several histories have covered the cultural aspects of that era, including Artemis Cooper, *Cairo in the War, 1939–1945*;[163] Mursi Saad el Din and John Cromer, *Under Egypt's Spell: The Influence of Egypt on Writers in English from the 18th Century*;[164] Jonathan Bolton, *Personal Landscapes: British Poets in Egypt during the Second World War*;[165] and Roger Bowen, *'Many Histories Deep': Personal Landscape Poets in Egypt*.[166] Lawrence Durrell was one of the prominent figures in the British literary scene during World War II, but his *Alexandria Quartet* is highly imaginative and only tangentially related to that port city.[167] Olivia Manning's wartime novels, often called the "Levant

Trilogy," are more descriptive of the British community in Cairo and can be compared with the famous Cairo trilogy of Naguib Mahfouz.[168]

Egypt's religious minorities were often viewed in the same light as the foreign communities, but they deserve and have received their own historical treatment. Some examples are Tariq al-Bishri, *al-Muslimun wa-l-aqbat fi itar al-jamaʻa al-wataniya*;[169] Barbara Lynn Carter, *The Copts in Egyptian Politics*;[170] Gudrun Krämer, *The Jews in Modern Egypt, 1914–1952*;[171] Shimon Shamir, ed., *The Jews of Egypt: A Mediterranean Society in Modern Times*;[172] Mustafa El-Feki, *Copts in Egyptian Politics*;[173] and Michael Laskier, *The Jews of Egypt, 1920–1970: In the Midst of Zionism, Anti-Semitism, and the Middle East Conflict*.[174]

After the passing of ʻAbd al-Nasser's Arab socialism and Sadat's open door to capitalism, new attention was paid to Egypt's economic history during the eighties. A detailed study was Alan Richards, *Egypt's Agricultural Development, 1800–1980: Technical and Social Change*.[175] Focused on the liberal age is Robert L. Tignor's *State, Private Enterprise, and Economic Change in Egypt, 1918–1952*.[176] Tignor shows that the Egyptian government played a key role in strengthening Egypt's nascent corporations. He has also written on Britain's ongoing involvement in Egypt's leading industry, *Egyptian Textiles and British Capital, 1930–1956*.[177] These issues have been further explored in Robert Vitalis, *When Capitalists Collide: Business Conflict and the End of Empire in Egypt*.[178] A major spur to capitalist development was Talʻat Harb's creation of Bank Misr, on which see Eric Davis, *Challenging Colonialism: Bank Misr and Egyptian Industrialization, 1920–1941*.[179]

Egyptian social history includes a study of the civil service by Monte Palmer, ʻAli Leila, and El Sayed Yassin, called *The Egyptian Bureaucracy*,[180] and of civil society by Robert Bianchi, entitled *Unruly Corporatism: Associational Life in Twentieth-Century Egypt*.[181] Lawyers are depicted by Farhat J. Ziadeh in *Lawyers, the Rule of Law, and Liberalism in Modern Egypt*[182] and by Donald M. Reid in *Lawyers and Politics in the Arab World, 1880–1960*.[183] Doctors are covered by Amira El Azhary Sonbol in *The Creation of a Medical Profession in Egypt, 1800–1922*,[184] Nancy Gallagher's chapter in the present volume depicts a very different history for Egypt's women healers. On engineers, see Clement Moore Henry, *Images of Development: Egyptian Engineers in Search of Industry*.[185] Business leaders are chronicled and criticized in Malak Zaalouk's *Power, Class, and Foreign Capital in Egypt: The Rise of the New Bourgeoisie*,[186] which includes an introductory section on the Egyptianization of business before 1952. Robert Springborg described a politician, Sayyid Marʻi (1913–1993), who has wielded power from the monarchical era through the regimes of ʻAbd al-Nasser, Sadat, and Mubarak.[187] Magda Baraka has depicted Egypt's wealthiest families in *The Egyptian Upper Class between Revolutions, 1919–1952*.[188] A lighter touch, which nonetheless conveys profound truths about how (and why) Egypt's society has changed since 1950, can be found in Galal Amin's *Whatever Happened to the Egyptians?*[189]

The strengths and weaknesses of Egyptian society were exposed by its response to three epidemics that struck during the 1940s, narrated in a book by Nancy Elizabeth Gallagher, *Egypt's other Wars: Epidemics and the Politics of Public Health*.[190] Contrary to popular belief, Egypt's peasants were and are politically active, as suggested by Samia Kholoussi in the present volume, and as investigated in some detail by Nathan J. Brown's *Peasant Politics in Modern Egypt*.[191] Even before the 1952 Revolution, the government tried to serve the peasants by establishing social centers, the brainchild of Dr. Ahmed Hussein (1902–1984), as told by Amy J. Johnson in *Reconstructing Rural Egypt*.[192] His wife's career, described in Amy Johnson's chapter, was in part an extension of his ideas and policies. Mine Ener's *Managing Egypt's Poor and the Politics of Benevolence, 1800–1952* covers mainly the nineteenth century but does include a section about state policies toward vagrants and beggars between 1919 and 1952.[193]

Egyptian and foreign writers must be cautioned not to assume that the rules and realities of family life were purely patriarchal and static in this or any other period of Egyptian history. Hanan Kholoussy's chapter in this book, which treats the efforts of the Egyptian state to establish a model for the modern family, builds on earlier work by Beth Baron[194] and Philippe Farguès.[195] Issues of personal rights and civil status have become ever more embraced by the Egyptian legal system, whose evolution and influence on other Arab countries is treated in Nathan J. Brown, *The Rule of Law in the Arab World*.[196]

The period from 1919 to 1952 was one of rapid educational growth and much competition among Egypt's institutions of higher learning. The rivalries are shown in Lois Arminé Aroian's *Nationalization of Arabic and Islamic Education in Egypt: Dar al-'Ulum and al-Azhar*.[197] A. Chris Eccel's *Egypt, Islam, and Social Change: al-Azhar in Conflict and Accommodation* gets into broader issues regarding religion's role in Egyptian society but covers extensively the changes within al-Azhar in 1919–52.[198] Though focusing mostly on the post-1952 years, Gregory Starrett's *Putting Islam to Work* contains valuable sections on the use of Islam in 1880s–1952 Egyptian schooling as a means to further British colonial or Egyptian modernist agendas.[199] 'Abd al-Mun'im al-Jumay'i's *al-Jami'a al-misriya wa-l-mujtama', 1908–1940*[200] and

Donald M. Reid's *Cairo University and the Making of Modern Egypt* cover the rise of Egypt's leading secular university.[201] Although at times it resembles a company history, Lawrence R. Murphy's *The American University in Cairo: 1919–1987* is well-written and beautifully illustrated.[202] Secondary education received some attention in Georgie D.M. Hyde, *Education in Modern Egypt: Ideals and Realities*;[203] and Amir Boktor, *The Development and Expansion of Education in the United Arab Republic*.[204] One private school has recently been described in detail in *Victoria College: A History Revealed*.[205]

The articles in *Re-Envisioning Egypt* by Barak Salmoni and Misako Ikeda extend the treatment of the content and politics of education in this period. On the attempts by historians and school textbook writers to frame Egyptian history from a nationalist perspective, see Gabriel Piterberg's exploratory piece "Tropes of Stagnation and Awakening in Nationalist Historical Consciousness."[206] For a work focusing in particular on the 'Urabi episode's continuing re-interpretation by nationalist historians and pedagogues before, during, and after the constitutional monarchy era, see Thomas Mayer's *The Changing Past*.[207] In a similar fashion but topically broader, Zaki al-Buhayri examines the historical narratives of 1920s–50s school textbooks as compared to the 1950s–80s era,[208] while Donald M. Reid focuses on Egyptology as a discipline disputed by Egyptians and foreigners, in "Nationalizing the Pharaonic Past: Egyptology, Imperialism, and Egyptian Nationalism, 1922–1952."[209] The output of Egypt's academic historians is compared with the popular nationalist histories of 'Abd al-Rahman al-Rafi'i by Yoav Di-Capua.[210]

Women's history moved to the forefront of Egyptian historiography during the nineties with the publication of Leila Ahmed's *Women and Gender in Islam*,[211] Margot Badran's *Feminists, Islam, and Nation: Gender and the Making of Modern Egypt*,[212] Cynthia Nelson's *Doria Shafik, Egyptian Feminist: A Woman Apart*,[213] Selma Botman's *Engendering Citizenship in Egypt*,[214] and Marilyn Booth's *May Her Likes be Multiplied: Biographies and Gender Politics in Egypt*.[215] One error for non-Egyptian writers is to conflate the feminist movement with the agendas of most Egyptian women. There were Muslim women activists who differed with Huda Sha'rawi and the Egyptian Feminist Union, notably Zaynab al-Ghazzali, who wrote memoirs, *Ayyam min Hayati*,[216] recounting her founding role in the Muslim Sisters Organization. See also Azza Karam's *Women, Islamisms, and the State*.[217] Recent work by Mona Russell and Barak Salmoni has examined gender in 1919–52 Egypt through the lens of national and nationalist education.[218]

Since the arts were one of the main opportunities for women in Egyptian society during that era, it is hardly surprising that we need to consult publications in related fields of history, such as Liliane Karnouk's *Modern Egyptian Art: The Emergence of a National Style*,[219] Karin van Nieuwkerk's *"A Trade Like Any Other": Female Singers and Dancers in Egypt*;[220] Virginia Danielson's "Artists and Entrepreneurs: Female Singers in Cairo During the 1920s,"[221] as well as her *The Voice of Egypt: Umm Kulthum, Arabic Song, and Egyptian Society in the Twentieth Century*;[222] Mustafa Darwish's *Dream Makers on the Nile: A Portrait of Egyptian Cinema*;[223] and Sherifa Zuhur's *Asmahan's Secrets: Women, War, and Song*.[224] Zuhur has edited two sets of papers on Middle Eastern culture: *Images of Enchantment*[225] and *Colors of Enchantment: Theater, Dance, Music, and the Visual Arts of the Middle East*,[226] including articles on the comic actor 'Ali al-Kassar, the singer Farid al-Atrash, the dancer Tahia Carioca (as remembered by Edward Said), and press cartoons. Caroline Williams' contribution to this volume analyses in detail the artistic output of Egypt's painters and sculptors, while Andrew Flibbert's chapter stresses the importance of the 1919–52 era in the development of the Egyptian cinema. The most general history of Egyptian cinema, edited by Magda Wassef, is *Égypte: 100 ans de cinema*.[227] Shaun Lopez in his contribution to this volume has drawn our attention to a heavily publicized crime that is remembered by most Egyptians and remains part of the popular culture. Broader issues of this subject are treated in Walter Armbrust's *Mass Culture and Modernism in Egypt*.[228]

Literature is by far the dominant form of Arabic culture in Egypt, and much can be learned about Egyptians' lives and feelings during the 1919–52 era from reading novels or short stories written in or about the period. This essay will cite just a few guides: Hamdi Sakkut's *The Egyptian Novel and Its Main Trends from 1913 to 1952*,[229] Roger Allen's *The Arabic Novel: An Historical and Critical Introduction*,[230] and Mustafa Badawi, ed., *Modern Arabic Literature*.[231] A novel that is often cited for its depiction of Egyptian rural life in the 1930s is Tawfiq al-Hakim's *Yawmiyat na'ib fi al-aryaf*.[232]

The signing of the Anglo-Egyptian Treaty in 1936 did not end Britain's power over Egypt. The last of the proconsuls, Sir Miles Lampson, who became Lord Killearn in 1943, has two sets of published diaries: *The Killearn Diaries, 1934–1946*,[233] and M.E. Yapp, ed., *Politics and Diplomacy in Egypt: The Diaries of Sir Miles Lampson, 1935–1937*.[234] For Britain's role in Egypt during World War II, we continue to consult Jean Lugol's *Egypt and World War II: The Anti-Axis Campaigns in the Middle East*[235] and George Kirk's *The Middle East in the War*.[236] Compare these with 'Asim al-Dissuqi,

Misr fi al-harb al-'alamiya al-thaniya.[237] It is time for younger historians to write about what was, after all, both a bitter experience for Egypt and the turning point in Britain's war with Germany. The trauma was Britain's ultimatum to King Faruq, which has been discussed in Charles D. Smith, "4 February 1942: Its Causes and Its Influence on Egyptian Politics and on the Future of Anglo-Egyptian Relations, 1937–1945";[238] Gabriel Warburg's *Egypt and the Sudan: Studies in History and Politics*;[239] Muhammad Anis, *4 Fibrayir 1942 fi tarikh Misr al-siyasi*;[240] and Laila Amin Morsy, "Indicative Cases of Britain's Wartime Policy in Egypt, 1942–44."[241] In the present volume, Malak Badrawi notes this incident's impact on parliamentary politics and legislator-monarchy relations. The postwar effort by Ernest Bevin and Isma'il Sidqi to resolve Anglo-Egyptian differences is recounted in H.A. Rahman's *A British Defence Problem in the Middle East: The Failure of the 1946 Anglo-Egyptian Negotiations.*[242] Peter L. Hahn treats the period of Anglo-Egyptian relations when the Americans became involved in *The United States, Great Britain, and Egypt, 1945–1956.*[243] Egypt's defeat in the 1948 Palestine War is analyzed by Fawaz Gerges.[244] Analyses of that final paroxysm of Egyptian frustration before the 1952 Revolution, Black Saturday, are treated in Anne-Claire Kerbœuf's article in this volume; but see also Muhammad Anis' *Hariq al-Qahira fi 26 yanayir 1952 'ala daw' watha'iq tunsharu li-awwal mara.*[245] Accounts of the Cairo fire recently filled a special issue of an Egyptian magazine.[246]

As the heady years of Gamal 'Abd al-Nasser receded into memory, historians and surviving participants resumed their investigation of the causes and effects of the 1952 Revolution, leading to a number of books, edited volumes, and memoirs, e.g., 'Abd al-Latif al-Baghdadi's *Mudhakkirat*;[247] Ahmad Hamrush's five-volume personal and at times partisan account, *Qissat thawrat yulyu*;[248] P.J. Vatikiotis' *Nasser and his Generation*;[249] Salah Nasr's *Mudhakkirat Salah Nasr: thawrat 23 yulyu*;[250] Mohamed H. Heikal's *Cutting the Lion's Tail: Suez through Egyptian Eyes*;[251] the memoirs of 'Ali Sabri as related to 'Abdallah Imam;[252] Joel Gordon's *Nasser's Blessed Movement: Egypt's Free Officers and the July Revolution*;[253] Kirk Beattie's *Egypt During the Nasser Years*;[254] Shimon Shamir, ed., *Egypt from Monarchy to Republic: A Reassessment of Revolution and Change*;[255] Khaled Mohy El Din's *Memories of a Revolution: Egypt 1952*;[256] and Tewfik Aclimandos' *Officiers et Frères Musulmans.*[257]

One of the ongoing issues associated with the 1952 Revolution is the degree of Egypt's commitment to Arab nationalism and the Palestinian cause both before and after that event. Works written in English include Thomas Mayer, *Egypt and the Palestine Question, 1936–1945*;[258] Joseph P. Lorenz,

Egypt and the Arabs: Foreign Policy and the Search for National Identity;[259] James P. Jankowski, "Egypt and Early Arab Nationalism, 1908–1924;"[260] Ghada Hashem Talhami, *Palestine and Egyptian National Identity,*[261] which uses the Palestine issue to chronicle Egypt's shift between its local and Arab identities; Israel Gershoni, "Rethinking the Formation of Arab Nationalism in the Middle East, 1920–1945"[262] Ralph M. Coury, *The Making of an Egyptian Arab Nationalist: The Early Years of Azzam Pasha, 1893–1936;*[263] Abd al-Fattah Muhammad El-Awaisi, *The Muslim Brothers and the Palestine Question;*[264] and Michael Doran: *Pan-Arabism before Nasser: Egyptian Power Politics and the Palestine Question.*[265] Rami Ginat's *The Soviet Union and Egypt, 1945–1955* explores an important aspect of late monarchical Egypt's increasingly autonomous foreign policy, with ramifications for the post-1952 era.[266]

Histories of Cairo are numerous, and for the 1919–52 period the best remains Janet L. Abu-Lughod's *Cairo: 1001 Years of the City Victorious.*[267] Recent scholarship has added valuable works to some aspects of that history, including Trevor Mostyn, *Egypt's Belle Epoque: Cairo, 1869–1952;*[268] John and Kirsten Miller, eds., *Chronicles Abroad: Cairo;*[269] Tarek Mohamed Refaat Sakr, *Early Twentieth-Century Islamic Architecture in Cairo;*[270] Samir W. Raafat, *Maadi 1904–1962: Society and History in a Cairo Suburb* and *Cairo, the Glory Years: Who Built What, When, Why, and for Whom?;*[271] Nina Nelson, *The Mena House: A Short History of a Remarkable Hotel;*[272] Max Rodenbeck, *Cairo: The City Victorious;*[273] André Raymond, *Cairo;*[274] and Maria Golia, *Cairo: City of Sand.*[275] What about Egypt's second city, the legendary Alexandria before the 'Abd al-Nasser years? Newly published is Michael Haag's *Alexandria: City of Memory.*[276]

Closely related (but not limited) to Egypt's cities are the impressions of foreign visitors, of which a judicious selection was made by Christopher Pick for *Egypt: A Traveller's Anthology.*[277] A magnificent new book, illustrated with period photographs, is Alain Blottière's *Vintage Egypt: Cruising the Nile in the Golden Age of Travel.*[278] The Association for the Study of Travel to Egypt and the Near East, which meets semi-annually in Britain, is publishing books about travelers to Egypt, and in the future may cover those in the 1919–52 period.[279]

How have Egyptians viewed their own past? A very detailed and thoughtful study of Egyptian historiography has recently been published: Anthony Gorman's *Historians, State and Politics in Twentieth-Century Egypt: Contesting the Nation.*[280] Recent attempts to write Egypt's history include a two-volume edited work with many collaborators, including Selma Botman and Joel Beinin for the 1919–52 period, *The Cambridge History of*

Egypt[281] and single volume works by established historians: Afaf Lutfi al-Sayyid-Marsot, *A Short History of Modern Egypt*;[282] Arthur Goldschmidt Jr., *Modern Egypt: The Formation of a Nation-State*;[283] and James P. Jankowski, *Egypt: A Short History*.[284] The era covered by the present volume is treated by a well-written general history by Selma Botman, *Egypt from Independence to Revolution*.[285] For the period just prior to the 1952 Revolution, see Derek Hopwood, *Egypt: Politics and Society, 1945–1990*.[286]

To conclude, the trajectory of the historiography of modern Egypt has gone from basically amateur recording of Egypt's past or current condition to professional and often highly specialized analyses. The traditional focus on Egyptian politics, economics, and foreign relations has not vanished. Rather, it has gradually broadened to include ideas, values, religious organization, societal changes, gender relationships, education, and culture. Even 'culture' is no longer limited to the poetry and prose of educated people, but includes folktales, vernacular poetry, popular songs, dance, drama, cinema, radio, and television. Although this essay has shown that scholarly and popular treatment of Egypt between the two revolutions has been extensive and ever more varied, ample room remains for further documentation and new historical interpretations.

Notes

1 The three volumes of *Tamhid* were followed by seven volumes of *Hawliyyat*. Cairo: Matba'at Shafiq, 1926–30. See also 'Abd al-'Aziz al-Rifa'i, *Ahmad Shafiq al-mu'arrikh* (Cairo: al-Dar al-Misriya, 1964).

2 Cairo: Maktabat al-Nahda al-Misriya, 1947–51. On al-Rafi'i, see *Mudhakkirati 1889–1951* (Cairo: Dar al-Hilal, 1952).

3 Cairo: Maktabat al-Nahda al-Misriya, 1946.

4 3 vols. in 6; Cairo: al-Matba'a al-Amiriya, 1912–36.

5 *L'Égypte: aperçu historique et géographique, gouvernement et institutions, vie économique et sociale* (Cairo: Imprimerie de l'Institut Française d'Archéologie Orientale, 1926).

6 New York: Charles Scribner's Sons, 1927. This work was part of a series called "The Modern World: A Survey of Historical Forces," ed. H.A.L. Fisher.

7 London: Edward Arnold, 1928; reprinted New York: Russell & Russell, 1969. A shorter work, which may have been an abridged version, is Elgood's *Egypt* (London: Arrowsmith, 1935).

8 London: Macmillan, 1933–34.

9 Cairo: The American University at Cairo, 1933. New York: Russell & Russell, 1968.

10 Paris: Paul Hartmann, 1937. This was the first volume in the Collection du Monde Islamique series.

11 2nd ed.; London: Oxford University Press, 1939.

12 London: J. Murray, 1940.

13 Paris: G.P. Maisonneuve, 1951.

14 Cairo: Maslahat al-Ihsa' wa-l-Ta'dad, 1909– .
15 London: Longman's, Green, and Co., 1938.
16 London: Constable, 1952.
17 London: Oxford University Press, 1947. In Thomas Naff, ed., *Paths to the Middle East* (Albany: State University of New York Press, 1993), 147–48, Issawi describes how this book came to be written and how it was banned from Egypt by King Faruq's regime. He tells a similar story in Nancy E. Gallagher, ed., *Approaches to the History of the Middle East* (Reading, UK: Ithaca Press, 1994), 57.
18 London: Oxford University Press, 1954. A further revision, *Egypt in Revolution*, appeared in 1963.
19 Paris: Éditions du Seuil, 1956. The English translation by Francis Scarfe was published by London: Methuen, 1958 and New York: Criterion Books, 1958.
20 2 vols. Paris: R. Julliard, 1959–60.
21 Le Haye: Mouton, 1957.
22 Cairo: Renaissance Bookshop, 1952. On Barawy, see Roel Meijer, *The Quest for Modernity: Secular Liberal and Left-Wing Political Thought in Egypt, 1945–58* (London: RoutledgeCurzon, 2002), 66–95.
23 Cairo: Imprimerie Misr, 1955.
24 Washington: Public Affairs Press, 1955; Buffalo, NY: Smith, Keyes, and Marshall, 1958. It is popularly thought to have been ghost-written by Muhammad Hasanayn Haykal. Afaf Lutfi al-Sayyid-Marsot asserts, however, in "Survey of Egyptian Works of History," *AHR* 95 (1991): 1425, that Tom Little was its author. Another theory is that the book was written by a committee under 'Abd al-Nasser's direct supervision, primarily by Amin Shakir, but with some participation by Haykal, which he may have exaggerated.
25 Garden City, NY: Doubleday & Co., 1955. Naguib acknowledged the assistance of Leigh White.
26 New York: The John Day Co., 1957.
27 Chicago: Scholars' Press, 1954.
28 Cairo: Maktabat al-Nahda al-Misriya, 1959. This stage of al-Rafi'i's career is discussed by Jack A. Crabbs Jr. in Shimon Shamir, ed., *Egypt from Monarchy to Republic: A Reassessment of Revolution and Change* (Boulder: Westview Press, 1995).
29 Tel Aviv: Israel Oriental Society, 1954.
30 New York: Frederick A. Praeger, 1953. London: The Cresset Press, 1954. "John Marlowe" was the pseudonym of a British businessman named George Collard.
31 New York: Macmillan, 1955.
32 London: Ernest Benn Limited, 1958. New York: Frederick A. Praeger, 1958.
33 London: Ernest Benn Limited, 1967. New York: Frederick A. Praeger, 1967.
34 London: MacGibbon & Kee, 1962.
35 Cambridge: Arlington Books, 1959.
36 New York: McGraw Hill, 1960; London: A. Barker, 1961; Israel: Steimatsky's Agency, 1960.
37 London: Oldhams Press, 1960.
38 Paris: Librairie Plon, 1962. Ahmed Abul Fath was an editor of the popular Wafdist daily, *al-Misri*, which was closed by 'Abd al-Nasser's government in May 1954. After being arrested, tried, and briefly imprisoned, he was allowed to go into exile. He was the brother of the editor-in-chief, Mahmud Abu al-Fath (1885–1958).
39 New York: Frederick A. Praeger, 1960.
40 Bloomington: Indiana University Press, 1961.
41 Jerusalem: Israel Universities Press, 1969.
42 Beirut: Khayat's College Book Co-operative, 1956, trans. John F. Brown and John Racy.
43 London: Oxford University Press, 1969.
44 Paris: L'Harmattan, 1983, reprinted 2001.
45 Cairo: Matba'at *Ruz al-Yusuf*, 1982.
46 Reading, UK: Ithaca Press, 1998.

47 Beirut: Mu'assasat *al-Risala*, 2001.
48 Allahabad (India): Kitab Mahal, 1967.
49 London: Third World Centre for Research and Publishing, 1982.
50 Cairo: General Egyptian Book Organization, 1999.
51 New York, Berne, and Frankfurt am Main: Peter Lang, 1985.
52 Richmond, UK: Curzon, 2000.
53 *International Journal of African Historical Studies* 15 (1982): 625–49.
54 Cairo: Maktabat al-Anglo-al-Misriya, 1963.
55 Cairo: Dar al-Kitab al-'Arabi, 1966.
56 *Khamsin 'aman 'ala thawrat 1919*, with an introduction by Muhammad Hasanayn Haykal but no authors identified (Cairo: Dar al-Kitab al-Jadid, 1969).
57 Cairo: Dar al-Kitab al-'Arabi, 1968; 2nd ed. Cairo: Maktabat Madbuli, 1983. Reprint Cairo: General Egyptian Book Organization, 1998.
58 Beirut: al-Watan al-'Arabi, 1973. Reprint Cairo: General Egyptian Book Organization, 1998.
59 Paris: Gallimard, 1967, trans. Jean Stewart as *Egypt: Imperialism and Revolution* (London: Faber & Faber, 1972).
60 London: Tom Stacey Ltd., 1972, and London Editions, 1976. Indianapolis: 1st Books, 2002.
61 London: Weidenfeld and Nicolson, 1969. Subsequent editions have been published by that publisher and by Johns Hopkins University Press in 1980, 1985, and 1991.
62 Berkeley, Los Angeles, and London: University of California Press, 1977.
63 London: Ithaca Press, 1979.
64 Cairo: Dar al-Hilal, 1984.
65 Cairo: Center for Political and Strategic Studies, 1995.
66 Cairo: Mu'assasat al-Ahram, 1975.
67 Berkeley: University of California Press, 2003.
68 Cairo: Maktabat al-Nahda al-Misriya, 1952.
69 Beirut: Khayat, 1965.
70 London: Mansell, 1982.
71 Reading, UK: Ithaca Press, 1994. Huda is the eldest daughter of the late President Gamal 'Abd al-Nasser.
72 Cairo: Center for Political and Strategic Studies, 1995.
73 London: Oxford University Press, 1960.
74 Cambridge: Harvard University Press, 1961. London: Oxford University Press, 1961.
75 London: Oxford University Press, 1962. Cambridge and New York: Cambridge University Press, 1983.
76 London: Croom Helm, 1976.
77 Cairo: Dar al-Fikr al-'Arabi. The volumes most relevant to the period are about Amin al-Rafi'i (1959) and 'Abd al-Qadir Hamza (1963), vol. 9, on Muhammad Husayn Haykal, was probably never published.
78 *Tatawwur al-sihafa al-misriya*, 3rd ed. (Cairo: Maktabat al-Adab, 1951).
79 *A'lam al-sihafa al-'arabiya* (Cairo: Maktabat al-Adab, 1944).
80 See *Tarikh al-waqa'i' al-misriya, 1828–1942* (Cairo: al-Matba'a al-Amiriya, 1942); *Jaridat al-Ahram: tarikh wa fann 1875–1964* (Cairo: Mu'assasat Sijill al-'Arab, 1964).
81 New York: Oxford University Press, 1995.
82 Cairo: al-Dar al-Misriya li-l-Tiba'a wa-l-Nashr wa-l-Tawzi', 1958.
83 Cairo: al-Dar al-Misriya, 1958.
84 Cairo: al-Dar al-Misriya, 1957.
85 Paris: Éditions du Seuil, 1962, trans. Charles Lam Markmann as *Egypt: Military Society: The Army Regime, the Left, and Social Change under Nasser* (New York: Random House, 1968).

86 Paris: François Maspéro, 1969, trans. Michael Chirman and others as *Class Conflict in Egypt, 1945–1970* (New York: Monthly Review Press, 1973). "Mahmoud Hussein" was a pseudonym for 'Adil Rif'at and Bahjat al-Nadi.

87 Cairo: Dar al-Thaqafa al-Jadida, 1975.

88 In Walter Z. Laqueur, ed. *The Middle East in Transition* (New York: Frederick A. Praeger, 1958).

89 London, New York, and Toronto: Oxford University Press, 1962.

90 Chicago and London: University of Chicago Press, 1969.

91 *Al-Haraka al-'ummaliya fi Misr, 1899–1952* (Cairo: Dar al-Katib al-'Arabi li-l-Tiba'a wa al-Nashr, 1967).

92 Princeton: Princeton University Press, 1987.

93 Berkeley, Los Angeles, and London: University of California Press, 1986.

94 Albany: State University of New York Press, 1994.

95 Roger Owen and Sevket Pamuk, *A History of Middle East Economies in the Twentieth Century* (Cambridge: Harvard University Press, 1998).

96 New York: Frederick A. Praeger, 1956.

97 Cairo: Dar al-Thaqafa al-Jadida, 1975.

98 Beirut: Sharikat al-Amal, 1972.

99 Cairo: Dar al-Thaqafa, 1975.

100 Syracuse: Syracuse University Press, 1990.

101 Syracuse: Syracuse University Press, 1988.

102 London and Atlantic Highlands, NJ: Zed Books, 1984. The English translation of the French original was done by Bob Cumming. Henri Curiel was the founder of the communist faction known as Hadeto, or the Egyptian Movement for National Liberation.

103 Berkeley and Los Angeles: University of California Press, 1990.

104 London: RoutledgeCurzon, 2002.

105 The Hague: Martinus Nijhoff, 1969.

106 Edited by P.M. Holt and published by Oxford University Press in 1968, the volume contains papers given at a conference on modern Egyptian history sponsored by London University's School of Oriental and African Studies in April 1965.

107 Stanford: Hoover Institution Press, 1975.

108 London: Al Saqi Books, 1985.

109 London and Totowa, NJ: Frank Cass, 1989.

110 See James Jankowski and Israel Gershoni, eds., *Rethinking Nationalism in the Arab Middle East* (New York: Columbia University Press, 1997).

111 London: Robert Hale, 1967.

112 New York: McCall Publishing Co., 1970. The British edition bore the subtitle *The Ten Faces of Farouk* (London: Michael Joseph Ltd., 1969).

113 London: Quartet, 1989.

114 New York: Carroll & Graf Publishers, 1991.

115 Cairo: Maktabat Madbuli, 1989, revised 1998.

116 London: H. Jenkins Ltd., 1936.

117 Cairo: *Ruz al-Yusuf*, 1973.

118 Cairo: Mu'assasat *al-Ahram*, 1982.

119 Cairo: Matba'at Hijazi, 1936.

120 Beirut: Dar al-'Awda, 1975; Cairo: Maktabat Madbuli, 1975.

121 Markaz Watha'iq wa Tarikh Misr al-Mu'asir, 1987– .

122 Elie Kedourie, ed., *The Chatham House Version and Other Essays* (London: Weidenfeld and Nicolson, 1970; Hanover, NH: New England Universities Press, 1984).

123 *Mudhakkirati fi-l-siyasa al-misriya*, vols. 1–2 (Cairo: Anglo-Egyptian Bookshop, 1951–53) and vol. 3, intro. and ed. Ahmad Haykal (Cairo: Dar al-Ma'arif, 1977). Do not confuse this author with the former editor of *al-Ahram*, Muhammad Hasanayn Haykal.

124 *Islam and the Search for Social Order in Modern Egypt* (Albany: State University of New York Press, 1983).

125 *Al-Duktur Muhammad Husayn Haykal* (Cairo: Matba'at Misr, 1958).

126 Sa'id 'Abd al-Raziq Yusuf 'Abdallah, *Mahmud Fahmi al-Nuqrashi wa dawruhu fi-l-siyasa al-misriya* (Cairo: Maktabat Madbuli, 1995).

127 Malak Badrawi, *Isma'il Sidqi 1875–1950: Pragmatism and Vision in Twentieth Century Egypt* (Richmond, UK: Curzon, 1996). See also Isma'il Sidqi, *Mudhakkirati* (Cairo: Dar al-Hilal, 1950).

128 Lanham, MD: University Press of America, 1986.

129 *Tarbiyat Salama Musa* (Cairo: Dar al-Kitab al-Misri, 1947), trans. L.O. Schuman as *The Education of Salama Musa* (Leiden: E.J. Brill, 1960).

130 *Contemporary Egypt: Through Egyptian Eyes* (London and New York: Routledge, 1993).

131 Many editions of this dictionary are extant. This writer uses the fifth edition, published in eight volumes by Dar al-'Ilm li-l-Malayin (Beirut, 1980). Newer editions exist, augmented by other Arab writers.

132 The first edition was published between 1949 and 1963 by various Cairo printing houses. It was reprinted in Beirut by Dar al-Gharb al-Islami in 1994.

133 Beirut: Jam'iyyat Ahl al-Qalam, 1956. Other volumes were printed by various publishers between 1950 and 1983.

134 Cairo: Dar Nahdat Misr li-l-Tab' wa-l-Nashr, ca. 1968.

135 Cairo: Dar al-Shuruq, 1997.

136 Cairo: Middle East News Agency, 1997.

137 Boulder: Lynne Rienner Publishers, 2000.

138 Lanham, MD, and Oxford: Scarecrow Press, 2003. Cairo: The American University in Cairo Press, 2004.

139 London: Grant Richards, 1935.

140 London: John Murray, 1938. Jarvis's books were often banned from Egypt.

141 London: John Murray, 1949. As chief of the Cairo police, Russell witnessed many of the confrontations between the British and Egyptian demonstrators. See also Ronald Seth, *Russell Pasha* (London: William Kimber, 1966).

142 London: Robert Hale, 1957.

143 New York: Walker, 1966. London: Michael Joseph, 1967.

144 London: John Murray, 1970. Reprinted London: Stacy International, 2002.

145 *Hayati* (Cairo: Maktabat al-Nahda al-Misriya, 1950). Leiden: E.J. Brill, 1978, trans. Issa Boullatta.

146 London: Ariel Books for BBC, 1983, paperback edition 1985.

147 New York: Simon & Schuster, 1987.

148 New York: Harper Collins, 1994.

149 New York: Farrar Straus Giroux, 1999.

150 Rome: Instituto Storico Domenicano, 1996. Paris: Éditions du Cerf, 1996.

151 London and New York: Zed Books, 1999, trans. Sherif Hetata.

152 Spennymoor: The Memoir Club, 2002.

153 2 vols.; Cairo: Matba'at Misr, 1934.

154 Cairo: General Egyptian Book Organization, 1988.

155 Cairo: Dar al-Shuruq, 1992.

156 *Qissat hayati* (Cairo: Dar al-Hilal, 1962).

157 *Hadhihi hayati* (Cairo, Dar al-Hilal, 1963).

158 Princeton: Princeton University Press, 1970.

159 London: Weidenfeld and Nicolson, 1971.

160 Beirut: Maison Naaman pour la Culture, 1981.

161 London: J.M. Dent & Sons, 1988.

162 London: Ithaca Press, 1988.

163 London: Hamilton, 1989; London: Penguin, 1995.

164 London: Bellew Publishing, 1991.

165 New York: St. Martin's Press, 1997.

166 Madison, NJ: Fairleigh Dickinson University Press, 1995.

167 Lawrence Durrell's *Alexandria Quartet* consists of *Justine* (New York: Dutton, 1957), *Balthazar* (New York: Dutton, 1958), *Mountolive* (New York: Dutton, 1958), and *Clea* (New York: Dutton, 1960). The London publisher of the novels was Faber and Faber.

168 Olivia Manning, *The Levant Trilogy* comprises *The Danger Tree* (New York: Atheneum, 1977), *The Battle Lost and Won* (New York: Atheneum, 1979), and *The Sum of Things* (New York: Atheneum, 1981). Naguib Mahfouz's Cairo Trilogy consists of *Bayn al-Qasrayn* (Cairo, 1956), trans. William Maynard Hutchins and Olive Kenny as *Palace Walk* (New York: Doubleday, 1990); *Qasr al-Shawq* (Cairo, 1957), trans. William Hutchins and Lorne and Olive Kenny as *Palace of Desire* (New York: Doubleday, 1991; and *al-Sukkariya* (Cairo, 1957), trans. William Hutchins and Angele Botros Samaan as *Sugar Street* (New York: Doubleday, 1992).

169 Cairo: Dar al-Wahda, 1982.

170 London: Croom Helm, 1986.

171 Seattle: University of Washington Press, 1989.

172 Boulder and London: Westview Press, 1987.

173 Cairo: General Egyptian Book Organization, 1991.

174 New York and London: New York University Press, 1992.

175 Boulder: Westview Press, 1982.

176 Princeton: Princeton University Press, 1984.

177 Cairo: The American University in Cairo Press, 1989.

178 Berkeley, Los Angeles, and London: University of California Press, 1995.

179 Princeton: Princeton University Press, 1983.

180 Syracuse: Syracuse University Press, 1988.

181 New York and Oxford: Oxford University Press, 1989.

182 Stanford, CA: Hoover Institution Press, 1968.

183 Minneapolis and Chicago: Bibliotheca Islamica, 1981.

184 Syracuse: Syracuse University Press, 1991.

185 Cambridge: Massachusetts Institute of Technology Press, 1980.

186 London: Zed Books Ltd., 1989.

187 *Family, Power, and Politics in Egypt: Sayed Bey Marei—His Clan, Clients, and Cohorts* (Philadelphia: University of Pennsylvania Press, 1982).

188 Reading, UK: Ithaca Press, 1998.

189 Cairo: The American University in Cairo Press, 2000. The pictures by Golo are as delightful as the text. Also see its sequel, *Whatever Else Happened to the Egyptians? From the Revolution to the Age of Globalization* (Cairo: The American University in Cairo Press, 2004).

190 Syracuse: Syracuse University Press, 1990.

191 New Haven and London: Yale University Press, 1990.

192 Full title: *Reconstructing Rural Egypt: Ahmed Hussein and the History of Egyptian Development* (Syracuse: Syracuse University Press, 2004). Do not confuse Dr. Ahmad Husayn with the man of the same name who founded and led Misr al-Fatat.

193 Princeton: Princeton University Press, 2002.

194 "The Making and Breaking of Marital Bonds in Modern Egypt," in Beth Baron and Nikki Keddie, eds., *Women in Middle Eastern History: Shifting Boundaries in Sex and Gender* (New Haven and London: Yale University Press, 1991).

195 "Terminating Marriage," in Nicholas S. Hopkins, ed., *The New Arab Family* (Cairo: The American University in Cairo Press, 2003).

196 Cambridge and New York: Cambridge University Press, 1997.

197 Cairo Papers in Social Science, vol. 6, Monograph 4; Cairo: The American University in Cairo Press, 1983.

198 Berlin: Klaus Schwarz, 1984.

199 Gregory S. Starrett, *Putting Islam to Work: Education, Politics, and Religious Transformation in Egypt* (Berkeley: University of California Press, 1998).

200 Cairo: Markaz al-Dirasat al-Siyasiya wa-l-Stratijiya bi-l-Ahram, 1983.

201 Cambridge: Cambridge University Press, 1990.

202 Cairo: The American University in Cairo Press, 1987.

203 London: Routledge and Kegan Paul, 1978.

204 Cairo: The American University in Cairo Press, 1963; also note his earlier work, *School and Society in the Valley of the Nile* (Cairo: Elias' Modern Press, 1936).

205 Written by Sahar Hammouda and Colin Clement and published in 2002 by The American University in Cairo Press. Former Victoria students include Amin Osman, Edward Atiyah, King Husayn, Omar Sharif, and Edward Said.

206 In Jankowski and Gershoni, eds., *Rethinking Nationalism in the Arab Middle East.*

207 Thomas Mayer, *The Changing Past: Egyptian Historiography of the Urabi Revolt, 1882–1963* (Gainesville: University of Florida Press, 1988).

208 Zaki al-Buhayri, *Tarikh Misr al-hadith wa-l-mu'asir fi muqarrarat al-madaris al-misriya* (Cairo: Dar Nahdat al-Sharq, 1990).

209 In Jankowski and Gershoni, eds., *Rethinking Nationalism in the Arab Middle East.*

210 "'Jabarti of the 20th Century': The National Epic of 'Abd al-Rahman al-Rafi'i and other Egyptian Histories," *International Journal of Middle East Studies* 36 (2004), 429–50.

211 New Haven and London: Yale University Press, 1992.

212 Princeton: Princeton University Press, 1995.

213 Gainesville: University Presses of Florida, 1996.

214 New York: Columbia University Press, 1999.

215 Berkeley, Los Angeles, and London: University of California Press, 2001.

216 Cairo: Dar al-Shuruq, 1982.

217 New York: St. Martin's Press, 1998.

218 Mona Russell, *Creating the New Egyptian Woman: Consumerism, Education, and National Identity, 1863–1922* (New York: Palgrave, 2004); Barak A. Salmoni, "Women in the Nationalist-Educational Prism: Turkish and Egyptian Pedagogues and their Gendered Agenda, 1920–1952" *History of Education Quarterly* 43: 4 (2003); "The Limits of Pedagogical Revolution: Female Schooling and Women's Roles in Egyptian Educational Discourse, 1922–1952," in Tom Ewing, ed., *Revolution and Pedagogy* (New York: Palgrave, 2004).

219 Cairo: The American University in Cairo Press, 1988.

220 Austin: University of Texas Press, 1995.

221 Beth Baron and Nikki Keddie, eds., *Women in Middle Eastern History* (New Haven: Yale University Press, 1991).

222 Chicago and London: University of Chicago Press, 1997.

223 Cairo: The American University in Cairo Press, 1998.

224 Austin: Center for Middle Eastern Studies, University of Texas, 2000. Asmahan, the sister of Farid al-Atrash, was regarded during her short lifetime as the rival of Umm Kulthum.

225 Cairo: The American University in Cairo Press, 1998.

226 Cairo: The American University in Cairo Press, 2001.

227 Paris: Institut du Monde Arabe, 1996.

228 Cambridge and New York: Cambridge University Press, 1996.

229 Cairo: The American University in Cairo Press, 1971.

230 2nd ed.; Syracuse: Syracuse University Press, 1995.

231 Cambridge and New York: Cambridge University Press, 1992.

232 Cairo: Matba'at Lajnat al-Ta'lif, 1937, trans. Aubrey (later Abba) Eban as *The Maze of Justice* (London: Harvill, 1947).

233 Edited by Trefor E. Evans (London: Sidgwick and Jackson, 1972).

234 Oxford: Oxford University Press, 1997.

235 Trans. A.G. Mitchell (Cairo: Société Orientale du Publicité, 1945). The original version was *L'Égypte et la deuxième guerre mondiale* (Cairo: R. Schindler, 1945).

236 London, New York, and Toronto: Oxford University Press, 1952.

237 Cairo: Arab Institute, 1976.

238 *International Journal of Middle East Studies* 10 (1970): 453–79.

239 London: Frank Cass, 1985.

240 Cairo: Maktabat Madbuli, 1982.

241 *Middle Eastern Studies* 33, no. 1 (1994): 91–122.

242 Reading, UK: Ithaca Press, 1994.

243 Chapel Hill: University of North Carolina Press, 1991.

244 In Eugene Rogan and Avi Shlaim, eds., *The War for Palestine* (Cambridge: Cambridge University Press, 2001).

245 Cairo: Maktabat Madbuli, 1982.

246 Majid M. 'Ali Faraj, "Hariq al-Qahira ba'd 50 Sanatan," *Misr al-mahrusa* 26 (2002).

247 2 vols.; Cairo: al-Maktab al-Misri, 1977.

248 Cairo: Maktabat Madbuli, 1977–84.

249 London: Croom Helm, 1978.

250 3 vols.; United Arab Emirates: Mu'assasat al-Ittihad, 1986–99.

251 London: Andre Deutsch, 1986.

252 *'Ali Sabri Yatadhakkar* (Cairo: Mu'assasat *Ruz al-Yusuf*, 1987).

253 Oxford and New York: Oxford University Press, 1992; Cairo: The American University in Cairo Press, 1996.

254 Boulder, San Francisco, and Oxford: Westview Press, 1994.

255 Boulder, San Francisco, and Oxford: Westview Press, 1995.

256 Cairo: The American University in Cairo Press, 1995. The Arabic original, *Wa al-an atakallam*, was published by *al-Ahram* in 1992. This work has been analyzed by Didier Monciaud, "Ideology, Identity, and Commitment in the Autobiography of Khalid Mohieddin" in Mary Ann Fay, ed., *Auto/Biography and the Construction of Identity and Community in the Middle East* (New York: Palgrave, 2001).

257 Cairo: CEDEJ, 2002. Available from the same publisher is his *L'Égypte dans le siècle, 1901-2000* (2003).

258 Berlin: Klaus Schwarz Verlag, 1983.

259 Boulder, San Francisco, and Oxford: Westview Press, 1990.

260 In Rashid Khalidi et al., eds., *The Origins of Arab Nationalism* (New York: Columbia University Press, 1991).

261 New York: Praeger, 1992.

262 Jankowski and Gershoni, eds., *Rethinking Nationalism in the Arab Middle East.*

263 Reading, UK: Ithaca Press, 1998.

264 London and New York: Tauris, 1998.

265 New York and Oxford: Oxford University Press, 1999.

266 London: Frank Cass Publishers, 1993.

267 Princeton: Princeton University Press, 1971.

268 London and New York: Quartet Books, 1989.

269 San Francisco: Chronicle Books, 1994.

270 Cairo: The American University in Cairo Press, 1993.

271 2nd ed.; Cairo: Palm Press, 1995 *(Maadi)*; Cairo: The American University in Cairo Press, 2004 *(Glory Years)*.

272 Cairo: Palm Press, 1997.

273 New York: Alfred A. Knopf, 1999.

274 Cambridge, MA, and London: Harvard University Press, 2000, trans. Willard Wood.

275 Cairo: The American University in Cairo Press, 2004.

276 Cairo: The American University in Cairo Press, 2004. Michael Haag also annotated the 1982 British edition of E.M. Forster's *Alexandria: A History and a Guide*, with an introduction by Lawrence Durrell.

277 London: John Murray, 1991.

278 Paris: Flammarion, 2003.

279 Not yet available to this writer was Deborah Manley and Sahar Abdel-Hakim, eds., *Traveling through Egypt from 450 B.C. to the Twentieth Century* (Cairo: The American University in Cairo Press, 2004).

280 London and New York: RoutledgeCurzon, 2003.

281 Cambridge and New York: Cambridge University Press, 1998. The second volume, covering the period from 1517 to the end of the twentieth century, was edited by M.W. Daly.

282 Cambridge: Cambridge University Press, 1985.

283 Boulder: Westview Press, 1988; 2nd ed., 2004.

284 Oxford: OneWorld, 2000.

285 Syracuse: Syracuse University Press, 1991.

286 3rd ed.; New York: HarperCollins, 1991.

18   Conclusion

Roger Owen

The monarchical period covered by this book lasted only thirty-three years, less than a generation and a half. And yet, as the contributions to this book amply demonstrate, these three decades are critical to an understanding of Egypt's twentieth-century trajectory, of the paths taken and not taken. The period started in a spirit of great optimism generated by the 1919 Revolution and what must have seemed like the almost miraculous success in getting the British to abandon their eight-year-old protectorate—which succeeded creeping occupation since 1882—for a more indirect form of influence. Like much else in modern Egyptian history this moment of enthusiasm is not much remarked upon today. Nevertheless, the strong sense of excitement about the achievement of partial independence can still be felt when reading the newspapers and fiction of those days, as members of the educated elite turned with passionate concern to those basic questions facing any newly independent country: What is Egypt? Who are the Egyptian people? And, what should be their political, economic, and social goals? For me this is nicely epitomized by the five characters on view in Mahmud Taymur's 1917 short story, "Fi al-qatr." Two (a clerk/effendi and a student) are sitting facing forward (the future), two (an Azhari *shaykh* and a Circassian pasha) sit backwards, and a village *'umda* straddles both ways, as they all engage in an intense discussion of the future of Egyptian education.[1]

What is not always properly comprehended either is the sense of confidence with which such questions were now able be addressed. There was the confidence, newly enforced by the discovery of Tutankhamun's tomb in November 1922, of belonging to one of the world's oldest, if not *the*

oldest, civilization. There was the confidence inspired by having a king, a parliament, and, above all, a constitution. And the confidence based on the presence of a solid corps of professional politicians, diplomats, journalists, doctors, lawyers, engineers, and administrators who had come to prominence during the British occupation, many from the growing number of middle class families which had benefited from the increased cotton-based prosperity of the pre-World War I years. Perhaps their most important contribution was the way in which they not only kept the process of government and administration going through frequent crises and changes of cabinet, but also—like Ahmad 'Abd al-Wahhab at the Ministry of Finance—how they made substantial contributions to policy formation as well.

Another good example of this new administrative elite is the doctor/diplomat, Muhammad al-Gindi, who, with the help of a colleague, Dr. A.H. Mahfouz, was largely responsible for placing hashish on the League of Nations' list of banned narcotics during the international opium conference held at Geneva between November 1924 and February 1925. One can imagine the pride in his voice as he reminded the delegates on 2 December 1924, just ten days after Sa'd Zaghlul's humiliating resignation in the wake of the Lee Stack assassination, of the fact that this was the first time his country had been represented at a conference organized by the League of Nations by "two purely Egyptian delegates."[2]

This was just the tip of the iceberg. The country's inter-war civil service was headed by a group of skilled officials whose abilities, *inter alia*, to manage the national accounts, repair the damage to the irrigation system by pre-war over-watering, and introduce an efficient system of protective tariffs as soon as the last of the capitulatory trade treaties expired in 1930, have all seldom received proper recognition. Furthermore, as Malak Badrawi's contribution to this book sensibly suggests, they operated with an admirable degree of probity and accountability. As Badrawi's chapter also demonstrates, parliamentary life was not only maintained in spite its many vicissitudes, but was usually carried out in a responsible fashion which most previous writers on Egypt's political history have chosen to overlook. Meanwhile, the country enjoyed a rich cultural and artistic life, whether in literature, cinema, or popular music, which was the envy of the rest of the Arab Middle East. And it was to Egypt too, that the other Arab states tended to turn for advice from that country's educationalists, jurists, and professors of constitutional law.

As is well-known, this achievement was immediately called in question by the shabby and sometimes violent politics of much of the post-World

War II period, beginning with the assassination of Prime Minister Ahmad Mahir in February 1945. In part Egypt seemed to be paying the price for its geographical situation, with its foreign-controlled Suez Canal and its close proximity both to strife-torn Palestine in the east and Egypt's would-be colony of Sudan to the south. But it was also suffering grievously from its unresolved social tensions and from the inability to find a place in its political system for one of the country's other major contributions to the modern Middle East, the enormously successful religious-cum-social movement, the Muslim Brothers.

Nevertheless, as is also well-known, many aspects of the monarchical period's rich educational and intellectual life remained at the service of the revolutionary regime that followed. And if some of its brightest jewels like the jurist, 'Abd al-Razzaq al-Sanhuri, were sidelined immediately, others like the novelist Naguib Mahfouz or the journalist, Muhammad Hasanayn Haykal, are still part of the Cairo cultural scene. Others again, for example, the journalist/intellectual, Ahmad Lutfi al-Sayyid and the singer Umm Kulthum, were honored under the three successor presidents with funeral processions the size of which rivaled those of any of the military politicians, with the exception of Gamal 'Abd al-Nasser himself. More was put to sleep in 1952 than the consciences of many of these same intellectuals, as Tawfiq al-Hakim so memorably suggests.[3] What was also lost was the ability to maintain belief in many, though not all, of the real achievements of what had come before.

Knowledge of Egypt's rich pre-revolutionary literary tradition was, of course, well-preserved in the works of such giants as Yusuf Idris, Yahya Haqqi, Fathi Ghanem, and, above all, Mahfouz. I should also note that much of the work done in my own field, economic history, was largely exempt from such strictures on the grounds that it was very much in line with revolutionary policies of national development. And that much of the excellent work of the pre-1952 period by A.E. Crouchley, 'Ali al-Giritli, Charles Issawi, and others was both preserved and elaborated upon in the 'Abd al-Nasser decades and beyond by Hussam 'Isa, Samir Radwan, 'Asim Disuqi, and others including the doyen of them all, Bent Hansen. But, sadly, these are best seen as the exceptions which also prove the general rule.

Many of the reasons for this sorry situation are relatively well-known. But they are still worth mentioning because they remain so powerful and pervasive. One, of course, is the ideology of the 'Abd al-Nasser regime itself, beginning with the views of its leader. Such views dealt not only with the corruption of the monarchy and the problems of trying to run a one man/one vote democracy in a predominantly peasant country. Also, more tellingly, regime ideology emphasized the incompleteness of the 1919 Revolution and the need to complement it with an equally comprehensive social revolution as well.[4] Such views were then elaborated in greater detail in the new school textbooks of the late 1950s, which still continue to inform the thinking of most of Egypt's own historians.[5]

A second reason is the revolution's emphasis on the pre-existing nationalist motif of the country's history being defined by a constant struggle against outside forces, most notably the British. Hence most historians' reduction of pre-revolutionary politics to the three-cornered contest between the palace, the British residency/embassy and the Wafd.

Two other reasons are also important. The first is the willingness to see the whole monarchical period in terms of its humiliating end, as if it vitiated everything that had come before. Hence Afaf Lutfi al-Sayyid's title, "The Failure of Egypt's Liberal Experiment, 1922–1936" or even Albert Hourani's decision to end his Arab "liberal age" in 1939. Tawfiq al-Hakim is probably more to blame when he remembered the movement to revive the 1923 Constitution in the mid-1930s not as the glorious achievement it really was but as just the lead-up to more mischief by the new king, Faruq, and his irresponsible advisers.[6] Moreover, once liberalism, or its absence, is taken as the touchstone of the monarchical period, other biases creep in, such as the repeated over-emphasis on the supposedly "fascist nature" of few of the Egyptian political movements in the 1930s—once again something that stems more from present concerns than a desire to revisit past realities.[7] The second reason 1919–52 accomplishments are seen as anomalies is the still strong influence of what might be called the Lawrence Durrell syndrome; that is the blinkered vision which sees the lives of the foreigners and foreign minorities as much more interesting and important than those of the vast majority of Egyptians themselves.[8] That such views are not just confined to those writing from abroad is attested, *inter alia*, by the use made of Durrellian quotes to illustrate the photographs on display in the exhibition of Alexandria's history in the city's much-praised new library.

One last reason deserves consideration even if it has not yet received the attention it rightly deserves. This is the attitude of educated Egyptians to their own national history, an attitude which, by and large, seems to view the whole period after 1923 as part of a present best left to journalists, like Muhammad Haykal, or to gifted amateurs like Samir W. Raafat.[9] There is some excuse for this, given both the poor state of the national archives and the jealousy with which ministries established in the monarchical period, like the Ministry of Social Affairs, still seem to view their records as containing politically explosive material. But it cannot help a people wishing either to understand its own history or to use it to find some firm ground in terms of models, achievements and a better-realized sense of the strengths and weaknesses of its great men and women.

As Arthur Goldschmidt also laments in the present volume, scholarly biographies of the most important political figures of the period are in particularly short supply. While we know quite a lot about Sa'd Zaghlul, Isma'il Sidqi, Abd al-Rahman 'Azzam, Ahmad Husayn, and others, we remain much more in the dark when it comes to the public life of such important figures as Fu'ad Sirag al-Din and Makram 'Ubayd. The same is also true for the lives of those who participated directly in the overthrow of the monarchical regime, notably Gamal 'Abd al-Nasser himself, for whom the lack of a good biography was not only richly lamented in the Cairo press on the occasion of the fiftieth anniversary of the revolution (2002), but was also deemed an impossible task in current circumstances of secrecy surrounding the whereabouts of his official papers.

Now, over fifty years after the overthrow of the monarchical regime, it is certainly more than time to attempt a wholesale re-evaluation of those three vital decades: time to ask new questions, time to challenge much of the conventional wisdom which passes for knowledge of the period, time to examine how it compares with what came before and what came after. This book is undoubtedly a good beginning. It is informed by large intentions and by a large view of history which goes beyond the narrowly political or the narrowly economic to include important contributions to the history of Egyptian education, culture, and gender. It contains important forays into a revisionist account of the practices of parliament and of the military. And it contains works by scholars from a number of disciplines and a number of different countries, including, most important of all, Egypt itself.

Nevertheless, this is just a beginning. For one thing the groundwork still remains to be done on some of the period's most important aspects: on the political and social role of the monarchy, for example; on the links between the lives of the majority Egyptians and those of the members of the foreign minorities in their midst; on the courts of law; and on the control and management of the large Egyptian agricultural estates known as 'izbas. This is not to deny the value of several important groundbreaking works: Magda Baraka on the cultural aspect of class relations, Reem Saad on peasant memories of their "liberation" at the hand of the 1952 Agrarian Law, Robert Ilbert on the divisions within Alexandrian society in the 1920s, not to speak of the truly revisionist work of Robert Vitalis on Egyptian family business and that of Ellis Goldberg on the impact of the use of children as agricultural laborers, as well as a number of the contributors to this particular volume. But illuminating though they all are, they just touch the tip of an iceberg consisting of all the institutions, relationships, practices, and processes which make the monarchical period so important, interesting and, in its own special way, unique. Such considerations lead me to see the contributions collected together in *Re-Envisioning Egypt* as a call to arms. So let me use the remainder of this conclusion in setting out what I see to be some of the most important methods, uses, and insights which might help to guide us in the task ahead.

The first suggestion concerns the crying need to place the period in its world historical context by the use of judicious comparison (of the compare and contrast type) with states in a roughly equivalent state of political and economic development. The period began with all the high hopes of international cooperation focused on the League of Nations and on either a return to democratic practices, or their new emplacement in what Michael Mazower in *Dark Continent: Europe's Twentieth Century*, describes as a "belt of democracies—stretching from the Baltic Sea down through Germany and Poland to the Balkans—all equipped with new constitutions drawn up according to the most up-to-date liberal principles." And yet, as Mazower also reminds us, twenty years later all had become dictatorships, with the addition of Spain, Portugal, and Italy in the west of Europe.[10] Meanwhile, in the Middle East itself, the practice of electoral politics and the public accountability of politicians was certainly more open and regular in Egypt than in Turkey, Iran, and the few Arab states which had a similar system, with the possible exception of Lebanon.

One could perhaps also make the case that one of the banes of the Egyptian system, the constant revising of the rules governing candidacies, voter eligibility, etc., owed something to the well-accepted nineteenth-century British and West European 'liberal' practice of defining citizenship, and therefore the right to vote, in terms of age, gender, education, and property. Viewed from any of these optics the Egyptian experience looks a great deal less bad.

The same might also be said for the early attempts to institute measures of social welfare described in this work by Amy Johnson and Scott David McIntosh. Once again a comprehensive international comparison might reveal that the Egyptian measures, though partial and underfunded, were at least the equal to those proposed elsewhere in the Middle East and perhaps just as progressive as those pursued in many parts of Europe before the new emphasis on 'welfarism' ushered in by the Second World War.

Lastly, European experience suggests that the establishment of a constitutional monarchy requires a considerable amount of time before the right balance can be struck. And while Elie Kedourie was right to point to the final draft of the 1923 Constitution as a "compromise between (King) Fu'ad's desire for unfettered power and the views of those of the (Constitutional) Commission who stood for unfettered sovereignty," this does not mean that compromise was impossible.[11]

Another set of international comparisons concerns Egypt's experience of two of the great global events of the period, the world depression and World War II. While the impact of the latter is quite well-known through the works of Nancy Gallagher, Robert Vitalis, Timothy Mitchell, and many others, the global depression's impact on Egypt still poses a number of as yet unanswered questions. Why, for instance, did it have much less of an influence on the political system than Europe? Although some might wish to see a rough equivalency between the brief 'dictatorship' of Isma'il Sidqi, 1930–33, and Europe's swing to the right after 1929, in fact the search for an Egyptian strongman had begun some years earlier and was quickly to exhaust itself in the powerful movement for the restoration of constitutional life, 1935/36. Perhaps this was because, in economic terms, the depression lasted a much shorter time than in most of Europe. This shorter duration made Egypt's experience more like that of Latin America, where the continued export of cash crops (like cotton) produced a new surge in national income after 1935.[12] Egypt was also like the rest of the non-European world in the way that, as Dietmar Rothermund has shown, the costs of the depression were born largely by the vast majority of the poorer peasants.[13] Hence the sharpening division between rich and poor made worse by landowner control of the Senate. The implications of this division, like the politics surrounding the revisions of the land tax in 1935/37 and 1949, have been less well-explored than the effect it had on the various attempts initiated from the late 1930s onward to alleviate rural poverty.[14]

A second suggestion concerns the new perspectives, which might be opened up by a closer look at the links between the monarchical decades and what came before and after. With its essential features framed, as many might see it, between a world war and a revolution, it is not always possible to distinguish what was new and special about it from the continuities which existed both with what came before and what came after. Here, at least, is an opportunity for asking new questions.

One such question concerns the observation that the economic and social programs put forward by Egypt's nationalist parties just before and just after World War I were developed very much as a critique of the British occupation—especially its policies toward industry and education—and its refusal to encourage the establishment of Egyptian rather than foreign-controlled financial institutions. This was very much the thinking behind the creation of Banque Misr as well as the tariff reforms of 1930 onward, even if, as Robert Vitalis has amply demonstrated, the bank was much less a purely Egyptian enterprise than has commonly been supposed.[15] But what about the failure to follow through on the criticism of British educational policy? Textbooks remained little changed until the mid-1930s, and the division into two systems, one for the urban dwellers and one for the rural poor, was not abolished until the laws of 1949 and 1951.[16]

Turning now to question that might be asked relating to the legacy of the monarchical period, a key issue still very much unexplored is that of the nature of civil society as it existed in 1952. On the whole it seems to be one in which there was freedom of speech, in which private property was respected, in which the rule of law obtained. It also consisted of a set of institutions such as the universities, the press, and a large number of professional associations relatively free from government control. But clearly, this is not the whole story. Attempts by the government in power to intimidate sections of the press began as early as the first Zaghlul cabinet in 1924; pressures put on rectors and professors included Sidqi's dramatic dismissal of Taha Husayn from his post at the Egyptian University; the ability of workers to found unions was heavily circumscribed. All this was long before the emergency regulations put in place at British insistence at the beginning of World War II. Of course, none of these restrictions had anything like the impact as those that followed the military coup of 1952 when the very basis for an independent political, economic, and associational life came under systematic attack from an authoritarian regime. Nevertheless, the subject is sufficiently important to merit academic attention, the more so at a time when Egypt itself is still cursed with an Emergency Law—first enacted in 1958, imposed in 1967, and in effect almost continually since then—and still trying to find ways to create institutions and associations strong enough to withstand the baleful influence of the pre-Nasserite state.[17]

Two other approaches are worth considering. The first involves the employment of certain counter-factual hypotheses to challenge various pieces of conventional wisdom. For one thing, the method itself always provides a useful challenge to all those explanations which rely on notions such as the inevitability of a nation's chosen path, to the neglect of the study of paths not taken. This is all the more important in the Egyptian case because of the huge effort made by the early 'Abd al-Nasser regime to justify its revolution in terms of its being the only answer to the country's economic and social crisis. For another, the method allows us to return to certain historical questions from a new perspective.

Joel Gordon's notion of the Wafd's "Last Hurrah" is one of the few attempts that I know of to use the method which any success.[18] True that his central question—might the successful implementation of the policies of the 1950 Wafd cabinet's four reforming ministers have been enough to avert the 1952 coup?—is a little crude. True too that Gordon does not push the question to its limits by asking what a successful Wafdist government might have looked like if it had managed to stay in power long enough, not only to avert the coup but also to put its stamp on the Egypt of the early 1950s. This, in fact, is a question I ask myself every time I pass the Tahrir Square's Mugamma' building in Cairo, a monument not to the 'Abd al-Nasser regime, as many suppose, but to the Wafd's minister of interior, Fu'ad Sirag al-Din. The latter might, in slightly different historical circumstances, have been able to create his own army-backed single party regime. Nevertheless Gordon's use of the counter-factual method to assess the importance of some of the key social issues of the time is an interesting one, as is its evaluation of the power of the forces preventing substantial change.

The last approach is also one that is beginning to receive some attention. This is the challenge to the old notion of Egypt's basic homogeneity, a country with a strong central administration, a dominant form of agricultural practice, and a people squeezed into the narrow strip of flat land along the Nile with very little regional or local difference. As is well-known, the main challenge to such a notion has come in recent years as a result either of the growing interest in how to rewrite the history of the nation state in the era of globalization or, more locally, in the perception of the people of the Sa'id (Upper Egypt) as being somewhat different in character from their Lower Egyptian cousins. However, few writers have looked at its possible implications for the monarchical period other than through the lens provided by the differences in land-holding and agricultural production between north and south, for example, or the role played by the southern large estate owners in the establishment of the Bank Misr. There has also been attention to the particular conditions that contributed to the extreme poverty in southern villages observed by those trying to combat the great malaria epidemic of 1942.[19] Many non-regional differences are equally worthy of analysis, as are the assumptions of a basic divide between old and new Cairo illustrated, among others, by several fictional works by Yusuf Idris—though nicely challenged by Nelly Hanna.[20] Be it town and country, men and women, rich and poor, Egyptian and foreign, and, in the case of Yusuf Idris again, village and 'izba, the assumptions of a binary system of fundamental difference seem to have a particular hold over the Egyptian historical imagination.[21]

As with many other aspects of Egypt's long history, there is much work to be done. And as is happening successfully in the field of Egyptian archaeology, it is vital that it be done, wherever possible, in partnership with the country's own historians. This is not an easy task. For a number of powerful reasons, exchange between the scholarly community inside and out has become more and more difficult in recent decades. Politics has something to do with it. Just as important, however, has been the parlous state of many Egyptian universities and libraries with little money to buy books and scholarly journals or to send academics abroad to conferences in Europe and the United States. As a result, the national and international groups of historians have drawn apart, using their own particular paradigms and methods and, for the most part, knowing little about what the other group is writing or saying. Indeed, we may have reached such a stage where, in Egypt itself, the very decision to concentrate attention on the monarchical period is challenged as a foreign effort to undermine a basic part of the national narrative.

What to do? Let us hope that this book is translated as soon as possible into Arabic. Let us hope that its ideas and reassessments will be taken seriously enough in Egypt to provoke counter hypotheses, while providing those outside with information about the current state of Egyptian academic thinking and research. And then let us hope that all this can then be discussed with our Egyptian colleagues in seminars and conferences in Cairo, Egypt's provincial universities, and elsewhere, as a basis for new thinking and new research.

Notes

1   "Fi al-qatr" in Muhammad Taymur, *al-Juz' al-awwal: wamid al-ruh* (Cairo: General Egyptian Book Organization, 1971).

2   Quoted in *Egyptian Gazette*, 2 December 1924.

3   Tawfiq al-Hakim, *Return of Consciousness*, Bayley Winder, trans (New York: Oxford University Press, 1985), 21–22.

4   For example, 'Abd al-Nasser himself in his *The Philosophy of the Revolution* (Cairo: Dar al-Ma'arif, n.d.), 23–25.

5   Barak A. Salmoni, "Pedagogies of Patriotism: Teaching Socio-Political Community in Twentieth-Century Turkish and Egyptian Education" (Ph.D. diss., Harvard University, 2002).

6   *Return of Consciousness*, 8.

7   For example, Israel Gershoni, "Confronting Nazism in Egypt: Tawfiq al-Hakim's Anti-Authoritarianism 1938–1945," *Tel-Aviver Jahr-Buch Für Deutsche Geshichte* (Tel Aviv: Institut für Deutsche Geschichte, Tel Aviv University, 1997), XXVI, 136–42.

8   For example, Robert Mabro, "Nostalgic Literature on Alexandria," in Jill Edwards, ed., *Historians in Cairo: Essays in Honor of George Scanlon* (Cairo: The American University Press, 2002), 237–66.

9   For example, Samir W. Raafat, *Cairo, the Glory Years: Who Built What, When, Why and for Whom* (Cairo: The American University Press, 2003).

10 *Dark Continent* (New York: Random House, 1998), 4–5.

11 "The Genesis of the Egyptian Constitution of 1923," in P.M. Holt, ed., *Political and Social Change in Modern Egypt: Historical Studies from the Ottoman Conquest to the United Arab Republic* (London: Oxford University Press, 1968), 346–61.

12 Rosemary Thorp, "Introduction" in *Latin America in the 1930s: The Role of the Periphery in World Crisis* (London: Macmillan, 1984), 2–3.

13 *The Global Impact of the Great Depression, 1929–1939* (London: Routledge, 1996), 80–81.

14 Roger Owen, "Large Landowners, Agricultural Progress and the State in Egypt, 1800–1970: An Overview with Many Questions," in Alan Richards, ed., *Food, States and Peasants: Analyses of the Agrarian Question in the Middle East* (Boulder: Westview Press, 1986), 72–73.

15 *When Capitalists Collide: Business Conflict and the End of Empire in Egypt* (Berkeley: University of California Press, 1995).

16 For example, Misako Ikeda, "Sociopolitical Debates in Late Parliamentary Egypt, 1944–1952" (Ph.D. diss., Harvard Univesity, 1998), 198–204, 235.

17 See Law no. 162 of 1958 Concerning the State of Emergency (as amended).

18 Joel Gordon, "The False Hopes of 1950: The Wafd's Last Hurrah and the Demise of Egypt's Old Order," *International Journal of Middle Eastern Studies* 21 (1989), 193–214.

19 Eric Davis, *Challenging Colonialism: Bank Misr and Egyptian Industrialization 1920–1941* (Princeton: Princeton University Press, 1983), chapter 2; Nancy Gallagher, *Egypt's Other Wars; Epidemics and the Politics of Public Health* (Syracuse: Syracuse University Press, 2002), chapter 2.

20 Nelly Hanna, "The Urban History of Cairo Around 1900: A Reinterpretation," in Edwards. ed., *Historians in Cairo*, 189–202. For one work by Yusuf Idris, see his *Qa' al-madina* (Cairo: Sharikat Markaz Kutub al-Sharq al-Awsat, 1964).

Selected Bibliography

Abdalla, Ahmad. *The Student Movement and National Politics in Egypt, 1923–1973*. London: Al Saqi Books, 1985.

Abdel-Malek, Anouar. *Egypt: Military Society*, trans. Charles Lam Markmann. New York: Random House, 1968.

Abu Shadi, 'Ali. *Waqa'i' al-sinima al-misriya fi mi'at 'am: 1896–1995*. Cairo: al-Hay'at al-'Amma li-l-Shu'un al-Mutabi' al-Amiriya, 1997.

Ahmad, Jamal Mohammed. *The Intellectual Origins of Egyptian Nationalism*. London: Oxford University Press, 1960.

'Ali, Sa'id Isma'il. *Wijhat nazarin fi fikr Isma'il al-Qabbani al-tarbawi*. Cairo: Dar al-Thaqafa li-l-Tiba'a wa-l-Nashr, 1974.

——. *Ta'rikh al-fikr al-tarbawi fi Misr al-haditha*. Cairo: al-Hay'a al-Misriya al-'Amma li-l-Kitab, 1989.

Alleaume, Ghislaine. "La production d'une économie 'nationale': remarques sur l'histoire des sociétées anonymes par actions en Égypte de 1856 à 1956," *Les Annales Islamologiques*, T.XXXI, Cairo: IFAO, 1997, 1–16

Ammar, Hamed. *Growing up in an Egyptian Village: Silwa, Province of Aswan*. New York: Octagon Books, 1966.

Anderson, Benedict. *Imagined Communities: Reflections on the Origin and Spread of Nationalism*. London: Verso, 1983.

Anderson, James N.D. *Islamic Law in the Modern World*. New York: New York University Press, 1959.

Anis, Muhammad. *Hariq al-Qahira*. Beirut: Mu'assasa al-'Arabiya li-l-Dirasa wa-l-Nashr, 1972.

Arasoughly, Alia, ed. *Screens of Life: Critical Film Writing from the Arab World*. vol. I. Quebec: World Heritage Press, 1996.

Armbrust, Walter. *Mass Culture and Modernism in Egypt*. Cambridge: Cambridge University Press, 1996.

——, ed. *Mass Mediations: New Approaches to Popular Culture in the Middle East and Beyond.* Berkeley: University of California Press, 2000.

Arnaud, Jean-Luc, Le Caire. *Mise en place d'une ville moderne 1867–1907.* Paris: Acte Sud, 1998.

Ayalon, Ami. *The Press in the Arab Middle East.* New York: Oxford University Press, 1995.

Badrakhan, Ahmad. *al-Sinima.* Cairo: al-Halabi Press, 1936.

Badran, Margot. *Feminists, Islam, and Nation: Gender and the Making of Modern Egypt.* Princeton: Princeton University Press, 1995.

Baraka, Magda. *The Egyptian Upper Class between Revolutions, 1919–1952.* Oxford: Ithaca Press, 1998.

Baron, Beth. *The Women's Awakening in Egypt: Culture, Society, and the Press.* New Haven: Yale University Press, 1994.

Beinin, Joel and Zachary Lockman. *Workers on the Nile: Nationalism, Communism, Islam, and the Egyptian Working Class, 1882–1954.* Princeton: Princeton University Press, 1987.

Berque, Jacques. *Egypt: Imperialism and Revolution*, trans. Jean Stewart. New York: Faber, 1972.

Booth, Marilyn. *May Her Likes Be Multiplied: Biography and Gender Politics in Egypt.* Berkeley: University of California Press, 2001.

Botman, Selma. *Egypt from Independence to Revolution, 1919–1952.* Syracuse University Press, 1991.

——. *Engendering Citizenship in Egypt.* New York: Columbia University Press, 1999.

Brown, Nathan. *The Rule of Law in the Arab World: Courts in Egypt and the Gulf.* Cambridge: Cambridge University Press, 1997.

Buhayri, Zaki. *Tarikh Misr al-hadith wa-l-mu'asir fi muqarrarat al-madaris al-misriya.* Giza: Dar Nahdat al-Sharq, 1996.

Caulfield, Sueann. *In Defense of Honor: Sexual Morality, Modernity, and Nation in Early Twentieth Century Brazil.* Durham: Duke University Press, 2000.

Chatterjee, Partha. *The Nation and its Fragments: Colonial and Postcolonial Histories.* Princeton: Princeton University Press, 1993.

Choueiri, Youssef M. *Modern Arab Historiography: Historical Discourse and the Nation-State.* London: RoutledgeCurzon, 2003.

Cochran, Judith. *Education in Egypt.* London: Croom Helm, 1986.

Cossery, Albert. *Les hommes oubliés de Dieu.* Paris: Joelle Losfeld, 1994.

Coury, Ralph M. "Who 'Invented' Egyptian Arab Nationalism?" *International Journal of Middle Eastern Studies* 14: 249–81 and 459–79, 1982.

Cvetkovich, Ann. *Mixed Feelings: Feminism, Mass Culture, and Victorian Sensationalism*. New Brunswick, NJ: Rutgers University Press, 1992.

Daly, M.W. *The Cambridge History of Egypt (vol. 2, Modern Egypt from 1517 to the End of the Twentieth Century)*. Cambridge: Cambridge University Press, 1998.

Darwish, Mustapha. *Dream Makers on the Nile: A Portrait of Egyptian Cinema*. Cairo: The American University in Cairo Press, 1998.

De Certeau, Michel. *The Practice of Everyday Life*. trans. Steven Rendall. Berkeley: University of California Press, 1984.

Deeb, Marius. *Party Politics in Egypt: The Wafd & Its Rivals 1919–1939*. London: The Middle East Center, St. Antony's College Oxford, 1979.

Denœux, Guilain. *Urban Unrest in the Middle East: A Comparative Study of Informal Networks in Egypt, Iran and Lebanon*. New York: State University of New York Press, 1993.

Dobry, Michel. *Sociologie des crises politiques*. Paris: Presses de la Fondation Nationale des Sciences Politiques, 1992.

Doran, Michael. *Pan-Arabism before Nasser: Egyptian Power Politics and the Palestine Question*. London: Oxford University Press, 2002.

Duggan, Lisa. *Sapphic Slashers: Sex, Violence and American Modernity*. Durham: Duke University Press, 2000.

Erlich, Haggai. *Students and University in the 20th Century Egyptian Politics*. London: Frank Cass, 1989.

Esposito, John L. *Women in Muslim Family Law*, 2nd ed. Syracuse: Syracuse University Press, 2001.

Favre, Pierre, ed. *La Manifestation*. Paris: Presses de la Fondation Nationale des Sciences Politiques, 1990.

Fillieule, Olivier. *Stratégies de la rue: les manifestations en France*. Paris: Presses de Sciences Politiques, 1997.

Franco, Jean. *Plotting Women: Gender and Representation in Mexico*. New York: Columbia University Press, 1989.

Gallagher, Nancy Elizabeth. *Egypt's Other Wars: Epidemics and the Politics of Public Health*. Syracuse: Syracuse University Press, 1990.

Gershoni, Israel and James Jankowski. *Redefining the Egyptian Nation, 1930–1945*. Cambridge: Cambridge University Press, 2002.

——. *Egypt, Islam, and the Arabs: The Search For Egyptian Nationhood, 1900–1930*. New York: Oxford University Press, 1986.

——, eds. *Rethinking Nationalism in the Arab Middle East*. New York: Columbia University Press, 1997.

Ghali, Mirrit. *Siyasat al-ghad.* Cairo: Matba'at al-Risala, 1938. (Trans. Isma'il R. el Faruqi. *The Policy of Tomorrow.* Washington, D.C.: American Council of Learned Soceities, 1953.)

Ghurbal, Muhammad Shafiq. *Tarikh al-mufawadat al-misriya al-britaniya, 1882–1939.* Cairo: Dar al-Qalam, 1952.

Goldschmidt, Arthur. *Modern Egypt: The Formation of a Nation State,* 2nd ed. Boulder: Westview Press, 2004.

Gorman, Anthony. *Historians, State, and Politics in Twentieth Century Egypt.* London: Routledge Curzon, 2003.

Habermas, Jurgen. *The Structural Transformation of the Public Sphere: An Inquiry into a Category of Bourgeois Society,* trans. Thomas Burger. Cambridge: Massachusetts Institute of Technology Press, 1991.

al-Hadari, Ahmad. *Tarikh al-sinima fi Misr: al-juz' al-awwal min bidayat 1896 ila akhir 1930.* Cairo: Nadi al-Sinima bi-l-Qahira, 1989.

Halbwachs, Maurice. *La Mémoire Collective.* Paris: Presse Universitaire de France, 1950.

Harris, Christina. *Nationalism and Revolution in Egypt: The Role of the Muslim Brotherhood.* Standford: Hoover Institution; 1964.

Hasan, Ilhami. *Muhammad Tal'at Harb: ra'id sina'at al-sinima al-misriya, 1867–1941.* Cairo: General Egyptian Book Organization, 1986.

Hassanein, Nasser Galal. *al-Ab'ad al-iqtisadiya li azmat sina'at al-sinima al-misriya.* Cairo: General Egyptian Book Organization, 1995.

Hatem, Mervat. "The Enduring Alliance of Nationalism and Patriarchy in Muslim Personal Status Laws: The Case of Modern Egypt," *Feminist Issues* 6, 1: 19–43, 1986.

Heyworth-Dunne, J. *Religious and Political Trends in Modern Egypt.* Washington, D.C., 1950.

Hopwood, Derek. *Egypt: Politics and Society 1945–1981.* London: George Allen & Unwin, 1982.

Husayn, Taha. *Mustaqbal al-thaqafa fi Misr, 1938.* Cairo: Dar al-Ma'arif, 1993. (Trans. Sidney Glazer. *The Future of Culture in Egypt.* New York: Octagon Books, 1975.)

Issawi, Charles. *Egypt at Mid-Century: An Economic Survey.* London: Oxford University Press, 1954.

Jankowski, James. *Egypt: A Short History.* Oxford: One World Publications, 2000

——. *Egypt's Young Rebels. "Young Egypt": 1933–1952.* Stanford, California: Hoover Institution Press, 1975.

Johnson, Amy J. *Reconstructing Rural Egypt: Ahmed Hussein and the History of Egyptian Development.* Syracuse: Syracuse University Press, 2003.

Kerbœuf, Anne-Claire. "La restauration du centre-ville: enjeux sociaux et historiques d'un projet urbain," *La Lettre d'information* 4, April 2003, Observatoire Urbain du Caire Contemporain, CEDEJ.

Kedourie, Elie. "Egypt and the Caliphate, 1915–52." In *The Chatham House Version and Other Middle Eastern Studies.* London: Weidenfeld and Nicolson, 1970: 177–212.

Landau, Jacob M. *Studies in the Arab Theater and Cinema.* Philadelphia: University of Pennsylvania Press, 1958.

Mahfouz, Naguib. *Midaq Alley.* Washington, D.C.: Three Continents Press, 1977.

——. *The Beginning and the End.* Cairo: The American University in Cairo Press, 1985.

Mansfield, Peter. *The British in Egypt.* London: Weidenfeld and Nicolson, 1971.

Mara'i, Farida, ed. *Sahafat al-sinima fi Misr: al-nisf al-awwal min al-qarn al-'ishrin.* Ministry of Culture, National Film Center. Cinema Files (1) Cairo: Lotus, 1996.

Marsot, Afaf Lutfi al-Sayyid. *Egypt's Liberal Experiment: 1922–1936.* Berkeley: University of California Press, 1977.

——. *A Short History of Modern Egypt.* Cambridge: Cambridge University Press, 1985.

Matthews, Roderic D. and Matta Akrawi. *Education in Arab Countries of the Near East.* Washington, D.C.: American Council of Education, 1950.

Mayer, Thomas. *The Changing Past: Egyptian Historiography of the Urabi Revolt, 1882–1983.* Gainesville: University of Florida Press, 1988.

Maza, Sarah. *Private Lives, Public Affairs: The Causes Célèbres of Pre-Revolutionary France.* Berkeley: University of California Press, 1993.

McLaren, Angus. *A Prescription for Murder: The Victorian Serial Killings of Dr. Thomas Neill Cream.* Chicago: University of Chicago Press, 1995.

Meriwether, Margaret and Judith E. Tucker, eds. *Social History of Women and Gender in the Modern Middle East.* Boulder: Westview Press, 1999.

Mernissi, Fatima. *Beyond the Veil: Male-Female Dynamics in a Modern Muslim Society.* Bloomington: Indiana University Press, 1987.

Mitchell, Richard P. *The Society of the Muslim Brothers.* London: Oxford University Press, 1969.

Morsy, Soheir A. *Gender, Sickness and Healing in Rural Egypt: Ethnography in Historical Context.* Boulder: Westview Press, 1993.

Murray, David. *Colonial Justice: Justice, Morality, and Crime in the Niagara District, 1791–1849.* Toronto: University of Toronto Press, 2002.

Naguib, Mohamed. *Egypt's Destiny: a Personal Statement.* London: Doubleday, 1955.

Nelson, Cynthia. *Doria Shafik, Egyptian Feminist: A Woman Apart.* Gainesville: University of Florida Press, 1996.

Owen, Roger. *Lord Cromer: Victorian Imperialist, Edwardian Proconsul.* London: Oxford University Press, 2004.

Pascal, Jacques, ed. *The Middle-East Motion Picture Almanac, 1946–47 / al-Dalil al-sinima'i li-l-sharq al-awsat.* 1st ed. Cairo: S.O.P. Press, 1947.

Pollard, Lisa. *Nurturing the Nation: The Family Politics of Modernizing, Colonizing, and Liberating Egypt, 1805–1923.* Berkeley: University of California Press, 2005.

al-Qabbani, Isma'il Mahmud. *Siyasat al-ta'lim fi Misr.* Cairo: Lajnat al-Ta'lif wa-l-Tarjama wa-l-Nashr, 1944.

——. *Dirasat fi masa'il al-Ta'lim.* Cairo: Maktabat al-Nahda al-Misriya, 1951.

Radwan, Abu Al-Futouh Ahmad. *Old and New Forces in Egyptian Education.* New York: Columbia University, 1951.

al-Rafi'i, 'Abd al-Rahman. *Muqaddimat Thawra 26 Yuliyu.* Cairo: Maktaba al-Nahda al-Misriya, 1957.

——. *Fi a'qab al-thawra al-misriya* (After the Egyptian Revolution). vols. 1–3. Cairo: Dar al-Ma'arif. 1951.

Ramadan, 'Abd al-'Azim Muhammad Ibrahim. *Tatawwur al-haraka al-wataniya al-misriya.* vols. 2–4. Cairo: Dar al-Kitab al-'Arabi, 1987.

Raymond, André. "Le Caire," in *L'Égypte d'aujourd'hui, permanence et changements, 1805–1976.* Paris: Centre National de la Recherche Scientifique, 1977.

——. *Cairo.* London: Hardcover, 2001.

Reid, Malcolm Donald. *Cairo University and the Making of Modern Egypt.* Cambridge: Cambridge University Press, 1990.

Richmond, J.C.B. *Egypt, 1798–1952: Her Advance Towards a Modern Identity.* New York: Colombia University, 1977.

Russell, Mona. *Creating the New Egyptian Woman: Consumerism, Education, and National Identity, 1863–1922.* New York: Palgrave Macmillan, 2004.

Sa'd, 'Abd al-Mun'im. *Mujaz tarikh al-sinima al-misriya.* Cairo: Matabi' al-Ahram al-Tijariya, 1976.

Sadoul, Georges, ed. *The Cinema in the Arab Countries.* Beirut: UNESCO and Interarab Centre of Cinema and Television, 1966.

Safran, Nadav. *Egypt in Search of Political Community: An Analysis of the Intellectual and Political Evolution of Egypt, 1804–1952.* Cambridge: Harvard University Press, 1961.

Salmoni, Barak A. "Women in the Nationalist-Educational Prism: Turkish and Egyptian Pedagogues and their Gendered Agenda, 1920–1952," *History of Education Quarterly* 43: 4 (2003).

Shaham, Ron. *Family and the Courts in Modern Egypt: A Study Based on Decisions by the Shari'a Courts, 1900–1955.* Leiden: E.J. Brill, 1997.

al-Sharqawi, Galal. *Risala fi tarikh al-sinima al-'arabiya.* Cairo: Maktabat al-Nahda al-Misriya, 1970.

al-Sharqawi, Gamal. *Hariq al-Qahira: "qarar ittiham jadid."* Cairo: Dar al-Jil li-l-Taba'a, 1976.

——. *Asrar hariq al-Qahira fil-wathaiq al-siriya al-britaniya.* Cairo: Dar al-Shuhdi li-l-Nashr, 1985.

Smith, Charles D. "The Crisis of Orientation: The Shift of Egyptian Intellectuals to Islamic Subjects in the 1930s," *International Journal of Middle East Studies,* vol. 4, no. 4 (October 1973).

Smith, Sydney. *Mostly Murder.* London: George G. Harrap and Co., 1959.

Sonbol, Amira El Azhari. "Introduction," in Amira El Azhari Sonbol, ed., *Women, the Family, and Divorce Laws in Islamic History.* Syracuse: Syracuse University Press: 1996: 1–20.

Starrett, Gregory. *Putting Islam to Work: Education, Politics, and the Transformation of Faith.* Berkeley: University of California Press, 1998.

Szyliowicz, Joseph S. *Education and Modernization in the Middle East.* Ithaca: Cornell University Press, 1973.

Talhami, Ghada Hashem. *The Mobilization of Muslim Women in Egypt.* Gainesville: University of Florida Press, 1996.

Tawfiq, Sa'd al-Din. *Qissat al-sinima fi Misr: dirasa naqdiya.* Cairo: Dar al-Hilal, 1969.

Terry, Janice. *The Wafd, 1919–1952: Cornerstone of Political Power.* Third World Centre for Research and Publishing, 1982.

Thoraval, Yves. *Regards sur le cinéma égyptien.* Beirut: Dar al-Mashriq, 1975.

Tignor, Robert. "The Economic Activities of Foreigners in Egypt, 1920–1950: From Millet to Haute Bourgeoisie," *Comparative Studies in Society and History* 22, July 1980.

——. "Bank Misr and Foreign Capitalism," *International Journal of Middle East Studies* 8: 2 (1977), 161–81.

Tripp, Charles. *Contemporary Egypt: through Egyptian Eyes. Essays in honor of P.J. Vatikiotis.* New York and London: Routledge, 1993.

Vatikiotis, P.J. *The History of Modern Egypt from Muhammad Ali to Mubarak*, 4th ed. Baltimore: Johns Hopkins University Press, 1991.

———. *Egyptian Army in Politics: Pattern for New Nations*. Bloomington, Indiana: University Press, 1961.

Wassef, Magda, ed. *Égypte: 100 ans de cinéma*. Paris: Éditions Plume and Institut du Monde Arabe, 1995.

Walkowitz, Judith. *City of Dreadful Delight: Narratives of Sexual Danger in Late-Victorian London*. Chicago: University of Chicago Press, 1992.

Zaalouk, Malak. *Power, Class and Foreign Capital in Egypt. The Rise of a New Bourgeoisie*. London: Zed Books, 1989.

Zayid, Mahmud. *Egypt's Struggle for Independence*. Beirut: Khayats, 1965.